J. C. FURNAS

Voyage to Windward

The Life of
Robert Louis Stevenson

"Speak of me as I am; nothing extenuate,
Nor set down aught in malice."

—*Othello* V, ii

WILLIAM   SLOANE   ASSOCIATES
Publishers   *New York*

The author wishes to thank Charles Scribner's Sons for permission to quote material from THE LETTERS OF ROBERT LOUIS STEVENSON, Selected and Edited with Notes and Introduction by Sidney Colvin; Copyright 1899 by Charles Scribner's Sons, Copyright 1927 by Lloyd Osbourne.

Typography and format designed by
LEONARD W. BLIZARD

Manufactured in the United States of America
Published simultaneously by
George J. McLeod, Ltd., Toronto

For Jorgen

when he grows up

I like biography far better than fiction myself; fiction is too free. In biography you have your little handful of facts, little bits of a puzzle, and you sit and think, and fit 'em together this way and that, and get up and throw 'em down and say damn, and go out for a walk, and it's real soothing; and when done, gives an idea of finish to the writer that is very peaceful. Of course it's not really so finished as quite a rotten novel; it always has and always must have the incurable illogicalities of life about it. . . . Still, that's where the fun comes in.

—Stevenson to Gosse, *Letters:* IV, 191

This book has been an ambition for fifteen years and a task as exacting as enjoyable since 1946, when I found myself living for months in Vailima, the house that Louis built to live—and die —in.

It has taken years and dollars and 30,000 miles of travel. To keep the record clear, the only places where he spent important time that I have not seen are Davos and the Marquesas.

Hundreds and hundreds of thousands of words of unpublished letters and manuscripts of his and his intimates have gone into the compost. This was more than mere checking: Thanks to luck and others' help, new information here first explodes the legends, mostly discreditable, that had been allowed, for lack of facts, to grow up round Stevenson.

It has amounted—strangely—to living with the man. As we returned from Edinburgh, talking nothing but Stevenson during the ten days' voyage, my wife warned me: "We'll probably be setting a place for him at dinner when we get home."

Throughout I have worked to high standards of accuracy and discretion in assessing the validity of data, both old and previously unknown. My training has been that of reporter rather than scholar. All-round reliability probably has not suffered.

The reader may take it for granted that each unqualified statement of fact is based on sound documentary or oral evidence, laboriously cross-checked. All mere probabilities, surmises, guesses, are clearly indicated. Numbered notes clarify minor issues, give supplementary definitions, or identify sources.

—J. C. F.

Acknowledgments

Both friends and strangers have generously helped me on this book— so many that to list them completely risks the inadvertent discourtesy of unintentional omission. In thanking the few here named, who were concerned with actual research for me, I should like to be considered to have thanked all: Mrs. Anne Roller Issler of Napa, Calif.; Mr. and Mrs. William Cogswell of Honolulu, T. H.; Mr. Colin Simpson and Dr. G. Mackaness of Sydney, Australia, Mr. D. K. H. Parsons of London; Mr. F. J. H. Grattan of Apia, Western Samoa; Mr. Leonard G. Usher of Suva, Fiji; Miss Caroline Dunn of Indianapolis, Ind.

Owners of Stevensoniana who have been most obliging include Mr. Flodden W. Heron, Mr. John Howell, Mr. Gordon A. Block jr., Mr. Frank A. Thomas. In giving me access to his remarkably rich collection of Stevensoniana, Mr. Edwin J. Beinecke has greatly forwarded my project. The substance of the book's original contribution to knowledge of Stevenson comes from his material and from that of the National Library of Scotland, where Mr. M. R. Dobie was of enormous help. Mrs. Muriel Mirylees, Curator of the Robert Louis Stevenson Museum, Edinburgh, Scotland, has kindly provided many of the illustrations. Special gratitude goes to my host at Vailima, Lieut.-Col. F. W. Voelcker, then Administrator of the Mandate of Western Samoa.

Thanks for research facilities of varying scale are due to the New York Public Library, the Princeton University Library, the Yale University Library, the Harry Elkins Widener Memorial Library, the University of California Library, the Henry E. Huntington Library, the library of the Harvard Club of New York City, the Library of Congress, the Municipal Library of Bournemouth, the Indiana State Library, the Indiana State Historical Society Library, the Public Library of New South Wales, the British Museum, the National Archives, H. M. Public Record Office.

Public or private institutions that have courteously answered in-

Acknowledgments

quiries make an extraordinary list; each item deserves thanks: The U. S. Department of State; the U. S. Weather Bureau; the Cunard-White Star Line; the New Zealand *Herald;* the Office of H. M. High Commissioner for the Western Pacific; the Consulate-General of the Netherlands (New York); the National Tuberculosis Association; the American Telephone & Telegraph Company; the Office of Lyon King-at-Arms; the U. S. Coast Guard; the U. S. Military Academy; the California State Department of Public Health; the Pennsylvania Railroad; the Museum of Modern Art.

Permission to quote previously unpublished letters of Stevenson's has been accorded by the estate of the late Lloyd Osbourne, through the courtesy of Mr. Lou Osbourne, Executor. Permission to quote letters of Henley's from John Connell, *William Ernest Henley,* has been accorded by Constable & Company.

The editorial assistance of Miss Helen Stewart (of the William Sloane Associates) and of Mrs. Elizabeth C. Moore is gratefully acknowledged; the latter having edited the manuscript, read the proofs, and prepared the indexes.

In research, weighing of issues and evidence, organization, editing, and enthusiasm, my wife has been a major collaborator.

Contents

Prologue

WE CHILDREN used to find the shells of locusts abandoned on the bark of the big red maples. Legs, abdomen, thorax, and head were all there, light and empty in transparent chitin.

Behind glass in the Stevenson Museum at Saranac Lake, New York, is preserved a black velveteen jacket, the sprig of heather in its upper pocket annually renewed by admirers of its long-dead owner. A robust girl could not possibly struggle into this narrow garment. Its wearer must have been an animated ribbon, with long arms, narrow chest, and, to judge by the lace-up boots in another case, long narrow hands and feet. Below lies an embroidered skullcap, the kind that goes with a meerschaum pipe. Art students wore those when Stevenson was young in Paris.

These are the shell of a man, cast skins as personal as a fingerprint. The locust always grew another shell of the same general pattern; through all his stages Robert Louis Stevenson always owned a velvet jacket. He wore it at the prompting of his adolescence, which was prolonged. That he retained it to his death signifies that a man may mature without necessarily ageing. Always shrewd, usually unflattering, in comment on himself, he said of a suggested resemblance between him and the Shelley of Dowden's *Life:* "a Shelley with less will and no genius; though I have had the fortune to live longer and (partly) to grow up." [1] Some thought it a reproach to him, some an honor, some a self-betrayal that, when he died suddenly at the age of forty-four, he was still growing.

Several, including Henry James for eminence, saw his life as a novel that its hero would have valued—a notion with illustrative merit. The story is both kinetic and ironic. Much of its detail has style. And, like most who knew him, the hero found the character of Robert Louis Stevenson fascinating. But implication that he himself helped to construct the story is rather pretty than pertinent. This life was active as a water bug, romantic as an elopement, wide-ranging as a tramp ship, dramatic as a duel to the death, even, as he would have liked it, moral as a tract, after his own morality, that is. But it is not in his own literary manner. *The Adventures of a Changeling* was not among the novels aborted by his unexpected death.

Nor is it fiction, say Balzac advising with E. M. Forster. All of it actually happened to a perverse, handicapped, brilliant, fertile, and brave man. Launched among turbulent emotions, urged toward uncongenial callings, subject to strange diversions of energy, haunted by illness, he nevertheless sailed a course that, charted fifty years later, has the asymmetric consistency of great composition. With the centenary of his birth, much fresh evidence, clearing up important passages in his life that were hitherto obscure, has come available. This novel of actuality, this case history with the values of fiction, demands full retelling.

He wrote *Treasure Island, A Child's Garden of Verses*, and *The Strange Case of Dr. Jekyll and Mr. Hyde*—a "boys' book," a "children's book," and a shocker with gross moral and psychological meaning. The first two have long been accepted as proper to young minds and tastes. Presently, in a naïf parallel, Stevenson himself came to be regarded as a hero specially suited to the juvenile:

. . . one of the most amiable, kind-hearted, affectionate and gentle of men, high and pure-minded, and possessing an indescribable charm of manner. He looked essentially at the bright side of things, even in times of sickness and trouble; he was excessively humourous and witty, and regarded life more or less from the comic standpoint. He was simple in his habits and mode of living and was a devoted son and husband; he was loved by all who knew him.[2]

Thus once fluted an amiable lady-writer, probably with no wish to crowd in so much flagrant misrepresentation, merely following the fashion of confusing Stevenson with the curate of Assesmilk-cum-Worter. Unluckily, between such distortion and inevitable efforts at "debunking" that followed, the man himself and most of his works have come to be undeservedly neglected. The world has too few people who can write like that, and too few men of such bowels.

His favorite figure in *The Pilgrim's Progress* was Valiant-for-the-Truth because he died willing "my courage and skill to him that can get it." For Stevenson this might have been a better epitaph than "Dig the grave and let me lie . . ."; though it was appropriate enough to put "Requiem" on his grave in Samoa, as he had once suggested. For his courage and skill—a doughty skill as artist in words and people, an apt courage of self-realization under grave emotional and physical strains— are farther salient than the gladness and weariness of those famous verses.

Meredith and Barrie knew what they were doing when they tried to put certain aspects of him into novels.[3] Henry James stated the principal reason for writing about Stevenson, recalling that, when asked why they had chosen a certain model, painters would always answer: "Character! Character is what he has."

The House of Eld

The Gyve Is Riveted

> The world is so large and I am so small,
> I do not like it at all, at all.
>
> —Early version of "Happy Thought," in
> Balfour, *Life:* I, 40, footnote

ROBERT LEWIS BALFOUR STEVENSON,[4] sickly only child of prospering upper middle-class parents, was born November 13, 1850—the dead middle of the Victoria-dominated century—in Edinburgh, cultural and political capital of Scotland. Each component of that statement left its mark on the boy.

Thomas Stevenson, his father, was a brilliant, eccentric, and independently devout civil engineer, specializing—like his brothers, father, and grandfather before him—in marine lighting and harbor- and river-works. As consultants to the Commissioners of Northern Lights, their firm had ringed Scotland with lights and breakwaters. The Bell Rock Lighthouse (successor to the Inchcape Bell of Southey's ballad) and the Skerryvore Lighthouse off the Hebrides were only the most brilliant of their monuments—peers of the Eddystone in the history of engineering, each an advance in the art of defying the stupendous forces of wind and sea. The mosaic frieze in the National Portrait Gallery in Edinburgh shows Robert Stevenson, Thomas's father, among Scotland's greatest—Carlyle, Sir James Simpson, Lord Kelvin—pointing to a model of the Bell Rock light with a gesture like Banquo's dumb-show boast of the kings to be born of his line. Thomas Stevenson was particularly noted for his inventions improving the optics of sea-lights and for textbooks on waves and currents.

Though this strong family tradition was a factor in the conflicts between the engineer and his obstinate son, Louis never overreacted into losing his great pride in his family's brilliance in work demanding integrity, intelligence, and incalculable devotion. He dwelt fondly on his father's passionate interest in currents and stresses, his grandfather's stubborn victories over fractious workmen and angry salt water and his quaint fancy of laying out a principal highway entering Edinburgh along the theory of Hogarth's Line of Beauty. Time and again, in verse and prose, fiction and autobiography, Louis harked back to the technical glories of his forebears as if he had been an exiled Highlandman asserting the prestige of his clan.

A few generations earlier these Stevensons (a name common in Edinburgh) had been petty bourgeois, ". . . decent, reputable folk, following honest trades—millers, maltsters, and doctors" [5] whose ancestors had been small farmers. Scots might feel that fact less of a stigma than Englishmen, but it was not insignificant. True, Grandfather Robert had come far enough up in the world to receive grant of coat-armor, showing a lighthouse and the motto "Coelum non solem" [6]—an ironical blazon for Louis, who was always seeking out the sun for his health and, in his elders' eyes, had showed strong disposition toward the other place. It was nevertheless gratifying that his mother's people, the Balfours, had always been gentry; "kent folk," ramifying into eminent Lowland and Border clans, they happily diluted Great-grandfather Smith, who got into engineering by way of an odorous business in lamps and illuminating oils.

Margaret Isabella Balfour's father was minister of the Established Kirk at Colinton, austere, revered, learned shepherd of a parish now reached by Edinburgh streetcars, well within the metropolitan aura even then. From this family tree other parsons leaned out to edify rigid congregations: one had caught a stinging flick from Burns's "Holy Fair." [7] By Lou's day, however, the secularizing times had diverted the children of the manse into less reverend careers. Little prestige was lost: Brother George became Physician in Ordinary to the Queen for Scotland; Brother John, high in the medical service of the

East India Company, was last man out of Delhi when the Mutiny broke; Brother James was engineer to the Crown Colony of New Zealand. Their sisters married other such. The family tomb-inscriptions at Colinton make a long list, for Meg was youngest of thirteen. (So was Thomas, though Stevenson viability was lower.) But genealogy has deservedly lost interest. The point here is that, though from backgrounds of dissimilar savors, Louis's immediate forebears on both sides were comfortable and mattered substantially to the world about them. He could never be a self-made man like Great-grandfather Smith. The very shining solidity of the bed he was born in, still preserved at the 8 Howard Place Museum, spells solid economic foundations. He would have to seek out hardship deliberately and go to some trouble to escape automatic respectability.

Engineer, physician, Calvinist theologian—serious Scots are known as such throughout the English-speaking world. Louis had all three of those elements smelted into his life from the moment he opened his blue eyes which, baby-fashion, quickly turned dark hazel. He could have been a standard article, lean, long-legged credit to engine room or surgical theater, hard-headed but sentimental, not always sober on Saturday, usually at church next day. But, both emotionally and physically, he was born to trouble as the sparks fly upward.

His mother may have encouraged both aspects. "The minister's white-headed lassie," as Colinton knew her, was fair and tall, gentle, shrewd, and graceful, with great bright gray eyes and a mouth that stayed tinged with a smile even during time-exposure photographs. She had had her son early enough still to be much of a gay, tender girl with him. In one of his earliest memories, Grandfather Balfour is coming to visit and mother and son are skipping upstairs hand in hand, singing "Let's all go up to Gatty's room." When Thomas was away at suppertime, son and mother had special dishes disliked by the master of the house and innocently conspired to treat themselves to the top of the cream instead of stirring it to thrifty uniformity.

The Balfours reckoned Meg notably sweet-natured, nervously eager to muffle up disagreements, ornamented by genuine piety and humorous optimism. Under stress of Lou's postadolescent antics, she could show hysteria and sometimes unworthy suspicions; but under such circumstances neither pattern is abnormal.

Not long ago Lou's having been an only child would have been thought significant. Currently psychologists are not so sure on this point. Why there were no more children is obscure —perhaps simple failure of fertility, though both family lines were prolific; or intentional deprivation because Thomas's young wife was "not strong"; like her father in his time, she had a "weak chest." As a young man, the Rev. Dr. Balfour had spent long intervals in the Isle of Wight, which was supposed "good for" consumption. But at that he lived to the age of eighty-three. Several stays in the South of France, Menton notably, helped Meg to best similar symptoms,[8] but her case was stubborn; in 1863 she still had twice to take her cough and feverishness to the Riviera and all through Louis's childhood she was accustomed to stay invalidwise in bed until noon. Eventually she proved to be her father's daughter—sailed on a small yacht for cannibal islands at the age of fifty-nine; took her share of champagne, getting no tipsier than others, when the King of Hawaii was a guest; rode horses for the first time in her life; and, when near seventy, learned to ride a bicycle. But, in the decade 1854-64, the time when Louis needed a normally hearty mother most and a domestic example of disability least, she supplied the latter.

What with doctors rife among the Balfours and this sort of history, it is probable that parents and upper servants both were too illness-conscious for Lou's good. His growing years were studded with family expeditions to German spas or English resorts undertaken, no doubt with ample discussion, for the health of father, mother or himself. When barely three, he came one day to his mother anxiously asking: "Do you think I'm looking very ill?"—though there was nothing perceptibly wrong with him. In his bitter twenties he wrote Mrs. Sitwell: ". . . I come of a gloomy family always ready to be frightened about their precious health."

Both physical and emotional factors may have underlain his becoming a juvenile invalid. The known hereditary factor in tuberculosis—a matter of inheriting not the disease but the lack of relative immunity to the bacillus—tempts speculation as to how much Louis had his forebears to thank for his frailness. But there is small reason to believe that tuberculosis itself attacked him in the days of the Land of Counterpane. Heaven knows what it actually was. Diagnosis is still no exact science; a hundred years ago it consisted even more flagrantly in relying on vocabulary to conceal uncertainty. Family tradition united with photographs to show him as originally a plump and pretty child, the contemporary frock for prosperous small boys helping him to look like a chubby little girl. But upper respiratory ailments, rough with coughs and fevers, soon attacked savagely. After a siege of something labeled "croup" [9] at the age of twenty-nine months, the round, fair-haired baby turned scrawny, bug-eyed, pigeon-breasted, with a jangled nervous system and a genius for running fevers.

The eccentricity of his bone-structure—no narrower man ever cast a shadow—rouses suspicion of a major endocrinal upset.[10] His eventual height, about five foot ten, was the only normal detail of his skeleton. This extraordinary attenuation—he once described a tapeworm of which he had been relieved as like himself even more in shape than in face—cannot have been inherited. His mother was normally proportioned, his father was made like one of the firm's granite lighthouses. Nor can the cause have been nutritional, for Louis had the same, or better, diet on which they had been reared. Yet all his life he was "a bag of bones, a very lath for leanness," [11] and probably would have got little good out of conscientious use of the bar-bells that were supposed to develop his chest. "To use a Scotch word," wrote Eve Simpson, ". . . he had a 'shilpit' look, which is starveling, crined, ill-thriven, all in one and more." [12]

Some biographers, notably the weather-minded British, make much of the baneful effects on him of Edinburgh's raw and strenuous winds, chill fogs, and persistent rains; the place is, after all, in the latitude of central Labrador, and British heating methods are inconsistent and inadequate. Nobody celebrated more fervently than Louis the brutal qualities of that notorious climate. Conversely, waking in Orange on his trip south in 1873, he skipped about the room for joy over the gush of sunshine in the window. In 1853, as Thomas prospered, he gave up the well-sheltered house at 8 Howard Place and took a larger, markedly exposed house across the way at 1 Inverleith Terrace (long since demolished) from which damp and chill had frightened the previous tenant. There, says this theory, Lou's health was permanently impaired. Not until he was six did the family shift, after their doctor had condemned the place as bad for him, to a large house snugged between neighbors, facing south into the sun across gardens, at 17 Heriot Row—the effective Stevenson home with the famous lamp before the door.

True to the New Town of Edinburgh, all three houses were stone-built, solid as powder magazines but with only open fireplaces to modify the climate. The Scottish feeling about room temperatures, still strong, had moved prosperous people to use gas-lighting at first only on stairs and in corridors because it "uncomfortably overheated" drawing- and dining-rooms. To the modern layman it sounds as if, whatever ailed young Lou, the special shortcomings of any given dwelling merely exacerbated it. No doubt the move to 17 Heriot Row was advisable; but the child promptly came down with a severe "gastric fever" that confirmed his chronic debility.

Such ailments were difficult to cope with in an age that knew so little of sanitation, immunology, and dietetics. A modern doctor would have wrought doughtily with vitamins and inoculations, perhaps introduced the parents to the elements of psychosomatic medicine. As it was, whether the occasion were a drop in the barometer or a drop in resistance, coughs, chills, fevers, aches, and pains paraded interminably through the bright-eyed, big-beaked little creature who so often lay awake dreading the bitter east wind as an ominous threat:

> . . . the horrible howl of the wind round the corner; the audible haunting of an incarnate anger about the house; the evil spirit that was abroad; and, above all, the shuddering silent pauses when the storm's heart stands dreadfully still for a moment. O how I hate a storm at night! . . . I always heard it as a horseman riding past with his cloak about his head, and somehow always carried away, and riding past again, and being baffled yet once more, *ad infinitum*, all night long.[13]

His parents dutifully found him nurses. The first two did not stay, the third was found drinking gin in a pub while Lou, wrapped in a shawl, slept on the bar. (I wish I could thus account for his eventual taste for Edinburgh's "shebeens.") The fourth, arriving as the family moved to Inverleith Terrace, was a clear-skinned, rock-loyal daughter of a Fifeshire fisherman, already experienced, with the lovely, utterly Scottish name of Alison Cunningham—the "Cummy" of the Stevenson legend. Photographs of her in old age, when sentimental pilgrims came to honor the dedicatee of *A Child's Garden*, show her handsomer than most queens; the elder Kirstie of *Weir of Hermiston* may be a partial portrait. Lou, she told literary trippers, was "like other bairns, whiles very naughty." [14] Her love for him and his for her were clear as her own complexion. He seldom wrote better than in describing her care for him, the sleepless, feverish, wailing little bundle of nerves and germs, "troubled with a hacking, exhausting cough, and praying for sleep or morning from the bottom of my shaken little body":[15]

> She was more patient than I can suppose of an angel; hours together she would help console me in my paroxysms; and I remember with particular distinction how she would lift

me out of bed and take me, rolled in blankets, to the window, whence I might look forth into the blue night starred with street lamps and see where the gas still burned behind the windows of other sickrooms . . . where also, we told each other, there might be sick little boys and their nurses waiting, like us, for morning.[16]

For generations this institution of the substitute mother has done strange things to upper-class British children, perhaps to their parents in repercussion, often to "Nanny" herself. In Louis's case, however, what with a half-ailing mother and a three-quarter-ailing child, a Cummy was very definitely indicated.

People noting the French-like gestures with which the grown Louis talked were not aware that he had acquired so non-British a habit from Cummy, whose hands flew as she spoke till the day of her death. That was only one lifelong influence. For so sickly a child schooling was often impracticable. Long illnesses, long absences at health resorts, made Louis by definition a dislocated pupil. He had a taste of a tutor at six, but he was seven before he could read—a backwardness curious in a man to whom reading was almost a vice in adolescence; it may connect with the fact that, for a writer well at home with Latin roots and European languages, he was a poor speller.[17] It was Cummy, by no means uneducated in the rural Scots tradition, who grounded him in ideas and rhetoric. Her strong, true voice sang him country balladry and the inspired doggerel of the Metrical Versions of the Psalms that, carrying the authority of Scripture for Scots Presbyterians, rang in Louis's ears all his life.[18] She eased his wakefulness by reading aloud from the Bible and Bunyan or with tales of the "killing time," when dragoons hunted Covenanters in the heather and made martyrs whose histories are saved from smugness only by a self-righteousness of appalling dignity. Rung out in strong and somewhat archaic Scots, this was strong stuff, particularly because Cummy read ". . . the works of others as a poet would scarce dare read his own; gloating on the rhythm, dwelling with delight on assonances and alliterations." [19]

Her material was not always so august. Cummy also hankered after, and sometimes inserted into the curriculum, the penny-paper serials written for the Victorian servant. Lou grew avid after swoons and wicked baronets and honest old fathers. If overcome by the author's bald intention merely to entertain, which was sinful, Cummy might drop the story in the middle:

> Yet neither she nor I were wholly stoical; and when Saturday came round, we would study the window of the stationer and try to fish out of subsequent woodcuts and their legends the further adventures of our favourites. . . . Each new Saturday I would go from one news vendor's window to another's, until I was master of the weekly gallery and thoroughly digested "The Baronet Unmasked," "So and So approaching the Mysterious House," "The Discovery of the Dead Body in the Blue Marl Pit," "Dr. Vargas Removing the Senseless Body of Fair Lilias." [20]

Their ghosts should still be visible in New Town streets: Cummy shawled and bonneted, ramrod-straight, nose a little blue with wind and color high; Lou also high-colored but watery-eyed with chill, gloved, muffled with flannel round his head against his chronic earache, quivering half with pleasure and half with the cold that, in Scotland, so seldom baked out of his small bones.

This warm, stern, merry reality—she danced for him as well as prayed at him, and was fond of a pawky joke—was a shaping force far superior to that of the sweet-voiced ladies who came to call and smiled foolishly over Lou's precociously grave vocabulary and the primly facile gestures of "the dear little baby hands." [21] But Cummy also presented drawbacks. Too many walks ended in Warriston Cemetery, which, though not so brutally gloomy as the Old Calton and Greyfriars which Louis would haunt later, was morbid enough in company with a pious country girl. With the Metrical Version of the Twenty-Third Psalm in his head, Lou identified "Death's dark vale" with the long, damp, dark railroad underpass that bisects the place. And Cummy had too many pertinent tales of the "resurrection-men" whom Louis would eventually work into "The Body-Snatcher." In fact, graveyards played too large a part in his small consciousness. Colinton Manse, Grandfather Balfour's house, lies between stream and churchyard, and the children used fearfully to peer into chinks in the retaining wall that banks the dead off from the sunny lawn.

Worst of all, even beyond the devout fears implicit in most Christian creeds, Cummy retained lively rural superstitions. Like many a child's nurse before or since, she provided over-rich material for night fears. Her Devil was personal, immediate, often got up as the Black Man of country tales—the glimpse in "Thrawn Janet" shows what Lou's imagination did with him; thirty-five years later his mother, encountering the fear of Tahitian children for white faces, would recall her small son's terror of "the b'acky man." [22] Doubtless Cummy did not altogether believe in him herself, but her tales of him had been concocted by people under no such skeptical handicap. In time Louis could share Burns's familiarity with Auld Hornie and write his own "Address to the Deil" with wit and point. But to the child the Black Man could not be seriocomic. He fathered a pattern of nightmares and delirious hallucinations—fever lay down with Lou night after night—that soaked the child in the sweat of terror.

True, he might have invented his own horrors if Cummy had given him none ready-made. But she had also imposed on him, for mordant, a highstrung religiosity. One of his favorite games was playing church, himself as minister in a pulpit made of an upturned chair; when he once added paper "bands" for verisimilitude, a playmate's mother tore them off as sacrilegious. [23] He was only thirty months old when Cummy seriously expected him to take more patiently to prayer as sequel to a serious illness: [24]

I would not only lie awake to weep for Jesus . . . but I would fear to trust myself to slumber lest I was not accepted and should slip, ere I woke, into eternal ruin. I remember repeatedly awaking from a dream of Hell, clinging to the horizontal bar of my bed, with my knees and chin together, my soul shaken, my body convulsed with agony. . . . I piped and snivelled over the Bible, with an earnestness that had been talked into me. . . . Had I died in those years, I fancy I might perhaps have figured in a tract.[25]

For the only thing grim about Cummy was her faith, learned under the elaborate expoundings of Calvinist divines in cold seaside churches. As Scottish households then went, the Stevensons' was not stiff. Sabbath was duly observed, with irreligious play and reading banned, but Lou's mother lightened it by sewing a tiny pack on the back of a wooden doll so the child could play *Pilgrim's Progress*. Other days such snares to the light-minded as cards and wine were countenanced, and family prayers were mere informal Bible-reading. Cummy, however, sniffily mistrusted cards and dinner parties and took ardent sides in theological quarrels among Presbyterian sects, infecting Lou with hairsplitting partisanship. There was a family tale of how, at an astoundingly tender age, he adjured his cousin John Smith, come to Edinburgh for a Kirk Assembly, to have nothing whatever to do with a certain theological iconoclast. When traveling with the family on the Continent in 1862-63, Cummy insisted on sowing tracts attacking the Pope in Catholic churches visited. So, long before he could read, Lou was two-thirds of a bigot, quoting Scripture about millstones and the nethermost depths of the sea for those holding false doctrine. This acute early attack of the disease evidently immunized him in later life; certainly, once in a position to form his own opinions, he showed small taste for bigotry.[26]

In a modern child from an educated family such behavior would now be outrageous. It was abnormal then, but not alarming by definition. In 1856 intelligent people could still take precocious religiosity as mere accentuation of something desirable in itself. To reproach Louis's parents for failing to see such holy pipings as morbid is to ask an anachronistic attitude. Thus, though his mother was eventually shocked to hear from her grown son the terrors he owed to Cummy, though even at the time she sometimes forbade his being exposed to the juiciest aspects of Calvinism, this phase seems usually to have struck his parents as tenderly amusing. For they were seriously religious: She was daughter of the manse and an enthusiastic amateur of foreign missions; her letter-diary of life at Vailima ends on a touchingly true note of faith. Thomas was an able amateur theologian who read his favorite Latin fathers for pastime while traveling and published on the Scriptural evidences of Christianity in a style soberly similar to that of his authoritative works on harbor engineering.

Their queer little devil of a son was soon moved by acute apprehension of sin to experiment with blasphemy, deliberately going off by himself to say the unsayable, so far as he could conceive it, reaching for the unforgivable thing to see if being eaten by troops of bears necessarily followed. Even in late adolescence he frightened himself badly by meticulously carrying out a formula for summoning the Devil which he had encountered in a book. No doubt Mr. Hyde, kept alive and growing by progressive acknowledgment of the charms of sin, was born of Cummy's influence. Louis was too apt a pupil, she too incisive a teacher. All his life the Metrical Versions of Job's despair, the close inquiries and bleak replies of the Shorter Catechism, the arbitrary, legally unimpeachable pessimism of the Westminster Confession, put phrases in his mouth and shaped his thinking. All this is plain to a biographer not reared in Scotland; fully to understand it probably requires being born north of the Tweed.

Scott says that the lower orders of his day spoiled their young children. In their higher station Louis's parents were open to the same charge, partly through tenderness or perplexity.

That Lou's mother would be tender was plain in her face. As he
developed there was a touch of doting in her pride in him;
guests recalled that she was capable of listening raptly for an
hour while he paced the room, monopolizing the conversation
with a rehearsal of one of his early essays. Tom Stevenson's
square boots and square thick eyebrows and square cheek-
bones were not so obviously philoprogenitive in implication,
but his eyes showed affection and harkening humor. It was he
who dubbed the baby "Smout"—Scots for the small fry of
salmon. When Smout's "nervousness" reached a peak in fever
or loud weather, the last resort was for his father to sit at his
bedroom door and hold audible conversations of great patience and drollery with imaginary persons. Presently the run
of his resonant voice and the distraction of his fictions would
set the child off to sleep well before the master of the house
had to dress and breakfast and be off to the family office.

That does not sound like the stock Victorian father, rebellion
against whom was an automatic and picturesque spiritual duty;
nor does Louis's freely exercised privilege of debating practically anything, no holds barred, with the head of the family
at the Stevensons' always highly conversational dinner table.
The boy's letters home in his late teens abound with cheeky
teasing of his father about illegible handwriting and such
round phrases as "I think what you say about the diving is
nonsense." [27] Biographers who have seen Thomas as *cliché*—pious, rigid, harsh—and have explained Louis's vagaries as natural
reactions anticipating *The Way of All Flesh* can have known
very little about either party. In later years Louis zestfully recalled how his father's occasional gregarious charm had filled a
country inn in 1880:

I have rarely been well received among strangers, never if
they were womenfolk; . . . it pleased and amused me to
be a sharer in my father's popularity, and in the public sit-
ting-rooms to be the centre of delighted groups of girls; the
stormy and tender old man with the noble mouth and the

great luminous eyes, had, almost to the end, so great a gift of pleasing.[28]

The fact is that, for all his solidity of look and profession, Thomas seems to have been an unstably inclined deviant held by his own will to duty as maturity imposed it on him. His theological hobby may have sprung not so much from intellectual taste as from need to brood over the blacker Calvinism to the point of melancholia, varied by fits of gaiety involving extravagant jokes or the outgoing charm described above. Before he died, society recognized his achievements by making him president of the Royal Society of Edinburgh. But he consistently refused lay office in the Kirk to match his worldly position; in senses that he never openly defined he considered himself unworthy. Among his private benevolences was substantial support of a "Magdalen Institution" for "fallen women"—a fact which, with more malice than plausibility, has been cited to show undue guilt-feelings consequent on early dissipation. There was nothing out of the way about such a charity—only his championship of that Victorian underdog, woman, extended to the extravagant contention that any woman should have divorce for the asking and no man be allowed divorce at all. All his life Louis was incurably solicitous of women, even bitterly despising W. S. Gilbert for such brutal caricatures of middle-aged spinsters as Katisha and Lady Jane.

On his daily walks Tom Stevenson had two amusements: making friends with dogs—he maintained blasphemously that dogs had souls—and stopping schoolboys to ask what they were learning out of that load of books, then smilingly advising them to drop the whole thing and learn only what seemed good to them —or, if that suited better, nothing. As Apologist for Idlers young Louis would write:

Sainte-Beuve, as he grew older, came to regard all experience as a single great book, in which to study for a few years ere we go hence; and it seemed all one to him, whether you should read in Chapter XX, which is the differential calculus, or in Chapter **XXXIX**, which is hearing the band play in the gardens.[29]

But it was through his original father rather than any Frenchman that he first met such an attitude. Thomas cheerfully admitted having been an "idle eager sentimental youth",[30] a consistent truant from the old High School with utter scorn for teachers, process of learning, and subjects taught.

So eminent and useful a citizen could afford the sardonic pleasure of adducing himself to show that schools were mostly nonsense. Mathematics bored him; an engineer without mathematics was unthinkable. Yet, by thinking problems through with small help from symbolic formulae, using inner feel for how water, wind, and light semed to want to act, trusting to his pocket Molesworth—rebound in antique Spanish leather—for ordinary calculations, and to learned friends for translating his inspired guesses into transmissible terms, he became celebrated as inventor of intricate optical apparatus. Such eccentricities meant, of course, that he was also deviant in politics, a radical zealot against privilege. Only he was nothing of the sort. His politics were sound Tory. The one thing he hated more than Mr. Gladstone was a revolutionary prophet.[31] But he also maintained that the country fared best when the Whigs had a perilously large minority in Parliament to keep the ministry singing small.

He did not carry his prejudices so far as to object when Lou went to school late in his sixth year. But the boy knew well enough what the kindly chief of 17 Heriot Row thought of schoolmasters, exercise-books, and multiplication tables. It naturally followed that he was the despair of pedagogues and denounced them all his life, in and out of season, in the tone of voice that he usually reserved for bankers, *fonctionnaires*, and California brandy. "Bummkopfery" was the young fellow's name for all meticulously uninspired scholarship.

Even without this (to say the least of it) negative conditioning and the handicap of illness, this child as "old-fashioned"

as Paul Dombey stood small chance of successful pupilage anyway. Cummy took him by the hand to his nearby "beginners'
school" at Cannonmills and there, if the way had been cold
and wet, "changed his feet" for him before his schoolmates—a
guarantee that he would be, as a schoolmate recorded, "butt of
the school." [32] His owlish, grown-uppish talk and strange ugli-
ness did the rest. Though play under a nurse's eye in the private
Queen Street Gardens[33] was indicated for children of his background, his regimen seems rather to have based on walks exclusively with Cummy, who had a countrified standoffishness.
No wonder that, as Miss Masson said, he grew up "precocious,
interesting, affected, and egregiously egotistic." [34]

He made twitchy efforts to adjust. Once, spurred by a pious
work called *Ministering Children*, about prosperous infants
benefiting underprivileged infants, he accosted an obviously
underprivileged small street-boy with a lame foot: "Would you
like to play with me?" The proletarian cripple cursed him with
adult fluency and stalked away. Lou may have learned something from that. Sent at ten to the Edinburgh Academy, new-
ish school for gentlemen's sons, he carried his *clackan*[35] like the
rest and rattled it boisterously on area railings as he hurried to
school. But that was protective coloring at best. When well, he
was fond of physical action—canoeing, walking, riding, swim-
ming—but seldom of sports with a competitive feature, perhaps
because they pitted him against strange, readier, and alarm-
ingly uncouth mates. He could not even warm up to golf, already the tribal ritual of upper- and middle-class Scots, in
which Walter Simpson, a crony of his youth, was adept.[36] Fishing appealed to him until, having caught thirty trout in a day
with rod and line, he suddenly sickened at the evident misery
of the flopping fish and gave up the sport for life.

Scorned by their peers, whom no bluff can mislead, such
children are known types. They do not know how or when to
lubricate social situations by an aggressive poke in the nose,
physical or moral. If they try violence in desperate imitation
of what seems called for, they seldom prove their point, as Lou

found out on at least one occasion recorded by a schoolmate with a long memory. Another schoolmate recalled him as a small boy apart from the others, his wide straw hat burst, the rim pulled down over his shoulders like an obscene collar, weeping in a passion of outrage over what arbitrary malice had done to him. It fits in too well that, as a child, he was beautifully amenable to his best clothes and behaved so nicely at children's parties that admiring mamas dubbed him "the little Frenchman." [37]

There was stray, broken-up tutoring at various resorts in Britain and on the Continent, and a few dismal months at an English school in suburban London. The last few years before, at sixteen, he entered the University, saw him at a special Edinburgh day-school for backward or delicate young people, which went in for such radical innovations as admitting girls and assigning no home-work—all helping to single the boy out as a poor emotional risk.

In his childhood summers, however, when troops of Balfour cousins gathered at Colinton Manse, he had playmates under predigested circumstances, and did better. Doubtless in compensation for his troubles with outsiders, his pecking-level here was fairly high. The cousins had a game of exchanging "curiosities"—odd souvenirs, bits of childish junk—each trade involving painful whacks on the hand, the deal falling through if the victim flinched. When he had the better of the bargain, the others remembered, Lou took stern glee in whacking, but he seems to have taken his own whacks with Spartan calm. For William Archer's small son he later recalled his prowess at hide-and-seek: ". . . not a good runner, I was up to every shift and dodge—I could crawl without any noise through leaves . . . it used to be my favourite boast that I always *walked* into the den." [38] Cleverness also made him leader in make-believe, turning wash-baskets into boats, inventing the dread Giant Bunker who, however often the allied cousins stalked and killed him, always revived to lurk again in the shrubbery.

For all these comradely doings, however, one need only

read *A Child's Garden*—an uncanny piece of reconstruction
—to see Lou as still basically "The Child Alone," burying the
grenadier alone, floating boats in the stream alone. He badly
needed third-person intimacies. Starting late and clumsily, he
would not find them until an age at which most boys are growing beyond them. In the meantime, because he was too greedy
of play and company, an hysterically intemperate day with the
cousins at Colinton would send him to bed for forty-eight hours.
At home, if his parents were incautious, romping games would
give him sleepless nights and subsequent days of nervous misery.

Egocentric as a cat, twitchy as a monkey, inattentive and irregular—not altogether a prepossessing youngster. Though
technically "spoiled," however, he does not seem to have shown
the peevish tantrums and self-seeking demands of the typical
prosperous "spoiled child." Since we take his word as to the
priggish little blasphemer, we can also take it as to a certain
rueful sweetness of disposition: "I had a great fund of simplicity, believed all things and the good rather than the evil,
was very prone to love and inaccessible to hatred, and never
failed in gratitude for any benefit I had the wit to understand." [39] Bits from his mother's Baby Book confirm this description.

Under the circumstances he could easily have been a little
monster, as skewed in personality as he was in body. That he
was not must mean that his emotional stamina was high and
that there was more than spoiling in his rearing. Cummy's love
for him certainly had its own realism. Something saved him
from the logical consequences of the way things deferred to a
superlatively important small boy at 17 Heriot Row, where
people devotedly wrote down what he said in little books,
where, when he was well, all was as reassuring as the Twenty-
Third Psalm. Exploring outside that utter familiarity would
be felt—and most rewardingly—as intemperately keen adventure. Thinking back thirty years later, perhaps of the time he
quakingly burglarized an empty house because he had dared
himself to do it, Louis wrote:

I was a particularly brave boy—this I think of myself . . .
and plunged into adventures and experiments and ran risks
that it still surprises me to recall. But, dear me, what a fear I
was in of that strange blind machinery in the midst of which I
stood; and with what compressed heart and what empty
lungs I would touch a new crank and await developments! I
do not mean to say I do not fear life still; I do; and that terror
(for an adventurer like myself) is still one of the chief joys
of living.[40]

Edinburgh as he first saw it, as one still sees it for that matter,
is simply the most striking principal city in the English-speaking world, New York not excepted. It must have been almost
as astounding before, in the late eighteenth century, it genteelly rebelled against smells and tumbledown gloom, and expanded into the New Town. When Louis was born the process was still going on, demolishing perpendicular slums here,
building stone-cut mansions backed by horizontal slums there.
But the principal features were the same as now:

Up the backbone of a ridge toward the huge blocky Castle
advances a procession of spires and harsh gray-black buildings
still close in spirit to the artificial cragginess of the former Old
Town. The Calton Hill, topped with a spurious "ruin," makes
a bizarre finial; beyond it Arthur's Seat shows the independent dignity of an isolated volcanic cone. Edinburgh has an
extraordinary amount of sky. Its light, sometimes as if reflected from a gray-iron mirror, sometimes swimmingly sunny,
is just right for the geometrical decorum of the New Town.
To the southwest the Pentland Hills cushion the horizon. To
the north, when the air is clear, lie the widening estuary of the
Forth, the remote loom of the Highlands, the indefinably extensive coast of Fife.

The Old Town retains many "closes"—steep, squeezed alleys,
often overbuilt into mere tunnels, falling left and right from
the High Street as reminder of what the nobility and gentry
of Scotland once considered fit to live in—proper setting for

Deacon Brodie, skilful thief and workman and patron saint of
double-livers; for Major Weir, the urban warlock, his devilish walking stick running ahead of him down the greasy-wet
steps; for turbulent and gnarly John Knox, spiritual father
of Scotland—all of whom Louis celebrated. Even in the New
Town, presumably built to Regency taste for elbow-room and
classic regularity, Edinburgh is devious and surprising. Streets
dip and twist into sudden intimacy with the ravine of the
Water of Leith or fly over it on lofty bridges. Solemnly stone-
lined avenues drop, lengthen, and open to frame views of Fife
or the Pentlands in a fashion that only San Francisco can equal.

In Lou's time Princes Street cannot have seemed quite so
droll a museum of the ugliest Victorian architecture, but it
already had the astonishing *vue d'optique* of the Old Town
spread before it and looked into the gorge overhung by the
Castle Rock, so like a Salvator Rosa background pampered
with lawns and gaudy flower beds. Any reasonably comprehen-
sive view of this city is unique. No two elements are ever on the
same level, none is horizontal, the composition has the planes
of a junk heap and the skyline of a smutty fairyland.

It was long ago when the child was first becoming aware of
this bizarre marvel, longer ago than the modern feel of much
of his career implies. The Crimean War was the first news that
penetrated to him; earnestly he played soldier and prayed for
the troops, founding a romantic admiration for soldiering that
he never lost. In that decade railroads and iron ships were
still marvels. Not for thirty years would technical changes now
taken for granted put telephones into his fiction and prepare
his copy on typewriters. Mere gas, decorative but ineffective,
strung rows of fireflies over the city's hills and prospects;
gingerly experiment with electricity would not come for
thirty years either. "With ladder and with light" the lamp-
lighter scuttled from post to post as dusk came on. It sounds
much older still to hear that, when Louis was born, a few sedan-
chairs still survived—so much older than the fact that he was
still in skirts when Darwin and Wallace published the explo-

sive works that would revolutionize the thinking he grew up
with and provide a bitter idiom for reciprocally disembowel-
ing battles between himself and his father.

It was hardly the designers' fault that, built during the
Napoleonic wars when seasoned timber was scarce, 17 Heriot
Row eventually suffered sagging floors. Otherwise—if one neg-
lects bad heating, insanitary plumbing, and wasteful use of
cubage—such ample New Town mansions, ranked in gracious
duplication, cared for by servants working for a pittance, were
well engineered. The Stevenson house still looks out, practically unaltered, on Queen Street Gardens, green and primly
private; the stair well is still chilly and beautiful; the neighborhood is still full of the eminent advocates and judges who
man the town's first and most respectable industry. Take auto-
mobiles off the street and the memorial plaque from the wall
and Louis, coming home tomorrow, would see no reason not to
try his latchkey.

The country for twenty miles round this house was the topo-
graphical placenta that nourished him. Often and far though
he traveled, he remained a mash fermented in the Lothians,
even if distilled by a French alchemy. I do not know at what age
he began to find this environment as such stimulating. Perhaps
his first turn of wonder at familiar things—the writer's and
painter's disease—came from the brilliant names of places in
and about Edinburgh: Cannonmills, Morningside, Comely
Bank, Fairmilehead, Portobello, Goldenacre. . . . Certainly
his first gloating over local detail—a habit that would enrich his
life—occurred at Colinton. The house was merely old and gray
and substantial. But the "well of sunshine" on the south lawn;
the lethal shadow of the great yew still standing against the
stable wall, defying grass to grow beneath it; the Water of
Leith pouring between river wall and wooded bluff—all roused
receptiveness in this small, self-centered soul. Colinton was
then a country village deep in its ravine, living on small water
mills manufacturing paper and snuff and looking for all the
world like a set for a Barrie novel. The snuff-mill's pouring

sluiceway was culminating glory for the miniature rapids that led exploring children up- and downstream. It was the same stream that led along Warriston Row to the cemetery, but that prosaic and befouled urban watercourse never seemed identical with Colinton's. Brawling water to lull the ears, steeping sunshine for born-chilly back and shoulders, refuse paper-pulp and snuff pungent in the nose, brown shallows and creamy little cascades for the eyes—such things were grateful education for the senses. In later life Louis had no use for fresh water standing still; he tolerated the stuff, he wrote Henry James, only in motion or else well qualified with whisky.

The annual contrast of gloom, chill, and illness at home with sun, warmth, and relative health at Colinton in summer came to an end in Louis's tenth year with Grandfather Balfour's death, which exiled the cousins from their common paradise and left Louis as sun-hungry as a pumpkin vine. His family's alternate solution of the problem where to summer turned his attention to the sea—his other lifelong obsession.

The new railroad was enabling Edinburgh to work farther east along the Firth in search of sea breezes during what Scotland considers warm weather. The Stevensons tried Portobello, Prestonpans—where Lou first mounted a pony—inland Peebles, where he rode much, finally settling on North Berwick, where the Firth opens wide to the sea, then undergoing transformation from fishing village to resort complete with rambling hotels and golf courses. In Louis's day its advantages were merely a proudly beautiful coast working up in emphasis through rhythmic beaches backed by North Berwick Law to the rousing melodrama of Tantallon and the Bass Rock. Against this backdrop Edinburgh's young built sand castles and splashed in the North Sea—which Lou liked—or, when older, roamed cliffs and dunes on their own strange amusements. Here the boy apparently began to learn more or less how to get on with strangers of his own age. The early adolescent of "The Lantern-Bearers" had advanced far beyond being merely bullied by contemporaries. Years later the men who had been boys with him on the links recalled him as a not unaccepted member of the community, as apt as anybody to climb precarious rocks or tap on timid householders' windows after dark or dabble in (that fine Scots word) skulduddery.[41]

That was sheer gain. Here also he seems to have turned conscious observer. Detail now gathered came back firm on demand because firmly realized at the time, in contrast with the total-recall impressionism of Colinton and *A Child's Garden*. Wind, tide, dunes, and thwarted trees in *The Pavilion on the Links;* birds and giddy height and basking isolation on the Bass in *Catriona;* five-sensed mental photography prepared him to write of them in Monterey or Samoa as if he had been there only the day before. It has often been pointed out that Stevenson practically never wrote of a place while there, even preferred backgrounds far away and different from where he happened to be. This is implicit in his early discovered and perpetually valued gift of remembering a feeling, unmarred by his turning self-conscious about it—at, I should guess, the age of fifteen or so.

It was certainly not lively at thirteen. In 1863 the Stevensons, including a girl-cousin and Cummy, set out to winter on the Riviera, Louis's first prolonged journey. In view of his later renown in travel books, the results were astonishingly meager. He sketched a few picturesque Mentonese on the flyleaf of Cummy's diary;[42] remembered the breath-demanding staired streets of medieval Rocquebrune, the smell of lemon blossoms, the picturesque shabbiness of the guard escorting the carriage into Rome, the scenery of the Brenner Pass, which he eventually worked into "Will o' the Mill"—a small bag for eight months and thousands of leisurely miles in places so unlike Scotland. No traces whatever survive of the next winter, which mother and son also spent on the Côte d'Azur.

Impression had been far greater a year or so before when, accompanying his father on a tour of lighthouses, the boy had unexpectedly learned that they were to cross Magus Muir in Fife. That meant much indeed to Cummy's pupil in Covenanting history—Magus Muir, where Balfour of Burleigh and his troop of cold-drawn fanatics dragged the archbishop from his carriage and piously killed him. Bookish and emulous, Louis was already writing away at historical romances in the vein of Scott. Hackston of Rathillet, the accessory who stood by, approving the deed but feeling privately bound not to lay a hand on the old man in either pity or injury, was the hero who possessed him—not Balfour, though the leader was a distant relative. This appealed where the charred loaves of the Romans' baking at Pompeii had not. It appears that the weedy boy's hyperaesthesia would have to grow out from home in widening circles.

His last summer before the University saw the Stevensons taking Swanston Cottage for summer use. As Flora Gilchrist showed St. Ives, the place is visible from the Castle—a sprinkle of gray stone in a scatter of trees among fields reaching up to the eastern spur of the Pentlands, Caerketton's raw scars of detritus directly behind and above, like a huge sighting-mark. Though a golf course now stretches behind it, and a scurf of new villas has crept out from Fairmilehead, sheep and hay are still going concerns at Swanston. In Louis's time it was pure country cheerfully near the city. Long walks had already taught him the Pentlands, as well as the lyrical view from Queensferry, where David Balfour would be kidnapped, and the sluggish haven at Cramond where Roman galleys had moored. But in these Swanston summers, when any glance out of his bedroom window showed the great hills looming over the tame garden, he fell in love for the first time. For the next twenty-seven years these "hills of home" were his symbol of youth, Scotland, reality come close. Again the Covenanters helped: Rullion Green, where Dalziel drove the faithful like a sheep-killing dog, was a few miles one way; the Pentlands gave their name to the whole tragedy that culminated in the battle. But the most precious place was secretly hidden: Glencorse Church, tangled in woods on its bluff over the meadow:

Do you know where the road crosses the burn under Glencorse Church? Go there, and say a prayer for me: . . . See that it's a sunny day; . . . stand on the right-hand bank just where the road goes down into the water, and shut your eyes, and if I don't appear to you! [43]

It is a stream of no special quality in a tranquil, shady spot. But nothing makes a place special like having been young and broody there.

Changeling

O, I wad like to ken—to the beggar-wife says I—
Hoo a' things come to be whaur we find them when we try,
The lasses in their claes an' the fishes in the sea.
—*It's gey an' easy speirin'*, says the beggar-wife to me.

—"The Spaewife"

H E HAD already been writing for years. Not all the young and broody who do that keep it up for life.

There really are people—if rarer than is often assumed—who *have* to write. Why they put such extravagant value on words is still obscure. Lump it with the way of a serpent on a rock. The force of the urge can be disproportionate to the talent challenged—it also haunts the frustrated hack, the precious amateur, the hair-trigger reporter. But, whatever his caliber, this never-flagging love affair between himself and the components of the dictionary is one sign of the born writer.

In the future that Louis envisaged schooling, earning, loving had no major portions. He was committed to writing as fatally as a vendetta-haunted Corsican is to vengeance.

It boded well for his calling and election that, when comparison was at all possible, others' verbal successes impressed and excited him more than his own. That was more or less true of him all his life. He read with greedy eclecticism, the shrewd generosity of the writer's perfect reader. The galvanics of the *Family Paper* soon sublimated into a higher power of zest for Scott and Dumas. At 17 Heriot Row there was much reading aloud of both sacred and profane material; the knotty rumblings of the English Bible were excellent preparation for the "terrible black stormy day" when Louis's mother read *Macbeth* to the child "and I had newts and snakes and others to crawl up and down my spine." [1] "I cannot say I thought the experience agreeable . . . to be thus ravished by a giant . . . " [2]

But it was ravishment, not fidgeting incomprehension, and a landmark in the boy's life, never marred by his amusement at discovering years later that his mother had expurgated the porter's lines in the knocking scene. Shakespeare early enticed him into the harmonies and violences of the other great Jacobeans, Webster in particular. Louis was earnestly trying to imitate *The White Devil* at an age when most boys of his station were sturdily reading either nothing or W. Harrison Ainsworth.

But he liked Ainsworth too. He could wolf down *Samson Agonistes* today and *Fleurs du mal* tomorrow; simultaneously worship Bunyan and learn the early Swinburne by heart; absorb Mrs. Todgers's idea of a wooden leg right on top of Spencer's definition of evolution, sandwich bites of Montaigne between lumps of Walt Whitman. It is dizzying to deal with a taste that eventually bestowed superlatives on *The Paston Letters, Crime and Punishment, Cashel Byron's Profession, Typee, Roderick Hudson, The Sorrows of Werther*, and *Sigurd the Volsung*. This voraciousness did not come of that modern reluctance to exist to oneself without reading, smoking, listening, or looking that properly annoys Aldous Huxley. Louis's was active reading, antennae always at full stretch, following the author with appropriate glee while coolly heeding successive occurrence and attempted solutions of technical problems. But he was never the pedantic student of literary conventions, so often mistaken for a critic. Instead of evolutionary botanist, he was wine-taster, vineyardist, and Bacchante combined. So, though he had strong and sometimes unworthy likes and dislikes, he lacked what could be fairly called prejudice. And, in final token of arriving at freedom of his craft—a privilege too indiscriminately bestowed in his day as in ours—he consistently relished work of character alien to his own aims. This came of early seizure with a rare kind of ambition that, to many, will seem getting the cart before the horse: "It was not so much that

I wished to be an author (though I wished that too) as that I had vowed that I would learn to write." [3]

The case has a history, of course. There was Cummy's taste for resounding statement of impressive ideas. Louis's father had a habit, infecting an imitative little son, of putting himself to sleep with self-told tales of stagecoaches and highwaymen—Victorian equivalent of the Wild West; insisted on pungent and precise expression of anything he chose to say; and kept a stern fatherly eye on the way the boy wrote in his letters home. When Louis was six, an uncle offered a prize among the cousins for the best History of Moses; Louis's dictated entry—his illustrations showed the Children of Israel wearing top hats and smoking pipes, both of which Thomas Stevenson did on occasion—won a special award. But most of the small Stevensons and Balfours met such stimuli, whereas few of them followed Smout over the fence separating the "creative" from the solid professions. The child had long been gabbling to himself rhapsodies that he called "songstries" in involved rhythms of some originality—at least as his father, secreted behind the bedroom door, took them down. Though one cannot account for talent, it is fascinating to watch and describe.

So much for talent. Intelligence is not essential to a writing career, though it helps. Through his mother's record of Louis's first years runs a thread of spontaneous, logical inquiry uncommon so long before schooling, the light glancing along a sort of edge unusual in the run of bright sayings of the children. His rearing—or perhaps the theology-mindedness endemic among Scots—posed most of this thinking-aloud in religious terms: At three, hearing that sheep and horses knew nothing of God, he wanted the Bible read aloud to them. He was troubled by a sober fear that he would be unable to play "nicely" on his harp in Heaven. Told of the "naughty woman" anointing Christ's feet, he asked why God had seen fit to make her naughty? a question that, after sonorous laboring, even the Westminster Confession leaves unanswered. Again, if God had lent man His Holy Spirit, how could He remain good? Before he was six, Louis had deduced from Christ's dying to save mankind in general that he, Louis Stevenson, must be saved in particular and so need no longer doubt whether he was good or qualified for salvation—a point on which the end of Ignorance in *The Pilgrim's Progress* may soon have reëducated him. This was no infant prodigy, but the intellectual faculty does seem to have been unusually lively, making him a solemnly unexpected child, given to sweet reasonableness when apart from other children. Having girded on a new toy sword, all glowing brass and gleaming tin, he was distressed when, to guard against drafts, they made him put on that most unmilitary garment, a shawl. "Do you think it will look like a night march?" he asked.

Actual scribbling began as soon as he learned to write at the age of six, though he long preferred to dictate when Cummy or his mother would stand amanuensis. At two of his schools he took the lead in schoolboy magazines in manuscript, a surviving example of which has him imitating the *Family Paper* tradition in a serial called *The Banker's Ward;* other efforts were in the tradition of "boys' stories" of ships, islands, post chaises, and precipices. Then, as he entered his teens, he began the process later described too well and too fully for the good of his reputation:

I was always busy on my own private end, which was to learn to write. . . . Description was the principal field of my exercise; for to anyone with senses there is always something worth describing. . . . But I worked in other ways also; often accompanied my walks with dramatic dialogues, in which I played many parts; and often exercised myself in writing down conversations from memory. This . . . only taught me (so far as I have learned them at all) the lower and less intellectual elements of the art, the choice of the essential note and the right word: things that to a happier constitution had perhaps come by nature. . . . there was perhaps more profit, as there was certainly more effort, in my secret labours at home. Whenever I read a book or a passage that particularly

pleased me, in which a thing was said or an effect rendered
with propriety, in which there was either some conspicuous
force or some happy distinction in the style, I must sit myself
down and set myself to ape that quality. I was unsuccessful
and knew it; . . . but at least in these vain bouts, I got some
practice in rhythm, in harmony, in construction and the
coordination of parts. I have thus played the sedulous ape
to Hazlitt, to Lamb, to Wordsworth, to Sir Thomas Browne,
to Defoe, to Hawthorne, to Montaigne, to Baudelaire and to
Obermann. . . .

That, like it or not, is the way to learn to write; whether
I have profited or not, that is the way. It was so Keats learned,
and there never was a finer temperament for literature than
Keats's; it was so, if we could trace it out, that all men have
learned; . . . But that is not the way to be original! It is
not; nor is there any way but to be born so. Nor yet, if you are
born original, is there anything in this training that shall
clip the wings of your originality.[4]

I quote this at such length because some critics, choosing to
disregard the unanswerable comment on "originality," have
used that "sedulous ape" as proof of Stevenson's unimpor-
tance; whereas, to be impregnable, the position lacks only
clearer distinction between conscious and unconscious imitation. What Louis did with his eyes open most writers, larger
or smaller, do with some illusion of spontaneity. Both are
good approaches. Such ground-breaking pioneers as Whitman
or Joyce must develop third approaches, or fourth or fifth for
all I know; but this immersion in the idiom of one's predecessors worked magnificently for Homer and Shakespeare and
fairly well for Louis. This was not the only time that his witty
frankness about himself was to be used against him. My only
objection to the passage as it stands is that it omits several of
his traceably significant models or molding influences: Carlyle,
Thoreau, Walter Pater, whose informally graceful skill in the
biographical essay is so evident in Louis's early articles on

Villon and Charles d'Orléans,[5] which take the reader into the subject with the smoothness of stepping on a slow escalator.

Self-apprenticeship was well under way when, in his sixteenth year, he first appeared in print. Proud of his son's bookwormish Covenanting lore, Thomas Stevenson encouraged him to drop Scott-like romances set in "the killing-time" and write instead a factual account of the incidents culminating at Rullion Green. The consequent *The Pentland Rising*, a slender pamphlet published at Thomas's expense, is dim, smothered, and blocky, the best of it consisting of extracts from Cummy's favorite Patrick Walker; but even so it reads more like the work of a clumsy and superficial scholar of thirty than that of a gangling boy, just reaching his full height. How few successful writers of our—or Louis's—time had first publication subsidized by an approving father! But that does not imply lack of friction as Thomas's son circled nearer and nearer to exclusively literary aspirations. Louis and his father paid equal shares in bitterness for every farthing of the thousands of pounds required to crutch the promising invalid into independence.

The difficulty—superficially at least—was that Louis wanted exclusively to write, to do nothing but lead ideas and actions down the ecstatic dance of words for forty or fifty years; whereas, to his father, writing could be little more than an admirable hobby. That he had subsidized his son's first publication did not mean that he approved of authorship as a profession. The great Scottish writers—and, until recently, English too—had typically combined writing with stabler incomes, Carlyle being one of the few exceptions. Scott had been an eminent law-officer with a private income; Burns a farmer presently seeking government appointment as exciseman; Robert Fergusson had a routine office post, Allan Ramsay was a bookseller. . . . Recent exceptions on the other side of the Border, such as Dickens, had shown that meager education and exuberant talent could distil wealth and eminence out of exclusive writing for a living. But the elder notion that writing was either starveling hack-work or else an amusement of prestige to which gentlemen trained for more serious business might condescend was still strong among educated Britons imperfectly familiar with literary affairs. In any case it was hardly conceivable that Robert Stevenson's grandson would not enter the old firm. No harm in writing—but the boy would unquestionably take that busy and responsible place in the world befitting a Stevenson and an engineer.

All things considered, the position was reasonable. Louis was aware enough of Thomas's fairness to enrol willingly at sixteen as student of engineering at the University of Edinburgh. All he would learn there was indirect, through people he met, sidelines that enticed him, subjects of study that determined him promptly to reject them. By being all that writing promised not to be—formal, prosy, tender of unstimulating mediocrity—the University did much to confirm his determination to write.

During vacations Thomas sent Louis for experience to the firm's works in progress. At Anstruther he enjoyed splashing round in work boats and exploring the sea bottom in a diving suit among weeds and fishes. But he was scandalously unprofessional, having to write his father asking the number of pounds in a ton—a datum that should have been as firmly in his mind as the rhyme-scheme of an Italian sonnet. Apropos of the working sketches necessary before photography, he confessed: "When I'm drawing I find out something I have not measured or, having measured, have not noted, or, having noted, cannot find." [6] He spent feverish evenings in his lodgings on a deathless and endless poem, *Voces Fidelium*, and truthfully scribbled in a notebook presumably reserved for the study of geometry:

> My candle goes not out by night
> And many a time
> I worked into the morning light
> To find a rhyme. . . .

> I labour harder at my trade
> Line upon line discreetly laid
> The filium travelling grade by grade
> From verse to verse
> Than Adam laboured with his spade
> After the curse.[7]

In the whole picture his parents could have found consolation only in his showing, by nocturnal devotion to *Voces Fidelium*, that there was no lazy bone in his strange body.

Louis jumped at tours of inspection round Scottish lights and harbors in the government yacht *Pharos* because, if you please, a similar trip with Grandfather Robert had moved Scott to write *The Pirate*. Seeing the wild Hebrides and Orkneys gave him that gruesome sense of the menace of these seas that underlies "The Merry Men" and *Kidnapped*. During several weeks on Earraid (Eilean Aros of "The Merry Men") when it was quarry and base for the building of the Dhu Heartach light, he grew most familiar with the seaweed on the rocks, the great boulders marching down into the sea like troops of cattle, and the senseless, ominous runes that wrote themselves far out on the water during calms. But these were hardly the kind of data and experience that his father had in mind.

As Louis grew older, father and son cultivated stormy discrepancies of approach during their long walks together out of 17 Heriot Row or some country inn. On the bank of Allan Water or on a dune behind Gullane Sands, Thomas would point out the stream undercutting here, laying down a sandbar there; the headland diverting the swell yonder, meaning that a groin elsewhere might build land . . . seeking to share with his son his own intimacy with the dynamics of mineral debris under stress of moving water. All the while Louis was intent on the sinister backsucking of the undertow or the raised pitch of the voice of the current narrowing between rocks. Never did two people look at the same things with such different eyes.

Years later, however, it proved to have been not altogether futile. Having absorbed some of his father's professional terms in spite of himself, Louis's writing often showed an engineer's—or topographer's—eye. Though born of a map, *Treasure Island* needs none for elucidation; the text alone gives all anybody could ask of the lay of the hills and the set of the current out of the anchorage behind Skeleton Island. The divinity student of "The Merry Men" is all engineer when determining where in Sandag Bay the wreck must lie. Both this and *The Pavilion on the Links* show their author to have been, though willy-nilly, " . . . trained to study seas from the land with a view to seamen's dangers." [8] Middle-aged in Samoa, Louis could even manage some rough surveying on his own jungle property, delighted as a child when his triangles proved out properly.

All that the University could give the heedless monomaniac of 1867, however, was unsupervised leisure. Until then Louis, as child of the house, was supposed to be at home when otherwise unaccounted for. Now, as student, he was entitled regularly to depart after breakfast, and walk across the ridge of the New Town and the spine of the Old to the gracious, sooty quadrangle housing the equalitarian-tending seat of learning that so vividly expressed Scots acuteness and Scots penury. There tenacious country boys in patched clothes, living on oatmeal and aspiration, fought for learning on the same benches as the broadcloth-warm sons of bankers, advocates, and generals. This environment, apparently less spiteful than it might have been, was bound to do Louis good. But he had only meager opportunity to observe his fellows at lectures or examinations—because he was seldom there. Instead he was religiously outdoing his father in studied truancy. His one piece of upper-classman advice to a young cousin entering the University consisted of a reliable method for getting credit for attending classes without actually doing so.

Conventional studious habits were always alien to him. A tutor who read Latin with him recalled how he rejected dictionaries, insisting on learning unfamiliar words solely from context—a method with certain long-run advantages but not leading to high standing in class.[9] The hour for Greek or trigonometry too often found him moping in Greyfriars Cemetery near the University. His sense of Covenanting history kept him obsessedly aware that on these gravestones they signed the Covenant; there under that columned cupola lies "Bluidy Mackenzie"; there in the lower corner stands the doggerel-inscribed tablet, complete with stone footnote, to the tragic fanatics whom Mackenzie so grimly sent to slaughter. Even on a sunny day cheerfulness is difficult in Greyfriars. On wet days, such as Louis often saw there, with damp and mold greasily smeared over the lopsided skulls and tasteful friezes of thigh-bones that decorate its ancient monuments, the suggestion is markedly suicidal. It apparently suited some of the boy's moods.

Rutherford's pub—"The Pump"—catering to students offered more cheer and less external moisture. Louis was there frequently but not dangerously so, since, perhaps on principle, Thomas Stevenson kept him on ten shillings a week pocket-money until he was twenty-three years old, a sum that, even in 1870, did not permit large dissipations. When the weather was supportable—in Edinburgh this means that one is neither soaked to the skin nor blown off one's feet—the potential Apologist for Idlers took his umbrella and permeated the most picturesque of cities. While professors, dry in both senses, expounded leverage or the binomial theorem, he was learning Edinburgh as thoroughly as a cab-driver or policeman. Hawk-nosed and stooped, the spring in his step belying his apparent frailty, "restless and questing as a spaniel," [10] he drifted from Portobello to Corstorphine, from Leith to Morningside, down every close off the High Street, up between Salisbury Crags and Arthur's Seat, through every frigid, stinking court down Greenside, where "lands" ten stories tall still remind the outsider what life could be like before elevators. He looked about when that suited, humped along in unseeing absorption when it did not, eagerly exposed himself to

place and weather in order further to cultivate his own acquaintance.

For this sort of education classrooms were pointless. He
was learning what people looked like, talked like, acted like in
queer corners, intentionally hypersensitive about it: "I don't
like being so sensitive in town," he presently wrote Mrs.
Sitwell, ". . . for the impressions are more often painful than
agreeable." [11] He might amuse himself today by slipping a half-
penny into the pocket of a ragged boy asleep on the grass;
tomorrow by borrowing the outfit, including bag of greasy
bones, of an old-bones man, presumably to see how it felt to
be a quasi-outcast. Presently he was dabbling in spirit-
ualism. . . . [12]

Most of the time he was doleful and lonely, given to crises
of gloom, lacking a confidante, for he was still the socially
spoiled child. Gross eccentricities of dress were yet to come,
but he was already a curious figure, standoffish, silent, exuding
tacit scorn likely to put off both the earnest and the gay among
students. He was living off books, sucking his own paws, bur-
rowing within himself, leaning over the bridge that crossed
the railroad in the gully below Princes Street and yearning
southward with the rushing, smoking trains. If not too prolonged, such a period can be healthy, provided it is voluntary.
The misanthrope *malgré lui* is pitiable. Louis needed rescue.
In view of the scorn of respectability that he was already developing, it is amusing that it was his family's conventional
social prestige that helped him out of the slough in time.

The University contained—still contains on the same basis—
a literary and debating club, the Speculative Society, electing
members from among undergraduates of presumed intellectual promise. It appears that the weekly meetings, held by
candlelight, evening dress mandatory, carried flavor; take that
on faith, for no outsider has ever attended a session. In Louis's
time it was pretty well a gentlemen's sons' affair, a known name
as well as brains implicitly required for election. In spite of
his misanthropy, Louis's standing as Lewis Balfour's and

Robert Stevenson's grandson combined with rumors that, though unprepossessing, he was clever, to admit him to the Spec. He particularly relished the fact that, having its own rules independent of the University, it permits smoking; and that, among the striking number of Scots eminent at the bar or in literature who have joined it in youth, Scott is conspicuous, his ill-spelled minutes of a meeting still hanging on the walls of its snug room.

Louis's first meeting was not propitious. He was snubbed during preliminaries, made his maiden speech in a passion of diffidence, was further snubbed in the interval when members traditionally adjourn to The Pump, and snubbed again after adjournment, walking glumly home by himself. But eventually his readiness in give-and-take—he was a poor formal debater—and his zest for parliamentary sword-play worked him out a valued place. He was once one of five rotating presidents, a meager honor but spelling general acceptance among the members. He wrote a fellow-member: "O, I do think the Spec. is about the best thing in Edinburgh." [13] (This was meant as a compliment, though, in view of some of his opinions of Edinburgh, it might have been faint enough praise.) It is highly appropriate that the British ensign flown on the *Casco* now hangs over the principal fireplace of the Spec.

Much of Louis's affection for it derived from its bringing him friends, a thing he had never had before, in demonstration of how rewarding comradeship could be. Thenceforth he collected friends, sank heavy emotional capital in them, gave and accepted important services, and grieved bitterly when death or quarrels took them away. His times allowed *friend* a significant warmth greater than ours now permit. Our comradeships between young men may be equally close, but explicit acknowledgment is rarer; whereas in the 1870's, particularly in intellectual-aesthetic circles, "friends" were gloatingly added up and acknowledged claims not dissimilar to, though less formal than, those of blood-brothers in preliterate cultures. Let no fool try to read perversion into the above. It is difficult to comprehend Louis's relations with Bob Stevenson or Henley or Henry James without understanding precisely what was meant and not meant by his ability frankly to write, "I love you, Henley, from my soul."

These new friends of Louis's, appearing at Heriot Row to take a place at dinner or a cup of tea at supper, had played as children in Queen Street Gardens or the equivalent, had well-considered parents and irreproachable sisters. James Walter Ferrier, for instance, was son of an eminent professor of philosophy at St. Andrews; Sir Walter Simpson (Athelred of "Talk and Talkers," often irreverently called The Bart.) had recently come into the baronetcy honoring his late physician-father for exploring the anaesthetic uses of chloroform. . . . Louis loved them like brothers and, whether leaping up to make a mischievous point of order at the Spec. or extravagantly preaching Whitman over beer at Rutherford's, was warmly loved in return.

Their net influence, however, was not so steadying as their social standing seemed to promise. It was a time of shifting values —as indeed most times have been for several hundred years—and, though the University contained plenty of stable youngsters, Louis had signally failed to choose them for intimates. Ferrier, for instance, was wittily and warmly erratic in behavior and temperamental in tastes, and died in his thirties as climax of a sort of cultivated Rake's Progress. Louis averred that Charles Baxter, who became his special colleague in extravagant scorning of University, city, Kirk, state, and cosmos, had the personality of Samuel Pepys and the conversational style of Congreve—a combination ill calculated to please Edinburgh. (Michael Finsbury of *The Wrong Box* embodies the stocky *sang froid*[14] with which Baxter went through strange antics with Louis.) Professors lecturing chill classes were annoyed when Louis, slight and insolently supercilious, and Baxter, bulky and insolently solemn, would enter, listen a few minutes, exchange glances of pitying contempt—and then casually leave. They amused themselves by making up impressive packages of trash and sending them to eminent citizens, spent whole afternoons buying quack remedies from street-hawkers in order to enjoy their patter, and bestowed picturesque *alter egos* on each other: Louis was Johnstone, a drunken and dishonest elder of the Kirk, Baxter was Thomson, his close friend and comparable whited sepulcher. For the next twenty years any given letter of Louis's to Baxter was likely to break into Johnstone's rich Scots letting Thomson know the latest about the state of his purse and peculations or whorings.[15] They found and made a cult of a shady pub run by a screamingly bad-tempered publican named Brash—Louis's sonnet-sequence, "Brasheana," includes some of his more skilful local verse. When in funds they often drank too much. When penniless they went to "The Republic," the small house where Simpson's sister looked after him and a couple of other young bachelors, and talked one another blue in the face.

Baxter remained not only Louis's legal and financial mainstay but the lifelong focus of bibulously bright memories. In 1875 he was addressee of a Burns-inspired epistle:

> . . . Sae let us in the comin' days
> Stand sicker on our ancient ways—
> The strauchtest road in a' the maze
> Since Eve ate apples;
> And let the winter wet our cla'es—
> We'll wet our thrapples—[16]

as well as of Louis's elegy on a dipsomaniac clerk of court of his and Baxter's acquaintance:

> . . . Whusky and he were pack thegether,
> Whate'er the hour, whate'er the weather,
> John kept himself wi' mistened leather
> An' kindled spunk.
> Wi' him there was nae askin' whether—
> John was aye drunk. . . .[17]

The whole atmosphere is in what Louis wrote on hearing that Baxter was planning to marry:

I wish you a rare good time and plenty of children . . . the past looks very delightful to me; the past when you were not going to be married and I was not trying to write a novel . . . the past where we have been drunk and sober and sat outside grocers' shops on fine dark nights, and wrangled in the Speculative, and heard mysterious whistlings in Waterloo Place, and met missionaries from Aberdeen; generally the past. But the future is a fine thing also in its way; and what's more, it's all we have to come and go upon. So, let us strike up the Wedding March, and bedeck ourselves with the loose and graceful folds of the frock coat, and crown ourselves with Sunday hats as with laurel; and go, leaping and singing and praising God, and under the influence of Champagne and all the finer feelings of humanity, towards that adored edifice, or secular drawing-room, from whence you, issuing forth, shall startle mankind with the first splendours of the wedded Chawles. Proudest moment of my life, C.B.[18]

As in other respectable towns, organized vice in Edinburgh was all the grimier for pretense that it was not there. How much Louis's cronies were involved I do not know; but it is certain that his early researches took him into inexpensive and slatternly "howffs" that shaded off into "shebeens," a background used in *The Misadventures of John Nicholson*.[19] These were the natural prowling-ground of the town's inferior whores. Under the nickname of "Velvet Coat," Louis once recorded, he was rather popular in such dens, a tribute to his personality rather than to his purse. He took pride in being hob and nob with a circle ". . . continually changed by the action of the police-magistrate,"[20] and in friendly relations with madams: "I have been all my days a dead hand at a harridan, I never saw the one yet that could resist me."[21] However self-conscious, this is education, though Louis felt obliged to tell himself that these petty criminals and shatteringly dislocated tarts were sounder than many of the respectable. One of these congenial trollops early took from Velvet Coat his virginity and a shilling or so;

perhaps it was the "robust, great-haunched, blue-eyed young woman of admirable temper and, if you will let me say so of a prostitute, extraordinary modesty," [22] with whom he had a comradely drink years later just before she sailed as an emigrant to the States. Such initiation into full-dress erotics was the custom of the country, probably observed by a large majority of Louis's social peers in youth. In Scotland in 1869 it would have been difficult to come effectually to grips with a girl of his own stratum this side of marriage; and, had he tried and succeeded, her sense of degradation might have warped both for life. Even so, bought-and-paid-for experience was a poor substitute. He was lucky to get away as he did, relatively unscathed, able thirteen years later to describe chastity soberly as "the real curse of a man's life in our state of society—and a woman's too, although, for many reasons, it appears somewhat differently with the enslaved sex." [23]

His own decency—and he was a very decent person—quickly made him an angry protestant against mistreatment of prostitutes:

> . . . if you can make it convenient to be chaste, for God's sake avoid the primness of your virtue; hardness to a poor harlot is a sin lower than the ugliest unchastity. . . . The harm of prostitution lies not in itself but in the disastrous moral influence of ostracism. . . . Hunted religionists become cruel and inhuman, just as ostracised harlots do. . . . A Jew, a Christian, a Mormon, a Thug, were proud of the reproach, and wear the bye-word as a distinction; while you may make many a prostitute cry by merely naming her trade to her.[24]

Accosted one evening by a middle-aged and bedraggled whore, he made an elaborate gesture of dropping a shilling where she could see it so she could pay for her lodging without directly taking charity as a derelict no longer attractive. Though the device was self-conscious and clumsy, the young fellow was as solicitous about it as another might have been about getting his fiancée across a muddy street without dirtying her dainty high boots.

No doubt he derived some of this attitude from Whitman, perhaps some even from the Gospels. Such influences hardly discount the essential chivalry, in the best sense, of such behavior. By fits and starts, more consistently as he matured, Louis showed much of what E. M. Forster called "the educated heart." He intervenes, futilely enough but generously, when he finds a crazy old street-preacher jeered at by street-loungers; he spends most of a night looking after a lost child; he reproaches himself bitterly because it has taken him so long to make up his mind to apologize to a servant for having spoken to her rudely. His courtesy, which often struck Englishmen as foreignly elaborate, had some of this quality: "I remember his gracious kindly manner," wrote one of Baxter's staff years after Louis's visits there, "and his exquisite courtesy. He talked to me, an apprentice on a three-legged stool, as if I had been the most eminent W.S. in Edinburgh." [25]

For all Louis's humaneness toward harlots, however, there was also a morbidity, a steeping sense of gloomy evil, in his explorations of vice. Ten years later he said that the worst of a serious Presbyterian rearing was that it "put a point on lust." [26] As hinted previously, this had begun in his pious infancy:

> Do I not know how nightly, on my bed
> The palpable close darkness shutting round me,
> How my small heart went forth to evil things . . .
> And how my spirit beat
> The cage of its compulsive purity;
> How—my eyes fixed,
> My shot lip tremulous between my fingers
> I fashioned for myself new modes of crime,
> Created for myself with pain and labour
> The evil that the cobwebs of society,
> The comely secrecies of education,
> Had made an itching mystery to mewards. . . .[27]

There may have been more than mere maturing biology in his impulse, growing as the cat found the way to the dairy, toward Edinburgh's dives.

Sins were categorical then, and Sin an entity, hot, dark and monolithic—the dynamic aspect of Evil, black opposite number of the Holy Ghost. Without such concepts Louis might never have written "Markheim" or *Jekyll*. For him a flavor of deliberate emotional destructiveness attached to what he felt as evil, will suddenly married to appetite in a fashion startlingly personified in Mr. Hyde. It could also mean obsessed despair, as when Jekyll dozed off in the park and woke to see Hyde's quasi-animal paw where his large, white, clean hand had been. "I am by nature what they call a very bad person and very greedy of sensation," Louis wrote as a young man, "a poor one if there is not a fine one to be had." [28] That is not so much accurate description as record of how it felt to try to escape from Calvinism to hedonism. Said Chesterton with brilliant accuracy: "Puritanism gave him the key of the cellars rather than the halls of Babylon." [29]

This chimes-at-midnight period must not, however, be envisaged—irresponsible speculation has often so described it— as a welter of drink and a perpetual tumble of frowsy wenches, with Louis "a particularly sordid sinner." [30] Several things make this implausible: He was usually short of money and seldom robust enough for major orgies; nor does it sound like dissipation on the grand scale that, in the very middle of this presumedly drunken, lecherous period, he is found writing that he has missed dinner at home for the first time in a year.

The second wave of biographers of Stevenson used ingenious selection from his early verses salted with the least reliable types of gossip to endow the boy with a desperate and emotionally maiming affair with a blacksmith's blonde daughter (or perhaps a brunette prostitute from the Highlands) whom he romantically nicknamed "Claire." It was most gratifying to find, in Louis's previously inaccessible letters to Mrs. Sitwell, resounding proof that "Claire" as such never existed. Appendix

B gives the details of this really egregious error, the finest example of how to transmute surmise into assumed fact since Samuel Butler so sardonically "proved" that Wordsworth murdered Lucy.

Even more cautious biographers have seen Louis ostracized from respectable Edinburgh on account of his flagrant roistering. This too fails to stand up. His parents duly continued to give "young dinners" well attended by the nicest young bourgeois as Louis's guests. His best friends were, as noted, sons of the best-considered people. No youngster with unmistakable crimson in his reputation would have been permitted a conspicuous part in the Jenkins' theatricals (described later). "I never saw him not greeted in any society he chose to enter," wrote Lord Dunedin of Louis, "though from his own wishes he did not enter society much." [31] Edinburgh had had plenty of practice in looking the other way in such matters, provided young fellows kept within normal range of vice. I suspect that such misconceptions as to the degree of Louis's ostracism came of his own highly colored accounts, sharpened by conscious Bohemianism, of what a misfit he was in the Athens of the North.

Some of his early—and highly autobiographical—verses reach toward a crude sensuality, as in this experiment in "*Petits poèmes en prose*":

I walk the street smoking my pipe
And I love the dallying shopgirl
That leans with rounded stern to look at the fashions; . . .
I love night in the city,
The lighted streets and the swinging gait of harlots.
I love cool pale morning,
In the empty bye-streets,
With only here and there a female figure,
A slavey with lifted dress and the key in her hand,
A girl or two at play in a corner of waste-land
Tumbling and showing their legs and crying out to me loosely.[32]

It is unsettling to be young, male, and fascinated by both Whitman and Baudelaire. Fugitive verses catalogue successive layers of clothes peeling off until "Forth leaps the laughing girl at last" [33]—indication of date, identification of girl both lacking. It is all scanty, but there is no question that much of such verse unpublished until well after Louis's death justifies Colvin's describing him as "a man beset with fleshly frailties, strong appetites and unchecked curiosities." [34]

At least once he had to face the fact that, even in casual carnality, there were two personalities in a kiss. A conscience-ridden little confession to Mrs. Sitwell brings into focus the hypersensitive youth facing this reality:

> . . . I have been thinking a little of my wretchedness when your letters did not come; and the whole business knocked unpleasantly at my conscience. I too let letters go unanswered until they ceased to come from a person to whom the postage even must have been a matter of parsimony; left them unanswered on purpose that they might cease. O God, a thing comes back to me that hurts the heart very much. For the first letter she had bought a piece of paper with a sort of coarse flower-arabesque at the top of it. I wish you would write cruelly about this—I wish you would by God! I want something to make me take up arms in my own defense—no I don't. Only I could not help writing to you because it is in my mind—on my heart; and I hope you won't hate me for it. Only one thing gives me pleasure and it is a very faint one. I never showed the letters to anyone, and some months ago they became insupportable to me and I burnt them. [35]

A cruder youngster would never have thought twice about it. For this and other causes Louis was sick of himself often and often and occasionally put it pointedly into verse:

I have left all upon the shameful field,
  Honour and Hope, my God, and all but life . . . [36]

All day the sea was on one hand,
  The long beach shone with sun and wet—

We walked in trio on the sand,
My shadow, I, and my regret! [37]

Yet it is not true, as sometimes hinted, that he altogether eschewed respectable girls who did not afford him indecorous privileges. In his twenty-first year he is writing to Cousin Bob about a narrow escape from committing himself to an apparently irreproachable girl. The "Duddingstone" verses of the same period also have him "drowned in love" while skating with a girl hand in hand; since Duddingston Loch was where all proper Edinburgh skated, he would hardly have gone there with a dubious partner. This may have been the same young woman mentioned in "A College Magazine," ". . .with whom my heart was at that time somewhat engaged, and who did all that in her lay to break it." [38] Other verses, e.g., "The relic taken, what avails the shrine," may record the demise of some of these affairs.[39]

Since there is no sign that his parents ever challenged his taste for dissipation, the gossip that trickled home about him must have been highly dilute. They can have seen only that his health, his studies, and his spirits were blatantly poor much of the time. He was receptive and had a potentially educated heart quite early; but in this phase he was also confessedly deep under the influence of Hazlitt's querulous, egocentric "On the Spirit of Obligations," which takes so dim a view of human relations. Had he continued in the directions there charted, which apparently appealed to some of his impulses, he would never have been more than a twitchy aesthete of possible talent—a sort of very minor Swinburne. But he was lucky. At the right juncture he acquired a salutary elder friend who not only neutralized some of the more exuberant influences of Baxter, Ferrier & Co. but also shocked him back into the long road toward integrity. Louis was too solid a character altogether to be accounted for by his friends' influences. But he was a resultant, a collaboration between himself and people impinging intimately on him; and this new man was first item in a cast of persons that, as one becomes acquainted with it as Louis's emotional entourage, shows great style and pungency.

It was a woman who brought this about. In 1868 Anne Jenkin, wife of the professor of engineering at the University, was having tea with Louis's mother in the candle-lit drawing-room at 17 Heriot Row. A high, resonant voice out of the deep shadow suddenly joined their talk, giving Mrs. Jenkin, who prided herself on social and aesthetic sensitivity, a sense of rich momentousness. Young Louis had already struck the vein of impetuous brilliance of speech that made him one of the renowned talkers of his day. As she left, a tall, thin figure opened the door for her and she first received the full impact of his convex, high-colored face and great brown eyes full of hasty life. On reaching home she burst out to her husband about this "young Heine with a Scottish accent." [40] Louis would have wriggled with joy to hear her, for Heine had recently become one of his literary heroes.

A woman of presence, if not beauty, and, according to some who saw her, a remarkable amateur actress, Mrs. Jenkin had a salon of respectable Edinburghers sharing her and Fleeming's interest in matters theatrical, musical, philosophical, and literary. Their house was fitted for regular temporary conversion into a theater for their annual play—Shakespeare, Sophocles, Molière perhaps—a great event. The atmosphere *chez* Jenkin was, I am told, a trifle precious, and Jenkin, watching his wife's acting, was overinclined to turn to bystanders with "My God, to think that wonderful woman is my wife!" But it did young Louis great good to be added to this coterie, which a contemporary described as "an oasis in a desert of convention and prejudice." [41] Jenkin never made an actor of him—too wooden on stage, he was allowed only minor parts, the Duke in *Twelfth Night*, Sir Charles Pomander in *Masks and Faces*. But he delighted in the rich costumes that went with such roles and in the champagne-supper that always followed a performance.

Though Mrs. Jenkin was presumably the magnet of the group, it was her husband who specially befriended the boy and so gained himself the most sympathetic of biographers. Louis's *Memoir of Fleeming Jenkin*, lovingly free of the affectionate cant that his subject would have denounced, shows a learned Admirable Crichton crossed with Darius Green. Before taking his academic post, Jenkin had laid more miles of submarine cable than Louis had read books and was a pioneer in applying electricity to transportation. He worked most of his life on a play that would reinterpret Patient Griselda for all time; was a brilliant ice-skater, a fine dancer, a fair actor, enough of a biologist to have had a correction accepted by Charles Darwin and to have written a scientifically significant work on fecundity. He mounted his Greek dramas in costumes that he designed himself on a new theory of classical dress evolved after studying Greek statues and draping live models. Merely from brief press descriptions of Edison's earliest model, he constructed a practical phonograph—Louis talked broad Scots into it and was with difficulty restrained from teaching it how to swear. I am told on excellent authority that some of Jenkin's philosophizings that Louis remembered skilfully anticipate some aspects of such modern philosophers as Whitehead. His harangues on the necessary blood-and-marrow relationship between craft and fine art probably did much to fix Louis's attitude toward creative skills.

This was Cockshot of "Talk and Talkers": "Something of a Herbert Spencer who should see the fun of the thing . . . bottled effervescency, the sworn foe of sleep . . . ," splatteringly able to outdo even Louis at his own wonderful new game of speculating in seven directions at once. Gosse, fellow-member of Jenkin's and Louis's at the Savile Club, wrote, a little silkily:

His only irritating quality, perhaps, was his vociferous omniscience. . . . In Jenkin's presence . . . Stevenson . . . seemed to be resisting an instinctive tendency toward veneration, which Jenkin, to do him justice, was on his part always anxious to break down.[42]

Veneration was certainly there and deserved. Jenkin's union
of mercurial brilliance with a first-class brain privileged him to
call Louis on the carpet whenever necessary without risking
the nose-thumbing reaction that almost anybody else would
have elicited. Once he knew him well, the brittle, scornful youngster never dreamed of not respecting Jenkin—even
respected the man's original and well-thought-out piety. The
way they learned each other illuminates both: To stay in the
University Louis had regularly to secure certificates of class-
attendance from so many professors. Bluff and blarney worked
on the famous and eccentric Professor Blackie, though the boy
might not have been near his Greek class for months. But Jenkin, though already Louis's occasional host, was a gnome of a
man unable to mince words:

"It is quite useless for you to come to me, Mr. Stevenson," he
said. "There may be doubtful cases, there is no doubt about
yours. You have simply *not* attended my class." [43] Unscrupu-
lously brash, Louis pled his father's anger and disappointment.
With a shrewd feeling for what would most corrode this facile
cub, Jenkin gave him both the certificate—on condition that he
never use it to qualify for a degree—and a haunting feeling that
only superior manners had kept him from making it clear what
a dirty business he thought it: "That was the beginning of my
love for Fleeming; I never thought lightly of him afterwards." [44]

Another passage shows how nicely Jenkin had the boy's
measure: Louis had put him a problem of conduct. Jenkin asked what Christ would have advised? Nothing unkind or
cowardly, said Louis, withdrawing to ground as high as possible. True, said Jenkin, pouncing— ". . . nor anything amusing." The tangled process of Louis's growing up may well have
begun at that moment.

This was, in fact, the elder brother of much experience and
some wisdom whom Louis should have had to cuff him into
shape from birth. Already a young atheist, rejoicing in the impertinence of Voltaire, Louis here found a devout man skeptical even of atheism, admitting the friability of social conven-

tions without exhorting free souls to flout them—drily remarking instead that the rebel must be "either very vain or very wise." Louis once undertook to convince him that a given human being could be "irredeemably bad," finally adducing an example that Jenkin had to admit convincing. "That is a bad man," he said. "I wonder if it isn't a very unfortunate thing for you to have met him. . . . This badness is such an easy, lazy explanation. Won't you be tempted to use it, instead of trying to understand people?" [45] On his part, Jenkin's young comrade was wise enough not to let the touch of smugness that some found in the man cause him to reject his ninety-nine parts of sense and salt.

This colt-breaking was imperfect because the animal's mouth was already hard and its heels restless when it arrived. But, in grave gratitude, Louis eventually wrote his other principal mentor: "My dear Colvin, I owe you and Fleeming Jenkin, the two older men who took the trouble, and knew how to make a friend of me, everything that I have or am." [46] Hearing that in the other world, Jenkin probably wagged his leprechaun's beard, wiped his bright eye, and resumed his experiments in improving the design of celestial harps and revising the harmonies of the choral music sung round the Great White Throne.

It was most fortunate that Mrs. Jenkin had been impressed and that her husband was perspicacious enough to like the boy. Many did not, particularly students outside his special circle. Growing affectations combined against him with his reputed intellectual extravagance. Seeing Louis make one of his rare appearances in the University quadrangle, a classmate waited as he approached and then announced: "Ah! here comes the Gifted Boy!" [47] Gloatingly Henley recorded that, as he got this story, Louis's vaunted cleverness could produce no reply. I doubt if Whistler and Shaw between them could have thought of one for him.

The Gifted Boy

It's strange that God should fash to frame
The yearth and lift sae hie,
An' clean forget to explain the same
To a gentleman like me.

Thae gutsy, donnered ither folk,
Their weird they well may dree;
But why present a pig in a poke
To a gentleman like me?

—"The Counterblast Ironical"

THOMAS STEVENSON would have done well to consult Jenkin and perhaps learn that an engineer as gifted as himself thought it useless to urge Louis into the family tradition. But such a step, in any case unlikely to occur to Louis's independent father, might have done small good. For Louis was on the verge of another unsettling, if enriching, phase:

By 1870 Cousin Bob (Robert Alan Mowbray Stevenson, son of Uncle Alan, three years Louis's senior) appeared from Cambridge with a degree and a hunger to paint. The pair had already been close in childhood, when Bob lived the winter of 1857-58 at Heriot Row; his incisive sister Katherine was also a special playmate. Louis frequently harked back to Bob's and his make-believes: Sugar or milk on porridge set them on tales of countries under heavy snow or subject to gradual flood. They invented two imaginary islands, Encyclopaedia and Nosingtonia, each requiring a map and the concoction of elaborate and tumultuous history. It was Bob who introduced Louis to the fun of coloring the printed scenes and characters of Victorian toy theaters, the occasion of "A Penny Plain." Later years, however, had taken Bob and Katherine to France. Half old playmate, half picturesque stranger, Bob now returned, long, lean, dark—"so odd and foreign-looking" [1] that, in 1875, Belle Osbourne called him a gentleman-gypsy—brimming with words, attitudes, and ideas acquired in France and among fledgling aesthetes at Cambridge, pouring all of it over Louis just as the younger was most apt for deviancy.

Second sight would have moved Thomas to have his eccentric and charming nephew kidnapped and held for ten years on the Bass Rock. For the instability that plagued Stevensons struck this branch harder: Bob's father, Thomas's brother, early brilliant in the family firm, succumbed at forty-five to "a sudden shattering of the nervous system" [2] that immobilized him professionally and personally the rest of his life. An obsessed recluse for thirteen years, he died before his children were grown. It is hardly surprising that Bob was always queer as Dick's hatband and Katherine little less so, both with great charm. Louis used facets of Bob's character in "The Young Man with the Cream Tarts," Somerset of *The Dynamiter*, and, according to his wife-to-be, certain aspects of Prince Otto.

People well acquainted with both cousins sometimes sounded as if talking of Sherlock and Mycroft Holmes. Gosse called Bob "that exquisite troll of genius" [3] in a tone that he never quite applied to Louis. Louis a brilliant talker? ah, you should have heard Bob in his great days. This is backed by Louis's description of Spring-Heel'd Jack in "Talk and Talkers":

> In the Spanish proverb, the fourth man necessary to compound a salad is a madman to mix it: Jack is that madman. . . . He doubles like the serpent, changes and flashes like the shaken kaleidoscope, transmigrates bodily into the view of others, and so, in the twinkling of an eye and with a heady rapture, turns questions inside out and flings them empty before you on the ground, like a triumphant conjurer. [4]

Louis write well? not so well as Bob might have if early committed to pen instead of brush. Louis charming? Bob was irresistible: ". . . a rarer brain, a more fanciful and daring humour, a richer gusto, perhaps a wider knowledge, in any event a wider charity," [5] wrote the invidious Henley, intimate of both. Yet it was Louis who met fame and a degree of fortune; whereas Bob, after going through his small patrimony in imaginative ways, drudged for a living in minor universities. His painfully wrought book on *Velasquez* was well thought of; but, for every one who knew of it, ten thousand knew of John Silver and Dr. Jekyll.

Henley's latter-day bile eventually moved him to say that Bob ". . . taught Louis to drink and think" [6]—which was inaccurate. Anybody close to Jenkin had had ample contact with thinking. Any crony of Baxter's had already well explored the other activity. What Bob actually did was intimately to crystallize Louis's as yet amorphous impulses. The chief point in things happening, he told Colvin, was to see what Louis would say about them. Observing the intertwining of their fancies as they schemed out the *New Arabian Nights*, Louis's wife-to-be would describe the pair as "component parts of one individual somehow disrupted by a cataclysm of nature." [7]

They shared the pure exuberance of heedlessness and mutual admiration. Pawning a pair of trousers to raise railroad fare home on a certain occasion, Bob gave the pawnbroker the alias of "John Libbel," which popped into his head at the moment. Louis and he later agreed that the name was somehow perfect for a chronic customer of pawnshops and whirled into a cult of "Libbelism" that seems to have consisted in attributing to the nonexistent Libbel anything and everything calculated to astonish the steady-going. Edinburgh was flooded with Libbel's shabbily printed calling cards with shady-sounding notations on them; mysterious messages for him were left at lodging-houses; eminent citizens were harassed by strange letters from him; rumors about his being sought as heir to the great Libbel fortune were fostered. . . . Never were such friends as this pair, never was such sport as walking out from Fairmilehead together on a crisp moonlight night, dancing on the highway out of sheer high spirits, singing, talking, shouting, living six-teen to the dozen.[8] In sending Bob to Colvin, Louis proudly described him as "just such another mutton only somewhat far-ther wandered or perhaps with a little more mire on his wool." [9]

Specifically Bob enlisted Louis in the cult of creative Bohe-mia, which afforded both a set of catchwords and a range of mag-niloquent ambitions. The good life, it appeared, meant bril-liant iconoclasm underlain by single-hearted devotion to an art; generosity and *esprit de corps* among the emancipated in united front against dull conformists; cultivation of ever more acute sensibilities; and, as outward and visible sign of inner en-lightenment, an eccentric garb. Tired as a metal spring too of-ten compressed, but still spasmodically tempting those taken with the arts who need to dramatize themselves, this Bohemia is still with us. It is hard to realize that, in Bob's and Louis's day, it was relatively new.

While they were being born, *Scènes de la vie de Bohème* was defining it by example, riveting on the poverty-ridden art-ist the label that the Middle Ages applied to gypsies, the exotic free wanderers possessed of uncanny knowledges and skills, al-ways to be mistrusted but sometimes to be envied their foot-loose independence. Murger's sentimentality thus rewrote the role of the Goethean or Byronic artist—well-born, upstage, Satanically mysterious—into something between Autolycus and Villon anomalously endowed with a heart of gold.

The tradition admirably suited youngsters of slim resources and humdrum origins struck with aesthetic ambition: Velvet-eens were inexpensive; *vin ordinaire* cheaper than vintages; slack-jawed, pretty models who posed by day and stayed the night were more accessible than sylphs or duchesses. Since such artists lacked the resources to live in many respects like the well-nourished *bourgeois*, they made it a moral obligation to do nothing whatever *à la bourgeoise*—a simple criterion, easily applied, embarrassing only aspirants with too many francs guiltily concealed in their pockets. Some aspects of the cult are admirable: It offers the second-rater a thrifty set of self-glorifying values, and frees the first-rater from certain demands on money and time clogging to the artist's feet. Years later Louis made the distinction:

> The true Bohemian, a creature lost to view under the imaginary Bohemians of literature . . . The Bohemian of the novel, who drinks more than is good for him, and prefers anything to work, and wears strange clothes, is for the most part a respectable Bohemian, respectable in disrespectability, living for the outside, and an adventurer. But the man I mean lives wholly in himself, does what he wishes and not what is thought proper, buys what he wants for himself and not what is thought proper, works at what he believes he can do well and not what will bring him in money or favour.[10]

But it took time to appreciate the conformity of eccentricity; and meanwhile Louis was eager to follow wherever the cult led.

From looking askance at the *bourgeois*, Bohemia evolved a somewhat self-righteous contempt for him. The subhuman lives of bankers, parsons, politicians, merchants, and other crass scramblers after vanities were condemned as being hypocritical as well as humdrum. Unconscious travesty is often good definition; hot in this phase and very young, Louis wrote:

> Hail! Childish slaves of social rules
> > You had yourselves a hand in making!
> How I could shake your faith, you fools,
> > If I but thought it worth the shaking. . . .
> I take my old coat from the shelf—
> > I am a man of little breeding,
> And only dress to please myself—
> > I own, a very strange proceeding.
> I smoke a pipe abroad, because
> > To all cigars I much prefer it,
> And as I scorn your social laws,
> > My choice has nothing to deter it. . . .

O fine, religious, decent folk,
　In Virtue's flaunting gold and scarlet,
I sneer between two puffs of smoke—
　Give me the publican and harlot. . . .[11]

Unless it has been much slandered, Edinburgh was a nourishing medium for this frame of mind. It had a scattering of the Bohemian-minded: artists of integrity like Sam Bough, whom Louis liked, and literary hacks of frowsy pretensions living on the fringe of subsistence. Many of its prosperous burghers were glibly able to enter the Kirk without qualms on Sunday after a week of pettifogging and a Saturday night of greasy debauch. Edwin Muir has noted how the deprivations of fanatical Calvinism ". . . did little to abate the national appetite for drink and fornication." [12] In his *Velasquez* Bob wrote of:

> the private, reactionary effect of that life of repression and humbug upon a decent, genuine man. That you may not think at all or act for yourself, is to add the very zest of piracy to experiment in life and originality in thought. Where public profession is manifestly a lie, and public manners a formal exaggeration, life becomes a chest with a false bottom, which opens into a refuge for the kindlier, wiser, and more ardent among human beings.[13]

It sounds strikingly as if Louis's leading pilot into Bohemia had helped considerably to formulate his disciple's lifelong sense of an abiding duality in the world of conduct. None of these attitudes can be logical, of course. For, once the notion of transgression gives place to that of self-fulfilment, one should feel only pity, nothing like contempt, for the secret sinner still stifling in his ugly mask.

The elder Scots vernacular poets had encouraged this contempt. First Fergusson, then Burns imitating and transmuting him, used racy Scots to show Elder Sneckdraw failing to let his left hand know what his right hand fondled or when his right elbow bent. All Scotland knew, and most of it applauded, the slashing razor-work of "Holy Willie's Prayer," however inconsistent it was with "So gently scan thy fellow-man." Sometimes it seems, in fact, as if Scots valued their egregious hypocrites as much as the foulness of their climate and the beauty of their vistas. Louis sometimes half-identified himself with Fergusson, "the poor, white-faced, drunken, vicious boy" [14] from St. Andrews who drank too much after office hours in Edinburgh's noisome closes. He might not have so clung to this hero if Fergusson's life, as he conceived it, had not so anticipated Murger's set of *clichés*. Had he written the essay on Fergusson early planned, its title should have been "The Harbinger of Scottish Bohemia."

Bob was made quickly free of Louis's little group of serious scoffers: Ferrier, Baxter, and, to some extent, Simpson, though he seems to have cared less for the party-line of manifest enlightenment. Louis tried to persuade Bob to collaborate with him on *Monmouth: a Tragedy*. True, Bob was a painter, not a writer, but then genius was genius. The finished draft—punctuated, if not stimulated, by violence, inspired by Swinburne but developing a blank verse queerly anticipating that of Edwin Arlington Robinson—was prefaced by verses lamenting that the author had lacked such gifted help. Bob, who had funds, as Louis often did not, showed the youngster what he knew of the fine points of French wines—a study that Louis thenceforth pursued whenever he could afford it. It was Bob, I suspect, who offered him Balzac and Baudelaire to supplement Dumas and Montaigne. And Bob was a chief founder of the L.J.R.,[15] a miniature club organized by September 1872, to meet weekly in a pub (with Burns associations) in Advocates' Close and, gloves off and flaming swords wheeling, lend important subjects all the brilliance latent in the two Stevensons, Ferrier, Baxter, and a couple of other teething archangels.

Having already inaugurated a pipe[16] and written a sonnet to it—sometimes Louis is unmistakably created by Booth Tarkington—he now had a velveteen jacket and wideawake hat, like Bob's, and a navvy-style neckerchief for cravat; he had for some time worn his hair long to ward off colds. Thus Edinburgh usually remembered him, concluding, like Sampson, that it was "a love of pose together with an ingrained artificiality that made him wear long hair and velvet coats" [17]—the uniform of his order, so to speak, a tradition of the time to which Edinburgh was insufficiently inured. As Chesterton shrewdly said: ". . . poor Stevenson is to be remembered as a fool because all the fools are forgotten except Stevenson." [18] He told people that he wore such an outfit "partly from a hankering after social experiment and adventure and a dislike of being identified with any special class or caste," [19] which is more ingenious than convincing.

This self-conscious figure hooted at by Edinburgh street-boys hooted back in due form. The young fellow who had tried flirting with girls of his own stratum and reproached Cummy with forgetting his dress boots when packing his bag now considered both dress boots and giggling misses ridiculous, if not obscene. He took to turning up at what evening parties he saw fit to attend in a dress-coat and blue flannel shirt, a practice not always well received. He submitted to full conventional "blacks" only to satisfy the rules of the Spec.; otherwise to cajole or browbeat him into proper garments might recoil on the cajoler. They got him into frock coat and silk hat to attend a Royal Academy exhibition; but the hat proved too small, so he carried it in his hand and walked Colvin to the hall declaiming Milton all the way with highly conspicuous flourishes of hat and arm.

In the winter of 1871-72 he was active in an undergraduate *Edinburgh University Magazine*, which saw four issues before the editors' funds were exhausted.[20] Louis's contributions, outnumbering those of the other backers—the writing of a boy of twenty who some day will write very well—sometimes contained germs of later work. The summer after he reached his majority his father refused to let him shift to Cambridge as a fairly transparent means of getting away from home. But he was permitted to visit Germany with Simpson, studying the Germans' "cursed mutter-sprache" [21]—he appears always to have found German clumpy and muddy—and seeing much opera in Rhineland towns. Germany took little hold on him. He probably best remembered reading parts of a German translation of Burns to a patient and polite German family.

Music looked as if it might strike roots: he was obviously hoping soon to grow as hypersensitive to sounds as he already was to words. He exalted *"Einst, O Wunder . . ."* above all songs—he reverted to this twenty years later in *The Ebb-Tide*—and wallowed in Beethoven and Wagner with Baxter at concerts in Edinburgh. He persuaded girl-cousins to play and sing *Lieder* all day long. The rest of his life a principal amusement consisted in tinkering with tin-whistle or piano and setting himself to get the hang of counterpoint. A modern phonograph would have been a godsend to the boy, musically without much skill but hopeful of understanding. As it was, he seems to have set concerts and opera on a footing with other arts only at this early juncture, and was never moved to take his own performances as more than a whimsical hobby. Bob kept him ever more conscious of sculpture and the graphic arts, of course. His rhapsodies about the female figures from the Parthenon pediments are, one may say, more extraordinary than aesthetic in approach, tying in as much with his involvement with Mrs. Sitwell as with the sculptors' probable intentions. But he had a sound if, at the time, fashionable taste in Japanese prints, and, so far as I can discover, never made the equally fashionable error of admiring the Pre-Raphaelite painters.

During these and the few following years he produced sheaves of verse, bits of which, varying in quality, are included above and will illustrate much to follow. Unscrupulous selection of a few lines here and there might hint that he was a potential poet of merit too early devoted to prose:

> . . . the folded valley lay
> In a stream of sun and odour
> That sultry summer day.

> In the highlands in the country places,
> Where the old plain men have rosy faces
> And the young fair lasses
> Quiet eyes . . .[22]

But the conglomerate assays too poor to imply any masterly bent. Louis truly defined himself in 1883—and there are exceptions too—as "A kind of prose Herrick, divested of the gift of verse. . . ."[23]

It is nevertheless pleasant to see the youngster so openly at work exploring a beloved field through learning by imitation. Keats, Tennyson, Herrick, Swinburne, Morris, Arnold are identifiable, and in many cases neither imitator nor model comes out ridiculous. Beyond that it is the biographer rather than the critic who thanks these rhymed juvenilia for surviving. Louis used verse largely as a second stage of acknowledging emotion in order to deal with it.

The son of the house was not the only Stevenson now doomed to obsessions and anxieties during solitary walks abroad. Thomas Stevenson was an equally gifted brooder.

Certainly Thomas must long have been uneasy over those outrageous clothes; the peripheral bits of gossip that loyalty could not wholly discount; and Louis's flashes of violent opinion or apparently hostile comment during the brisk conversations that characterized the Stevenson dinner table. Each day no doubt his mother would be worse dismayed by the findings of her quick glances of perception. What had become of the quaint, bright, pious, ailing little creature in the blue pelisse that Cummy made for him, holding out thin, tiny hands for his white gloves, piping hymns that he learned so nicely, loving papa and mama so transparently? The long, bony-faced youth in his place was febrile even in his flashes of gaiety, lounged tragically, babbled hysterically, came home figuratively smelling of alien incongruities, and often seemed to have lost all sense of identification with his family. This was the other side of Gwynn's unquestionably sound statement about Louis at this period: "He was surrounded by too many and too intimate solicitudes; he had to trample his way to freedom over the tenderest affections and the most devout beliefs." [24]

Perhaps Thomas was reassured in the winter of 1870-71 by Louis's managing the application to prepare a paper "On a New Form of Intermittent Light for Lighthouses," read before and awarded a silver medal by the Royal Scottish Society of Arts.[25] If so, the shock was the greater two weeks later when, during a walk to Cramond with his father, Louis served final notice that he could not and would not go into engineering. There are hints of a storm, then a compromise acceptable all round: Louis should study law, an august vocation with a lively Scots tradition of affinity with letters. Let him go steady enough to qualify for the bar; then, in a young advocate, writing on the side would not be objectionable. That autumn Louis took the University's examinations preliminary to legal studies and allowed himself to be installed in the office of a respectable Edinburgh law firm to learn conveyancing. He seems to have appeared for work fairly regularly for some while. But how useful he was as gentleman-clerk to Skene, Edwards & Gordon may be fairly gauged by the surviving fact that five errors were found in one two-page document that he copied.

So far neither parent knew the worst: that he was whoring after gods so strange that, in any sense intelligible to Calvinists, they were not gods at all. The child of the midcentury had come on Darwin and Herbert Spencer. Thenceforth he could never again sit in any church in a frame of mind proper to Lewis Balfour's namesake, for whatever residual faith he had had in revelation and formal Christianity was dead. He saw the authoritarian obscurantism of all Christian theory as a mere rhetorical trick, and had none of Jenkin's instinct to penetrate through extreme skepticism to the point of *credo quia impossibile*. The same was happening to thousands like his cronies in the L.J.R. and would soon happen to hundreds of thousands. Louis eventually found a sort of religion of his own, but it took years of shaking down and, at best, the result could never have pleased the theology-minded master of 17 Heriot Row.

No doubt both Darwin and Spencer would have regarded this disciple with more misgiving than pride.[26] To say the least of it, his tone was more shrill than scientific:

> Priest, I am none of thine and see
>> In the perspective of still hopeful youth
> That truth shall triumph over thee—
>> Truth to oneself—I know no other truth.
> I see strange days for thee and thine, O priest,
>> And how your doctrines, fallen one by one,
> Shall furnish at the annual feast
>> The puppet-booth of fun.
>
> Stand on your putrid ruins—stand,
>> White neck-clothed bigot, fixedly the same,
> Cruel with all things but the hand,
>> Inquisitor in all things but the name. . . .[27]

Such rebellion consisted as much in throwing stones at the windows of empty houses as in ridding the Temple of graven images. Here is the young fellow describing a thunderstorm:

> As though my God fell down a pair of stairs. . . .
> I lay in bed with a Voltairean smile,
> The terror of good, simple guilty pairs. . . .[28]

A Voltairean smile at twenty-two, Lord help us.

Such tingling iconoclasm readily spread into social issues. In France next year Louis wrote to his father denunciations of proposals to reduce the income tax and use laws against conspiracy to suppress labor unions. And once more he wrote verses:

> By sunny market-place and street
> Wherever I go my drum I beat,
> And wherever I go in my coat of red
> The ribbons flutter about my head.

I seek recruits for wars to come—
For slaughterless wars I beat the drum,
And the shilling I give to each new ally
Is hope to live and courage to die.

I know that new recruits shall come
Wherever I beat the sounding drum,
Till the roar of the march by country and town
Shall shake the tottering Dagons down. . . .[29]

He often referred later to this period, his time of sampling
Utopias and trying stubbornly to find reassurance in their
promises. But to describe his eventual political bent would be
premature here. At the moment it was the fuses of matters religious that were burning short:

Our generation may have difficulty understanding how cata-
clysmic religious issues could be a hundred years ago—particularly to good Scots Calvinists, whose zealously studied Westminster Confession saw holy duty in condign, secular punishment for heresy, not to mention agnosticism. To some commentators on Louis the storms that occurred between him
and his father on religious grounds seem so implausible a cause
for such passion that they have assumed it was Louis's dissipations that actually lay behind them. To your great-grandfather,
however, there would have been nothing out of the way in the
fact that the boy's creeping irreligiousness wrung his parents'
hearts as if he had turned alcoholic or swindler. "If a man does
not hold Christianity," Louis wrote, quite accurately, of his
father, "he must be to him ever a knave, a madman, or an in-
considerate and culpable fool." [30]

On January 31, 1873, in the shivering middle of the hopeless
Scottish winter, "My dear papa was in a devil of a taking" be-
cause he had found a copy of the impudent constitution of the
L.J.R. To Louis he promptly put

. . . one or two questions as to beliefs, which I candidly answered. I really hate all lying so much now—a new-found

honesty that has somehow come out of my late illness—that I could not so much as hesitate at the time; but if I had foreseen the real hell of everything since, I think I should have lied as I have done so often before. I so far thought of my father, but I had forgotten my mother. And now! they are both ill, both silent, both as down in the mouth as—I can find no simile. . . . If it were not too late, I think I could almost find it in my heart to retract, but . . . am I to live my whole life as one falsehood? Of course, it is rougher than hell upon my father, but can I help it? They don't see either that my game is not the light-hearted scoffer; that I am not (as they call me) the careless infidel. . . . I am, I think, as honest as they can be in what I hold. I have not come hastily to my views. I reserve (as I told them) many points until I acquire further information, and do not think I am thus justly to be called "horrible atheist", and I confess I cannot exactly swallow my father's purpose of praying down continuous afflictions upon my head.

. . . What a *damned* curse I am to my parents! as my father said "You have rendered my whole life a failure." As my mother said "This is the heaviest affliction that has ever befallen me." O Lord, what a pleasant thing it is to have just damned the happiness of (probably) the only two people who care a damn about you in the world. . . .

I think if Cambridge could be managed, it would be the best thing. A little absence is the only chance. Imagine, Charles, my father sitting in an arm-chair gravely reading up Butler's Analogy in order to bring the wanderer back. . . . If all that I hold true and most desire to spread is to be such death, and worse than death, in the eyes of my father and mother, what the devil am I to do?

Here is a good heavy cross with a vengeance, and all rough with rusty nails that tear your fingers, only it is not I that have to carry it alone; I hold the light end, but the heavy burden falls on these two. . . .[31]

So, after warning sputters, the fat was in the fire at last. One can only surmise how, for the next five months, it flared up and spattered these three thin-skinned people; but this single letter gives much of the essence: Louis aghast, embarrassed, trying to handle as a problem for his unshaped intelligence a matter that, for all three, was almost wholly emotional; his parents, also aghast, trying to heal with emotional storm wounds created by ideas, but Thomas also certain that, if the intellect could only get the matter properly before the boy, he could not resist orthodoxy. The one thing certain is that the emotional pitches were quiveringly high.

As often happens in crises including fear as well as wrath, readjustments followed: Thanks to no discretion of his own, Louis came out of this round better off. He was given a study of his own next his bedroom on the top floor of 17 Heriot Row, which had been recently remodeled for greater space, and, toward the end of summer, was accorded a long and momentous visit to a married cousin in Suffolk of whom he was fond. These concessions, obviously emollient, probably cost Thomas's conscience much. He often acted with brittle foolishness in assailing Louis, said stupid things, forced issues stupidly; but then he was not playing a hand at cards, he was putting himself and his son through the meat-grinder, chewing up his own nervous tissues every time he turned the handle—which does not lead to calm judgment. The next few years must have been doubly painful to him because the boy's patent needs often made a fool of a father's plain duty to be loving but stern. Every time Thomas failed to disown Louis, instead giving him rope for therapeutic reasons, conscience could and probably did call him a moral coward. The Victorian father has had much well-deserved abuse. Here we, as well as Louis, who was much more confusingly involved, may allow that an honest, intelligent, and unstable man duty-bound to the role of Victorian father sometimes deserved compassion.

Five weeks after the explosion, still drugged by the weariness of battle, though his breath was back in his body, Louis wrote what sounds almost like an obituary:

I think now, this 5th and 6th of April, 1873, that I can see my future life. I think it will run stiller and stiller year by year; a very quiet desultorilly [*sic*] studious existence. If God only gives me tolerable health, I think now I shall be very happy. . . . I shall never be a great man, I may set myself peacefully on a smaller journey; not without hope of coming to the inn before nightfall. . . .

Desiderata
I. Good-Health.
II. 2 to 3 hundred a year.
III. O du lieber Gott, friends!

AMEN
Robert Louis Stevenson[32]

Man proposes. For years to come his life would be increasingly turbulent; his health no better, then far worse; finances sometimes close to the mark; studiousness nothing remarkable. The one item notably to materialize was "friends."

It is a strange reflection that "on this 5th and 6th of April" the boy was already 135 days into the second half of his life.

Louis's stay in Suffolk was, as aforesaid, momentous, but, in all logic, that must wait. He returned to find that, in his absence, he had given his father another shock:

A young cousin of Louis's who was dying had summoned Uncle Tom. He could not die easy, he said, without warning him how Bob, whom he called a moral "blight" and "mildew," was wantonly corrupting Louis. (Doubtless this was further reflection of the L.J.R.) It is difficult to see much ridiculous about a deathbed, and the youngster did die. But I get a shiver of cynical comedy out of this minor scene of taletelling under circumstances bound to lend impertinent dignity.

In any context it must have been shattering for a father to

hear that his nephew was poisoning his son's immortal soul. But presently an oddly grateful comfort emanated from this information. The cousin's story made Bob the cause of it all, enabled Thomas to see Louis as mere victim, thank God, no longer spontaneously a spiritual villain.

"It is a Lord's mercy," Louis wrote later, "I was not home, or things might have really come to a climax." [33] That note of relief was premature. Thomas met Bob on the street and proceeded to have it out. Louis wrote Baxter:

> There is now at least one person in the world who knows what I have had to face and what a tempest of emotions my father can raise when he is really excited. The war began with my father accusing Bob of having ruined his house and his son. Bob answered that he didn't know where I had found out that the Christian religion was not true but that he hadn't told me. And I think from that point the conversation went off into emotion and never touched shore again. . . . my views according to my father are a childish imitation of Bob, to cease the moment the mildew is removed; all that was said was that I had ceased to care for my father and that my father confessed he was ceasing, or had greatly ceased, to care for me. . . . They shook hands; my father wished him all happiness, but prayed . . . that he should never see him between the eyes again. . . . no practical issue except the ludicrous one that Bob promised never to talk religion to me any more. . . . he had no idea that there was that sort of thing in the world, although I had told him often enough—my father on his knees and that sort of thing. . . . I learn that my mother had hysterics last night over it all. [34]

That scene on the street, between iron railings and curbstone, passion boiling out of the older, sturdier man, bitter expostulation dripping from the high-strung youngster, is unmistakably a steel engraving to illustrate a Victorian novel.

Louis indignantly rejected the notion that his fine new opinions were mere echoes of Bob. His father doubtless set that down to mistaken loyalty. But the boy did not mistake the convenience of the theory:

> . . . my father I believe has some of the satisfactions consequent on a good auto-da-fe now he has finally quarrelled with Bob and banished him. And although it seems mean to profit by what my own heart feels anxious to resent, I am only too glad of any peace between us although every moment of it were to cost me a finger.[35]

Father and son soon risked resuming their long walks together. However self-consciously, Louis was trying to keep his mouth shut.

It would have puzzled Thomas to learn that Bob, the atheistic "blight," was already off on a new tack, trying to persuade Louis that, after all, the soul was immortal. As his lunging movements show, Thomas was sadly puzzled anyway. A dangerous instinct made him tell Louis that he had permanently alienated his mother. Worse, he sometimes succumbed to the impulse to pick at the boy, probing for further degeneration. They quarreled, for instance, over a hypothetical case of whether a dead man's heirs should permit publication of letters that, under unscrupulous presentation, might harm his reputation—suppose me the deceased and you the heir, was Thomas's rash way of putting it. "Publish!" said Louis; such things are sure to come to light some time and better while the heir is alive to examine them. Thomas was "utterly crushed, and tauntingly reproachful. . . . O, it was miserable—utterly miserable." [36]

Late in September Mrs. Stevenson went visiting, leaving the pair uninsulated from each other. Things grew worse than ever:

> He said tonight "He wished he had never survived." . . . "A poor end," he said, "for all my tenderness." And what was there to answer? "I have made all my life to suit you—I have worked for you and gone out of my way for you—and

the end of it is that I find you in opposition to the Lord Jesus Christ. I find everything gone. I would ten times sooner see you lying in your grave than that you should be shaking the faith of other young men and bringing ruin on other houses as you have brought it upon this." . . . "I thought," he said, "to have had some one to help me when I was old." [37]

As scene after scene dragged on without climax, the cleavage between Bob's villainy and Louis's imitativeness began to blur: "They think the offense originally wilful; . . . no protestations of regret can be of the value of so much breath in their eyes . . . I see no daylight in front of us . . ." [38] Louis recognized that, were he not emotionally involved, he could play his cards better: "I cannot help getting friendly with my father (whom I *do* love) and so speaking foolishly with my mouth." [39] But he was probably nearer the dynamics of the thing in:

I tell you this is just a mere trial of nervous strength between us. The weakest will die first, that is all; and I don't know whether to wish for the one alternative or the other. Both seem horrible; but not much more horrible than the unsightly, hopeless present. [40]

Eighty years later one is tempted to see in this deadly wrestle of father and son an antagonism that, had it not found vent in terms of religious heresy, would have had to express itself in terms of business or marriage.

Artificial respite came in November. On a railroad journey Louis and his father encountered the Lord Advocate, chief law officer of the Crown in Scotland, a family acquaintance. Hearing of Louis's plans to be a lawyer, he advised him to go to the English bar—an opinion taken quite as seriously as the source deserved. This gave Louis the moral equivalent of his get-away-from-home-to-Cambridge scheme. Only half-perfunctory examinations stood between him and one of the Inns of Court in London, four hundred miles from Heriot Row. Unless I badly misread him, his head immediately filled with Pendennis, Warrington, and The Back Kitchen.

But a recent attack of throat infection had weakened him and daily family torture had no doubt hampered proper convalescence. On arriving in London to take examinations, he had a physical collapse. Alarmed friends sent him to the eminent Dr. (later Sir) Andrew Clark, who promptly forbade exams—his outlandish patient was down to 118 pounds—and ordered him on a fattening diet pending further study. With suspicious offhandedness Louis wrote his mother that it was "a bore about the exams," [41] and promised her a written report from Clark as soon as the case was well digested.

His parents came to London promptly, but even so too late. Graduate of Edinburgh and Aberdeen, pious (he wrote *The Physician's Testimony for Christ*) and a temperance-crusader (he wrote *An Enemy of the Race*, meaning alcohol), Clark was no man for the Stevensons to disregard; and he had already spoken: He had feared "consumption" in view of the patient's "weak chest" and family history, but there was no definite sign of it. Until the boy was built back in shape to reduce the risk of consumption, however, study of law or any other exacting activity was out of the question. He needed rest, good food, undemanding climate—say the Riviera; London or Scotland impossible.

Louis's mother mentioned firmly that she had already thought of taking Louis to Torquay—a place that, the British climate being there sufficiently mollified for palms to grow, was popular for "lung" cases. But this mid-Victorian physician, necessarily ignorant of modern psychiatry, merely studying the whole human animal under his gaslight, seems to have had a firm grasp of the clinical point that, for some ailments in some patients, no complication is more ruinous than too much family. Mothers, he said, merely make people fancy themselves worse. It would be the Riviera—and alone. Louis had every reason to have written so enthusiastically: "Clark is a trump." [42] A year later Mrs. Stevenson confessed that she had thought it all a put-up job between Louis's friends and the doctor.

Clark was probably shrewd enough to see that his patient did not share his parents' dismay over sentence of exile. But he can hardly have been expected to understand that this geographical therapy, so crisply outlined in the evil murk of London, was the first major step in making a man of a spidery, flat-chested youth "with wide-open, lamp-like eyes," [43] whose hands flickered like a Frenchman's as he talked.

Monsieur Est Bien Jeune

> Prudence is a wooden Juggernaut, before whom Benjamin Franklin walks with the portly air of a high-priest, and after whom dances many a successful merchant in the character of Atys. But it is not a deity to cultivate in youth.
>
> —"Crabbèd Age and Youth"

THREE months previously another cousin had affected Louis's zigzag course. Headed for the beach by natural corruption, he was clawed off by Jenkin; diverted by Bob toward shoal-water, he was now swept toward the channel by people named Sidney Colvin and Fanny Sitwell. To those ill acquainted with sailing, a vessel beating to windward always looks erratic.

This cousin Maud (a Balfour) was wife of the Rev. Churchill Babington, a Cambridge professor and rector of Cockfield, Suffolk. A guest of the Babingtons' during Louis's visit in late summer of 1873 was their close friend Mrs. Sitwell, who was a "wonderful woman"—a thing hard to define but easy to recognize in person—and certainly the most decorative of all major influences on Louis's life. Henry James, Joseph Conrad, E. V. Lucas were greatly to admire her. Sir Osbert Sitwell recently wrote of her intelligence, charm, and patrician beauty even in old age. The late John Garvin said of her: "Beauty like hers was genius. . . . Divining intuition like hers was genius. Vitality like hers was genius." [1] Louis was almost the first, but by no means the last, promising youngster to profit by her powers as spiritual catalyst.

Almost twelve years his senior, she was born Frances Jane Fetherstonhaugh of Protestant gentry long settled in Ireland.

Her father sounds like a character out of Samuel Lover, training his boys and girls to jump any fence that offered and never to expect more than sixpence to bless themselves with. Special dearth of sixpences when Fanny was four years old moved him to take his brood to Germany, where living was supposed to be cheap. There German schooling endowed little Fanny with cultivated tastes. Then the revolutions of 1848 sent them all scurrying back to Ireland. Within a few years, as fortunes refused to mend, father and two of the boys joined the Australian gold rush. They found no gold; but father found a living as police magistrate on the Buckland River, where his sporting skills made him popular, and the family were sent for.

At seventeen Fanny came home to marry a left-behind fiancé, the Rev. Albert Sitwell of the Church of England, and set off with him to take up a chaplaincy in Calcutta. By the time her first child was born, she had lived in Ireland, Germany, Australia, and India—for a receptive mind an education in itself. Presently she brought her surviving boy child home from the sanitary hazards of India; Sitwell followed to assume a country vicarage. There was domestic trouble of an unidentified nature, attributed to Sitwell's "unfortunate temperament and uncongenial habits." [2] The matter must have been serious, for the Victorian wife did not lightly leave her husband. Sweet but no Griselda, Fanny abandoned Sitwell, taking her son Bertie with her, in 1873. Ensuing frictions also remain vague. Legal separation, leaving her custody of the boy, was probably arranged by 1875. The times and the British divorce law being what they were, divorce seems not to have been sought.

Cultivated friends helped Fanny to a livelihood in translating, reviewing, and acting as secretary to the College for Men and Women, Sloane Square, London, an institution to uplift the working classes that had taken the startling step of instructing men and women together. [3] One of her closest friends was Sidney Colvin, essayist and art critic, then Slade Professor of Fine Art at Cambridge, later Curator of Prints at the Brit-

ish Museum. For some twenty-five years, in fact, in an acknowledgedly noncarnal arrangement that apparently involved neither scandal nor occasion for it, she acted as hostess for Colvin's
entertaining in London while living apart from him. Sitwell's
death, freeing her, did not occur until 1894. Hampered by meager income and needy relatives, Colvin could not marry her until 1901. The lady was then sixty-two. Today that story sounds
like warped nonsense. For proper correction, consider that it
occurred in the period that flowered in George Bernard Shaw.

Garvin did not exaggerate her beauty. She was widely admired with a sort of voluptuous awe. Photographs show a
Mona Lisa-like mouth—she scolded Louis for mentioning the
resemblance—a fragile, aquiline nose, eyes of Eurasian darkness and softness, famously pretty little feet and hands; the
whole as if Burne-Jones had painted a buxom young *rani*. Her
affectionate patronage of creative youth lay behind Louis's
later reference to

> . . . a lady whose generous pleasure—perhaps I might say,
> whose weakness—it was to discover youthful genius. With a
> little good will and a little friendship genius is mighty easily
> supplied.[4]

Only, the lady being so lovely and youth often susceptible, difficulties were predictable. Stopford Brooke, biographer of Tennyson, said that Mrs. Sitwell had had more men in love with her
than any other woman he knew.[5] Said Colvin in a passage
particularly worth noting:

> In the fearlessness of her purity, she can afford the frankness
> of her affections, and show how every fascination of her sex
> may in the most open freedom be honourably secure. Yet in
> a world of men and women, such an one cannot walk with-
> out kindling once and again a dangerous flame before she is
> aware. . . . she never foresees these masculine combus-
> tions, but has a wonderful tact and gentleness in allaying
> them, and is accustomed to convert the claims and cravings of

passion into the lifelong loyalty of grateful and contented friendship.[6]

There lies the key to Louis's first great love and its tenuous history. To us, of course, Colvin's comment sounds as curious as her and his quasi-*ménage*; but there is small reason to doubt the facts of either. The cultural climate of 1870 differed widely from ours and, perhaps to an extent now hard to grasp, made its own sense. These people believed implicitly—hence, to a certain degree, effectively—in the force and emotional workability of explicit, conscious moral principles and self-evident motives. We know better now, on good grounds, some of which Louis's later writings would curiously anticipate. Our knowing better obliges us constantly to probe for the unconscious self-deceptions that, they tell us, often underlie and vitiate rigid behavior. But it may also tempt us into bunglingly neglecting the validity and the self-bolstering quality that such graceful renunciations as Mrs. Sitwell's once carried. Utter belief in technical chastity as a moral and aesthetic value could greatly have minimized the ill effects of thwarting biological impulses.

In proof, Mrs. Sitwell's catalytic friendships with young men did last after she waved her emergency wand over them, did somehow sublimate and consolidate on supra-erotic grounds. No doubt it cost the lady much thus to disguise from her fastidious self the basic meaning of her young worshippers; but at least she seems to have spared them "Sir, how dare you!" when the emergency broke. That it all involved hypocrisy or conscious deprivation, that she ever slipped into carnal congress with Louis or any other disciple—as some have implied on no grounds but cynical presumption—is most unlikely. There really have been more things in heaven and earth than are dreamed of in diagnoses suggested by the *Contes drôlatiques* and substantiated by dilute Freud.

Release, however temporary, from crises at home probably lent Louis special effervescence when, in velveteen jacket and straw hat, knapsack on back, he arrived at Cockfield Rectory.

At this period he was closely related to a style of youngster already rife in British universities and later imitated in the States with pious Anglophilia—very young, very witty, very impulsive, very cultivated, very promising, very picturesque, very high-strung, very generous, and oh, so very sensitive. Rupert Brooke was peak of the development. Louis's essential charm in his Scottish version of that role seems to have been marked if sociably egocentric; years later a lady-interviewer came near explaining it: " . . . he assumed that you too were alertly alive; . . . that you would understand and share his interest in all interesting things." [7]

Mrs. Sitwell's son instantly liked this limber stranger who looked like an anthropomorphic insect sired by Don Quixote. In a matter of hours the boy's mother had stamped Louis "genius" and was writing Colvin to come at once, here was "a fine young spirit" to be cherished. Colvin's arrival completed the team that would sponsor Louis emotionally and professionally.

> . . . this most trusty and noble-minded man . . . paved my way in letters; . . . set before me, kept before me, and still, as I write, keeps before me, a difficult standard of achievement. . . . had the tact and wisdom to suffer me to be very much myself; to accept and cherish what was good in me; to condone much of what was evil; and whilst still holding before me a standard to which I could never quite attain, neither to damp nor disgust me of the trial.[8]

As this book proceeds, I must say justifiably harsh things of Colvin as literary mentor and editor of Louis's *Letters*. They need not obscure the great, generously motivated, and generously accorded services that Colvin did Louis the rest of his life, nor the extent to which, when tensions had died down, he understood the nature of his protégé.

Louis was a trifle awed by this trim-bearded, slight, severe man whose writing in the *Fortnightly* he already admired, whom he knew to have been a principal founder of the bril-

liant new Savile Club in London. Colvin had both temperament and means for scolding and persuading "this slender,
slovenly, nondescript apparition" [9] into producing writing
that could be duly printed in organs carrying prestige in the
right places. Within a couple of months an essay called
"Roads," Louis's first paid contribution, had been agonizingly
completed, refused by the *Fortnightly*, and accepted (subject
to revision) by the *Portfolio*—all at Colvin's prodding behest.

Pledging his connections and reputation to Louis's service,
Colvin soon went back to his post from Cockfield, but not soon
enough to escape a "treat" for a hundred children on the
Rectory lawn, during which he accidentally hit a small boy
with a cricket ball and Louis blistered a finger cutting sand-
wiches wholesale. Mrs. Sitwell stayed on at the Rectory. So
did Louis.

In the most decorous of figurative senses, she ravished the
boy, who was susceptible enough anyway and just then specially apt for extravagant sympathy because of his conviction
that he had alienated both his parents. Lady and lad made lazy,
sunny expeditions with their hosts, read German together, sat
under trees, Louis with his head on her knee while she stroked his
lank, yellow-brown hair and he told of his literary ambitions,
his family troubles, his Edinburgh friends. They laughed sometimes in the intervals of smiling raptly, for Mrs. Sitwell is said
to have been witty. This went on for weeks, Cousin Maud and
the Rector apparently beaming approval in the background. It
was not always peaceful; once, finding that the lady failed to
share his enthusiasm for newcomer Robert Bridges's early
poems, Louis threw the book across the room and stormed out
of the house, not returning ruefully to apologize until several
hours later. But sympathy easily interpreted that as the de-
monstrativeness of genius. When Louis departed for a visit to
Colvin and then Edinburgh and the "blight" crisis, he was suf-
fused with a sense of transcendent identification with a person
outside himself such as he had never before experienced.

Fortunately for biographers, it was still the era of letter-writing. Apparently Louis and the lady projected a book in which passages from the letters that he would write to her, full of soul and devotion, would reappear transmuted into great literary and emotional significance. The scheme was short-lived, nor was any such arrangement necessary to encourage him to drown her in correspondence. Only amputation of the right hand could have prevented a severe case of logorrhea in so pen-broken a devotee as Louis. Letter after letter to Mrs. Sitwell on Mrs. Stevenson's sober "17, Heriot Row" note paper ran twenty to twenty-four sides, closely written in a hand changing to match the crises in Louis's moods. These documents are essential to understanding young Louis. His salient angles fairly burst through his struggle to say everything absolutely everything, to a lovely lady of thirty-three graciously pleased to be his good angel.

By my great good luck, this is the first biography of Stevenson to work from the full text of Louis's cryptic, quasi-love letters to Mrs. Sitwell as well as those to Colvin, Baxter, Bob, et al. Later editions of the *Letters* give large extracts from the Sitwell letters, but Colvin's frequent editorial excisions suppressed many of the more ecstatic passages as well as much "my dear" and "dearest." [10] Here, under choice of equally significant passages, I use previously unpublished material from the original letters which, until recently, were under embargo imposed by Colvin's will.

As soon as Louis reached Edinburgh the ink began to swirl and bubble:

> I must write you a little word again before I go to bed; although my last is not so many miles in its southward journey. Blessings on the trains that go all night, through rain and moon-glimpse, over the sleeping country to bring people so near together. . . . I hope more in the strong inspiration of your sympathy than ever Christian hoped out of his deity. . . . I want our friendship, my own dearest freind [*sic*] to be the faithfullest, most candid that has ever been.[11]

Within a few days the Florence Nightingale motif:

> It is a thing to thank God for, that there should be someone
> like you, carrying so bright a lamp of comfort up and down
> our dim life, bringing priceless sympathy to one and to an-
> other, giving it widely and painlessly like the good sun.[12]

In mid-September the lady enclosed some violets; Louis
swallowed one—while kissing it, I assume—and wrote her
about it with elaborate playfulness. Seeing in a shop a gold
trinket engraved *Phil. 1, 3* ("I thank my God upon every re-
membrance of you"), he recommends the text as summarizing
his feeling for her. He calls her "meine schöne, liebe Freun-
din" who has upset his scheme of living:

> . . . be long suffering with me. . . . you have spoiled a
> certain rough, vulgar and courageous volunteer in the war
> of life who went south some two months and a half ago and,
> since you have put a new heart of flesh within him, you must
> help to keep it warm with sympathy.
> . . . think how much you have been to me *alone* without
> thought of others, without thought of how many dark lands
> the white moon has looked healingly down into . . . O
> blessed life, O madonna mia—no!—nostra—look down a little
> gladly on us all.[13]

He was young and she a delicate woman reared in the era of
The Princess. Both are easily forgiven their inability to see
how ill the word "friendship" suited the context.

Since the lady was still technically married, some precau-
tions were observed. Her letters were addressed to Louis at the
Spec., where he collected them from the porter; occasionally
she advised him to write in such a tenor that the letter could be
shown to others, which he sometimes managed. But it took
much urging to get him to burn the accumulated mass of her
letters, and he long held out the first and the latest to carry as
talismans. Accidental gaps in the series of her-to-him meant tremendous storms, culminating in a few days; for instance:

NO LETTER. Now this is very funny. I should have thought you would have answered my Tuesday's letter; I felt sure you would not have lost an hour in answering Monday's note; and yet, thank God, you are not ill, or Maud would have heard of that. What can this mean, old man? She could not be so brutal as to give you no hint, as to let the whole correspondence cease without a word, and you go day after day up to the college and come back again with the heartache. And what can it be? O God, God, God [each "God" is more despairingly scrawled] . . . Oh this poor letter that will never be read. . . .[14]

Then it all proved to have been the fault of the Spec.'s porter, a man I do not envy when Louis found that the letters had been there all along. Still, all was well. His Madonna, the moon of his delight that knew no wane, was still ever so graciously embosoming Louis in spite of her own troubles. For Sitwell was somehow behaving badly, about the separation, no doubt. She told Louis enough to put him in a rage: "If only that man would break his neck!"

This child of his time was presently singing a popular contemporary scientific-literary motif:

If I never saw you again, and lived all my days in Arabia, I should be reminded of you continually; you have gone all over the house of my mind and left everywhere sweet traces of your passage. It is not possible that our two minds should quite cease; I believe with Theophile Gautier—not a grain of dust that has ever been through my brain in these latter days, but will leap and thrill and waken to recollections if the wind should blow or the rain should wash it anywhere near you. It is very *living*, this matter; we let ourselves still be blinded by the old stories that it is something dull and cold and clayey only half-awakened for a while by the strong impulse of the soul. Dreams and delusions! It is this matter that thinks and thrills and is shaken all through with delicate sympathies, that is obedient to music and colour and love.

Oh I am proud—I am *glorious!*—that I am made of this honourable stuff.[15]

Mrs. Sitwell too had a weak respiratory tract. No doubt Louis's and her reciprocal uneasinesses over each other's health strengthened the bond between them—though, heaven knows, it was hardly necessary. Louis was curiously proud of having been first to notice that she felt unwell one afternoon at Cockfield; this, he deduced, showed special affinity between them. He repeatedly exhorts her to be well, to get well, to avoid falling ill, denouncing her ailments for their brutal presumption in visiting such as she, passionately turning hypochondriac for two, rejoicing with her in the prospect of a stimulating "change of air" in visiting her married sister in Paris. This was solicitous and unselfish of the boy. But he could also display an actorishly innocent self-absorption:

> I had yesterday news from Bob that nearly took me out of the body with pleasure. He is really making progress; the fellows at the school of art in Anvers seem to think he will get on; . . . O I say, it makes me feel well, that. If he does well, I shall do well too. You can fancy how excited I was; it is the first hope I have had given me.[16]

Devotion sometimes tempted him to invidiousness:

> There were two English ladies with me in the carriage going to Italy under the guidance of a man; all three stolid, obtuse, and unemotional. It did make me angry to think that a third of the money that will be spent hawking these dull creatures through all that is sunny and beautiful would suffice to take you, with all your eager sensibilities and quick nerves.[17]

At times, however, his dependency, so intimate in the dependent, has a dignity that defies bathos of content:

> Your sympathy is the wind in my sails. You must live to help me and I must do honour to your help. . . . If some of us

are spared there will be at least eternal honour to your name.
. . . No, your name will never be quite forgotten but wherever there are humane men and noble women, the one will
wish that they could have lived where they could have
known you, and the others will set you before them as
a model. *There*. If you don't believe that, it is because you
doubt those whom you have inspired; and that would be
rude.[18]

This was the support that held him together in spite of illness
and shattering conflicts at home.

The Stevensons were understandably taken aback when, join-
ing Louis in London to investigate Clark and his diagnosis,
they found that, in Mrs. Sitwell and Colvin, the boy had acquired a spiritual family without their knowledge or consent.
Louis's mother showed her annoyance when, his last Sunday in
London, Louis went to church with Mrs. Sitwell instead of his
own parents. But this intruder was a lady, charming, and an
intimate of the irreproachable Babingtons—Thomas openly admired her—and Colvin sounded reassuringly respectable. Parents and friends joined amicably to see their common problem
off.

On his twenty-third birthday Louis would be steeping in sunshine at familiar Menton. Alone, not solicitously accompanied. In bright, easy-going, stimulating France, where many
things were presumably better ordered, not in wet, cold, exacting Scotland. His farewell to Mrs. Sitwell said:[19]

I do look forward to the sun and I go with a great store of
contentment—bah! what a mean word—of living happiness
that I can scarce keep bottled down in my weather-beaten
body. Do be happy.

Ever your faithful friend

R.L.S.

The patient unquestionably needed building up of body as
well as soul. He was shockingly emaciated, with a grim history

of feverish "colds," and "nervous exhaustion," spells of facial *tic*, dyspepsia, and cold feet. When consulted on the Riviera, the famous Dr. Bennet (prophet of the area for tuberculosis) agreed with Clark that, though there were no overt symptoms of the disease, lesions might nevertheless exist. Beyond the emotional aspect that Clark had so well in mind, to relegate Louis to the Côte d'Azur was sound: If he did have undetected TB, this was supposed to be the best place for it; if not, warmth, rest, sunshine, and dry air would benefit his respiratory troubles as well as his nervous system, and spare him the extra burden of Edinburgh's winter infections.

Social history—in both senses—lies behind the resorts of Southern France. Fashion has frequently settled on localities—Saratoga, Vichy, Bath, Carlsbad, Cannes, Torquay—first conspicuous because local waters or air were presumed "good for" genitourinary troubles, constipation, or "lung-trouble." About a century ago doctors perceived—or thought they did, which is enough—that sunny, dry places near the sea promoted "cures" of consumption. Ventnor (in the Isle of Wight), Madeira, Hyères took on scientific significance. Solemn controversies over optimum distance from salt water and height above tidemark were carried to great lengths. Hotels were built to house invalids prosperous enough to live for health. Then came the invalids' families to discover that healthy places were often pleasant for expensive loafing. . . .

In Louis's day Menton was in the first stage of boom by the cult of climatotherapeutics. The East Bay was thick with small hotels and pensions for different lengths of purse; the West Bay was expanding toward Cap Martin; between them the semiperpendicular medieval town was being squeezed into a compactness even greater than that originally imposed by pirates and fortification-minded princes. Up the precipitous mountains that block off north winds and—so they said—reflected sunshine back on the dwellings at their feet climbed terraces of orange, lemon, and olive trees to assure visitors from colder places that this was paradise at last. Bone-shivering

Louis would have been grateful for such a climate if the local sights and sounds had been those of Pandemonium—whereas, of course, the world has few such lovely coastlines.

There for a generation had come the sick and dying from Poland and Russia, England and Scotland, Denmark and Sweden, even America. Some improved, some lingered hopefully, many died—having waited too long to try the virtues of the climate, said the doctors peevishly. Death was specially hard to forget because the enclosures of the old castle squatting on a spur above the town had been tactlessly converted into a most conspicuous cemetery. Catholic Poles and French had consecrated ground in the center; heretics paved the lower ramps between the outer circumvallations. There they still lie elbow to elbow: Sorensen, Griffiths, Mackenzie, Brown-Smitherinton, Hauptmann, Pozanski—Scandinavian parsons, Indian Army subalterns, Irish gentlewomen, a ghastly number dying young, their tombstones soaking in the sunshine that they sought too late. The invalid climbing by carriage or donkey to rest on a blanket in the open air as instructed looked down on this fortress garrisoned by death. On returning to his pension, his eyes, irresistibly uplifted to the hills, saw institutionalized death looming over him. This "Château des Morts" and the rush of odor from the lemon blossoms were among the things that Louis found he remembered from his stays there in his early teens. It was a queer place to begin to live in.

Since subjects of Queen Victoria were the largest group among the invalids, English was Menton's second language. The pharmacies sold English quack remedies, English tweeds warded off the chill that follows the sun's descent behind Cap Martin, English manners infested the hotel smoking-rooms. There was much staid carriage-riding, picnicking, strolling, and acquaintance-pursuing among so many "wounded soldiery of mankind . . . all shut up together in some basking angle of the Riviera, walking a dusty promenade or sitting in dusty olive yards." [20] The prevailing atmosphere was tepidly apprehensive. Who had just arrived hopefully was more discussed than who had just disappeared regrettably.

From Avignon en route Louis had written: "I am back again in the stage of thinking there is nothing the matter with me, which is a good sign; but I am wretchedly nervous";[21] and he was much the invalid after arrival. The doctors allowed him opium as soporific and cough-suppressor (taken as laudanum, I suppose); being literary, he wrote Mrs. Sitwell about the hallucinations that it produced. He was already deep in the Menton tradition of interminable clinical detail:

> I have been very tired all day; lying outside my bed and crying in the feeble way that you recollect. . . . I finished up my day with a lamentable exhibition of weakness. I could not remember French, or at least I was afraid to go into any place lest I should not be able to remember it, . . . I walked about the streets in such a rage with every person who came near me, that I felt inclined to break out upon them with all sorts of injurious language; . . . If you knew how old I felt! I am sure that this is what age brings with it—this carelessness, this disenchantment, this continual bodily weariness. I am a man of seventy; O Medea, kill me, or make me young again![22]

That last touch was used in "Ordered South." Louis died too young to know whether the general premonition was correct or not.

As rest and sunshine brought snatches of well-being, he sought out people and activity and began to cultivate his sensibilities by reading George Sand—an excellent means to the purpose; for some months he addressed Mrs. Sitwell as "Consuelo." His reading aloud of "Out of the cradle endlessly rocking . . ." so affected a fellow-boarder named Dowson that he wept and promised never again to neglect Whitman. "I think," Louis wrote his Consuelo, "if I read that to a person; and the person remained quite callous that I should tomahawk the person." [23] (Dowson's little boy, with whom Louis studied geography and played dominoes and pickaback, was named Ernest and eventually wrote—in his fashion—that poem to Cynara.) Soon Louis had the courage to write his father a long declaration of moral independence, knowing that it might mean "ultimate rupture." The immediate result was a telegram: "Quite satisfied with your letter—keep your mind easy."[24] Months later he learned that his parents had concluded that he was out of his mind and had to be humored at all costs. He even began to develop misgivings about using unearned money, developed later in "Lay Morals";[25] and determined to "go into an office of some sort" [26] if Colvin, soon to visit him, saw too little hope of his earning living expenses by writing.

Colvin and Louis met again as if pledged to intimate harmony in an arranged marriage. Their determination to be lifelong, fast friends easily survived the awkward fact that both were smitten with and dependent on the same lady, sometimes writing to her from opposite sides of the same room. Louis never challenged Colvin's priority with Mrs. Sitwell. He seems to have felt that his elder derived special rights from having known her longer as well as from collaboration with her on Louis Stevenson.

Toward the end of 1873 they moved to the Hotel Mirabeau in the East Bay, seeking escape from "the Pavillon lot of horrid English" [27] and greater progress in French, since all at the Mirabeau spoke it consistently. Within a month a genial French painter assured Louis that he had never heard an *Anglais* with less foreign accent, which naturally delighted the budding cosmopolite. The company also included a Francophile American couple with a small daughter whose pretty disposition set Louis deliberately noticing and analyzing children;[28] and a pair of noble Russian sisters, each with a child, whose gay attacks on Louis's egocentric peace of mind dizzied him most educationally. That he came out of the Eastern Question—as he called the ensuing complications—with any grace at all speaks well for his growing dexterity with people.

The elder, Mme. Zassetsky, was an ironic, impulsive, hag-ridden, backhanded kind of Slavic liberal, mother of ten and alleged author of successful Russian comedies. This strange youngster intensely amused her. She took him to sit to a Menton photographer, saw him posed, then said: *"C'est mon fils. Il vient d'avoir dix-neuf ans. Il est tout fier de sa moustache. Tâchez de la faire paraître,"* [29] and fled giggling. Bewilderment went with amusement. Both she and Mme. Garschine, her sister, told Louis candidly and often that they had never seen anything remotely like him and could make no sense of him at all.

Bewilderment was mutual. Russian plays and novels had not yet educated Western Europe in the cryptic antics, emotional and physical, of whatever the Russian temperament may be. Broken in only to Victorian ladies and Scottish queans, Louis was ill prepared for the emotional nudity with which this pair flung themselves into situations. "They do what they want with perfect frankness," [30] he wrote Mrs. Sitwell in awe. After Mme. Zassetsky had flown into a screaming rage at Mme. Garschine's small daughter, an unpleasant brat of eight, she turned "with the sublimest nonchalance" [31] and told him and another guest that this was her own child, not Mme. Garschine's at all, though the girl did not know it; by previous agreement Mme. Garschine had taken her at birth to make up for her own child-lessness. The tale was notable; but what left Louis reeling was the instantaneous, actresslike succession of moods and the exhibitionistic renunciation of privacy. He grew very fond of Mme. Zassetsky's acknowledged child Nelitchka, "a little polyglot button of a three-year-old." [32] But how to feel toward Mme. Garschine was soon a problem that not even Mrs. Sitwell could make head or tail of.

The readiest solution was that this impulsive creature past her midthirties but still attractive, alienated from her husband, wanted to seduce him for his *beaux yeux*. Even at twenty-three Louis was not fatuous enough to believe that. Complacency about the other sex was never one of his failings.

Yet the theory that she was playing with him for lack of any more absorbing occupation was crasser still. Perhaps the lady herself did not know her motives. This youngster was as alien to her as she to him. Mere curiosity as to what he would do may have moved her so ostentatiously to make him sit by her, cast sheep's eyes at him, shift the talk so dizzyingly from speculation on the most abstruse subjects to warm personalities. . . .

At their villa—the Russians merely ate at the Mirabeau—they gave him samovar-tea, which he found pointless, and caviar, which he thought dull, and classic and folk-Slavic music, which was ravishing; he sent home for a collection of Scots folk songs for them to try. In bursts of sudden confidence *tête-à-tête* Mme. Garschine told him of her fame at home as a last-resort midwife in league with the Devil (her serfs thus accounting for her failure to go to church), and otherwise flooded him with extravagant ideas in an idiom of rich mental compost and uninhibited impulse. One such talk, they two alone in the villa, culminated in a confession that she was *"amoureuse de Christ"* [33] and should have been one of the women who loved and followed Him. On a drowsy Riviera afternoon with blinds closed against the sun, such talk is hazardous. A sillier youngster full of George Sand might easily have succumbed. But, though the word fits him now and again, Louis was not quite that silly. I like to picture the scene: the lady "graceful and refined, and only good looking after you know [her] a bit," [34] rhapsodizing in spluttering French, eyes rolling, forehead a little damp, breathing a little ostentatious; and Louis touched, no doubt swayingly inclined, but unable not to wonder inhibitingly whether sometimes, after he had left, the Villa Marina did not ring with cultivated laughter as the two sisters discussed this so *drôle jeune Ecossais.* . . .

They tried everything. Mme. Garschine probed sweetly into his "passion"—i.e., Mrs. Sitwell—and, though apparently unable to fathom the exact relationship, expressed relief at hearing that she was "impressionable" and not at all "Scotch." In her sister's presence Mme. Zassetsky read Louis's palm and, with eloquent coyness, refused to reveal his immediate future. But young Malvolio's instinct was to suspect it was a trifle too much of a game in another language. ". . . Since my illness," he wrote Mrs. Sitwell, "I have been unspeakably timid and blushful. . . . and I suppose that is where the humour of the thing lies." [35] Eventually the Russians relented, grew relaxedly maternal. For the rest of his stay they and Louis were greatly charmed and charming friends, the relationship strongly cemented by their firm and frequently expressed belief that he was really brilliant.

It all helped to confirm his lifelong fascination with women's irresponsibilities, which crops out again and again in such of his characters as the Countess von Rosen,[36] and always saved him from the fictioneer's temptation to pose as the Man-Who-Understood-Women. To him women were attractive, aesthetically commanding, but basically inscrutable, like cats. Their antics interested him vastly, their grace and warmth and occasionally appalling directness of mind instructed him, their appeal to his maleness always fluttered in his path with opportunistic overtones, if less imperiously as he grew older. But, for all his popularity with harridans and his depictions of such skilful ladies' men as Alan Breck and St. Ives, the root of the matter evaded him. He seems to have been subject to a feeling, cognate to preliterate notions, that women are somehow "uncanny," charged with magnetic but hazardous qualities not altogether of this world. This is poor preparation for straightforward, youth-to-youth falling in love. No boy carrying on so windily about the figures from the Parthenon pediment and "unconscionably bored" by the conversation of young girls stood much chance of finding a conventional object for his affections in Victorian Scotland.

In any case the Eastern Question helped him to refit. January brought many improvements, always in his own terms. He finished "Ordered South," his first work worth reading for any but clinical reasons, was juggling with an essay on Victor Hugo that would sell to the august *Cornhill*, and planning "Four

Great Scotsmen"—Knox, Hume, Burns, and Scott—a project that bore fragmentary fruit for the next ten years. In February Mme. Zassetsky, still puzzled though tensions had died away, heard him explaining certain arbitrary tricks of memory that interested him and said: ". . . with her little falsetto of discovery, 'Mais, c'est que vous êtes tout simplement enfant!' This *mot* I have reflected on at leisure and there is some truth in it. Long may I be so." [37] It was evident that, as he wrote his Madonna: "Look here, do you know I am really getting better?" [38]

At this period Colvin introduced Louis to Andrew Lang, who remembered him, not favorably, as

> . . . more like a lass than a lad, with a rather long, smooth, oval face, brown hair worn at greater length than is common, large lucid eyes . . . slender, agile frame . . . "Here," I thought, "is one of your aesthetic young men, though a very clever one." [39]

Though they were good and mutually respecting friends later, there could be a profound moral in the fact that Louis also disliked Lang at first on somewhat similar grounds: "too good-looking, delicate, Oxfordish . . . a la-de-dady kind of Scot." [40] Louis's costume may have played its role here, for he was now sporting a new hat, "a brigand sort of arrangement," [41] and a swashbuckling cloak that Colvin sent him, by request, from Paris:

> . . . the most admirable of all garments. For warmth, unequalled; for a sort of pensive, Roman stateliness, sometimes warming into Romantic guitarism, it is simply without concurrent; . . . [42]

That was to his father. In spite of the ever ominous relations between them, Louis could grin sturdily in Thomas's presence at his own absurd self. But, if maturity consists in knowing as well as appreciating oneself, it was still far away. On his way home from Menton he was in a strangely recessive mood, writing to Mrs. Sitwell:

I should like to live alone in a country inn always, not too far away from people to come occasionally and see me; an inn with a garden in which I could sit when there was sun, and fine big trees about it. That is my ideal now, and to settle down there for good among books and papers.[43]

There was better prognostication in the fortune that the loose-lipped old eccentric told him at Dunoon in 1870: that he should go to America and thereafter be much upon the sea.

In order to meet Bob in Paris, Louis started homeward prematurely, in the spring of 1874. Paris was rawly cold. Down he came with a roaring headache, heavy sweating, and a recurrence of *tic*, but he did not turn tail and run for sunshine. As soon as the weather relented he was going home, predicting, with nonchalance close to cynicism: "Going home not very well is an astonishing good thing for me. I shall simply be a prince." [44] Headache or not, he worked away on Victor Hugo and his and Colvin's plans to collaborate on plays: Diana of the Ephesians, burning temple, pagan rites . . . now there was a subject for a major drama! Heaven knows where Colvin's literary judgment was. Happily for both, the project proved abortive.

As predicted, home was relatively calm. Thomas was relieved to find his son apparently sane after all, his wife at finding groundless her previous fears that Louis's suspicious exit had meant he was gone for good. They granted a dignified allowance—eighty guineas a year, seven pound a month, which, though not large for a gentleman's son, would then have supported many a laborer. In return Louis went on with his law and broached no schemes more disturbing then trying—and failing—to get leave to study Roman Law at Göttingen with a brilliant young Russian relative of Mme. Zassetsky's whom he had met in Menton. Summer was to see a cruise in the Inner Hebrides in a small yacht chartered by Simpson.

But in June he visited London. Intoxicated by being in the presence of his Consuelo, he found further self-deception temporarily impossible and brimmed over. The voltage had been piling up anyway. With risky semifrankness he had already written, after reading too much in Tennyson's *Maud*: "Only just tonight I cannot write any half words. I can think of nothing but how much I love you and how happy it makes me that I do so. I would not give up my love of you for eternity." [45] Even though, in their terms, major "love" was not necessarily carnal-minded, that passage was fair warning to both, setting the scene for the June explosion.

Nobody knows just what was said where or when. But Louis's subsequent letters indicate that the lady ably and warmly convinced him that it could never be—on higher general grounds as well as because she was still technically married. Passages previously quoted have hinted at the notion, apparently orthodox among her protégés, that none of them was privileged to monopolize, by making physical the spiritual privileges that all others—e.g., Colvin—needed as badly as Louis. Her immaterial favors were a sort of public trust with herself as trustee, her material favors inaccessible by definition—a position that Colvin too apparently accepted in whatever understanding he and she presently reached. Louis seems actually to have gone forth into the night apologizing for his presumption instead of raging with frustration. He was "filled with shame," called himself "poor and selfish," and wrote in worshipping capitulation:

> Should I have been good enough, unselfish enough, to have let you follow without trammel the obvious way of your destiny, as the helper of all men, of the *Sun* (as I used to phrase it, do you remember, in old days) that is to shine on all, do good to all, encourage and support all? I fancy not; it is better as it is. . . . I am afraid, had I been more fortunate, you had been less useful, and so, on the whole, the sum of help had been diminished. [46]

The young lover of the Utilitarian century was thus reconciled to defeat in the name of the greatest-good-of-the-greatest-number.

But no such intellectual jokes can discount the violence of the feeling, or the loyal courage with which Louis took his medicine. By the time he was away in the yacht, waiting out a storm in the beautiful harbor of Oban:

> . . . my health is better. I work like a common sailor when it is needful, in rain and wind, without hurt, and my heart is quite stout now. . . . I believe in the future faithfully. . . . I shall be a man yet, dear, and a good man, although day by day, I see more clearly by how much I fall short of the mark of our high calling; in how much I am still selfish and peevish and a spoiled child.[47]

Never mind the vocabulary—that is not bad for an overarticulate young fellow with much "spoiled child" about him just deprived of what for almost a year had been his fundamental, if probably unconscious, desire. In a crude sense he might have done better to renounce the whole relation as torturingly uncandid. But no such gesture was possible in a youth of his stamp then and there. The proof is that, through the faith that both he and the lady had in the validity of such terms, the relation remained vital and viable.

Verses duly recorded the crisis:

> Fear not, dear friend, but freely live your days,
> > Though lesser lives should suffer. Such am I,
> > A lesser life, that what is his of sky
> Gladly would give for you, and what of praise.
> Step, without trouble, down the sunlit ways.
> > We that have touched your garment are made whole
> > From all the selfish cankers of men's soul,
> And we would see you happy, dear, or die . . .[48]

Most gratifyingly calm.

But Mrs. Sitwell's continuing ailments kept him guiltily suspecting that, added to her other troubles, his outburst had been the particular cause. Presently his cousins' difficulties were added to his own: Bob almost died of diphtheria. Kather-

ine insisted on marrying a man reputed to be an atheist, which
involved Louis in disputes with his father that both should
have been spared. This was the period when his "kobold look"
and gaunt-stalking figure on the hill-paths convinced country-
people round Swanston that he was somewhat touched in the
head. The exception seems to have been John Todd, the brass-
lunged shepherd of "Pastoral," who became a harsh good
friend in his own time.

Eventually the poor devil fell on a *modus vivendi* of no great
originality. In the yacht he had experimented with the mother-
motif as saving formula for his passion. By August he writes:
"You need not fear any bother from this child except petulant
moments," [49] and by Christmas he is composing whole orato-
rios on the theme:

I do not know what longing comes to me to go to you for two
hours and tell you plainly you have another son. This letter
will not speak to you plainly enough; and you must eke it
out with what you know of me, madonna, and you do know
that I love you dearly—; and think of what I should say to
you if I were there; and what I should look like as I saw you
again out of the body with delight; and how childish I should
be for very pleasure; and so, if you love me, this letter shall be
to you as a son's Christmas kiss. . . . You must be happy; I
will not have a sad deity in my chapel, she must be all smiles
and peace and must look eloquently out of her eyes. And she
must not know what doubt is. Nor need she doubt just now
on my account; for I do feel all that she could wish, happy
and good and industrious. So—there's a hymn to myself by
way of conclusion.

And now let us put out the tapers for a while (for we must
be thrifty in this chapel and the priest needs some of them
to study by, so that he may be a worthy priest); only the
little red heart-shaped lamp, let us leave burning, just before
the shrine; it has not been extinguished since it was first
lighted, eighteen months ago among the summer trees; and

it is the rule of my order that it must be kept ever trimmed
and bright; so that the priest himself may warm his hands at
it when he is sad, and others perhaps, seeing it through the
window, may have the better courage for life.

So, madonna, I give you a son's kiss this Christmass [*sic*]
morning, and my heart is in my mouth, dear, as I write the
words—

> ever your faithful friend
> and son and priest
> ROBERT LOUIS STEVENSON[50]

Earlier he had set her off as "mother of my soul" from Mrs.
Thomas Stevenson as "mother of my body";[51] later he enlarged on that perhaps too pellucidly: " . . . my mother is
my father's wife; . . . the children of lovers are orphans." [52]

An instrument gauging such tensions might well have shown
him worse off than ever. His only hope was to mature past
the point where fictional maternity seemed to express emotion. He had to grow into self-weaning. Not even Mrs. Sitwell's
clever handling could hasten that—if, indeed, she actually
wished that effect. But in the meantime he never slipped from
terms of son-and-mother. Burningly swoony as were the thousands of words he wrote to her in his chill hideaway at the top
of 17 Heriot Row, his performance was always unimpeachable.
Self-censorship is plain in one instance: In a preliminary draft
of verses occur the stanzas that have been taken as one proof of
Louis's relation with the lady having been carnal:

> If I had wings, my lady, like a dove,
>   This hour should see my soul at rest,
> Should see me safe, my lady, with my love,
>   To kiss the sweet division of her breast, . . .
>
> If I could die, my lady, with my love,
>   Die, mouth to mouth, a splendid death,
> I should take wing, my lady, like a dove,
>   To spend upon her lips my all of breath, . . .[53]

But, when copying the verses off to mail to her, Louis cut the first stanza quoted and cobbled up a new one that shifted "sweet division" from her breast to her coiffure. Even as revised, true, it is hardly the sort of apostrophe that mothers often receive from sons. But it did not absolutely violate the oath to behave himself that she had apparently extracted from him in June. If they two saw fit to suffer these ambiguities, strangers can hardly complain; though occasionally truth struggled out from under cover, as when Louis wrote in January 1875: "It is not one bit like what I feel for my mother *here*. But I think it is what one *ought* to feel for a mother. . . . That's a lie; nobody loves a mere mother as much as I love you, madonna." [54] Even when tangled in artificialities that he could not afford to analyze, Louis was still unable altogether to deceive himself.

The writer of a "love story" is permitted a lopsided hero and can neglect to keep the reader reminded that, during erotic developments, the principals usually continue to work, eat, and converse with third parties. The biographer must weave into high, middle, or low passion accounts of how Louis Stevenson, wayward law student, lived his life while his soul was forcing its cork.

His law studies actually progressed: he even mildly relished the intellectual challenges of law and once stood third in a certain small class. His father had promised him £1000 from his patrimony when he should pass advocate (i. e., qualify at the Scottish bar as equivalent of an English barrister). In mid-July 1875, wearing evening dress in the morning as custom required—a fellow-aspirant told him he looked like a drunken Irishman on the way to a funeral—Thomas Stevenson's son was formally acknowledged to possess the learning and integrity to plead for justice for his fellowman. When ceremonies were all over, his parents drove him back to Swanston in the open family carriage, Louis sitting on the folded top with his feet in the seat, whooping the news of his new dignity to all passers-by. Presently the façade of 17 Heriot Row carried a brass plate:

R. L. Stevenson, Advocate. Jenkin wrote him: "Accept my hearty congratulations on being done with it. I believe that is the view you like to take of the beginning you have just made." [55]

He made a few professional gestures—clubbed with several other new advocates to hire a common clerk, handled a complimentary brief or two from family friends. [56] The principal duty of the tyro Scots advocate, however, is to promenade the magnificent medieval hall where Parliament sat before the Union. Louis appreciated the glow of the fireplaces that try to warm the great hollow of the vault; the Daumier-like couples passing to and fro, agent and advocate clinging together in the half-gloom like insects mating on the wing; the crowd of statues and portraits commemorating great and long-dead judges in scarlet robes. But temptation to turn active professional rapidly passed if Louis ever felt it. (Baxter did so, thereby saddling himself with lifelong troubles, cheerfully endured, as Louis's man of business.) He remained fond of law and lawyers, as his many sketches of legal characters and situations show; his enforced contact with such matters helped him to honor his art with Prestongrange and Hermiston. His widow eventually drew a pension of sixty-odd pounds a year from group-insurance consequent on his passing advocate. That was all Thomas ever got for the thousand pounds that Louis's legal education and fees probably cost him, in addition to the thousand advanced on Mrs. Stevenson's jointure.

There had been more future in Louis's election, in June 1874, to the Savile Club, founded in 1868 on the un-British principles of any member's being obliged to chat with any other without introduction, and of insisting on a "mixture of different professions and opinions." [57] Louis probably owed this rather to Colvin's good offices among his fellow-founders of the Savile than to marked reputation in literature, for so far neither quantity nor quality of publication had been impressive. Louis proved, as Gosse said, "the most clubbable of men," and became one of the Savile's institutions whenever he was in

London, among such cronies as Colvin, Gosse, Henley, and Jenkin and such useful acquaintances as Walter Pollock, W. K. Clifford, and George Saintsbury. A writer can go a long way, even clear to the top, without such connections, but they do no harm whatever.

His showing to date—"Roads," "Ordered South" (in *Macmillan*'s), and a review of Lytton's *Fables in Song* for the *Fortnightly*—was very meager for paper and ink consumed. On he toiled with the doggedness of the chronic aspirant that has so little to do with degree of talent. He tried "John Knox and His Relations to Women" on the Spec.;[58] only the first page or so is fair Stevenson. His "Victor Hugo" was enough better to sell to Leslie Stephen for the *Cornhill*, but it was two years before he again appeared in those pages. Critics have sometimes accused him of writing before he had anything to say. Actually in his earliest paid work his brains were well ahead of his skill in statement. He had some shrewd points to make about Hugo's vulgar if able melodrama, but the handling is clotty and pedestrian, cramped by reference to rather than use of connotations, needlessly formal structure, sentences that fail to run. Not yet could he strike up apparently in the middle of a bar and dance sure-footedly to a conclusion structurally sound though indeterminate—much as bagpipes behave. His feel for aimed words as part of his life was not yet a reflex as reliable as the grip of a horseman's knees or a golfer's left hand—as it later became.

But certain writers' stigmata are already there: impatience with his elders for one. Noble as he thought *The Ring and the Book*, he was presently reviewing Browning's *Inn Album*[59] with high presumption, comparing the poet's procedures in this work to those of a conductor who should upset the music-stool when he knew there was a false note coming. Seeing "Roads" in print months after he wrote it, he could already say Ah me, I can't write like that any more, henceforth I can hope only to make minimum sense. And, like the writer in *The Sea Gull*, he regretted his inability to be moved by a sunset without automatically speculating on how best to handle the thing verbally; to Mrs. Sitwell:

> I saw a woman come out of a shop the other day on the oppo-
> site side of a wide street, and dear, I thought it was you. . . .
> I noticed afterwards (how brutal one has to be if one wants to
> be an artist) that I had put my hand to my heart.[60]

His parents' satisfaction with his passing advocate gave him a sort of claustrophobia, for he could feel small hope of health in his relations with Mr. and Mrs. Thomas Stevenson:

> I have discovered why I get on always so ill, am always so
> nasty, so much worse than myself, with my parents; it is be-
> cause they always take me at my worst, seek out my faults and
> never give me any credit. . . . I am always bad with them
> because they always seem to expect me to be not very good;
> and I am never good because they never seem to see that I am
> good.[61]

There is the Pontifex aspect—not to be overemphasized—of Louis's family troubles.

Further imperiling the relation, the winter of 1874-75 brought Thomas to a severe emotional crisis, perhaps of a sort familiar in men of fifty-six. His normal alternations of gay and dark moods—"My father is such fun here . . . always skipping about . . . speaking to all the girls and telling them God knows what about us all" [62]—gained such momentum at the bottom of the swings that he grew miserably surly, rude and vindictive. The sinister memory of brother Alan's years of psychosis was probably what moved Thomas wisely to consult doctors, but they were little help. In time he became himself again, but while thus haunted he saw fit to torture himself and Louis about the ethics of inherited money. They were soon drowning each other beyond their depth:

> I have finally bade adieu to inheriting any money. I must
> learn to live by my own pen or something. I promised my
> father (as I think it was entirely his right, and mind you, it

was on no prompting from him, nor has he any notion how serious the words were for me) that I shall never use a farthing of his money unless I am a Christian. He was talking of the duty of leaving money to children; and then he said "Of course, there were certain conditions that preceded the call of the blood; for instance did he think he had a son who thought as Tyndall thought, he could not leave his money to him; he only held it in trust for the views in which he believed." So I said to him that I should reckon any person a thief who would use another man's money in such circumstances. And he said fervently "And a damned thief too.". . . for me it will, of course, supersede the terms of any will written in ignorance, doubt or misapprehension. . . . I shall not construe this promise too tightly. I shall not let myself starve, of course; but beyond that must try to be an honest man.[63]

The famous thousand pounds, advanced presumably to set Louis up as advocate, though there were no formal strings attached, found Louis with little of it left at the end of three years and precisely no legal practice. It had gone on getting away from home as much as possible; on wine and new asparagus now and then; on books; on loans to less fortunate friends, for Louis often liked people who were hard up. Thus two guineas paid for a canvas by Bloomer, an American painter-friend, as a mutually acceptable device for curing emptiness of the pocket. Sizable sums went to Bob, who was coming to the end of his patrimony; to Henley; to Colvin, who had a meager salary and needy close relatives and regularly paid interest and sometimes worked off a little principal. Some went to Bob's sister, whose atheist husband proved unfortunate. (Anomalously enough, Louis was one of Katherine's trustees.) This was a generous young fellow, if sometimes heedlessly so. The trait stayed with him all his life. When he died, a letter signed only "H." came to the London *Times*:

Seven years ago I lay ill in San Francisco, an obscure journalist, quite friendless. Stevenson, who knew me slightly, came

of the most intelligent short criticisms of him and his earlier work. At Stephen's table Louis reëncountered Edmund Gosse, met first years before on a Hebrides steamer,[66] now to develop into a cardinal member of the inner circle round R.L.S.[67] Then, in February 1875, Stephen, coming to lecture on mountain-climbing in Edinburgh, took Louis along to visit another young unknown—William Ernest Henley, a patient in the old Edinburgh Infirmary, whose boldly irregular verse had caught the editor's notice. The jovial bull of a young fellow ". . . sat up in bed with his hair and beard all tangled and talked as cheerfully as if he had been in a King's palace";[68] he had been spending suffering weeks in making friends with two small boy-patients who shared his room, in studying languages and polishing up some notable poems about hospital-life.

To many of us Henley may now be only the man with the bloody but unbowed head or the King in Babylon who had so anachronistic a Christian slave. In his day he was far more: Gloucester-born, never prosperous, the Henley boys were talented—Anthony an artist whom Louis was to know in France; Teddy an ambitious young actor whom, to his great regret, Louis would also know; William Ernest self-dedicated to literature. His wit, energy, and pluck were equal to Louis's own under even greater demands. For under the bedclothes his burly body ended in mutilation—one foot had been amputated to check tuberculosis of the bone, the other too would have gone if Henley had not brought it to Edinburgh's great Joseph Lister, pioneer of asepsis, one of the great surgeons of the century. Each of Lister's periodic scrapings of the bone meant prolonged postoperative agony. But doctor and patient had the bowels for this inquisitorial ordeal that saved the foot.

Doggedly navigating with stick or crutch, slouch-hatted, fabulously bearded, drinking like a comradely fish, Henley became a landmark in literary London—critic, editor, poet, spottily learned, quarrelsome as a musketeer, fond as a woman of ill-natured gossip, talking like a fire-hose, detested here, greatly loved there—particularly by young men whom he helped to launch, such as Wells, Kipling, Yeats. Louis made him partial original of John Silver, as well as Burly of "Talk and Talkers." In 1875 his name was still to make and Louis helped his approaches to people in the right places. In grateful return Henley would be Louis's unpaid literary agent[69] and aesthetic cathode for twelve years.

Friendship blazed up as soon as hands were shaken. They were "my dear lad" and "my dear boy" most rewardingly until Henley's growing malice, probably stimulated by some of the overtones of Louis's marriage, estranged them. Now, as soon as Henley could sit up, Louis brought him an armchair from 17 Heriot Row, carrying it across town on his head for momentary lack of cab fare. He took him on the first carriage drive he was allowed:

> I had a business to carry him down the long stair, and more of a business to get him up again, but while he was in the carriage, it was splendid. It is now just the top of the spring with us. The whole country is mad with green. To see the cherry-blossom bitten out upon the black firs, and the black firs bitten out of the blue sky, was a sight to set before a king. You can imagine what it was to a man who had been eighteen months in a hospital ward. The look of his face was as wine to me.[70]

Louis is sometimes thus visible at prime moments—exultantly sensitized, jubilantly generous, so embracingly at home with emotion that the word "happy" seems niggardly. These fits of hyperconscious pleasure were almost worth their price—times when, in a phrase of which he was significantly fond, the black dog was on his back, or when illness renewed its temporarily loosened hold. In one such black period Henley established Louis—just then reluctant to be ill at home—in his grimy lodging near the University and took comradely care of him. It was all among friends—Louis had just been working what legal connections he had to get copying work for Henley.

Letters to Mrs. Sitwell soon begin to read in a new idiom:

You need not be afraid, madonna. My dear, I will be as much to you as I can. I do not deny that somehow I am happier; and I do not deny that I am glad of it.[71]

A year later he was able to spend a few days in London en route to France without visiting her, and never told her until months later:

"I once went down Southampton Row and felt in a fine flutter in case you should come out of Casino Place. I daresay you know a great deal more about me now, as I know much more of you; and both of us must have learned something of the inscrutable ways of fate. How dark and foolish are the ways in which people once walked, thinking them lit up with eternal sunlight, and what we now see to be so much gauze and cardboard, imperishable masonry! . . . God help us all, amen. For I do cling a little to God, as I have lost all hold on right and wrong. You cannot think things both right and wrong, you know; the human mind cannot do it, although I daresay it would be devilish clever if you could; and when you come to a stone wall in morals, you give them up and be d——d to them. I beg your pardon, but that's the only English idiom which explains my meaning. So I say, I cling to God; to a nice, immoral old gentleman who knows a bit more about it all than I do, and may, sometime or other, in the course of the ages, explain matters to his creature over a pipe of tobacco; nay, and he may be something more than this, and give one that sense of finish and perspective that can only be had one way in the world. I daresay it's all a lie; but if it pleases me to imagine it——[72]

The lady may well have sighed over these tinges of bitterness and harried impoliteness. In almost sure token of weaning well in operation, Louis, now twenty-five, was drafting something "which I should not suppose you would like," [73] to be called "Virginibus Puerisque," along lines that he had discontentedly sketched in February.

I don't believe I ever shall love anyone else although I know the world's experience against me and I dont know but what a good dull marriage with a good dull girl would be a good move.[74]

I like to think that it was during Louis's visits to France this jangling year that he saw Dumas' *Le Demi-Monde*. The flavor of the piece, which treats women as props rather than as people partly breathing their own private climates—an approach that he always detested—gagged him. Thirteen years later he told what occurred:

On my way down the Français stairs I trod on an old gentleman's toes, whereupon with that suavity which so well becomes me, I turned and was about to apologize, and on the instant repenting me of that intention, stopped the apology midway, and added something to this effect: No, you are one of the *lâches* who have been applauding that piece. Said the old Frenchman, laying his hand on my arm, and with a smile that was truly heavenly in temperance, irony, good-nature and knowledge of the world, "Ah, monsieur, vous êtes bien jeune!" [75]

As he neared twenty-four, Louis had warned his mother that the rest of his life he would be often absent and affectionately reproached her with having had a tramp for a son. He kept his word: in 1886 he could list 210 towns of the United Kingdom and Europe in which he had slept one or more nights. It meant deep-sprung discontent. By definition the tramp is the dislocated man, succeeding, even when intelligent, only in rationalizing his suspicions of rooted people. In 1878 Louis candidly acknowledged that

> . . . There's nothing under heav'n so blue
> That's fairly worth the travelling to.
>
> On every hand, the roads begin,
> And people walk with zeal therein;

And wheresoe'er the highways tend,
Be sure there's nothing at the end.

Then follow you, wherever hie
The travelling mountains of the sky,
Or let the streams in civil mode
Direct your choice upon a road;

For one and all, or high or low,
Will lead you where you wish to go;
And one and all go night and day
Over the hills and far away![76]

His day-long prowlings in the Lothians had long grown into walking trips lasting several days: alone in the north of England; with Simpson in the Black Forest; alone in Buckinghamshire. . . . Following his itineraries on a map shows that he was by no means one of " . . . your athletic men in purple stockings who walk their fifty miles a day," [77] though, when in motion, his eager long legs could do up to twenty-five miles a day on occasion. It speaks well for his basic stamina that he came back four inches larger round the waist from a long stretch of snowy tramping in southwestern Scotland. He somewhat self-consciously exulted in "the purely animal pleasure, the sense of physical well-being, the delight of every inhalation, of every time the muscles tighten down the thigh." [77] Under the influence of George Borrow he even planned to buy a caravan with "plenty of accommodation for two, or perhaps three, a stove for wet weather, etc. Yachting on dry land . . ." [78] But he remained a pedestrian.

That was acceptable. The solitary pedestrian is the perfect egocentric. Even when with Simpson, Louis often arranged to travel out ahead of him, rejoining him in the evening for sociability. (It was this arrangement that got him arrested and thrust into a damp jail as a suspected Prussian spy, as told in "An Epilogue to *An Inland Voyage*.") Thus he could steep himself undistractedly in details of topography and casual conversations, like an impressionist Boy Scout qualifying for a merit badge in Observation. Borrow and Hazlitt, two of his literary heroes, and Whitman as apostle of the Open Road, had lent literary *cachet* to walking. The trip finished, the mixture precipitated, Louis wrote about it as closely and atmospherically as he could contrive, answering his own self-challenge: ". . . a book about a journey from York to London must be clever; a book about the Caucasus may be what you will," [79] and often somebody was willing to print the result. This congenial way of pursuing one's chosen craft fathered many of his break-in early writings and his first two books, *An Inland Voyage* and *Travels With a Donkey*.

His skill was approaching professional firmness. By early 1876 whole passages were surefooted:

> The snow lay on the beach to the tide-mark. It was daubed on to the sills of the ruin; it roosted in the crannies of the rock like white sea-birds; even on outlying reefs there would be a little cock of snow like a toy lighthouse. Everything was grey and white in a cold and dolorous sort of shepherd's plaid.[80]

Though "Forest Notes," his second sale to the *Cornhill*, was, as he told Colvin, "too sweet to be wholesome," [81] it has bits of texture;

> . . . a picnic party seated under a tree in the open. The old father knitted a sock, the mother sat staring at the fire. The eldest son, in the uniform of a private of dragoons, was choosing out notes on a key-bugle. Two or three daughters lay in the neighborhood, picking violets. And the whole party as grave and silent as the woods about them! My friend watched for a long time, he says; but all held their peace; no one spoke or smiled; only the dragoon kept choosing out single notes upon the bugle, and the father knitted away at his sock and made strange movements the while with his flexible eyebrows. They took no notice whatever of my friend's presence,

which was disquieting in itself, and increased the resemblance
of the whole party to mechanical wax-works. Certainly, he af-
firms, a wax figure might have played the bugle with more
spirit than that strange dragoon. And as this hypothesis of
his became more certain, the awful insolubility of why they
should be left out there in the woods with nobody to wind
them up again when they ran down, and a growing disquietude of what might happen next, became too much for his
courage. . . .[82]

This emergence as craftsman showed further sloughing of imitativeness. One could confidently pick either passage as Stevenson out of quite a confusing literary puzzle.

By 1877 his *Cornhill* connection forever spoiled his amateur
status by attracting his first known "fan"—an Australian called
A. Patchett Martin who sent Louis his own volume of verse,
A Sweet Girl Graduate, and Other Poems;[83] Louis's highly
pleased reply favored his admirer with a memorable definition
of George Eliot as "a high, but, may we not add?—a rather dry
lady." [84] In the seventy-four years to follow, too many personally admired Louis on the strength of his printed writings.
But the first touch of flood was welcome.

Better in France

But then no disgrace is attached in France to saying a thing neatly; whereas in England, to talk like a book is to give in one's resignation to society.

—*An Inland Voyage*

I<small>N THE</small> spring of 1875 milder, trans-Channel climates were again recommended. Off Louis went, with Bob as veteran intermediary, to the country that had become a passion with him. Three times he had visited Germany; he had hoped to visit Mme. Garschine in Poland and to see the Spain that Borrow and Napier had written about. But in practice, every time money coincided with opportunity, he went straight to France.

He had his share of the reversedly snobbish British feeling, inevitably affecting Americans, that the French was a more cultivated culture affording the English-speaking world sharp, eloquent, and negligently graceful lessons in food, drink, manners, *joie de vivre*, intellectual honesty, and minding one's own business. It has been an influence quite as fertile as it has been absurd in unhappy contexts. But Louis was never the frustrated schoolmaster the far side of the Channel, wallowing in an uncritical sense of how green it was. After seeing as much of France as of Britain between 1875 and 1883, he sent Simoneau, his great French friend in California, a double column of generalities which, whether accurate or not, show no blind worship of either nation:

The English	The French
hypocrites	free from hypocrisy
good, stout, reliable friends	incapable of friendship
dishonest to the root	fairly honest
fairly decent to women	rather indecent to women[1]

France made him something of "a dainty feeder" like Loudon Dodd. Trying to qualify Louis as *gourmet* is pointless. He showed few earmarks of the devoted, intense savorer of great dishes. But he had a catholic palate, which is uncommon among Britons, and his enthusiasm over sweet corn and sweet potatoes in the States betokens more than the mere gastronomic Francophilia that sometimes appears in the English. In Louis's mind, delicate omelets, gently savory salads, and portly, ghastly-white French asparagus, that most voluptuous of vegetables, were coupled with good wine. His growing proficiency in the language he also felt as a privilege. He had begun learning French from a tutor in Menton in 1864; perhaps in despair, the man neglected grammar and merely trained his pupil to talk, a thing to which Louis was usually more than willing. Thus, when French was among the subjects in which he had to qualify for his law course, he took his first look at a French grammar the night before and passed on the strength of oral proficiency alone. His letters in French—to Simoneau, Rodin, Marcel Schwob—show minor errors, I am told. But there is no question of his feeling admiringly at home in this elegant tongue, taking pleasure in the way the man in the street handled it, as well as in the way Daudet, Baudelaire, Musset, Charles d'Orléans, Villon, Béranger, and Dumas wrote it.

Several scholars have tried to identify the influence on his writings of Louis's loving intimacy with French and French literature. Barring his experiments in archaic French verse-forms —a literary fad of his time—the direct influence seems to me hardly major. Some of his early tales had a French touch as well as French background: were the paganism a trifle more sententious, "The Treasure of Franchard" would have anticipated Anatole France. "A Lodging for the Night" has a high and valuable flavor of Balzac—the harsh little literary curiosity is still shapelessly cunning and, for all its didactic dialogue, strangely alive. The figure of Villon naturally fascinated him, though in a markedly clinical fashion; Louis would probably have been genuinely shocked by the distortions of *If I Were*

King. And that is about all. The sounder point is that the young
fellow distilled out and assimilated French literary ideals,
rather than ideas, to his own Scots-English idiom. He did not
imitate Flaubert's excellent one-pearl-at-a-time style nor yet
the tawdry, specious word-embroidering of *Salammbô;* he did
apply the doctrine of the *mot juste* most organically to his own
needs. He did not imitate Villon; but he did derive from that
most eccentric of first-class poets the hope of making the *mot
juste* kick like a pistol in addition to being *juste.* . . .

This taste for French writings was selective, no mere gaping
at Gallicness *per se.* Racine he found "damned standard"[2]
—a dismissal as apt as his later complaint that Swinburne had "literary diabetes."[3] He emphatically denounced Zola but, when
his strictures are analyzed, they come not so much from shock
at the persevering Frenchman's material—which was the occasion of his notoriety in Louis's time—as from technical disapproval of his sloppy techniques and apparent neglect of selec-
tivity. When Zola did what seemed to Louis better work, he
could find a great deal in *Le Débâcle,* and, reading *L'Œuvre,*
write Henley gloatingly:

> The first four or five chapters are like being young again in
> Paris; they woke me like a trumpet. Does Bob remember the
> martyrdom of St. Stephen with petits-pains? The man who in-
> sured his old mistress? The very moral of him is here. . . .[4]

Generalized zest for France is clear in his enjoyment of provincial street-names: ". . . Boulevard (if you please) de
Belles Manières; streets of the Five Bridegrooms, the Ancient
Palace, the Good William, the dead, of God's Oven, . . ."[5] This
country was like being on stage with character-actors of uniform talent, from the yokel through the Jack-in-Office to the
singing chambermaid and the philosophical old father, not
quaint in the tourist's or the Francophile's sense, but all alive
with a spirited explicitness, the cast reading their improvised
lines with a dash matching the pungency of their scenario:

The wine was excellent. When we made the judge our compliments upon a bottle, "I do not give it to you as my worst,"
said he. I wonder when *Englishmen* will learn these hospitable graces.[6]

Louis admired equally an old lady of adroit obscenities in Le
Puy and the innocent pride and courage of the strolling players
at Barbizon who were the germ of "Providence and the Guitar."
Eve Simpson, who was then in a position to know, says that
Louis went trouping for a while with these strollers; he is said
to have sent the originals the money that he was paid for the
story. But then he was always sensitive to the emotional risks
taken by public performers, automatically laid open to the possible jeers of the cash customers a thousand times an hour.

As in the above quotation, Louis was given to comparisons
often unfavorable to Scotland, oftener to England. His dismayed dislike for that latter country and nation grew as he saw
more of it and the world. He was, of course, as loyal to King and
country as a Greenwich pensioner; but, whereas the Englishman is loyal primarily to England, the Scot is so primarily to
the Crown. So for Louis the region south of Tweed could remain principally a dank corridor to Europe, an habitation for
friends, living or dead, a cultural puzzle, and a steady irritation. Loudon Dodd's reaction to Stallbridge-le-Carthew in *The
Wrecker* is not that of an American aghast at the opulence of
British stolidity; it is Louis Stevenson still marveling at the
prestige that can attach to human vegetables. At Frenchmen
in France he was sometimes wildly angry; in England, Englishmen and their ways made him feel like a cat in a dog-
pound. Though he revered and reveled in what Shakespeare,
Milton, and Defoe had done with their eloquent Topsy of
a language; though he admired or liked such highly English
figures as Pepys, Wellington, and Dr. Johnson; nevertheless
the face and heart of England remained smugly and snugly
strange to him. Too many Englishmen's attempts at courtesy

were rude; there was too graceless a condescension in many of their ways.

Americans often share this difficulty with Scots. Whether Stevenson or his American stepson wrote the lines, Louis certainly relished Davis's snarling at the back of the patrician zealot of *The Ebb-Tide:*[7] "Here's the real article, I said, and I don't like it; here's the real, first-rate, copper-bottomed aristocrat. *'Aw! Don't know ye, do I? God damn ye, did God make ye?'* . . ." Of Louis's two best-drawn English characters, Silver was a highly integrated cutthroat and Huish the slimiest little rat ever bred in a London sewer. The London of the *New Arabian Nights* and *Jekyll* is a mere geographical convention; whereas the Paris of "A Lodging for the Night" and *The Wrecker* is felt almost as intimately as he felt Edinburgh.

But—again the distinction—he was fierily British. Overhearing a flamboyant Frenchman abusing the British in a café, Louis crossed the room and slapped his face. *"Mais vous m'avez frappé!"* ejaculated the Frenchman. *"À ce qu'il paraît,"* [8] said Louis, hovering, and the incident closed, perhaps because his opponent was paralyzed with astonishment at finding this exotic-looking creature British. In Honolulu in 1893 he flew into a violent rage, for which he soon apologized, merely at mention of an English writer who had abused the Royal Family in print. His temper was proverbial anyway. "The Old Man Virulent" was a family name for him. One reminiscer saw him smash a bottle of spuriously labeled wine against a restaurant wall. Another could never forget his blistering, voluble rage when a bank in Clermont-Ferrand denied knowledge of the British correspondent-bank on which Louis's drafts were drawn. Colvin made a distinction significant of the young fellow's personality: he was devastating as an army with banners when he cut loose with no tactical purpose, but he did not have the knack of "putting down insolence by greater insolence." [9]

France was to be the scene of his personal and professional emancipation. Bob's guidance made him free of the jargons and customs of the polyglot artists' colonies of Montparnasse, where

Bob was most enjoyably spending his patrimony and learning something about painting too. His studio on the Boulevard St. Michel was headquarters for British, Americans, and French of various degrees of achievement and solvency, mostly from the *atélier* of Carolus Duran. Will Low, American student with whom Louis made great friends, nostalgically recorded this brave new world, where one man lived in a stairway closet and another, temporarily flush, dined sumptuously at Lavenue's, the Montparnasse restaurant that became Louis's symbol of expensive elegance in food,[10] and a third was so unavoidably shabby that he was refused entrance to the Luxembourg. This was not Bohemia laboriously attempted in stony Edinburgh but the original Bohemia in earnest in a town of pale sun on stucco, as well established as the turbulent and messy Paris markets. Fifteen years later Louis recalled every smell, every plump of rain, every toothful of red wine in describing Loudon Dodd's ups and downs. The only missing detail is what happened to Louis when—if, rather—he engaged personally in the pursuit of "that extinct mammal, the grisette."

Like many of his cronies, Bob spent much of the summer painting in the relative coolness and quiet of the neighborhood of Fontainebleau. Louis went along and returned again and again, in person and in his writing. There he found his wife and there, quite as importantly, he consolidated his early literary phase. The relation between him and the region is so intimate that it is hardly figurative to say one half expects to see him striding down the dusty, shady avenues of the forest of Fontainebleau, with Charles d'Orléans in one pocket, a half-empty bottle of wine in the other, and the ugliest and most sociable mongrel in Barbizon skirmishing at his heels.

The founders of the "Barbizon School" were already gone. But the colony of disciples sprung up round their feet was still in the vigorous stage preceding the plague of tourists that often follows. Here the aspirant, respectful of the *milieu* that had stimulated Corot and Millet, came to apply in summer what he hoped he had learned in Paris during the winter, living frugally in catch-as-catch-can pensions, working by day if the light suited, talking obsessively about his own and others' work by night—Bohemia *al fresco* inspiring Louis and Bob to rig out in peasant blouses and wooden shoes for fun as well as for thrift. Louis found artists admirable company. He even tried his hand again at sketching and had an occasional fit of this pastime the rest of his life:[11] "The results are so comic, Henley,"[12] he wrote in 1878. But the best of it was that the place contained no writer, so he could freely choose to vegetate, experiment with the other fellow's craft, or tinker with his own in an atmosphere just far enough removed from his own kind of shop-talk. How this advanced his development is implicit in his "Fontainebleau" of eight years later:

This purely artistic society is excellent for the young artist. The lads are mostly fools; they hold the latest orthodoxy in all its crudeness; they are at that stage of education, for the most part, where a man is too much occupied with style to be aware of the necessity for any matter; and this, above all for the Englishman, is excellent. To work grossly at the trade, to forget sentiment, to think of his material and nothing else, is, for a while at least, the king's highway of progress. Here, in England, too many painters and writers dwell dispersed, unshielded, among the intelligent bourgeois. These, when they are not merely indifferent, prate to him about the lofty aims and moral influence of art. And this is the lad's ruin. For art is, first of all and last of all, a trade. The love of words and not the desire to publish new discoveries, the love of form and not a novel reading of historical events, mark the vocation of the writer and the painter. . . . he is already in a second stage when he begins to use his pretty counters for the end of representation. In that, he must pause long and toil faithfully; that is his apprenticeship; and it is only few who will really grow beyond it, and go forward, fully equipped, to do the business of art—to give life to abstractions and significance and charm to facts. In the meanwhile, let him dwell much among his fellow-craftsmen. . . . They alone can behold with equanimity this fingering of the dumb keyboard, this polishing of empty sentences, dull and literal painting of dull and insignificant objects. Outsiders will spur him on. They will say, "Why do you not write a great book? paint a great picture?" If his guardian angel fail him, they may even persuade him to the attempt, and, ten to one, his hand is coarsened and his style falsified for life. . . . But the time comes when a man should cease prelusory gymnastics, stand up, put a violence upon his will, and for better or worse, begin the business of creation.

I cannot judge how much of that holds good of modern art students. It does formulate Louis's transition into his second stage. Deliberate imitation survives in him at this point only in such elaborate, and pleasant, literary jokes as Mr. Worldly Wiseman's conversation in "An Apology for Idlers." [13] He now had some of his tools and an urge to use them so devotedly that his fingers would wear individualized dents in their handles. In the next couple of years the world of English letters was infiltrated by what seemed to watchful readers highly idiosyncratic, if often slight, writing from a young Scot whom you sometimes heard about from Stephen or Clifford. (It is mistaken to see Louis's rise to prominence as anything but very gradual; in the early '80s Morley refused him one of the *English Men of Letters* series on the grounds that he was too little known.) Like most distinctive writers, he sometimes parodied himself.[14] But he could also show salt and thunder when most unabashedly stretching after writing up to his ambitions of the day:

> . . . for youth and all ductile and congenial minds, Pan is not dead, but of all the classic hierarchy alone survives in triumph; goat-footed, with a gleeful and an angry look, the type of the shaggy world; and in every wood, if you go with a spirit properly prepared, you shall hear the note of his pipe. For it is a shaggy world, and yet studded with gardens; where the salt and tumbling sea receives clear rivers running from

among reeds and lilies; fruitful and austere; a rustic world, sunshiny, lewd and cruel.[15]

Further betokening growth, his output of absurdly long letters slacks off; henceforth his logorrhea channels more directly into his work. Further still, his attention turns toward narrative.[16] By the winter of 1874-75 he is planning a whole volume of tales with enticing titles, most of which were either never written or have failed to survive: "The Two Falconers of Cairnstane," "A Country Dance." . . . (If the quality was no higher than that of *When the Devil Was Well*, of the same period—a murky and motionless piece of melodrama with a Boccaccio-like plot and setting—the world missed little.) This is seeking to add another dimension to his craftsman's universe. The shift from the rhetorical dynamics of exposition to the emotional dynamics of fiction is bridged in due time by the appearance of "A Lodging for the Night" and "Will o' the Mill"—narrative essays, so to speak—showing a very good grip on his trade. In its kind "Will" is wonderfully consistent in style and feeling.

The coincidence of this new firmness of style with his previously noted sour contemplation of possibly marrying "a good dull girl" may be no accident. For personally, as well as professionally, he was approaching a corner that he would have to turn or slide into the ditch. In August 1876 the *Cornhill* published the first section of that article that Louis had defied Mrs. Sitwell to like. Its successive parts, published over several years, probably written at wide intervals, nicely illuminate the darts and swoops with which a bright young man approached and reconciled himself to the notion of marriage. Marriage was

a sort of friendship recognized by the police; . . . if they only married when they fell in love, most people would die unwed; . . . the Lion is the King of Beasts, but he is scarcely suitable for a domestic pet.

And more ominously, it was also

. . . a step so grave and decisive that it attracts light-headed, variable men by its very awfulness. . . . It seems as if marriage were the royal road through life, and realised, on the instant, what we have all dreamed on summer Sundays when the bells ring, or at night when we cannot sleep for the desire of living. . . . But this is a wile of the devil's. To the end, spring winds will sow disquietude, passing faces leave a regret behind them, and the whole world keep calling and calling in their ears.[17]

To whatever extent these remarks, already in proof when the crucial event occurred, reflect Louis's frame of mind, they show a young man amusing himself with regarding marriage as a potentiality to which one must become reconciled in season, like having to shave or turn to spectacles—with which, as his letters to Mrs. Sitwell show, he had been familiarizing himself, as a matter of theory, for some time. Reality was waiting for the theorizer, and the shape it took was that of a person who was neither good in any conventional sense, nor dull nor a girl.

Round July 1, 1876, Louis arrived at Barbizon to hear the distressing news that women, respectable women, neither models nor mistresses, had invaded the magic circle—not Barbizon itself, but bad enough, Grez, the riverside branch of the colony, on the near bank of the Loing across the forest. Bob Stevenson, they said, had gone to scout and, if necessary, eject the intruders by well-known means always at hand which had usually worked on objectionable men. But Bob had remained at Grez and merely sent back word that the invasion seemed benign. Amused and alarmed, Louis set off for Grez to rescue Bob from whatever Circean wiles had beglamored him.

As he remembered it in after years, he arrived at Chevillon's pension as dinner was being served and looked in at the half-door opening on the garden from the dining-room. His eyes sought and singled out the chief intruder—a small woman, well composed, lucidly pretty, with eyes that people said looked like those of a man sighting a pistol.

Over the Windmill

The Blind Bowboy

> We had rumours of you . . . vague, though they blew
> note of a wife and had thunder in them . . . Is she
> American—Californian—Scottish washed in Pacific
> brine?
>
> —Meredith to Stevenson, June 16, 1880

MEREDITH's first guess was right: This compact, glowing-eyed young matron was American. The importance of this could be over- but also understated. Fifteen years later Louis signalized it in affectionate doggerel about his wife and her daughter:

> From European womankind
> They are divided and defined
> By the free limb and the plain mind,
> The nobler gait, the naked foot,
> The indiscreeter petticoat; . . .[1]

Here the transatlantic thread is first conspicuous in the Stevenson pattern. Like that of most educated Europeans, Louis's previous knowledge of the States had been fragmentary: The melodrama of *Uncle Tom's Cabin* had impressed him as a child. At various intervals he had been entertained or influenced by Cooper, Whitman, Hawthorne, Poe, and Thoreau, and learned to despise Benjamin Franklin. In 1872 he maintained before the Spec. the generous thesis that American literature was already on a par with British. At Menton he quarreled with an expatriate American fellow-boarder over continuing American surliness after settlement of the *Alabama* claims. And he had made warm friends of several American art students in Paris and Barbizon.

Little of that could prepare him for a woman who was a Hoosier, an adventuress in the polite sense of that damaged word, and an attractive example of a type that the United States was then exporting to the astonishment, sometimes the admiration, of Europe. It owed much to dilute Mary Wollstonecraft and George Sand. But, thanks to freer relations between the sexes in the States, its American exemplars usually needed to use their elbows less. Poorer taste and lower stability developed it into such as Victoria Woodhull and Adah Isaacs Menken. Better circumstances produced such more palatable phenomena as Fanny Van de Grift Osbourne.

On both sides her people were from around Philadelphia, of long-settled Swedish and Dutch colonial stocks.[2] Her dark complexion encouraged tales, probably more picturesque than accurate, of Latin or gypsy admixture. The Vandegrifts sound like a high-tempered, strong-minded crew. (They spelled—and still spell—the name "Vandegrift"; during her first visit to Europe Fanny endowed herself with the more aristocratic-looking "Van de Grift.") Jacob, her father, was a young runaway. Returned to his family, he was sent west to start fresh in Indianapolis, the rawly new capital of Indiana, where he did well enough in lumber and real estate to own a small red brick house on the northwest quadrant of The Circle, next to Henry Ward Beecher's new wooden church; then to build a row of cramped brick apartment houses that proved an excellent investment; finally to buy a fat 180-acre farm in Hendricks County after becoming purchasing agent for the Vandalia Railroad.[3] His photograph shows a composed, perceptive face above grave Sunday clothes; but, for all his success, money never stuck to his hands.

A family legend about Fanny's mother, Esther Keen, shows such integrity that one hopes it is true: On his deathbed, it runs, Jacob told a daughter that Esther, a trig, small-footed Philadelphia girl somewhat his elder, had been under a cloud when he courted her. On his proposing she had honorably warned him that she had already been married and divorced; he had a right to know, but nobody else should. He married her at once without asking questions: admirable behavior for five generations ago.

Frances Matilda was born to Jacob and Esther on March 10, 1840, eldest of five sisters plus a Jacob jr.[4] Mother and baby were baptized by Beecher in an interdenominational ceremony near the Kentucky Avenue bridge across White River in April 1842. This made little Fanny nominally a Presbyterian like Louis—only American Presbyterianism as watered down by such spiritual press agents as Beecher was hardly so gnarly an affair as the Kirk of Scotland.

In most respects the Indianapolis of the 1840s could not have less resembled the Edinburgh in which Louis would be born. The place was flat as your hand and only twenty years old, instead of thirty centuries, laid out by a disciple of L'Enfant in converging avenues imposed on a gridiron that made it an even more ironical "city of magnificent intentions" than Washington. It had plenty of ironweed, stumps, whisky, loose women, and shoddy shacks, and floods of tobacco juice as brown as the spring floods of Fall Creek and Pogue's Run. Also present were energy, sapped by "fever 'n' ager"; enterprise braked by an elementary economy just turning from cattle-running to farming; ambition slowed down by the National Road which, bisecting the town, too often tempted intending residents farther westward; and refinement, imported as books and furniture from southward and eastward, but diluted by the dense ignorance of the bulk of the population—for, not without reason, the more settled areas of the nation then took "Hoosier" to typify adenoidal uncouthness. At worst the town was growing like a promising if hammerheaded colt; and, lying as it did on an artificially chosen site between two streams of population—one up from Kentucky, another across from the Yankee-ridden north of Ohio—it had the stimulus of marked divergences in attitudes and folkways.

Girls from such families as the Vandegrifts were likely to be good cooks. Fanny was even imaginative and eclectic about it, eagerly assimilating whole schools of cookery that had little in common with fried chicken, elderberry pie, and her grandmother's pepper pot. She had a temperament apt for skills—was an excellent seamstress in a day when skill with the needle had to be extreme to be notable, and an avid gardener with five green thumbs on each tiny hand. Otherwise she leaned toward nonconformity, toward the talented tomboy-ugly duckling, that narcissistic androgyne who would supply so many misunderstood but eventually triumphant heroines for girls' books, from Jo March to Rebecca of Sunnybrook Farm. Her elders approved of her "temperance" drawing of "The Drunkard's Home," but not of her sacrilege in dramatizing *The Pilgrim's Progress.* She was given to traipsing the woods with a boy-cousin and, when Sam Osbourne first saw her at sixteen, already three parts of a young woman, she was gallivanting round the Vandegrift yard on stilts. Former playmates recalled sitting on the cellar door after supper while she improvised ghost stories. Perhaps her taste for raw head and bloody bones, prevalent in her later writings, came from her redoubtable grandmother who startled the child by snatching herself baldheaded in preparing for bed—the old lady wore a wig—and filled her with grisly tales.

It belonged in the syndrome that she should be precocious in letters, reading at an age so early that friends of the family were alarmed. She attended the Third Ward public school and the old high school on University Park, not the Misses Axtells' select Female Academy; but her formal schooling probably had small significance. On internal evidence most of her education came from reading whatever came to hand, much of it of quality. Like Thomas Stevenson, Jacob Vandegrift preached latitude in education. Fanny was as welcome to read *ad lib* as she was to tramp the woods and blacken her fine-boned hands with walnut juice.

Her complexion may have encouraged her tomboyishness and the tinge of blue in her stockings. Her "golden shoulders" and "tawny knees" might attract Louis, but in 1855 Indianapolis required fair skin, whatever the hue of hair or eyes. Smoky-dark hair—eyes "full of sex and mystery" [5] with a hint of gold-stone in their darkness—face justly compared to the young Napoleon's for neoclassic symmetry—these could not make up for her unhappy swarthiness. Fanny's grandmother tried washing the child's face with harsh soap, only to give over in despair, saying, "She's that color by nature—God made her ugly." A girl-child hearing that often readily seeks compensation in eager claims to talent. In time, however, she proved attractive enough. She was sparklingly pretty when she wanted to be. Her kind of demure pertness frequently appeals to American men, and her short-leggedness was less handicap in that day of bell-shaped, ground-length skirts, beneath which peeped out the exquisitely small feet, size 4-D, that were her pride all her life.

Always an ardent self-dramatizer, she left an autobiographical fragment that curiously misrepresents the "pioneering background" of her childhood. Her parents were actually both city-bred, transplanted to a growing new town after their temperaments were set. However raw, life in Indianapolis was in no sense "pioneering." A single generation of development made huge differences in these mushrooming Midwestern communities. No rifle stood by the Vandegrift door in case of prowling redskin varmints. To be precise, when Fanny was seven years old, the town had some 3000 inhabitants, six hotels, over a hundred retail stores, twelve schoolhouses, six mills and two foundries, and the recently built Madison & Indiana railroad. There were a newspaper, amateur theatricals—though local sentiment distrusted them—and a local poetess, Sarah T. Bolton, who wrote recognizable verse in the intervals of helping a cultivated but feckless husband operate a tavern. Fanny admired Mrs. Bolton, or perhaps merely the idea of a resident poetess; she spoke of the lady's verses as "known wherever the English language is read." [6] The barest hint of what is now called "the creative" always made her nostrils twitch.

In later years her will to believe that her father had worn a coonskin cap and lain in canebrakes while Injuns prowled their margins probably enabled her to take genuine pioneering in Nevada and the South Pacific with admirable courage and efficiency. One to the frontier born was naturally more ingenious and less timorous in the face of risk and deprivation. Certainly the practical crudities, as well as the illusions, of her early experience, which must have included rail fences, homemade soft soap, sassafras tea, hog-killings, and the diverse uses of corncobs, as well as a silk dress for Sunday, were handy training for keeping house with Louis on Apemama or at an abandoned silver mine on Mt. St. Helena.

Louis Stevenson was mustering tin soldiers on the counterpane at the age of seven years and forty-one days when his future wife was marrying her Samuel Osbourne on the day before Christmas 1857—a young marriage, the bride seventeen, the groom twenty-one, but not noticeably so for the period. Fanny Sitwell was marrying at much the same time. There is no point in laboring the striking parallels of detail between these two women who were closer than any others to Louis: The same given name and nickname; the same age, same dark complexion, same famous pretty feet, same bluestocking leanings, same history of disastrous marriage and one small son dying. . . . The thing is too pat except for psychiatrists, to whom I leave it with compliments.

Samuel C. Osbourne was a long, fair, charming Kentuckian then secretary to the governor of Indiana, later deputy clerk of the state Supreme Court. The arid rigors of his "snortin' Methodist" parents seem to have made him an amateur atheist, and, though educated at the Methodists' new Asbury University at Greencastle (now DePauw), he remained a stubborn doubter, urging his wondering small daughter to look hard at churches, for, in her lifetime, they would all disappear. But he was a youngster with ability and the Vandegrifts had reason to think this early disposal of their eldest a good omen for Josephine, Elizabeth, Cora, and baby Nellie all stair-stepping along behind.[7] I assume that the Osbournes' first years in their house on Michigan Street were happy. They soon had a girl-baby named Isobel, "Belle" for short, a dark, quick, square-faced little creature fine-built like her mother and grandmother.

In 1861, however, Sam went to war in the 46th Indiana and, like numerous young men before and since, in a manner of speaking never returned from soldiering. His story feels like fundamental instability encouraged by the dislocations of war and thenceforth flawing his behavior at crucial junctures. Commissioned captain but never assigned a company, he resigned after six months—hardly the expected thing—and presumably resumed his civilian career; at least in July 1863 he is in Indianapolis enrolling in the "home guard" Indiana Legion hastily raised to oppose "Morgan, Morgan the raider, and Morgan's terrible men." Next winter he left wife and family to escort his consumptive friend and former comrade-in-arms, George Marshall (already married to Josephine Vandegrift), to California in search of health. The pretext for restlessness was tenable if quixotic; but, when Marshall died at Panama, Sam proceeded to California without pretext. He can hardly have been shirking the dangers and hardships of soldiering. A Sierra mining camp, though perhaps less hazardous, was about as rough as warfare, certainly nothing to attract a timid man. The fact seems rather to be that he had small talent for staying anchored or organized.[8]

With honorable promptness he sent for wife and child as soon as he was well settled. Fanny was game. Gameness was her salient characteristic. Throughout life she took such emergencies as emotional duties, sometimes groaning because the flesh was weak, but always plucky. This generally commendable quality was certain specially to appeal to Thomas Stevenson's courageous son.

Her trip to San Francisco (rail to New York, no doubt on a pass secured through her father's connections; steamer to Aspinwall; rail across the Isthmus; steamer again to San Francisco) was not what it would have been before the Panama Railroad was built, but, in sheer miles and days, it must have sounded like a formidable project. At the end Sam took his far-traveled dependents to their new home—Austin, a raw silver camp on the Reese River in Nevada.

There the matured tomboy learned to placate the local Indians, who were supposed to be, and may well have been, dangerous, with coffee and imperturbability; to roll and smoke cigarettes; to handle a heavy revolver; to cook, wash, and clean for flannel-shirted and bearded men with little but fire and hot water. Her department went well; Sam's did not. Presently they abandoned Austin, which had taken most of Sam's ready money, to try their luck in Virginia City—prototype of the Wild Western silver town, site of the Comstock Lode, stock-and-stencil background for "colorful" writing about Mark Twain. Even the soberest records of the place are incredible. But there it actually was, abounding as per invoice in shootings, whores, red-eye, and quick fortunes.

It also contained a leaven of men and a few more women inclined to respectability. Still game, Fanny made jerry-built quarters comfortable, conjured up tasty dishes from the dull and expensive contents of kegs, barrels, and bags. Sam returned to his old trade as clerk for what passed locally for courts. It looked as if the Osbournes were finally settled in—of all places —Virginia City.

But Sam's instability broke out in a fresh place. Whether his taste ran to clandestine affairs with amateurs or to the town's numerous and, by most accounts, attractive fancy women, he grew careless about where he slept. Quickness to resent injury was conspicuous in Fanny. There was an explosion. Sam threw up his job and went prospecting in the Cœur d'Alenes. Fanny and small daughter returned to San Francisco to await his return.

Hotel life exhausted their funds before he was heard from. News finally came, as a substantial rumor that Indians had killed him. Fanny went into mourning, took a furnished room, and, representing herself as French, began to support herself and daughter with her clever needle. But one day at the door was a big, fair-haired man in boots and breeches shouting at Belle: "Is that my little girl?" Resilience, charm, frailty, and all, Sam was home again on borrowed money. Belle adored Sam, and so did her mother. In 1868 there was a fair-haired son, Samuel Lloyd Osbourne.[9]

Sam dived into the bubbling San Francisco of politics and mining stocks and came up with a post as court stenographer at ten dollars a day and pickings—then a comfortable income—and status as a known figure about town and popular member of the new Bohemian Club. He bought Fanny a cottage with a large yard across the Bay in Brooklyn (now East Oakland), where she settled down to garden and tend her children. But the marriage never recovered health. Belle remembered an evening when Sam, reading *Vanity Fair* aloud, reached George Osborne's betrayal of Amelia, and Fanny burst out: "I wonder, *Captain Osbourne*, you can read your own story!" and Sam shouted: "My God, woman, can't you ever forget?" Belle was sent from the room to be spared heaven knows what. This or other such quarrels ended in Fanny's taking the children to her parents in Hendricks County. She did not return until next year, bringing Sister Cora with her, to make a third trial of Sam.

Back in the cottage with money enough and a servant, she developed her bluestocking streak—set up a rifle-range, dabbled in the new art of photography, made friends with local cultural figures such as Oscar Weil, musician; Virgil Williams, founder of the San Francisco School of Design, husband of Dora Norton, a painter; and Timothy Rearden, lawyer, expert on Low German though of Irish extraction, and chief of the Mercantile Library. She also wrote stories to show to Rearden. When Belle, who seemed talented, went young to Williams's art school, Fanny went along and won a silver medal for drawing. In the '70s San Francisco desired local poetry and fine arts to be as notable as local barroom nudes; Fanny thus acquired a tinge of aesthetic *parvenu* that would cling to her the rest of her life. It also fits rather too well that, at this time, she had her first recorded accesses of the second sight—"psychic powers" if you prefer—that she considered herself to possess. Eventually Birge Harrison, American artist recalling knowing her in France, obligingly ascribed to her ". . . a mysterious sort of over-intelligence." [10]

She also bore a second son, Hervey, whose beautiful fair hair was allowed to grow into long curls. It was all in vain. The cottage was buried in roses, the children were bright, communion with "creative" people was delightful. But Sam was at it again. In 1875 Fanny left him again. This time—much water having flowed under the tenuous bridge of her alleged talents—she went 4000 miles beyond the tree-fretted horizons of Indiana to study art in Europe, taking along all the children and a San Francisco maiden lady, who doted on Hervey, as chaperone and governess. The whole party must considerably have puzzled Europeans, who had not seen many female art students, and very few indeed with growing families clustered round them.

The scheme was not too costly. Fanny probably had railroad passes for all across the continent and seems to have secured transatlantic passages for $170. Osbourne appears to have been well reconciled to subsidizing his family on a minimum basis so far away for almost three years to come. According to his letters, he missed them; but it may also be noted that, not long after Fanny departed, the neighbors had reason to believe he had installed a lady-friend in the Oakland cottage.

Fanny tried Antwerp first. But the famous Academy did not admit women. Alarmed besides by an epidemic of "Antwerp fever," she shifted her brood to Paris, where the Atélier Julian admitted women students able to pay, in contrast with other *atéliers* that admitted strictly on merit. Fanny's presence in the life-classes adequately chaperoned Belle. The almost naked male and utterly naked female models troubled them, she wrote Dora Williams, only when, at the end of the sitting, they dressed in full view, chatting the while with the instructor. Fanny's drawing was praised for charming simplicity. Surviving work of hers shows that she had at least a pedestrian handiness with charcoal and brush, as was likely in a determined woman fond of color, deft with needle or firearms, among stimulating examples produced by interesting people. Her oil painting (now in the 8 Howard Place Museum in Edinburgh) of the bridge at Grez particularly indicates how cleverly she acquired the mannerisms and conventions of the Barbizon School. She sometimes showed signs of not taking her art very seriously, but she was certainly apt enough to make it plausible for her to inhabit this great, jabbering, stimulating city of Paris, feeding herself and young on smoked herring and black bread for economy, while expanding her soul in artistic expression.[11] It is often stated that Fanny was paying her own way with writing during this adventure. But her only such sale that anybody has been able to trace was a pleasant enough and highly moral fairy story in *St. Nicholas* with which she supplied an artist acquaintance who had a commission from the magazine to find something to illustrate. Her letters home make it very clear that Sam was her major source of income throughout her stay in France.

This harmless, almost pretty comedy was shattered by the prolonged illness and horrible death of Hervey; the doctors called his trouble scrofulous tuberculosis. His agonizing ordeal lasted long enough for Sam to arrive at the deathbed; Fanny's letters home dwelt morbidly on the savage details. Sam stayed on for weeks, but did not take his family back with him.

In the interval the party had spent some time, as recuperation for Fanny, who showed the strain of the boy's death in physical debility and occasional loss of memory, at Grez, a sleepy riverside village in the Fontainebleau belt of summer art colonies. It had been fatefully recommended by an American student of sculpture whose father had sent him to learn sculping in order to keep in the family a certain lucrative contract for sculpture on a public building—one original, of course, of Loudon Dodd in *The Wrecker*. After Sam's departure, Fanny, with gray already touching her dark hair, Belle, just turned seventeen, ". . . a bewitching young girl . . . with eyes so large as to be out of drawing," [12] the governess, who soon found things too primitive and went home, and Lloyd, towheaded and eight years old, returned to Grez. They had liked its being frequented by British and Americans; its being cheap to get to and thrifty to stay at; its *pension* backing on a long, shady garden down to the shining river half choked by sedge; its high, gaunt old church, jagged bit of old castle, heavy-piered medieval bridge that had been painted a thousand times. They also had liked the particular people they had met there.

The sculptor had promised that their few fellow-pensioners would be more decorous than those at the rowdy Barbizon colony, or at least willing to assume a virtue in view of the presence of so charming a mother and daughter. The most alarming—and most attractive—specimen was a versatile Scot famous in Montparnasse as "Bob" Stevenson. Musician, painter, scholar, he was said to have squandered a large fortune in a few years and only recently to have somewhat reformed from a career of epic debauchery. Some pronounced him a trifle mad and dying of his excesses.[13] His skill at boating, developed at Cambridge, made him center of life at the aquatic Hotel Chevillon, where the Loing was handy for skiffs and canoes. At Grez, Sam Osbourne had met both Bob and his gaunter cousin Louis, Walter Simpson and his eccentric painter-brother Willie, who used to get sociably drunk with his bull-terrier on absinthe—it finally killed the dog but not Willie—O'Meara, the talented Irishman on whom Belle looked very kindly, and the others. Fanny's husband seems to have had no qualms about leaving his semi-wife unchaperoned among these young fellows, so his impression must have been favorable.

It is a question whether Belle or Fanny enjoyed that summer more heartily. Belle had plenty of admirers to buoy up her vivacious self; Fanny, petted and spoiled by all, was known in the village as "*la belle Américaine.*" When she felt sickly, the men competed as to who would take her on a daily constitutional or carry her umbrella and painting kit to her "motif" of the day in the forest or along the river. Though she could not swim, she gamely donned what passed for a bathing suit in 1876 and, shrieking and splashing, shared the artists' sports of canoe-capsizing and tilting afloat in wash tubs; there was always somebody handy to fish her out in time. It was excellent therapy for recovery from the shock of Hervey's death. But her long letters home of this period soon lack the stigmata of deep grief. Her references to the boy are brittle or exhibitionistic; her tone throughout the correspondence with Rearden, in fact, is that of a crude coquette. As her stay in Europe continued, she began to learn more subtle social techniques, of course, and it is doubtful that her relations with the young fellows at Grez were as tinged with coy presumption as her approach to Rearden, else she might not so have charmed them. And charm them she did. The cultivated tomboy, still at the height of her original and striking beauty, flattered by the boys' insistence on making studies of her mouth and arms, was eating her white bread in amusingly unladylike gulps. It was a long while before any more was heard about going back to America.

Fanny's first impressions of Louis cannot have been deep. Within a few days of their meeting he returned to Scotland, and was not back in France until early autumn, for the *Inland Voyage* expedition. So that the idyllic summer of falling in love—at first sight, it is sometimes said—was not that of 1876. In any case, Fanny's early interest concentrated on Bob, who did stay on at Grez and was more and more admired for his looks, wit, learning, grace, and talent. Louis drew notice only as junior member of "the two Stevensons," of whose brilliance the British-American art colony was so convinced.

It was all quite innocent, however. Even when in October, Bob and Fanny lost themselves in the forest and the Chevillons grew alarmed, the conversation distracting them into missing the path had been merely brotherly: to be precise, Bob had been earnestly recommending his cousin Louis to the lady's attention. Some of the artists squiring her about were, he assured her, unreliable; he himself was a poor lot; but, for all his strange antics, she would find Louis brilliant, sound, and wholly rewarding. Thus, at the next opportunity, Fanny looked much harder at the "other Stevenson" than, dazzled by Bob, she had yet cared to. Students' gossip had also considerably decorated Louis: he was not only a great writer *in posse* but come of parents who were cousins and threatened with hereditary insanity —no doubt a construction from Thomas's recent troubles and Bob's father's psychosis—and eventual heir to a great fortune, though he would probably not live to enjoy it. There is dazzle, some invidiousness, and much gratitude in the tone in which Fanny wrote home about these successive opportunities to come in contact with such picturesque brilliance.

In October Fanny and brood returned to Paris. Doctors advised her not to do housework yet, so she established herself in a Montmartre apartment in the same building as several other English-speaking and respectable women pursuing the creative. Thither came O'Meara to see Belle, and Bob Stevenson, familiarly bringing Louis. By January Louis was giving "5 rue Douay"—Fanny's address—for forwarding. He first mentioned Fanny to his mother in an account of a studio party given by a wealthy art student so prim that the refreshments included no intoxicants: "One of the matrons was a very beautiful woman indeed; I played old fogy and had a deal of talk with her which pleased me." [14]

As acquaintance deepened, Fanny was alarmed by Louis's tendency to hysterics if he laughed heartily or, moved the other way, burst into tears. The favored cure for his hysterics was to bend his fingers backward until the pain penetrated his consciousness. Once, when escorting Fanny in a cab, Louis had such a fit and demanded that she apply the remedy. As she hesitated, he seized her hand and demonstrated so painfully that she had to bite his hand until it bled; then he apologized most humbly on the grounds that, when hysterical, he was not responsible for what he did. (This is Fanny's story—the reader may believe it if he likes; in any case it shows that Louis's temperament had struck her as extraordinary.) Bob's behavior had already prepared her for anything that either of "the two Stevensons" might see fit to do. He too was likely to enter a room and fall on the floor and weep violently over some detail of existence. It would take analysis more skilled than mine to determine how much of this pair's behavior was neural necessity and how much part of their cult of untrammeled reaction.

That winter Louis—and Bob, I presume—daily joined the various lodgers at 5 rue Douay for a frugal dinner at a *crèmerie*. Perhaps by now he was the more conspicuous cousin in her eyes. When both were away in midspring, each wrote her a letter asking her to write the other because, poor devil, he was said to be dying. Fanny had already positively diagnosed what ailed Louis as tuberculosis, three years before doctors found any reason to do so. She decided not to go home that spring after all.

She spent the summer of 1877 altogether at Grez. Louis was there a great deal until well into July. There—this is surmise of high probability—he found a gracious, slow, silent, sunny place to fall in love in. At table he sat next to and monopolized Fanny, talking volubly with loose, wide gestures. Every morning, carrying her painting outfit, he went with her in equal monopoly, and the other boarders were grateful to him for thus freeing Belle for time with them. After Fanny badly hurt her foot in some river escapade she lay in a hammock on the bank, watching the fun and, Belle noted, growing prettier every day. The cause may have been the process that Louis celebrated in print the following winter:

. . . the ideal story is that of two people who go into love step for step, with a fluttered consciousness, like a pair of children venturing into a dark room. From the first moment when they see each other, with a pang of curiosity, through stage after stage of growing pleasure and embarrassment, they can read the expression of their own trouble in the other's eyes. There is here no declaration so called; the feeling is so plainly shared that, as soon as the man knows what is in his own heart, he is sure of what is in the woman's.[15] In reminiscence he soon came to believe—and for all I know, with virtual accuracy—that he fell in love with her the moment he saw her at the dining table at Chevillon's, her husband at her side. But full acknowledgment of that possible fact seems to have waited for an afternoon in a boat on the Loing below the bridge at Grez, commemorated in fugitive verses:

> . . . On the stream
> Deep, swift and clear, the lilies floated; fish
> Through the shadows ran. There, thou and I
> Read kindness in our eyes and closed the match.[16]

Louis spent the latter half of the summer in Scotland, but by late September was back in France, his mail addressed to Fanny's new lodging at 5 rue Ravignan. This may have been mere continuation of a previous convenience; but Louis soon made it more intimate by going nearly blind with a severe eye-infection. Fanny promptly took him in and nursed him. Neither could know that this portended ten years of much the same situation. But it must have further cemented whatever degree of development the relationship had reached. On November 1 Louis's failure to improve had her so alarmed that she telegraphed Bob to come and take him home. When Bob failed to respond—I do not know where he was—she herself packed Louis up and, telegraphing ahead to Colvin, took him to London for help. Louis began to recover. Fanny's foot injury became so troublesome that it needed surgery, so Mrs. Sitwell took her solicitously in for convalescence. Colvin and Louis's Madonna petted and politely flattered Fanny. When she forgot Louis's caution not to be caught smoking in Mrs. Sitwell's rooms, her hosts did not scold but instead sent out for tobacco and papers and had her teach them how to roll cigarettes for her. She also met Henley and Leslie Stephen, who came to call one afternoon. Nobody but Fanny recorded first impressions; but even through the twists of her hypersuspicions one can see that this first experiment in association with Louis's sponsors went well—better than the later history of the group might lead one to expect.

Bob eventually turned up in bad shape himself. Now well recovered, Fanny conducted him back to Paris where she and friends gentled him into a sounder frame of mind. By January Louis was in Paris again. This may well have been the occasion of Fanny's and his becoming actual lovers. It had certainly occurred before spring of 1878, when Louis is writing Henley from Edinburgh:

> . . . the weather is so dark that I have to light the gas all day long; but then life's not possible for a *positively*, not negatively lonely man without it. . . . I'm a miserable widower; but so long as I work, I keep cheerful, and I find I have no tendency to reproach God or disown the highly respectable solar system on account of my little irritations. . . . And do I not love? and am I not loved? and have I not friends who are the pride of my heart? O, no, I'll have none of your blues; I'll be lonely, dead lonely, for I can't help it; and I'll hate to go to bed where there is no dear head on the pillow, for I can't help that either, God help me; but I'll make no mountain out of my little mole-hill and pull no damnable faces at the derisive stars, as I think I had the honour of calling them somewhere; at least I know I called something derisive, and I daresay I was perfectly right.[17]

Not a discreet letter; but Louis and Fanny apparently made no secret of their relationship among his friends. It probably heartened Louis greatly to see the heedless calm with which Fanny threw her cap over the windmill; nor was he likely to miss the point, that, of their two caps, hers alone was indispensable. For women of her background extramarital love was then an unthinkable emotional luxury; yet she seems to have entered on it with great spontaneity.

The effect on Louis of wholly requited love was not altogether exultance. That same winter he was telling Baxter:

I am not so young as I once was; there is a relish of time in me. I find myself heavy and a little sad-hearted in comparison with the past; and above all laughter, that old incontrollable hyperbolical laughter that took you by the midriff and kept you crowing till the tears came . . . is all extinct. . . . But . . . though nothing can bring back the hour of splendour in the grass and glory in the flower, I pretend to be a pretty sound and merry liver after all. . . . We are a little too old for green sickness and Wertherism. If we haven't cleared our spirits of that unripe rubbish by this time, I wonder how we expect to die.[18]

It sounds like a step toward growing up. Nobody need be surprised to find that marriage, as a practical possibility, not a graceful subject for magazine copy, soon cropped up. Baxter received a hint from Paris in the spring of 1878. Louis gave himself far more than a hint in some surviving rough notes[19] eventually worked into Part II of "Virginibus Puerisque," probably written this winter of 1877-78. The final form, unpublished until after Louis married, needs quotation for both light on his anticipations of marriage and a famous sample of his consummated early style:

Times are changed with him who marries; there are no more bypath meadows where you may innocently linger, but the road lies long and straight and dusty to the grave. . . . with what temerity you have chosen precisely *her* to be your spy, whose esteem you value highest, and whom you have already taught to think you better than you are. You may think you had a conscience and believed in God; but what is a conscience to a wife? . . . To marry is to domesticate the Recording Angel. Once you are married, there is nothing left for you, not even suicide, but to be good. . . . And yet when all has been said, the man who should hold back from marriage is in the same case with him who runs away from battle. . . . ere you marry, [you] should have learned the mingled lesson of the world; that dolls are stuffed with sawdust and yet are excellent playthings; that hope and love address themselves to a perfection never realized, and yet, firmly held, become the salt and staff of life; . . .

This wry performance on the piccolo of an air usually considered solemn or ecstatic, following as it does so closely on the letters quoted above, probably amounts to Louis's farewell to one aspect of his youth. It is not so sophomoric as critics ill acquainted with his history have sometimes thought. This salutary habit of looking at himself slantwise eventually enabled him to mature after the sort of early history that too often prevents maturity. For the Louis who had so far lived so stormily and jauntily marriage was obviously absurd; very well, he was inclined to marry. Obviously then he was no longer the same Louis; very well, odd but there it was. He had immersed himself in Mrs. Sitwell with conscious rapture, continually congratulating himself: "Bless me, how sensitively hard I am taking all this!" This affair was quite another thing. He was still marveling over its imperiousness when writing young Haddon in 1882: ". . . true love will not allow you to reason about it. . . . that love which may befall any of us on the shortest notice and overthrow the most settled habits and opinions." [20]

Perhaps because the thousand pounds had dwindled so far, Louis apparently gave his parents some notion of this fresh complication in his life. He wrote Mrs. Sitwell from Paris:

I have two invalids instead of one to look after, and I feel so tired you wouldn't believe. . . . I have had a deal of writing and telegraphing to my people; they are behaving awfully well; and perhaps that is not the least of my troubles. It takes some of the wind out of my sails; I am ashamed to be stiff, where I find them so full of concession. [21]

Soon he was asking Mrs. Sitwell and Colvin to mediate in his behalf with Thomas Stevenson—a shrewd choice, for Thomas had admired the lady in 1873 and could afford to credit any assurances she might give that, however distressing the situation, this person who had taken hold of Louis was no trollop. In February 1878, at Louis's request, Thomas came to Paris to look into the affair personally: ". . . don't be astonished," Louis wrote Colvin, "but admire my courage and Fanny's. We wish to be right with the world as far as we can." [22]

Whether Thomas then met Fanny, whether he was made privy to the extent of the relationship, I do not know, but suspect that No answers both questions. In any case, Louis was soon telling Mrs. Sitwell that things had gone relatively well. The terms of the treaty have not survived, but might be surmised; the game of either party may be divined: Everybody was willing to temporize in the hope that time would reduce strains. Just what strains needed reducing could not have been agreed on, but neither party would have wanted this clarified. Assurance of minimum support for Louis was probably exchanged for a promise to do nothing rash or overtly scandalous. Perhaps Thomas told himself that politeness, not shouting, was better therapy for a twenty-seven-year-old son in love with a much older married woman—if so, this was a highly civilized attitude for a Scots *paterfamilias* of the day. He may have leaned, of course, on the brute fact that Louis and Fanny could not marry—she was still Mrs. Samuel C. Osbourne. For all these possible maneuverings, Louis and he were friends about it, which is very clear in the letter that Louis soon wrote him—half-religious, half-self-analyzing, concluding:

I have taken a step toward more intimate relations with you. But don't expect too much of me. This is a rare moment, and I have profited by it; but take it as a rare moment. Usually I hate to speak of what I really feel, to that extent that when I find myself *cornered*, I have a tendency to say the reverse.[23]

It is hard to pin down just when Fanny determined to return to California and somehow resolve her personal tangle. The cause—or one cause—may have been Sam's cutting off support. By June 1878, Louis was in Paris to stay a good while as secretary to Jenkin, who was judging at the Exposition. At this time he is trying to raise sums of money— £100 via Baxter, £350 mentioned to Henley as an optimum amount—that suggest some sort of domestic financial emergency. Later the Osbournes are all in London in lodgings, and Fanny is enjoying taking part in the scramble of manuscripts and proofs consequent on Henley's becoming editor of *London* with Louis as mainstay contributor.[24] Lloyd remembered Louis in great detail: almost respectable in a stiff new blue suit, volubly scheming the *New Arabian Nights* with Bob and Fanny—the germ of *The Suicide Club* was Bob's—dashing off copy to fill holes in the paper; spending too much on cabs; carrying a loaded walking-stick for the melodramatic feel of it. . . . The final sketch is of Louis seeing them all off on the boat train for the States, and walking away, long and miserable, without looking back.

The whistle of that train must have carried all the way to Edinburgh and caused great relief in a certain elegant drawing-room with an Adam fireplace and a street-lamp just outside the window. Thomas had sound reason to believe that he had won his game of wait-and-see. The strange woman was gone, and 6000 miles was a propitiously great distance. He could not know that for months Louis had been considering himself emotionally, if not legally, married.

In early September he returned to France for the walking trip through the Cévennes that became *Travels With a Donkey*, in a state of tranquillity that may reflect a sense of long-needed emotional orientation: " . . . for the first time for near a year I feel something like peace," he wrote Baxter. "It is like gold—yea, much fine ditto; it is like the dew of Hermon, or the pomade on Aaron's whiskers." [25] But peace did not mean reconciliation to Fanny's being away: " . . . lots of [*Donkey*]," Bob was told, "is mere protestations to F. . . ." [26] Next winter the nature and extent of his feelings were made clear to Colvin:

. . . to F I never write letters. . . . All that people want by letters has been done between us. We are acquainted; why go on with more introductions? I cannot change so much, but she would still have the clue and recognize every thought; . . .[27]

A great change indeed from his inky loquacity with Mrs. Sitwell! He speaks of a recent tendency to go speechless for days, explaining: "Perhaps I have more in my heart; perhaps I have been spoiled by a very perfect relation; and my heart, having been coddled in a home, has grown delicate and bashful and will not cross the door." [27] And by the summer of 1879, the separation close to a year old:

> I can do no work. It all lies aside. I want—I want—a holiday; I want to be happy; I want the moon or the sun or something. I want the object of my affections badly anyway; and a big forest; and fine breathing, sweating, sunny walks; and the trees all crying aloud in a summer wind and a camp under the stars.[28]

Part of the work that "lay aside" was *The Story of a Lie*, which Louis finished while crossing the Atlantic "in a slantindicular cabin with the table playing bobcherry with the ink-bottle." [29] It is interesting only for the figure of "The Admiral" and for being Louis's first effort to handle father-son conflict. He read a draft to his mother, whom Dick Naseby's troubles with the Squire amused. She might not have smiled had she seen them as portending a new objectivity in Louis's chronic troubles with his own father. The cutting-off layer had begun to form, in emotional fact, not self-conscious principle alone, though it would soon have to tear prematurely and so raggedly, not cleanly. Passionate disagreement had grown so familiar at 17 Heriot Row that Louis had begun to take it as a condition of the universe and so could begin to purge of the toxins of adolescent dependency. High time at the age of twenty-eight!

I have no reliable clue as to when, in writing "The House of Eld," Louis styptically stated these troubles; but I incline to agree with Colvin that it was drafted before he left for America. In this long fable, a fetter is riveted to each child's right ankle as soon as he learns to speak. It hurts and is unhandy, but such is the custom of the country. When Jack, the hero, sees fetterless strangers passing through, he asks brash questions. His elders answer that fetterless people are hardly human, nor can the strangers themselves assure him that, in their country, lack of fetters makes people happier. But, after Jack finds a boy of his own age secretly dancing with his fetter laid aside, he determines to overthrow the custom. It is decreed and enforced, it appears, by a wizard living in the middle of a great forest who is clever at disguising himself in the shape of others, but is readily identified because, when crossed, he gobbles like a turkey. Jack finds the wizard's house and, while searching it, meets his uncle the catechist, who affectionately praises his daring but advises him to go home and forget his mission. As Jack demurs, his uncle gobbles like a turkey, and the boy is miserably obliged to kill him. Then his father appears and orders him home, is forced to give the fatal sign, and is killed; then his mother. This third killing disposes of the wizard for good and all, and Jack's fetter falls of itself from his ankle. He sets off homeward, victorious but still badly shaken by the wizard's vivid disguises. On the road he finds all fetters gone from people's right ankles. But now all wear fetters on the left ankle: " . . . that was the new wear, for the old was found to be a superstition." And, when he reaches home, he finds his father, his mother, and his uncle all lying dead of the wounds he visibly inflicted on them. The moral, if one exists, appears in a concluding gnomic rhyme:

> Old is the tree and the fruit good,
> Very old and thick the wood.
> Woodman, is your courage stout?
> Beware! the root is wrapped about
> Your mother's heart, your father's bones;
> And like the mandrake comes with groans.

In these last few months as son of the house Louis also completed a long-standing article on Robert Burns that Scotland still holds against him.[30] As a Scot, he naturally took Burns as the major phenomenon that he is; as a writer, he exulted in Burns's brilliance; but he also felt moved somewhat to rub his country-men's noses in the fact that Burns had frequently behaved like a self-conscious tomcat—an aspect of the man that they had pre-ferred to neglect. The title, "Some Aspects of Robert Burns," clearly disclaims intention to do Burns in the round. The text expands on it: "Mr. Carlyle has made an inimitable bust of the poet's head of gold; may I not be forgiven if my business should have more to do with the feet, which were of clay?" Scotland answered No!

For Burns was—and still is—the Scottish national symbol-deity, a thing Americans can best understand by thinking of Abraham Lincoln. The apotheosis had occurred in the cen-tury ornamented by Thomas Bowdler. So the effect of publicly stating that the man who wrote "Had we never loved sae blindly . . ." made a cult of wenching had about the same ef-fect as if American newspapers next February 12 should loudly remind readers that Lincoln was the richest source of dirty stories in Illinois. Victorian admirers of Burns focused on mountain daisies, mice, "The Cotter's Saturday Night," and the miraculous love lyrics and tried to forget that the verses con-taining "To see ourselves as ithers see us" are entitled "To a Louse."

People who know far more than I about Burns and the Scot-land of the eighteenth century stoutly maintain that Louis's interpretation of Burns's erotic history is unsound. Certainly his organization of the essay was unwise: Toward the end comes superlative admiration for the man's genius. Midway is warm admiration for the native dignity that enabled Burns so be-comingly to survive acclaim as a plowman-poet in Edinburgh drawing-rooms. But the aspect first treated is the sexual athlet-icism that, Louis believed, clogged the poet's emotional heels most of his life. After this portrait of the village *roué*, the rest might as well have never been written; nor need have been, since Burns's quality and integrity hardly needed further comment among readers of the *Cornhill*.

While preparing it, he had written Gosse that he had drawn up ". . . a kind of chronological table of [Burns's] various loves and lusts and have been comparatively speechless since . . . there was something in him of the vulgar, bagman-like, professional seducer." [31] The essay says: "He sank more and more toward the professional Don Juan . . . plumes himself on the scandal at the birth of his first bastard." With some insight, Louis sees this alleged Don Juanism doubly damaging because even it was inconsistent, callousness varying with sporadic loyalty to tinge successive affairs with falseness. But he made too little effort to discern how it was that this nature's nobleman of balance, self-respect, and good taste could be capable of such instability and poor taste in love. The result cannot, however, be called priggish, a word sometimes applied. Louis was deploring not fornication as such, but what he took to be a self-vaunting exhibitionism that could not claim the sort of frank intention about erotics that he respected in Walt Whitman. In his preface to *Familiar Studies* he gave the back of his lean hand to those assuming that here he had been smugly deploring wickedness:

> If Burns, on the facts dealt with in this study, is to be called a bad man, I question very much whether . . . I . . . have ever encountered what would be called a good one. . . . When we find a man persevering, indeed, in his fault, as all of us do, and openly overtaken, as not all of us are, by its consequences, to gloss the matter over, with too polite biographers, is to do the work of the wrecker disfiguring beacons on a perilous sea-board; but to call him bad, with a self-righteous chuckle, is to be talking in one's sleep with Heedless and Too-Bold in the arbour.

What then was the root of the angered dismay with which he lashed out at his subject? I suspect that it reflects the extreme, perhaps exaggerated, sense of respect for women as such, chaste or promiscuous, old or young, that Louis had from his strange father. Don Juan has less than none of that. In 1884 Louis told young Haddon: " . . . any man who believes himself to be worthy of a wife's love, a friend's affection, a mistress's caress, even if venal . . . is worthy of nothing but a kicking." [32] Shocked to find himself concluding that the man who wrote "Still gentlier sister woman" was riddled with Don Juanism, he considered himself entitled to annoy Scotland with his less-than-rounded conclusions.

Caledonia was very stern and wild about it. When, after Louis's death, it was proposed to erect a monument to him in Edinburgh, many of her citizens bitterly protested "on this ground alone, that he here writes disparagingly of Burns." [33] English readers apparently received it more cordially. At least that was the word from Gosse when the November *Cornhill* of 1879 appeared. But Louis was not on the ground to receive either kicks or congratulations. In August he had received a cablegram from Fanny. Nobody knows what was in it—perhaps only that she was ill and perplexed and needed him. Whatever it said was enough, however. Tearing himself away with a ripping sound audible in the Savile Club as well as in every room of the House of Eld, Louis Stevenson, ill himself, close to penniless, the black dog crouched smotheringly on his bony back, sailed for America.

The Gates of Darkness

> . . . then, if not before, you can no longer hang back,
> but must stride out into life and act.
>
> —Stevenson to Haddon,
> *Letters:* II, 87

O NLY posthumous cross-examination of Fanny, Sam
Osbourne, Thomas Stevenson, and Colvin could determine the exact circumstances of Louis's departure.

The mechanics at least are clear: He went to London, thence
back to Scotland, sailing from Greenock August 7, 1879, in the
Devonia of the Anchor Line—not, as often said, an "emigrant
ship" but a regular liner carrying the prosperous in first class,
the less prosperous in a second class dismal for even that un-
luxurious day, the least prosperous, mostly emigrants, in steerage. For thrift and to gather material for a travel book Louis
had planned to go emigrant-style the whole way. But he needed
the money that *The Story of a Lie* would bring; so, to secure use
of a table to write on, he paid a few pounds more for second
class, which gave him ready access to steerage and enough seasick squalor in its own right. On August 18 the ship came alongside a North River pier. The evening of the following day Louis
departed, along with numerous immigrants, by coach-train
probably on the Pennsylvania Railroad from Jersey City. Eleven
days later he was in Oakland.

Tactics are vague: Some surmise that, her divorce being imminent, Fanny had summoned him to marry her; that his parents violently opposed marriage; that, feeling honor-bound to
make an honest woman of her, Louis defied them; that they

refused him funds for the trip; that his going outraged his London friends; and that he sailed gloomily committed to a marriage of duty, not inclination.

This crudely oversimplified little drama does not seem to have occurred. Common sense and knowledge of Louis applied to information contained in newly available letters tell a likelier story:

To the prime question, why did he insist on going? the answer is charmingly simple: He was in love with Fanny and most disturbed by the vacillations of purpose that she seems to have shown after returning to California, evident in two passages from Louis's letters; one to Henley in the spring of 1879: "I have parted company with half of man and nearly half of myself. . . . I now know that I can suffer and not be permanently embittered or warped: . . . God keep me brave and single-minded";[1] the other to Bob the day Louis sailed: "F. seems to be very ill. At least I must try and get her to do one of two things. I hope to be back in a month or two; but . . . it is a wild world."[2] That is not the tone of either a self-exiled prodigal or a cooling lover honorably responding to the prehensile reproaches of a "wronged woman." Sentimental blackmail would have been wasted on Louis, nor was Fanny the one to try it. Had her values enabled her to feel "wronged," she would more probably have shot the man than pled with him. In Louis's view—and in hers too, no doubt, off and on—a supra-legal bond between them already existed. If her circumstances and confusions were fraying that bond, as looked likely, Louis would serve them both by rushing to inspect and repair it. The possibility of marriage with her was already in both minds, of course. But that Louis considered it a definite objective of this trip is not so sure. Just before landing in New York he wrote Colvin:

At least if I fail in my great purpose, I shall see some wild life in the West and visit both Florida and Labrador ere my return. But I don't yet know if I have the courage to stick to life without it [presumably a definite arrangement with Fanny]. Man, I was sick, sick, sick of this last year.[3]

None of it sounds as if make-an-honest-woman-of-her as such were salient in either mind.

Previous speculation here turned to a mixed prescription: Victorian horror of marriage to a divorcee; British dislike of the idea of an American daughter-in-law; regret that Louis had not chosen a nice girl from round the corner; disapproval of the eleven-year difference in age; or all together, as explaining Louis's family's strong stand against him. Most of those items are dubious. There is every indication that Fanny had yet to decide on divorce; and, if Louis was not talking marriage to his intimates, he would hardly do so to his parents. (In any case, as lifelong proponent of divorce-at-will for women, Thomas could hardly object to a divorcee.) Five months later, when marriage was decided upon, he wrote Baxter: "I own I was surprised at the vivacity of my father's feelings; for I went so completely out of my way to prepare him, that I did not imagine he could be taken unawares." [4] But the word is "prepare" not "inform." The one solid clue to Louis's parents' outraged agony lies in a letter of Thomas's asking Colvin's help in coaxing Louis to return:

> For God's sake use your influence. Is it fair that we should be half murdered by his conduct? I am unable to write more about this sinful mad business. . . . I see nothing but destruction to himself as well as to all of us. I lay all this at the door of Herbert Spencer. Unsettling a man's faith is indeed a very serious matter." [5]

This is clarifying. Self-persuaded, the year before, that if let alone Louis's scandalous but distant affair would burn out, Thomas had accepted Mrs. Sitwell's mediation. Thus to take Fanny as a temporary indiscretion of a young fellow in France, that notorious hotbed of indecorous *liaisons*, enabled Thomas to live with his sense of shock. Fanny's going so far away

from Louis had furthered his illusion of security. This was now
brutally destroyed. A few words of hers on a piece of coarse
paper from the post office—if only Louis had passed that cablegram down to posterity!—had changed Louis from a readjust-
ing if troublesome son into a zealot bent on the worst end possible—a trip to God knew where to resume deliberate sinful-
ness. Here was the deservedly disastrous consequence of
attempts cannily to temporize with the flesh and the devil.

So, in his parents' eyes, Louis must have seemed like a re-
lapsed Tannhäuser, as a storm of bewilderment, sick anger,
and hysterical prayer blustered up and down the smooth, cold
stairwell of 17 Heriot Row. This was certainly the most doleful
couple in Edinburgh that winter; Thomas even thought of
moving out of Scotland to avoid gossip. But even so Louis was
not cast out. His parents' love for him, however possessive—as
most love is—took small damage either from the shocks to
which he subjected it or from their failure to comprehend his
actions. They made threats of disinheritance but apparently
more as a way of getting him back than to express revulsion.
Their campaign to persuade him to come home soon had them
hopefully assuming that only lack of money could be keeping
him in the States, and trying to get money to him via Baxter.
With the same purpose, word that Thomas was desperately ill
was relayed to him in October. Louis grimly responded that
Fanny too was seriously ill and "I won't desert my wife" [6]—a
phrase most significant seven months before marriage actually
occurred. In one sense it was Louis who had cast his parents
off, perhaps from momentary revulsion against people who
thought what he was going to do amounted to such crass sinful-
ness. Yet, within eight weeks of sailing, he asks Baxter most solicitously for word of Thomas: "Since I have gone away I have
found out for the first time how much I love that man; he is
dearer to me than all except F." [7] It is also notable, as Mrs.
Issler recently pointed out,[8] that in his meager luggage was a
copy of Thomas's book on the evidences of Christianity.

His departure had many earmarks of being a flight. The visit to London was presumably to take counsel with friends. He booked his steamer passage under the half-hearted alias of "Robert Stephenson." To Baxter alone he entrusted an address: c/o Jos. D. Strong,[9] Monterey, Calif., to be given to "no one, not even the Queen." [10] He was in rather worse physical condition than usual, but ignoring such things was an old story to him. He had at most some thirty pounds in his pocket and a credit for £150 that Baxter had somehow arranged—very well, future sales of writing would have to cover living expenses when travel and living had exhausted that.[11]

His London circle seem to have put his poverty, his poor condition, and his quixoticism most candidly before him. Loving him as the most stimulating of comrades and the most promising of young writers, they were outraged by his proposing to abandon them on a sentimental wild-goose chase; to cut himself off from helpful contacts at the Savile at just the time he most needed them; to risk his fragile person to take lame aid and comfort to a woman apparently not altogether sure just what she wanted of him. Neither Colvin nor Henley was a mincer of words. But, when Louis remained stubborn, neither did they cast him off. They said goodbye, if not godspeed, at St. Pancras and carried on as his informal agent-advisors in the British market. Gosse remembered "the dismal clammy evening when we bid one another farewell at the corner of Berkeley Square and [I] betted sixpence with myself that I should never see your face again." [12] For all the depressing weather and his friends' misgivings, however, Louis was still Louis: he spent his last ten minutes with Gosse inquisitively knocking at the door of a reputedly haunted house to see if the spectral tenant would answer.

His farewell note to Colvin, written at sailing and enclosing a note for Thomas that I wish had survived, was black enough:

I have never been so much detached from life; I feel as if I cared for nobody, and as for myself I can't believe fully in my own existence. I seem to have died last night. . . . I can say honestly I have at this moment niether [*sic*] a hope, or fear, or an inclination; except a mild one for a bottle of wine, which I must resist. . . . I have just made my will and am reading Aimard's novels! Que le monde est bête! God bless you all and keep you, is the prayer of the husk which once contained

R.L.S.[13]

In *The Amateur Emigrant* and *Across the Plains*, Louis duly made copy of his journey. None of his friends liked either work,[14] and he found both bitter drudgery himself. This unanimous reprehension is hard to understand now. True, the little books—balder, harsher, stringier than the idiom in which he had worked so far—are not characteristic early Stevenson. But both, the *Emigrant* particularly, are work of prophetic merit, besides giving a record of the trip that inhibits paraphrase.

The biographer can only note the educational effect of the amateur emigrant's enforced and prolonged rubbing of elbows with squalor and defeat at a time when his own depressing crisis made such experience bite deep. Louis had occasionally visited working-class groggeries, peered into slum windows, disputed with proletarian doctrinaires. But such explorations by a self-conscious student of human beings could not avoid a touch of young Haroun-al-Raschid exploring the depths of Bagdad. Once, trying to behave suspiciously in rough clothes in order to get arrested in London, he had found no policeman willing to do more than wish him "Good night, sir," and advise him to go home.

On the *Devonia*, however, he could not at will disengage himself from her dingy steerage passengers and return to the amenities of Heriot Row or Colvin's Hampstead lodgings. So gradually there protruded and rubbed against him the direct knowledge that to be penniless was more miserable than picturesque; that economic disaster was cruel to individuals as well as abstractly depressing to masses; that alcoholism was incapacitating, not jolly; and that, for daily wear forward in the steerage, Louis Stevenson required much revision. For days he hardly dared open his mouth for fear of giving unintentional offence. As a Scot, reared in the relatively equalitarian traditions of Scots education and church government, he may have felt all that more readily than if he had been an Englishman of equivalent stratum. But hitherto his lively distrust of the Victorian caste system, which was by no means weak in Scotland either, had been academic. Now it was as practical as unwashed humanity. As calmer weather cheered up the steerage and set it fiddling and singing:

Through this merry and good-hearted scene there came three cabin passengers, a gentleman and two young ladies, picking their way with little gracious titters of indulgence, and a Lady-Bountiful air about nothing, which galled me to the quick. I have little of the radical in social questions, and have always nourished an idea that one person was as good as another. But I began to be troubled by this episode. It was astonishing what insults these people managed to convey by their presence. They seemed to throw their clothes in our faces. Their eyes searched us all over for tatters and incongruities. A laugh was ready at their lips; but they were too well-mannered to indulge it in our hearing. Wait a bit, till they were back in the saloon, and then hear how wittily they would depict the manners of the steerage. . . . There was no shadow of excuse for the swaying, elegant superiority with which these damsels passed among us, or for the stiff and waggish glances of their squire.[15]

Further, Louis had thought of emigrants as energetic Vikings setting out to ransack a new world for wealth; whereas the *Devonia*'s random sample, including odd Continentals as well as Scots, Irish, and English, were mostly down-in-the-mouth, drink-ridden, inept failures, slackly seeking in the New World the stamina and efficiency that they had not shown in the Old. He nevertheless immensely liked several of his fellow-passen-

gers and seems to have been liked in turn—a relation nearer
reality than his experiences with their likes in his rambles as a
picturesquely questing youth. A sense of immediacy and grave
actions hung over the ship like her own smoke. Anomalies were
always plentiful with Louis. Here he first encountered un-
cushioned reality as prelude to the most impractical episode of
his whole life.

His first view of America consisted largely of precipitation.
New York was having two days of sticky, heavy summer rain:
"One sees it's a new country," he wrote Colvin, "they are so
free with their water. I have been steadily drenched for twenty-
four hours; waterproof wet through." [16] That was unlucky for
a man with a weak respiratory system bent on a grueling trans-
continental journey. He had no time for prophylactic rest
because the letter from California that was waiting for him in
New York indicated that Fanny was again seriously ill. Nor did
it help to have no introductions and be shabbily soaked when
calling on publishers with manuscripts. But, to judge from the
brisk front that he put up in writing Henley from New York, his
spirits were better than his circumstances:

> I have passed the sea with comparative immunity, having
> only lost a stone and got the itch. . . . and am now sending
> a story as long as my arm to the vile Paul. . . . The voyage
> was otherwise great fun; passengers singing and spewing lust-
> ily; and the stormy winds did blow.
>
> My news is bad. . . . F. has inflammation of the brain and I
> am across the continent tonight. Last night I did not close an
> eye, but sat on the floor in my trousers and scratched myself
> from ten p.m. to seven, when I rose much better for the ex-
> ercise. A little Irish girl just bursting into figure but dirty, is
> now reading my book aloud to her sister at my elbow; they
> chuckle and I feel flattered . . . Now they yawn and I am in-
> different; such a wisely conceived thing is vanity. [17]

All this, of course, in the exceedingly cheap West Street room-
ing-house described in the *Emigrant*.

The departure was sodden, crowded, and murky. Next morning the sun was out and the Pennsylvania Dutch country green and rich. Taking a fancy to the name "Susquehanna," like Coleridge before him, Louis used it as springboard for verses proclaiming great changes in himself and a conviction that ". . . God me yet shall bring/To lands of brighter air." [18] As the train clicked its cindery way through Ohio:

No man is any use till he has dared everything; I feel just now as if I had, and so might become a man. "If ye have faith like a grain of mustard-seed". . . Just now I have faith as big as a cigar-case; I will not say die, and do not fear man nor fortune.[19]

The instinct was very probably sound; it had been then or never for making his own life without regard to Heriot Row. As the emigrant cars to which he changed at Council Bluffs dangled and trundled through Nebraska, he sat on the coach-roof in his shirt sleeves and told Henley:

I can see the track straight ahead and straight behind me to either horizon. Peace of mind I enjoy with extreme serenity; I am doing right; I know no one will think so; and don't care. My body, however, is all to whistles.[20]

No doubt some of his good spirits came of a commendable impulse agreeably to disappoint his Job's comforters. If so, retribution was at hand. His body was rebelling. Appetite went; then sleep, unless he used the laudanum that he had brought with him. Presently illness combined with the razeed lunar landscape of Nevada to produce a semidelirious and tortured stupor. Immigrant-train conditions were murderous for people stronger than Louis. The cars were wheeled Black Holes, badly lighted, worse heated and ventilated, requiring passengers to sleep on bare boards laid from seat to seat, gradually developing stenches that drove those with nostrils out to the hazards of riding on platforms or roofs. The reappearance of green the other side of the crest of the Sierra seems to have struck Louis and his fellow-sufferers as a personal blessing:

> I had one glimpse of a huge pine-forested ravine upon my left, a foaming river, and a sky already covered with the fire of dawn. I am usually very calm over the displays of nature; but you will scarcely believe how my heart leaped at this. It was like meeting one's wife. I had come home again—home from unsightly deserts, to the green and habitable corners of the earth. Every spire of pine along the hill-top, every troutly pool along that mountain river, was more dear to me than a blood-relation. . . . The sun no longer oppressed us with heat—it only shone laughingly along the mountain-side. . . . At every turn we could see further into the land and our own happy futures. At every town the cocks were tossing their clear notes into the golden air, and crowing for the new day and the new country.[21]

Early next morning a shaky and skeletonized Scot dragged his valise—containing principally the ten volumes of Bancroft's *History of the United States*—to the platform at Oakland and inquired how to get to a place called Monterey. It was a clear, chilly day crossing the ferry. San Francisco was at its extraordinary best, but he saw little of it, not being there for sightseeing; his perspicacious sketches of "yon distressful city" [22] came later. The Southern Pacific took him to Salinas, the primitive narrow-gauge trundled him into Monterey. There, according to Mrs. Anne Fisher, a miraculously close student of Louis's Monterey period, his first act was to buy a stiff drink—a thoroughly understandable impulse.

The modern visitor is incessantly reminded that Monterey was the pre-Gringo capital of California. It had never been more than a middle-sized village, for Spanish, and then Mexican, penetration of Upper California was lackadaisical, composed only of missions, soldiers, and cattle, all sparsely spread. In 1879 this backwater was still being drained, not yet flooded, by the American exploitation that had long boomed San Francisco. A few down-at-heel Mexican families of dignified *hacienda* tradition kept up the light-opera notes of lace mantilla and guitar. A few Italian fishermen had arrived. Shore-whaling dragged on, and a small and squalid colony of Chinese did some shark-fishing. But most of Monterey's meager cash-in-pocket came of purchases made by outlying ranchers of no great prosperity. Enterprise, in the shape of newspaper, money-lending, and transport, was largely Gringo.

The Pacific Ocean, principal phenomenon thereabouts, supplied the smells down by the long old Custom House, the northward view of wide beach swept by blowing sand and spray, the winds that torture the cypresses into shapes deservedly loved of photographers, and the tremendous spectacle—of the sort Louis loved best—of the smoking surf out at the Point, irresistibly eloquent of the impetus of thousands of miles of deep water. Louis had no reason yet to know that this same ocean 6000 miles to the southwest, a blue metal rim high against a sky burning with sun, would be one of the last things he would see before he died. Nor yet that he would immortalize this scenery in the aromatic, booming coast of *Treasure Island*, or that among the live-oaks along the railroad, "crouching, hardy, . . . the kind of wood for murderers to crawl among," [23] John Silver would stun and butcher the honest hand.

Fanny was boarding with an old Mexican family, along with her sister Nellie, accounted the gentlest of the brood, young Lloyd, and Belle, then being warmly courted by Joe Strong. Their wish to marry was no secret. Fanny discouraged it in the hope of a son-in-law with better economic prospects than those of a young artist. Just before Louis arrived, the young people had solved this minor complication of Fanny's life by an elopement. But the major problem remained thorny. Sam Osbourne seems to have been agreeable to Fanny's settling in Monterey while she considered her situation. He came down some week ends to see his children and discuss matters with his wife; the more they talked, the more confused they were. Lloyd remembered Fanny's voice coming sharp out of a murmured conversation in the next room: "Oh, Sam, forgive me!" Both had a good deal to forgive, and Fanny a great, great deal to think about in between whiles. Sam's contributions were the sole support of herself and children, and she had small taste for the scandal that divorce would create in both San Francisco and Hendricks County. Her indecision is understandable. At such crises in their lives people determine on clean-cut actions more readily in novels than in real life.

Once Louis was there, his very presence pressed for decision. Fanny tried telling people the implausible story that he was a literary friend from England on a lecture tour of the States. If his condition on arrival—physically exhausted and debilitated, financially crippled, with no concrete prospects—dismayed her, it is hard to blame her. Once his family had withdrawn support—and Fanny had always been clearly aware of Thomas Stevenson's high solvency—life with Louis was not likely ever to be economically sound on even a minimum basis. Nobody knows what passed in their first interviews. But within a week Louis hired a horse and light wagon to go gypsying in the hills, ostensibly seeking health, actually for reasons hinted in a letter to Baxter: "My news is nil. I know nothing. I go out camping . . . and now say good-bye to you, having had the itch and a broken heart." [24]

This was the first time he unquestionably came near dying. The rigors of the immigrant train exacted payment. Ranchers found him lying in the open, collapsed, half-unconscious.[25] They kept him alive and mending until he could creep back to Monterey with some chance of surviving; in return he acted as schoolmaster for the little girls of the ranch in the absence of their ailing mother. He had no illusions as to how close a call it had been. The earliest version of "Requiem" now appears in a letter to Colvin, seriously suggesting it be used for his epitaph.

This same letter says "I want to be married . . ." [26] and

tells Colvin what he had written Baxter six days earlier, only five weeks after the breaking of his heart and flight to the hills:

> In coming here I did the right thing; I have not only got Fanny patched up again and in health, but the effect of my arrival has straightened up everything. As now arranged there is to be a private divorce in January . . . and yours truly will be a married man as soon thereafter as the law and decency permit. The only question is whether I shall be alive for the ceremony.[27]

Perhaps it was Louis's nearly dying that finally determined Fanny to divorce a pleasant and prospering philanderer in order to marry a rickety economic casualty whom she loved.

In further token of Louis's reticence to his friends before sailing, Colvin seems to have protested bitterly against the idea of marriage: By January—remember that San Francisco-London mails were then a matter of over two weeks at best—Louis is replying to him with ominous calm: ". . . by what you say about marriage you leave me in wonder. What else should I do? Do I not want to have all rights to protect my darling?" [28]

For over three months, while these dispositions were brewing, Louis inhabited the old town on a steadily dwindling purse and with ominous ill health. His work on the *Emigrant* was hampered by weakness forcing him to lie down between pages; by digestive upsets, toothache, lack of sleep reflecting perplexity, as well as the steady torture of the "itch" on his hands, so conspicuous that landladies took it for a dangerous disease and were reluctant to rent him lodgings. Weight and spirits were low, and the local doctor, a Luxemburger at whose house Louis paid for room during most of his stay, could do little for any of his ailments. Days and weeks passed, Fanny back and forth from Oakland, Osbourne driving them all, no doubt including himself, distracted by backing and filling about the divorce.

Fortunately Louis found friends: not only Dr. Heintz but

also Bronson, recently arrived editor of the weekly Monterey *Californian;* Adolfo Sanchez, gentleman-bartender, whose Latin good looks and charm prevailed on Nellie Vandegrift to marry him—hence the "little Louis Sanchez" of *A Child's Garden;* and closest of all, Jules Simoneau, a big-hearted, derelict Frenchman who ran the restaurant where Louis ate, grateful for a Gallic touch in cookery. Simoneau looked after Louis when he was worse than usual, played chess with him, extended him credit with such unostentatious delicacy that this "dear and kind old man" [29] became for Louis a symbol of comradely benevolence.

The slenderness of Louis's resources was gnawingly inconvenient, but Monterey was used to penniless people. A friendly conspiracy among Simoneau's handful of boarders—the smallness of the sum shows how poor they were themselves—raised two dollars a week to enable Bronson to hire Louis as part-time reporter on that salary. The only surviving item of his work covers a local festival culminating in a special Mass for the local moribund Indians at the old Mission; Louis reworked some of it in one of his short essays on the region.[30] He never knew— the contributing boarders would have lynched anybody betraying them—that his miniature salary was disguised benevolence.

They had apparently concluded that this skinny stranger was a man to tie to. He had gone far out of his way to befriend a half-demented and alcoholic old Indian who was the butt of local juvenile delinquents. Delightedly he helped to plaster the town with placards denouncing the penurious parish priest as "Padre Dos Reales" (Father Two-Bits).[31] It's a pleasant thing to think of Louis and the boys and Simoneau swapping lies so much to their mutual respect over omelet and cheap red wine in the back room.

But the more respectable strata of Monterey—which did not include Simoneau's customers—gossiped eagerly about this untidy and dejected stranger's devotion to that pretty Mrs. Osbourne who smoked cigarettes and had the daughter who eloped with that blond artist, whose husband came down fairly often but mark my words, something mighty queer is going on there. Chewing over Fanny and Louis in later years, Monterey developed some lurid fictions, one of which ignored the facts of human gestation and the calendar: I need mention only the minor tale of how Louis took to heavy drinking during his stay. In view of all that ailed him and his affairs, few could have blamed him if he had. No doubt he did use brandy to keep coughing down and resilience up. But, just as he had had neither the health nor the money for all the high-low life sometimes attributed to him in Edinburgh, so he certainly did not have the money for weeks of consistently heavy drinking in Monterey. No developing alcoholic could have still had almost $200 left when, in December, he quit Monterey for San Francisco.

Whenever the ache in his bones and the flooding weariness in his muscles eased a little, Louis used legs and eyes to good effect in walking, walking, walking. He explored the arid graces of Pacific Grove and had grave technical discussions—for he retained at least the vocabulary—with the lighthouse-keeper at the Point. During a long walk on the Bay-beach he told Lloyd Osbourne, now eleven years old, that he was going to marry Fanny. While walking out to see a smoldering forest fire, he risked a mobbing by setting a match to a moss-hung pine to test the inflammability of the moss. It ". . . went off simply like a rocket; in three seconds it was a roaring pillar of fire," and the volunteer fire-fighters were near by:

> I have run repeatedly but never as I ran that day. At night I went out of town, and there was my own particular fire quite distinct from the others, and burning as I thought with an even greater spirit.[32]

Louis never quite outgrew such lapses into mischief. At Vailima, Belle and Fanny never knew when he would have a spell of chuckling teasing of the same monkeylike quality as this devastating experiment. To this extent Collins was probably justified in writing that he retained "infantile" [33] traits all his life.

Monterey interested him, but he did not make the mistake of taking it as characteristic of the States, nor did it specially attract him. The success with which the Gringo had elbowed the Mexican aside struck him as indecent, and, as between the two, he preferred the grave, ceremonious Latin to "absolutely mannerless Americans." [34] The decay of the Mission—which, he contended, should be restored, if only as a profitable tourist attraction—and the consequent degradation of its Indian wards depressed him as much as the surviving Indians' singing of old Catholic chants delighted him. His account of their annual return to the roofless church showed great insight and proportionate regret for their decay.

Ever since he had sailed from the Clyde—though he can hardly have so conceived his attitude—he had been tempted away from personalized work toward impressionistic but relatively objective reporting. It was that element which probably made his *Emigrant* and *Across the Plains* unacceptable. In this field he had much to learn, nor was he close to learning it until shortly before he died. To diminishing degree he always lacked the reporter's skill in pursuit and distinction of significant fact as such, and proper sense of the body of observation necessary to a conclusion. Thus, his account of these Indians hangs in limbo because he had little information on the curious relation between Spanish missions and the supine aborigine. Within a few weeks of landing in New York he had projected a novelette to be called *A Vendetta in the West* built round a character named Arizona Breckenridge; since all he knew of the West was how it looked out of the dirty windows of an immigrant car, that authentic-sounding name would probably have been its only appropriate detail.

His account of Monterey—a swift sketch of rocks, pines, surf, and the dying local ways—makes all later descriptions sound tourist-trappish, except *Tortilla Flat*, which is a cartoon. His paragraph beginning "The one common note of all this country is the haunting presence of the sea . . ." has besides the spherical gravity of a good Wordsworth sonnet. But a professional stickler for fact finds regrettable touches: Hereabouts, says Louis, forest fires discourage later rain—a pseudo-scientific superstition to which Tom Stevenson's son should have been skeptically alert. In the Eastern States, he predicts, the melting-pot will turn out a breed predominantly British, on the Coast almost anything will result; whereas, as he wrote, the flood of European, non-British immigration was reaching toward its peak and exactly the contrary was already observable to anybody who had been more than thirty-six hours in the East. Without ever visiting Mexico, he writes of ". . . that high-pitched womanish alto which is so common among Mexican men." For all he knew, Mexican men had the voices of bass bullfrogs.

This reproach is lightened by consideration of the free-wheeling traditions of his time, the sort of thing that Holmes satirized in quoting "Our Sumatran Correspondent." Since Louis had never had any experience on the names-dates-and-places press—a momentary effort to get employed by the London *Times* had come to nothing in 1879—it is a wonder he stayed as close to fact as he did.

Much as he admired the Pacific, he came to hate its cold, saturating fogs regularly creeping inshore to make him cough and shiver. Gossip eddying round Fanny and him was a steady irritation. "To live alone in such a hole," he wrote Henley, "the one object of scandal, gossip, imaginative history—well, it was not good." [35] In late December 1879, he left Monterey with unflattering joy. Fanny had already gone. The new arrangement was: She would live in the Oakland cottage, which was legally her property, while a divorce proceeded. Osbourne would support her until she remarried, she in return would not hurry the marriage, lest it double comment by coming too close on the divorce. Louis would live across the Bay in San Francisco and meet her at discreet intervals for dinner in side-street restaurants. No conceivable arrangement would have been exactly practical. But it did look as if the miseries of uncertainty were relieved. After a couple of other efforts to find lodging he could afford, Louis got himself well settled in a thrifty furnished room in the house of a good-natured Irish landlady at 608 Bush Street.

Then Osbourne lost his post and, never having been one to save, could no longer afford even temporary support of Fanny. It looked as if Louis's resources, meager though they were, would have to supply the Oakland household as well as himself in San Francisco. He wrote Baxter to sell the books he had left behind at home and forward the proceeds—and pulled in his belt. To crown his blessings Colvin and Henley, in a "correspondence that would have taken the heart out of Mark Tapley," [36] were showing high dissatisfaction with the writing that he had been sending back. They may have been right, however shortsightedly, to fret over the *Emigrant*. But their verdict on *The Pavilion on the Links*, Louis's most elaborate fiction to date, was most gratifyingly reversed in a higher court when Stephen bought it for the *Cornhill*. From September to spring this was the one bit of good news that the poor devil received from across the Atlantic.

The fact was that Colvin, Gosse, and Henley had, with all good intentions, formed a committee of three to bemoan Louis's past wilfulness, present predicaments, and potential involvements, and if possible to bully him into coming home. Colvin and Gosse were gentler about it; the tone is least admirable in Henley's letter to Colvin in February 1880:

Don't defer expostulation because he is ill. On the contrary, it is absolutely necessary that he should be brought to see that England and a quiet life are what he wants and must have if he means to make—I won't say a reputation—but money by literature. We shall pass off all he's done, but I won't answer for much more. Come back he must and that soon. Married or unmarried—je m'en fiche. . . .

I don't believe that our letters . . . will have any effect at

all in diverting him from his project [i.e., marriage]. He has
gone too far to retract; he has acted and gushed and excited
himself too nearly into the heroic spirit to be asked to
forbear his point. All we can hope is to make him get through
his book quickly and come back quickly. . . . You may expect that Louis will resent our criticism of his last three
works. . . . but I think it right that he should get them: et
avec a confident expression of hope for the future, and as
confident a prediction that Monterey will never produce
anything worth a damn.[37]

Under the circumstances Louis's mildness in reply, after
some anguished yelps, is rather surprising.

Close as it was kept from Louis, a tinge of "that woman" was
already strong in his friends' intramural correspondence. No
doubt they all set Fanny down as hardhearted as well as prehensile when they learned, from a letter of Louis's, that he had
not seen her at all on Christmas Day, dining glum and lonely in
a cheap restaurant; whereas the reason probably lay in Fanny's
delicate diplomatic situation in Oakland: it would hardly have
done for her to disappear, leaving Lloyd and Nellie and perhaps Sam, come to have the day with his son, for a mere secret
Christmas rendezvous across the Bay.

San Francisco then abounded in cheap tables d'hôte, so Louis
was not faring too badly on seventy cents a day—breakfast and
supper of coffee and a roll bracketing a full-course lunch including half a bottle of cheap red wine and a toothful of brandy.
But Fanny's needs—though Osbourne was soon supplying
more than had once looked likely—bled away at his slim purse.
Late in January he had to cut down to a twenty-five-cent lunch,
a step announced to Baxter with rather a grunt than a whine:
"I have great fun trying to be economical . . . as good a game
of play as any other." [38] Fortunately he had fallen softly in his
lodging. Mrs. Carson[39] had at first been suspicious of this odd-
looking stranger, but was soon feeding him odd snacks and
cheering him with woman's gossip as he sat, smilingly inter-

rupted, at his writing table. With dismay she noted his growing thinness.

Even though his health gave small margin of resilience, Louis was working: on his essay on Thoreau, the abortive *Vendetta*, a first effort at *Prince Otto*, abortive essays on William Penn and Benjamin Franklin. Penn's *Fruits of Solitude* attracted him as much as Franklin repelled him, the politic sage of Philadelphia being his standing symbol of bourgeois smugness and pickthank caution. He even began an autobiography, "an odd book," he told Henley. "I began it that I might have something posthumous, like an insurance, for my survivors." [40] It remains an invaluable fragment.

For distraction Mrs. Carson's lean, shivering lodger, huddled in a loose ulster, walked up, down, and around the city's hills, finding this long-before-the-fire San Francisco of sand lots and square-riggers too fantastic for credibility. Loudon Dodd's San Francisco, like his Paris, was Louis's. Still with reportorial ambitions, Louis thought of an article on the proto-Fascist Dennis Kearney and his strange powers and stranger entourage. Fortunately he dropped the scheme, producing instead his impressionistic sketches of the city—jerry-built, beautiful in spite of its marble fronts and wooden sidewalks, already strangely aged. This is another *locus classicus*. Twenty times a year some hack writes another "colorful" description of "Old San Francisco" without coming close to these few thousand words. The first public monument ever erected to Louis stands appropriately in Portsmouth Square, where he often took the sun. The picturesque but most unseaworthy and storm-tossed caravel that crowns it well symbolizes the state of his affairs at the time.

He sometimes visited the Strongs' studio—Louis always liked the young artist, burden though he later became—and made friends with Charley Stoddard and Fanny's friends the Williamses. Coming home to find this queer creature calling on his wife, Virgil Williams took him for a brazen panhandler who had wheedled his way in and determined to throw him out at Dora's first sign of uneasiness. On better acquaintance Williams secured Louis privileges at the Bohemian Club, the library of which he found useful. The legend that he tried to be a stringman on a local newspaper, only to be fired when his copy had too much atmosphere and too few names, dates, and places, has been exploded. But he did get a few dollars for some small literary pieces in the San Francisco *Bulletin*, which Mrs. Issler has identified.[41]

He was hungry and unhappy, his teeth rotting, his pocket steadily emptying; but at least the divorce was an accomplished fact not long after the first of the year,[42] which, since it made marriage possible, was backhandedly cheering: ". . . as few people before marriage have known each other so long or made more trials of each other's tenderness and constancy," he wrote Gosse, ". . . I do not think many wives are better loved than mine will be." [43] True enough; but these happy thoughts did not prevent well-founded forebodings, already described to Gosse from Monterey:

I have the peculiar and delicious sense of being born again in an expurgated edition which belongs to convalescence. It will not be for long; I hear the breakers roar; I shall be steering head first for another rapid before many days; . . . I am going for thirty now; and unless I can snatch a little rest before long, I have, I may tell you in confidence, no hope of seeing thirty-one. My health began to break last winter, and has given me but fitful times since then. This pleurisy, though but a slight affair in itself, was a huge disappointment to me, and marked an epoch. To start a pleurisy about nothing, while leading a dull, regular life in a mild climate was not my habit in past days; . . . I believe I must go. It is a pity in one sense, for I believe the class of work I *might* yet give out is better and more real and solid than people fancy. But death is no bad friend; a few aches and gasps, and we are done; like the truant child, I am beginning to grow weary and timid in this big jostling city and could run to my nurse, even although she should have to whip me before putting me to bed.[44]

As spring came on, Mrs. Carson's younger boy, Robbie, fell gravely ill with pneumonia. To aid the kindly woman who had both house and child to care for, Louis took on much of the nursing. As the case grew more desperate and affecting, the amateur nurse, full of pity and fatigue, wrote Colvin: "O, never, never, any family for me! . . . I did all I could to help; but all seems little to the point of crime, when one of these poor innocents lies in such misery." [45] This was another facet of his mistrust of the parental impulse, which had once moved him to advise Charles Baxter to castrate himself if ever he felt it coming over him.

Not unnaturally Louis collapsed as soon as the child turned the corner toward recovery. A San Francisco doctor had the wit to discern that, whatever the import of his pulmonary symptoms, the high, fluctuating fever came partly from malaria.[46] Quinine cleared up this complication and probably made the difference between life and death.

As he struggled toward convalescence, Fanny moved him to a hotel in Oakland where she could more handily watch over him. As that proved expensive, she defied convention by installing him in her own cottage, with Nellie as nominal chaperone. Before that, however, a landmark had been reached—his first definite hemorrhage from the lungs. Bluidy Jack had arrived.

". . . consumption it has to be some time," [47] Louis had written Gosse earlier that winter. The disease that henceforth made his life a subtle battle has been loaded with all kinds of significance, sometimes spiced by doubt that he had tuberculosis at all.[48]

In 1880 modern means of exact diagnosis of tuberculosis did not exist, but the tragic series of hemorrhages that began in Oakland leaves small room for reasonable doubt. The California doctors, Uncle George Balfour, the great Dr. Ruedi of Davos all agreed. Though it is possible that Louis had had lesions undetected for years, neither Clark nor the equally expert Bennet had previously found definite symptoms. The histories of his mother and grandfather hint that he had inherited inadequate resistance to the bacillus. Then—for a well-founded guess—the combination of physical debility and shattering emotional problems that had heaped themselves on him since he had left Edinburgh finally opened the way for major infection. Henceforth for many weary years the camera focuses on the fragile man propped up in bed writing, writing, and defying one of the most sinister of human diseases to keep him from being notably close to a whole human person.

There is still no "cure" for tuberculosis, though newer antibiotics may offer some hope. Modern therapy relies on prolonged bed-rest and diet, often supplemented by surgery. It is dismally probable that a good modern sanatorium could have made Louis an "arrested" case—as near as medicine dares come to speaking of "cure"—inside eighteen months, provided it could have kept so mercurial a temperament as consistently flat on the back as necessary. But in his time therapy was still dangerously encouraging exercise at the patient's first return of energy and relying overmuch on special atmospheres—sea-air as at Menton; high air as newly popular in Colorado and Switzerland; dry air as in deserts; conifer-scented air; germ-free air as in dry cold. Thus Uncle George Balfour equipped Louis with a pine-oil respirator; the victim loathed its man-from-Mars effect, but did not question the theory. It is a tribute to Louis's essential stamina that, in spite of all such well-meant misconceptions, he did achieve "arrest" and died not of tuberculosis, as most people assume, but of cerebral hemorrhage.

His times had other curious notions, some still prevalent among laymen if disappearing among physicians, about the emotional effects of tuberculosis.[49] For instance, an assumed increase of *libido*, due to mysterious effects of the infection, helped such as Hamilton to enrich their juicy hints of Louis's early sexual excesses. In his case the more decorous welcomed the theory that tuberculosis is cryptically associated with genius, particularly literary genius, conspicuously including Louis on lists of examples—the Brontës, D. H. Lawrence, Keats, and others. The poor logic back of this position would embarrass a reasonably alert chimpanzee, but that has not prevented speculative doctors—and some commentators on Louis —from seeing tuberculosis as an asset for him, not only because it presumably forced him to write to relieve the tedium of being bedridden—as if Louis Stevenson ever needed such a spur —but also because the by-products of the tuberculosis germ actively stoked the fires of inspiration. Worse still, the old notion of the *spes phthisica*—the pitiful, semi-automatic cheerfulness supposed to characterize the consumptive clear to their last gasp—also survived as pat explanation for Louis's resilience and kinetic "optimism" as mere pathological symptom, like the hallucinations that go with brain tumor. The facts are, of course, that Louis's most fruitful periods coincided with better health more often than not, and that not even those doctors most taken with the theory could apply it to his consistent and fecund pluck—". . . in no sense a pathological state of mind," wrote Munro, in refreshingly unprofessional language, ". . . no spes phthisica but a conquest of the spirit." [50]

Current conservative psychiatry tends rather to see tuberculosis accentuating personality traits already present—the schizoid type withdrawing farther, the stable personality often rallying into higher stability. . . . So, Louis had always been impishly stoical—tuberculosis made him more so. He had always been hypochondriacal—the ever-present hazard of hemorrhage and the subtler, slower shifts in less dramatic symptoms now focused his attention even more closely on how-do-I-feel. He had always had reckless streaks—now perhaps they did not occur oftener but, when they did, physical penalties were heavier: "O to be able to get out and get wet and not spit blood next day!" [51] he wrote Bob from Davos.

The enthusiast in the new science of psychosomatic medicine has not yet tied tuberculosis firmly to a definite emotional type. But he is understandably tempted to wonder not so much what effect the disease had on Louis as what Louis's emotional history might have done to encourage the disease. Much could be made—probably too much—of his letter to Gosse from San Francisco about death being "no bad friend." For his realization that death might mean rest never moved him to turn his face to the wall. If die he must, however, he saw some advantage in it, and, if it had to occur, could take the fact objectively. One night at Hyères, Fanny, roused to find him hemorrhaging copiously, was flustered and clumsy about preparing the indicated ergotin. Louis took bottle and spoon, steadily measured out the dose and then wrote her a note: "If this is death, it seems an easy one." [52]   J. A. Symonds saw fit to lament this aspect of this patient: "I am not hopeful about him. He does not seem to have the toughness of instinctive energy of self-control . . . which I possess, of lying still when I find my centre of vitality attacked." [53]   It was Symonds, not Louis, who died of TB.

Emotional repercussions cannot, however, be altogether ruled out of the game. There is some evidence that, though a person can and often does develop tuberculosis without emotional prelude, a curiously high proportion of cases first show active disease during or not long after prolonged emotional crises.[54] For what it is worth: Between leaving Scotland and marrying Fanny, Louis was a one-man emotional maelstrom; whereas before that period evidence of active tuberculosis is very weak.

When he came to die, he had Bluidy Jack practically beaten to a standstill. But forty-four is an early age to die of cerebral hemorrhage. Some physicians associate it with too heavy and too prolonged tensions in earlier life. Louis had certainly had his share of such. Perhaps the emotional tangles that may have helped tuberculosis to establish itself in 1880, only to be defeated by his stamina and courage, were the same that finally carried the day by another avenue in 1894.[55]

His convalescence in Oakland was pleasanter for the presence of Nellie, his blue-eyed and sweet-tempered sister-in-law-to-be. With her he studied Spanish, a tongue in which her love-affair with Sanchez interested her, and washed dishes, developing elaborate techniques for polishing glassware. She acted amanuensis for him in preliminaries to *Prince Otto* and, in due season, found it dedicated to her. Later there was some graceful blank verse in *Underwoods*, regretting that there had been too little opportunity for Louis to know her still better.

What the household then lived on is not known; at least rent was no problem. In December Louis had written Baxter: ". . . with my parents all looks black," [56] and had since had no cause to change his mind. In February he told Henley: "I am glad they mean to disinherit me; . . . I always had moral doubts about inherited money, and this clears me of that forever." [57] So the stimulus was the greater when—perhaps in consequence of Baxter's commission to sell Louis's books for desperation money—Louis received a cable from Thomas: "Count on £250 a year" and word that an advance draft was on the way. That probably did more than twenty doctors could have. The fundamental affection between father and son had conquered bitterness. Thomas even refrained from making conditions about the strange woman, except to suggest delay between divorce and marriage. With money in hand, Louis could drop distasteful uneasiness about Osbourne's solvency, have his rotting teeth removed, and supply decent subsistence for Fanny, Nellie, Fanny's three saddle-horses, and Lloyd's vacation homecomings from his school at Sonoma.

Even so his slowness in convalescence moved Fanny to hasten marriage. Nellie and Louis both recorded that Fanny thought this "a marriage *in extremis*." Writing to Fanny's brother a few months later in the curious role of stranger in the family accounting for himself, Louis admitted:

I know I am on my trial; if I can keep well next winter, I have every reason to hope the best; but on the other hand, I may very well never see next spring. In view of this, I am all the more anxious she should see my father and mother; they are well off, thank God, and even suppose that I die, Fanny will be better off than she had much chance of being otherwise. . . . I am an author but I am not very likely to make my fortune in that business, where better even than I are glad to get their daily bread.[58]

They were married on May 19, 1880, with Dora Williams as the only attendant, at the San Francisco house of a Scots Presbyterian minister named W. A. Scott, who was president of the local St. Andrews Society. In addition to the conventional ten dollars, Louis presented Scott with his father's little book on the evidences of Christianity.

From here on the road would be anything but straight, not exactly dusty—nor long, as such roads go.

The Williamses had a small bucolic "ranch" toward the head of the Napa Valley, where Mt. St. Helena towers up into the sunshine. Their influence determined the newlyweds to see whether moderate altitude and air drier than that of the fog-haunted Bay region would help Louis. The original party included a sentimental setter named Chuchu, whom Louis genially spoiled, and two of Fanny's nippy little horses. Later it was joined by Lloyd and, off and on, by Nellie or Joe Strong, of whose skill with omelets Louis greatly approved.

It was a curious honeymoon, taking them first to Calistoga, a thermal development below Mt. St. Helena where Sam Brannan, the flamboyant Mormon renegade, had tried to create a California Saratoga. With this strange settlement as headquarters, they sought out the right location at greater altitudes. This proved to be an abandoned silver mine across the mountain shoulder, close by the stage road and stage tavern where, in still habitable mine buildings, they could settle down rent-free, 2800 feet or so above sea-level. Louis naturally loved the whole idea and was already planning a book on experiences to come which, as *The Silverado Squatters*, was to be his first sizable contribution to an American publication.[59]

The place was a rattling wilderness of particolored rubble with vegetation just beginning to creep back and a tremendous view of miles on miles of valley across tree tops. The departing miners had left old clothes and broken equipment, window-panes were few in the bunkhouse and the office. Louis was small use at reactivating practical details, being notoriously, like his father, what the Scots call "a handless man." But clever, ingenious, determined Fanny hung this and nailed that back together until a somewhat airy and rickety habitability became a fact.

I have too good sense to try to epitomize Louis's own account of life at Silverado. During my visit to the site in 1948 I found that the mine platform would still have been identifiable even if the clubwomen of Napa County had not placed there an inaccurately inscribed granite marker in the shape of an open book showing a stanza of "In Memoriam: F.A.S.": "Doomed to know not winter, only spring. . . ." Past tourists have chipped off bits for souvenirs, but they say in the neighborhood that few come any more, and postcards sold at Calistoga show the marker only in a one-sixth vignette barely visible to the naked eye. Louis underemphasized the steepness of the trail down to the Toll House, which, since his time, has burned down, been rebuilt, and is again ruinous. The beating sun and aromatic flora still persist, as, I am told, also does the extraordinary spectacle of the fog's mimicking of Noah's flood in the valley. But the trees have now grown so high before the platform that they pretty well spoil the valley view. I have visited every place in the world (except Davos) where Louis spent more than casual periods of time. Perhaps because of the special immediacy and pungency of his writing about it, one feels more Stevenson in the air at Silverado than anywhere else except in Edinburgh and environs. This even excludes Vailima, the house in Samoa where he lived for years and died.

The *Squatters* was written in Switzerland by dogged drudgery. It reads strong and on the spot, as of a man ransomed from extinction, breathing and smelling all the deeper for previous uncertainty as to whether these sensuous physical privileges would continue. His character-work on the Jewish[60] storekeeper and the poor whites—the best he ever did outside fiction—has the mordancy not of photography but of drawing, which lends significance to resemblance.

This adventure—which amounted to camping out with the help of a shed-roof and a cookstove—was temporarily interrupted by diphtheria striking both Fanny and Lloyd in a mild form, forcing retreat to Calistoga and undue strain on Louis. But each day saw either minute progress or only minor setbacks. By July it appeared not too impracticable to think of taking him home to Scotland. The Panama route was ruled out, probably because of the yellow-fever and malaria hazards of the Isthmus. Louis hated "that miraculous and really insane invention, the American Railroad Car," [61] but was willing again to use it eastward across the continent. He was eager to obey his parents' injunction to bring them his new wife, whose letters to them, written with both care and charm, sending them a photograph with the disarming note that it was much prettier than the original, had gone far to cement relations.

Louis was depressed and apprehensive when in late July he exchanged the sunny dryness of the mountain for San Francisco. But luck was good all the way. With a short stopover in Chicago, Louis, Fanny, and Lloyd made New York without mishap, sailing on the Inman-Royal Mail's *City of Chester*. This was his only sea voyage of which Louis left no vivid record, from which I surmise that top-class on a conventional steamer miserably bored him. On August 17, 1880, only 375 days after that strange sailing on the *Devonia*, the tug came alongside at Liverpool and Colvin clambered aboard. Louis's parents had come down from Edinburgh and were waiting ashore.

Reporting to Henley, Colvin noted that Louis looked better for his new teeth, which seem somewhat to have improved the shape of his mouth, but was ". . . weak and easily flustered . . . so small . . . you could put your thumb and finger round his thigh." He also went out of his gloomy way to express doubts "whether you and I will ever get used to [Fanny's] little determined brown face and white teeth and grizzling (for that's what it is) grizzling hair." [62] Among Louis's friends, Colvin was more loyal to Fanny than most. But it could never have been said that he liked the assignment.

In view of the Victorian attitude toward divorce, it is almost miraculous—and highly creditable to third persons—that the marriage met practically no social onus strong enough to be recorded. The only such difficulty of which traces survive Louis brought on himself: William Dean Howells, then editing the *Atlantic Monthly*, having already corresponded with Louis about verses of his that the *Atlantic* had bought, was urged by both Louis and Louis's friends to visit him at St.-Marcel in 1882. But before Howells could consummate plans, Louis read *A Modern Instance* and, concluding that its author's notions of marriage were ominous, went out of his quixotic way to explain to Howells how precisely to insult his prospective host if he wanted to:

Dear sir, I have just finished reading your last book; it has enlightened (or darkened?) me as to your opinions; . . . I find myself under the unpleasant necessity of intruding on your knowledge a piece of my private life.

My wife did me the honor to divorce her husband in order to marry me.

This, neither more nor less, it is at once my duty and my pleasure to communicate. . . . after the kindness you showed me in your own country and the sympathy with which many of your books have inspired me, it will be a sincere disappointment to find that you cannot be my guest; for I assure you I desire to know no one who considers himself holier than my wife.

With best wishes, however it goes, believe me
Yours truly
ROBERT LOUIS STEVENSON[62]

Howells is not altogether to be blamed for never answering this extraordinary communication, which, to a cautious mind, would seem to imply that visitors to St.-Marcel would need well-oiled dueling pistols. But a more adventurous type would have immediately boarded a train for France to have a look at its writer.

Louis's mother had already told a woman-cousin, ". . . doubtless she is not the daughter-in-law that I have always pictured to myself," [64] and doubtless she was not. But, in support of Fanny's well-engineered letters, Louis too had written his parents from Calistoga: "If you can love my wife, it will, I believe, make me love both her and you the better." [65] For whatever reason, things went most swimmingly. I have no record of the exact events when Louis presented Jacob Vandegrift's eldest daughter to his parents, but there is no question that the cordial aroma of fatted calf pervaded every cubic inch of 17 Heriot Row and that Fanny and Lloyd were welcomed with admirable grace and warmth. Louis's firm taking it for granted that his wife would be on the same footing as himself was good tactics but probably unnecessary. For, in a respectful way, Fanny had her own best foot forward, and that was often a very good best indeed.

What the Stevensons expected is hard to guess. What they saw was a trig, short, soft-spoken, comely, and intense woman of great stage-presence obviously able to take her own part, obviously devoted to their son, making herself at home without overstepping. On finding that Thomas disapproved of them, she readily gave up white stockings; but she also charmed him by pertly calling him "Master Tommy" and talking back to him with quasi-masculine common sense. He named her "Cassandra" for her emotional pessimism and "The Vandegrifter" to signalize her exotic origin. Louis's mother—who was, after all, only ten years her new daughter-in-law's senior—was soon taking Fanny through cupboards and trunks, showering items from her own gently luxurious wardrobe on Louis's wife and showing her the accumulations of Louis's respectable clothes that he had practically never brought himself to wear.

It went to Fanny's head like champagne at 20,000 feet. Though the Vandegrifts had been well off, life in Indiana had not had the layers on layers of fat and quilting that 17 Heriot Row implied. She gleefully used some silk-net underwear that had been bought for Louis years before, dressed him up in smoking jackets and dressing gowns that he had hardly known existed, breathlessly dramatizing for herself this swift transplantation from relative penury in raw San Francisco to relative affluence in ages-old Edinburgh. There were several women folded away in Fanny, unfurling in response to appropriate stimuli. One of them was this Hoosier *bourgeoise* ecstatic over accumulated gentility. Louis noted it with the grin that he reserved—and that often stood him in good stead—for females being specially female.

Fanny's handling of Louis impressed people. After studying her, Uncle George Balfour told his nephew: "I too married a besom and have never regretted it." [66] Walter Simpson gave Fanny a Skye terrier, his sister gave a specially procured Manx cat. When the household transferred to Strathpeffer for a few weeks in the Highlands, she approved the step and professed to believe that Louis was thriving in a climate that her American prejudices found dismayingly raw.

Louis knew better. From Edinburgh he had already written a friendly fellow-passenger in the *City of Chester:* ". . . I must flee from Scotland. It is, for me, the mouth of the pit." [67] Vague plans to return to California were gone like smoke. Uncle George was highly alarmed by his nephew's emaciation and the sounds in his bony chest. Menton again was indicated, or perhaps follow the new Swiss emphasis on high, dry altitudes where "germs"—those new-fangled things—were absent? So sun-thirsty, heat-hungry Louis, complete with Fanny, Lloyd, and dog—the cat proved impossible to house-train—was packed off to Davos, world-famous center of the latest treatment for consumption.

Weevil in a Biscuit

The Magic Mountain

> . . . when all is said, these fields of white and blots of
> crude black forest are but a trite and staring substitute
> for the infinite variety and pleasantness of the earth's
> face.
>
> —"Davos in Winter"

T HE next seven years were an industrious nightmare of
much fertility and occasional enjoyment.

The official fiction was that Louis's writings plus £250 a year
from his father would cover the costs of exile. Actually
expenses incident to Fanny and Lloyd, plus dismally heavy
medical bills, meant periodic requests for more. Lloyd remembered: "Fanny, I shall have to write to my father" as frequent
conclusion of family councils of war. These requests were sometimes apologetic, sometimes mere statement of need, never
querulous as, with the unfairness of the embarrassed, they
might well have been. Thomas responded generously. On the
average Louis may easily have cost him another £250 a year.

The journey to the Magic Mountain began poorly, with a
stopover in London, where the brethren's welcome was intimately glorious, the more so for their long-standing conviction
that they were never to see Louis again. A famous luncheon at
the Savile Club saw Gosse, Lang, Henley, Walter Pollock, and
much Burgundy present. Buoyed higher and higher, Louis grew
spinningly heedless: in a week of high living and reunions at the
Grosvenor, Fanny, Lloyd, and he ran up a bill of £46—an immense sum then, steep for a purse at all straitened even now.
Muttering hennishly, Colvin scraped up ten pounds to float
the party to Paris and arranged, via Baxter, for forty more to

meet them there as part payment of principal of his debt to Louis. (Louis asked his father to return to Baxter this sum, which he knew Colvin could not then spare.)

Fanny apologized to Louis's parents for having permitted such folly. Her lame excuse was that she did not know her way about with English hotels. The fact was, of course, that, separately or in cahoots, Louis and she could be quite heedless in money matters. Once they had to leave Paris long before they wished because Louis had forgotten a check for £100 in his pocket. . . . Once they two and Colvin ran out of funds in Marseille and clubbed their last francs to get Colvin to Paris to cash drafts while Louis lay "in pawn for a professor." . . . Once, receiving more than expected for book rights to *Treasure Island*, Louis spent an outlandish proportion of it on a set of Hokusai prints for Fanny. He had a right to say: ". . . if a man be not frugal, he has no business in the arts," [1] and so did Fanny. In these days of small earnings their scale of living was never extravagant. But their occasional outbursts of riotous living had much to do with their occasional penury.

After London Fanny was indignant about what "fiends disguised as friends" had done to Louis's health with overprolonged evenings of overstimulating talk, smoke, and drink. She wrote Louis's mother:

> . . . if we do not soon get away from London, I shall become an embittered woman. It is not good for my mind, or my body either, to sit smiling at Louis' friends until I feel like a hypocritical Cheshire cat, talking stiff nothings with one and another in order to let Louis have a chance with the one he cares the most for, and all the time furtively watching the clock and thirsting for their blood because they stay so late. [2]

These cannot have been restful occasions: Bob Stevenson swooping brilliantly, Henley flashing and booming like masked artillery from behind his whisky-impregnated beard, Gosse spurting and chortling, Colvin looking on like a slim, sententious mother-cat, and Louis swirling from one to another like a gypsy fiddler. Starved for his own kind of talk among men, like other starvers before him, he overindulged on reaching ample supply. Fanny seems to have done well enough. But people often recalled her as predominatingly a brooding listener, her amazing eyes shifting from one speaker to another but her solid little head almost motionless in a silence sometimes as ominous as it was respectful. Henceforth she had to struggle, not always successfully, against an instinct to glower at Louis's intimates. Coincidentally one feels in her from here on an impulse to go underground. She had always lived in her special world, but hitherto it had been overt; now it was almost secretly private, in-drawing, always potentially hostile, except where Louis as acknowledgedly hers was salient.

There was a flavor of last fling tingeing these evenings at the Grosvenor. Fortunately it came to nothing.

Crippling along on scanty funds, stopping to rest at Troyes and elsewhere, they took over two weeks to reach Davos Platz, far in the eastern prong of Switzerland. The place was hardly calculated to ginger up Louis's spirits: a long, high, bleak, windy valley among mountains rising to snow peaks, marred by hotels and châlets for invalids. There the tuberculous arranged their own lives, amateurishly responsible for observance of the regimens laid down by doctors. The great Dr. Ruedi put Louis on a gratifyingly modern diet, stressing milk and red meat—and the wine of the country, then considered particularly beneficial to the phthisical. The patient was by no means loath; whatever variations in therapy he encountered later, Louis clung firmly to the principle of plenty of red wine. He was much less pleased to be forbidden cigarettes and allowed only three pipes a day—I lack evidence for my suspicion that this rule was well honored in the breach—and only three hours of work.

The rest of the day went to rest or exercise, which consisted principally of walking drearily along the same paths day after day, meeting the same fellow-lungers at the same intervals, passing the same yellow splash of dog urine on the same snow-bank at the same time. Louis liked the thrills of tobogganing— this was just before skiing was introduced at Davos: ". . . though so obvious a member of the crock-company," wrote a fellow-exile twenty years later, "he would, whenever he had an ounce of strength to spare, insist upon a place with the ro-bust brigade." [3] Periodically the patients were exposed to wandering entertainers or ship's-concertish amateur perform-ances. Louis took part, but such occasions seem to have given him small sense of fun. Once he passed the brittle, dreamy ex-hilaration in which the altitude at first immersed him, Davos was insidiously depressing.

It did not stimulate work, as the relative pomposity of "The Morality of the Profession of Letters," written this winter, in-dicates. He did his best to make copy of the place, writing on the spot for once. But between the lines of his four short pieces on the Magic Mountain it is evident that he felt like a man in a trance floating with giddy resignation among the rings of Sat-urn. He experienced none of the fascination with such a moun-tain limbo devoted to the corrupt and dying that Thomas Mann made classical. Perhaps this indicates relative lack of morbidity in Louis's temperament. Davos, Lloyd wrote forty years later, was the only place where he ever saw Louis subject to "anything like mental inertia." [4] He did not like the landscape; nor his fellow-sufferers; nor the prospect of staying among them for the solid eighteen months that Ruedi advised; nor even the bus-tling, straight-coursed stream at the bottom of the harsh valley.

Fanny, however, long aware that she had her work cut out for her—she had already written from Calistoga that keeping Louis under control was "like angling for sly trout" [5]—found reassurance in this atmosphere, even sent to Zurich for a clock to time Ruedi's regimen precisely. Having cast a professional eye over her, Ruedi recommended a reducing diet, occasioning ribald comments from Louis. Fanny was never ill-naturedly sen-sitive about her tendency to stockiness. When the invalids did tableaux, she cheerfully took being paired with another stubby woman as Alice's Red and White Queens—from her temperament I assume Fanny was Red. Louis, ahem, was Raleigh laying down the cloak. Nor was she foolish about the discrepancy of age between husband and wife. The misrepresentation in her marriage lines is not the "forty years" but the word "widowed." Fortunately, since it would have been cruel, she was not present when a Davos landlady showing them rooms (Fanny gone upstairs, Louis staying below) said helpfully to Louis: "Your mother will be down soon." [6]

The new dog helped greatly to keep Louis in touch with life in this half-alive world. This "remarkably pretty, engaging, excitable, ill-behaved" [7] Skye terrier—the breed with which Louis had been reared—was christened Walter, for his giver; but a whimsical devolution of nicknames ended in his being called Bogue during most of his turbulent life. In gloomy weather at Troyes he cheered Louis by thoroughly polluting an ugly hotel carpet; Louis told Baxter that he grudged so much good manure to a foreign country. In Davos he bit Colvin for stroking him the wrong way; he once bit Fanny too. But for his six years —he died fighting, still in bandages from a previous overmatch —Fanny and Louis adored him. They buried him at Skerryvore with a Latin epitaph that Louis worked on as if it had been his own, in mournful memory of the impish eyes behind his absurd coiffure and the exultant energy packed into his small body. During one of her absences Louis writes Fanny:

Your Bogue is oppressive, affectionate and expository; he lets me alone till I sit in the arm-chair; but then (says he) my hour is come; . . . by windmilling, anatomical gesture, cat-mewing, pig-grunting and trebling, not forgetting rabbit-digging in his pantaloons, I shall constrain this man to conversation. . . . as for yourself, I adore you—on the whole and I am

Ever your
Louis [8]

Bogue often suffered horribly from canker of the ear.[9] During the day only the warmth of Louis's bony hand would check his terrified moaning, so the rest-dedicated invalid sat for hours holding his dog much as he had looked after Mrs. Carson's small boy. Thomas Stevenson would have done the same thing.

Vicarious parenthood was also fruitful. Louis and twelve-year-old Lloyd had got on well at Silverado—under amusingly gypsyish conditions. Life at Davos was more closely trammeled by weather, walls, and gossipy strangers, bound to arbitrary times, punctuated by crises—Louis's hemorrhages and fits of weakness, Fanny's troubles with her heart, which disliked the altitude, and her growingly surly abdominal tract. Under such strains, not to mention those of a "broken home," the boy persisted in candid hero-worship of Louis as a stimulating big brother. It survived even Louis's attempts to tutor him, though better judgment procured him local consumptive tutors glad to earn while treating their lungs. Better still, in April he was sent to school at Bournemouth.

The growth of this relation does not, however, justify Gosse's assertion that Lloyd's advent ". . . made an instant change in Louis Stevenson's attitude toward children." [10] Gosse's devotion to Louis seldom kept him from concocting such twittery ironies. Since he disliked the developing cult of the dead Louis as patron saint of the nursery, he had to believe that the man's taste for children came artificially and amusingly late. Actually, as Colvin noted, Louis had always taken an "exceptionally observing and loving interest . . . in young children." [11]—playing pickaback with Bertie Sitwell and Ernest Dowson, helping Nelitchka bathe her dolls, giving the ranch children lessons out back of Monterey, nearly killing himself over the Carson child. Since his writing "Child's Play" in 1878, this attitude had varied little. Its most poignant expression is in his letter to the wife of an old college friend on the death of a boy-baby to whom he had stood godfather:

I hope you will not trouble to write to me just now. This has been a very short story, but thank God, we cannot suppose it to be at all a sad one for the child.

"Yet shall poor Tom find pleasant weather," the song says, as good as many texts; and into that zone of quiet, the child has gone very straight. It is sad for you, and for Robertson; sad too, for me—for this was after all a little fellow on whom a childless man might look, in the future, with a half-sense of property; but happily not sad for him, who has escaped out of the snare, and gone straight home.[12]

Close though the pair were, however, Louis was never a father, not even a stepfather, to Lloyd. From devoted big brother he developed into something like chieftain to Lloyd's kinsman-retainer. Again, as in his being no husband as such to Fanny, this is no hint that the relation lacked pith. It does indicate that, in frequently renouncing the idea of children of his own, Louis's instinct was probably sound.

The supine dullness of the invalids inhabiting Davos's wooden cages afforded no parallels of Simoneau or roaring John Tod for Louis to chum with. The one sizable person sharing his tastes was John Addington Symonds, to whom Gosse had supplied introduction. Though their community actually included little but infected lungs and a love of writing, Louis and the lyric historian of the Renaissance made a determined effort at friendship. At first Symonds showed a little too nakedly his dismay over the gaps in Louis's education, and was understandably annoyed to find that Louis ". . . Hardly disguises his opinion that I cannot write poetry at all and am a duffer at prose." [13] Louis once said that knowing Symonds was "an adventure in a thornbush." [14] Mrs. Symonds reflected animus in vivaciously recalling for Margot Asquith her low opinion of Fanny's housekeeping.[15] Yet Symonds was soon urging Louis to undertake a scholarly study of the *Characters* of Theophrastus—a ridiculously inappropriate but apparently friendly suggestion; and consulting him, and Gosse through him, on selection for a projected anthology of English odes. With restraint admirable in two such nervous men under the prickling strains of confining illness, the pair kept their tempers to some purpose. Symonds dedicated to Louis his book of medieval students' songs, Louis gracefully responded with verses *à propos* (addressed to H. F. Brown, Symonds's companion-biographer), summed the man up with shrewd generosity: ". . . an invalid mind and character. But his mind is interesting," [16] and made him Opalstein of "Talk and Talkers."

Such counterirritants were needed. For this sinister, blood-spotted winter had brought old friends to Davos—Fanny Sitwell in charge of Bertie, who was dying of tuberculosis. The boy lingered much longer than was merciful for him or his mother.[17] Louis and Fanny helped as they could, marveling at how tragically well she held together. No doubt thus to see death creep up on connections so intimate, with so many connotations of summer at Cockfield, so many—actually only seven—years before, confirmed Louis's growing distaste for Davos and all its implications.

Ruedi insisted that, if Louis would remain through the second winter, an "arrested" case was probable. The experiment, however, was most improbable. Six months of Davos was all Louis could take at a dose; in view of his temperament even that was an achievement. He wondered openly at already having spent more time continuously in one spot than he had anywhere for eight years. So here he was, a fish out of water— the British colony at Davos suspected him for "his un-British courtesy of manner";[18] he was an economic anomaly as a family-man without assets drawing on his father with miserable reluctance; an apparent professional failure, for his recent work was pathetically scanty and ill thought of by his sponsors back in London. Even possible improvement in his health was small comfort in view of the chance, daily demonstrated among the invalids about him, that any moment fifteen minutes of bleeding might destroy fifteen weeks of hope. A dismal period—there survives a memorable picture epitomizing it: Years later a fellow-invalid wrote that he best remembered Louis as he looked returning from his pre-breakfast tobogganing, his narrow, hunched-up figure long and black against the low sun and the cold snow, the toboggan twitching absurdly along behind as his feet plodded homeward in a sort of rickety dutifulness—here was the most alive of men seen cold, alone, and tired half to death.

It speaks well for Ruedi's sympathy and authority, as well as for Fanny's persuasive powers, that, once he left in April 1881, Davos ever saw him again.

No invalid with so lively a sense of the Scottish climate—Louis pointed out how rich Scots is in raw, wet, windy words like "snell" and "blae"—would risk faulty bellows and shaky frame across the Channel in midspring. So Fanny and he spent a sentimental while at Siron's at Barbizon,[19] then some days round Paris, where they had a hypochondriacal scare over an epidemic. Arriving in Scotland in late May, they soon shifted, with Louis's mother, to a rented summer cottage at Pitlochry in the Highlands.

Though a zealous Scot, Louis had not hitherto cared greatly for the inconsiderable but lovely irregularities of terrain known as "the Highlands." Now, perhaps because it was not Davos, he came to love the loom of peaks called Ben Haggis, the subtle coloring of heather, the imaginative little "burns" that made pools and riffles as streams should, instead of rushing down a sort of badly made ditch like the stream at Davos. The weather was regrettably standard—"Here I am in my native land," he wrote Gosse, "being gently blown and hailed upon and sitting nearer and nearer to the fire"[20]—but, a miracle of which he had almost despaired, he found himself able to work again.

He planned a book on the Camisards, the French Calvinists in whom he had been interested ever since his Menton days. He began a series of horror tales—"crawlers" was the house-

hold name for them—to which Fanny would contribute. For a
professional, Louis was curiously given to collaboration with
the less experienced. It flew in the face of his theory that writing should involve assiduous apprenticeship, but it also slaked
his thirst for comradeship, and it was usually he who suggested
it—to Ferrier and Bob, the brilliant cronies; Fanny, the fascinated dabbler; Lloyd, the promising beginner. Collaboration
with Fanny appears again and again for the next eight years.
Most of the "crawlers" were never written or, like Fanny's
completed "The Shadow on the Bed," have not survived. But the
index of success was high: the scheme resulted in "Thrawn
Janet," often called Louis's finest short story, though the thick
Scots puts off many readers; and "The Merry Men," Louis's
shuddering compliment to the brutal, obscene hazards of the
ocean:

> "If ye had sailed it for as lang as me, ye would hate the thocht
> of it as I do. If ye had but used the een God gave ye, ye would
> have learned the wickedness of that fause, saut, bullering
> creature, and of a' that's in it by the Lord's permission; lab-
> sters and partans an' sic like, howking in the deid; muckle,
> gutsy, blawin' whales; an' fish—the hale clan o' them—cauld-
> wamed, blind-eed uncanny ferlies. O sirs," he cried, "the
> horror—the horror o' the sea!"

The words were crowding eagerly—the sure token of it is that
Louis was again cursing bad pens, sandy ink, waterproof blot-
ting-paper, and the vicious swindlers who foist them on white-
livered customers. Unsatisfactory as its conclusion may be,
"The Merry Men" has a quality making it easy to understand
why, on hearing his son read it aloud years later, Alfred Tennyson rasped out *ex cathedra:* "Hallam, remember we must have
this book in the house."

How much Fanny influenced Louis's aesthetic destiny is uncertain. He seems to have thought it a great deal. Miss Boodle
says that he told her Fanny's critical judgment was superior to

his own, which was polite if not necessarily sound. Fanny claimed—correctly, I am sure—to have agreed with Louis's father that Louis should publish nothing without her approval, this power to pass to the old gentleman if he should survive her. In itself that might mean little. A writer whose wife is better than supinely dull usually shows her all his production and she usually gets enough feel of the business to make admissible comment. But Fanny, hot after her pretensions, was not likely to remain a mere familiar touchstone.

Apart from actual collaboration, she sometimes brought about abortion or major modification of a piece of Louis's work. She early appointed herself not only mandatory first reader of a draft but last to abandon opposition to aspects of it that she disliked. Violently though he might react at the time, Louis wanted her to do just that. But this consultative power carried no veto. He could and did override her with impunity on occasion. For him, as her invaluable genius, unique among human beings, indispensable medium of her self-esteem, she could abandon infallibility without losing face with herself—often after grim battle, grudgingly at the time, but in the end without lasting animus. On the whole this arrangement worked better than might seem likely in view of the curiously vulgar flavor of Fanny's tales in *The Dynamiter*, which survived even Louis's rehandling, and of the few short stories that she wrote independently between 1884 and 1890.

August brought Louis a heavy cold and blood-spitting. The party abandoned Pitlochry for Braemar, the amenities of which Queen Victoria had advertised by choosing it as summer residence. Almost daily they saw the old lady of Balmoral driving out regardless of wind or rain while her red-nosed ladies-in-waiting shivered on the opposite seat. Inviting Gosse for a visit, Louis advised that, if he had had an uncle who sailed the Arctic, he had better bring the old man's outfit. With his cold had come chest pains, and enforced speechlessness, relieved by chess, a rap on the board meaning that he was too tired to go on. Lack of money forced taking Lloyd out of school. But, in the teeth of such physical and financial miseries, productivity remained high.

Amusing himself with Lloyd's paints and drawing paper, Louis developed a map of an imaginary island with an outline "like a fat dragon standing up" studded with swashbuckling names—Spyglasse Hill, Skeleton Island, etc. (He was highly map-minded, maintaining that a high-detail chart was better reading than most books.) The genesis of *Treasure Island* calls up many bits of Louis's past: his and Bob's imaginary Encyclopaedia and Nosingtonia; his tinkering at sketching; his father's improvisations. . . . Lloyd liked the yarn that developed. Thomas, up from Edinburgh when business allowed, took fire and, drawing on his own past as a youth in the lighthouse yacht, suggested the apple barrel, drew up the inventory of Billy Bones's chest, and "forged" the gnarly legends on the map as published. Every day Louis's pen strode confidently through another chapter to be read to an applauding audience of his parents, Fanny, Lloyd, and whoever else happened to be in the house. He is said to have read very well, his rich, flexible voice being a good tool for his narrative instinct. The only hearers who are reported ever to have disliked his reading were the suspicious Britons at Davos.

"If this don't fetch the kids, why, they have gone rotten since my day," [21] he wrote Henley, requesting a large, sound work on pirates for background. Then a visitor who heard some of it— Alexander Japp, expert on Thoreau, about whom Louis had corresponded with him—suggested a means to revenue quicker than book publication: He considered that James Henderson, editor of *Young Folks* (an English boys' paper in the high—or low—Victorian style, of greater respectability than most), might pay as much as £100 for *The Sea-Cook*, which was the original title.[22] After seeing a sample, Henderson commissioned the job at space rates, which eventually brought Louis a mere £34/7/6—"not noble," he granted, but cash in hand when badly needed, and the copyright for book purposes remained in the author's hands. Unaware of Louis's habit of dropping long jobs in the middle to be taken up months or years later, Henderson began to run the story in his issue of October 1, 1881, under the pseudonym of "Captain George North." This moral obligation to the calendar, Louis later asserted, was what forced him to finish the second half in Davos that autumn—his first full-length narrative.

Some of the brethren in London professed distress at the Gifted Boy's turning to hackery, even in disguise, for a publication of about the same aesthetic and intellectual standards as the *Tom Swift* series. Hearing of it from Henley, Louis let fly:

> To those who ask me (as you say they do) to do nothing but refined, high-toned bejay-bedamn masterpieces, I will offer the following bargain: I agree to their proposal if they give me £1000, at which I value *mon possible*, and at the same time effect such a change in my nature that I shall be content to take it from them instead of earning it. If they cannot manage these trifling matters, by God, I'll trouble them to hold their tongues, by God. . . . I will swallow no more of that gruel. Let them write their damn masterpieces for themselves and let me alone. . . . I am ever yours, the infuriated victim of his early books, who begs clearly to announce that he will be so no longer, that he did what he has done by following his nose to the best of his ability, and, please God Almighty, will continue to pursue the same till he die.[23]

This somewhat overstates Louis's beginning emancipation from the preciosity of his younger phases. Its very violence may somewhat betoken that he was not yet clear of it. The pseudonym on *Treasure Island* was mere professional caution—it might be bad for his general reputation to hack openly for the juvenile press, confounding himself with the regular brewers of watery trash about Australian diggers, valiant knights, and gallant seamen, imitators of puerile imitations of Scott, Cooper, and Marryat. But, as he read *Young Folks*, he was somewhat unnecessarily overamused by the style of *Sir Claude the Conqueror* (a serial overlapping *Treasure Island*), which he described as "like buttermilk and blacking." [24] And he did foster the legend, often overemphasized by his biographers, that the adolescent readers of the paper, trained in the shoddy galvanisms of its steady contributors, found *Treasure Island* distasteful. [25] Even when the book rights brought him (quoting Mr. Mantalini) "A hundred, jingling, tingling, golden, minted quid," [26] the largest single sum so far touched by a piece of his work, he thought it "a sight more than [it] is worth"; [27] he had expected perhaps £50. He was pleased, of course, when Lang told him that, as romance, the book stood only below the *Odyssey* and *Tom Sawyer;* but to word that Mr. Gladstone, whom Louis detested, sat up all night to read it and was recommending it on all sides, Louis snapped back that the Grand Old Man "would do better to attend to the imperial affairs of England." [28]

Gradually, however, the extraordinary merits of the work imposed themselves on even its author. He wrote Henley: "John Silver is quite a kind of a good third-rate part-creation . . . he has his moments has Long John. Let the Heathen rage; Long John'll do." [29] By 1882 he could say that he wished he could read *Treasure Island*—it sounded like the sort of book he liked—and was delighted when Henley sent him an antique pistol as a certified relic of "Barbecue"; certainly, Louis responded, the actual weapon that he passed to Jim at the treasure-pit. By 1890 he doubtless got nothing but pleasure from a letter from the newly rising W. B. Yeats assuring him that *Treasure Island* was about the only book that his seafaring grandfather had ever found any satisfaction in reading—he even read it "upon his death-bed with infinite satisfaction." [30]

A difficult transition—more credit that it was successfully made. Preciosity is a deep-seated complaint, and so is artistic arrogance. With years, Louis grew steadily less inclined to feel that, in writing, he was doing a favor to anybody but himself.

No fast best-seller, *Treasure Island* kept doggedly alive and built gratifyingly, perhaps fostered more by adults than by clamoring schoolboys, until, as Louis's fame expanded toward the end of the 1880s, it infiltrated the canon of books that every child is supposed to have read. Note how much good came out of Nazareth: I know of no more striking example of an artist's taking a cheap, artificial set of commercialized values—which is fair enough to the Victorian "boys' story"—and doing work of everlasting quality by changing nothing, transmuting everything, as if Jane Austen had ennobled soap-opera. It is dizzying to jump from *Don Zalva the Brave*, rich with inky cuts, to a bit from the next column of *Young Folks* doing Pew on the highway or Silver negotiating with Captain Smollett. The ingredients are utterly nonoriginal—even Billy Bones at the Admiral Benbow was half stolen, as Louis ruefully admitted some years later, by unconscious memory from Washington Irving.[31] But anybody needing example of the difference between fuzzy and hard-twist writing should read the original Irving and then what Louis did with the same materials filtered through discipline. He was clearly showing what it was to be steeped in Bunyan and Defoe, his masters in monosyllabic English narrative. The free, clear run of *Treasure Island*—the string pulling with a readiness that, to a writer, feels almost eager—first acknowledged him master of his craft.

Lest this should be taken to mean undue maturity, he was simultaneously pursuing a markedly unreal scheme. Thomas Stevenson had brought from Edinburgh not only enthusiasm for *Treasure Island* but also a project: The Professor of History and Constitutional Law at the University was retiring. The chair paid £250 a year for duties consisting solely of summer lectures, not even residence required in other seasons; selection of candidates lay among the Faculty of Advocates, of whom Louis was technically one. The income would be a godsend, the schedule permitted Louis's lungs to spend dangerous seasons abroad—why should he not turn professor?

Few questions have ever been so easily answered: He was at best an amateur in history and knew no more law than clung to him after years of devoted neglect of the subject. His reputation and scholastic record at the University had been poor. Few of his fellow-Advocates knew him, fewer still would remember him respectfully. The Scottish climate might not permit him regular lecturing even in summer. At thirty, he was certainly too young for the post. At least once Louis admitted that he was certain of defeat and told himself that he was standing only to get his name in the pot against future vacancies, when age, and perhaps improved reputation, might better his chances. But Thomas, whose grasp of matters academic had always been faulty, though some of his intimates were eminent professors, showed no misgivings. On other occasions Louis too took the scheme seriously, using young Lloyd as audience for impromptu lectures of dignified length on appropriate subjects.

So that autumn Thomas's credit with the learned and respectable was strained to gather testimonials in favor of Louis's candidacy "As Mr. Stevenson is at present on the continent, and cannot personally meet with the electors." [32] In view of Edinburgh's prejudices and Louis's appearance, his absence was probably sound tactics. The result Balfour called "a tribute to the ingenuity of the human intellect." [33] Three St. Andrews professors and the Vice-Chancellor, plus the Professor of Humanity at Edinburgh, strove like gentlemen to make Louis sound qualified without actually having to say that he was. Jenkin, be it noted, furnished no testimonial, but his advice, that English names would outweigh Scottish, set Louis vigorously working the oracle south of the Border: Symonds assured the Advocates that Louis would ". . . handle grave studies with the fine touch and attractiveness that belong to a master of expression"; Lang called Louis "the most ingenious and refined writer of his generation" who would engage "the affections of any class of young men with whom he might be thrown";[32] Colvin, Gosse, Stephen tried to make it sound as if an assiduous and brilliant writer of unstable health and mercurial disposition were just what Constitutional Law had been needing all along. Even the clergy appeared in due proportion: Babington from the Church of England and Cambridge, the Scottish Kirk augustly represented by the ministers of St. Giles' (Edinburgh's equivalent of St. Paul's) and St. George's, Edinburgh.

Charles Guthrie, rising advocate and old friend from the Spec., obligingly handled Louis's interests, though his doing so might imperil his reputation for sober discretion. In the election (which recommended to the chiefs of the University) the winner received eighty-two votes, the runner-up fifty-one; Louis was a poor fourth with nine.

He was already high in the Alps at work on *Prince Otto,* a notably flighty and unhistorical work, and, so far as I can discover, never again referred to the matter. But this turn of his attention to responsible history had consequences: His father encouraged him to plan a serious account of the eighteenth century in the Highlands, which suffered severe economic and social dislocations as Scotland entered the full current of the modern world. (Louis knew no Gaelic; first he professed to believe that knowing it was unnecessary for the scheme, then made an abortive effort to learn it.) This set him on the rumor-ridden mystery of who killed Colin Campbell of Glenure; and that eventually begot David Balfour, Alan Breck, Eli Hoseason, Barbara Grant, Tod Lapraik, and glib, valorous, and shameless James More. Louis's vagaries usually turned up somewhere in his work.

The second winter at Davos was more private. The Stevensons rented a wooden châlet—rather like a New York elevated station on a mountain slope—near the hotel where the Symondses awaited the completion of a permanent home. The new quarters were as bleak as all else. But they afforded Lloyd room for his printing press and, in the lower story, which was difficult to heat, ample floor space for a new game:

From a military family-friend Louis had received Hamley's *Operations of War*—a still recognized summary of the strategy, tactics, and logistics that Victorian soldiers developed out of the great campaigns since 1800, rich with maps and resounding names like Wellington and Moltke, written with a leisurely clarity akin to that of Darwin. Louis had been long attracted by, if seldom earnest about, chess, and by the picturesque moral devotion of soldiering—remember, the charge of the Light Brigade still outweighed, in literary convention, the fetid, feckless campaign that had included it. In a famous and unmistakably childish passage, Louis once professed to a consistent ambition to have been leader of a horde of irregular cavalry.[34] Deeply as certain phases of Tolstoi later affected him, he never forgave the great Russian for his disrespectful picture of strategists in *War and Peace*. It is strange indeed to find Louis Stevenson, who had never yet heard anything more warlike than the sunset gun from the Castle, lecturing a former captain of artillery from the siege of Sebastopol on the trenchant niceties of war.[35] (Inconsistently enough, he highly approved of Zola's war scenes.) Now, in the chilly-to-freezing semibasement of the Châlet am Stein, gathering hints from professional soldiers relegated to Davos, he set his ingenuity to work on a German-style was game that sounds like immense fun.

It had skill—popguns fired printers' "ems" from Lloyd's font of type, and the boy's superior accuracy sometimes checked Louis's superior planning; luck—data on strength and condition of opposing forces were scattered over the "theater of war" on face-down cards, to prevent reconnoitering cavalry from knowing just where the more valuable information might lie; variations in quality of troops—some corps of lead soldiers, solider on their bases, stood fire that routed less staunch regiments; censorship and misleading news releases—the correspondence that Louis supplied to the Glendarule *Times* and the Yallobally *Record* is fine, if sometimes ferocious, travesty of British war correspondence of the period. When the *Record* suggested that General Osbourne be court-martialed, the editor was

. . . hanged by order of General Osbourne. Public opinion endorsed this act of severity. My great-uncle, Mr. Phelim Settle, was present and saw him with the nightcap on and a file of his journal round his neck.[36]

Louis always loved not so much making believe child-style —some biographers have missed the point—as the fun of making believe, which is another matter. A child enjoys being a pirate specifically; some adults enjoy the general proposition of dressing up for and acting the part of pirate; a few can do so without condescending toward either themselves in the part or the part itself. In an anecdote which I hope is not apocryphal, Louis is watching a child play boat and, wearying of it, climb out of the armchair that had been acting as boat, and walk away. "For heaven's sake," Louis calls after him, "at least swim!" That is genuine technique in play.

Johnstone and Thomson and John Libbel gradually acquired colleagues thrown out sporadically by Louis's imagination to be played with in his letters with comparable consistency and care:

Old Mr. Pegfurth Bannatyne is here staying at a country inn. His whole baggage is a pair of socks and a book in a fishing-basket; he borrows even a rod from the landlord. . . . I naturally asked him about Hazlitt. "He wouldnae take his drink," he said, "a queer, queer fellow." But did not seem further communicative. He says he has become "releegious" but still swears like a trooper. . . . He once met Borrow; they boxed; "and Geordie," says the old man chuckling, "gave me the damnedest hiding." Of Wordsworth he remarked, "He wasnae sound in the faith, sir, and a milk-blooded, blue-spectacled bitch forbye. But his po'mes are grand—there's no denying that." [37]

The same taste for doing things amusingly brown begot the Davos Press. While at school in California, Lloyd had acquired a small printing press and set up a miniature paper called *The*

Surprise. For its issue of June 1, 1880, the convalescing Louis offered *Not I*, a bit of unblushing doggerel. The press came along to Davos, where Lloyd earned a little pocket money by printing menus and concert programs for the hotel. Somehow he acquired some crude cuts of scenes of violence, to match which he wrote and set up a ripsnorting Western tale, *Black Canyon*. Louis was quickly at his door with a revised version of *Not I* and more doggerel in the same vein; but the verses had to go unillustrated because all available cuts were already committed to *Black Canyon*. So he took fine-grained wood from Lloyd's fret-wood outfit—apparently what the States called scroll-saw work—and, with a pocketknife, occasionally gashing his fingers, embarked on a series of baldly impudent woodcuts and verses to match—putting William Blake in his place, he wrote Henley. Joseph Pennell once saw fit to praise the composition and vigor of Louis's blocks, but I suspect that they are to be taken just about as seriously as the verses attached. It was good occupational therapy and hygienically far preferable to blue-knuckled hours on one's knees in a chilly room; but that had little to do with the case.

In this period he leaned much on Henley among his faraway coterie in Britain. Each new issue of the *Magazine of Art*, which Henley began to edit in late 1881, meant a monthly "cricket"—brief and often acid comment from Louis on each item in the number, which gave him, no doubt, a feeling of needed participation in more active lives. Henley seems highly to have valued the "crickets." Along with them often came much of Louis's most elaborate fooling—occasionally ribald, sometimes merely effervescent in strange tricks of the pen that could easily imply red wine, the best of these outbursts were most successfully outrageous. For instance, when Colvin—the severe, the monitory, the responsible—visits Louis at Kingussie in the summer of 1882:

The Garden Angel [Colvin] . . . has quite surprised me by his rowdy conduct. He insists on raking out at night with a big stick and a white great-coat tally-ho-ing down the street of this long village and rattling with his cudgel in the doors. He is the Hero of the bar-parlour; the young men and maidens follow him like a piper. I sit in a rose garden in a bath chair now making a little water colour sketch and from time to time laying my paints aside and waking the echoes of the mountains with my silvery flute. . . . Meanwhile up comes the uproarious Archangel, swinging his sprig of oak, and "D—n you," says he, "what the d—l do you sit puking at there? Here's a set of jolly boys come in for a drink with us by G—d; and d—nme if you shall skulk, d—nme if you shall!"

In consequence of this opposition of tastes we see little of each other. I question if these excesses can ultimately benefit his health; but he seems decided on urging on his Wild Career.

Yrs ever
HENRY BISHOP[38]

Or, protesting against the contemporary fashion of having artists illustrate magazine verse with the text in illegible "rustic" lettering, Louis runs on for the edification of Will Low:

We live in a rum age of music without airs, stories without incident, pictures without beauty, American wood-engravings that should have been etchings, and dry-point etchings that should have been mezzotints. I think of giving 'em literature without words; and I believe if you were to try invisible illustration it would enjoy a considerable vogue. So long as an artist is on his head, is painting with a flute, or writes with an etcher's needle, or conducts the orchestra with a meat-axe, all is well; and plaudits shower along with roses. . . .[39]

Those hearing from Louis in flightier moods never knew how letters would be signed: Dummle, Blood & Fargo . . . el caballero melindroso . . . George the Pieman . . . George North, my old Lord Tushery (when deep in *The Black Arrow*)

. . . The Hired Bard (when reporting the astounding sum of
$75 paid by *Manhattan* for verses to be decorated by Will
Low) . . . or a string of abstract characters that, Balfour truly
says, are "worthy of Bunyan's own invention":[40] "Mr. Muddler/
Mr. Addlehead / Mr. Wandering Butterwits / Mr. Shiftless Inconsistency / Sir Indecision Contentment." Louis was pleased
when Henley Bunyanesquely dubbed him "Fastidious Brisk":

> Excellent is Mr. Fastidious Brisk. . . . I say, Bunyan could
> make names. You may add him to your list of men of genius;
> he has that surprising air of being commonplace and plain
> sailing and being quite master of himself and not in any rush
> that they all have. I would say Shakespeare, Molière, Chau-
> cer (Molière's young first cousin) Fielding, Scott, a little
> lower because of bad work and laziness; Balzac, a little lower
> by reason of an unsound temper—the lark was dead in his
> bosom. After these come the geniusettes, the djinis: two will
> suffice—de Musset and Bunyan. And we have to go to the
> Essayist sort of people for the next level of excellence, Mon-
> taigne, Wordsworth. Close behind the ranks of geniuses are
> one or two hangers on: a curious instance is Le Sage, almost
> a man of genius, yet not a bit a djini. The Djinis are always a
> little high, a little rank, a little spicy; as it were with origi-
> nality. . . . Byron, if he had not been a dandy, promised to
> take to genius. If a djini, or any small card, tries to take to
> genius, he is at once detected; he becomes dull. . . .[41]

This may have approximated Louis's famous talk—lacking, of
course, the sweeping gesture and the essential give-and-take.

He often broke into doggerel; for instance, Henley has mentioned a critic's speaking of "Stevensonism"; amused and
irked, Louis replies:

> Stevensonism, it seems, exists
> Although to Stevenson unknown,
> By eager men with toes and fists
> Either upraised or overthrown.

> To whom is this new gospel known
> That puts the elder faiths to rout?
> Broad is its blood-red banner blown—
> Pray tell me what it blows about? . . . .[42]

Learning that a publisher of one of his books, losing all back stock in a warehouse fire, collected full insurance without paying his authors royalties to match, Louis grew ebulliently slanderous:

> . . . . Hi O to be a publisher
> And be allowed to cheat
> For the law that sits on you and me
> Lies down and licks his feet.[43]

Warned by Henley that some day a respectable man would write a biography of him:

> Chapter 2, youth in Edinburgh, is like to be a masterpiece of the genteely [sic] evasive. . . . I seriously suggest that you should write a blackguard supplement . . . The best name for your work and perhaps for me is the Christian Blackguard.[44]

As per invoice, time brought both—the evasion and Henley's blackguard supplement.

Toward Christmas 1882, Fanny's internal troubles sharpened into what sounds like a gall-bladder attack. Lloyd escorted her to Berne for special doctoring, followed by gradual recovery. Lonely and gloomy, Louis went to meet them in Zurich as they returned, standing the trip well, but on reaching Davos again, falling and badly injuring a knee. Both Fanny and he spent New Year's Eve ill in bed, kept awake by "shouts of stifled laughter all through the watches" [45] and a little later:

> . . . still lame . . . must resign myself to stationing on my behind. . . . non-getting on with work damps me also; my people seem dry of coins; we spend too much; this place makes and keeps my wife ill. . . .[46]

Even so the winter's work improved on sterile 1880-81. Louis completed drudging at *Silverado*, progressed with *Otto*, and did some solid work in such essays as "Talk and Talkers" and the fine bit on Bagster's *Pilgrim's Progress* for Henley's magazine. He read eagerly for a tentatively commissioned biography of Hazlitt; this, however, came to little because, the more he learned of the personality of his great literary admiration, the more dismayed he became. *Liber Amoris* finished him off. His dropping the project on such grounds infuriates Hazlitteans, but Louis said little about it. By now he was better prepared to find that a man can write with the pith of a sage and the effortless follow-through of a good golfer and yet be personally hysterical and whiningly petty. It was good judgment not to pursue work on a man whose every other action stung the biographer with distaste. He consoled himself with planning a biography of Wellington that Lang would presently commission for a series of *English Worthies*. The Iron Duke and Louis had little enough in common, but he had long valued the figure as admirable character work, just as he relished Braxfield and Admiral Duncan; now his absorption in military techniques clinched the match. It was probably just as well that only a few pages of preface ever came of it.

At least the New Year brought physical hope. In April: "My lungs are said to be in a splendid state. . . . Taïaut! Hillo! Hey! Stand by! Avast! Hurrah!" [47] Ruedi consented to see him descend from Davos, prescribing the South of France "fifteen miles as the crow flies from the sea, and if possible near a firwood." [48] Louis had a talent for nostalgia. He could hanker after almost any place that he had ever known well. But not the Magic Mountain. He blotted that out from his universe like an outraged father expunging a son from the family Bible. He was delicate, but he was not "life's delicate child."

Happy Once

> . . . To make this earth, our hermitage,
> A cheerful and a changeful page,
> God's bright and intricate device
> Of days and seasons doth suffice.
>
> —"The House Beautiful"

However hopeful Ruedi's prognosis, disease still dictated where and when. At both Stobo and Kingussie the Scottish "summer" brought bad weather and hemorrhages. When there was sun, Louis sun-bathed—which, clinicians now know, was distinctly bad for him. In the autumn Louis and Bob—recently married to a "new woman" with a job and an intellectual tolerance of a week-end husband—went to spy out the land in the Midi, Bob amusedly passing himself off as Louis's servant. At Montpellier an alarming hemorrhage struck. Fanny, left behind on account of illness, hastened to relieve Bob in charge. As soon as Louis was again fit for activity, exploration continued. Outside St.-Marcel, a semi-industrial suburb of Marseille—a city that Louis liked for style, bustle, and comely women—they found what they wanted:

Only a few miles beyond the southern hills of knobby white stone, the sea was nearer than specified. But the Campagne Defli was a sunny, gracious, spacious house looking south on a warm valley down which a convenient railroad ran to Marseille. The prospect was dusty, aromatic, composed with unpretentious cunning, vegetation stuck where it would earn its way and, in consequence, look well—the kind of dry, highly stylized countryside that Van Gogh loved to paint; not far to the northeast, in fact, he was even then committing to canvas masterpieces that would probably have sadly puzzled Bob and Louis. Fanny exulted to Dora Williams over the impressive gateway and olive orchard, the filtered water and dozens of cupboards of the "château" they had found. Louis exulted generally.

But the climate, or something, was not for him. He drooped, seeped blood, and accomplished little. His physical recalcitrance so gnawed at Fanny that the next emergency—a local epidemic of an enteric fever that she took to be typhus—sent her into panic. She insisted on Louis's fleeing to Nice while she closed the house and followed. Telegrams that he promised to send en route failed to reach her. Handicapped by both inadequate French and growing hysteria, she set off to seek him. Her letter to the Symondses about her subsequent experiences sounds like a bad dream; I suspect that much of it was just that. She had a tale of a corpse left to bloat at the gate on the morning Louis was to leave, and another of how police and railroad officials assured her that Louis must be already dead and, for sanitary reasons, so hastily buried that she would never learn where. . . . Any of it is conceivable, but all of it sounds too much like the authoress of certain tales in *The Dynamiter*. Though she never lied for practical advantage, Fanny sometimes justified her dreads with details that happened never to have existed—what psychiatry calls "retrospective falsification."

The flight from St.-Marcel proved a happy catastrophe. Casting about for a safer haven, the Stevensons fell on Hyères, then a renowned resort for the tuberculous. It was another Menton a few miles from the sea—the modern town grown up at the skirts of the steep, stone-harsh old town under a formidable medieval fortress; new hotels for prosperous invalids already built and more building. . . .

On the line between new and old, where the slope becomes abrupt, in the rue de la Pierre Glissante—the Street of the Sliding Stone was sure to attract Louis—was a Swiss châlet with a history: Designed as a model small house for a Paris exposition, it had been bought by a well-to-do citizen of Hyères and rebuilt here on his own land.[1] The floor plan gives strange notions of what the nineteenth century considered good design: two tiny rooms in front on the first floor, two on the second, the rear of the squares allotted wastefully to storage, and a stuffy first-floor kitchen partly dug into the slope. But the acre or so of steep garden planted with semitropical flora—oranges, palm, cactus—was a great attraction, and Louis and Fanny do not seem to have minded the front veranda's being practically on the street. Just able to afford the rent, for eighteen months they took rapt satisfaction in being lords of the villa "La Solitude" in "Highairs-the-Palmtrees," even going the length of primly printed notepaper. For Mrs. Sitwell Louis described his

> . . . loveliest house you ever saw, with a garden like a fairy story, and a view like a classical landscape. . . . Eden, madam, Eden and Beulah and the Delectable Mountains and Eldorado and the Hesperidean Isles and Bimini.[2]

and for Will Low:

> . . . a most sweet corner of the universe, sea and fine hills before me, and a rich variegated plain; and at my back a craggy hill, loaded with vast feudal ruins. I am very quiet; a person passing by my door half startles me; but I enjoy the most aromatic airs, and at night the most wonderful view into a moonlit garden. By day this garden fades into nothing, overpowered by its surroundings and the luminous distance; but at night and when the moon is out, that garden, the arbour, the flight of stairs that mount the artificial hillock, the plumed blue-gum trees, that hang trembling, become the very skirts of Paradise. Angels I know frequent it; and it thrills all night with the flutes of silence. Damn that garden;—and by day it is gone.[3]

A plaque on the veranda of La Solitude now reminds visitors that eleven years later Louis wrote: ". . . I was only happy once; that was at Hyères." [4]

It was not the society of stuffy invalids that made him so. The Stevensons' few friends were a French wine merchant, a local English pharmacist with literary leanings, and the local doctors whom Louis consulted. Nor yet markedly better health: hemorrhages were frequent, malaria recurred, he had attacks of savage sciatica and an eye infection that kept him long sightless under bandages. (Fanny tried to persuade herself that inability to read was good for him.) Nor lack of personal troubles: Strains internal to the family firm were threatening to force Thomas Stevenson into early retirement and diminished income, hence impairment of Louis's emergency resource. Far worse, James Walter Ferrier, whom Henley called "our Athos," died shattered by drink and tuberculosis—the first breach in Louis's circle. Though Louis understood that dying was the kindest thing Ferrier could have done for himself, the culmination of the tragedy nevertheless buried him in rebellious gloom; he wrote Henley:

Alas, boy, we begin to come into the trade winds of Death. All our friends will go dying . . . But poor J. W.—though I don't know that he is poor—but my poor past, and the poor world, to lose the kind face . . . tell me how he went. My poor, besotted gentleman. O, what regrets, what regrets! . . . I wish to God I could have gone to his funeral even. Christ pity us: the hearse to take him away, that old fount of laughter. . . . Thinking over this wrecked and still brave life, I grow to think of him more and more with honour. Few have made such a plunge; but few, having lost health, hope and pride, would have made so fine a stand. . . .[5]

Fanny forbade him to write at all about the death, since doing so left him dangerously shaken. Nevertheless the birds in the garden, the produce of Fanny's plots planted with American vegetable seeds, the blue and yellow coastal plains and sea, all made for an elation probably based on inscrutable factors. During his vacation visits Lloyd noticed that Louis's sense of being harmoniously established even extended to costume—he had grown a little French tuft on his chin and was wearing the short *pèlerine* cape.

By a minor blessing Fanny secured the perfect retainer-servant in Valentine Roch, a strong, fair, intelligent French-Swiss whom Louis called "Joe" when she behaved prettily and "Thomasine" during streaks of contrariness. Soon serving notice on Fanny that she would never quit them, she kept her word for six years. When Valentine fell ill, Fanny nursed her as solicitously as if she had been Louis. At Bournemouth later, when Fanny would be away, Valentine defied local gossip by sleeping by the fire in Louis's room to be instantly on hand if hemorrhage should strike.[6] Her relation to her employers was about that of country-cousin helping more august relatives, "one of the family" in most senses. On hearing that Edmund Yates had been convicted of criminal libel in London, Louis insisted on a bonfire in the garden, and maid joined master and mistress in dancing madly round it hand in hand.[7] The exertion gave him a well-deserved relapse. Soon ashamed of his uncharitable reaction to Yates's disgrace, he wrote Henley: "After all, we are all gaol-birds—loose." [8]

Hyères being more accessible than Davos, friends came more readily: Henley (Louis offering to help with his traveling expenses), Colvin, Bob, Ferrier's sister after her brother died. The doll's house of a châlet—plates had to be reached over people's heads at dinner—was inadequate, but guests could stay at the Hôtel des Iles d'Or on the next street-level down. In early 1884 Louis even risked a trip to Nice to foregather with Henley and Baxter more commodiously. A few days laid him low with all his old ailments plus a kidney infection that brought Fanny flying; to Louis its "dull, drowsy pain" ominously implied "the creak of Charon's rowlocks and the miasmas of the Styx." [9] Baxter and Henley had perforce gone their way, so, when British doctors at Nice told Fanny that some man friend had better stand by in case Louis died, she imperiously telegraphed Simpson to come at once, and was furious when he did not instantly jump to the whistle all the way from Edinburgh. By the

time she could secure Bob instead, Louis had mended enough
for her to support him by easy stages back to Hyères. Convalescence was dismally slow, and his report to Bob a few weeks later
bleak-minded, if not discouraged:

> . . . looking slowly up, after some abominable back-casts in
> which "pain, pain, forever pain" played a loathesome solo.
> Now I dislike pain. I am not one of those who triumph over
> the carrion body, frail tabernacle, wicked carcase or what
> you please; but when Pain draws a lingering fiddle-bow, and
> all the nerves begin to sing, I am conscious of an almost ir-
> resistible temptation to chime in, alto: L'Invitation à la Boo-
> Hoo. . . . I am now shorn of my grog forever. My last habit
> —my last pleasure—gone. I am myself no more. Of that lean,
> feverish, voluble and whiskyfied zany Scot who once sparked
> through Britain, bent on art and the pleasures of the flesh,
> there now remains no quality but the strong language. That,
> at least, I shall take gravewards; my last word, it's like, will
> be an execration; the hired nurse, the weeping widow and
> the anxious medical attendant, shall be embraced in one all-
> round and comprehensive detonation, and at a breath the
> *Temper* that was known as R.L.S. will flit from its discarded
> tenement.[10]

This caper prompted Fanny to prohibit further independent
junketings with cronies. Louis's trip to Montpellier with Bob
had collapsed him, now this reunion in Nice had been nearly
fatal. (He was not shorn of his grog forever, of course; next
year at Bournemouth the evening tray with glasses and whisky
was once more an institution.) But she sometimes overstepped
herself in her ensuing program of encouraging people to visit
Louis at Hyères where she could keep an eye on him. When
Baxter was considering postponement of a long-promised visit,
she belabored him with written accusations of bad faith that
would have been extreme if he had defaulted on a trust. She
was equally ill advised in having subscribed to *The Lancet* in
her quality of amateur physician. Handiness with bandages

Peter A. Juley & Son

The second of two portraits of Robert Louis Stevenson done by John Singer Sargent at Bournemouth. Fanny's costume is East Indian, donned to lighten the color scheme. The bare feet that go with it seem to have caused rumors that she attended London dinner parties barefoot. This picture is considered by many of those who knew Louis to be the best portrait of him ever done.

Louis's mother, Margaret Isabella Balfour Stevenson. Clearly brings out the similarity of her profile to Louis's; although, between emaciation and—until he had radical dentistry done in 1880—his poor alignment of teeth, the profile worked out much more attractively in her.

Louis's father, Thomas Stevenson.

Mrs. Stevenson with Louis who is wearing the conventional, little-girlish clothes of upper-class Victorian children in the 1850's. The plumpness and prettiness were soon lost, probably through systemic illnesses.

The Stevenson Museum, Edinburgh

The Stevenson Museum, Edinburgh

Thomas Stevenson with Louis at the age of about seven.

The Stevenson Museum, Edinburgh

Louis in the middle teens, probably the year before he entered the University of Edinburgh. Evident retouching adds to the untypical effect of conventionality.

Gordon A. Block, Jr.

Self-portrait of Louis. The thick, waving hair—Louis's own hair was always lank—and the costume indicate that he drew himself in theatrical get-up, with wig, probably for one of the Jenkins' amateur productions.

Fanny Vandegrift Osbourne at approximately the time when she me
Louis.

Married by me at my residence 19th May 1880
Robert Louise Stevenson born Edinboro, Scotland,
            and   White ingr, 30 years old, reside
                                in Oakland, Cel
Fannie Osbourne (born Indianopolis, Indiana,
                                40 year, widower, White resig in
witnesses   Oakland
Dora N. Williams
Anna Sate. Certificate to be sent to Mrs Virgil Williams
£10.00 m   719 Geary Street. City.

Record of Louis's marriage to Fanny in the register of the officiating
clergyman. Fanny disguised the fact that she was a divorcee, bu
candidly admitted her age.

"The Precarious Mill," a wood-cut carved by Louis with a pocket knife. It and others were done for *Moral Emblems*, first printed and published in Davos by the then twelve-year-old Lloyd Osbourne.

"The Pirate and the Apothecary," Scene the First, from *Moral Tales*.

"The Pirate and the Apothecary," Scene the Third.

Louis, taken by a professional photographer at Bournemouth, complete with velvet jacket, long hair, and poetic pose appropriate for the literary man. The mourning band could be for Fleeming Jenkin, possibly for Thomas Stevenson.

The Stevenson Museum, Edinburgh

Lloyd Osbourne, Louis's stepson, taken in San Francisco before the *Casco* sailed.

The Stevenson Museum, Edinburgh

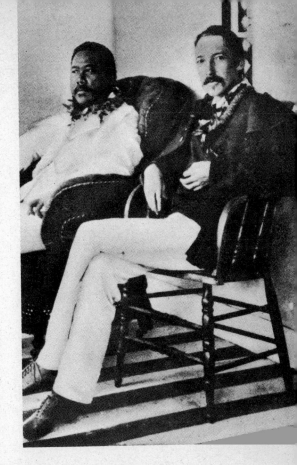

Louis and Kalakaua, King of Hawaii. Fore-shortening makes the king look less than the giant he was. This is probably the photograph the Stevensons used to impress South Sea chiefs with the party's importance.

Below: at Waikiki, Hawaii, about 1889. *Standing:* Mrs. Thomas Stevenson; Belle Strong, Louis's stepdaughter. *Seated:* Ah Foo, the cook; Louis; Fanny; Lloyd Osbourne.

The Stevenson Museum, Edinburgh

Above: Vailima, first stage, taken before Louis's workroom was built. Louis is leaning on the second-floor railing. *Left to right on lower level:* Mrs. Thomas Stevenson's maid, Mary; Mrs. Thomas Stevenson; Lloyd Osbourne; unidentified guest; Samoan servant; Fanny; Samoan servant; Belle Strong. *Below:* Vailima, with second unit completed, more or less as the house remained until Fanny sold it after Louis's death. His workroom is the second-floor veranda enclosure at the right.

Right: Louis and Tuimaleali-ifono, a principal Samoan chief and a good friend of the Vailima household. Louis is dressed for riding down to Apia on business.

Below: Fanny and a Samoan servant before the second-floor fireplace at Vailima—these fireplaces are still the only ones in Samoa. On formal occasions the servant would have covered her bosom. Fanny wore the elaborate *holoku* to eliminate the necessity for corsets.

Portrait of Louis done at Vailima by Count Guglielmo Nerli, globe-trotting Italian artist. Fanny disliked it, saying that Nerli tried too hard to do the author of *Jekyll*.

National Portrait Gallery, Edinburgh

Party at Vailima in Louis's last year. The band of H.M.S. *Katoomba* came up for the entertainment. The Samoans' axes show that they have been performing one of the local ceremonial dances with weapons. *On the veranda:* Belle Strong (white dress, dark sash); Bazett Haggard (beard), brother of H. Rider Haggard and H. M. Land Commissioner in Samoa; Louis (dark jacket); Graham Balfour; Fanny (dark dress).

Tattersall, Apia

Tattersall, Apia

U.S.S. *Vandalia*, *Trenton*, and *Nipsic*, wrecked by the hurricane described in *A Footnote to History*, shortly before Louis first saw Apia. Three German warships also were destroyed. The wreck of the German *Adler* is still holding together today, high above water.

Sydney, 1893; Fanny, Louis, Belle, Mrs. Thomas Stevenson. Belle Strong's exotic darkness gave rise to a rumor in Samoa that she was Louis's daughter by a "native." His mother is wearing the conventional Victorian widow's cap. *Freeman & Co., Sydney*

To C.B from R.L.S.

Louis in 1893.

The Stevenson Museum, Edinburgh

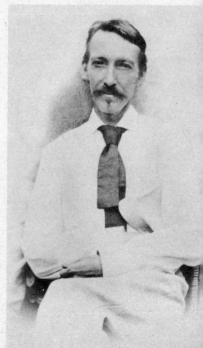

The last good portrait of Louis.

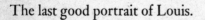

The Stevenson Museum, Edinburg

Augustus Saint-Gaudens Memorial

Medallion of Louis in characteristic attitude when working in bed, done by Augustus Saint-Gaudens in 1887-88. Verses in background are text of "Youth now flees on feathered foot . . ." A larger version, full length, much inferior, was used as the Stevenson memorial in St. Giles's, Edinburgh.

Robert Louis Stevenson's tomb on top of Mt. Vaea, as shown on a modern postage stamp of the Trusteeship of Western Samoa.

and home remedies was on the whole useful in mining camps and, later, trading schooners. But it was unfortunate when her avid reading of medical articles persuaded her to bar vinegar from Louis's salads because some arbitrary British F.R.C.P. had decided that vinegar was unwholesome. Her self-confidence sometimes led her even farther, into tenuous or fantastic theories or folk and quack remedies. When Simoneau's Mexican wife brought California herbs that the Indians thought good for "lung complaint," Fanny showed considerably less skepticism than even politeness required.

This did social damage when she jumped at the conclusion— it happened accidentally to be sound—that colds were infectious. Since colds were associated with Louis's breakdowns, she went to great and tactless lengths to isolate him from anybody with cold-symptoms. A person with a cold was humorously labeled a "pizon sarpint" and summarily exiled, which infuriated people who, in 1880, had no reason to agree with her inspired guess as to the etiology of upper respiratory infections. At the time it was largely her word against that of the medical profession. In such a case she was never one to hesitate to hew to her own line, let the chips fly as far as Harley Street if they liked. So Bob, Colvin, Baxter, Henley, and Louis's parents were frequently glowered at, or ejected after somewhat painful severities, because they seemed suspiciously sniffly, her solicitous dogmatism blinding them to the chance that she might be right and, if so, such extra protection might mean higher safety for her patient.

Yet the besom's acerbity and lack of perspective need not be exaggerated. She was not unrelaxed when writing Louis's mother that the little girl with the curl could well have been a Stevenson; that even Bogue was infected with this wildly vibrating temperament; that she perpetually marveled at the way the clan kept up so high a head of steam. Nor should one ignore the morbid conditions under which she had to carry out her abiding purpose of what she thought of as keeping Louis alive as long as possible. Here he was huddled into a shawl even at meals—or flat on his back, bronchi oozing blood, arm strapped to his side to discourage further hemorrhage, forbidden to speak. . . . The code of hand signals that he developed is eloquent of the strains to which Fanny as well as her patient was subjected:

1. The crooked forefinger begs explanation, criticism, elucidation, opinion.
2. Violent pantomime is to be answered not by remarks on the dumb person's impatience but by a statement of what you understand him to wish.
3. The case of the dumb is one of great inconvenience and suppressed wrath. When he has made you a sign you have failed to follow and he shrugs his shoulders, drop it *forever*. . . .[11]

This places Fanny, harassed, perplexed, and apprehensive, in Louis's immediate background—face hard set as she scrambles for the ergotin that may forestall death or doses out the dangerous morphia or aconite that doctors recommend but Louis loathes; or aware, as she watches Louis climb the garden stairs, that he is being a touch too active, gingerly about calling to him again, afraid not to, suspecting that, the rest of whatever life he manages to secure, no six months will pass without his again hearing Charon's rowlocks. She was pitifully grateful for bits of hope, such as, from a London doctor specially sent to look Louis over at Hyères in 1884:

The doctor says, "Keep him alive till he is forty, and then although a winged bird, he may live to ninety." But between now and forty he must live as though he were walking on eggs, and for the next two years, no matter how well he feels, he must live the life of an invalid. . . .[12]

Renewed sense of accomplishment, good work done in the teeth of the worst handicaps yet, may have made up much of his "happiness" at Hyères. There Louis brought *Otto* close to completion; in "A Penny Plain" and "The Character of Dogs" and (in fiction) "The Treasure of Franchard," showed that he could still put witty charm into print; disdainfully but practically kept revenue coming in with *The Black Arrow* for *Young Folks*; and drafted much of *A Child's Garden of Verses*. This was no heavy eighteen months' work, but of good quality on the average and significant of coming shifts in his techniques. Though Louis never added up in a manner convenient for aspirant Ph.D.s, it is informative to take stock of him as writer in these years:

Prince Otto (its first phase had been *Semiramis*, an aborted comedy of his early twenties) had long been Louis's Penelope's Web. It was to be a romance of ideas laid in a mythical German principality, scenery out of recollections of the Black Forest, human values somewhere between a Landor dialogue and a French conversation-piece. An appalling assignment, and Louis was distinctly not the man for it. His revival of the scheme in San Francisco in 1880 was delayed reaction to his having met George Meredith at Box-Hill in 1878. Somewhat to the mystification of his neighbors, Meredith had pronounced Louis a creature of whom the world would hear worthily and often. Older and younger man liked and admired each other in a gracefully self-conscious way and, in a manner of speaking, *Otto* was Louis's return of the compliment, as well as the last gasp of the "sedulous ape." His end-product was clearer than Meredith, for Louis had a knack, sometimes betraying him, of being clear at all costs. But it too successfully shared the Meredithian vice of making a ballet out of the novel and, though swimmingly precious, managed to miss the genuine passion of preciosity that makes *Richard Feverel* brilliant reading.

Ability to admire *Otto* has been said to be the test of the true Stevensonian—say rather "fanatic." This was not the vein in which Louis's future lay or ever had lain. Its one service to him was finally to get off his laboring chest the impulse to spin words and ideas for their own sakes. Yet he retained a sneaking affection for the work, noting owlishly in the copy that he inscribed for Dr. Trudeau:

> This is my only love tale, this Prince Otto,
> Which some folks like to read and others *not* to.[13]

George Moore said that Stevenson was not a romantic at all, a point sounder than the bilious witness. Louis used action not for empathy but to illustrate moral dilemmas, a habit from which *Otto* suffered sadly. Throughout its sprightliness moral paradoxes obtrude like angular bones through a silk shirt. Intended to be exquisite, it succeeds only in being finicky, the sole success being the jarring, bitter flavor of Sir John Crabtree. Even so it is pleasant to listen to the born writer exulting to Henley when he thinks he feels his skill cantering smoothly under him:

> The chapter of Otto that I drafted today has pleased me . . . c'est la guerre si ce n'est pas magnifique . . . it has entrails and it smiles . . . Yesterday I was low over it; today it's all gold sun, blue mountain and the rainbow hope. . . . To feel as I felt today, when I turned the corner of my story, was the reward of a lifetime. It came next, and but some thousand miles behind, love.[14]

The merits of "The Treasure of Franchard" are in pregnant contrast: Its idiom is as light-footed, its ideas quite as pleasingly skewed, but the fabric comes out all of a piece, almost as well integrated as *Treasure Island*. Neither Otto nor Dr. Desprez is supposed to be primarily flesh-and-blood. But Desprez is a significant comedian of delightfully high competence, whereas Otto is Hamlet translated into porcelain, small and strange against the markedly ugly issues of the story. Merrily Desprez lubricates the ironies of sententiousness, almost rejoicing in being so decoratively thoughtful a fool; whereas Otto always draws away from the implications of what he does not do. Louis even made the crowning error of a last-minute effort to turn his heroine, until then a mere queen in the chess game, into a warm-to-the-touch woman.

Certainly Louis at work on *A Child's Garden*—a project born of his happening on a Kate Greenaway book in 1882—was another matter altogether. It was excellent escape from the red-soaked handkerchief and the taste of organic iron in the mouth—total recall of a childhood (much of that spent in bed, too) drifting to the surface in shrill, angular, and often highly engaging verses. Assiduously he filed and tinkered and up-ended chains of rhyming words. The completed collection was dedicated to Cummy, who, he assured her, alone would recognize all the data. He was reconciled to seeing the book taken principally as an excuse for illustration, ". . . without which no child would give a kick for it." [15] But his great fondness for "the ragged little regiment" also made him work obsessively over proofs, layout, and title, which at first rang the changes on "Penny Whistles." He was at least half right in predicting that the book would please the public more than it would the run of publishers, for this time painstaking solicitude was rewarded. *A Child's Garden* made Louis part of the universally recognized body of English quotation, along with Shakespeare, Pope, Benjamin Franklin, and Isaac Watts.

Though quality has little to do with such immortality, the *Garden* has quality anyway. Much of Louis's soul was buried here. Manner often matched matter: from "The squalling cat and the squeaking mouse/The howling dog by the door of the house/The bat that lies in bed at noon/All like to be out by the light of the moon," to the apostrophe "To Minnie" in which, somewhere in the middle, Louis begins to bow his fiddle all the better for stumbles marking catches in the throat.[16] "Inspired doggerel," true; but the inspiration is often quick, cool and sweet to the bottom of the lungs, and carries a wit of content and form that justifies Sampson's distinction:

. . . not (as too easily supposed) a book of verse for children, but a book of verse about children. Children, of course, like many of the pieces, but essentially the poems are the disclosure of a child's mind. . . . Never was there a set of playful verses about children more completely free from mawkishness. There is no attempt to make them songs of innocence.[17]

For that sort of thing the *Garden* contains too many backhanded flicks of the essential Louis: the wistful cynicism of "The World is so full of number of things"; the contention that the dirty child is wicked, "Or else his dear papa is poor"; the original etiology of "Naughty children, crying babies/All grow up to geese and gabies,/Hated as their age increases/By their nephews and their nieces"; the insidious assumption that, however interesting their lives may be, the "Little Indian, Sioux or Crow" must often "Have wearied *not* to be abroad." The moralist had free entry to Victorian writing for and about children, but in Mrs. Barbauld's—or Canon Kingsley's—terms, not these. Louis's content in such passages was, in fact, so alien to his age that the world has ever since agreed to miss the point and interpret "The World is so full . . ." as simple-minded optimism.

Much of *The Black Arrow* was worked out during a summer stay with Louis's parents at Royat, the miniature hill-spa that the Empress Eugénie created as foil for her husband's sponsorship of Vichy.[18] Borrowing flavor from the quaint sordidness of the *Paston Letters*—a work that Louis relished for bedside browsing—background from the fens and beaches of eastern England, he kept damning the job as artificial "tushery" but also hacking away at it—in both senses—with an energy that gave great briskness and proved highly popular with the readers of *Young Folks*. Most critics read the book out of the canon with even more zeal than they apply to *Otto*—it is almost incredible that the same man wrote both these very minor works. Fanny refused to read it. But at that, three generations later D. B. Wyndham Lewis called it, with equivocal admiration, "the best study of the mediaeval world . . . ever put on paper by a nineteenth century Calvinisto-Agnostic." [19] The fact is, the thing is by no means altogether hackery. The living eye in the head of the tapestry-huntsman; Sir Daniel as a leper; the weasel-in-armor sketch of Gloucester—at least one can wish such hackery were commoner, and that more Victorian historical fictions had succeeded as well in getting out from under the Kotzebue touch in Scott's medieval romances.

Even here the troubled and troubling moralist insinuates himself. The conventions of the "boys' story" were based on Rights and Wrongs. To enlist the hero with the White Rose should have made the Red a villainous cause by definition, the White candid indeed. But Louis drily lighted up the futilities of medieval dynastic wars by having Dick admit choosing sides by accident and by allowing him to leave the war before it determines; by the appalling figure of Gloucester, chief of Dick's party, in contrast with the vaguely glimpsed integrity of his particular opponent, the Earl Risingham; and by showing the result of all the intriguing and bloodshed to be widespread ruin as well as the restoration of the heroine and his insignificant estate to Dick. The triumph of Right, if it can be considered to occur, is chillingly incidental.

The story opens with Tunstall hamlet taking news of impending battle as pure calamity, no thought of "Up Brackley!" Says a shivering woman: ". . . the ruin of this kind land. If the barons live at war, ploughfolk must eat roots"—the reverse of the coin that Morris so wistfully minted in *A Dream of John Ball* a year or so later. Grimmest are the episodes of the shipman: Having stolen old Arblaster's vessel for an amphibious raid, Dick wrecks it and with it all the skipper's laboriously acquired resources. Reappearing as lucky young lieutenant of the conquering Gloucester, he finds Arblaster among prisoners about to be hanged merely for existing. He spoils his new credit with Gloucester by begging the old man's life and considers that he has thus evened scores for the loss of the ship. But that sentimentality is not allowed to stand:

"An I had my ship," said Arblaster, "I would 'a' been forth and safe on the high seas—I and my man Tom. But ye took my ship, gossip, and I'm a beggar; and for my man Tom, a knave fellow in russet shot him down. . . . Nay, let be. Y' ave played the devil with me and let that content you." . . . shambling away with bowed head across the snow, and the unnoticed dog whimpering at his heels; and for the first time [Dick] began to understand the desperate game that we play in life, and how a thing once done is not to be changed or remedied by any penitence.

To this harsh little sermon, which would certainly never have come into the head of a good fifteenth-century Catholic—and which editors should have cut as out of tone with the rest of *Young Folks*—Louis added astringent heresy about the Robin Hoodish outcasts of his story. Barring drink, Will Lawless, unfrocked monk and proclaimed outlaw, has been Dick's bold, loyal ally, none better at one's back in a tight place. But, when Dick offers to entrust him with papers crucial to his fortune, Lawless refuses even knowledge of where they are hidden:

"I am a kind old Christian and no traitor to men's blood, and no sparer of mine own in a friend's jeopardy. But, fool, child, I am a thief by trade and birth and habit. If my bottle were empty and my mouth dry, I would rob you, dear child, as sure as I love, honour and admire your parts and person!"

Few "boys' stories" include the moral that it is possible and sometimes convenient to like a man immensely without being able to trust him.

Louis was no formal moralist, bolstering principle by self-evident truth or eternal verities. Moralizings were merely implicit in his incurable introspectiveness. He was chronically fascinated by "the war in the members"; by the need to choose courses of action without better guide than dubious guessing as to consequences; by the spectacle of people, himself included, struggling to do right while lacking both intelligible notions of what "right" is and the emotional thews and sinews necessary for such a feat. He shows clear influences from the New Testament, which he knew like a parson; from Spencer, as his father was so bitterly aware; from Scots Calvinism, of course, though he recommended the Shorter Catechism to his parents on what must have struck them as the impertinent grounds that it taught children "fine style and some austere thinking";[20] with touches from Montaigne and Marcus Aurelius. Only a madman could synthesize those. Louis never tried; but, sometimes deliberately, sometimes in passing, he incessantly sifted through his inquisitive fingers the issues raised by the words "should," "must," and "wish." Not infrequently he set down self-guiding maxims of gnarly toughness: "Acts may be forgiven; not even God can forgive the hanger-back." . . . " 'Do I love?' said Loveless; and the echo laughed." . . . "Great-heart was deceived. 'Very well,' said Great-heart."

Occasionally his terms were concrete. At Menton he first grew uneasy about spending unearned money and tended to regard it as a sort of loan from society somehow to be repaid penny for penny. Even though it was principally illness that kept needs far ahead of earnings, the moral anomaly of his semi-dependence gnawed at him all the while his father lived. Toward the end of the Hyères period, he told Mrs. MacMorland, a good friend at Davos:

> . . . my position as a fraudulent bankrupt is the only thing undeniably civilized about me. I have been ill; I have done no work for eight months [which was not true]; I have about ruined my father; and as I have never answered a letter or paid a debt, I am in self-defence obliged to glory in my abasement, and wrap myself in the Pirate Flag. . . . a Devil Incarnate, an Unrepentant Bilk and Bandit, A man who lacks but the opportunity to Ruin Empires.[21]

This burlesque does not vitiate the feeling underneath. Note that, in Louis's terms, he eventually squared himself with society: First and last he probably cost Thomas Stevenson something like £10,000—a respectable inheritance in itself. But the earnings of his last ten years, which developed a plantation for Fanny and dependents and supported them in the interval —never mind the soundness of the investment—more than repaid the world's general fund for Thomas's contributions. This attitude was more notable then than it would be now. Beneficiaries of Victorian upper-class incomes seldom questioned the justice of their advantages, and would have looked queerly at Louis's revision of his "Lay Morals" during this period:

> I suppose that in the course of ages, and through reform and civil war and invasion, mankind was pursuing some other and more general design than to set one or two Englishmen of the nineteenth century beyond the reach of needs and duties. . . . At this rate, short of inspiration, it seems hardly possible to be both rich and honest; and the millionaire is under a far more continuous temptation to thieve than the labourer, who gets his shilling daily for despicable toils.

Politics too are concrete, and Louis was never more the moralist than in his political attitudes. These are tricky to formulate: Thomas, as noted, was an eccentric Conservative. At sixteen Louis duly voted for Disraeli and against Carlyle (who won) in the students' election of a new Rector for Edinburgh University, and then cheered the victor. But his adolescence naturally included radical social and political notions, for which he never apologized:

> I look back to the time when I was a Socialist with something like regret. I have convinced myself (for the moment) that my own scheme would not answer; and all the other schemes I ever heard propounded would depress some elements of goodness just as much as they encouraged others. Now I know that in thus turning Conservative with years, I am going through the normal cycle of change . . . I submit to this as I would to gout or grey hair; . . . I do not greatly pride myself on having outlived the fairy tales of Socialism.[22]

If the above has a strange ring, remember that, to Louis's generation, the word Socialism meant Morris rather than Marx. Even while falling out of love with radicalism, he kept harassing his father with denunciations of such middle-class stupidities as laws to suppress trade unions or abolish income tax: "Is there no shame about the easy classes?" he wrote hotly from Menton.[23]

This had little to do with doctrine or party, much with his preference for "decency." The MacMahon government in France offended his nostrils like the first-class passengers in the *Devonia*. Though duly despising Mr. Gladstone, he considered Mr. Disraeli a nauseating opportunist. His crowings over Lord Roberts's victory at Peiwar Kotal in December 1878 should have labeled him imperialist—only, when Britain and the Boers rehearsed at Majuba Hill for their full-dress war twenty years later, Louis wrote: "This is a damned, dirty, foul job of ours in the Transvaal," [24] and, in a paper apparently intended as a letter to some newspaper:

> I am . . . literally grilling in my blood about this wicked business. . . . It is no affair of ours if the Boers are incapable of self-government or not . . . that we have been . . . fairly beaten [is occasion for] honourable submission.[25]

Twelve years later he took the same road to concluding that the only decent course open to the Powers was to get out and stay out of Samoa. Henley would readily turn ecstatic imperialist and embrace Kipling, the press agent of Empire. Louis remained in an inconsistency that is baffling until one sees that his eye was always on decency instead of policy, necessity, or opportunity—decency determined for each case like the law of fraud.

Thus he was personally outraged by the Fenian dynamitings and the Land League boycotts; and, being attracted to "Chinese" Gordon, the Christian adventurer, and repelled by what he thought of as Gladstone's Uriah Heepishness, was devastatingly hard hit by the hesitations and irresponsibilities that made Gordon the martyr of Khartoum. Gordon's end remained for him a permanent symbol of the viciously meaningless wrongs implicit in things-as-they-are. Somewhere he acquired Gordon's last message, written in Arabic on a cigarette paper, and kept it as a relic at Vailima.

Preoccupation with decency, asking great men to observe in public affairs the same standards expected of the man in the next house in private affairs, is a poor clue to politics-as-they-are, since it focuses on individuals and individual actions. When Louis chose to think of politicians at all, his comments were acid:

> Parnell is an attorney; Foster a wooden moralist; Randy [Lord Randolph Churchill] a journalist; Northcote a very honourable muff; Chamberlain a swindler; and Gladstone a man of fog, evasions . . . and a general deliquescence of the spine.[26]

People often adopt a political creed or party out of violent revulsion against the pilots or the projects of its rivals. Louis was guarded against that by suspicion that those on the side of what might be taken for angels could be just as smug, intolerant, sly, and cruel as the plumpest Philistine. Disgustedly he described the French *librepenseur*:

> I met the other day one of the new lay schoolmasters of France; a pleasant cultivated man, and for some time listened to his ravings. "In short," I said, "you are like Louis Quatorze, you wish to drive out of France all who do not agree with you." I thought he would protest; not he! "Oui, monsieur," was his answer. And that is the cause of liberty and free thought! But the race of man was born tyrannical; . . . you see the old tyranny still active on its crutches; in this land, I begin to see the new, a fat fellow, out of leading-strings and already killing flies.[27]

"The Day After Tomorrow," his only formal pronouncement on such matters, was shrewd, amateur summary of intelligent forebodings of the analogy between the paternalistic state and an army enlisting all at birth:

> . . . *laissez-faire* declines in favour; our legislation grows authoritative, grows philanthropical, bristles with new duties and new penalties, and casts a spawn of inspectors, who now begin, notebook in hand, to darken the face of England. It may be right or wrong, . . . but . . . it is Socialism in action; and the strange thing is that we scarcely know it. . . . a few disclosures . . . of what the freedom of manufacturers, landlords, or shipowners may imply for operatives, tenants, or seamen, and we not unnaturally begin to turn to that other pole of hope, beneficent tyranny. . . . if Socialism be at all a practicable rule of life, there is every chance that our grandchildren will see the day and taste the pleasures of existence in something far liker an ant-heap than any other previous human polity. . . . We cannot trust ourselves to behave with decency; . . . and the remedy proposed is to elect a round number of our neighbors, pretty much at random, and say to these, "Be ye our conscience; make laws so wise and continue to administer them so wisely, that they shall save us from ourselves and make us righteous and happy, world without end." . . . There are great truths in Socialism; . . . and if it came and did one-tenth part of what it offers, I for one would make it welcome. But . . . the first thing to grasp is that our new polity will be designed and administered (to put it courteously) with something short of inspiration. . . . this golden age of which we are speaking will be the golden age of officials. . . . So that upon all hands we may look for a form of servitude most galling to the blood—servitude to many and changing masters—and for all the slights that accompany the rule of Jack-in-Office.

Louis knew Jack-in-Office as fragmentarily but as well as the hobo knows the railroad detective. Pondering the contemporary radicalism of syndicates and communes, he goes on to suggest that boredom may spawn political *morcellement* and internecine wars, which, in view of the monolithic trend of the modern social-service state, was very poor prophecy. But the early part of his argument demonstrates that, right or wrong, he had a firm grasp of his apprehensions. Few of his contemporaries managed to mistrust the *fonctionnaire* equally with the self-righteous, flint-skinning *entrepreneur* on the identical grounds that both were tyrannical and obscene.

"The House of Eld" shows him feeling cultural forces as frames to live in. Montaigne and Spencer had early taught him that specific right and wrong are matters of geography. So his universe was primarily the theater of his and others' quests for individual integrity with subjective moral goods as integrating, if insubstantial, fixed points. Objective criteria are indefensible. His last draft of "Lay Morals" sometimes anticipates Veblen in both doctrine and vehemence:

> Life at any level among the easy classes is conceived upon a principle of rivalry, where each man and each household must ape the tastes and emulate the display of others. . . . I should count myself a nincompoop indeed to lay out the colour of a halfpenny on any fancied social decency or duty. I shall not wear gloves unless my hands are cold, or unless I am born with a delight in them. . . . Are you sure you prefer cigars at sixpence each to pipes at some fraction of a farthing? Are you sure you wish to keep a gig? Do you care about where you sleep, or are you not as much at your ease in a cheap lodging as in an Elizabethan manor-house? . . .

Heavy influence of Thoreau, no doubt; but Louis scouted and scorned the asceticism that underlay Thoreau's gospel of self-sufficiency. For him the flesh—and the devil too, for that matter—were avenues to a higher integration.

He kept hoping to see life as a series of choices which, whether expressed in conventional or unconventional terms, required free will as at least necessary illusion, the essential as-if. What readers called "romance" in his fiction usually drama-

tized this against archaic backgrounds. What admirers took
for "romance" in his life was merely the curious consequences
of his own choices worked out under conditions of illness and
scanty shillings. Well aware that the shape-giving fixed points
were irrational, he wrote dialogues in which fictional characters voice their suspicion that their ostensible reasons for
given actions were actually the author's notion, readily changed
to suit his whim. But, back on stage, the puppets continue to
act—and to feel while acting—as if autonomous, self-responsi-
ble. Much of this is translatable into modern terms of unconscious impulse, rationalization, and so forth. Louis lived too soon
for acquaintance with that terminology. But, when you peer inside, his is no less and no more of an explanation.

The chief moral goods that held his world together were de-
ceptively simple: loyalty, for instance, a highly personal and
necessarily irrational value. David Balfour deliberately risks
his neck by not denouncing Alan. And fairness: he risks it
again by insisting on testifying for an innocent man railroaded
for political ends. Much of Louis's devotion to things Japanese
came of the excitant effect on him of Japanese standards of loyalty. The intransigence of the Forty-Seven Ronin, the miseries
that came on Yoshida Torajiro, give the range of his ambitions
for this virtue. Conversely, his most strongly felt villains, Ballantrae and Huish, scorned and thwarted loyalty and fairness. Yet
Ballantrae had a sort of black-for-white integration of his own
that his creator readily respected.

His own conclusions often amused him: In "A Dialogue on
Character and Destiny," Count Spada, the villain, twits the
General of the Jesuits: "It is pure Calvinistic election, my dear
sir, and, by your leave, a very heretical position for a church-
man to support." Child of the manse, Louis always showed
strong marks of Calvinism. His was a stern universe. Its egocentricity (in the geometric sense) and demands on free will
matched his conviction that the primary relation is between
an atomic individual as one entity and the rest of everything
as the only other. He was prepared to get the worst backlash-

ings of both free will and determinism, since the Calvinist is
not permitted, by his peculiar relation to God, to be either a
passive tool of fate or the exultant pilot of his own course. This
is a lonely position—lonely as the man leaving all behind to
scramble toward the Celestial City. It can hardly be mistaken
for a Christian universe, though Louis had a formidable sense
of the positive aspect of the Sermon on the Mount. His relish
for sinful man was too mundane. The Christian cannot afford to
relish Judas; Lucifer he may perhaps, but not Simon Magus,
James More, or "The Admiral." Nor yet so indignantly renounce the idea of reward in an after-life; he wrote Gosse
about Jenkin's death:

> . . . if I could believe in the immortality business, the
> world would indeed be too good to be true; but we were put
> here to do what service we can, for honour and not for hire;
> . . . The soul of piety was killed long ago by that idea of re-
> ward. Nor is happiness, whether eternal or temporal, the re-
> ward that mankind seeks; . . . his soul is in the journey; he
> was born for the struggle, and only tastes his life in effort and
> on the condition that he is opposed. . . . how can he be re-
> warded but by rest? . . . when we die there can be no quiet
> for mankind, but complete resumption into—what?—God,
> let us say—when all these desperate tricks will lie spell-
> bound at last.[28]

Such quasi-Oriental heresy would move even a Quaker to cry
out in horror.

His egregious charity sometimes deceived such unwary divines as Kelman into seeing him close to the skirts of Christianity. Charitable he was: Brutality and all, Hoseason is allowed
to be a considerate son and, once his word passes, a scrupulous
smuggler of men or brandy. There is a flash of pity for Mr.
Shuan, frozen drunk after committing murder, and for the shy-
ster Bellairs, even a touch of shivering solicitude for Mr. Hyde.
But, closely weighed, this is no Christian charity, rather a cor-

dial and ironic chivalry—always a pagan institution. It comes not of the sacramental doctrine that all share potentially in salvation, but of the feeling that all are comrades in the human race, some worse off than others, none in good case—a pessimistic extension of Original Sin untempered by ability to take redemption seriously. It implies not forgiving unto seventy times seven, which is Christian; nor that life itself is vigorously interesting, which is Shakespearean; nor that, if all were known, ample excuses would extort a soothing forgiveness, which is the welfare worker's moral staff. This says, bleakly and abruptly, that there is nothing to forgive, only sporadic occasion to exult over a feat of integrity in despite of reason and probability: " 'Do you forgive me?' . . . I have never yet been able to discover what forgiveness means. . . .'Do you understand me?' God knows; I should think it highly improbable." [29] Written in his late twenties, this has genuine intellectual delicacy that he never lost. Under stress of emotion he could forget it all and agonize about forgiveness like anybody else. But reduce the shock, give him time to touch ground, and he climbed back again to an overwhelming sense of the rank impertinence of whatever forgiveness might mean between man and man.

It is impossible to understand the many people who have chirped of his optimism. He knew better: in describing his grandfather:

> A profound underlying pessimism appears, upon inquiry, to be the last word of the Stevensons. It does not usually depress them; they are cheerful enough; they have a great gift of enjoyment; but their sense of the tragedy of life is acute and unbroken.[30]

So did "J.F.M.," whoever he was: "Stevenson's message (so far as it was delivered) appears to be that of utter gloom." [31] Stuart Sherman was one of the few to see clearly that Louis was phetic of some still lively modern attitudes:

a modern gospel, based on self-knowledge and self-acknowl-edgment, boldly individualistic, with independent stand-ards of honor and loyalty. . . . the real distinction between Stevenson and the moderns is that, while they devote them-selves to elaborate diagnosis he devoted himself to the elabo-ration of therapy.[32]

By the mid-'eighties his brash agnosticism was fading. "Lay Morals," the bare existence of which so annoyed Henley, prom-ised a liberal use of the word *God* that, he assumed, would dis-tress "the conscientious atheist, that strange and wooden rabbi." [33] But the end of the fragment still found him ponder-ing honesty, God so far pretty well neglected. At Bournemouth his passing affair with Tolstoi may have helped to restore the concept. At Vailima he wrote prayers for family worship—a matter to be gone into later. But he never assimilated the no-tion of salvation, even in its hyperlogical Calvinist sense. And the only one of the Seven Deadly Sins that ever struck him as necessarily sinful was Sloth, *accidie*—turning away from the glories of life, sulking at dawn, eating without relish.

He once defined conversation as consisting of incessant com-ment on I being I, you being you, and various other people being dimly understood to be neither. God as an august *vis-à-vis*, such a You in capitals, he never found. What he meant by "God" was at most a metaphysical possibility necessarily im-plied by certain hypotheses that were probably as tenable as any others. His basic moral axiom had no backing from so ten-uous a support: It was mere imaginative self-respect that sub-jective-I should keep his own nose as clean as he can manage while trying to promote the well-being of objective-Others—particularly as individuals, not as too readily abstracted masses. Everything beyond that he suspected of being tendentious non-sense:

We should be clearly persuaded of our own misconduct, for that is the part of knowledge in which we are most apt to be defective. . . . Even justice is no right of a man's own, but a thing, like the king's tribute, which shall never be his, but which he should strive to see rendered to another.[34]

Such remarks of his aid in understanding how he could frequently think of Henley without backbiting and live loyally and rewardingly with Fanny—and with himself. Japp, the midwife of *Treasure Island*, complained that Louis suffered from "a desire to be over-just" [35] and had none of Carlyle's "healthy hatred of scoundrels." That sort of thing can be carried to excess. But in intelligent moderation it can produce what would even now be thought highly civilized attitudes.

The Tragic Woman and the Flimsy Man

> . . . remember the pallid brute that lived in Skerryvore
> like a weevil in a biscuit.
>
> —Stevenson to Colvin,
> *Letters:* IV, 44

CHOLERA drove the Stevensons from Hyères in early
summer, 1884, never to return to the steep little garden
and the dining-room panels that Fanny had cleverly painted
à la Japonaise. Epidemic or not, Louis had been nibblingly restless. The winter before, he had been greatly taken by an American publisher's scheme for a tour of and book about the Aegean
Islands. Necessary advances had been estimated; the doctor had
approved; but financial and other complications forbade. Fanny
and he went north instead.

The problem of therapeutic geography was again acute.
Hyères had done him small good. The spring after his flirta-
tion with death at Nice had seen a hemorrhage that Fanny
ranked as the worst yet, and epidemics were much too likely
under the local French-Italian sanitary standards, none too
good even now, far more startling then. The unquestionable
charm of La Solitude had proved to be symbolically underlain
by a complex of seeping cesspools.

By autumn Bournemouth, midway along the English Channel coast, was chosen for the winter's experiment in keeping
Louis alive. The diverse reasons were all sound: For a generation the place had been known as good for consumption; the
neighborhood had sea air, mild temperatures, coniferous woods,
heather to appeal to the exiled Scot. Reputation for general
salubrity had attracted prosperous retired people—generals, ad-
mirals, upper civil servants or the widows thereof—to build

villas called "Cathay" or "Lorna Doone" in which to outwit death. Not a cheering environment; but Louis was long used to places in which much of the population daily played heads-or-tails with the undertaker.

Lloyd had been tutoring there with an expensive clergyman. When Louis and Fanny visited him, the spot seemed to suit Louis. His parents also liked it—an important point, for southern France was too far away as the threat of disintegration gathered over Thomas Stevenson. Already sixty-six busy years old, he was coming apart in what seems to have been progressive cerebral hemorrhage. His talk, which had always delighted and influenced Louis with its precision and apt flashes, now often broke off in fumblings and searchings. Stubbornly he left sentence or thought unfinished rather than end without the word that would not come to him. At intervals he was much himself—as when, having taken *The Innocents Abroad* to read in bed, he refused to go on next day on the grounds that it could not be good for a man his age to laugh so hard. But, though his fits of brooding may not have come more frequently, when they did they lasted longer. As disability progressed, he clung more to his son, fundamentally so like him, now so well reconciled—a dependence deepened by his reliance on Fanny, whom he treated as distinctly a daughter. He would sit pouring out his wild dreads to her until Louis approached, then visibly pull himself together and try to resume his old pungent decisiveness, to get the old steering intelligence back into his eyes. Probably worst for Louis's mother, who was constantly with him, this was bad enough for all. For the next thirty months the old people were often in Bournemouth or at other resorts considered good for Thomas, Louis in solicitous attendance whenever his own health conceivably permitted. Not infrequently the invalid was a pathetic nurse for the older man.

This intimacy of father and son was apparently their reward for pretty complete explosion of emotion. There had been small inhibition about the passion of exile in which Louis had sailed for America in 1879; still less about the passion of righteous repudiation and disappointment with which Thomas saw him go. Decks thus cleared, adrenalin thus neutralized, both parties better realized in the following winter apart how fitting and mutually bracing had been the relationship so despairingly dismantled. The nearer extinction Thomas drifted, the oftener he was moved hesitantly to call Louis "my dearie." The strong voice that had been so comforting outside the child's bedroom door was uncertain; the prehensile brain, hungry for ideas and dynamics, that had lent Louis the gift of quaint clarity, was now unsure; the broad, sturdy face was going flabby, the head set uncertainly. . . .

Spent in lodgings and then a rented house, the winter had proved the climate of Bournemouth not discouragingly hostile. So, when Thomas expressed his dependence on Louis and wife by offering Fanny a house there and £500 toward furnishings, she set about looking for premises to buy. A retired naval officer wanted to sell "Sea View," his villa secluded on the cliffs of Westbourne; and here Fanny was, proprietress of British soil, yellow brick and blue slates, with an acre or so of garden between house and the brink of Alum Chine, a picturesque, shaded gully slashed in the chalk cliff; a well-inhabited dovecot; and few near neighbors, for the area was only beginning to develop. She used Thomas's bounty for a Sheraton dining-room, yellow silk cushions strewn on a long window seat in the dressing-room, and ingeniously elaborated paths and terraces down the Chine.

Louis readily followed her in savoring ownership. He renamed the place Skerryvore in honor of the family masterpiece of engineering and, at the street entrance, installed a model lighthouse religiously lighted every evening; in the garden was a ship's bell. He said that the drawing-room was ". . . so beautiful that it's like eating to sit in it . . . there I sit like an old Irish beggarman's cast-off bauchle in a palace throne-room. . . . I blush for the figure I cut in such a bower." [1] Several bits of verse reflect his wonder at his own satisfaction with householding, complete with dog, big yellow cat, and pigeons—the cat's zeal in eating the pigeons was matched only by Colvin's zeal in hoping that the dog would eat the cat. The youngster who had warned his mother that her son was a tramp could also show a streak of house-pride—in fact, had already drawn up for his own amusement a sketch of "The Ideal House" that, for the times, sounds strangely modern and, to some extent, influenced the design of Vailima.[2]

The semi-doddering society of Bournemouth—"that nest of British invalidism and British Philistinism"[3]—saw little of the Stevensons. They made local friends notably only in the barber who came to trim Louis's long hair; the family of Sir Henry Taylor, literary lion-hunter and retired Foreign Office official, of whose regally pungent wife Louis was most reverently fond; and the Shelleys—Sir Percy, gentle, elderly son of the poet, being an addict of amateur photography and amateur theatricals. Lady Shelley saw in Louis such resemblances to her celebrated father-in-law that she seemed almost to suspect reincarnation—an analogy, remember, that stirred Louis to sarcastic self-analysis. In this form it was embarrassing; nor were the grosser details clear: Shelley was sentimentally beautiful, Louis at best brilliantly styled like a grotesque walking stick; Shelley a major rhapsodist, Louis barely a poet at all. . . . This may have been merely an awkwardly stated tribute to the quasi-feminine charm of personal presence that both seem to have shown. In any case these Bournemouth friends contributed to the Stevenson legend: for the next several years interviewers reporting on Louis mentioned the strange, reddish, ink-spotted garment that he wore receiving them in bed—this was the South American poncho that Lady Taylor gave him, precisely the right thing for the purpose. Sir Percy photographed Louis in it: one plate looks the astral body of himself, the other like a character out of *Jane Eyre*.

Henry James was a more significant acquisition. The acquaintance began—auspiciously—on the literary level. James's "The Art of Fiction" in *Longmans'* roused Louis to "A Humble Remonstrance." Both essays are good work: James was the more intensively experienced, Louis the more analytic, student of the vertiginous craft-art (or art-craft, if you like) of fiction. I do not know what James knew, through mutual acquaintances, of Louis before this autumn of 1884. Until then Louis's opinion of James, derived from his earlier writing, had not been ecstatic. He granted "a supreme knack of neatness" [4] but found *Washington Square* unpleasant and called its author "a mere club fizzle." [5] Fanny admired her countryman rather more, defending him lengthily, though in condescending terms that would have made James writhe. She may not have felt so strongly as Louis the weakness possibly implicit in James's transplantation, which set Louis on satirical verses for Henley's eye:

H. JAMES

Not clad in transatlantic furs
    But clinking English pence
The young republic marks me hers
    In no parochial sense.

A bland colossus, mark me stride
    From land to land, the sea
And patronize on every side
    Far better men than me.

My books that models are of wit
    And masterworks of art
From occident to orient flit
    And please in every part.

Yet I'm a sentimental lot
    And freely weep to see
Poor Hawthorne and the rest who've not
    To Europe been like me.[6]

Personal contact was another matter. The "Remonstrance" was excellent recommendation to a man who loved his field—canorous Stevenson moving with witty leisure from point to point with a logic that reminds one of the structure of a Burke oration:

Life goes before us, infinite in complication; attended by the most varied and surprising meteors; appealing at once to the eye, to the ear, to the mind—the seat of wonder, to the touch—so thrillingly delicate, and to the belly—so imperious when starved. . . . To "compete with life," whose sun we cannot look upon, whose passions and diseases waste and slay us—to compete with the flavour of wine, the beauty of the dawn, the scorching of fire, the bitterness of death and separation—here is, indeed, a projected escalade of heaven; here are, indeed, labours for a Hercules in a dress coat, armed with a pen and a dictionary to depict the passions, armed with a tube of superior flake-white to paint the portrait of the insufferable sun. No art is true in this sense; none can "compete with life"; not even history, built indeed of indisputable facts, but these facts robbed of their vivacity and sting; so that even when we read of the sack of a city or the fall of an empire, we are surprised, and justly commend the author's talent, if our pulse be quickened. And mark, for a last differentia, that this quickening of the pulse is, in almost every case, purely agreeable; that these phantom reproductions of experience, even at their most acute, convey decided pleasure; while experience itself, in the cockpit of life, can torture and slay.[7]

James wrote Louis a cordial appreciation that would have mollified Thomas Carlyle.[8] Louis's answer began a running discussion of their common literary concerns—the breath of life to both—that continued, in person or on paper, until Louis's death. Both had struck and would gracefully hold a note of ad-

miring friendliness on an even footing. It is understandable, if
amusing too, that thenceforth Louis was a hearty and heartfelt
admirer of James's work.

In the spring of 1885, James, bringing his ailing sister to
Bournemouth, called on the Stevensons. A servant mistook him
for a tradesman come to apologize for a crime of omission; but,
once that was got past, professional acquaintance moved on
into deep personal regard. A large armchair from Heriot Row
in which, evening after evening, James sat, listened and talked
while Louis paced, chain-smoked, drank, and talked, was formally christened "Henry James' chair." He came to love Louis
like a perspicaciously cultivated maiden aunt with a beard.
Louis loved and respected him with, apparently, no further
grinning at his expatriation. To Fanny, James was deferential,
articulate, and politely gratified when she made an occasion of
giving him American dishes for dinner; she wrote Dora Williams
that he looked exactly like the Prince of Wales.

Other stimulating people included John Singer Sargent,
who came to paint Louis at the behest of patrons, Mr. and Mrs.
Charles Fairchild of Boston.[9] Louis wondered that the marvelously Europeanized Sargent should bother to call himself an
American, but liked his innocent lack of ceremony and trenchant work. Hence that famous portrait of Louis the peripa-
tetic talker, half-caricature, all personality, the incredibly gan-
gly man with the stringy mustache pacing like an attenuated
puppet charged with electricity, Fanny to one side, cut in half,
garbed in East Indian fabrics for decorative color, one tiny
bare foot showing.[10] Gosse said that this and the St. Gaudens
medallion best convey the man, and Louis was no easy model.
As Greenwood noted from his numerous photographs, Louis's
face and manner had a baffling streak: ". . . the most threateningly elfish face that I have ever seen in print or paint." [11]
That, no doubt, instead of a twittery touch, was what Symonds had meant when nicknaming Louis "Sprite."

William Archer was invited down, and became a friend, in
consequence of having written an article on Louis's writings

that—though Archer apparently knew the facts to the contrary —postulated great robustness to account for his subject's exultance. Louis's letters of protest show him articulately plucky without undue impulse to boast about it. Such new acquaintances were excellent for his aesthetic health. His physical health had other needs. From London also came frequently —too frequently, Fanny thought—Henley, Bob, and Bob's sister Katherine Stevenson de Mattos. Their advent always filled Fanny with dread, in fact, for Louis alone was hard enough to discipline. Colvin was considerate, James exceedingly so, but Bob was usually in too deep perplexity to be discreet and Henley was no man to take a hostess's hint to drink up and depart lest Louis tire. That was not the way things had been "hard by the old Bristo' Port" when two young fellows with their way to make had talked all they liked and drunk as much as they could pay for. Nor could Fanny reconcile herself to the way Louis's father and mother would stay for days or weeks, Thomas dragging on Louis's strength.

An invaluable close look at Skerryvore, through rather a naïf medium, exists in *RLS and His Sine Qua Non*[12] by Adelaide Boodle, a young Bournemouth gentlewoman who played the violin and had literary impulses. The presence of a picturesque author strongly attracted her, but she was given to understand that his health forbade visits. The Stevensons' move to Skerryvore, close to the Boodles' own house, was too much for her. Heart in mouth, card-case in hand, she nervously brought Mama to call. When the door was not instantly answered, Mama burst into panicky tears. Glooming in old clothes over heaps and tangles of their newly arrived worldly possessions, Louis and Fanny seem to have welcomed the diversion. Tea was managed, and the young lady's respectful shyness—her book makes her sound very sweet—won her permanent privileges. She was allowed to coach Louis in his new game of one-fingering the piano; introduced him futilely to the violin; ran errands for Fanny; ransacked the Boodle books for items that Louis had not read; and dutifully disappeared at the lift of an eyebrow warning her either that Louis was tired or that Henley or Gosse was expected.

Her prime purpose was to sit at Louis's feet. Fanny would countenance no such strain on her patient, so Miss Boodle focused on Fanny as a cultural-emotional crutch and was not rebuffed. The great man being inaccessible, this sprightly devotee took his spouse as a great woman—intellectual, creative, spiritually lofty. When Miss Boodle asked permission to show Louis her scribblings for his opinion of whether she should persevere, Fanny said no, my dear, he would slash them to ribbons and break your heart—may I take you in hand? For Fanny was a writer too, in consequence of having sold that fairy story to *St. Nicholas* and worked with Louis on *The Dynamiter*; she was about to confirm it by selling a short story to *Scribner's*. In a few years these literary aspirations of hers would have tragic consequences. At this point note only the higher leapings of Miss Boodle's awe as her sibylline heroine spoke negligently of tossing off a story to make money needed for some ill and penniless friends. The atmosphere is best conveyed by her description of Fanny's eyes:

> . . . each depth that you reached was clearer, clearer, clearer, full of yearning kindness that one's heart might draw from inexhaustibly in time of need . . . But how those glorious eyes could flash with righteous anger![13]

Actually, of course, Fanny was duty-bound to insulate Louis. It was generous of her to help the girl, she really did need the £30 from *Scribner's* for hard-up friends from Hyères, she certainly knew far more than her pupil about writing. But she might have been a touch less comfortable in her role of genius-partner; less dramatic about keeping inquisitive callers from acquiring the "interview" sort of data—such people she labeled "spies" and instructed her protégée in the art of keeping talk flowing without vouchsafing anything to lewd curiosity; less beatified in telling the girl that Louis had enjoined her to live after him to supervise his biography. The Boodle recollections, set down after forty years, are no ideal source; she was evidently capable of believing Fanny's tale of how Ginger, the cat who so annoyed Colvin, daily took part of his food to a down-on-his-luck stray in the vicinity. But she does leave an all-too-recognizable picture of Fanny, possessiveness rampant, suspicions well extended, overweeningness creeping up on her.

In time Miss Boodle gained her heart's desire. Through Colvin (I assume) Louis was approached about teaching a weekly course for young writers at the British Museum. Needing a sympathetic guinea-pig on whom to try out possible lectures, he cast the girl in the role that Lloyd had played for the abortive Professor of History and Constitutional Law. She reveled in the short course of precept and practice in which he immersed her, setting her authors to imitate in the "sedulous ape" technique, soundly calling Latin and French better studies than English grammar for the aspirant to English prose. He obviously liked his pupil and enjoyed hammering out issues on this flattered little anvil. When the family quit Skerryvore, she was honored with the responsibility of seeing that the tenants did right by the cat and the pigeons; Louis wrote her affectionately and frequently under title of "The Gamekeeper."

The Museum course came to nothing; Louis's health would never have permitted it anyway. The three Bournemouth years brought him to his longest period of low ebb. Hemorrhages struck at random like red lightning; each convalescence was ominously long. "Change of air" was usually disastrous, though Louis went when he could to one health-resort or another to be with his father on demand. A trip westward to see Thomas Hardy—personally lukewarm toward Louis, who wanted to dramatize *The Mayor of Casterbridge*—meant collapse in a hotel in Exeter. As a rule Louis's optimum hardihood consisted in dining at the Taylors' or the Shelleys' or, in good weather, walking in cloak and broad hat along the cliffs to stare at the sea. Lloyd remembered his silent despair when, one overdamp day, Fanny found him in outdoor rig and ordered him—no doubt properly—not to dare go out. But he kept hoping to

live up to his defiant "I was never bored in my life." When too
seedy to write, he tinkered with the piano. When taking to bed
as too seedy for that, he modeled wax figures of no recognizable
merit with his flickery hands. "I am in sculpture," he wrote
Gosse, "what Mr. Watts is in painting . . . both of us pre-oc-
cupied with moral and abstract ideas." [14] Perhaps on that account he made a failure of trying to learn to knit.

Nevertheless at Skerryvore were delivered "Markheim," the
final versions of the *Garden*, *Kidnapped*, *Jekyll*, "On Some
Technical Elements of Style in Literature," and "The Day After Tomorrow," as well as the potboiling "Body-Snatcher," the
spottily brilliant *Memoir of Fleeming Jenkin* and the misbegotten "Olalla"—a notably versatile list. The "Technical Elements" is no less fine work for its demanding that the reader
have some knack in writing in order to understand what it is
not talking about. *Jenkin* was both obituary for and preface to
the assembled papers of the imaginatively rigid little engineer,
done with perspicacity and affection. And *Kidnapped* (which
cut an even stranger figure than its predecessors in *Young
Folks*) broke new ground, not only scoring a fair commercial
success but making its author feel well qualified in long fiction.
He glowed with pride in its character work. For the first time,
he said, his creations had taken matters into their own hands
like living people. Gosse considered it ". . . one of the most
human books I ever read, the only romance I know in which
the persons have stomach aches and sore throats and have not
cast iron physiques that feel nothing." [15] In Dr. Trudeau's presentation copy Louis wrote, as of 1888:

> Here is the one sound page of all my writing,
> The one I'm proud of and that I delight in. [16]

But *Jekyll* was the crucial item: Though Louis dreamed the
germ of it, that was no guarantee of quality; the same was true
of "Olalla." Waked from a nightmare by Fanny, he protested
that she had broken off "a fine bogy-tale" and soon proceeded to
develop it. Hearing his first draft, Fanny insisted that it would

be better as an allegory, not a mere "crawler." After violent protest, Louis burned the draft and completely rewrote, opening up the allegorical aspect. It took such hold of him that he finished the rough in three days—a tremendous stint of work.

He had long sought to express the war-in-the-members, the duality of human orientation that, as original sin, Calvinism insisted on and that Freud would melodramatically label the death-wish. It had been the theme of "Markheim," as also of "The Travelling Companion," which, written at Hyères, had been refused by a publisher as "a work of genius but indecent" and was finally burned by Louis because ". . . it was not a work of genius, and *Jekyll* had supplanted it." [17] His dream had unquestionably been working toward the duality-motif, though at first he had consciously wanted to use only the horrible machinery of its simple symbolism. Fanny probably did him an aesthetic favor in protesting and, in view of the frantic fervor of his rewriting, an emotional favor as well. But this haste did not mean hasty-seeming writing. *Jekyll* is the essence of concision without choppiness, that most difficult literary attainment—fear in a single glimpse of an eyeball, evil in a few sharp sounds. One actually knows little of Mr. Hyde: his hands were hairy, Jekyll's clothes hung on him, the mere sight of him was paralyzing. . . . Symonds was shocked:

> I doubt whether anyone has the right so to scrutinize "the abysmal dregs of personality." . . . At least . . . he ought to bring more of distinct belief in the resources of human nature, more sympathy with our frailty. . . . Louis, how had you the "ilia dura, ferro et aere triplici duriora" to write Dr. Jekyll? [18]

Others were most profitably startled. Fanny did Louis great economic service also in forcing the revision. Had the allegory been less baldly spelled out, it might have been merely another occasion for admiration of Louis in the right circles. He had long been known, was growing even well known—but it was *Jekyll* that exploded him into fame among people outside the writing business. Pulpits took *Jekyll* up; edition after edition sold out at a shilling a copy on railroad newsstands; in a matter of months Jekyll-and-Hyde was a proverb throughout the English-speaking world, as much so as Falstaff or Old Mother Hubbard. The same would probably have happened if the story had been only a quarter so well handled, for it was the content, ferociously symbolizing something that most members of Western cultures feel with some acuteness, that attracted so many shillings.[19] By carrying her hotly contested point, in fact, Fanny did as much as Henley and Colvin combined toward Louis's permanent place in world literature, as well as toward the prosperity of his last eight years. Since, though sweepingly popular, *Jekyll* was by no means a cheap piece of work, this can be set off against the unproved possibility that she sometimes kept Louis from risking material offensive to Mrs. Grundy. It does not, however, wholly justify her claims to be a literary strategist. There is luck in presumption as well as in games of chance.

All through the Bournemouth period, in fact, the sequel to one of her strategic mistakes wasted Louis's time and energy, strained relations with one of his best friends, and, by outraging Fanny herself, no doubt helped her emotional tone to deteriorate. As far back as 1878 Louis and Henley had been working on a play, *Deacon Brodie,* based on Louis's young attempt to dramatize the historical Edinburgher who had been a sober cabinetmaker by day and a mastermind burglar at night. (Duality again—the Deacon had fascinated Louis ever since he had learned, as a child, that the chest of drawers in his room was of the criminal's making.) They aimed it at Henry Irving; after some futile years of whittling at it, Henley tried to tailor it to suit Teddy (Edward) his actor-brother. Periodically, besides, Louis and he launched on other plays, which Henley sadly listed in his attack on Louis in 1901—*Ajax* and *The King's Rubies,* for instance, took much time before aborting. Both liked the fun of stagecraft, little though either knew about it, and Louis was readily persuaded that the theater could lead to the large earnings that, so far, neither Henley nor he had derived from writing.[20]

When Fanny began to sit in council, she was eager as Henley and gave Louis no chance to cool off on play-writing. Her whole chronically self-convinced soul backed her belief that the box office was the gate to wealth and eventual security. In Bournemouth she pored so intently over their play, *Admiral Guinea*, that she had most of it, all parts, by heart. The last spring in Bournemouth she prodded Louis into working with her on *The Hanging Judge*, a play finished in Saranac. Louis's interest might not have flagged anyway; or, if it had, Henley's thunderous persuasion might again have swept him away, for Louis loved both Henley and the comradeship of collaboration. But Fanny's influence was immediate and continuous, and (though later she tried to deny it) the responsibility for futile months of play-writing was considerably hers.

Proud of knowing his way in London, Henley handled the contacts with managers. Down in Bournemouth, receiving reports and visits from Henley and even a visit from Beerbohm Tree, who thought he might be interested in their *Macaire*, Louis had his share of the passive sort of hope deferred that maketh the heart sick. For—greatest folly of all—they went on messing with plays after *Brodie* proved a feeble vehicle in provincial tryouts. Louis often wasted himself on projects that came to nothing, but at least those of his own begetting sometimes left him with valuable technical experience. These irreplaceable weeks and months taught him nothing, and it may be significant that, once he got out of Henley's neighborhood, he never again spontaneously laid hand on a dramatic treatment. Almost any Stevensonian must grudge the absence of what he might have written if Henley and Fanny had not been so enthusiastic.

Macaire reworked an elderly French vaudeville for cynical fun. *Beau Austin*, a Regency piece, hinged on a moral decision of the heroine's so tenuous that perplexity as to her precise motive precludes much audience-sympathy. *Admiral Guinea* shows the melodramatic Pharisaism of a reformed slaver; all it has is the theatrical advantage of a clever bit of business involving a blind man (David Pew, borrowed from *Treasure Island*) and a burning candle. All have been produced, usually in experimental curiosity after Louis's death; the best commercial fate of any was the inexplicable success of *Brodie* for a short run in Chicago.

English dramatic literature would feel much the same if all these plays vanished tomorrow. As the work of writers-for-print they should at least read fairly well. Actually they do not, for, however ineptly, Louis and Henley knew that the stage was different, that they must try to work in terms of action explicit, and, though they failed, did not attempt the mechanisms of printed fiction. Shaw used a production of *Brodie* in 1897 as occasion for abusing the London stage, adducing its authors' failure to "effect a lodgment" as proof that said London stage was dead; he also admired their *Macaire* (in print) in contrast to Irving's production of an earlier version. When his approval boils down, however, it is largely amusement at seeing this notable pair so devoted to an insignificant idiom, plus a high opinion of the quality of prose in the dialogue—not, be it noted, their dialogue as structural contribution to an actable script. This virtue—if it be one in a play—appealed to Shaw, whose own inability to write poor prose so often protruded awkwardly from his own plays.

Pinero, more of a dramatist than any of these three, pointed out one of Louis's and Henley's troubles: they were acknowledgedly trying to inject aesthetic quality into the old conventions of the "transpontine" British popular stage, that highly stylized hash of thefts from French and German melodramas seasoned with Dibdin and Tom Moore that was the Crummles' stock-in-trade. Louis called it "Skeltery" in grateful reference to the "books of the play" packaged with the characters and sets for his childhood toy theater so wittily handled in "A Penny Plain." The sets specified for *Guinea* are pure Skelt; so are the cracksman scene in *Brodie* and the inn courtyard in *Macaire*.

Except *Beau Austin*, plots and action patterns are also Skeltery, unable to take the greater intensification that the collaborators asked of it. This was a blind alley, all the more so for their error, as noted by Pinero, of using only the transpontine drama's puerile tactics while neglecting its often admirable strategy. In "A Penny Plain," remember, Louis considered the sport of *Skelt's Juvenile Drama* gone when sets and characters were painted and set up—performance of the script he thought boring. This explains the failure, which is nevertheless ironical: In *Treasure Island* Louis had succeeded just where these plays failed—there he really had transmuted the presumably cheap into literature.

Already an editor accustomed to wringing copy out of dilatory contributors, temperamentally intemperate in habits, opinions, and friendships, Henley had too little notion of what Louis was and was not good for. In this period Colvin had to scold Louis and Henley into dropping a scheme to turn principal contributors to a new Conservative review projected by people with more money than judgment. (Henley later ran a Conservative weekly well, but usually left the "leaders" to hands more politically adept.) Crippled, often ill, he probably thought it fair enough that Louis should take plays as seriously as he himself did, and invest in them as much time and energy as he, who was equally busy earning a living and had no prosperous father. And fair it was—provided Louis remained equally eager and that other work, which promised better, did not suffer. Louis later maintained that, toward the end, he had thrown good time and energy after bad merely to uphold Henley's stubborn hands. This may be somewhat distorted afterthought; perhaps loyalty did help to keep him on the dramatic lay. However that may be, Fanny was the weak spot:

As more and more work on plays produced neither prestige nor revenue, she was having the distasteful experience of seeing her judgment proved all wrong. Her dismay—which she preferred not to face squarely—seems partly to have turned into resentment of Henley, for the worse the fiasco, the more

Henley demanded. She had already fixed him in her mind as prime sinner against the interests of Louis's health. It was only a short step, of a sort that she usually found easy, to smell positive sabotage in his resounding schemes. It probably did not help that Lloyd hero-worshipped Henley—not Colvin the gentle and scholarly nor James the suave and sympathetic, but this rowdy, roaring, hairy, bulky Old Man of the Sea on Louis's frail back, always (as she saw it) borrowing money, exhausting the household's whisky and, what was worse, exhibiting inability to take Fanny very seriously as literary consultant, not even while she too was mad about plays. Sensitive as a woman, and apt to backbiting, Henley could not fail to feel this silent but rodent grudge. It did not improve his solicitude for the woman whom he had privately denounced ever since the day Louis had sailed for the States.

Fanny might well have fallen out with him anyway. She stayed on unruffled good terms to her death with Henry James alone among Louis's good friends; he alone had not known the pre-Fanny Louis. With others the pattern often was: Immense enthusiasm on first meeting, her infallible intuition taking her right into the hearts of their wholly admirable characters; then developing suspicion, sometimes ably veiled; but sooner or later, months or years, she would suddenly hoist the black flag, luff across the man's bows, and pour hysterical broadsides into him. Perhaps because he was the most feminine of the crew, Gosse was first: Within a few weeks of meeting him Fanny wrote Dora Williams that she and Mr. Gosse were secretly at daggers drawn because she had given him as good as she got when he had somehow tried to discredit her. In view of Gosse's style of malice she was probably right in predicting that he would never forgive her. Simpson, Henley, Katherine de Mattos, Baxter, Colvin, were assailed in that order over the years, the second and third in a slashing squadron action that was not primarily Fanny's fault.

In "Virginibus" Louis had noted that marriage "often puts old friends to the door"; but Fanny's behavior to that end feels more deep-rooted than the mere social dislocations that may normally follow marriage. Too often her explosions released astounding pressures previously unsuspected. Each such outbreak left the corners of her mouth more emphatically turned down, her gaze broodier, a more hagridden effect in her attitudes.

In early days at Bournemouth she could work off steam on Sam Osbourne whom she suspected, no doubt with reason, of trying to steal Lloyd as the boy matured. Twice Sam came abroad to see his son, once took him on a walking trip from which, Fanny averred, the boy returned heavily, if temporarily, vulgarized. His support of his son, she bitterly pointed out, consisted in buying him a bicycle that he badly wanted; or, having acquired a ranch in California, in trying to induce him to come and learn to operate it. Grim though the episode was, there is no mistaking Fanny's relief when—in the most literal sense—Sam disappeared. His second wife had had his usual supper awaiting his return from late work at his office, but he never arrived to eat it. Barring a dubious rumor that he had been seen in South Africa, nobody to this day knows whether Sam Osbourne's bones are at the bottom of San Francisco Bay or decently buried on St. Brandan's Isle. Fanny charitably surmised that he had eloped with some woman; but she did profess to pity the deserted wife and was kind to her, even gave her money, she said, when they met in San Francisco in 1888. At the time of the disappearance Louis gave Lloyd funds to help her meet her emergency.

This left Fanny in sole possession of her son. Belle was 7000 miles away in Hawaii, where Joe Strong had gone to paint. (A letter from her suggested that Fanny call on her friends, the Queen of Hawaii and the Princess Liliuokalani, who would be in London for the Jubilee in 1887.) But Lloyd was close at hand, valued for himself, as a valuable second ligament to Louis, and as reassuring link with Louis's parents, who were highly pleased with their step-grandson; while at Edinburgh University working for a B.Sc. the boy lived at 17 Heriot Row.

Reared as he was among the hypochondriacal, however, he developed ailments that interrupted his schooling with a cruise for health to the West Indies. Then his eyes began to fail so ominously that doctors thought blindness probable. Courageously he began to learn to run a typewriter, so that sightlessness would not isolate him more than necessary. Fanny recalled that it must have been nearsightedness, not insensitivity, that had caused him to be so bored with scenery as a child. Fortunately proper lenses saved his eyes; the natives of various Pacific islands sometimes used his gleaming glasses as basis for his "native name."

Gadgetry was his passion: printing press, camera, magic lantern, bicycle, eventually the automobile. But the irregularity of his education and the magnetic preoccupations of Skerryvore inclined him toward writing as a career. Louis was eager to embark him on a catch-as-catch-can apprenticeship. He was highly articulate to Henley about his affection for "the Port Admiral," as he called the tall, big-boned, fair-haired, myopic boy. When Lloyd was holidaying in the Scilly Isles, Louis solicitously packed and sent him a parcel containing a lump of coal, an empty matchbox, a cat's bell, an iron spoon, and several other items sufficiently silly for a Scilly destination. It was a good, if original, relationship, and meant steadily more to Louis.

Fanny worked fiercely at her landscaping down Alum Chine. Put her in Oakland, Hyères, or Westbourne and she was ordering seeds and plants, improving and innovating. She was solidly committed to her high-shouldered, hidden-away house. But, as the months became years, Louis's zest in it waned and he lost whatever small impulse he might ever have had to write "I was happy again—that was at Skerryvore." For him a certain morbidity had begun to cling round those secretive eaves. The third winter Henry James received a short letter that recommended itself to a novelist by its overtones, both of the writer and of a flashingly temporary situation:

My wife . . . is a woman (as you know) not without art:
the art of extracting the gloom of the eclipse from sunshine;
and she has recently laboured in this field not without success. . . . It is strange: "we fell out my wife and I" the other
night; she tackled me savagely for being a canary-bird; replied (bleatingly) that there was no use in turning life into
King Lear; presently it was discovered that there were two
dead combatants upon the field, each slain by an arrow of
the truth, and we tenderly carried off each other's corpses
. . . . here are the kindest recollections from the canary-
bird and from King Lear, from the Tragic Woman and the
Flimsy Man.[21]

Louis sometimes swore at Fanny when, between toxicity and
weakness, he was half out of his head in night emergencies of
his illness. The fact that the relation between them easily survived such outbursts is one of the few conventional aspects of
this marriage between a semi-invalid "Of passion, impudence,
and energy" and the woman whom Henry James called a
"poor, barbarous and merely *instinctive* lady." [22] Most biographies of Louis blur Fanny over as vaguely but gleamingly perfect or else slander her on inadequate evidence. Only a masoch-
ist or a gross cynic could have lived three months with such a
Gorgon as she is sometimes made to seem; whereas Louis was
neither martyr nor cynic—lived with her fifteen years—dedicated to her his last and finest book.

Biographers, of course, are seldom fair to their subjects'
wives if they show any distracting features. The convention is
that the spouse of a "creative" man is obligated to be strictly
nurse, manager, and mistress, a sort of cherished aide-de-camp,
allowed no effort to be person in her own right. Any influences
of hers on his work are *lèse majesté*. Her illnesses or her tactless-
ness in complicating his life with offspring, any intrusions of
her tastes in people, dwellings, or drinking habits, are taken as
selfish warpings. She-bedfellows, friends, colleagues the artist
may have. But a wife unwilling to remain a cipher inspires

cries of interference, busybodiness, frustration. Call it the Livy Clemens complex.

Such subscribers to what Lang called "fudge about the rights and privileges of genius" [23] will never make sense of Louis and Fanny, or of numerous other marriages that they may encounter. For the institution of marriage is embarrassingly diverse. As practiced, if not always envisaged, among English-speaking people, it is much more flexible than, say, the relation between parents and children. The only consistent feature is legal cohabitation. Its theoretical purposes are to beget a posterity (*cf.* Moses); to canalize concupiscence (*cf.* St. Paul); to organize families (*cf.* Westermarck); and to lend special emotional significance to a regular routine of rest, nourishment, and social life (*cf.* Russell). A given marriage may neglect any of these, or all, yet the parties are still married and would be startled—and so would a court be—were it claimed that they are not.

Thus Louis and Fanny did not want children, and their marriage remained what it had begun—a legalized *ménage* turning into not so much a partnership as a true symbiosis. They two were as different and functionally complementary as the fungus and the alga in a lichen on a sterile rock. Fanny was the medium whereby Louis lived daily life, he was the source of values and stimuli that maintained her illusion of accomplishment. For at least their first fourteen years, their two sets of roots were notably thrifty in association and, even later, never lost mutual rewardingness. Both set great store by memories of the "romantic" conditions of their courtship, both liked the Bohemian life migratory and untidy well enough to be easily reconciled to living it for reasons grimmer than usual—health-seeking at any cost in dislocation. Comfort, regularity, alignment with any body of *mores*, whether of Edinburgh or Indiana, would have been little regarded in any case, so they readily subordinated these, as if by common consent before the parson, to work and therapy.

Several times Louis spoke of his marriage as "good for" him, as if Fanny had been a tonic or a species of bath. The attitude does not sum up his position, but there is truth in it. Without her physical devotion he might well have died before accomplishing much. Without her emotional devotion, which carried all the warmth of pride and admiration and hero-worshipping solicitude, he might have made both himself and "some good, dull girl" miserable or sunk into the bachelor wearily committed to semimechanical philanderings.

Those were the factors that made this marriage work. What of the other warmth? the way in which personality-in-love can so square and cube the higher values of personality by physical expression? Evidence of how it was with these two strange but integrated people cannot be expected to abound in letters or even surviving gossip. The Louis of Grez and Paris may well have been much of the "youthful, gay and burning bridegroom" when both Fanny and he were well. But there can hardly have been much of that in the enfeebled Louis of Silverado, Davos, Hyères, or Bournemouth—though obviously, since a pregnancy was suspected at Hyères, there must have been occasion for it. Later, though Louis was much healthier in the Pacific, the debts of the flesh must often have been impracticable. Adequate privacy did not exist during months in the *Casco*, the *Equator*, and the *Janet Nichol*. Love will find a way, as many a shamed girl has found. But a marriage that so readily deprives itself of convenient opportunity for such long periods can hardly have made a point of intimacy. That this collaboration of temperaments was consistently a marriage of bodies in the same degree is dubious.

But to conclude that it therefore lacked validity or seemed inadequate to its principals is to ignore the potentialities of human adjustment. When the Rev. Dr. Scott uttered those portentous words: "I now pronounce you man and wife," he might have added: ". . . and legally privileged to be jangling but mutually supporting comrades, impatient adoration on her side adjusted to inquisitive and resigned affection on his." That suited both. Louis's world—a rewarding place for all its lacks—began as and, in some aspects, continued to be the ideal world of Berkeley, apprehended by a single subjectivity with a possible God somewhere beyond as projecting medium. Fanny might have been a wife, for a while may have been one for Sam Osbourne. Louis was not and could never have been a husband. He was too positively conscious of the issues. At the second-cabin table in the *Devonia*, on his way to join Fanny in the teeth of all discretion, he established that once for all in writing:

> . . . the woman I love is something of my own handiwork; and the great lover, like the great painter, is he who can so embellish his subject as to make her more than human, while yet by a cunning art he has so based his apotheosis on the nature of the case that the woman can go on being a true woman, and give her character free play, and show littleness or cherish spite, or be greedy of common pleasures, and he continue to worship without a thought of incongruity.[24]

Admirably, even generously, perceptive—but no attitude conducive to the act of faith, however partial and temporary, essential to the great lover in any meaning of the words. It was nevertheless an attitude well calculated to assist in staying married—and on the whole happily—to Jacob Vandegrift's eldest daughter. Chesterton was shrewd in writing of this relation: ". . . it is no disrespect to either to say that in both, psychologically speaking, there was an element of patching up, as well as of binding together." [25]

The salutations of the few surviving letters that Louis wrote Fanny carry overtones that might have distressed a different sort of woman in another sort of relation: "My dear Dutchman . . . My dear fellow . . . My dearest little man . . ." True, one finds also "My dearest girlie . . ." and such closings as "I shall be damn glad to get you back again and meanwhile send you a kiss." [26] But most of them fit rather too well with Fanny's early comments to Dora Williams on her new husband's loving-kindness—they sound somewhat as if Louis were a new son-in-law turning out even better than she had hoped.

The psychiatry-minded may incline to see this as a mother-son relation. But there were practically no gross coincidences between Fanny and Louis's mother: Fanny was untidy, aggressive, presumptuous, irreverent, broody and swarthy, thick and short, her somewhat theatrical style of beauty worlds away from Meg Balfour's delicate sweetness of face. Had the mother-son constellation of emotions bulked large, Louis would occasionally have drifted into the "mother" motif with Fanny, as he so significantly had with Mrs. Sitwell and, once momentarily, with Mme. Garschine. Nothing of the sort appears. The unusual note, in fact, is the way his letters to her sound almost like Damon writing to Pythias. It is also significant that, whereas he had afforded Mrs. Sitwell quite a lofty pedestal, Fanny got hardly a footstool.

Some who knew her well have told me that she was a tremendous personage; certainly Miss Boodle thought so. But the record that she left in letters and elsewhere helps one to understand why so close an observer as Louis was never tempted to see her more than life-size. "Steel-true" she was to him. But the artless and charming lady-Bohemian of Grez should not soon have been writing home from Europe that young Lloyd was to be reared strictly as a "gentleman," that contact with Sam Osbourne pollutes the boy's "gentility," that he has taken most gratifyingly to shuddering at the very word "Bohemian." The emancipated American addict of the creative should not so thoroughly have suppressed her native Hoosier accent that still living British witnesses recall little, if any, trace of "American" in her speech.[27] The amateur cosmopolite should not so early have developed the theory that facility in acquiring languages shows a coarse mind, perhaps as satisfactory explanation of her own inability to get the hang of French. . . .

A more timid woman might have kept more such symptomatic babble to herself. But, though she could be circumspect enough with Louis's parents in a simple emergency, Fanny's long-term sense of how what one says sounds to others was not too reliable. This went with her fundamental infallibility, so evident that it hardly needed claiming. Her opinions were modes of elementary right. Disagreement with them was not intellectual give-and-take but moral or intellectual sabotage. After strikingly short acquaintance, Fanny knew more about a given person that did God, the doctor, or the person himself —all of which helped her to be so good a hater that a striking proportion of her last will and testament is devoted to denouncing her first daughter-in-law.

After reading more hundreds of thousands of words of her letters than are ever likely to see print, I must conclude, however, that she often succeeded in keeping her less worthy aspects well away from the brilliant, ailing young fellow on whom her private cosmos centered. And, on those occasions when discretion failed—when the *parvenue*, the opinionated presumer, or the overweening bluestocking did peep in—Louis had well prepared himself to absorb any jar that he felt. His own dicta were altogether pertinent: ". . . the most masculine and direct of women will some day, to your dire surprise, draw out like a telescope into successive lengths of personation." [28] Love need not suffer though its lady-object ". . . show littleness or cherish spite or be greedy of common pleasures."

On Louis's side, beyond this wry realism about the uncanny sex, the basic reënforcement of this marriage, or whatever it was, lay in his conviction of its essential worth as institution. It was not that the woman he espoused could do no wrong but that, first and foremost, it was she whom he delighted to honor. The attitude has a medieval savor, but is generous in its own way and was certainly indispensable to this relation. Nor did it preclude equality of footing within itself. Louis's last word on marriage was his most grateful and wisest:

Marriage is one long conversation, chequered by disputes. The disputes are valueless; they but ingrain the difference; the heroic heart of woman prompting her at once to nail her

colours to the mast. But in the intervals, almost uncon-
sciously and with no desire to shine, the whole material of life
is turned over and over, ideas are struck out and shared, the
two persons more and more adapt their notions one to suit
the other, and in process of time, without sound of trumpet,
they conduct each other into new worlds of thought.[29]

This was written at Davos eighteen months after Louis became
a married man. He had learned much in so short a time.

That was a foul winter of 1886-87. Jenkin had died in June
1885, but work on the *Memoir* kept death in Louis's mind.
Thomas Stevenson's condition was flagrantly worsening. And—
whether this was further cause or mere effect—Louis had fallen
on the inspirational phase of Tolstoi and was unhygienically
immersed in that specially morbid species of amateur Christianity; he was in no shape to resist the great Russian's harpings
on guilt-feelings.

A shattery feeling pervades all that he did in this period:
He reverted to Libbelism, conniving with Baxter elaborately
to harass newspaper advertisers of patently dishonest intentions. He alarmed Fanny by becoming obsessed with music—
badgering Henley and Bob for hints on harmony, trying little
compositions of his own, exhausting himself in picking out
Lully, Bach, and Rameau at the piano. His tinkering with music was usually a valuable recuperative hobby, but it now
looked so much like withdrawal that Fanny was probably right
to feel disturbed. He frightened Colvin who, unexpectedly
coming up behind him in the garden, saw him turn ". . . a
face of utter despondency, upon which seemed stamped
for one concentrated moment the expression of all he ever had,
or might yet have, in life to suffer or renounce." [30] Then, in final
token of grave strains, he fell on the strangest scheme of his
whole life:

The Irish hell's broth of crooked questions and cross answers
was bubbling lively in the mid-'eighties. Louis was sure to

view any action of Gladstone's government as criminal nonsense and, in *The Dynamiter*, had strongly, if with mistaken
backhandedness, made clear his attitude toward Fenian violence. Irish resistance had again taken the form of mobbing
people of unpopular religion, opinions, or economic status.
During one such incident a farmer named Curtin had been
killed and a member of the mob killed in turn. In retaliation
his farm and surviving family, mostly women, were boycotted—
then a process of social, economic, and physical blockade that
made life close to impossible. Whatever the rights of the Land
Leaguers' cause, this ugly and ill-advised persecution of be-
reaved women lost nothing in the British press. Louis determined that he, Fanny, and Lloyd would dramatize the immor-
ality of it all by moving in with the Curtins and, with Tolstoian
refusal to countenance evil, die or survive in token of resistance to the forces of darkness. At illuminating length he wrote
Anne Jenkin about his motives:

. . . my work can be done anywhere; hence I can take up
without loss a backgoing Irish farm; . . . writers are so much
in the public eye, that a writer being murdered would . . .
throw a bull's eye light upon this cowardly business; . . . I
am not unknown in the States, from which come the funds
that pay for these brutalities: . . . *Nobody else is taking up
this obvious and crying duty* . . . You will not even be murdered, the climate will miserably kill you, . . . Well, what
then? . . . the purpose is to brave crime; . . . My wife has
had a mean life (1) loves me (2) could not bear to lose me
. . . But what does she love me for? . . . she must lose me
soon or late. . . . am I not taken with the hope of excite-
ment? I was at first. I am not much now. I see what a dreary,
friendless, miserable, God-forsaken business it will be. . . .
am I not taken with a notion of glory? I daresay I am. Yet I
see quite clearly how all points to nothing coming, to a quite
inglorious death by disease and from the lack of attendance;
or even if I should be knocked on the head as these poor

Irish promise, how little anyone will care. . . . I do not love this house-keeping, house-tending life of mine. . . . The cause of England in Ireland is not worth supporting. . . . I am not supporting that. Home Rule, if you like. . . . [But] populations should not be taught to gain public ends by private crime. . . . for all men to bow before a threat of crime is to loosen and degrade beyond redemption the whole fabric of man's decency.[31]

An extraordinary document slashed off late at night when Louis should have been healingly asleep.

That he meant it all is very likely. That he also knew he was being a fool is clear. That he would carry it out in spite of knowing that he was three parts of a fool to do so was all too probable. Fanny was game: Louis quoted her: "It is nonsense, but if you go, I will go." Forty years later Lloyd surmised that it all came of Louis's ill-realized but desperate wish to get away from Skerryvore at all costs—which, as far as it goes, is shrewd. A confirmed theorist might see a quasi-suicidal impulse: At low ebb emotionally, half-convinced that a disintegrating death awaited him within a few months or years, Louis wished at least to die to some purpose.

This strange story never got beyond the prologue. Two of his elder influences saved him: Jenkin—for, had the exacting revision of the *Memoir* not been still to finish, Louis might have set off for Ireland in April 1887. And Thomas Stevenson —in May he died.

Louis and Fanny hurried to Edinburgh but not in time for Thomas to recognize his son. Yet he was still dressed and upright. Having always maintained that dying in bed was indecorous, he now stuck to his principles and met death in self-respecting broadcloth and cravat—"That was his constant wish; also that he might smoke a pipe on his last day." [32] As for life, he had always considered it "a shambling sort of omnibus taking him to his hotel." [33]

His funeral was said to have been the largest such private occasion that Edinburgh had ever seen. Louis had caught cold and Uncle George refused to permit him to go to the cemetery, so the son of the house gloomed at home in the high, gray old mansion that he was unwittingly inhabiting for the last time. He paid his respects to death by finishing his ballad of "Ticonderoga," the base-legend of which Thomas and he had recently discussed.

By June the *Contemporary Review* had his accurate, wistful, and proud obituary of "my dear, wild, noble father." [34] Miss Boodle was told that he hoped best to remember him "as a man of fifty, lying on a hillside and carving mottoes on a stick, strong and well; and as a younger man, running down the sands into the sea near North Berwick." [35] Ferrier . . . Jenkin . . . Thomas Stevenson. Having taken three in less than four years, death would now rest for seven.

The Gates of Gold

I am become a name.

—*Ulysses*

THOMAS STEVENSON's death apparently snapped the spell. The Stevensons' emotional emergency put the Curtins out of Louis's head. Now chief of the house, he plainly found it tonic to write to his mother, after returning to Skerryvore, that, if legal delays with the estate left her short, he could lend her £100 at any time.

For a while it looked as if Thomas's eccentric financial dispositions had left the bulk of his resources to the Scottish Kirk. But in the end his wife had a very comfortable life income. The original will, written at the time of the "damned thief" episode, left Louis only the £3000 mandatory in his mother's marriage settlement. A codicil added in the Hyères period gave him disposal and life income after his mother's death.[1] He was also adjured to look after Brother Alan's children when they were in straits, an injunction that presently proved awkward to obey. Louis was annoyed when the press averred that his father's death had left him rich. But even so, £3000 was a reassuring sum to lodge with Baxter to be cared for. Nobody yet knew that £2000 of it would charter a yacht for cruising the Pacific.

Bluidy Jack called again at Skerryvore in July. But the doctors thought they detected a flicker of new vitality:

. . . they all say . . . You ought not to be in such a state of health; you should recover. Well, then, I mean to. My spirits are rising again after three months of black depression; I almost begin to feel as if I should care to live; I would, by God! And so I begin to believe I shall.[2]

Louis had no intention of pursuing recovery at Skerryvore, now that nothing detained him in Britain. He had long pondered the remark of a doctor to Lloyd that, for more than one year, the climate of Great Britain was a slow poison. Fanny had occasional twitches of impulse to visit her family in the States and her property in Oakland; the cult of mountain-cure for tuberculosis had arisen in Colorado, where Ruedi had seen lung-rotten farmers resuming life with full vigor. It was decided to rent Skerryvore for extra revenue and try the next winter in Colorado or New Mexico. Lloyd was eager to go Wild-Westing, Valentine loyally agreeable, Fanny game, though aghast at leaving her plantings and terracings to probably neglectful tenants. Louis's mother, who seems readily to have transferred to Louis the serene dependence that made her a good wife, chose to go along. She was fifty-eight years old in a day when this was old age. But her new widow's caps were crisp, her back straight as a Scotch fir, her step light as a girl's, and off she went to Colorado. Naturally, since she was with Louis, she never laid eyes on Colorado. Before Scotland saw her again, she had entertained cannibals and faced shipwreck in lonely waters.

To transport five people 4000 miles would be costly. Seeking thrifty means, Fanny found the Wilson Line taking passengers out of London to New York via Le Havre on an inexpensive semi-freighter basis. She inspected and found satisfactory one of these ships lying down the Thames, so all booked passage on the late August sailing of a sister ship, the *Ludgate Hill*. At this juncture Colvin and Fanny seem to have become somewhat embroiled, which Louis found depressing if probably temporary; he wrote Colvin from Bournemouth:

. . . here I am in this dismantled house hoping to come tomorrow . . . this time of my life is at an end; if it leaves bitterness in your mind, what kind of a time has it been? . . . If you can find it in your heart to forgive me: I shall go with the more peace. If not, my dear old friend, time will bring it about. There was no essential unkindness in any of our minds;

some muddle, some trouble . . . and it has spattered you;
. . . I wish we could have left with a godspeed; but if that
may not be, I know you will forgive us before long. . . . I
have told Fanny, who was cut to the heart with fear and alarm,
that I would disculpate her. It was certainly not her doing,
beyond meddling; wherein I cannot excuse her; and if we have
grown to count on your indulgence very largely, yours is the
fault. I wish I had a word of peace to take to her tomorrow.
. . . I am still your most grateful, most admiring, and
most affectionate friend, without change—perhaps without
enough. . . . Yours, my dear soul from the bottom of my
heart

RLS

P. S. The last day—the last evening—in the old house with a
sad but God knows, nowise a bitter heart; and wish I could
say with any hope.[3]

Whatever the occasion of unpleasantness—it sounds as if somehow connected with Colvin's standing resistance to Louis's
crossing the Atlantic—this brought him generously round. It
was Colvin who accompanied the party on board ship as farewell escort.

This second departure for America had less drama, since
Louis now had an intelligible purpose—to return after regain-
ing health in a therapeutic winter. What commotion there was,
Louis himself furnished in his East End family hotel—he called
it "Todgers', as ever was, chez Todgers, Pecksniff Street"[4]
—by proclaiming on a Sunday, when such things were difficult,
that he had immediate need of a solicitor, witnesses to his will,
and a copy of Hardy's *The Woodlanders* to read during the passage. Arrived on board next day he found that Henry James had
sent a case of champagne as remedy for seasickness. As the ship
was towed down the river, Louis was seeing his last of Britain—
but there was no way he could know that.

At Le Havre the ship loaded a small consignment of apes for
transatlantic zoos and a large number of horses, some stowed

so intimately near the passengers that their long, sad faces peered into the saloon windows. Louis was comically indignant, Fanny scolded because the shipping office had given no hint that the ship was to be a floating stable; the "great bucket of iron" rolled all the way and, for all that champagne could do, prostrated Fanny and Valentine. But, fortunately in view of what the next few years would bring her, "Aunt Maggie" proved a good sailor, and Louis, who had left seasickness behind in his twenties, picked up hand over hand. He made friends with apes, officers, and hands indifferently, was full of jokes, skipped busily round dosing seasick shipmates with champagne, exulted in a northward shift of course that gave him a glimpse of Newfoundland, and began to speculate ebulliently on making Japan, instead of Colorado, eventual goal of the trip.

New York, eleven days out, was heaped with good omens. The boarding pilot proved to be nicknamed "Hyde" in contrast to his better-natured partner "Jekyll." The first people up the gangway were Will Low, overjoyed to see his old comrade from Barbizon, and that very useful man, E. L. Burlingame, editor of *Scribner's*, eager to talk business. In telling Mrs. Jenkin that he was "not unknown" in the States, Louis had understated farther than he knew. In an uproarious style that Britain had not attained, *Jekyll* had made him as famous as James G. Blaine, and—however anomalously in a ship reeking of horse manure—he had arrived just when the uproar was highest. The town was full of publicity for Richard Mansfield's self-starring production of T. R. Sullivan's stage version of *Jekyll*, for which the great actor-manager (contrary to the American custom of the time with dramatized foreign stories) was actually willing to pay Louis mild royalties. Already a hit in Boston, it was to open in New York the next week.

A *Herald* reporter noted Louis's queer hat and his resemblance, he said, to a Van Dyck painting. At the Victoria Hotel on Broadway, where Sargent's friends, the Fairchilds, had reserved rooms for the party, the press swarmed thicker. Louis held up through four interviews before pleading fatigue. In spite of Fanny's "spy"-mindedness and his own misgivings, he managed to accommodate the boys by saying that he liked New York exceedingly as "a mixture of Chelsea, Liverpool and Paris";[5] through them besought Americans to buy only authorized editions of his work—international copyright and the scandal of American pirate-publishing was then a lively subject—said a good word for Grover Cleveland, though "I am not in love with any form of government," and loyally extolled Henry James's latest work. Next day, taking along a cold that he had caught off the Banks, he fled with Lloyd to Newport, whither the Fairchilds had invited any and all of the party.[6] Louis's hosts do not seem at all to have minded his staying in bed practically all the time. They had already sent a carriage to the pier and arranged to pay the party's bill at the Victoria.

Money began to heap up to match fame. *Scribner's* bid $3500 for a year's worth of essays on any subjects Louis might choose. The hyperkinetic Sam McClure, rising paragon of the American periodical press, offered $10,000 a year for what would now be called a weekly column in the New York *World;* he also made an excellent price for *The Black Arrow* for his own syndicate, provided he could drop the first five chapters and call it *The Outlaws of Tunstall Forest.* These were excellent prices sixty years ago, when the dollar bought more in both beefsteak and literature. Louis's arithmetic failed intelligibly to convert dollars to sterling, but vagueness did not flaw his awe of such sums—he had been accustomed to think £250 (say $1200) a good year's earnings. Only five years before, his father had bought back the copyrights of the *Virginibus Puerisque* volume, *An Inland Voyage*, and the *Donkey* for a mere £100.

Firmly he refused the *World* on the sensible grounds that he probably wasn't worth all that and certainly could not manage a weekly assignment—an attitude that startled McClure almost as much as did Louis's willingness to decapitate the *Arrow.* Then, cheerfully incredulous, he closed with *Scribner's:*

I am sure it will do me harm to do it, but the sum was irresistible . . . I am like to be a millionaire if this goes on, and be publicly hanged at the . . . revolution. . . . a godsend to my biographer if I ever have one.[7]

The good fairy was dipping in with both hands: Beneath the *Jekyll* clamor, *Kidnapped* and *Treasure Island* were doing well in authorized editions that paid royalties. When last in the States, Louis had been snubbed by editors' office boys as well as by shipping agents, railroad employees, and hotel clerks. Now, only eight years later, he was cockered up in luxurious hotels, solicitously entertained by millionaires, and offered private railroad cars. On his return from Newport a sculptor friend of Low's named St. Gaudens, whom Louis greatly liked, began a medallion of him, propped in bed, cigarette in hand.[8]

It is not wholly true that the States "discovered" Stevenson. But it was the American public—rather, American publishers—who first paid him on something approaching a modern scale. Their eagerness did have the flavor of "Chicago making culture hum" that Chapman tasted in it. McClure wanted Louis, exactly as Sam Goldwyn later wanted Maeterlinck, because he was a "name," because the byline of the author of *Jekyll* would be a feather in the *World's* yellow cap. But it was most convenient for Louis and, for a man thus shot into relative affluence, he kept his head well. Fanny, too, apparently took it in stride. And presently, in another kind of recognition, Louis was one of nine annually elected to London's august Athenaeum Club "as being of distinguished eminence in Science, Literature, or for Public Services." [9] Though he put the Athenaeum on his calling cards, he soon tried to resign, probably to avoid the annual dues.

Fresh information made Colorado seem needlessly—and expensively—far, as well as possibly too high for Fanny's heart. The famous Dr. E. L. Trudeau of Saranac Lake had recently attracted attention to the Adirondack Mountains of upper

New York State, several thousand feet up, cold much of the year, as good tuberculosis country. Inquiries made it all sound admirably to Louis's purpose, so Saranac was determined on. Within a few days of the return from Newport the party took the river steamer to Albany, Louis delighted with his first sight of the famous American autumn foliage. The railroad west from Plattsburg would not reach Saranac Lake until December, so the last twenty miles were covered in a buggy over roads such as they had not seen since California. Close to the village they rented from a local guide-trapper-hunter most of his rambling "cottage"—"a hatbox on a hill"—with their own entrance and kitchen.[10] Thus supplies and Trudeau were near at hand, while communication by mail with New York editors and transatlantic steamers was a matter of only a couple of days. After hearing that, on occasion, "cold" in Saranac meant —40°F., Fanny went to Montreal, the nearest city, to buy buffalo coats, sealskin boots, and fur caps for all. In these shaggy, bulky garments Louis looked and was pleased to feel like a survivor of the Franklin expedition.

Trudeau found no active disease in him; it had certainly been present and might recur, he said, but Louis was a marginally "arrested" case, a verdict specially impressive because Trudeau was already using sputum-examination in diagnosis. Later in the winter the addition of koumiss to his diet gratifyingly fattened the patient up. But for all the intense little doctor's aid and comfort, Louis did not get on so well with him as he usually did with physicians. Shown round Trudeau's laboratory, where the future of American tuberculosis-therapy was then being determined for the next two generations, Louis objected to its organic messiness. "Your light may be very bright to you," Trudeau said Louis told him, with wounding insouciance, in a metaphor indicating that he was then working on "The Lantern-Bearers," "but to me it smells of oil like the devil." [11] The rudeness apparent in this unilateral, though responsible, account is puzzling. Unless angry, Louis was usually most courteous. The incident is salutary reminder that occasionally people of genuine stature, not merely stupid *bourgeois*, found his renowned charm less than irresistible.[12]

The village, which lived on trapping, pioneer "lungers," and the tag-end of lumbering, had small opportunity to vote yes or no on Louis. Relations between the hat-box and local people consisted mostly of purchases, which once led to a sharp row with the local butcher over a dubious roast. Louis was showing a misanthropic dislike of even so much as meeting passers-by when on his occasional walks. In exploring ways for the Fairchilds to come visiting, he wrote acidly of ". . . hours of . . . unavailing inquiry in this damned, ignorant, helpless den of a hamlick."[13] The others sometimes saw the outside world: Aunt Maggie and Lloyd visited the Fairchilds in Boston;[14] Fanny visited her sister in Danville, Ind., returning by way of the Bellamy Storers[15] in Cincinnati. But Louis holed up and wrote in his little corner room and, at prescribed intervals, donned buffalo coat and fur cap to pace the narrow veranda, the cold peppery in his nose; only now and then did he risk skating, which he loved, or a dash of sleighing.

What he saw of the neighborhood daunted him. Tumbled and too low for sublimity, the Adirondacks are like the bleaker Highlands or the Cévennes furred out with timber, harsh with broken stone, impersonally inimical as the sea but without its broad, simple effects. Though fires roared all day at Baker's, the house walls popped with contractions as the cold clutched and pounced. Louis made a botch of the finale of *Ballantrae*, but not specifically of his handling of this subzero wilderness.

Possibly because this was the least active life he had ever led, his improvement persisted. For fifteen months between Skerryvore and Tahiti he had no recorded hemorrhage—his longest respite since TB had been diagnosed. But it was technically unfortunate that inactivity gave him such meager opportunity to become acquainted with the States. True, Fanny was helpful when he made efforts to try American characters and backgrounds—the pillow is a great teacher of cul-

tures as well as languages. Louis's occasionally sound general-
izations about America—such as the megalomania of the street
plans of new American towns—must often represent rather
Fanny's knowledge than his own. His best handling of Americans was his fine group portrait of the Hansons, that generically
squirrel-shooting frontier cluster of ne'er-do-wells squatted on
the Silverado mining claim—the sluggish giant epitomizing
"oaf" and "loaf"; and the formidably silent, preternaturally
woodcrafty head of the house, lean and potentially violent,
with the grave manners of dispossessed royalty, are fundamental
American figures. He could hardly so soon have depicted them
so well without drawing on Fanny's lifelong awareness of such
"trash" in the background of her girlhood.

His luck was never so good again in this field. *The Wrecker*,
written in collaboration with Lloyd, has some merits, but no
American with an ear can forgive the succession of notes struck
too flat, too sharp, or just violently out of range[16] in the depiction of Loudon Dodd and Jim Pinkerton, its American central
figures. Louis was fascinated by American turns of speech, of
which his letters sometimes show traces; the man who read
Huckleberry Finn straight through with dazzled wonder and
then read it straight through again in awe obviously felt the virtues of the American idiom. But his grasp of it was as faulty as
his handling of the Boehm flute, and, perhaps through hyper-
expatriation, his American-born family failed to help him.
Though his formal education was latterly British, Lloyd had
spent three years in the States as refresher during his teens;
heaven knows where Fanny and he were when Pinkerton's
speeches were being read aloud. At any rate the man who did
so double-dyed a Briton as Sir John Crabtree, so essential a
Frenchman as Dr. Desprez, so vivid a colonial as Wiltshire,
never had a hand in a sound fictional American. His opportunities had been too cramped: even the Americans he knew well
consisted too much of Brahmins like the Fairchilds or expatri-
ates like James and Sargent.

Pinkerton (drawn from McClure) best brings out this fail-

ure. His presumably American go-getterism is that of an Englishman in a manic state, like Uncle Ponderevo; he has the
American awe of European culture in the fashion of a *Punch*
cartoon; and his talk is occasion for nothing but despair.
"Throw all this down!" this sharpshooter in the San Francisco
of the 1870s is made to write, "Have you never set up an advertisement?"

Louis fitted more easily into other aspects of America. He
liked her dishes, as noted, and at Calistoga had taken very
kindly indeed to ". . . the playful, innocuous American cocktail. . . . lo! veins of living fire ran down my leg; and then
a focus of conflagration remained seated in my stomach, not un-
pleasantly, for a quarter of an hour." [17] As "Ticonderoga" had
already shown, he greatly fancied Indian place names and
complained that not more had survived. He called the States
"a good place for kindness" [18] and, unlike most Britons, showed
little tendency to regard Americans as curiosities; this was true
long before he met Fanny, long before his American market
became his principal economic resource.

Ballantrae was the winter's major project, broken by departure in April, lamely finished in Tahiti and Hawaii to maintain serialization in *Scribner's*. Louis early suspected that the
later sections, planned in Saranac, would be inferior, so the
break cannot be blamed for its unevenness. Yet the book is
too strongly and darkly laid on the canvas to be rejected for its
technical sins. Sureness ably masks the extravagance of the
stage business, and the morality was bleakest yet. A father and
two sons allow political and dynastic considerations to align
them in positions false to all three. Exploiting this falseness
with exquisite skill and malice, the elder and stronger brother
destroys all three. There is no pseudo-Greek tinkering with
Destiny. The original decision is responsibly made, bitterly
italicized at the time by the younger: "If we were playing a
manly part, there might be sense in such talk. But what are we
doing? Cheating at cards!" The Master is evil free will incar-
nate. Had it been he who married the girl and the cadet who

went out in the Forty-Five, Durrisdeer might well have seen stormy times anyway. But, as the weaker characters band together against him, they come so close to saving themselves that one sees the scale tipped toward ruin solely by the basic, irreclaimable error.

The monthly essays for *Scribner's* went well—after all, they included "Pulvis et Umbra," "Beggars," "A Chapter on Dreams," "The Lantern-Bearers." [19] Suppressing his dread of deadlines, Louis had copy well in time. The only casualty was "Confessions of a Unionist," an effort to show the American reader that an intelligent and well-meaning subject of Queen Victoria could think British rule in Ireland indecently stupid and yet oppose immediate Home Rule—much the attitude that Louis had already sketched in defending his Curtin project. *Scribner's* had the article set up in type before—dreading public reaction, I suppose—they thought better of it. Louis's letter to Burlingame consenting to suppression was a model of open-minded courtesy.

The article had also included his accusation that no American paper, not even the New York *Evening Post*, the sober organ that seems to have been his Stateside newspaper, had tried intelligently to report the Unionist position. This further elucidates his dislike and mistrust of newspapers on both sides of the Atlantic. Two years before, in England, he had called the press ". . . the mouth of the sewer, where lying is professed, as from a university chair, and everything prurient, and ignoble, and essentially dull, finds its abode and pulpit." [20] In the States gossip about his appearance, diet, plans, and family had printed many errors of fact: seeing himself described as "fleshy" seems to have rankled as much as those London paragraphs about his having inherited a fortune. In June 1880, interviewers in San Francisco could not even agree on what hotel he was inhabiting. His opinion of the turgid style of the newspaperman of the day was understandably low, and the approach to celebrities struck him as bafflingly ridiculous: "Mr. Stevenson expressed his opinion in a kindly but earnest way that the American system of interviewing was 'awful folly.'" [21] But, beyond such tenable points, he does seem to have felt that strange British dread of "the press" that was shared among staider strata of well-to-do Americans. Favorable or unfavorable or neutral, publicity was in itself something obscenely distasteful and degrading. This was one of Louis's few definitely bourgeois traits, straight from the inward-drawing architecture of Heriot Row. And Fanny, of course, took it all five times as keenly as he, reacting more and more violently against publicity all the rest of her life.

Though seldom so explicit as "Unionist" and "The Day After Tomorrow," the *Scribner's* series plainly showed Louis's new urge to lean on ideas more and his own personality less. Sixty years later the ideas do not always seem wisely selected. Like most of his contemporaries, he had been greatly taken by the "eugenics" that Galton had popularized for fifteen years. To us the notion that, through heredity, ancestors determine gait and emotional bias as well as eye-color is more like tendentious nonsense every day. But in Louis's time such ideas were augustly endorsed and taken as seriously by intelligent people as the basic tenets of psychiatry are today. (I mean no equation of relative validity; this merely describes a parallel wide acceptance by laymen unqualified to judge in either case.) He could hardly be expected to mistrust a body of doctrine accepted by people far more learned than he, particularly when it met his standing need for a sense of identity with the past. So, in "Pastoral" and "Gentlemen," he publicly enjoyed the thought that both his grandfather of the Bell Rock and the Darwinians' Missing Link—whom he irreverently christened Probably Arboreal—lived in him organically, in moral bent and stubborn passion as well as in physical structure.

Many used Galton to bolster upper-class notions of inborn aristocratic superiority. With characteristic good will Louis took it rather to mean that innate integrity and capacity descended to shrewd, skilled, and active Scots peasants as well as to the high and mighty. This seemed obvious in his own ancestry, which, trying to understand himself better, he was now exploring, eager to confirm his suspicion that "Stevenson" had been an occasional alias of the red-headed sept of McGregor. But the more he explored his family tree, the more prosaic it became. Even the French barber-surgeon supposed to have come over with Cardinal Beaton grew dubious. . . .

Other contemporary pseudo-scientists supplied him solace with their new emphasis on "racial traits." The Aryan has now glimmered out. Whether he was fair or dark, round- or long-headed, European or Asiatic in origin no longer matters, since the odds are several thousand to one against his ever having existed as anything but a possible linguistic entity. In Louis's day, however, the Aryan's various branches—Celt, Latin, Teuton, et al.—were considered highly identifiable counters in the game that Galton invented. People looked for—and naturally saw—"Celtic traits" in Welshmen; expected—and naturally felt—"Teutonic stolidity" in big-boned, fair Yorkshiremen; and so forth and so forth, as pleased as their descendants now identifying father-fixations in their friends. Our mothers and fathers still talked that sort of thing. By now physical genetics are hard enough put to it without having to establish a "Celtic type," let alone associate it with a tendency to see small supernatural beings. But sixty years ago Louis and his biographers both readily saw in him a mixture of Celt and Teuton, like Scotland in general, his moral sense coming from the latter, his mercurial creativeness from the former, just as his coloration originally mingled fair hair with dark eyes.

Though such notions tempted the harsh into the Hitler brand of "racism," they merely heightened Louis's respect for other races, encouraged him rewardingly to feel that race traits in Polynesians or Japanese were as venerable as in Lowland sons of Vikings. "We are all nobly born," he wrote, "fortunate those who know it; blessed those who remember." [22] A truly civilized man still tends to derive civilized conclusions from even smug nonsense.

Posterity must nevertheless consider him better advised

when he anticipated, rather than followed, the intellectual crotchets of the Western world. "Pulvis et Umbra," ruefully but admiringly depicting the plight of man, that "ennobled lemur," in an impersonal, materialistic, luridly menacing and yet essentially insubstantial universe, was a more cogent and considerably better written sermon than Bertrand Russell would later set down in "A Free Man's Worship." [23] It elicited anguished protests from readers, but Louis kept his hand on the plow, for the child who had played church—no doubt the hereditary result of coming of a long line of parsons—still clung to the game of preaching without the trappings, even candidly labeling one of the *Scribner's* series "A Christmas Sermon." This loose summary of his moral world to date would have been near the death of his clerical ancestors. Its epitaph for even the best of men was: "another Faithful Failure"—a joyous and tinseled thought for Christmas. But readers of the Messrs. Scribner's cultivated publication were probably already numbed by Louis's preceding doubts as to the salubrity of conscience-searching—a vice to which he himself was prone—and of the ethics of being one's brother's keeper—which he was often tempted to but seldom guilty of:

> It is probable that nearly all who think of conduct at all, think of it too much; it is certain that we all think too much of sin. . . . To make our ideal of morality center on forbidden acts is to defile the imagination and to introduce into our judgments of our fellow-men a secret element of gusto. If a thing is wrong for us, we should not dwell upon the thought of it; or we shall soon dwell upon it with inverted pleasure. If we cannot drive it from our minds—one thing of two: either our creed is in the wrong and we must more indulgently remodel it; or else, if our morality be in the right, we are criminal lunatics and should put our persons in restraint. Gentleness and cheerfulness . . . are the perfect duties. And it is the trouble with moral men that they have neither the one nor the other. . . . If your morals make you

dreary, depend upon it they are wrong. I do not say "give them up," for they may be all you have; but conceal them like a vice, lest they should spoil the lives of better and simpler people.

In 1888 it was strong stuff to ask readers to weigh failure and frustration and say "perhaps something is wrong with Mrs. Grundy and the Ten Commandments."

Nor were his readers in a position to see that, in "A Chapter on Dreams," his realistic introspection raised a spirit at which contemporary psychology was merely hinting; which, within a couple of generations, would leave the Ten Commandments in ten thousand fragments. No scientific document, this was merely a writer's account of the possible role of his unconscious in fictioneering, but all the more striking since the label "unconscious mind" was yet to be invented. When he needed a story, Louis was saying, he often found it in sleep, as powers personal to and yet independent of his waking self told him usable tales. For conversational purposes he called these forces his "Little People," his "Brownies," who were

. . . near connections of the dreamer's beyond doubt; . . . share in his financial worries . . . share plainly in his training; . . . only I think they have more talent; . . . can tell him a story piece by piece, like a serial, and keep him all the while in ignorance of where they aim.

That is pretty good for 1888, but it goes rather farther; they

. . . do one-half my work for me while I am fast asleep, and in all human likelihood, do the rest for me as well, when I am wide awake and fondly suppose I do it for myself . . . [they] have not a rudiment of a conscience.

For these descriptions Louis may have had hints from Hazlitt's theory that dreams obscurely dramatize what one would like to do and from Lamb's guesses at an amorphous, pre-"dreamwork" magma for nightmares. He unquestionably had more than hints from the detailed commentary on *Jekyll* that he received from F.W.H. Myers, the Taylors' eminent psychical-researching friend. But the above intensely shrewd observations were Louis's own, concluding a vague but pregnant passage on an aspect of the unconscious that many modern psychiatrists, those strange and wooden rabbis, condemn themselves to do without: these "Brownies," he said, besides declining to put morals on their fables, were often found "conveying hints of life's larger limitations and that sort of sense which we seem to perceive in the arabesque of time and space." His explorations in this line are important not so much because they anticipated the general mind of a later time—though this they brilliantly did—as because they illuminate the acumen with which he peered at his own behavior.[24]

Psychiatry might find even better pickings in the Brownie-invented plot in the "Chapter" that Louis abandoned because ". . . it soon became plain that in this spirited tale there were unmarketable elements." The story sketched is, in fact, a sort of mirror-image *Hamlet*, involving a young man who murders his father and, when the narrative breaks off, is well on the way to a love affair with the old gentleman's young second wife. One of the strange things that happened posthumously to Louis was the result of his using the term "Brownies." He meant the Brownie of British folklore, the "lubber fiend," capriciously clever, sometimes malicious, sometimes helpful, of *A Midsummer Night's Dream*. But unhappily Palmer Cox was currently using the word to label his jolly little sprites with feathered caps. So that certain women writers, all too taken by the whimsy of it, were soon archly telling how dear Louis Stevenson had used stories that his sweet little Brownies told him while he slept; whereas he makes it so clear that plots delivered in his dreams were often what weaker spirits would have called formulated nightmares—the evil brown dog that caught flies with his paw like a human being; the blood-lapping lady used in "Olalla"; . . . and, whether marketable or not, were about as jolly as *The Cenci* or a sadistic German fairy tale.

This is a long way from Louis waiting for spring at Saranac. Happy the winter that had no history. Lloyd was whacking away on the typewriter at an extravaganza to eventuate as *The Wrong Box*, a swirling farce involving a game of Hearts with the corpse of a misidentified invalid as the Queen of Spades, that hugely tickled Louis. First encouraging the writer, he soon determined to give it a rewrite himself as the first collaboration between them, though it proved hard to sell even with Louis's name on it. Most critics reject it as even worse error then *Otto* or *The Dynamiter*; personally I think it excellent good fun. There was also a novel about the Indian Mutiny being planned between Louis and Lloyd which never saw light. This notion of publicly collaborating with Lloyd had the minor advantage of securing American copyright for Louis through the boy's American citizenship. . . . The Fairchilds came visiting in a private car, arriving with colds; Fanny forbade them the house until they could show her clean handkerchiefs through the window. . . . Old Dan Bandmann, veteran second-rate actor, came with his stage version of *Jekyll*, which seems to have ended with the repentant doctor's being snatched up to heaven like Little Eva. Louis liked Bandmann, whatever he thought of the improvement on his story. Aunt Maggie noted with approval that this was the only guest at Saranac who ever said Amen to her grace before dinner. . . .

Even when history began again, it was benign. McClure had come several times to skate with Louis and keep his foot in the door. Once he managed to hypnotize his man into promising him a novel in contravention of Louis's agreement with Scribner; all hands behaved well about it, and the matter was adjusted without broken bones. But that was only one of McClure's irons in the fire that roared up the chimney at "Baker's" without warming the room much. The Stevensons had been dreaming of a yacht voyage ever since landing in New York. Pleased to find herself so good a sailor, Aunt Maggie thought of financing a charter herself. McClure translated this into an offer to pay handsomely for travel letters from such a voyage for syndication—in effect financing it by instalments. Perhaps Lloyd could take photographs to make slides for Louis to use on a lecture-tour booked by McClure's lecture bureau; a recording phonograph might pick up the noises of wind, sea, natives, and whatever. . . .

The Aegean Isles leaped into focus again, along with Bermuda, the Azores, and all sorts of geographical garnish on the assumption that a yacht could be found on the east coast; remember that the Panama Canal did not yet exist. Or if the yacht were Pacific-based . . . the Marquesas, the Galápagos, Guayaquil immediately began dancing reels in Louis's and Lloyd's heads. Laying in Findlay's sailing directories, they also studied the Indian Ocean for good measure, dreaming of the island of Paul and Virginia while the wind shook the cottage and twisted the icicles crashing to the ground.

Fanny was game; that can be kept standing in type. Valentine was willing. Aunt Maggie was eager. It seems never to have occurred to anybody in this household to feel misgivings about taking a widow of sixty on a long cruise in a small ship in an era lacking radio—not even to the old lady herself. Nor did anybody mention the risks implicit in removing Louis from possible contact with doctors for weeks or months at a time.

As spring approached, McClure combed the Atlantic seaboard for yachts. Late in March Fanny left to visit Indiana and the Coast, with instructions to look into yachts out of San Francisco. A few days earlier the emotional weather had changed, almost precisely with the equinox, though Fanny knew nothing of it when she left. Thanks to Henley, Louis was headed into his worst storm since he had sailed in the *Devonia*.

The Case of the Pomeranian Dog

Thou hast not half the power to do me harm
That I have to be hurt.

—*Othello:* V, ii

HAD Fanny seen Henley's misbegotten letter before she left for California, no conscientious psychiatrist could have answered for either her or Louis.

This *casus belli* in its squareish envelope, carrying what had been Queen Victoria's profile before either Louis or Henley was born, set off one of the most discussed literary-men's quarrels of the latter nineteenth century and seriously affected the reputations that both left behind them. Damage was the greater because the facts were long locked up in a file of the pertinent Henley-Stevenson letters that Baxter preserved for posterity. Even those few writers who saw them confined themselves largely to mutterings about how they did not ". . . leave any stain on the character of either Henley or Stevenson." [1] This was discreet but inaccurate and served only to keep speculation spinning faster. John Connell's recent and highly valuable life of Henley published much of this previously mysterious correspondence. But Connell did not have access to supplementary material that tells the rest of the story and, for the first time, explains why, seven years after Louis's death, Henley chose hysterically to desecrate the grave. The affair is most eloquent of the characters of all concerned—a sort of prism breaking them down to fundamental colors. It also contributed considerably to Louis's maturity. Never again was his heart so conspicuous on his sleeve.

Fanny's brashness furnished the materials. Henley's malice

furnished the occasion. And Louis's low emotional flash-point furnished the explosive.

The trouble with many friendships is that the parties fail to stagnate. When Louis and Henley first met, Henley had not yet been overspurred by the literary-journalistic cliquery that, as he elbowed farther into his career, so suited his harsher qualities. His flair for likely newcomers and his effervescence as he developed are more striking because most of the time he was in physical pain, or at least major discomfort, from violent enteric troubles as well as his disablement. No doubt that exacerbated his lashings-out at intimates.

To the end he was a reverberating person of large scale, a rousingly considerable figure in his "maimed masterfulness," as Louis defined the quality that suggested John Silver. But, as I see him, he also tended to become a sort of brassy Micawber in letters; and along with his Micawberism—perhaps coming from his consistent failure to earn in proportion to his immense capacities—went a fatal tendency to shoulder himself into his good friends' lives. Louis was by no means the only literary chum with whom Henley quarreled. Fastidious Brisk exulted in intimacy, used friends as confessional and sounding-board; but he avoided Henley's somewhat feminine habit of intrusion, which so often made trouble as successive Arabs woke to find their tents smotheringly full of camel. These strains were half expressed as Louis resisted Henley's stubborn enthusiasm about plays, as Fanny glowered when Henley disregarded her discipline, as both she and Louis made efforts to ration the guest's whisky at Skerryvore. But, worse than all that, Louis was in the process of steadily becoming, whereas Henley's temperament, though gaining momentum, was not maturing. He acted himself with growing vigor and skill, but the role was the same all his life. His motives were punitive but his observation was correct when he complained in print that the Louis who came back from California was not the Louis who had departed from St. Pancras the year before.

Besides, Henley's centripetal ego—Louis's was centrifugal—made him a greedy gossip, an indiscreet scorner, a backbiter frequently tempted beyond regard for the cordialities of friendship. Soon after Louis and his crew got Henley elected to the Savile, the new member needed cautioning from his sponsor: ". . . we do hope . . . you will not . . . keep up dissensions. . . . Beware of . . . whispering, smoking-room corner young men. A man's in a club to be fair guid day and fair guid e'en with all." [2] This fits with Colvin's telling Baxter that Henley was always the loudest at the Savile in disparaging Louis's later reputation, and boded ill in conjunction with Fanny's growing defensiveness in her snug, built-snugly-round-Louis castle at Bournemouth.

Some have seen generalized jealousy in Henley's outburst. I see it as cruel contempt for, rather than actual jealousy of, Fanny alone. True, Louis was entering on a phase of economic rewards and wide readership that Henley would never touch; but there are no signs of anything more serious than comradely jeering at Louis's fattening bank balance, which Louis too thought anomalously absurd. The small, irregular financial drain that Henley represented may have heightened Fanny's irritation, not Louis's. In all fairness such "loans" were no more than, as unpaid agent, Henley had earned thrice over, nor did either party ever envisage them so coldly. Up to the morning when Henley's letter arrived at Saranac, Louis would cheerfully have got killed or gone bankrupt for Henley, and there is no reason to doubt the converse.

The bond had even survived Teddy Henley's antics as lead and storm center of a company touring the States with *Deacon Brodie*. His talents, though possibly considerable, were certainly eccentric. Some American reviewers expressed surprise that two writers so eminent should have signed a play with which they could have had so little to do. Louis loyally wrote stiff notes to editors averring that the authors considered *Brodie* well worth signing. Except in Chicago *Brodie* proved a dejected weakling. By December Teddy was suggesting that

Louis guarantee the troupe's expenses for six weeks. Then he tried to borrow direct, receiving only pointed assurance that Louis would pay Mrs. and Mrs. Henley's passage home. Then he was making headlines: He and two fellow troupers tried to play the conquering Briton in a Philadelphia bar; people were hurt in the ensuing brawl and the actors were lucky to get off with fines. Then he allowed himself to be jockeyed out of a New York booking and the enterprise collapsed altogether. Too late Louis learned that Teddy had never given his sanguine brother any hint of difficulty, so that the catastrophe fell on Henley in shocking reversal of what he had been led to expect.

But ripples from that should have disappeared by March. Louis had just arranged for McClure to meet Henley during a trip to England and, it was hoped, employ him as transatlantic literary scout. Henley was asking Louis to do an article on their common friend, Rodin.[3] The last few years had seen sharp quarrels between them, ostensible causes now undiscoverable. But apparently Louis's apologies in the first and Henley's in the second had healed all. Louis knew that Henley considered him unethically quixotic for having refused full payment for a story that he thought below standard. Henley knew that Louis thought him sometimes unbecomingly his own worst enemy. But they were—for both a word of imperative magic—*friends*. The Envoy to Henley's *In Hospital*, written that same March, had heavily played on the very word as applying with ultimate intimacy to Louis, himself, and Baxter.

So the devil put into Henley's big freckled hands *Scribner's* for March 1888, containing Louis's "Beggars" and "The Nixie" by Fanny Van de Grift Stevenson, her third published short story, a fantasy about a poetic young man meeting in a railroad carriage an eerily feeble-minded young woman who turns out to be a watersprite. Her first parent had been Katherine de Mattos, Louis's astringently brilliant cousin, who outlined the tale to Louis and Fanny one evening at Henley's. Her version made the girl merely an escaped lunatic; she rejected Fanny's eager suggestion of the nixie-motif. She also rejected Fanny's rash offer of collaboration and—being literary too and a great close friend of Henley and his London circle[4]—tried her hand alone. All Henley's efforts to place her manuscript were futile. Further prodded by Fanny, Katherine grudgingly handed her the plot to do as she liked with, and Fanny's version proved salable to a magazine presumably not insensible to the value of her husband's surname. This success, where his protégée and he had failed, was well calculated to rankle in a man who had small use for Fanny to begin with. He instantly wrote Louis a letter glaringly headed "*Private and Confidential*," teasing him about his recent election to the Athenaeum and proceeding:

I am out of key to-day. The Spring, sir, is not what it used to be. . . . Enfin! Life is uncommon like rot. *C'est convenu.* If it weren't that I am a sort of centre of strength for a number of feebler folk, I think I'd be shut of it dam soon. . . .

I read the *Nixie* with considerable amazement. It's Katherine's; surely it is Katherine's? There are even reminiscences of phrasery & imagery, parallel incidents—que sais-je? It is also better focussed, no doubt; but I think it has lost as much (at least) as it has gained; and why there wasn't a double signature is what I've not been able to understand. . . .

Louis, dear lad, I am dam tired. The Chatelaine's away. The Spring is spring no more. I am thirty-nine this year. I am dam, dam tired. What I want is the wings of a dove—a soiled dove even!—that I might flee away and be at rest.

Don't show this to *anybody*, & when you write, don't do more than note it in a general way—By the time you *do* write, you will have forgotten all about it, no doubt. But if you haven't, deal vaguely with my malady. Why the devil do you go and bury yourself in that bloody country of dollars and spew? . . . However, I suppose you must be forgiven, for you have loved me much. Let us go on so to the end. . . . We have lived, we have loved, we have suffered; & the end is the best of all. . . . Forgive this babble, and take care of yourself & burn this letter.   Your friend,

W.E.H.[5]

All in Henley's usual letter-style—tags of French and abusive affection as it slides unobtrusively, almost daintily, into the comment on "The Nixie" and away again. (My excisions do not alter either pacing or spirit.) Louis took it as an agonizing insertion and withdrawal of a skillful blade:

My dear Henley,

I write with indescribable difficulty; and if not with perfect temper, you are to remember how very rarely a husband is expected to receive such accusations against his wife. I can only direct you to apply to Katherine and ask her to remind you of that part of the business which took place in your presence and which you seem to have forgotten; she will doubtless add the particulars which you may not have heard. . . .

I am sorry I must ask you to take these steps; I might take them for myself had you not tied my hands by the strange step of marking your letter "private and confidential." . . . I wish I could stop here. I cannot. When you have refreshed your mind as to the facts, you will, I know, withdraw what you have said to me; but I must go farther and remind you, if you have spoken of this to others, a proper explanation and retraction of what you shall have said or implied to any person so addressed, will be necessary.

From the bottom of my soul I believe what you wrote to have been merely reckless words . . . but it is hard to think that anyone—and least of all my friend—should have been so careless of dealing agony. . . . This is the sixth or seventh attempt that I make to write to you; . . . You will pardon me if I can find no form of signature; I pray God such a blank will not be of long endurance.

ROBERT LOUIS STEVENSON[6]

So far there is a case for an unhappy misconception: Henley's private-and-confidential and burn-this-letter could have been mere precaution against others' learning of his gloomy mood and need of a "soiled dove." But nowhere in the later correspondence is there any hint that, on Louis's protest, Henley withdrew his embargo. Louis seems eventually to have taken the matter up with Baxter, Katherine, and Fanny in distant San Francisco in the teeth of Henley's injunction. Certainly anybody knowing Louis well must have expected explosions: His temper was famously high; his standards of personal honor higher still, and, by definition, his wife's honor included his own. My necessary conclusion is that, being emotionally at low ebb, hence unusually susceptible to his meaner self, Henley was indulging in hit-and-run backbiting on a topic that had long irritated him, i.e., Fanny in general. It is significant that he took occasion from a misunderstanding in business correspondence to patronize Louis's letter: "I know not whether to laugh or cry over it. . . ." and to disclaim ". . . any suspicion that my remarks upon the *Nixie-Watersprite* could possibly go near throwing our lives into separate tragedies. . . ." [7] But it took him a month longer to vouchsafe a round disclaimer in a tone signally failing to match that of Louis's reaction:

My dear Lad:—Your letter is heart-breaking; & I do not know how to reply to it, for it convicts me (I now see) of a piece of real unkindness, unworthy of myself and of our old true friendship. You may blame me in the bitterest terms you will for the cruel blunder I made in opening my mind to you; and I shall not complain, for I deserve them all. . . .

You must not believe, though, that I struck to hurt. I did not. I thought the matter of little consequence. It seemed right that you should know how it looked to myself, & that there might well be the end of it. I was elbows deep in the business from the first & I had (I thought) a right to make remarks. It was surely as well (I assumed) that you should hear of certain coincidences from me as well as from another quarter. That I had any feeling of unfriendliness is what I want now explicitly to deny. . . . Twice before (I want you to remember) you have put this same charge upon me; each time, as you know, to my astonishment. In this case, as in the others, I can truly say the amazement is the same. How much greater the distress has been I leave you to judge. . . .

. . . I could not answer your first letter. It put me (as it were) in the dock, and I preferred to keep silence until I could speak on the old footing, & in the old terms. Now that I can do that, I make haste to own that I spoke without a full sense of the regard that was due you, & that I beg your forgiveness.

. . . do not doubt me again if you can help it. Life is short enough, as it is; and you and I, dear Louis, should know better than to waste the good that is in it—the soul that we have made for ourselves—like this

Ever your friend
W.E.H.[8]

Nobody who knew Henley could have mistaken this nervous rhetoric for regret. At the bottom Louis noted, probably for Baxter's eye: "His original position carefully saved throughout; . . . even if he still thinks as he did, I think a kind spirit would have lied." Henley was capable of deep personal emotion for his wife and idolized small daughter; but here he may have betrayed another kind of deep feeling—the pleasure of insulting Fanny *via* Louis was too intimately visceral to allow honorable retraction to spoil it.

Both parties turned to poor Baxter as emotional stakeholder, a thankless role that he played well. When Louis wrote him about it all, his replies unhesitatingly endorsed Louis's position. The excuses that he put forward for Henley were hardly flattering, consisting as they did of pointing out Henley's egocentric insensitivities and necessarily imperfect acquaintance with behavior expected among gentlemen. He finally came round to feeling that, culpable though Henley was, Mrs. de Mattos was even more so. But he stuck loyally by his huge affection for both parties, made no move to break with Henley, and readily offered to act between them in necessary correspondence, since it was so plain that neither could write the other without torture.

To Baxter, 3000 miles away, Louis put everything he was feeling on paper at a word-liberal length eloquent of shock. In letter after letter he sifted his conscience for Baxter, making much of motes in his own eye to reconcile the situation with his view of loyal friendship, but never able to blink the almost cynically masked malice, toward himself as well as Fanny, of Henley's original action. His despair was all the greater when Katherine de Mattos twistingly refused to confirm Louis's version of the events behind "The Nixie," not on the grounds that it was untrue so much as because she felt quite ill about it all and preferred not to be questioned. To Louis's protest she returned only three lines of huddling withdrawal into convenient mystery: "That was best. I am afraid to speak or breathe. There is devilry in the air," [9] that gave Louis some excuse for being tempted to think the world had suddenly gone mad; to Baxter again:

I fear I have come to an end with Henley; the lord knows if I have not tried to be a friend to him, the lord knows even that I have not altogether failed. There is not one of that crew that I have not helped in every kind of strait, with money, with service, . . . and every year there is a fresh outburst against me and mine. . . . And I have forgiven, and forgiven, and forgotten and forgotten and still they get their heads together and there springs up a fresh enmity or a fresh accusation. . . .

I can't say it's anger that I feel, but it is despair. My last reconciliation with Henley is not a year old—and here is the devil again. I am weary of it all, weary, weary, weary. . . .

It will probably come to a smash; and I shall have to get you to give the poor creature an allowance, pretending that it comes from Hamilton Bruce or—anybody but me. Desert him I could not; . . . but whether I can continue to go on cutting my hands and my wife's hands is quite another question. . . . I see myself in a thousand ways unwise and (as my way is) sometimes harsh, and often foolish with my mouth. . . . . On the other side, there have been, I think there still are, some warm feelings; they have never been warm enough to make him close his mouth; even when he knew he could hurt me sorely, even to the friends whom he knew I prized.

. . . to you, I do devoutly believe, he will be the old, affectionate, fine, big heart of a fellow whom we have both loved. . . .

Well, God bless us all—and Henley in the first rank, though I think I will let him bless him during my discreet absence—for the future . . . I do care for Henley . . . and all his fine spirit and courage and geniality and loyalty—though to me, of these late days, he has not been loyal—and his rich temperament which was a fund of pleasure to me, all of which are now only subjects of regret.[10]

And later:

Suppose that I am insane and that I have dreamed all that I seem to remember, and that my wife has shamefully stolen a story from my cousin, was this the class of matter that a friend would write to me? God knows if I heard ill of Henley's wife, I should bottle it up in my heart from him, not write it to him in the midst of fulsome protestations of love; . . . If this be friendship, I am not robust enough to bear it. If it be want of tact, it is strangely like want of heart. . . . Katherine's attitude absolves him of three parts of what I had against him, but the fourth part that remains—that willingness to seethe up against me and mine in my absence and that heartless willingness to wound me—was it seems the fact that I most keenly felt.[11]

He says—for the first time—that he wished he had died at Hyères: ". . . the happy part of my life ended there." [12] At the close of May, with the much desired yacht presumably arranged for, he was still wrung and incredulous: "O, I go on my journey with a bitter heart. It will be best for all . . . if the Casco goes down with me." [13] Then, in reversal, he made a perspicacious point about the Henley clique that Fanny called "the Shepherd's Bush gang":

> I think I perceive that I injure these people by treating them with too great delicacy, which they misconstrue—and what drives me wild, misconstrue to the disadvantage of my wife. . . . Well, I mean to beat the crowd. I *will* have a good time on the *Casco*; it means a hard heart; well, harden it, O Lord! and let's be done." [14]

Pluckily he struggled against the smugnesses of anger and self-pity: "I am . . . the most purely unhappy card on the ground," he writes Baxter from Manasquan, "—or so my egotism thinks, when there are (I daresay) a thousand who might envy me." [15]

Lloyd, of course, was desolated by this breach between his Number One and Number Two heroes. Fanny had early made a gallant effort to keep herself in hand, even sending a nominally cordial message to Katherine while Louis was seeking testimony. But, alone in San Francisco, with pressure mounting up, she finally broke into tumult specifically charging treachery. Louis admitted that, through the itch to meddle with Katherine's story, Fanny was somewhat to blame for the trouble. But he reproached her only with disparity in temperament; he wrote her:

> I envy you flimsy people who rage up so easily with hate; the days go, and this is the more dreadful to me. Excuse my little bitterness with "flimsy," it is a tap in return for my thousands, and don't believe it, dearest.[16]

He was fortunate to be incapable of the spiralings into unreality reflected in a letter of Fanny's to the long-suffering Baxter: She never wanted to see England again, she wrote grimly; she had done her best with Louis's friends and now the "foreigner" had her reward. Though tempted by poisons available in drugs she was taking, she felt obligated to live on for Louis. If she ever did return to "perfidious Albion," she would smile dutifully at his friends but secretly wish that her smiles were poisons to wither them slowly. In her bitter despair, she said, there might be a threat of insanity. . . . The poor woman was paying dear for her droopy little story. She was already too given to hypersuspicion and convictions of collective persecution, had far too little of Louis's salutary need to think as well as feel through the bruising tangle.[17]

Louis meant his protestations of still valuing Henley, so the relation was not cleanly cut, advisable though surgery might have been. The publication of Henley's collected verse brought a letter to Baxter from San Francisco, making Louis's position cordially if not precisely clear:

> I wish you would tell Henley how heartily I have enjoyed his verses. My wife and I were both rejoiced to see him at last do something worthy of himself. . . . I . . . am to quote one in an article. . . . It is easy to send a last word to you; but just in case of accident I wish to send one to W.E.H. also. These words will do "Auld Lang Syne" . . . I am going to have a job to enjoy myself; but I'll try.[18]

His inclusion of Fanny may not have been wholly nominal either. At least she was simultaneously writing Baxter an apology for her previous intemperate attitude, blaming it at least partly on anxiety over a possibly malignant growth in the throat, which had required an operation. In 1890 Louis sent Henley money via Baxter. Henley's new *Scots Observer*, backed by a group of Edinburgh Conservatives, including Baxter, began a series of "Modern Men" with a laudatory article on Louis by Andrew Lang. The paper also published the great hurricane chapter out of *A Footnote to History* and—with Louis making sure that Baxter considered it would not unduly imperil the publication—the libelous letter to Dr. Hyde, to be described later. A courteous message to Henley occasionally appeared in Louis's letters from the Pacific to common friends; sometimes there were even friendly notes from Samoa to 11 Howard Place about reviews read or books received.

But the old sores readily broke out. Henley's letters to others frequently show contemptuous little references to Louis. Louis had a fit of fury when Henley, moving to Edinburgh to take on the *Scots Observer*, failed to call on Mrs. Thomas Stevenson, who had temporarily returned to Edinburgh; and then relaxed enough to tell Baxter:

> I cannot describe the sense of relief and sorrow with which I feel I am done with him. No better company in God's earth and in some ways a fine fellow, a very fine one. But there has been too much hole-and-cornering and cliquing, and sweltering; and of late days, with all sorts of pleasant and affecting returns of friendship when we met, too much and a too visible jealousy of me. . . . Et puis après? So they both died and went out of the story, and I daresay young fellows short of a magazine article in the twentieth century (if our civilization endures) will expose the horrid R.L.S. and at last do justice to the missused W.E.H. For he is of that big, round, human, faulty stamp of man that makes lovers after death. I bet he has drunk more, and smoked more, and talked more sense, and quarrelled with more friends, than any of God's creatures.[19]

I submit that it is the measure of the relative stature of the pair that Henley could never conceivably have achieved such objectivity about the relationship.

Five months before his death, Louis reports to Baxter a letter from Henley ". . . which I thought in good taste and rather touching" but in which Fanny, with "that appalling instinct of the injured female to see mischief," saw possible prelude to a loan. Uncertain what to do should this prove correct, Louis writes: "He has had bad luck, of course; but then he has had good luck too and has never known how to behave under it.

. . ."; then decides that, if Henley should prove in drastic need, Baxter is to allow him five pounds a month at Louis's charges: "He can't starve at that; it's enough more than he had when I first knew him; and if I gave him more it would only lead to his starting a gig and a Pomeranian dog." [20] In 1901 the world was to hear more of that Pomeranian dog.

I do not know at just what juncture Louis pithily formulated the situation in one of the best of his *Fables*:

The Man and His Friend

A man quarreled with his friend.

"I have been much deceived in you," said the man.

And the friend made a face at him and went away.

A little later, they both died and came together before the great white Justice of the Peace. It began to look black for the friend, but the man for a while had a clear character and was getting in good spirits.

"I find here some record of a quarrel," said the Justice, looking in his notes. "Which of you was in the wrong?"

"He was," said the man. "He spoke ill of me behind my back."

"Did he so?" said the justice. "And pray how did he speak about your neighbours?"

"O, he always had a nasty tongue," said the man.

"And you chose him for your friend?" cried the justice. "My good fellow, we have no use here for fools."

So the man was cast into the pit, and the friend laughed out aloud in the dark and remained to be tried on other charges.

Henley did not achieve catharsis so readily. When he did, the process was a trifle too literal. Incomplete realization was probably his trouble. It is difficult to express something when one is unsure just what one wants to say about something one did not understand to begin with. By January 1891, he published verses:

> O, Time and Change they range and range
>   From sunshine round to thunder!
> They glance and go as the great winds blow
>   And the best of our dreams drive under:
> For Time and Change estrange, estrange—
>   And now they have looked and seen us,
> O, we that were dear, we are all-too-near
>   With the thick of the world between us. . . .[21]

So far, so good—"Time and chance happeneth to them all," and it is nobody's fault. But, as years passed, he never managed to look squarely at what had happened. This is clear in his strange comment when Louis's fragmentary *Weir of Hermiston* was posthumuously published: "I have my old Lewis back again!" The "old Lewis" whom Henley knew—if indeed he ever knew him—was not the sublimating creator who wrote *Hermiston*. He was older, nearer integration, farther than Henley from "the old Bristo' Port," farther than Samoa was from Kensington. But it pleased Henley to think that his boon companion and intellectual whetstone of the '70s was back, for, by definition, no other Louis had a right to be impressive.

Then, in 1901, Balfour published the official life of Louis, which the *Pall Mall Magazine* sent to Henley for review. Henley's biographer John Connell says that, though Henley took the assignment reluctantly, he flatly refused to tone his article down at the editor's request when it proved to be what even this thorough and sympathetic biographer of Henley calls "a brutal unguarded performance. . . . He wanted to savage Fanny . . . Parts of the essay were reckless; all of it was wilful. Parts were clever; its intention throughout was mercilessly cruel." [22] Even John Connell is puzzled, as all previous commentators were, by the scale of the bitterness shown. The difficulty was that neither he nor the others had the clue—lacking until all Louis's surviving letters to Baxter became available—the clue of the Pomeranian dog:

My view is that Henley read along in Balfour, snorting at omissions here, pricked by pangs of reminiscence there, until, far along in the second volume, he found a (slightly garbled) bit from a letter of Louis's to Baxter inserted as an example of Louis's generosity: "I hereby authorize you to pay when necessary £—— to Z——; if I gave him more, it would only lead to his starting a gig and a Pomeranian dog." [23] Balfour's text gives no hint of who Z—— was. I do not know how Balfour came to see this letter, nor yet how Henley knew, from merely reading the book, that he himself was Z——. Perhaps Louis had previously belabored him with Pomeranians and gigs as mutual private symbols of bourgeois extravagance. But that he did know is the only possible explanation for his cryptic fury over a reference that meant nothing to any less well-informed reader. He drags it panting into the review, saying, with quivering hate, that this attitude toward an object of solicitude ". . . scarce becomes the lips of a man who had several kennels of Pomeranians and gigs innumerable." [24] Fanny told Alice Meynell that Henley must have been drunk when he wrote this strange commentary that might well have been entitled *I and Stevenson*. Perhaps so, but not on alcohol; drunk with anger at the dead man who had spoken of him with such comradely contempt, he could not stop lashing galvanically at the body.

His convention of protest against Graham Balfour's reticences, which are not actually extreme for an official biography, was well handled at first: ". . . this Seraph in Chocolate, this barley-sugar effigy of a real man . . . is not my old, riotous, intrepid, scornful Stevenson at all." But presently he slips into a notable patronizing of the man who had helped to launch Henley, outstripped him in both prestige and popularity, and, most woundingly, tried to overlook encroaching disloyalties and presumptions:

At bottom Stevenson was an excellent fellow. But . . . incessantly and passionately interested in Stevenson. He could not be in the same room as a mirror but he must invite its confidence every time he passed; to him . . . the smallest of his discoveries, the most trivial of his apprehensions, were all by way of being revelations, and as revelations must be thrust upon the world; . . . his style is so perfectly achieved that the achievement gets obvious. . . ."

This is cool from the critic who praised *Otto* so lushly that even the author protested.

It was particularly abject to insist on spelling the name "Lewis" throughout cleverly—and falsely—so as to imply that, when Henley and his victim were first acquainted, it was written as well as pronounced so and that the French spelling was a later affectation. (Note that in Henley's letters at the time of the quarrel he himself then consistently spelled it "Louis.") It was worse to say

. . . if he wanted a thing, he went after it, with an entire contempt of consequences. For these, indeed, the Shorter Catechist was ever prepared to answer; so that, whether he did ill or well, he was sure to come out unabashed and cheerful. . . . where he was grossly interested, he could see but one side of the debate. . . . I learn of his nameless prodigalities—and recall some instances of conduct in another vein. . . .

None of this fits the young fellow who so agonizingly tried to understand his parents' attitude toward him, and the middle-aged man who spent weeks trying to concoct excuses for Henley's having accused his wife of plagiarism and private perjury. Until one sees the words on paper, it is hardly credible that Henley, speaking with the authority of a former intimate, should have been the only person who ever accused Louis of being stingy. . . . But then the "real Lewis" never came back from Monterey. Between the influence of the despised Fanny and the canting, vulgarizing influence of the States—about which Henley felt as bilious as Dickens—that lost *charmeur* who freely lent money with such casuistic selfishness had become a prig who prospered and wrote prayers and—being priggish— grew unworthily distressed when one of his best friends proved disloyal. "He set up a straw man," said Stuart Sherman of Henley, "bitterly complained that this straw man was what all the world except himself took for Stevenson and then he knocked the straw man down." [25] The only paragraph that does not induce some nausea in anybody with adequate knowledge of the relation is the last—where Henley, veteran of both privation and suffering, who knew much about courageous persistence in well-beloved work under handicaps, protested, as he had right to do, against canonizing Louis or any other man for writing "his best in the shadow of the Shade; for writing his best was very life to him." Then a curious climax, first impertinent, then exuding the last bile:

> Let this be said of him, once for all: "He was a good man, good at many things, and now this also he has attained to, to be at rest." That covers Sophocles and Shakespeare, Marlborough and Bonaparte. Let it serve for Stevenson; and for ourselves, let us live and die uninsulted, as we lived and died before his books began to sell and his personality was a marketable thing.[26]

There is the final shudder of relief as the soul finally empties. Henley wrote it when ageing and ill, not far from death himself. He had some reason, in spite of Sherman, to feel "insulted" by the already booming cult of R.L.S. as archangelic model for romantic but docile youth. The casuist who tries going beyond that, however, in excusing the "dear lad" for the rest of this review, has his work most colossally cut out for him. "To have a friend like Mr. Henley," wrote Frank Moore Colby in comment, "must add greatly to the terrors of the grave." [27]

The thing naturally raised a storm. Barrie advised Colvin not to reply and Colvin did not. Henley eventually convinced Walter Raleigh that he had been long-suffering with Louis and that his outburst was justified. But Lang languidly flayed him in the *Morning Post*,[28] and an anonymous hand in the *Saturday Review* took the whip to him with a vigor that may almost have penetrated his self-righteousness.[29]

The sad thing is that, had it not been for the Pomeranian dog, Henley might have managed to let his record of the "real Lewis" stand at its best—not inaccurate and by no means abjectly worshipping—in his portrait of the youth who stood by him so handsomely in the old Infirmary:

> Thin-legged, thin-chested, slight unspeakably,
>   Neat-footed and weak-fingered; in his face—
>   Lean, large-boned, curved of beak, and touched with race,
> Bold-lipped, rich-tinted, mutable as the sea,
> The brown eyes radiant with vivacity—
>   There shines a brilliant and romantic grace,
>   A spirit intense and rare, with trace on trace
> Of passion, impudence and energy.
> Valiant in velvet, light in ragged luck,
>   Most vain, most generous, sternly critical,
>   Buffoon and poet, lover and sensualist;
> A deal of Ariel, just a streak of Puck,
>   Much Antony, of Hamlet most of all,
>   And something of the Shorter-Catechist.[30]

The Place of the Name

The Isles of Voices

> . . . years sit upon me; it begins to seem to me to be a
> man's business to leave off his damnable faces and say
> his say.
>
> —Stevenson to Burlingame,
> *Letters:* III, 318

THOSE were the emotions bubbling under the scrawny
man who, because the cottage was full of colds, broke
up the Saranac establishment in late April and fled to New
York with his mother and Lloyd to await word from Fanny.
Plans had already been made to leave before the black-fly season, perhaps to return in summer for a camping trip, in the
event that yachts remained scarce. This was probably the period
during which young Edward Bok, then an understrapper at
Scribner's, visited Louis with proofs and reported him:

> . . . not a prepossessing figure . . . With his sallow skin and
> his black dishevelled hair, with finger-nails which had been
> allowed to grow very long, with fingers discolored by tobacco
> . . . a general untidiness which was all his own . . . an
> author whom it was better to read than to see . . . yet his
> kindliness and gentleness more than offset the unattractiveness
> of his personal appearance.[1]

It was certainly now that Louis managed an afternoon with
Mark Twain on a sunshiny bench in Washington Square, talking shop; the two corresponded sporadically during Louis's remaining years. Mark Twain recalled the ingenious gaiety of his
style, the effect as if there were no flesh on him between bones
and clothes, and—as usual—his extraordinary eyes.
When the thrifty Hotel St. Stephen proved too dismal for pro-

longed habitation, Louis asked Will Low to find him a place with
easier amenities. Low sent him to a boarding-hotel down the
Jersey shore at Manasquan as preseason guest. There Louis and
Lloyd were frequently visited by Low, Wyatt Eaton (an old
friend from Barbizon), and St. Gaudens, now working on casts
of Louis's hands. Henley's target seems to have shown few signs
of his inner misery; Bok had found him given to irresponsible
japes; at the shore he was eagerly sailing in a catboat and pleased
when he found that this insignificant craft could force a railroad train to wait while a bridge was opened for her passage. But
his nights were still sleepless and he had the additional burden
of finishing off the *Scribner's* dozen.

Just when it was most needed, came a joyful telegram from
Fanny in San Francisco: she had secured the *Casco*, a Coast-
owned schooner-yacht. Louis had already instructed Baxter to
get £2000 ready to finance the projected voyage, McClure's succeeding payments to replace the capital—a project that was duly
forwarded, though it can hardly have commended itself to Baxter's business judgment. On May 31, 1888, Louis, Aunt Maggie,
Lloyd, and Valentine left New York for California, making the
trip not too uncomfortably in Pullman cars. By June 6 Louis
was assuring a San Francisco reporter that "Jekyll" was pronounced with a long *e*. Another learned that he had not been
inside a theater since seeing *The Pirates of Penzance* in San
Francisco in 1880, that he heartily approved of international
copyright, and that San Francisco was ". . . the only city
which interests me in the whole United States." [2] He might
have added, but did not, that it was also the only one of which
he had much personal knowledge.

Fanny's telegram had overstated. The wealthy physician
named Merritt whose pride and joy the *Casco* was had qualms
about chartering her to a probably irresponsible literary man.
The deal was still contingent on his seeing and approving of
Louis and the rest of the party and on his being allowed to name
the sailing-master. Neither Louis's appearance nor his manner

was theoretically likely to convince a man already suspecting that authors were mostly feckless cranks.

Superstition makes great play with the gravitational pull of places on dedicated persons—the appointment at Samarra, the doom of "the place of the name" still strike down into the spinal marrow. Being a Scot, Louis had some—being a woman forbid with a hankering after the occult, Fanny had much—tolerance for the force which, though doubtless it does not exist, is identified as fate or destiny. When, after eighteen months of apparently aimless movements, the rolling stone at last deliberately determined to gather moss in Samoa, Louis wrote to Mrs. Fairchild:

> . . . now in 1890, I (or what is left of me) go at last to the Navigator Islands. God go with us! It is but a Pisgah sight when all is said: I go there only to grow old and die; but when you come, you will see it is a fair place for the purpose.[3]

As he already saw it, though he had so far been played on a long line, something or other was at last subtly bringing him up to the boat. It is his point, not mine; I do not insist on it. No doubt the series of arbitrary events that culminated in settling him in Samoa points toward unconscious choice stemming from a preconceived idea.

The idea was certainly of long standing. In late childhood Louis had met R. M. Ballantyne, author of boys' books seeking authentic background on lighthouse-keeping, whose healthy good nature and rich black beard parting on fine white teeth first moved the boy to be an author. He had already read and admired some of this personable hero's works; conspicuous among them, hence among the impressions made, was *The Coral Island*, a sort of *Swiss Family Robinson* involving only boys, laid on a South Sea island apparently near Fiji.[4] Doubtless Louis would soon have learned elsewhere to include the South Seas in his atlas of places reeking with picturesque adventure, along with the Malabar Coast, the America of Cooper's Indians, and the Great North Road of highwaymen and mail-guards' bugles. But early hero-worship of the author of this first principal document in the case certainly increased the emphasis.

In 1875, shortly before Louis's examinations for the bar, 17 Heriot Row saw another fateful visitor: a pleasant New Zealand government official named J. Seed. Louis's health came under discussion; Seed, a man of enthusiasms, kept the boy up till four in the morning exhorting him to leave at once for the South Seas, specifically Samoa, which he considered ideal for respiratory ailments:

> . . . told me that I had no business to stay in Europe; that I should find all I cared for and all that was good for me in the Navigator Islands. . . . beautiful places, green forever; perfect shapes of men and women, with red flowers in their hair; and nothing to do but study oratory and etiquette, sit in the sun, and pick up the fruits as they fall. Navigator's Island is the place; absolute balm for the weary. . . .[5]

Louis said that it sounded too far from friends and family. But the reference stuck: though Samoa was no such part of general European consciousness as Fiji (the traditional Cannibal Islands), it was probably Louis who nominated Samoa as setting for "The Hair Trunk," a mock account of an ideal commonwealth of Cambridge undergraduates on which he and cronies were to collaborate.[6]

In San Francisco in 1880 these stirrings revived when Louis saw Kanaka sailors in water-front bars and the rakish schooners that served San Francisco merchants trading to the South Seas. From the talk of barrooms

> . . . there began to piece itself together in my head some image of the islands and the island life; precipitous shores, spired mountain tops, the deep shade of hanging forests, the unresting surf upon the reef, and the unending peace of the la-

goon; sun, moon, and stars of an imperial brightness; man moving in these scenes scarce fallen, and women lovelier than Eve;
the primal curse abrogated, the bed made ready for the
stranger, and the guest welcomed, the boat urged, and the
long night beguiled with poetry and choral song.[7]

Here also he met Charles Warren Stoddard, plump, smiling
minor poet, highly sugared romantic and old Islands-hand, author of *Summer Cruising in the South Seas*, a collection of
swooning prose sketches already eminent in the South Seas legend.[8] Stoddard had Hawaii, Tahiti, the Tuamotu at his tongue's
end, Polynesian baskets, weapons and *tapa* on his walls, and
Melville on his shelves, and would have been quite at home at
Barbizon. Louis and he hit it off at once; soon Louis was giving
him literary advice in return for further infection with the
South Seas idea.

Now, eight years later, finding the long-sought yacht in the
Pacific finally pointed squarely at "the Islands." Atlantic craft
had been inexplicably scarce. Dr. Merritt's ship—schooner-yacht
ninety-four feet over-all, draft aft twelve feet, fitted out with all
the carved, tasseled, and mirrored luxury that the late Victorian
decorator could crowd in—was already in commission and had
recently made two short shake-down cruises; the doctor was not
at all sure that he wanted to use her himself that season. . . .
But, as aforesaid, he was chary of charter to an author, and Captain A. H. Otis, whom the doctor considered essential to any
deal, disliked what he called "fashionable yacht-sailing" and was
inclined to look for another berth.

Louis's charm carried the day with Merritt: "Why, Captain,"
he told Otis, "Mr. Stevenson seems quite as sensible a man as
you or I." [9] Aunt Maggie, the idea of whom had caused the
owner uneasiness, was also inspected and approved. The bargain—$500 a month, all repairs during voyage at Louis's ex-
pense, right to name sailing-master reserved—still hung on Otis's
willingness to sail. Fortunately, little though he liked such a
cruise in general, Otis had once had a look at the Islands and

never lost a twitching urge to go back that way. Interviewing Louis, he thus managed to persuade himself that this pigeon-breasted pen-pusher at least would not bore him with hifalutin literary talk during the voyage; and found that his wish to re-visit Polynesia could even overcome his understandable reluctance to have on board three women, one an old lady. No doubt considerably to his own wonder, he said Yes.

The *Casco* fitted out in Oakland Creek. Part of the interval Louis spent nursing a cold in the Occidental Hotel. One of his callers here was William Churchill, former U.S. consul in Samoa, whom he asked about possible places to settle in the South Seas, supposing J. Seed were right and the climate suited him. Churchill described a small plateau up the mountain behind Apia on the principal Samoan island of Upolu, reached by a steep path, watered by several streams, with a view straight north to the Aleutians if the earth were flat, overlooked by the conical bulk of a volcanic peak called Vaea. . . .

Belle Strong was temporarily in San Francisco, fresh from hobnobbing with Polynesian royalty in Honolulu. At her instance Fanny and Aunt Maggie had themselves made a wardrobe of *holoku* and *mumu*—the voluminous "Mother Hubbard" dress and under-dress that the missionaries had imposed on South Seas native women wherever possible. Belle's theory was that these very loose gowns, waistless, hanging straight from a yoked top, were cooler; and since they made corsets unnecessary, no doubt they were. By the same token they carried a flavor of the emancipated woman; for several years newspapers had been jeering at the Mother Hubbard gown as daringly free. The rest of her life Fanny wore *holoku*-like dresses most of the time. She had long been cutting her hair into a loose crop. Uncorseted, smoking incessantly, short-haired, she made a strange figure in the late 1880s and the following decades as well.

The Galápagos and Guayaquil, prominent in scheming done at Saranac, did not fit into practical navigation. The first leg of the voyage was finally determined as a run south-southwest to the Marquesas, easternmost outpost of the South Seas proper. After some nasty hazards, the ship came back to her doting owner. But Louis was not going anywhere outside the South Seas sphere of influence, try as he might, not ever again. Five thousand miles from the Golden Gate, Mt. Vaea was waiting for him. The underbrush that his grave-diggers would uproot was already growing lush and rank. Just as the Cameron was drawn to Ticonderoga to dree his weird, so Louis came at last to the Navigator Islands, Samoa, "the place of the name."

In further omen, Otis was so dubious of his bag-of-bones author's health that, before sailing, he secretly made sure that the ship carried everything necessary for proper burial at sea.

The actual departure was anticlimactic—successive anchorages down the Bay, successive farewell visits of friends, reporters, and so forth. But finally, early on the morning of June 28, 1888, the tug *Pelican* towed the laboring *Casco* outside the Golden Gate and cast her off to make the best of her way to the Islands of the Blest. There was a heavy swell; that first morning Aunt Maggie could not face smoked herring and mutton chops for breakfast; even Otis missed a couple of meals before his sea-legs returned; most of the first three days Fanny and Valentine were in their bunks. But the ship liked the weather, logging 256 miles the first twenty-four hours, a performance that some steamers of her time would have envied.

Being the original of Nares in *The Wrecker*, Otis was a slashing seaman. Doubtless he was gratified by the following nine days of favorable winds. He needed encouragement. He had sailed shorthanded; worse, he was the only soul on board fit to steer in really dirty weather, which meant that crew, passengers, and—by no means least affecting—the beautiful *Casco* would be practically derelict if he were washed overboard or dropped dead in one of his spells of black anger. But he had unlimited trust in the ship, in contrast with Louis, who considered her "over-rigged and over-sparred, and like many American yachts on a very dangerous sail-plan." [10] (Later Otis indignantly denied Balfour's statement that, built for racing, the *Casco* was unsuited for such a cruise; on the contrary, he averred, her fine sailing qualities had several times extricated the Stevensons, all unaware, from considerable dangers.) But all agreed that she was "a lovely creature; the most beautiful thing at this moment in Tahiti." [11]

For some weeks the beauty of the ship was about all that Otis and his charges saw eye to eye on. To be fair, his prejudice against this mixed lot of Jonahs and potential sea-lawyers proved not altogether unjustified. Fanny defied discipline by chatting with the man at the wheel; when, however, Otis risked verbal mayhem by trying sarcasm—"Please don't talk to him today, Mrs. Stevenson. Today I want him to steer," [12]—she seems to have knuckled under with uncharacteristic meekness. None of the women took seriously his orders to keep deadlights dogged down—until a sudden squall heeled the ship over and flooded hundreds of gallons of the Pacific into the snug cabin. Even serene Aunt Maggie annoyed the captain by insisting on grace at the table and by trying to discuss Louis's writings with him. He told her rudely that he had read only *Treasure Island* and— doubtless put off by its seamanship, which Louis readily admitted was "jimmy"—saw small reason to try another. When Fanny teasingly asked what he would do if Aunt Maggie fell overboard, he answered more gruffly than politely: "Put it in the log." [13]

Yet, as noon observation followed noon observation and the North Star sank lower and the water grew bluer and the breeze blander, these females ridiculous enough to come on such a voyage proved curiously tolerable. In small or in large emergencies —and the voyage supplied both—there was not a scream nor a fainting-fit among them. Aunt Maggie was not only a good sailor but a formidable whist-player commanding Otis's respect. Though half-seasick much of the time—20,000 miles of the Pacific in small vessels never cured her—Fanny pluckily stayed in harness, gave the cook badly needed supervision, doctored the hands' lacerated fingers and torn clothes. Louis, who, of course, had had some experience in seagoing yachts, knew better how to stay out of the way than Otis had dared hope. It must have been long before the captain could look round the cabin table at Aunt Maggie, calm and tidily starched; Fanny, gamely queasy and broodily solid; Valentine, wholesome and charming but as anomalous at sea as a Shetland pony; Lloyd, his new British accent as prim as his gold pince-nez—and not feel like the little old woman who wondered deary-oh-me can this really be I? But time worked its wonders, both ways.

At first his passengers liked nothing about Otis but his obvious sense of duty to and love for the ship. They thought him a martinet and much of a brute; Louis wrote home:

> We have had an awfae time in some ways, Mr. Baxter; and if I wasnae sic a verra patient man (when I ken that I *have* to be) there wad hae been a braw row, and ance if I hadnae happened to be on deck about three in the marnin', I think there would have been *murder* done. The American Mairchant Marine is a kent service; ye'll have heard its praises, I'm thinkin'; . . . [14]

In the Marquesas, however, Otis shipped a mate, which enabled him somewhat to modify his savaging of the hands. And somehow, for all their disparate ideas, backgrounds, and histories, mutual respect came to reign round the cabin table. The Stevensons had tamed their man.

Louis had sailed feeling that the trip was "too good to be true," but also aware that the black dog Henley had set on his back might spoil all. A surviving rough draft of verse says:

> Farewell, and when forth
> I through the Golden Gate to Golden Isles
> Steer without smiling, through the sea of smiles, . . .
> Why should I sail? . . .
> I have been young and I have counted friends.
> A hopeless sail I spread, too late, too late . . .[15]

The black dog was snatched away down the following wind that the *Casco* picked up off the Farallones. Louis took the first two legs of the cruise like a man drinking his way through a case of his favorite wine with a guarantee that each fresh bottle will excel the last. Blow high, blow low, this was being at sea on the most gorgeous and formidable of oceans. He stripped down to singlet and trousers, went barefoot (as indeed all did but Aunt Maggie, who left off stockings), turned roast-brown with high color glowing through; ate, drank, and exulted.

The North Atlantic had taught him "I am never well but at sea." But that considerable ocean as he knew it lacks the clouds strung along the horizon like mile-high ranks of pompous cherubim; the streaming trade wind, bland and firm; the nights when every star in the cosmos joins the conspiracy to make the Southern Cross look puny; the Titanically dignified swell beneath the ship as, under Otis's driving, she dipped her lee-rail toward her own shadow and fled into ever-warmer waters. It had been fifteen years since Louis had known the intimacy with the sea that no steamer with any freeboard can give. Loudon Dodd's feelings as the *Norah Creina* neared Midway Island are much less applicable to the colder waters in question than to the way Louis felt as the *Casco* made her southing:

> Day after day in the sun-gilded cabin, the whisky-dealer's thermometer stood at 84°. Day after day, the air had the same indescribable liveliness and sweetness, soft and nimble, and cool as the cheek of health. Day after day, the sun flamed; night after night, the moon beaconed, or the stars paraded their lustrous regiment. I was aware of a spiritual change, or perhaps of a molecular reconstruction. My bones were sweeter to me. I had come to my own climate, and looked back with pity on those damp and wintry zones, miscalled the temperate. . . . The blank sea itself grew desirable under such skies; and wherever the trade-wind blows, I know no better country than a schooner's deck.[16]

This was the honeymoon of the love affair with the Pacific that had begun when he saw the spindrift smoking beyond the lighthouse at Monterey. She soon forced a confession that her charm implied dread; that she could bruise and bully and weary the little forked creatures who courted her from the hollow of her broad hand:

> . . . yet the sea is a terrible place, stupefying to the mind and poisonous to the temper. . . . the motion, the lack of space, the villainous tinned foods, . . . I cannot say why I like the sea; no man is more cynically and constantly alive to its perils; I regard it as the highest form of gambling; and yet I love the sea as much as I hate gambling.[17]

There is a touch of the young Louis who, as Colvin saw with wonder when they two were in a runaway cab, got principally exultant joy from the experience.

Whatever lay behind this fascination, it was now altogether salutary. Henley became merely a thing to wince at when it crossed the mind, not an obsession so heavy that " . . . even when I don't think of it, [I] start up to wonder what load is at my heart." [18]

In the Pacific, islands are the merest flaws in the great spread of waters. Even those larger bear to the whole ocean the proportion of a small pea to a billiard table. But it was islands that the ship sought. Thirty days out Otis brought Nukahiva, in the Marquesas, up over the horizon well enough before sunrise to lay the most magical light on Louis's ". . . first South Sea Island . . . touching a virginity of sense." [19] His account of that landfall carries all the hush and wonder.

Wonder at such a sight was always spontaneous among far less acute and self-conscious observers. Explorers, whalers, missionaries all felt, and recorded as best they could what, through lack of previous preparation, may have hit Louis specially hard: He had been here and he had been there, but never before had he seen the high deep tropics. The Riviera is brilliant, not rich, semi-arid like the California that had made Louis's other approach to the kingdoms of the sun. Both present bold coasts and queer vegetation; but both are continental, whereas the compact

South Seas "high island" is implausibly isolated. The chart asserts it is there, you know people who have been there, to persist in incredulity would mean shipwreck; yet it is still difficult to believe in this discrete, majestic audacity. Besides, the thing is so patently a miniature world to itself, lushly innocent. The words that come to mind always imply untouchedness.

There is extra savor, as Louis already knew from books, in the fact that neither youth nor innocence has much to do with these islands, least of all the Marquesas.[20] It requires immense age to produce this boldness of profile and luxuriance of detail—beauty consequent on thrusting a well-composed cluster of volcanoes up from the sea bottom and then allowing rain and wind to attack them for millions of years. The more prolonged the weathering, the richer the soil into which volcanic detritus decomposes. Tropical temperatures, copious rain on the windward slopes, seeds brought by birds or men, end in an obscene welter of intercompeting vines, shrubs, and herbs.

Sailing directories and Melville's *Typee*—which he pronounced "a howling cheese"—had led Louis to expect corresponding savagery in the inhabitants. He had chosen the Marquesas as prelude because of the natives' reputation as "the most beastly population in the South Seas." [21] From whites' point of view they had recently deserved the epithet. Unlike most of their cousins, they were eager cannibals and had supplemented the usual Polynesian premarital sexual relations with a lively system of polyandry and a taste for intercourse with girl children long before puberty. Only recently had French efforts to tame them established a miniature and apathetic colonial government, the principal result of which was to infect them with lethal lackadaisicalness. This was a pity: rowdy though they had been, the Marquesans were still notable among Islanders for beauty of person and, in their day, had made perhaps the loveliest Polynesian artifacts.

In one tragic aspect, however, they were indistinctive: Neither skill nor occasional pugnacity had saved them from the general extinction then creeping over the Island peoples.[22] Wher-

ever courteous Marquesans took Louis, the great stone platforms on which houses had once stood were gradually drowning in jungle as death made further headway against life. He
was as ready to pity and reprehend this people's obvious destiny
as, on superficial acquaintance, he had been in the case of the
mission Indians of Monterey. As acquaintance grew less superficial, his sympathy beat up like an excited pulse. He had an excellent head; but his heart was always the elder brother.

The anchor was barely down when much of the dwindling
native population of Anaho—local port of entry, scattering of
shabby trading stores—swarmed on board. Their size, dark skins,
darker looks, and assumption of perfect right to make themselves
at home somewhat daunted the Stevensons, who knew several
true stories of ships "cut out" by natives. A great lowering
Marquesan openly sneered at them for their lack of interest in
fruit and baskets brought off for sale. But the self-possession of
the white party and the luxury of the vessel—one woman visitor
pulled up her *holoku* and ecstatically rubbed her bare behind-
side on the velvet cushions in the cabin—soon secured them respectful treatment. This was no cockroach-lively trading
schooner with a foul-mouthed skipper and a slippery supercargo
accustomed to swindling "Kanakas" [23] while keeping them in
their places; instead a shining wonder-ship, her owner wealthy
enough to travel for his own stately pleasure appropriately
attended by women of assorted ages and complexions plus an imposing son with glittering spectacles—and marvelously strange
devices. Lloyd's camera was no novelty to them, but the typewriter, on which a certain chief who knew the alphabet delighted
to punch out his own and others' names with his great, plump,
brown fingers, was unprecedented. Though, even with all good
will, the Stevensons could not avoid occasional blunders in Marquesan etiquette, their status was henceforth that of very high-
ranking chiefs indeed, entitled to every courtesy ashore.

In token of this the natives applied to Louis the name "Ona,"
which would also be used in Tahiti and Samoa. This is the Polynesian transmutation of "owner" (of the vessel), signifying

great wealth and high power, for it had long been evident that the owner could order around even so high a chief as Polynesians early assumed the sea-captain to be. It was roughly "The Rich Man." Another token was the readiness with which Paaeua, chief of Atuona, two miles down the shore, and his family "exchanged names" with the party. In Polynesian terms this act formally recognizes a stranger's standing. In theory thenceforward Louis's name was Paaeua, and Paaeua's new name was pronounced as close as he could come to "Louis."

That Louis as yet understood the nature of this acceptance is doubtful. But it was probably all the readier for such minor tactical advantages as his excellent French, which enabled him to be articulately courteous to both the better-educated natives and the shore authorities; his sympathy for underdogs; his naturally demonstrative good manners. The major factor, however, must have been the ship, representing wealth uncountable. To the Islander, other things being equal, great possessions naturally adhere to those whose great rank exacts special favors from the gods. Gilt mirrors; elaborately cushioned cockpit; lazarette full of such delicacies as salt beef, ship's biscuit, and sugar—Louis could have ridden fairly rough-shod and still have been solicitously cherished.

As it was, displaying dignity and courtesy (white style), the party were in a position to learn much. Louis explored the "club," where the few polyglot local whites drank all they could pay for of what the last schooner had left; the French governor, who acquainted him with the local penal system of letting convicts go home visiting at will; the Catholic missionaries, cheerfully serious about sweeping back the sea of native apathy and incomprehension. Best of all, on Hiva-Oa, the next island, he found "Prince" Stanislas Moanatini,[24] European-educated high chief, who did his cultivated best to bridge the gap between Louis and the Marquesas of former fact. They visited the disused ritual amphitheater, stone-paved and -seated, where (before nominal Christianity backed by guns had interfered) drums had boomed, dancers writhed, and dead man after dead man had been fetched in, cooked, and eaten; they called on the former "queen," now passively and most genteelly pious, tattooing showing only on the hands protruding from her Mother Hubbard—whereas, in her day, her deliriously tattooed legs had been the sight of the Marquesas; they entered the shady, ominously breathless coves where, not many generations before, life had so teemed that, even in these isles of plenty, famine always impended. Everywhere Moanatini told Louis the shapeless, sly legends attached to this headland, that house-platform, the obscenely shaped rock up the valley—in Parisian French but with the authenticity of a narrator whose emotions steer the translation. Thus Louis entered the Island world keenly aware of the immediacy and the tragedy of the native, and firmly convinced that higher-ranking Polynesians were great gentlemen.

Knowing this was luck, he fed his senses and synthetic faculties fat on it:

I . . . will tell you more of the South Seas after very few months than any other writer has done except Herman Melville. . . . I did not dream there were such places or such races. My health has stood me splendidly; I am in for hours wading over the knees for shells; I have been five hours on horseback; . . . This climate; these voyagings; these landfalls at dawn; new islands peaking from the morning bank; new forested harbours; new passing alarms of squalls and surf— the whole tale of my life is better to me than any poem.[25]

Every day he spent himself looking, asking, listening, noting, noting in a rough, nervous journal. When he woke at night in the cockpit of the yacht—he slept in the open whenever weather permitted—the lap of the water and the tiny, hesitating motion of the anchored ship making the loom of the island skyline shift unstably, reeked with the savor of limpid living. ". . . It is such a relief to him," Aunt Maggie noted, "to find he can keep so well in so enjoyable a climate, as he feared he might be condemned to places like Davos or Saranac." [26]

In the Marquesas the ship lost her ambiguously Oriental cook, who had fed the crew on cabin supplies and, once ashore, turned into an earnestly uncontrollable drunk; he remained behind in irons in the local calaboose. In his berth shipped a large and robust Chinese named Ah Fu whose history and personality recommended him to the Stevensons, and illustrate an odd angle of the South Seas:

As a child he had come to the Marquesas among coolies imported to work cotton plantations set up there when the American Civil War cut off the world's main cotton supply. Island cotton disappeared with the emergency, but many Chinese stayed, mostly failing to assimilate. Young Ah Fu, however, was almost as Marquesan as Chinese—outgoing, brawny, and bone-loyal, he stayed with the party during this cruise and the next, finally leaving for China with a beltful of gold to astound his family with the good fortune of this son of their ancestors. He was blandly adaptable enough to learn what his employers considered to be good cooking. But his vocabulary, crossing that of the beachcomber with Far Eastern pidgin, remained incorrigible.

Otis's new mate was a garrulous Pole reputed to be skilled in the treacherous waters of the Tuamotu between the Marquesas and Tahiti, parts of which exasperated explorers long ago had designated as the Pernicious Islands, the Dangerous Archipelago. This complex of great and small atolls—strange, friable loops of low-lying coral, practically awash, utterly unlighted—is in itself a great menace to navigation. Add strong and capricious currents to confuse dead reckoning; inaccurate charts; the relative helplessness on a lee shore of a vessel without auxiliary— and Otis's desire for a lieutenant personally acquainted with this ships' graveyard is understandable. But the Tuamotu can outguess any navigator. One chilly dawn the *Casco* found herself coming up hand over hand on a large atoll which, when identified, should have been thirty miles away. It was quite as nasty a moment as that in the Marquesas when moorings failed and it was touch and go whether the ship would answer her helm before she bilged on rocks dead ahead. Once again, however,

Otis won his game and, five days out from the Marquesas, she slid into the huge lagoon of Fakarava atoll. Picking her way among the coral "horseheads" with which such serene sheets of water abound, she anchored off the tiny settlement that was administrative center of all the Tuamotu.

Most of the inhabitants were away confirming family land-titles on other atolls. But Louis found enough stay-at-homes, official and otherwise—a half-Tahitian, half-French official named Donat was particularly charming and obliging—to learn something of the twists of Island religious life: The local native catechist, for instance, as devout as any Catholic mission could envision, was nevertheless a transported convict, respected in spite of his past. The local cult of spiritualists employed spirits who whistled, not rapped. A curious sect competing with Catholicism claimed nominal standing as Mormons, though Louis and Fanny could discern small resemblance to the institutions of Joe Smith and Brigham Young. . . .

All of it was dwarfed by the wonder of living on an atoll. The isolated culmination of a "high island" is unlikely enough. The mere existence of an atoll is so fantastic that it is obviously a stage trick; that it should be inhabited is simply incredible. In "The Isles of Voices" Louis would cleverly use the high-islander's amazement at an atoll to make it seem an emotionally appropriate destination for an Hawaiian version of the magic carpet.

In a state of nature it is all sand, sun, and scrub. Where men have been, it probably has coco-palms, as have most South Sea beaches. But the peculiarity of this outrageous setting is to be all beach—not a key buffering a continent nor a sand bar heralding a river, but an independent ring of coral detritus, continuous or broken into elongated islets, too low in profile to offer the security implied in the word "land"; too sterile to nourish much but pandanus and coconut; too dry to afford any but brackish water to which atoll-dwellers must specially adjust. Yet scores or hundreds of brown people have lived there for centuries.

Their opinion of their environment is pointless; few of them know anything else. The outsider with a wider set of references may gape at it for weeks. The sea beach is jagged with blocks of broken coral and thunderous with surf; the native, who knows war when he sees it, fears and avoids this battleground between the smashingly aggressive ocean and a stubborn barrier of precipitated calcium. The inside beach, margin of the lagoon—a shallow salt-water pond—offers lapping ripples and astonishing sunsets, supports bright fish and tolerates canoes gracefully, though its coral growths readily rip the bottom out of heedless vessels drawing any water to mention. A mere five minutes' walk in the slatted shade of coco-palms will take one from this stagnant peace to the hurly-burly of the outer beach.

Under a tropical moon it is easy to forgive such a setting its swarms of insects and its smell as of drying plaster. Louis needed no moon, being still the lone small boy on

> . . . a little eyot of dense, fresh-water sand . . . delighting to hear the song of the river on both sides, and to tell myself that I was indeed and at last upon an island.[27]

On Fakarava he was so indeed and indeed. The queerness of the lost, unlikely place was enhanced by its tingle of decay and corruption. This suspicion came into shuddering focus a year later when, on an atoll in the Ellices, Louis inquisitively broke off a jag of weathered coral and found it hanging full, like macaroni, of long, thick, blind, whitish worms.

The Fakaravans soon returned to their homes. But the opportunity to learn more about them and their taste in evil spirits —which ran to putrefying corpses flying through the air in broad daylight—was cut short by Louis's first menacing illness since Newport. Defiantly he wrote home that, thanks to the great strides his health had made in the Island climate, he would weather this cold without going to bed. It promptly took such hold that Fanny demanded a doctor. Finding that the nearest was in Tahiti, several days' sail southwestward, she bundled Louis on board and ordered Otis to make sail at once. He glanced at the weather, which was thundery, and refused. The modern schooner, with auxiliary, might have risked it, but the gusty flaws of wind that go with thunder could easily have swung the *Casco*, under sail alone, on a horsehead, marooning the party, sick man and all, for weeks. Fanny and the weather thundered and lightened together, but the ship did not sail until next morning, in propitiously flawless sun.

By the time they made Papeete, chief town of Tahiti, Louis was very low. Another hemorrhage before night, said the local French doctor. . . . Louis sent for Otis and gave exact orders about ship and charter in case he died, smoking a cigarette and speaking low and to the point. This lean romantic's lack of self-concern was so unaffected that it killed the skipper's last vestige of prejudice against the cruise. Come to summons, he was briefed and dismissed as if it had been a matter of deciding on the next port. True, Louis had had some experience in facing imminent death. But this did not altogether account for a courage so ready that it did not even bother to be grim.

The fatal hemorrhage did not appear, and what passed for a hotel in Tahiti was less commodious and noisier than the ship. Louis and Fanny moved into "a little bare one-twentieth-furnished house . . . with grated verandas" [28] near the site of the old calaboose where, forty years before, the French had jailed Melville and his co-mutineers. As Louis gained, then lost ground, Fanny and he developed as poor an opinion of the salubrity of Papeete as they already had of its social and political quality. This small capital of France's eastern Pacific possessions was a slack and corruptly depressing hole either to live or to die in. Louis and Lloyd significantly chose it as proper background for the semicriminal beachcombers of *The Ebb-Tide*. To leave would deprive Louis of doctors in further crises; but, in view of the known local medical faculty, this would be small loss. It would also check dispersal of the ship's crew: the new mate had already been turned off for excessive drunkenness, and three hands shed, two as drunks, one ill. The replacements were no nature's noblemen, but at least departure would force them to sobriety.

Much lovely country lay alongshore in both directions; few have ever been disappointed in the physical charms of this fig-ure-8 of an island sweeping up from the sea as graciously as the train of an Edwardian ball gown, classic since Bougainville's time as *locus* of the earthly paradise. According to the half-white Tahitian aristocrats whom Louis met in the intervals of illness, the smaller loop of the 8 was specially handsome, though its people were "almost as wild as the people of Anaho." [29] In view of how much the *Cascos* had liked Anaho, that settled it. They crawled back on board and, duly furnished with credentials to the local chiefs of Tahiti-iki, sailed for the far end of nowhere.

Taravao, where they first touched, was dull and full of insects. Exploring for likelier spots, Louis and Otis found only a dour Chinese who owned a wagon and horses but would not hire them to strangers. Fanny, accompanied by Valentine, disap-peared in the direction of the Chinese's shack and, after hours of representations in heaven knows what language, returned as-sured of unlimited use of horse and wagon on demand. Next day the party trundled off seeking "the largest native village and the most wild" [30]—characteristic specifications.

That took them to a principal village called Tautira, about as far from Papeete as one can get and stay on Tahiti. The long, jolting drive to this story-book village of "bird-cage" houses and clean lawns under coco-palms left Louis in very bad shape. But he had fallen softly. After some embarrassments, those introduc-tions from the great folks of Papeete brought them to the notice of "Princess" Moë, a high chiefess who prided herself on hos-pitality to whites of standing. At her behest the *Cascos* were cherished by Teriitera, local subchief (under his political name of Ori à Ori), who lent them most of his European-style house. Moë personally prepared for Louis a great South Seas dainty, raw fish in *miti* sauce,[31] an innovation that brilliantly roused the sick man's critically dwindled appetite. From the moment she fetched it, he began to mend. She might almost have claimed magical powers for her raw fish—it does taste essentially of the environment that had been so good for this scrawny stranger. From now on he lived in light flannels, swam in the lagoon, picked up weight and zest, proudly wrote home that, at feasts, he had applied four times for pork. Never again, so long as he stayed between the tropics of Cancer and Capricorn, would he sink so near the old sinister weakness.

The *Casco's* coming round to anchor in the lagoon mightily reënforced the party's standing. The name by which Teriitera introduced Louis at a feast in his honor was again simply "Ona." Wines and foodstuffs landed from the ship were noted with awe. When, with direct good breeding, Teriitera asked the price of the ship's champagne—first he had ever drunk—and was told, he said with simple gusto that such costly stuff was suited only for very great chiefs indeed and abandoned the notion of ordering some from Papeete.

For all the gaudy glories of the ship's cabin, however, the Rich One preferred to live ashore in a welter of precisely what he had come so far to feel:

> . . . here I was at last;
> Here found all I had forecast:
> The long roll of the sapphire sea
> That keeps the land's virginity;
> The stalwart giants of the wood
> Laden with toys and flowers and food;
> The precious forest pouring out
> To compass the whole town about;
> The town itself with streets of lawn,
> Loved of the moon, blessed by the dawn,
> Where the brown children all the day
> Keep up a ceaseless noise of play, . . .
> And late at night in the woods of fruit,
> Hark! do you hear the passing flute? . . .[32]

Though dying out, the Tahitians were less morbid about it than the Marquesans. And through all that occurred Louis felt dreamily buoyed up by steadily growing affection between his party and their gentle brown hosts: "God's best—at least God's sweetest works—Polynesians." [33] Taken literally, this is poor observation. But Louis was—and had a right to be—a little tipsy to find that all J. Seed had promised was real.

For there is another side to the Islander's eager respect for wealth/nobility/prestige which sometimes shocks our equalitarian-cum-medieval tradition. As beachcombers the Stevensons might well have been not so cordially treated; but it also seems to be true that Polynesians often manage to feel the love formally due to Rich Ones of reasonable decency. (It may help here to consider the deep affection that the British often manage to feel for the Royal Family.) These Tautira chiefs were of the Teva, a specially proud, able line with a lofty sense of *noblesse oblige*. When Louis asked Moë if Teriitera would exchange names with him, he was seeking—and duly received—recognition of his standing as equivalent gentry from a South Seas house of superlative standing. It is understandable that he was pleased deep in his bones to be even nominally a considerable chief in a primitive clan with the wild slogan: "Teva the wind! Teva the rain!" In parallel Fanny exchanged names with Moë, who proved both a gracious, graceful lady and a slashing player of High-Low-Jack-and-the-Game.

Teriitera was the pattern of that distinguished creature, the Polynesian great gentleman: six foot three in his huge bare feet, filling jacket and *pareu*[34] with breadth and brawn; the integrity and authority of his carriage and handsome mustache irresistibly reminded his guests of a middle-aged Guards officer. His French was adequate, if not so fluent as Moanatini's, his English fair, his thoughtful courtesy delicate and firm. When the party's fine ship disappeared in difficulties, leaving them short of ready money, Teriitera unerringly observed the full tenor of his sworn kinship with Louis, his new blood-brother. As long as the Stevensons chose to inhabit Tautira, whether willingly or not, they would lack nothing the place afforded—perhaps merely fish, coconuts, and plantains, but house and living were theirs by definition. When Louis told Teriitera of the full extent of the party's embarrassments, he was so cordially assured of the reality of these freely accorded privileges that whites and browns shed tears all round.

The trouble with ship and money came close to catastrophe. As Louis's strength returned, Otis prepared to sail for Honolulu, where money was waiting, as well as Belle and Joe Strong. One day, however, an idle glance aloft showed him the main-topmast badly sprung. Inspection proved that, sure enough, the spars were full of dry rot. Whoever had reported her sound to Dr. Merritt and Otis had blundered very badly. All went cold with apprehension after the fact. Suppose that topmast had gone during the masterly little dance round the center of a cyclonic storm of which Otis had been so proud ten days out of San Francisco; or during the squall that had laid her on her beam-ends. . . . In those lonely waters a dismasted ship might well have spelled burial at sea for Louis and everybody else too, most informally.[35] Risky though it would be if a squall came up, Otis took the *Casco* round to Papeete to move heaven and earth to get repairs at least begun. Off she went, treading on eggs, so to speak, leaving the cabin party to hope for the best.

At Papeete Otis found a ne'er-do-well admitting experience as ship's carpenter and willing to try to step new spars and fish old ones to justify attempting Honolulu. Fortunately the port afforded a wrecked barque from which sound spars could be bought. Otis made the deal at barely practicable expense and, unaware that Tahiti knows no such word, told his man to go at it lively. It took five weeks to cajole and bully the job to completion, while the exiles in Tautira swallowed steadily gloomier bulletins: more rot than suspected, greater expense, more maddening delays. . . . Louis worked on *Ballantrae* and studied Tahitian with Teriitera, Fanny learned local handicrafts, Aunt Maggie busied herself with prayer meetings among the local Protestant natives.

By late December, when the ship, reasonably seaworthy, reappeared, hospitality was still unflagging. On Christmas Day, the weeping heartfelt on both sides, the Stevensons went on board; Otis fired thirteen shots from his rifle in salute and dipped the ensign, and the *Casco* filled away for Honolulu and solvency.[36]

It was a miserable passage to Hawaii—calms and headwinds for weeks, day's runs averaging sixty to seventy miles. Otis grew morose, then miserable with double earache and irked by Louis's cheerfulness and liveliness in spite of the Pacific's bad manners. As the voyage stretched out, provisions ran short; it looked as if even the cabin table would be reduced to nothing but salt beef and hardtack. When he sensed dirty weather coming up astern, Otis's feelings were mixed. To lie-to and wait it out would further prolong the passage and, in view of the patched-up spars, offered its own risks anyway. To run before whatever blow was coming would save time, but it also committed the ship to the chance of being pooped by a following sea; and, once the decision to run was made, bringing her to might be out of the question. Otis put the issue up to Louis who, though little of a seaman, knew enough to appreciate it. Again, to the captain's wondering pleasure, this rickety landsman made a life-and-death decision without a qualm: Run for it, he said, and run it was.

Hands were lashed on deck, passengers theoretically forbidden to show their heads. But Louis and Lloyd sneaked a look at the situation at its tightest—the day Hawaii was sighted. In a letter Louis roughed out what would be one of the best bits in *The Wrecker*:

It blew fair, but very strong. . . . she carried her lee rail under water and flew. The swell the heaviest I have ever been out in . . . came tearing after us about a point and a half off the wind. We had the best hand . . . at the wheel; and, really, he did nobly, and had noble luck, for it never caught us once. At times it seemed we must have it; [the helmsman] would look over his shoulder with the queerest look and dive down his neck into his shoulders; and then it missed us somehow and only sprays came over our quarter, . . . I never remember anything more delightful and exciting. Pretty soon after we were lying becalmed under the lee of Hawaii, of which we had been warned; and the captain never confessed he had done it on purpose, but when accused, he smiled.[37]

They were becalmed for several days on short rations. The ship was thirty days out of Tautira when a change of weather finally brought her dancing past Diamond Head on a sparkling day. The Strongs were out to meet her in a shoreboat. For days she had been given up for lost. Casting his eyes aloft, Otis should have felt devout, had he been a religious man. As it was, all he had to do was sail his quasi-jury-rigged lady-love home, which he duly accomplished, and spend the rest of his life trying to make out what manner of man he had sailed for.

For six months Louis would be ashore. Voyaging had set him up like nothing since he was born, nor had anybody suffered on his behalf. As he wrote, Aunt Maggie had had "a Huge Old Time," [38] sea-bathing, learning to type as potential alternate for Lloyd, now planning to send the Tautira Protestants a silver communion service. Fanny's throat-growth had not returned. Lloyd was fit and enthusiastic. Ah Fu was blissfully attached to people whom he could love like a capable dog. Valentine was the only casualty—"the usual tale of the maid on board the yacht," said Louis. She packed off with her wages to California, married, and settled down. Years later she gave the impression that, though her devotion to Louis never flagged, she had found Fanny increasingly a trial.

Landfall

> Now, messmates, when my watch is up,
> And I am quite broached to,
> I'll give a tip to 'Evving
> Of the 'ansome thing to do:
> Let 'em just refit this sailor-man
> And launch him off anew
> To cruise among the Hislands
> With the dollars of Peru: . . .
>
> —"The Fine Pacific Islands"

Technically Hawaii was Polynesia too, but in some
respects the Honolulu of 1889 might have been Port-
land, Oregon. Horsecars trundled along its dusty streets, transpacific mail steamers tied up at its piers, rival newspapers
tried to operate Stateside-style though, for lack of cable communication, outside news was available only on "steamer day." It
even had the telephone, a device that Louis thoroughly disliked.[1]

For all these trappings of civilization, however, it was Hawaii
that first began to involve Louis practically in the Island world.
So far he had been merely deeply affected guest and spectator.
Now he slid gradually into acting as if he had a stake in the
Islands—a thing he had never done in France or the States, and
had on the whole eschewed in Britain. It was no deliberate involvement. Once his waiting mail assured him that he was
still solvent—a matter of some previous dubiety—he made plans
to return to the Western world: summer in England and Scotland, perhaps Madeira as regular winter prophylaxis. Life in
Tahiti tempted him, but the infrequency of the Papeete-San
Francisco mail brigantines made it impracticable for a writer

with Western literary markets. Besides, he was still counting on an occasional sight of old friends and familiar places.

He never loved Honolulu, with its large white houses for successfully intruding white men, and its callously evident degradation of the native. That was ungrateful, for Honolulu tried to treat him well. At Waikiki—then merely beach, coco-palms and scattered summer houses a quarter-mile beyond the end of the horsecar line—the party recuperated from the sea at Manuia Lanai, a small colony of buildings on a lawn between road and beach. Lloyd and Aunt Maggie inhabited the only structure that could be called a house—and, *haole*-style,[2] even that was mostly veranda. The larger of the two supplementary shacks was devoted to photography, painting, and whatever other odd activity needed room. The smaller and frowsier had cots and mosquito nets for Louis and Fanny, and a companionable mouse whose presence as earlier tenant Louis respected, taming him with bits from dinner. There on a plain table, with the surf on the reef in his ears, Louis finished his reworking of *The Wrong Box*, wrestled the stubborn *Ballantrae* into unsatisfactory conclusion, wrote "The Song of Rahero" and "The Feast of Famine" out of his gleanings from the Marquesas and Tahiti, and studied Hawaiian with a native teacher. For sea-bathing he had only to walk to the foot of the lawn, which gave on the beach and the view of reef and Diamond Head. For sociability he had so much company that, anomalously formal though it sounds, Fanny and he were driven to setting up regular "afternoons," so that disruption could be planned ahead for and concentrated in one wasted day.

The nearest neighbor, Henry Poor, part-native local politician, became a good friend and helped to attract Louis's notice to Hawaiian, thence to Samoan, affairs. Prime responsibility for that, however, lay rather with Louis himself and with Belle and Joe Strong. A merry and attractive young couple of cheerfully Bohemian tastes, already established several years in Honolulu with their small son Austin, they were closely identified with "the royal crowd"—the gayer, more worldly, less thrifty, horsier stratum of white and half-white society that supported and was often supported by His Hawaiian Majesty, King Kalakaua. Belle had designed the royal Order of the Star of Oceania and acted as undercover courier between Kalakaua and his chief minister —an implausible but very respectable-looking Mormon renegade —during the "Bayonet Constitution" revolution of 1887; Joe had recently been "official artist" of an Hawaiian embassy to Samoa. Louis made friends on the other side—notably "Father" Damon, eminent Protestant missionary—but only a few. He was already emotionally committed to Polynesians in general, sure to be annoyed by the blend of respectability and rapacity that characterized the antiroyal elements in Hawaii; and, supposing he had had any cautious reservations about "the royal crowd," would have suppressed them as ungenerous toward such warm young partisans as Belle and Joe.

Louis's liking for the tall, well-plumped-out King furthered the good cause. Though a bribe-seeker, an exhibitionistic spend-thrift, and a marked case of gracious megalomania, Kalakaua also had charm and dignity and, for all his infantilist dabblings in ancient Hawaiian religion and "science" (all Louis's party were made honorary members of the King's society for the propagation of heathen knowledge), marked intelligence. Within a week the *Casco* was entertaining the King and his sister with a party on board at which Louis read "Ticonderoga," Otis played the accordion, Belle did a dance, and Lloyd sang "The Fine Pacific Islands"—apparently all much to royal satisfaction. At Poor's native feast for the *Cascos* a few days later, Louis presented his majesty with a graceful set of occasional verses and a large yellow pearl from the Tuamotu. Thenceforth the royal carriage was frequently visible at the Stevensons' gate as token that the King was within, absorbing their champagne with bland impunity. Louis wrote Baxter about it:

> . . . a bottle of fizz is like a glass of sherry to him; he thinks nothing of five or six in an afternoon as a whet for dinner.

You should see a photograph of our party after an afternoon
with H.H.M. What a crew! [3]

Kalakaua talked well on Hawaiian archeology and sometimes
invited Louis to play cards and see revived *hulas* at his beach
house not far away; since the guest returned merely bored, I
suspect that, in the interests of good public relations, the night's
program was heavily censored beforehand.

If so, it was not the only measure taken by "The First Gentleman of the Pacific" to capture this world-famous writer so op-
portunely dropped into his large brown lap. Kalakaua was under
menacing pressures from Stateside influences—only four years
later the throne he sat on sank without a trace—and needed
countenance. Honolulu soon heard rumors that Louis had promised the King—or one of his intimates—to put before the world
his case as martyr to solicitude for his downtrodden people. For
once there was something in a Honolulu rumor. At least Louis
did consent to do the text for a book to show the world the
photographs that Joe Strong had taken of the recent Hawaiian
embassy to Samoa.

Kalakaua lived not as a simple gentleman like Moanatini, but
as much like Western royalty as he could manage: He had a
stone palace resembling a Midwestern courthouse with verandas; a royal box in a miniature opera house with electric lights;
a German bandmaster and a white-style national anthem; a wardrobe of frock coats and musical-comedy uniforms; a few score
soldiers handling a battery of high-wheeled field guns; and a
growing national deficit. Some of these had originated with his
predecessors; but the deficit and his ambitions toward a miniature imperialism were all his own.

Hawaii was then in the last twitching stages of being swallowed by the States. Between American missionary influence and
large-scale agriculture largely of American provenance, the natives were being supplanted by Oriental labor imported to do
what the natives did not care to do. Kalakaua's early diplomacy,

embarked on to bolster his position as a semi-usurper of very high birth, had tied the Islands closer than ever to the States. Whites owned most of the good land, Chinese worked it for them, Hawaiians stood by, sadly or sulkily.

Of late the King had grown unrealistically chauvinist, megalomanic, obscurantist—if you like, patriotic—seeking to revive old native ways and native powers through a sullen, sentimental movement encouraged by opportunists, some white, some half-white, of widely varying honesty and responsibility. (Among the best were Poor, Louis's neighbor at Waikiki, and A. S. Cleghorn, a Scot and friend of Louis's, who had married a native princess and fathered a very charming little Princess Kaiulani, heiress-presumptive.[4]) Tied in with his domestic nativism was Kalakaua's policy of "Primacy of the Pacific," which called on Hawaii, the most advanced native state in the Islands and focus of emulation among all ambitious Polynesians, to check white encroachment by forming a partly imperialistic union, rather like the Athenian Empire, of islands as yet nominally independent. That meant the Tonga group; the Gilberts, still uncertain between Britain and Germany; and Samoa, for twenty years a lively apple of discord for Germany, Britain, and the States. Under unscrupulous white influence Kalakaua had made the lunatic choice of Samoa as the place to begin.

Since imperialism, God save the mark, required a navy, Kalakaua equipped a small, elderly steamer with a few small guns, manned her with young native delinquents from the royal reform school, and dubbed her HHMS *Kaimiloa*. An embassy, including a half-native editor as chief, Poor as secretary, and Joe Strong as aforesaid, was sent to fish in the troubled waters of Samoa, where the three Powers were confusedly bullying three tenuous native factions, each headed by a "royal" great chief. But it was poor judgment—if, indeed, it mattered—to send the *Kaimiloa* to reinforce the embassy's prestige. She looked wofully puny alongside the obsolescent but imposing men-of-war that the Powers kept handy in Samoan waters, and her arrival accomplished little beyond encouraging the embassy's enthusiasm for strong drink. In the end the embassy had to borrow money to get home on, and the *Kaimiloa* was so disorganized by alcohol and indiscipline that she had to ship a local sailing master to make sure of making Honolulu instead of Davy Jones's locker.

In Samoa the Germans had used this intrusion as pretext for insulting Samoans and expelling American and British subjects in the course of badgering their respective consuls. I do not know who first gave Louis the story,[5] along with a general sketch of Samoan affairs, thus rousing him with both implied wrongs to Polynesian dignity and disregarded injury to British prestige. The second-hand data that he used in the manuscript to go with Joe's pictures sound as if Poor (the obliging neighbor) had been the principal source. Whoever it was, his clever balance between rueful frankness and injured dignity, masking much suppression of reality, bore immediate fruit. After a bare two weeks in Honolulu, Louis sent the London *Times* a sizzling letter—his signature practically guaranteeing publication, of course—denouncing the supineness of Britain and the States in allowing Germany to humiliate their consuls; and—this was the cream of it for "the royal crowd"—describing the Hawaiian embassy as having been sent "by a power of the same race . . . dismissed with threats and insults." [6] The tenor of the whole assured the world's most eminent newspaper that this spavined, hung-over diplomatic mission had deserved status and respect. It was generous of Louis; but it was also poor reporting, and later exposed his far more responsible writings about Samoa, after he had actually seen the place, to the charge that he was always going off half-cocked in blind partisanship for natives.

But the book of Joe's pictures and Louis's text was never to see the light. Its data went, in shortened form, into *A Footnote to History*—that classic in South Seas history that, merely in passing, reduces the embassy to the sodden burlesque that it really was. The completed manuscript of "A Samoan Scrapbook," however, gathered dust for sixty years until, just the other day, I found it in a batch of miscellaneous Stevensoniana in the great Beinecke Collection. Somewhere along the line of his edu-

cation after writing that letter to the *Times*, Louis apparently
learned that he had been intellectually swindled by "the royal
crowd." The change of tone between the "Scrapbook" and the
Footnote is unmistakable. My guess is that, between long talks
with Strong and better acquaintance with Samoa than can be had
from 1500 sea-miles away, the affair could not fail to look utterly different.

Still, there is no hint that Louis held this performance against
his Honolulu informants. He remained friends with Poor, and
persisted in amicable support of the Hawaiian throne. At Kalakaua's death, he wrote Liliuokalani, the sister who succeeded, a
handsome letter of respectful condolence and congratulation.
When the "missionaries" jostled the new queen off the throne
in 1893, he paid her numerous calls of friendship and com-
miseration during a stay in Honolulu. Dethroned royalty had a
great appeal to Louis's imaginatively romantic heart, and there
was small counterinfluence in the smug and cynical machinations
of those who contemptuously extinguished the Kingdom of Hawaii.

Why go so far into all this? Not least because the whole
contretemps tied Louis very close to Samoa months and months
before he ever landed there.

Having thus exploded indiscreetly to small purpose, within a
year Louis was exploding even less discreetly to more purpose:

Though pressed by work on *Ballantrae*, he nevertheless felt
bound to search outside Honolulu for copy for the McClure letters. Traveling alone to the Big Island, he acquired background
used later in "The Bottle Imp" and "The Isle of Voices," looked
at a ranch that he momentarily considered buying, saw tag-ends
of native life surviving in remote areas, and, as nominal member of the Scottish bar, acted as *amicus curiae* at a local native
magistrate's court. Then, in June 1889, he visited Hawaii's
leper colony:

In the midcentury leprosy had become a minor menace on
Hawaii. A colony for life isolation of lepers—then considered

essential to control of the disease—was set up on a peninsula on the northern coast of the island of Molokai, accessible only by sea or by difficult bridle-track. Life imprisonment appeals to few. Hawaii's difficulty in catching and transporting lepers made a noise in the outside world; well into the twentieth century, thanks to such romancers as Richard Walton Tully and Jack London—Fanny's melodramatic leper-tale, "The Half-White," anticipated them by a generation[7]—the name "Hawaii" carried the connotation "leprosy," much to the annoyance of *haoles*.

Once lepers were isolated, Hawaii was slack about their welfare. Sin, squalor, and violence developed in the colony. The soon-to-be-famous Father Damien, a Belgian missionary priest, volunteered to spend his life there, trying to ease physical ordeals and at least save some souls. After some years he contracted leprosy and, staying active as long as possible, died of it. There were proposals to erect a monument to so striking a martyrdom.

Honolulu did not take this altogether in good part. The behavior of Damien, a Catholic, had tactlessly called attention to the lack of feverish interest in the colony among dominant Hawaiian Protestants, who were sensitive to Catholics anyway: thirty-odd years previously local Protestant missionaries had abetted forcible ejection of Catholic missionaries from the Islands. During most of his ministry on Molokai nasty rumors about Damien circulated in Honolulu and were still lively when Louis sailed on the tiny interisland steamer for the dismal settlement of Kalawao-Kalaupepa, abiding place of the living dead.

In the ship were several newly caught lepers sentenced to exile and some nuns volunteering to share it. She reached the colony just at sunrise:

> . . . bleak and harsh, a little town of wooden houses, two churches, the sunrise, with the great wall of the pali [cliff] cutting the world out on the south. . . . I do not know how it would have been with me if the sisters had not been there. My horror of the horrible is about my weakest point; but the moral loveliness at my elbow blotted out everything else; and

when I found that one of them was crying, poor soul, quietly under her veil, I cried a little myself; then I felt as right as a trivet, only a little crushed to be there so uselessly. I thought it was a sin and a shame she should feel unhappy; I turned round to her and said something like this: "Ladies, God himself is here to give you welcome. I'm sure it is good for me to be here beside you; I hope it will be blessed to me; I thank you for myself and for the good you do me." . . . a great crowd, hundreds of (God save us!) pantomime masks in poor human flesh, waiting to receive the sisters and the new patients. Every hand was offered: I had gloves, but I had made up my mind on the boat's voyage *not* to give my hand; that seemed less offensive. . . .

People annoyed by Louis's occasionally overdramatized behavior should have been eavesdropping on this stiff little speech, as right as it was self-conscious. His apology contains much of the essential Louis:

> Partly, too, I did it because I was ashamed to do so, and remembered one of my golden rules, "When you are ashamed to speak, speak up at once." But, mind you, that rule is good only with strangers: with your own folks, there are other considerations.[8]

For eight days he lived in a passion of pity among these faces melting into bestiality, daily playing croquet—gloveless—[9]with leper-children and

> . . . yarning with old, blind, leper beachcombers in the hospital, sickened with the spectacle of abhorrent suffering, . . . touched to the heart by the sight of lowly and effective virtues among their helpers; no stranger time have I ever had, nor any so moving.[10]

The heavily Catholic atmosphere irked him: "The passbook kept with heaven stirs me to tears and laughter. One of the sisters calls the place 'the ticket office to heaven.'" But Damien had firmly embedded his church in the scene of his labors. Hearing much of the martyr on the spot, Louis summed up what he could learn:

> Of old Damien, whose weakness and worse perhaps I heard fully, I think only the more. It was a European peasant, dirty, bigoted, untruthful, unwise, tricky, but superb with generosity, residual candour and fundamental good humour; convince him that he had done wrong (it might take hours of insult) and he would undo what he had done and like his corrector better. A man, with all the grime and paltriness of mankind, but a saint and hero all the more for that.[11]

In Samoa six months later Louis was aghast to hear that a recent public denunciation of Damien's alleged gross vices might ruin the project of the monument. In Sydney two months later still he found the denunciatory document in an Australian church-journal—a letter from the Rev. Dr. C. M. Hyde of Honolulu to the Rev. H. B. Gage of Sydney in reply to an inquiry about Damien's reputation. Herein Hyde assured his brother in Christ that Damien had been a stupid and dirty person who had accomplished little actual good and hinted that his infection had come of sleeping with female lepers. When trying to arrange a cruise on a mission ship out of Honolulu, Louis had visited Hyde at the suggestion of "Father" Damon; the man seems to have been perfunctorily obliging. Now Louis read his letter with a sort of freezing awe at its superb lack of charity. For once "The Old Man Virulent" had a target commensurate with his temper. He picked up his pen and unexpectedly, most undeservedly, the Rev. Dr. Hyde became immortal.

This *Open Letter* . . . is often taken as primarily defense of Damien. When later regretting that he had so castigated Hyde in order to vindicate the martyr, Louis himself seems so to have conceived it. The error is promoted by Johnstone's doubts that Hyde's charges were well founded;[12] since Louis accepted most of them in substance, he may actually have been unfair to his client. After all, one hardly defends a priest against accusation

of fornication with "Suppose it true, who are you to bring
charges?" But his own hyperexcited study of Damien and his
work had so impressed him with how holily congenitally erring
man can act on occasion that it seems never to have occurred to
him to doubt Hyde's allegations. One might almost say that he
would have felt a touch of disappointment had they been dis-
proved. It was the exultant reversal of Jekyllism.

Beyond that, this model of deliberate insult as personal as a
love letter, this dismantling of a fellow-creature not with ax or
scalpel but with a razor-sharp butcher knife that flays as handily
as it disembowels, most magnificently arraigns Hyde as a type
of whited sepulcher, of gimlet-eyed Pharisee, of the general
scandal of diametrically un-Christian behavior among men holding posts in Christian cults. The horror, pity, and backhanded
self-reproach that had been pent up in Louis ever since his week
with the lepers now flooded forth in expression of his lifelong
hatred of the unco guid and his ever-deepening sense of human
beings' common ground in moral frustration:

. . . when we have failed, and another has succeeded; when
we have stood by and another has stepped in; when we sit
and grow bulky in our charming mansions, and a plain, uncouth peasant steps into the battle, under the eyes of God,
and succours the afflicted, and consoles the dying, and is himself afflicted in turn, and dies upon the field of honour—the
battle cannot be retrieved as your unhappy irritation suggests.
One thing remained to you in your defeat—some rags of
common honour; and these you have made haste to cast away.
. . . "Damien was coarse." It is very possible. You make us
sorry for the lepers who had only a coarse old peasant for their
friend and father. But you, who were so refined, why were
you not there, to cheer them with the lights of culture? . . .
"Damien was dirty." He was. Think of the poor lepers annoyed with this dirty comrade! But the clean Dr. Hyde was at
his food in a fine house. . . . I fear you scarce appreciate
how you appear to your fellow-men; and to bring it home to

you, I will suppose your story to be true. I will suppose—and
God forgive me for supposing it—that Damien faltered and
stumbled in his narrow path of duty; I will suppose that, in
the horror of his isolation, perhaps in the fever of incipient
disease, he, who was doing so much more than he had sworn,
failed in the letter of his priestly oath . . . The least tender
should be moved to tears; the most incredulous to prayer. And
all that you could do was to pen your letter to the Reverend
H. B. Gage. . . .[13]

True, Hyde had asked for it. But, in any exact sense, it was
scarce Christian of the assailant. It seems never to have occurred
to Louis that Hyde's scarlet if subtler sins against his professed
faith and avowed obligation could also move to tears or prayer.

Committed though he was to revision, he seldom wrote better
than in this diatribe thrown off, to judge from internal evidence,
with only minimum rehandling. The impromptu letters describing the lepers quoted from above have the same quality. The
rhythms spit and crawl like lighted fuses while never losing a
stateliness of pattern cunningly relieved by balder bits. The structure is as irregular as a castle built to fit asymmetrical terrain,
and equally satisfying to the sense of composition. Even the
rhetorical self-consciousness is an asset, since it gives a sense of
formidable technical control over tender or vindictive impulses.
Disproportion of provocation to reaction is supposed to be token
of unconscious motivation. No doubt there was such a factor in
both Louis's wonder at Kalawao and his anger at Hyde. But no
upward wellings could affect the excellent instrument that his
writing had become.

Even a lesser lawyer than Louis would have known that to
publish a letter so reeking of libel risked financial ruin. Louis
read it aloud to a family council and described the probability
that Hyde would sue and saddle the family with crippling dam-
ages. Without hesitation the family said Publish! Louis challenged action not merely in Honolulu, where he was hardly
vulnerable to suit, but in Australia and in Britain, where his

royalties were notably attachable. (In Hawaii it was published in *Elele*, a native-language newspaper, and further distributed through town as a throw-away—another token of how nativist forces valued Louis as a weapon against "missionaries.") He refused revenue from it; to one of his London publishers inquiring about republication and payment, he wrote: "The letter to Dr. Hyde is yours or any man's. I will never touch a penny of remuneration; I do not stick at murder, I draw the line at cannibalism." [14]

Actually Hyde contented himself with snorting about "Bohemian cranks" without suing. It was represented that, since his letter had not been meant for publication, the guilty party (if one existed) was Gage, who had printed without permission. These were poor tactics for cushioning the attack, for Hyde and his enemy were met on the enemy's grounds. Seven months later Louis's *peccavi* was significantly calm. He called his letter

> . . . barbarously harsh; if I did it now I would defend Damien no less well, and give less pain to those who are alive. These promptings of good humour are not all sound; the three times three, cheer boys, cheer, and general amiability business rests on a sneaking love of popularity, the most insidious enemy of virtue. On the whole, it was virtuous to defend Damien; but it was harsh to strike so hard at Dr. Hyde . . . and I have deeply wounded one of his colleagues whom I esteemed and liked. [15]

The spring was released, tension reduced. He had made another step toward full human responsibility.

The affair Hyde is anticipation. What most occupied Louis's consciousness in June 1889 was the prospect of wilder islands. Micronesia this time: ill-defined, sprawling groups, mostly atolls, lying north of the Equator, west of the Date Line—Marshalls, Gilberts, Carolines, Marianas, says big type on the map. The smallest type may say Makin, Tarawa, Peleliu, Bikini . . . but to most Americans those names were then meaningless. Mis-

sions and traders had been chipping away at them for a generation, but they remained least white-infested, nearest to preliterate behavior, least accessible of any South Sea Islands, outside
malarial Melanesia.

If her owners could overlook Louis's affinities with the un-
godly "royal crowd," it was theoretically possible for the Stevensons to sail in the *Morning Star*, the missionary auxiliary barken-
tine making regular rounds of God's service stations in Micronesia. But this was the marginal expedient—such passengers were
pledged to eschew smoke, drink, and all other worldliness. While
negotiations hung fire, Louis and Lloyd were at sailing directories again: the *Morning Star* might take them round the Gilberts and Marshalls, then drop them on Ponape, a high island
in the Carolines, to be voluntarily marooned

> . . . among a doubtful population, with a Spanish vice-gov-
> ernor and five native kings, and a sprinkling of missionaries
> all at loggerheads, on the chance of fetching a passage to
> Sydney in a trader, a labour-ship, or (maybe, but this appears
> too bright) a ship of war . . . try to fetch Fiji, hire a schooner
> there, do the Fijis and Friendlies, . . . make back by Tahiti
> . . . home; perhaps in June, 1890.[16]

Or one might somehow make Samoa for the west-bound Sydney
steamer. . . .

When the mission denied the Stevensons privileges in the
ship, they repined the less because an alternative had appeared:
the new trading schooner *Equator*, whose San Francisco owners
were amenable to a charter that would show the party much of
Micronesia without hampering her usual business. She would not
only permit drink, cards, smoking, and oaths, but would spare
the party the handicap of landing from the august and inhibit-
ing mission ship. As the schooner picked up copra[17] and palavered
with local chiefs and elders, Louis would learn a great deal about
normal Island life.

Except for Fanny, Louis's entourage was always changing. By
May, Aunt Maggie, who had an ailing sister, had gone home to

Scotland, hoping that Louis would follow next year. Daughter of the manse, she might have endured the sanctimonious *Morning Star*; but the *Equator*, which was to the *Casco* what a caboose is to a private car, should have been out of the question for her anyway. Joe Strong, whose chronic conviviality was a problem, came along to paint transparencies for lantern slides that Lloyd might use later on that lecture tour planned by McClure for Louis; in any case, it was a good way to get Joe out of Honolulu. Lloyd's camera also came along with Lloyd. Ah Fu was to be general utility man, much to his delight. Belle Strong and small Austin were sent to Sydney to wait for them all—six months, seven months, who knew how many?

They were already storing up a list of necessities that reads like equipment for Snark-hunting: revolvers; bad cigars; vegetable seeds; potassium permanganate; a portable organ; hammocks (obligingly knotted for them by the ratings of HMS *Cormorant*, then at Honolulu); a magic lantern lent by Damon to ingratiate them with the natives and an outfit of slides, mostly religious, some comic; for informal music, Louis's flageolet, to which he had graduated from the outright tin whistle, Joe's accordion, Fanny's guitar, and Lloyd's "taro-patch fiddle," which I take to have been a ukulele. Fanny's general sentiments about the scheme simultaneously involved two separate points of view no more sociable than Euclidean parallels; she wrote Mrs. Sitwell:

> . . . the usual risk from hostile natives, and the horrible sea, but . . . it is all such joy to Louis and Lloyd. . . . I hate the sea and am afraid of it (though no one will believe that because in time of danger I do not make an outcry—nevertheless I *am* afraid of it and it is not kind to me), but I love the tropic weather and the wild people and to see my two boys so happy.[18]

Meanwhile Louis was exultantly advising Baxter that the party might be out of touch for months or years, hence should not be written off ". . . till you get some certainty we have gone to

Davie Jones in a squall, or graced the feast of some barbarian in the character of Long Pig." As for addresses: "They have nae post-offishes at the Gilberts, and as for the Carlines! Ye see, Mr. Baxter, we're no just at the punkshewal *centre* o' civilization." [19]

His health was bubbling too. He thought Hawaii too cold for him, but rode twenty miles a day on poor trails on Molokai with no worse penalty than healthy weariness; no hint of hemorrhage since Papeete eight months before. It was daily more evident that anything keeping him in the Islands was better for him than anything forcing him to leave. Yet still he was planning "home."

With a punctuality unusual in sailing vessels in the least calendar-minded of oceans, the *Equator* turned up late in June. Reënforced by a brace of less respectable cabinet ministers, a basket of champagne, and part of the Royal Hawaiian Band, Kalakaua came to a farewell luncheon on board. Just about a year after clearing the Golden Gate, the Stevensons were off again. Never before had they so well answered a formula I have heard suggested for them: Part Sanger's Circus, part Swiss Family Robinson, part Peterkins.

The Honolulu *Pacific Advertiser* noted their departure with a paragraph ferocious even for the school of journalism that trained Mark Twain:

> Robert Louis Stevenson and party leave today by the schooner Equator for the Gilbert Islands. . . . It is to be hoped that Mr. Stevenson will not fall victim to native spears; but in his present state of bodily health, perhaps the temptation to kill him may not be very strong.[20]

The *Equator*, though small for even an Island schooner, was still too new to have the full conventional reek of copra and bilge, and her owners had duly altered her for the party, turning the skipper out of his cabin to build a second bunk therein for Fanny. The squarehead mate shifted to the spare bunk across from the cook's, while the captain supplanted him. The trade room[21] had two new bunks for Lloyd and Joe. I do not know how Captain Denis Reid had liked having the ship's business made secondary to the needs of an ailing writer accompanied by a woman and three others; whatever his original comments, he behaved well. The Stevensons were lucky in their sea captains. Only twenty-three, Reid was a Scot himself given to wearing the national bonnet even in the tropics, a good checker-player, and a fine seaman. His sole unfortunate trait was his knowing only two songs—"Annie Laurie" and "In the Gloaming"—and insisting on singing both whenever entertainment was afoot.[22]

Ah Fu was told off to cook in place of the New Zealand parson's runaway son whom Reid had shipped as cook at the last moment in San Francisco.[23] This strangely assorted ship's company got on well from the beginning. By the time they had reached Apia six months later, the afterguard all knew each other well enough to sing a special song: "Captain darling, where has your topmast gone?" in memory of a squall that, intruding on a dead calm, had caught the ship with all sail set and carried away her fore-topmast. One does not joke a seaman on such a subject unless one knows him very well indeed.

The only trading station that the Wightmans (owners of the ship) actually owned in the area was on Great Makin in the Gilberts. After landing stocks and picking up copra there, she went on a roving commission to trade supplies for copra with independent local traders who had so far managed to survive German encroachment out of Jaluit in the Marshalls. No arrangement could better have instructed Louis in how white men and their things and ideas impinged on brown men and their things and ideas.

The first lesson could have been the last. Makin had two competing trading stores and a native "king" who was an ugly brute even when sober. On the recent Fourth of July he had been got to relax the tabu on selling spirits to natives. The *Equator* arrived well after the Fourth, but the "king," his council, his wives, his largely naked bodyguard armed with repeating rifles, and most of his subjects were still getting more menacingly drunker. True, the stores could have refused to sell; but such actions had to be simultaneous and neither cared to risk loss of profit to the other or the chance that the screaming-drunk Makinese would thereupon storm both establishments. The solution was for the "king" to sober up enough to restore the tabu. Far from that, he was still sending to one store or the other for more *peranti* (brandy) or *din* (gin).

The *Equators* went ashore armed with both presents and revolvers. At one juncture they found it advisable to practice marksmanship most ostentatiously on the beach, Fanny firing her turn at the rows of target bottles then so prevalent on the island. Louis told it all—a South Seas nightmare done too well for synopsis—in an excellent chapter of *In the South Seas*. Sanity finally won, partly through his shrewd interview with the rival store manager; the tabu was restored, and the Makinese got clear of their colossal communal hang-over just in time to entertain a dangerous rival of the "king's" come for a visit of state from Little Makin. The ensuing ceremonies acquainted Louis with magnificent Micronesian singing and group dancing of far higher quality than Kalakaua's moribund *hulas*.

Then the ship was off again, peddling trade goods for copra. Louis and Lloyd learned the lore of false weights, watered copra, hostile speak-houses, native "wives," shipwrecks, square-face gin, "position-doubtful" reefs, barratry, piracy, and cheap firearms that underlay local economics. They met lepers, proven or suspected murderers, cheerful brown ladies who smoked corncob pipes 3000 miles from the nearest cornfield, white toadies to brown chiefs, and scrawny-necked missionaries in yellow boots and sun helmets. They ate muck, fried in the sun, developed superficial ulcers; but day after day, as Reid continued to ground them in what they were seeing, all were aware of being as poignantly alive as people well could be. That is specially valuable for a man who has spent half his life outguessing death. It was not just copy-hunting, but a daily more vigorous grasp of an extremely exigent reality.

The culmination was Apemama in the Gilberts, ruled by

"King" Tembinok', a shrewd, ruthless tyrant (in both modern and classic senses) whom only British men-of-war kept from being the Napoleon of the group. As it was, he ruled his atoll with vindictive terror, crack marksmanship, and an armed bodyguard of wives of all ages. Hearing much of him—he was as much a Pacific legend as Bully Hayes or Shirley Baker—the Stevensons hoped to stay on Apemama while the *Equator* made her duller rounds to other islands. This was no likely project; the only white to whom Tembinok' permitted residence was a renegade "prime minister" who lived in fear of his life. The only missionary ever to land had eventually been ejected, partly because he had dared to flaw the royal monopoly on copra by accepting presents of it from converts, partly because he had served his purpose of teaching the tyrant workable English. Life on Apemama was living uninsulated with a tiger.

But the tiger loved things as well as power. He personally boarded trading vessels—which lay well out in the lagoon to avoid suspicion of contraband trade with the natives, a thing attempted only at dead of night—and bought whatever took his catholic fancy. His thatched "palace" was stuffed with degenerating clocks, rusted weapons, fancy garments, and an awesome miscellany of gadgets that clever skippers had fetched along to tempt him. He bought and wore indiscriminately frock coats and ladies' evening gowns, top hats and sunbonnets, flowered cravats and red flannel drawers; but he scorned both trade-gin[24] and the legitimate spirits that he might have had for a price; his only tipple, of which he was very fond, was an implausible and corrosive imitation of Hennessy's brandy that traders stocked specially for this adipose and eagle-beaked connoisseur.

When he boarded the *Equator* for his usual buying spree, the Stevensons unwittingly gained a great tactical advantage against the time when Reid should broach their request to stay ashore. Seeking new acquisitions, the "King" fell on Fanny's dressing-case and announced he would buy it. Louis and Fanny refused to sell. When the "king" stormily insisted, they said very well, take it as a gift, and stubbornly refused payment. A gift it was.

"I shamed," said Tembinok'. By injecting a commerical tinge into relations between chiefs otherwise on their good behavior, he had lost a trick in South Seas etiquette; by forcing him to accept a valuable gift for which he had incautiously shown avidity, the Stevensons had gravely flawed his prestige. He could regain standing level with that of these obviously chiefly whites—he had been allowed to believe Louis close to Queen Victoria, and was impressed, as Islanders always were, by a photograph of Louis with Kalakaua—only by heaping them with favors and presents. Besides, Louis could give him much valuable information about white men's ways potentially useful in the polity of Apemama. So, duly enhancing the value of the concession by long hesitation and exhaustive scrutiny of Louis and Fanny, the famous tyrant formally admitted them ashore and bent all his power in their behalf.[25]

Ashore they went with all their gear: Ah Fu, camera, magic lantern, garden seeds, medicine bottles, typewriter. . . . At the tyrant's rasping orders scores of subjects scurried to collect a special village for the guests: "collect" is the word, for the local house is highly portable—a dozen men with shoulders under its thatched superstructure can shift it to any other properly aligned set of posts. Dwelling-house, eating-house, cook-house, and odd subsidiary shacks became a group christened Equator Town—doubly appropriate, since the Equator itself runs within half a degree of Apemama—shielded from the light-fingered or the inquisitive by an invisible line of tabu. The penalty for infringement, whether of formal tabu or mere orders, was likely to be a bullet in the back from the "king's" ready Winchester. One male (to learn white men's cooking) and several practically naked female servants were assigned to see that the party lacked nothing. And off sailed the schooner to call back at leisure.

Here too it would be foolish to paraphrase Louis's account of Tembinok' and his island in a section of *In the South Seas* in which even Colvin saw merit. Fanny planted lettuce and onions; the schooner being delayed by weather and accident, there was ample, rather anxious time for them to mature. (A large free-lancing schooner that called in the interval asked so much for a passage to Samoa that Louis refused; this was lucky, since she sank after leaving Apemama, only part of her crew surviving.) Since the voracious local mosquitoes did not observe the tabu, Fanny lined the principal house with a gigantic bag of netting, inside which life went airily and strangely on. Louis and Lloyd worked away on *The Wrecker*, their new mystery adventure founded on the queer story of the ship called the *Wandering Minstrel*,[26] and luxuriated in the thought of where they were.

Life was pervaded by the personality of Tembinok'—no sulky, numb brute like his opposite number on Makin but a man of intellectual vigor, curiosity, and, for all his childishness about gadgets, an adult approach to affairs. His mashed-in English, founded on the missionary's teaching, was incisive and fluent. His domestic policies showed the realistic foresight and the cynical reliance on *force-majeure* of a rising medieval baron. His greatest pleasure was to compose poetry which, to Louis's delight, he defined as "about sweethearts, and trees, and the sea— and no true, all-the-same lie." [27] Like Teriitera, having begun merely as a chief duly honoring equals, he ended in deep personal fondness for his guests as warm as theirs for him. Again the Island game of beggar-my-neighbor in terms of prestige became occasion for a valuable transcultural relationship.

When the *Equator* finally appeared and the party packed up, the dark and Dante-esque face of Tembinok' puckered with genuine grief; nor does the well-integrated Micronesian weep so readily as his distant Polynesian cousins. He had found a sort of younger brother in this strange lean white man of patent chiefliness—a quality that, in the expert judgment of Tembinok', Fanny also showed. Knowing only his own harem of loyal female animals, he marveled at her high status and qualifications: ". . . plenty chench" (plenty sense), was his astounded comment. Enthusiastically he accepted her design of a royal standard for him—green, red, and yellow, with a black shark in the middle in token of his legendary descent from a woman-chief impregnated by a shark-god.

Reid was now to drop the party in Samoa to pick up the mail steamer for Sydney, thence home for a visit only. It was a poor voyage. Lloyd was limping from a leg ulcer, Fanny none too well. In an emergency that saw the hands losing their heads and Reid entangled elsewhere, Ah Fu probably saved the ship by cutting a line adrift at the crucial moment. But the red wine held out, the various musical instruments remained operable, and Louis's birthday at sea was celebrated with due tunefulness and bibulousness. Now he was homeward bound, brown, fit, far-traveled.

The flaw in the plan, the unexpected significance soon to intrude, was that the cloud-masked mountains coming up hand over hand on the starboard beam on December 7, 1889, were the inner peaks of Upolu in Samoa.

Success that she was, the *Equator* had not resolved a gnawing problem taken on board as she sailed from Honolulu:

As first reader and last critic, Fanny had been on the warpath again. The issue this time was neither aesthetic strategy nor decency of content but the manufacturing and merchandising problem of how to handle the letters for McClure. She stated her position well if disingenuously in appealing to Colvin:

Louis has the most enchanting material that any one ever had in the whole world for his book, and I am afraid he is going to spoil it all. He has taken it into his Scotch Stevenson head . . . that his book must be a sort of scientific and historical impersonal thing comparing the different languages (of which he knows nothing, really) and the different peoples, . . . and the whole thing to be impersonal, leaving out all he knows of the people themselves. And I believe there is no one living who has got so near them or who understands them as he does. . . . I am going to ask you to throw the weight of your influence as heavily as possible in the scales with me. . . . otherwise Louis will spend a good deal of time in Sydney actually reading other people's books on the Islands. What a thing it is to have a "man of genius" to deal with. It is like managing an overbred horse. Why with my own feeble hand I could write a book that the whole world would jump at. . . . Even if I thought it a desirable thing to write what he proposes, I should still think it impossible unless after we had lived and studied here for some twenty years or more. . . .[28]

Few novelists could concoct a letter so eloquent of character as this jumble of presumption, sense, and misrepresentation.

Lloyd backed Fanny; Colvin apparently made the requested protest. Fanny's letter contrasts sharply with Louis to Colvin:

. . . material for a very singular book of travels: . . . strange stories and characters, cannibals, pirates, ancient legends, old Polynesian poetry—never was so generous a farrago. . . . The Pacific is a strange place; the nineteenth century only exists there in spots; all round, it is a no man's land of all the ages, a stir-about of epochs and races, barbarisms and civilizations, virtues and crimes.[29]

Her bill of particulars shows a curious fear of objectivity. "Impersonal" is twice used as a reproach; Louis's "stern sense of duty" may be all-in-the-family joking, but not her sense of outrage over his intention actually to consult previous writers who might throw further light on what he had been seeing. That objective sense demanded twenty years in the Islands is absurd exaggeration and contradicts her assertion that, after ten months in the Pacific, Louis understands Islanders better than anybody else alive. Apparently she wished Louis to apply to Tautira the mood of *Travels with a Donkey*, whereas Louis sought to exercise his brains as well as his sensibility.

Technical issues alien to Fanny the amateur may have been influencing him. The tools for the *Donkey* sort of job were still in hand; he might easily have satisfied her. No writer—except possibly the author of *Old Calabria*—was ever handier than Louis at keeping the reader comfortable while immersed in obscure geography and history.[30] You enjoy the *Donkey* about as much regardless of whether Camisards are garments or strong winds. But, once become interested in the heretics of the Massif Central for themselves as well as in Louis the hopeful traveler, and you at once perceive with what dry and scanty husks you were fobbed off. It is the poorest possible reporting because it was never intended to be reporting at all, which is fair enough.

In handling the Islands, however, this insouciant approach becomes technical fudging, as impressionistic writers on the area, from Melville on and down, always show. A clever tactician can handle the kiver-to-kiver Calvinist fanatics of France without elaborate background and still be intelligible because educated readers in the Western tradition are more or less familiar with cognate values: though they may never have heard of "Spirit" Séguier, they know John Brown or "Prophet" Peden. But the bases of South Sea behavior are alien to, if not always incongruent with, our ways of doing and feeling. To tell the unprepared Western reader about Kalakaua or Teriitera is to distort impressions to a degree repugnant to a matured literary conscience. In *In the South Seas* Louis skilfully symbolized these anomalies by selection and placing of those early encountered —the surly boarding party of Marquesans leading on to the tearful poor man with the rejected pig and on to the incomprehensible duties of the old wizard hired to braid old men's beards. And at that the reader gets none too much help among transcultural pitfalls. Louis should have furnished even more of such rich and informative summary as ornaments the opening of *A Footnote to History*. That there was so much such matter in *South Seas* is a credit to his stubbornness and sound instinct.

This might have been indeed a magnificent book if Fanny had not been snapping at his heels and Colvin baying at him from a frustratingly long distance. As it was, these two bakers pulling at a very sinewy devil skewed the work into a huddle of ill-assorted elements that, individually, are very well handled and invaluably immediate. Joseph Conrad highly approved of the book in even this mangled form.[31] But again Fanny was right commercially. After patiently running thirty-four instalments, the

New York *Sun* threw the deal back at McClure: ". . . not what they asked for," Colvin said, "not letters of incident and experience . . . but only the advance sheets of a book and rather a dull book at that." [32] The series had not been at all so popular as the decapitated *Black Arrow*. McClure complained that it had too much of Stevenson "the moralizer" and too little of Stevenson "the romancer." [33] Since moralizing hardly appears in the work—except in its able defense of cannibalism—this may merely have been the first explanation occurring to him. No doubt, like most great editors, he operated largely by the pricking of his thumbs, occasionally guessing wrong and then misleading himself and others by trying to account for his error.

Embarrassed, Louis pled that the *Sun* material had been meant only as a "first state," [34] and that some time rehandling would make a good, or at least solid, book of it. But merely getting the *Sun* copy into shape had almost broken his back during much of 1890, so the end-product was that shapeless selection in book form called *In the South Seas* that would take a generation to be only half-appreciated.[35]

Our point here is that, right or wrong in commercial tactics, Fanny had probably felt something important—and unwelcome—happening to Louis:

Previous schemes involving research and objectivity, such as the abortive history of the Highlands, had never disturbed her; whereas she was now outraged by his proposing "objective," "impersonal" treatment of the South Seas. Why?

The solution—this is bald surmise—is that, while reading up the Appin murder in 1880, he was still largely the Louis whom Fanny had married; whereas, while reading Fornander on Polynesians, he was undergoing a major shift toward greater maturity. Standing up with her before Dr. Scott, he was still much of the hyperaesthetic, egocentric gypsy who had thoughtlessly started a forest fire. That mischievously amusing youth never died; he always maintained residence and occasionally looked out of the window like the Bottle Imp looking dartingly out of the bottle—as the Governor of New South Wales, the Colonial Office, and the High Commissioner of the Western Pacific would be well aware within a few years. Most people, particularly such changelings as Louis, now and again show flashbacks to behavior patterns long abandoned for daily wear. But, as he passed the midthirties, Louis was growing with cumulative acceleration in directions previously only hinted at. The *ci-devant* stars of his private theater—The Gifted Boy, The Apologist for Idlers, Fastidious Brisk, and young Mr. Linger-after-Lust— had to crowd up into smaller and smaller garrets to make room for maturer versions of Louis. Some of these new roles were not always comfortable, but he played most of them well. Some greatly pleased Fanny; others greatly disquieted her.

Shrewdly self-aware though he was, perhaps not even Louis altogether grasped what was going on. So it is understandable that Fanny never articulately grasped it, could only fret over and react to it, expressing only in terms that disguised the fact her fear that somehow the ground was shifting under her feet. Thus her extreme uneasiness over *South Seas* may well have masked her reluctance to give up the young Louis Stevenson—fair-haired, magpie-brilliant, headlong, who, already in love with Fanny Osbourne, had used his trip in the Cévennes as a means to pouring experience over himself, who so slashingly denounced research and soberly objective judgment as trappings of "Bummkopfery." In view of his nearness to forty, his hair darkened to a heavy brown and showing sprinklings of gray, he had kept faith with her on such scores rather better than might have been expected of a chronic invalid. But now he was in effect seeking leave—of nobody in particular—to grow up relative to the world as the objective category of experience.

This approach to Fanny's difficulties may be wrong, though I think highly of it. It cannot be wrong to discern some such shift in Louis. The evidence is too striking. We have seen some of its obscure beginnings. Perhaps the Amateur Emigrant twitched the course a few points in this direction ten years before Fanny grew so troubled in Honolulu. By 1884, pondering his proximity to death at Nice, Louis hinted to Henley:

> . . . to return to daylight and the winds, I perceive I have grown to live too much in my work and too little in life. . . . a good fault for me; to be able to do so, is to succeed.[36]

True, but only because of physical handicaps and need of income. Suppose health improved and money came more readily?

By 1886 in Bournemouth, though Louis never lost his passion for the amenities and glories of the great art of writing, he sometimes saw it in new relation to other things; he wrote Gosse:

> As for the art that we practice, I have never been able to see why its professors should be respected. They chose the primrose path; when they found it was not all primroses, but some of it brambly, and much of it uphill, they began to think and speak of themselves as holy martyrs. But a man is never martyred in any honest sense in the pursuit of his pleasure; and *delirium tremens* has more of the honour of the cross.[37]

Within a year, he can say in "The Day After Tomorrow":

> Play in its wide sense, as the artificial induction of sensation, including all games *and all arts*, will, indeed, go far to keep [the man of the socialist future] conscious of himself; but in the end he wearies for realities.[38]

Next year he advised the "Young Gentleman Who Proposes to Embrace the Career of Art":

> Suppose it ill paid: the wonder is it should be paid at all. . . . To give the public what they do not want and yet expect to be supported; we have here a strange pretension and yet not uncommon, above all with painters.[39]

This is a heresy that many artists would call treason. On Parnassus the sensitive creator's right to a living in return for his pleasing himself cannot safely be questioned. But this heretic can hardly be accused of inadequate sympathy for artists or of ignorance of how the dismayed but stubborn creator feels about niggardly returns. Louis was merely extruding into a world wider than that of the youngster-author of *Voces Fidelium* who so itched and burned to write and write that law and engineering seemed criminal waste of time.

In later stages the thing is even clearer. After the *Equator* voyage he writes: "0.6 of me is artist, 0.4 adventurer. . . . since I have indulged the second part, I think the formula begins to change: 0.55 of an artist, 0.45 of the adventurer. . . ." [40] In 1893 he baldly asserts: "I ought to have been able to build lighthouses and write David Balfours too." [41] Will Low, loyal intimate of the Barbizon days, wailingly deplored this attitude and Louis cheerfully spurred him on to reply to the "Young Gentleman" in print. But there was no chance of his agreeing with his antagonist. Making a long-delayed adjustment to perspective, he could hardly regard the sensibilities of those with more consistent emotions about pretty painting. Low was not the man to understand how Louis could simultaneously look on artists and writers as people reveling in demanding play and yet feel all possible reverence for their greater works.

A negative heresy, demotion of the Holy Ghost, so to speak. But then, this was the member of the Trinity whom Louis never grasped.

There followed positive actions that would have interested even Mr. Worldly Wiseman—no febrile demonstrations about Gordon or the Irish Land League but efforts to relate Louis Stevenson to politics and markets as participator, not spectator. In that blundering letter to the *Times* from Honolulu this new-fledged citizen of the world, growingly conscious of responsibilities to mankind in general and to Britain and a Scots conscience in particular, was merely trying his new knife on the nearest tree.

The *Equator* provided another sort of impulse toward hitherto condemned reality: As Reid talked trading stations, tabu boy-

cotts, shell, copra, and the sunburned, cotton-clad exiles who
dealt in such things, Louis and Lloyd planned going into business—to buy or build a schooner to be called the *Northern
Light*, with Reid in command, and make living expenses for
the whole family by sailing the Islands as traders *de luxe*. Reid
liked his prospective owners and knew enough of Louis's resources and prospects to see it would be a good berth. Round
the table in the dwarfish cabin they planned how to fit up the
trade room, who would bunk where, how much Three Castles
tobacco and red wine to store; Jekyll, Hyde & Co. was suggested
as name of the operating firm. The project was dropped not because of suspected impracticability but because, as the projectors
learned more of island trading—the ethics of which were on a
par with the shoddy merchandise handled—it smelled too
strongly of petty swindling. In a given transaction both sides
of the counter understood that nothing—copra, calico, or coin—
was as represented. The decision was sound. But the point
here is that the last time Louis had dreamed of floating living
quarters, it had been the *Eleven Thousand Virgins of Cologne*,
which was to have no economic function whatever—a significant change from the weedy placidity of French canals to the
mighty and turbulent Pacific; from a floating hermitage for artists to the copra-bugs and greasy surf boats of the Island
schooner.

Why Scott and Mark Twain tried to combine writing with
being men of affairs I do not know. Louis's case sounds like improved health accelerating the approach of emotional maturity.
Seven years from Menton to marriage were concentrated apprenticeship at his craft. Ten years from marriage to Samoa went
half to consolidating his talent, half to staving off death, necessarily in insulation. Now the South Seas—that incredibly picturesque actuality involving gin, cannibals, and derelicts—coincided with health as opportunity to grasp at things that Louis
had previously thought to be only stage props. The grasp would
be clumsy in result but deft in detail. In London Colvin bewailed
the money, time, and energy wasted in Louis's Samoan involve-

ments with his "blacks and chocolates," for Colvin had small idea of what Samoa was like. It took Henry James to follow Louis's situation so thoroughly that Graham Balfour said he could take a First in Samoan affairs, and to understand, however wordily, that such distractions meant richer life and richer life meant better work. But it was rough on Fanny. She had sublimated her own sense of her overweening importance into an even stronger sense of the importance of her nursing, steering, advising, protecting Louis, because he was the brilliant, picturesque, prosperously reared, magnetic "creator" that she had always dreamed of being. His superb performance of the egocentric, sensitive, unworldly artist of fiction had been the foundation of the relation. Now he was again a changeling, in a fashion tending to dismay her—not that she could ever have admitted it—much as the metamorphosis of The Sick Child had dismayed Aunt Maggie. Since Bournemouth, Fanny had been contracting. Louis was in a new phase of expansion and, in a sense that did not preclude continued intimacy with his wife, he had to do it alone.

The importance of where a rootless man takes root and happens to die is almost equal to that of his birthplace.

As the *Equator* neared Samoa, the island of Upolu probably came first into view. Presently a man peering over the bulwarks could also have made out the poured-out heap of Savaii, the larger island to westward, much of it sterile from recent lava flows. Over the eastward horizon lies the craggy, old, middle-sized island of Tutuila, its broken-down, flooded crater being the best harbor in the group; still farther, the Manu'a group of scraps of islets. The highest proportion of arable land, hence the bulk of population and the principal white settlement, gives Upolu hegemony. As customary headquarters of the highest native chiefs, she also has highest prestige. In any case Upolu is no inconsiderable rock, being the size of Staten Island; but, as high islands go in the Pacific, her jungle-smothered mass rising tamely from the ocean, her elderly volcanic contours worn into somewhat characterless slopes, are not so striking as some that Louis had already seen.

Closing with the coral-girt north coast, he could have picked out white-plastered churches spaced grandiloquently alongshore and the bulging, huddled roofs of the elegant Samoan basket houses, perhaps through glasses even tiny brown figures indistinguishable from other Polynesians at this distance. Then here was Apia steaming in the sun, backed by a conical, furry-green hill called Mt. Vaea.

Long before anchoring, a prepared observer could have made out signs of the turmoil then centering attention on Samoa. Those unusually extensive plantations of coco-palms meant German ambition and enterprise. Most of the churches meant British Protestant missionaries. There was an American among the men-of-war riding gingerly within the break of the reef, yards squared like aggressive elbows. This harbor of Apia is a mere bottle-shaped, coral-defined pool, its only entrance a gap in surf-tormented coral kept open by fresh water from a small river here entering the sea; vessels with much draft of water lie well out toward the bottle-neck and lighter everything ashore. The flurry of taking the schooner into this navigational bag's end without creating an international incident by fouling a national ship probably absorbed Louis's attention while it lasted. Then the ship's boat took him and his ashore to seek quarters and information.

He already knew this frowsy, sweaty settlement as scene of the strange events of which he had written the *Times,* and was well aware that it still held the title of "Hell of the Pacific" inherited from Levuka when Fiji went respectable. It straggled for a mile or so along the beach between the horns of a shallow bight in the shore line; consisted of white-style, wooden, verandaed one- and two-story buildings housing both trading stores and traders; churches as principal features; native villages lying up the mountain and to either flank. It needed only false fronts, in fact, to look like a small western town strung along a railroad. But the view was of surfy reef and deep Pacific instead of arid plain and scurfy mountain. For water-tank and railroad siding, Apia had the pier and warehouse of the "German Firm," the *Deutsche Handels und Plantagen Gesellschaft für Süd-See Inseln zu Hamburg*, which had meant to be to the South Pacific what the East India Company had been to India. Making Germany still more salient in this tepid puddle was the astounding wreck of His Imperial German Majesty's corvette *Adler*—her red-rusty skeleton is still there—smashed on her beam-ends on the reef by the hurricane of eight months before: ". . . tossed up there like a schoolboy's cap upon a shelf . . . a thing to dream of." [42] Salvage crews were still working on the sunken or stranded wrecks of USS *Trenton, Nipsic,* and *Vandalia* and of HIGMS *Olga,* driven ashore by the same storm in spite of all their engines could do. These relics of recent high times naturally interested any Stevenson, however sterile his share of the family concern with what wind and waves could accomplish. As times grew high again, the unexpected arrival of a British man-of-war to call for orders would raise all too likely rumors that her mission was to arrest and deport a factious British subject named Robert Louis Stevenson. . . .

The sea-weary and shabby party wandered down "the beach" —meaning the main street of Apia, barrooms and churches on one side, salt water on the other—Lloyd wearing dark glasses and earrings and carrying his ukulele, Fanny in a broad straw native hat and carrying her guitar, no doubt because irreplaceable musical instruments could not be trusted with the boat's crew. Observing this equipment and Louis's invariably and Joe Strong's probably extraordinary appearance, the Rev. Mr. Clarke of the London Missionary Society took them for broken-down entertainers off the San Francisco steamer trying their luck in Apia. (The error was pardonable; next year a small circus arrived and had to sell its horses to raise passage-money home; Louis bought one for Aunt Maggie to ride.) If Clarke told Louis of his conclusion, it unquestionably delighted the author of "Providence and the Guitar."

Somehow they fell into the arms of a brisk Michigan-born

trader with a Samoan wife, Harry J. Moors, who offered to put them up and give all other assistance needed.[43] This man had a major hand in settling the Stevensons in Samoa. He was no petty swindler of savages on a remote island, but owner of a chain of outlying trading posts and, perforce, banker, factor, import agent, and local politician. No mouse squeaked or plot hatched without his getting some inkling. In Samoa business and politics were inextricable, for the "Long Handle Firm" was a mere economic arm of Berlin—oftener than not the German consul in Samoa had doubled as manager of the Firm's Pacific interests. Moors's ability to keep headway against the Germans vouches for his acumen. Hospitable, humorous, he readily charged himself with doing these strange and noted newcomers the favors of advice and adjustment that the old hand can always do the new chum in the Islands. No doubt he would have been just as obliging if Louis had offered him no potential advantages.

Under Moors's and Clarke's auspices the party rented a small cottage to live in while getting their bearings and arranging passage to Sydney. Louis began to seek material for the Samoan section of the *Sun* letters, in which Moors was most useful. The important development, however, was that, within a few weeks, Louis determined to buy and plant land in Samoa—a magniloquent replacement for the scheme of the abortive *Northern Light*.

This obviously rash decision might never have been made without Moors's countenance. True, there was a case for Louis's settling in Samoa: The political situation was deplorable and not likely to improve; the place offered few of Hawaii's conveniences; so far Louis thought both place and people inferior to Tahiti and its natives. But, for his health, he needed a permanent headquarters in the South Pacific; Hawaii was too cold, he cared little for its Westernized features, and he disliked it anyway. Samoa had regular mail steamers, Sydney to Auckland to San Francisco, plus regular German service to Australia. A cable entrusted to a mail boat's purser would reach London via Auckland within a week. Even Honolulu could not better that.

For health the muggy, populated beach was unsuitable. But the slope rises steadily behind Apia. A few hundred feet up, nights are cool and winds on the stimulating side of balmy—much like the being at sea in the tropics that suited Louis best of all. At Vailima he never had the fits of insomnia that had bothered him off and on since Bournemouth.

To turn landed proprietor and planter, however, instead of merely dwelling at optimum elevation, was another matter. Louis managed to think of it as potential security for his family. Fanny may have helped this curious notion to grow. She was so proud of her green thumb and her alleged pioneering background that, in her ears, "tropical plantation" sounded most enticing. Cocoa and pineapple were said to do well in Samoa; so might vanilla. Experiments in such cash crops could accompany sustenance cultivation of banana, chickens, hogs, cattle, and garden-truck. Having capably fostered growth and liveableness at Austin, Virginia City, Silverado, Hyères, Skerryvore, and Apemama, she thought wishfully of several hundred acres of tropical humus waiting to be put to work—an appetite that may have disqualified her as advisor to Louis. Yet it is hard to blame her. In her own semi-ailing person she took the brunt of the project as it materialized. When Louis's death cut off the necessary flow of new capital, she was well along toward creating her dream.

It was Moors who should have known—and advised—better, for arguments *con* were devastating: No man with health as shaky as Louis's should pioneer in the tropics or anywhere else. Political prospects justified nobody but a German in risking serious capital in Samoa. Cocoa eventually did well there, but in 1889 not even the German experts knew that it would pay; pineapple is an awkwardly perishable crop without a cannery at hand; vanilla was an unknown quantity. Labor supply was most unsatisfactory: Since Samoans have never yet worked steadily in large-scale agriculture, the Germans were using "blackbirded" (i.e., semi-kidnapped) Melanesians in a dragooned quasi-slavery that Louis could hardly stomach long. To provide for his family Louis's best means was to set Baxter to investing available surplus in solid British securities. As any disinterested businessman could have told him would happen, ". . . the plantation never paid its way, and never seriously promised to become self-supporting." [44]

Moors's disinterestedness may not have been complete. The local agent for anybody with such resources as Louis's would draw steady profits and commissions well worth while in the miniature Samoan economy. Moors may also have hoped, as had Kalakaua, that Louis's presence would help to draw English-speaking attention to a spot that his antagonists, the Germans, preferred obscure. He must have hugged himself daily when, in a few months, Louis was addressing to the *Times* or the *Pall Mall Gazette* a series of bitter and devastatingly detailed indictments of what all the Powers—but particularly Germany—were doing in and to Samoa.

Not completely heedless, Louis was aware that behind Moors's round blue eyes lay dubious collaboration with unsavory "black-birders" and that, for other reasons, caution was indicated. "It is not the least likely that it will pay," he wrote Baxter coolly, "(although it may); but it is almost certain to support life, with very few external expenses." [45] He reassured himself about Moors with the reflection that Louis Stevenson was hardly worth swindling—a point sounding shrewder than it was in that time and place; and apparently realized that even the Book of Proverbs recommends not muzzling the ox that treadeth out the corn. I have no reason to believe that Moors took unreasonable advantage; he certainly well earned his commissions in arranging for clearing, building, the importation of necessaries, and in teaching Louis the ins and outs of Samoa. But a man of his experience, acting strictly in friendly solicitude, could hardly have failed to have discouraged the project from the beginning, sharply and decisively.

The shelf up the mountain of which Churchill had told Louis eighteen months before was nucleus of the land that Louis bought: Nearly 400 acres of heavy high bush[46] three miles back of the port and some 800 feet above sea level, at approximately a pound (then $5—minus) an acre. Buildings eventually cost Louis £2000 more; road-making, clearing, stock, planting, and so forth probably had worked the whole investment up to £4000 when he died,[47] partly covered by £1500 from the sale of Skerry-vore, which was nominally Fanny's. Nobody else in Samoa but the German Firm had such sums readily at command. They bought a great deal:

> . . . three streams, two waterfalls, a great cliff, an ancient native fort, a view of the sea and lowlands. . . . It would be affectation to omit a good many head of cattle; above all as it required much diplomacy to have them thrown in . . . a good deal more forest than I have any need for; or to be plain the whole estate is one impassable jungle, which must be cut down and through at considerable expense.[48]

When the cattle were sought for, however, they were flagrantly not there, nor was there much reason to suppose they ever had been; and three years later only 300 of the acres proved ever to have belonged to the original seller.

Another kind of livestock, neglected in negotiations, proved more useful as well as possibly more substantial. Vailima[49] had and still has a local reputation as a great haunt of *aitu*, demong-ghosts of both sexes and nasty habits, one specially notorious as a succubus commerce with whom means death. The presence in the area of this creature and her colleagues was assurance that, whatever their other troubles as amateur planters, the Stevensons would suffer little from natives marauding after dark.

Nothing ties one down like landed property. But Louis still thought of going home, if only to visit and settle his affairs in the light of these new commitments. Deputing Moors to get a patch of jungle cleared and a temporary dwelling erected in it —which was faithfully accomplished—the Stevensons sailed for Sydney on the *Lübeck* in February 1890, for a reunion with Belle—Joe had gone ahead to join her—and then home via Orient or P & O.

To Louis large cities—and Sydney was as old as Cincinnati and as large as San Francisco—meant special wines, white tablecloths, and bookstores. But by now nobody in the party could muster costumes at all appropriate for Castlereagh Street. When they appeared at a first-class Sydney hotel, brown as gypsies, their luggage consisting conspicuously of Island calabashes and weapons, Louis and Fanny looking much as Clarke had seen them at Apia, the functionary on duty—apparently one of the few literate subjects of the Queen who had never read *Jekyll* —gave them the standard treatment for discouraging ineligible guests. Louis lost his temper in the fashion that people usually remembered shrinkingly the rest of their lives and shifted to a less pretentious hotel. All rejoiced uncharitably when, as the press played the great man up, the offending hotel found itself daily sending bushels of fan-mail over to Louis.

This was when and where Dr. Hyde was chopped into inch pieces. But Louis had barely begun to look round him, hobnobbing with local artists and newspapermen and hanging round Circular Quay, raiding bookstores for the servant-girl fiction that he loved to relax with, when illness struck. Low though the latitude was, mild though the antipodean summer can be, Sydney's gusty breezes and urban infections laid him low with the familiar constellation of troubles: fever, cough, headache, pleurisy, loss of appetite, severe hemorrhage—first since Papeete. After a later and equally discouraging experiment, Louis peevishly rechristened the province of which Sydney was capital "New South Pole." Prosperous admirers moved him into the august Union Club where he could be quieter. Fanny began to doubt that he would ever leave it standing up. The only measure that occurred to either was to get Louis to sea again up among the Islands.

From schooner to liner, shipping east and north out of Sydney should have offered wide choice. But the maritime unions had struck the port, no white seaman could sign on, the quays were clogged with dead vessels—and Louis might well die before the strike ended. Fanny set her jaw and began to present the unusual spectacle of a lady prowling the water front. Again her persistence turned up a possibility: Henderson & Macfarlane, a minor trading firm, had a small fore-and-aft-rigged steamer, the *Janet Nichol,* due out for the Islands and able to sail because her deck hands were all unorganized, beetle-browed Kanakas. The Scots names of both ship and owners should have been good omens. But the firm refused—understandably—to book a dying man and an eccentric woman who kept repeating stubbornly that it was a matter of life and death and neither of them would be any trouble.

Louis sank daily. Refusal continued. I know no more of how Fanny broke the owners down than of how she conquered the sulky Chinese at Taravao. But, when the ship sailed, Mr. and Mrs. Stevenson and Lloyd were on board. As they boarded, another passenger fell reeling drunk off the gangway and had to be fished out. Thus sobered he proved to be a Sydneysider right out of the *New Arabian Nights*—Jack Buckland, who spent a short period each year in Sydney playing spendthrift on the accumulations of a small funded income and the rest of the year vegetating penniless as a petty trader out in the islands; he was to be Tommy Haddon of *The Wrecker.* People with such implausible histories are still sometimes to be found in the South Pacific. The other passengers were one of the owners, who found he approved of the intruders after all, and Ben Hird, veteran trader known and respected from Sydney to Jaluit, who greatly advanced Louis's and Lloyd's education in Island affairs.

The cargo included a job lot of cheap fireworks which set themselves off after the ship left Auckland—Fanny intervened just as the hands were jettisoning a smoking trunk containing Louis's hoard of manuscript—and a shiny new pulpit for a mission church from which, on a convivial occasion, Louis preached a sermon on St. Jacob's Oil (a patent medicine of the day) that, fortunately for decorum, has not come down to us. He disliked the ship, a narrow-built dirty roller with a teakettle of an engine, and a cabin irksomely stuffy in a following breeze. But the prescription proved itself again. The moment latitude lowered and the breeze grew softer, he turned fit and energetic, though blood-spitting continued half through the voyage.

The *Janet*'s plodding rounds—Suwarrow, Tongareva, up into Micronesia again—allowed only limited time ashore in any given place but did show Louis such strange new things as the tiny ghost-town on Suwarrow. On the return run he left the ship at New Caledonia to look about him and hear French again. Invited to dine with the governor, he had to appear in a hastily constructed dress suit that made him look like a tramp comedian. The place had little other humor. *The Ebb-Tide* made passing use of the shudders Louis derived from the gray-faced convict band playing in the square in Noumea while the *fonctionnaires* sat over their *digestifs* in the cafés. Kalaupepa and Noumea were the two most "distressful countries" he ever saw.

Still fit, he rejoined Fanny in Sydney in August—and fell ill at once. The moral was unmistakable. Even *visits* home had to be renounced, as he wrote Henry James:

> I do not think I shall come to England more than once and then it'll be to die. . . . even here, which they call sub- or semi-tropics, I come only to catch cold. . . . The thermometer was nearly down to 50° the other day—no temperature for me, Mr. James: how should I do in England? [50]

This decision, dismal enough in itself, was further darkened by the outraged scolding to which it moved Colvin, who, for once unveiling his hostility to Fanny, seems to have let it be seen that he blamed her for it. Louis made it loyally and truthfully clear that the verdict was as much his as hers, and wrought hard to restore her to Colvin's presumed good graces:

> . . . if I tell you that she cried all night after reading your letter, it is simply to give you a measure of what she thinks of your opinion. And yet she knew all the time that you scarce meant all; she—and I—understand you as you understand me. . . . when it became more and more clear to me that I ought to stay in the tropics, my one trouble was about

you. . . . I said to Fanny: I cannot stay here, I must go home to Colvin. She said: He made me promise to keep you in any place that suited your health; . . . since I am speaking plainly for once, I bind it upon you as a sacred duty, and upon another beside you: should you be dangerously ill, I must be summoned. . . . I have a charge of souls. I keep many eating and drinking. . . . But I have to see you again.[51]

Fanny wrote how, in Samoa, Louis had been waking beside her at night to wonder aloud at the blessing of being able to live like other people, active and energetic. Both were hurt and troubled, no less so because living separately; Fanny was permitted only daily visits at the Union Club. She even went to the length of proposing that they give up the whole South Seas prospect and go home regardless. Louis wrote miserably to Mrs. Sitwell:

In the South Seas, I have health, strength. I can walk and ride and be out of doors, and do my work without distress. There are great temptations, on the other hand, to go home. I do not say it is to die—because I seem incapable of dying, but I know it is to go back to the old business. . . . remember that, though I take my sicknesses with a decent face, they do represent suffering, and weakness, and painful disability; as well as the loss of all that makes animal life desirable. . . . my feeling for my friends at home has pulled me hard; but can you wonder if the hope of . . . some snatch of a man's life after all these years of the sickroom, tempted me extremely? . . . If you blame me, I shall be surprised. If you do not, try and get Colvin, without giving him an idea that he has hurt us, to write a kindlier letter to Fanny.[52]

It is hard to avoid impatience with Colvin sitting in London, aware of how hungry Louis was for such friends as himself, how much Europe was in the marrow of the exile's bones, yet scolding a man prevented solely by physiological crippling from coming home to all those highly valued things. But Colvin never managed to divest himself of Gosse's frankly stated notion that the fruitful life literary could not be lived more than three miles from Charing Cross.

Often exiles, Scots are usually homesick in consequence. Louis's originality lay in his having deliberately to sentence himself.

Le Ona

> . . . there are always high and brave and amusing lives
> to be lived; and a change of key, however exotic, does
> not exclude melody.
>
> —Stevenson to Mrs. Fairchild,
> *Letters:* IV, 102

I N 1890 Henry Adams, seeking distraction from the recent death of his wife, traveled into the Pacific with his
friend John La Farge. In October they reached Samoa, where
their appropriately august letters of introduction secured them
great deference from Sewall, the U.S. consul. Adams found that
it also made him all sorts of a great chief in Samoan eyes
merely to state that USS *John Adams*—a man-of-war closely and
indiscreetly involved in recent Samoan squabbles—was named
after his great-grandfather.

Sewall soon took them up the mountain to call on the only
resident lion.[1] Adams wrote home about it voluminously:

. . . a clearing dotted with burned stumps. . . . a two-story
Irish shanty with steps outside to the upper floor and a gal-
vanized iron roof . . . squalor like a railroad navvy's board
hut . . . a man so thin and emaciated that he looked like a
bundle of sticks in a bag, with a head and eyes morbidly intelligent and restless . . . dirty striped pajamas, the baggy legs
tucked into coarse woollen stockings, one of which was bright
brown in color, the other a purplish dark tone. . . . a
woman . . . the usual missionary nightgown which was no
cleaner than her husband's shirt and drawers, but she omitted
the stockings . . . complexion and eyes were dark and
strong, like a half-breed Mexican. . . . though I could not
forget the dirt and discomfort, I found Stevenson extremely

entertaining . . . he cannot be quiet, but sits down, jumps up, darts off and flies back, at every sentence he utters, and his eyes and features gleam with a hectic glow. . . . looking like an insane stork . . .[2]

When asking them to breakfast later, Louis and Fanny encouraged La Farge and Adams to bring their own provisions. After Louis had cordially supplied him with invaluable introductions to the cream of Tahitian "royalty," Adams had the grace to feel slightly embarrassed over how he had enlarged on their "squalor." But he was doomed to proceed with invidious and inaccurate solemnity:

> Their mode of existence here is far less human than that of the natives and compared with their shanty a native house is a palace; but the squalor must be somehow due to his education. All through him, the education shows. His early associates were all second-rate; he never seems by any chance to have come in contact with first-rate people, either men, women, or artists. He does not know the difference between people and mixes them up as if they were characters in his New Arabian Nights. Of course he must have found me out at once, for my Bostonianism, and finikin clinging to what I think the best, must rub him raw all over, all the more because I try not to express it; but I suspect he does not know quite enough to hate me for it; and I am sure he would never have the finesse to penetrate La Farge, though compared with La Farge, I am a sort of Stevenson for coarseness. . . . The two characters in contact are rather amusing as contrasts; the oriental delicacy of La Farge seems to be doubled by the Scotch eccentricities of Stevenson who is as one-sided as a crab, and flies off at angles no matter what rocks stand in his way.[2]

It was too bad that Belle had not yet arrived, for her neat darkness gave rise to a rumor that she was Louis's daughter by a former non-Caucasian wife.[3]

Adams peevishly noted that, though Louis knew of La Farge, who was a hero of Will Low's, he ". . . had evidently not the faintest associations with my name";[4] suggested that some of what Louis had grandiloquently spent on too much land might have bought soap; labeled Fanny "a wild Apache"; and persisted in seeing Louis as vulgar end-product of a low rearing and un-stimulating friends. The intimate of such blown-in-the-bottle first-raters as Clarence King, John Hay, and La Farge—whose fame, Adams averred, would still be growing in 1990—had a nat-ural right intuitively to deduce the penurious slums of Heriot Row and the coarsening influence of such toadies as Jenkin, Meredith, Leslie Stephen, Fanny Sitwell, and Henry James. Per-haps the only thing that might have saved Adams from making such an exhibition of his less admirable side would have been to see "Athenaeum Club" on Louis's calling card.

Still, it is late in the day to feel the old urge to kick Henry Adams for a snob. Forgiveness is easier because this is a valuable picture of the Stevensons newly installed in their kingdom. The "board shack" was the temporary dwelling, to be camped in rather à la Silverado while a comfortable house was building. The "burned stumps" were presage of a huge lawn before the house. The pair were alone because Lloyd was in England ar-ranging shipment of civilized necessities from Skerryvore, Aunt Maggie was to return with him from Scotland, and Belle and Joe were waiting in Sydney until matters had somewhat shaken down. They were so dirty and sloppy because both were hard at weeding, planting, cleaning—Louis worked in singlet and trou-sers, with bare feet. Provisions were so short because all men-of-war had left port and it was no longer profitable for local sup-pliers to bring produce to Apia—which immensely complicated the problem of getting provisions up the rough track from town. (Lloyd once likened that track to a Highland river without the trout.) One day Louis and Fanny lunched on a single avocado; another lunch was a can of sardines, supper the same day a single breadfruit. Apparently it never occurred to Louis's low breeding to explain their privations or to excuse their grubbiness by the exigencies of settling down in a tropical wilderness. People should be more careful when entertaining Brahmins unawares.

Within weeks improvements were going ahead rapidly—and expensively. The track was widened, though in Louis's time it was never practicable for wheels in all weathers; in the meantime riding down to Apia amounted to a sort of steeplechase in slow motion. The immediate clearing was freed of stumps, and extensive cutting of brush discouraged the mosquitoes that had so tortured Adams.[5] Saddle horses for personal transport, pack horses for supplies, and ducks, hogs, chickens, and a cow had variously to be stabled, fenced, or penned. During a roaring rain the horses ate the palm-thatch off their temporary stable and were found with their heads protruding into the weather like the giraffes out of a Noah's Ark. An overgrown banana patch and an abandoned *taro*[6] patch were found and cleared into usefulness, and Fanny's truck-garden was already hoping for onions, green peppers, parsley, tomatoes, and asparagus; she was startled to find that, in this climate, string beans grew a foot long. What time Louis could spare from *The Wrecker* and *South Seas* and, as family man of business, riding on his brown pony, Jack, to Apia, he spent with a bush-knife cutting paths in exploration of his new domain or doggedly uprooting the poetic sensitive plant that is so nasty an imported nuisance in Samoa. Wryly he noted deriving a great glow of virtuous feeling out of doing a shilling's worth of manual labor and a feeling of an afternoon wasted if he earned ten pounds by assiduous writing.

Perhaps only a chronic invalid can appreciate his exultation in his new privilege of physical activity. He discreetly left ax and mattock alone; but even so he could spend hours sweating wet and breathing deep without imminent risk of hemorrhage or weeks of exhaustion to follow. It had been eleven years since he had done anything as strenuous as his rugged rides to the port. For that matter, it had been seventeen years since he had chosen a prolonged place of residence for any reason other than established renown among the consumptive. This was no Menton, Davos, or Hyères, thick with invalids, soft to the enforcedly idle, artificial as a prison or a school, but a highly complicated community, raw, petty, turbulent, and peevishly stimulating in its own right. Small wonder that he felt as if readmitted to the human race after years of exile, or that here in Samoa he matured so broadly.

The improvement could nevertheless be exaggerated; relatively alone could his rejoicing be understood properly. In 1893, a temporary fit of discouragedly considering himself "an ancient, lean, grim, exiled Scot" set him to writing to Meredith:

> For fourteen years I have not had a day's real health; I have wakened sick and gone to bed weary; and I have done my work unflinchingly. I have written in bed, and written out of it, written in hemorrhages, written in sickness, written torn by coughing, written when my head swam for weakness; . . . I am better now, have been rightly speaking since first I came to the Pacific; and still, few are the days when I am not in some physical distress. And the battle goes on—ill or well, is a trifle; so as it goes. I was made for a contest, and the Powers have willed that my battlefield should be this dingy, inglorious one of the bed and the physic bottle. . . . I would have preferred a place of trumpetings and the open air over my head.[7]

Fanny—that "haunting, indefatigable and diminutive presence in a blue gown . . . she comes in heated and bemired up to the eyebrows, late for every meal." [8] —was the terror of hired labor and the admiration of her vastly amused husband, sure and direct, whether right or not, about chickens or cocoa, pineapple or pigs or people. For her too Samoa was a consummation. Louis never quite shook off the dream of going home, or at least of meeting Colvin in Cairo . . . or Ceylon . . . or Honolulu. . . . The day he died he was speculating about a trip to the States. But, while he lived, Fanny left Samoa only once for reasons other than her own or Louis's health. I have an impression that, as years came and went, Vailima became an obsession with her, enabling her to sink ever farther within herself while still feeling that to do so was to continue as a function of Louis the all-important.

During this preliminary hurly-burly the looming, rank, and shadow-tangled rain-forest clogging his domain deeply impressed Louis. Its morbid qualities enabled him to sympathize with the emotions with which, one day, a Samoan employee burst out of the high bush sweating in fear because an *aitu* had molested him at work. But Louis's own Westernized feelings centered on the vicious vigor of these woods:

> . . . Thick as a mob, deep as a sea,
> And silent as eternity. . . .
> 'Mid vegetable king and priest
> And stripling, I (the only beast)
> Was at the beast's work, killing; hewed
> The stubborn roots across, bestrewed
> The glebe with the dislustred leaves;
> . . . Here and there
> I spied and plucked by the green hair
> A foe more resolute to live,
> The toothed and killing sensitive. . . .
> I saw him crouch, I felt him bite
> And straight my eyes were touched with sight.
> I saw the wood for what it was:
> The lost and the victorious cause,
> The deadly battle pitched in line,
> Saw silent weapons cross and shine:
> Silent defeat, silent assault,
> A battle and a burial vault.
> Thick round me in the teeming mud
> Briar and fern strove to the blood. . . .
> . . . with despair
> Competing branches pushed for air.
> Green conquerors from overhead

Bestrode the bodies of their dead:
The Caesars of the silvan field,
Unused to fall, foredoomed to yield:
For in the groins of branches, lo!
The cancers of the orchids grow. . . .[9]

"The Woodman"—suppose Marvell had fallen asleep reading Darwin in the jungle—ranks high among Louis's best doggerel.

In January 1891, Louis went to Sydney to fetch Aunt Maggie and, of course, fell ill there, with a high fever this time. On their return, the "squalid" phase that Adams saw proved too much for her; she went visiting relatives in New Zealand until the projected big house should afford better quarters. This was the great scheme:

It still stands, considerably altered by the Germans in the 1900s, as Government House of New Zealand's Trusteeship of Western Samoa. I lived there for weeks off and on in 1946-47 and heard how a former Administrator's lady had persuaded herself that she saw Louis's thin hand, and then his whole person, scribbling away in the corner which was once his workroom —visions supplemented by sharp rappings on the ceiling. In its rapping phase, at least, periodic use of rat poison exorcised the spirit. If Louis's ghost walks, it must be on the North Bridge of Edinburgh or the northern scarp of the Pentlands.

Louis and Fanny drew, redrew and reredrew plans for the house, Moors also playing the game; then from a Sydney architect Louis got some ideas that proved far too costly to begin; then local talent was called in and plans were settled on in the cubage-wasting, airy style of timbers and planking that characterizes white men's houses in the British tropics, using corrugated iron roofs and many verandas. Over the years, as money came available—the success of *The Wrecker* financed a second block of house instead of the projected trading schooner—Vailima grew *en échelon* of two contiguous units each of two stories. Its fireplaces—for warming Louis's sheets, it appears—are still, I believe, the only such things in Samoa. Aunt Maggie paid for the bathhouse and the concrete work and pipes to bring a copious water supply down from the mountain. Verandas lined the northern face toward the monochromatic and vastly extensive wall of ocean. Apia itself was invisible, but ships approaching were easily made out—the San Francisco mails, the little German packet, the New Zealand packet, war vessels taking post on this troubled station, trading schooners, big square-riggers fetching supplies to the Firm and taking away copra. Louis's room, built like a swallow's nest in the northwest corner of the upper veranda, where he lived like a sergeant in barracks with little but a cot and a work table, had the best of this view. The red iron roof contrasted handsomely with the dull blue siding. In the rear were cook shed and staff quarters, to south and west rose heaped-up, dark, lofty forest. The original shack was rebuilt to the east as overflow quarters, sometimes for guests, sometimes for Belle and Joe, sometimes a bachelor hall for Lloyd. Down the slope and to the left the principal stream plunged over a rocky shelf into a much patronized bathing pool.

These premises, rather like the nucleus of a large children's camp, often puzzled visitors who had heard London or Sydneyside gossip about Louis's barbaric palace of immense cost and splendor. In the South Pacific, of course, Vailima *was* a palace. In Fiji in late 1891 Fanny found Polynesians settled there already agog with tales of this miraculous edifice. And local whites were necessarily much stirred by the great expense of importing so much lumber and hardware, for sawmills are scarce and rolling mills nonexistent in the Islands; every nail, sheet of iron, pane of glass, and sliver of wood in Vailima came from the Colonies or the States. "We call these our marble halls," Lloyd told some visitors who had evidently expected something more imposing than a capacious wooden barrack, "because they cost so much." [10]

Both browns and whites were even more deeply impressed at the arrival of the contents of Skerryvore plus bits from Heriot Row: mahogany and rosewood furniture, family portraits, hundreds of books, chests of silver and linen, wineglasses, decanters, and mirrors, a cottage piano that came up from Apia on poles slung over the shoulders of a whole troupe of Samoans, a plaster cast of Rodin's *Le Printemps*, gift of the sculptor, from which missionary-shy Samoans averted their shocked eyes. . . . Not even the manager of the Firm or the chief missionary at Malua had so many costly things that shone and broke easily. (There was even a small ice-machine that refused to work, confining the household to occasional supply of ice from transpacific ships.) So dinner at Vailima was soon the great show of the island— massive silver, glowing red wine, shaded lights reflecting in the varnished redwood of the "great hall," Samoans with flowers in their hair serving with the serene hauteur appropriate to duty for a great chief, fuming braziers under the table to keep mosquitoes away from chiefly ankles. On great occasions the staff wore striped blazers and special *lavalavas*[11] of the Royal Stewart tartan, which Louis chose for colorful blending with their skins—a Samoan, Belle wrote with an artist's accuracy, is the same hue as a light bay horse.

Though committed to bare feet and *holoku* by day, Fanny was tinily majestic on occasion in gray silk or a black velvet-and-lace that Louis bought her in Sydney. Louis too rigged out elaborately for evening—a starched white mess jacket, pleated white silk shirt made in Sydney, black dress trousers, pumps on his narrow feet: "Slovenly youth, all right—not slovenly age. So really now I am pretty spruce . . . fresh shave, silk socks, O a great sight!"[12] Trips to Apia saw him in battered white yachting cap, white shirt, white trousers tucked into lace-up high boots—an effect as of an irregular military man in tropic kit. Though during the day at home he might dress about as sketchily as ever, his prejudice against complicated living and elaborate possessions had unceremoniously vanished. For some while it had not been much of an issue; after all, his favorite passage from Walt Whitman was: "Do I contradict myself? . . . Very well, then, I contradict myself." He liked this life and he loved "My beautiful forest, O my beautiful, shining windy house!"[13] When riding back from Apia at night, he ordered lights kept burning, no matter how long he delayed, so that he could see the glow of his own windows through the trees.

The track to and from Apia was soon worn deep as much by social visits as by delivery of goods—dinings back and forth, occasional public balls (for Louis was now an earnest if never a brilliant dancer), evenings sponsored by Louis and Fanny for the growing and dislocated population of half-Samoans. Louis averred that the whites of Apia, however heterogeneous, averaged higher in ability and intelligence than an equally random lot of the same size in Europe or the States. Most were somehow interesting, many made sound friends: Sewall, the U.S. consul; Ide, the U.S. Land Commissioner, later Chief Justice of Samoa (it was to his lovely daughter Annie that Louis gave that famous deed to his birthday to console her for having been born on Christmas); Haggard (brother of the romancer), the gaily indiscreet British Land Commissioner; Moors aforesaid; Stuebel, the German consul, with whom Louis stayed friends in spite of formal frictions; affectionately respected missionaries like Clarke and Newell—at Clarke's Louis met George Brown, the fighting Wesleyan, whom he liked immensely, and James Chalmers, the martyr-hero of New Guinea missions, whom he thought one of the greatest personalities he had ever known. . . .

Vailima saw a great variety of occasional guests: Ben Hird and Jack Buckland from the *Janet;* a vacationing actress named Fraser who wrote of Vailima: "Things are certainly allowed to occur here. Any attempt at order would be coldly received" [14] (it would probably have been no news to Miss Fraser that Fanny had quickly come to loathe her); Sydney Lysaght, friend of Meredith's, poetically touring; "Max O'Rell," the French globetrotter; Count Nerli, painter of several controversial portraits of Louis; Count Festetics de Tolna, Hungarian yachtsman; traveling journalists picking up a salable interview while the mail steamer was in port; people in hard luck. A consumptive musician who had tried to teach Louis the flute in Sydney appeared with his wife to try Samoa for his lungs; Louis found him the start of a livelihood and put the couple up until they secured quarters.

Again a tuberculous little Pennsylvania Quaker had to be given a hand just because he seemed badly in need of it; as also a derelict Scot with an honest story of misfortune. At Louis's death the acting U.S. consul wrote to Washington that the late Mr. Stevenson had been "the first citizen of Samoa and the center of its social life." [15]

Not that the Stevensons were universally popular. Ramrod-stiff Colonel de Coetlogon, who was British consul when Louis came, found this eccentric most dismaying. Louis retaliated by warmly praising in print the Colonel's record as honorable official and merciful organizer of and chief worker in an amateur hospital for Samoans wounded in the fighting that occasionally racked the islands. So unsparing a Good Samaritan could be as diffidently rude to Louis as he liked. His successor, Cusack-Smith, found Louis's series of letters to the *Times* personally irksome and developed a rather low opinion of the scribbling busybody who wrote them and joined movements to refuse taxes imposed by the triconsular government. But even he ungraciously endorsed the quality of Louis's reporting from Samoa:

> . . . while his language and some of his deductions are to be regretted his facts appear to be accurate on a somewhat hasty perusal.
>
> I fear that Mr. Stevenson's interest in Samoan affairs is commensurate with the amount of gratuitous advertisement he secures thereby.[16]

Louis's politicking also strained the patience of the gentlemanly German and the genial Swede who, as President and as Chief Justice, made a botch of governing Samoa for the Powers; but he could not avoid liking them personally. In a square dance at a public ball Louis and the Chief Justice—whom the squire of Vailima was just then moving heaven and earth to get recalled —found themselves dancing opposite. Each caught the other's eye and saw a flash of amusement there, and thenceforward, Louis wrote, ". . . we pranced for each other." [17]

Healthier, closer to generalized people than ever before, he rejoiced in wide cordialities. Of all Vailima's guests he best liked the officers and the ratings of British men-of-war on the station. The complement of HMS *Curaçoa* made such eager use of their standing invitation to Vailima that the road thither was dubbed "the Curaçoa track."

Those skirted and beflowered Samoan servants at Vailima are the key to the Stevensons' life there. At first, hearing from local whites of the natives' unreliability—confirmed by early experience of their own—they tried white supervisors outdoors and white servants indoors. Available talent, however, consisted largely of stranded ne'er-do-wells. In 1891 Fanny imported a Mohammedan cook from Fiji, from whom she learned a famous curry. Finding that, in her absence, Lloyd and Belle had made a pliable and promising cook out of a handsome young Samoan named Taalolo, she passed the confused Moslem on to Haggard and embarked on a consistent program of employing Polynesians for everything.

In those first few months, thinking Samoan men untrustworthy and Samoan women sluttish, she had doubted that she would ever come to like them. Louis too thought Samoans less self-respecting than Polynesians elsewhere, though pleasantly courteous; and, during his early visit to Tutuila, had been daunted by their leering pleasure in obscene references and lewd dances:

> No sense of shame in this race is the word of the superficial, but the point of the indecent dance is to trifle with the sense of shame; and that . . . the chief actor should be a maid further discloses the corrupt element which has created and so much loves this diversion; for it is useless to speak, the Samoan loves the business like pie.[18]

But two experimental native servants began soon to prove fitfully reliable: Lafaele (Raphael) and Henry Simele, a young chief from Savaii who attached himself to Louis to learn English, which he called "long explosions." Presently there appeared Sosimo, an ostensibly turgid and slow young fellow whose rapidly developing loyalty to Louis turned him into a devoted and flexible right-hand. By Christmas 1891, Vailima had five Samoans indoors and out; within a year the household numbered nineteen, including wives of some of the men, but not all Samoans: there was also a Tongan, from the colony that Shirley Baker's dictatorial regime had exiled, a Wallis Islander, a Fijian—and an ugly and ingratiating little Solomon Islander who turned up at Vailima pitifully half-starved and with the scars of long welts across his back, after running away from a German plantation. Louis hired his time from the Germans, fed him up and—in spite of the Samoans' strong prejudice against darker outsiders—installed him in the household, where he became a popular pet.

A group of his tribal enemies among the Germans' laborers waylaid and wounded this Arrick. Next day he spent hours in Fanny's room expressing appropriate emotions in a half-hypnotized war dance while playing a homemade one-string harp; he once asked Louis to lend him a gun with which to shoot his enemies among other runaways in the bush. Queer emergencies were frequent among such servants: Inexplicable magic threw one man into convulsions that only certain mystic herbs could relieve; another's wife caused social feuds and a sort of slowdown strike because she proved to be of disgracefully low social rank; another appropriated a pig to contribute to a feast in his nearby village. . . .

What held the staff together in the teeth of local probability was the complete glory of Vailima. At least this is my reading of the situation based on some acquaintance with the Islands: The more packing-cases were lightered ashore, the more "the beach" heard of barrels of red wine, acres of roofing, and trunks of fine raiment, the more the Samoans respected this thin but tallish *papalagi*[19] on the same principle that had first moved Marquesans and Tahitians. In writing "The Bottle Imp" Louis accidentally strengthened this impression. A missionary heard the plot from Louis and, thinking it cognate with certain Samoan notions (which it was) and perhaps a sermon against the things of this world (which it was not), translated the finished draft into Samoan for serialization in a missionary paper for natives.[20] It ran from May to December, roughly the same period as the blossoming of Vailima.

Now Islanders have small notion of deliberately concocted fiction admitted to be such. However misty or fantastic, their own tales are supposed to be at least constructions of actual events; they can hardly conceive of a novel as acknowledgedly untrue.[21] Hence as "The Bottle Imp" infiltrated the Samoans via those who practiced the literacy taught by the missions, Louis's wealth was readily assumed to come from his actual command of just such a magic bottle as that in the tale. Native inability to understand that Louis's writing was highly profitable encouraged the mistake. Even Teriitera had been startled and baffled to hear what sums *Kidnapped* had earned: "As they scarcely ever read themselves," Aunt Maggie wrote, "it must be . . . almost incredible to them that book-making should be a paying occupation." [22] Samoans on social-political visits, all eyes for the Burmese idols at the foot of the stairs, the piano, the shining great hall that was the glory of Vailima, sometimes broke down toward the end of the tour and asked if they might see the bottle?

Such occult powers added the prestige of the wizard to that of the chief. In the Islands a great chief's *mana* (roughly prestige-power-luck) can readily manifest itself in sorcery as well as in great possessions, for both are aspects of supernally attained powers. Fanny reënforced the notion: Her piercing and broody glance, masterful ways, skill with foreign plants (doubtless magical themselves), readiness with nasty-tasting and alien doses for ailing retainers—medicine being a branch of sorcery, of course—made her uncanny in her own right. By a schoolgirl trick involving the victim's feeling an inexplicable tap on his back while his eyes are closed, she persuaded a Samoan servant that she commanded a familiar spirit. "I am glad to say," she wrote Aunt Maggie's sister, "that the gossip among the natives is that I have eyes all round my head and am in fifty places at once, and that I am a person to be feared and obeyed." [23]

It all fitted handily well with the local reputation for *aitu*. The extreme Samoan view of Louis probably was: He lived untroubled in a land of ghosts and spirits, drew untold wealth from a demon in a bottle, and was deferred to by a woman who was a considerable witch in her own right; I have unavoidably made all this sound logical and definite, which it was not, but I cannot doubt some such element in Louis's local prestige. . . . Whites believing equally firmly in such things would have fled the premises. But Louis obviously exuded good will, sorcery does lend prestige in Polynesia, prestige is attractive in itself, and it was taken to be in Louis's own interest not to harm his own retainers. Fanny, in fact, was able to work cures on the servants by assuring them that no evil spirit could harm a man belonging to her as Louis's deputy.

Since Louis was soon "Le Ona" in Samoa too, prestige enabled him to utilize a suggestion of Clarke's that Samoan servants handled best on a basis of "family." [24] (Missionaries on local stations were accustomed to gather round them and educate natives in the same relation as that of the villager to his local clan and chief—a matter of the ethnologist's "extended family" including various social grades all related by blood or equivalent adoption, all owing services to the head of the family as expression of the family.) Samoans whom Louis might "adopt" would retain certain rights in their home villages, but their boast and social *raison d'être* would soon specially become their status in the "Tama Ona"—which Louis neatly translated for Colvin as "The MacRichies." This half-implicit, half-formal relation recruited the Vailima staff and held them to what must often have seemed to them strange requirements imposed by Louis as their white chief and quasi-parent. In November 1893, when, attending a festival in a body, the Vailima servants appeared in their blazers and tartan *lavalavas*, they were hailed by all others present as a genuine Samoan clan.

Not as employer demanding due performance, rather as elder invoking clan loyalties, Louis held councils to punish malingerers and fine offenders. "We don't have servants," Fanny told an interviewer after Louis's death. "We have families. . . . If you called the money you give your family for spending money 'wages,' they'd all leave you in a body." [25] Once this institution was well knit together, cooking, cleaning, care of animals—in which, like most Polynesians, Samoans are cruelly lax—even sweaty drudgery in bush or garden went in reasonably acceptable fashion; whereas other *papalagi*, committed to the wage relation, got little but smiling inefficiency. It was remarked with growing wonder; said the beach: "You never see a Samoan run except at Vailima." [26]

Notions as to men's and women's work differed, sometimes conveniently. A muscular male Samoan did Aunt Maggie's laundry, starching and fluting her crisp widow's caps with right Parisian skill. Taking these caps as tokens of rank, in fact, he preserved discards and appeared abroad proudly wearing the same headgear as Queen Victoria in her later portraits. But training often presented troubles: Instructed to take a bucket of water to the second floor, a new man unfamiliar with stairs took the bail in his teeth and shinned up a veranda post. Another planted Fanny's costly imported vanilla vines upside-down; trying to spare his pride in the job, she secretly replanted them properly; finding them reversed next morning, he hurriedly replanted them the wrong way again—an ordeal that they failed to survive. Reproached with not watering a horse, a third tried to persuade her that, though watering some horses might be necessary, this one came of a breed that never needed it.

But patience, incisive sympathy, jokes varied with dignified anger in season, worked wonders on the firm foundations of Le Ona's splendor. It is all clearest in the case of Elina, a dogged, somber Vailima underling who—deformity being shameful in Samoa—had disgraced his family by developing a wen on his neck. The local German doctor called it safely operable, but for long neither bribery up to five dollars nor calling him a coward would move Elina to permit surgery. When he finally gave in, Louis took him to his relatives in Apia for the job and personally administered the chloroform; the poor, terrified devil went under repeating, like a safeguarding charm: "I belong Tusitala . . . I belong Tusitala. . . . " The site healed well and, when wenless Elina next visited his clan village on Savaii, he came back with prestige completely restored and glorying in having been given a minor chief-"name." That is the handsomest and most loyalty-building way to be a patriarch.

The Stevensons all had Samoan names used partly in fun, partly to divert retainers from offhandedly addressing them as "Louis" or "Belle." Fanny was "Aolele"—flying cloud—for her perpetual skirmishing bustle; also "Tamaitai"—a rough equivalent of "madame"; also "O le Fafine Mamana o i le Mauga"—the Witch Woman of the Mountain. Belle was "Teuila"—adorner of the ugly—for her pleasant habit of impulsively making the staff little gifts of trinkets and scraps of cloth. Louis, of course, was "Tusitala"—usually translated as "teller of tales"; he rendered it literally as "Chief White Information." [27] His *kava*-name,[28] used to express his prestige at ceremonies with natives, was given him by Seumanu, a neighboring chief of high standing. In all native ceremonies the Stevensons wisely took care to observe the elaborate behavior expected of high chiefs. All studied Samoan, informally or with mission teachers. Lloyd became reasonally adept, Louis learned enough to make set speeches in form and to admire highly the beauties of a tongue so full of liquid, connotation-packed adjectives and verbs.

Growing sympathy with his own and other Samoans did not move Louis to idealize them as he had the Tahitians: ". . . like other folk," he said of them, "false enough, lazy enough, not heroes, not saints—ordinary men, damnably misused." [29] He knew that his retainers could never make head or tail of him or his life:

> . . . and my
> Brown innocent aides in home and husbandry,
> Wonder askance, *What ails the boss?* they ask,
> *Him, richest of the rich, an endless task*
> *Before the earliest birds or servants stir*
> *Calls and detains him daylong prisoner.*

He, whose innumerable dollars hewed
This cleft in the boar- and devil-haunted wood,
And bade therein, from sun to seas and skies,
His many-windowed, painted palace rise . . .
How can he live that does not keep a shop?
And why does he, being acclaimed so rich,
Not dwell with other gentry on the beach? . . .[30]

But grasp grew with sympathy and again he began to reap the rewards of Polynesians' transmutation of apparently crass respect into valid love and loyalty. His MacRichies became as warm—and on occasion as exasperating—as children are to parents. A common self-respect, a common trust in Tusitala's dignity and fairness, drew brown and white steadily closer.

It helped greatly that, as noted before, Louis's firm belief in the inheritance of personality traits never tempted him to race prejudice. "Of all stupid ill-feelings," he wrote of his first trip to California, "the sentiment of our fellow Caucasians toward our companions in the Chinese car was the most stupid and the worst. They seemed never to have looked at them, listened to them, or thought of them, but hated them *a priori*." [31] Handling Samoans, he ripened sympathy with a device that he had used in the Marquesas and Tahiti, telling himself that these social bonds were much like those among the Highlanders whose "barbarian" virtues he had long admired. Analogies between, say, *aitu* and kelpie, Mataafa and Cluny Macpherson, leave much to seek in ethnological accuracy. But they greatly forwarded Louis's task of comprehending his own clan-family-household-encomienda. These values soon became a principal part of his life, along with the theatrical kettledrumming of rain on the iron roof and the sweetness of waking in the presunrise tropical dawn to think out and note the work of the day. Many a morning's writing was ruined by the unexpected visit of a Samoan chief and retainers, necessitating *kava* and speeches on the veranda. But as one got the feel of these things, they acquired inner meaning. Once Sosimo, who was not usually on that duty, fetched Louis's early coffee along with an unexpected and prettily turned omelet. Louis asked who had made it. "I did," said Sosimo. "Great is your wisdom," said Louis in the proper form of approval. "Great is my love," said Sosimo. And that too was ceremony; only— this is difficult for both sentimentalist and cynic—it was also heartfelt.

Louis usually cut a queer figure but seldom more so than when presiding cross-legged over Samoan ceremonies with the gravity due Tusitala's *mana*—or when acting *paterfamilias* of the Vailima family. Though its components continued somewhat to change, the itinerant entourage now struck roots: Belle was permanent. (Little Austin was presently sent to school in Monterey; Joe Strong, whose instability and conviviality distressed everybody, himself included, was divorced and went Stateside, eventually remarrying happily, I am told.) Lloyd was permanent, having declined to go to Cambridge because Louis's expenses on account of others were too heavy. In midsummer 1892, came Graham Balfour, Louis's scholarly cousin and later his biographer, to stay for months before going schoonering in Micronesia. Noting his hosts' bare feet, Balfour turned up on the second day barefoot himself. Said Louis: "Why, he's the same kind of fool we are!" [32] and his status was assured.

Until sent to school, Austin had been making friends with British jack-tars; proudly conducting pack horses down to Apia; building forts on the lawn with Arrick, that ingratiating cannibal; playing the old Davos war game with Louis and Lloyd, Austin being known as General Hoskyns; taking desultory lessons in history and arithmetic from Louis and Aunt Maggie, whose Scots tongue was soon evident in the way he recited verses that she taught him. She also had charge of the books which, in that climate, need varnishing and constant attention, performed minor domesticities, and supervised the staff's religious observances, ringing the hand bell for prayers night and morning. Lloyd became business administrator, moaning to Baxter about the incomprehensibly primitive character of Louis's previous records. Fanny was general superintendent and horticulturist, spurring on the planting of cocoa for cash crop, trying coffee and the distillation of the *ylang-ylang* for sale to perfumers, sending away for experimental plants of huge variety. Belle was inside steward, managing the staff and buying supplies; then presently became Louis's amanuensis, paid a minor wage for taking his dictation of rough drafts. All but Aunt Maggie smoked like chimneys, rolling their own.

The rest of the establishment soon included Belle's cockatoo, which frequently bit Louis; Louis's brown pony; a sedate, broad-backed horse from the circus for Aunt Maggie; mares for Fanny, Lloyd, and Belle, who loathed horses but had no other way to visit Apia; two pack horses, two cows, a bull. "Is not this Babylon the Great which I have builded? Call it Subpriorsford." [33]

By Christmas 1892, it all felt consolidated enough for a Christmas tree—the pinelike, feathery ironwood made a plausible *Tannenbaum*—to the delight of the Samoan retainers. Louis was fond of special occasions with formal presentations, songs written to match, special things to drink, ceremonious fooling like that vanished sermon on St. Jacob's Oil. This relish for ceremony was a great asset in Samoa, never more so than when —shades of Thomas Stevenson's brash freethinker-son!—he led prayers in the great hall at Vailima. At Heriot Row an evening chapter from the Bible had been routine. Ever since Saranac Aunt Maggie had promoted grace at meals; Louis reported to her from Honolulu that they sometimes managed it even in her absence. But it was not only for his mother's devout sake that all the brown-skinned family trooped in to sing a hymn led by one of the women, then hear a chapter from the Samoan Bible, with Louis presiding on Sunday—and sometimes other—evenings. Only thus could the Vailima clan qualify as respectable. However short on Western-style moral niceties, the Samoan is long on formal religious observance. In native eyes it was a great feather in Louis's cap that his was the only nonmissionary white household in Samoa to bother with this rigid spiritual tooth-brushing.

This is the provenance of the *Vailima Prayers*, which, posthumously published, made so many wonder what touch of Salvation Army had come over the man in the tropics. Being himself, Louis naturally wrote these prayers for household use as well as he could and filled them with ethical values that he took seriously himself and considered Samoans to need—such as truthfulness, charity, industry. As Aunt Maggie sat serenely, her handsome head bowed, while grown-up Lou read prayers of his own composing to marginally converted heathen—he deferring to their borrowed theological plumage, they revering him as chieftain-priest-big brother—she must have recalled the times when, long before he was sent to school, the solemn mite had talked to her about growing up to be a missionary to the savages.

She may have had even further hopes when Louis joined the three ravishingly beautiful Ide sisters to teach classes in an Apia Sunday School for native and half-caste children. But the children merely wriggled dumbly at Louis as he talked, apparently not even understanding why he was there. Despairingly talked out, he offered sixpence to any child who would ask a question —no response. He raised it to a shilling—still no response. It took half a crown to get his question: "Who made God?"—and this routed him, never to return. In no case would he have kept up this holy project longer than he had every-evening attendance of prayers. For he had not gone pious in any conventional sense—he had merely abandoned dogmatism about his "Calvinisto-Agnosticism."

That was plain in his dealings with missionaries, his good friends among whom have already been identified. The simply selfless, if often crude, French Catholic missionaries in the Marquesas, the extraordinary story of Damien, the pluck of the native Hawaiian missionaries in Micronesia, had helped prepare him to admire burly George Brown and Chalmers's doughty saintliness. Already in 1890 he addressed the students at the Malua training school for native pastors on a favorite theme: "There is love, and there is justice. Justice is for oneself; love for others. It did not require any gospel to teach a man to love himself or be stern to his neighbors." [34] In 1893 he lunched with the New South Wales General Assembly (Presbyterian, hence highly flavored with Scots) and drew great applause with a non-sensical speech asserting his prerogatives as a congenital child of the manse.[35] Illness prevented him from following with a serious address to the Assembly; read to them, it proved to be a confession that Louis had come round to believing missions did more good than harm and would do still more were missionaries more tolerant of native ideas and more charitable toward the singularly godless whites of the Islands. Next year, answering Adelaide Boodle's announcement that she was entering mission work, he summed up what he had learned:

> You will like it in a way, but . . . The work is one long, dull, disappointment varied by acute revulsions; and those who are by nature courageous and cheerful, and have grown old in experience, learn to rub their hands over infinitesimal successes. However, . . . it is a useful and honourable career in which no one should be ashamed to embark. . . . Forget wholly and forever all small pruderies and remember that *you cannot change ancestral feelings of right and wrong without what is practically soul-murder.* . . . remember that all you can do is to civilize the man in the line of his own civilization, such as it is. And never expect, never believe in, thaumaturgic conversions. They may do very well for St. Paul; in the case of an Andaman Islander, they mean less than nothing. In fact what you have to do is to teach the parents in the interests of their great-grandchildren.[36]

Again, however, it is not religious at all, rather the attitude of a gentle-minded and perceptive colonial administrator versed in the issues of modern ethnology—small word of souls, much of behavior. Incurably interested in people, skeptic to the bone, Louis could not be drawn to recognizable religion even by the personal magnetism of the great missionaries whom he so admired. (Occasionally one encounters the assertion—magnificently without evidence and not even plausible in its ignoring of

Louis's emotional make-up—that he was gravitating toward conversion to Catholicism; it seems to have been started by people observing that he was as civil to Catholics as to anybody else.) What he loved in Chalmers was his integrity, his outgoing love for his fellow-man—for this was no character out of *Rain*; Chalmers was unmistakably a tremendous figure. Adept Stevensonians will be reminded of Louis's fable of "Something in It": A missionary is snatched away from preaching the nonexistence of the ancient Hawaiian gods by those very gods themselves; he is saved from annihilation of his soul only because he is so irksomely sea-lawyerish that they throw him back into the world like a noxious fish. Shake himself as he likes, he cannot deny that the experience was real. "It seems there was something in it after all," he says to himself, and doggedly rings the bell for service anyway. Louis wrote this in the middle of the very period when, according to biographers pondering the *Vailima Prayers*, he was degenerating back into the chirping piety of his childhood.

There was also the affair of the paper chase. Politics were slumberously quiet—for Samoa—in July 1894, and Louis embarked on a genially conscious effort "to live well with my German neighbors." [37] He breakfasted peaceably with the new (German) President of the Council, "a rather dreamy man whom I like," [37] and, to amuse the young fellows working for the German Firm, suggested a horseback paper chase. An innocent activity—except that Sunday was the boys' only free day. Too tempted by the idea of the invalid's riding several miles hell-for-leather, Louis neglected to tell Aunt Maggie about the scheme until it had gone too far for him to back out. He and Lloyd duly rode their course, gratifyingly coming in third and fourth. Next day Louis reported in a letter to Barrie:

> There was racing and chasing in Vailele Plantation
>   And vastly we enjoyed it;
> But, alas! for the state of my foundation,
>   For it wholly has destroyed it! [38]

What steps Aunt Maggie took I do not know. But the course had lain through several Samoan villages at more or less the hour of Sunday morning service and native pastors were aghast at seeing the rigid Sabbath decorum of their flocks shattered by this stampede of hard-riding *papalagi*. On Tuesday Mrs. Clarke, wife of Louis's good missionary friend, meeting Louis in Apia, scolded him severely for outraging native feeling and setting so indecorous an example to heedless youth—the godless local whites were always a thorn in mission-flesh—and demanded that, in the presence of the young Germans, then at hand on a near-by veranda, he apologize to her as representing missions.

Louis did it—probably with a rueful twist beneath his mustache—which I take to mean that he liked the Clarkes more than he valued his own dignity. The young Germans had the grace not to grin and that was that. Apia saw no more paper chases on Sunday, or any other day; nor yet much reason to suspect that the squire of Vailima was in any danger of overpiety. The nearest he came to religion was in harsh, jangled verses written in his last few years:

> God, if this were enough
> That I see things bare to the buff
> And up to the buttocks in mire;
> That I ask nor hope nor hire,
> Nut in the husk,
> Nor dawn beyond the dusk,
> Nor life beyond death!
> God, if this were faith? [39]

It is not very close. Aunt Maggie seems to have known it. After Louis's death her uneasiness about his religious attitudes moved her to demand that conventionally hopeful verses from Scripture be inscribed on the tomb instead of "Requiem" and (in Samoan) Ruth's speech to Naomi.

Nobody could live near Apia a week without entanglement in local politics. "I never saw so good a place," an Apia Irishman told Louis. "You can be in a new conspiracy every day!" [40] What traders one dealt with, who bought one a drink, the relative warmth of this or that "good morning"—all were assumed, and usually correctly, to carry partisan significance. Louis was a land-owner with a major stake in Samoa's future; took native interests much to heart; was a Briton with an American household; al-ready mistrusted the dominant Germans, as his first letter to the *Times* had shown; and was, besides, daily more inclined to help "spin the great wheel of earth about."

Part of the day Tusitala sat in his little clapboarded box dic-tating to pay for red Bordeaux from Noumea, Austin's schooling, 1500 cocoa trees, and a new tennis net. Another part of the day often saw Le Ona, chief and contemner of indecent politicians, riding down to Apia to attend a public meeting or consult Clarke about the tactical significance of some native ceremony or seek Moors's aid in some new device to goad Chief Justice Ceder-crantz into resigning. His letters contain railings against the "cursed idiots . . . I cannot bear idiots" [41] whose misgovern-ings drove him into political meddling. But Colvin's protest against such activity also produced a magnificent sweep of the pen:

Why, you madman, I wouldn't change my present installation for any post, dignity, honour, or advantage conceivable to me . . . . as for wars and rumours of wars, you surely know enough of me to be aware that I like that also a thousand times better than decrepit peace in Middlesex. I do not quite like politics; I am too aristocratic, I fear, for that. God knows I don't care who I chum with, perhaps like sailors best; but to go round and sue and sneak to keep a crowd together— never. My imagination, which is not the least damped by the idea of having my head cut off in the bush, recoils aghast from the idea of a life like Gladstone's, and the shadow of the news-paper chills me to the bone. Hence my late eruption was in-teresting, but not what I like. All else suits me in this (killed a mosquito) A 1 abode. [42]

Mail-service and climate had been his first reasons for choosing Samoa. Within a couple of years he told an interviewer that he chose it because it was "awful fun."

This is more understandable when one has some idea of what was going on in this "distracted archipelago of children, sat upon by a clique of fools." [43]

Samoa's troubles came of alien pressures aggravated by an indigenous political system—or social system, since it pervaded Samoan life—so ill adapted to centralization that outside efforts to use it always frustrated all parties.

The Powers—newly imperialistic Germany, sluggishly imperialistic Britain, sporadically imperialistic America—had intruded for reasons both strategic and economic. The States had long maintained shadowy rights on Tutuila and were further involved by past antics of American land sharks and quasi-official carpetbaggers. Mistrusting German ambitions in Micronesia and the big, potentially rich islands of Melanesia, Britain looked askance at German efforts to swallow up strategically located Samoa. For a generation Germany, seeking power in the Pacific partly for nuisance value, partly to bolster her stake in China, partly to forward exploitation of Melanesia, had had the major interest and called the tune, the other two merely braking her growing aggressiveness. Hence outbreaks of war among native Samoan factions in false situations due to alien intrigue. Hence the assiduous presence of the Powers' men-of-war in Apia harbor. The hurricane of March 1889 would never have had the opportunity to wreck all those ships if their commanders, each jealous lest another steal a march on him, had not too long delayed seeking sea room. It was truly said at the time that the value of the lost ships and lives would have bought all Samoa.

In the Treaty of Berlin of 1889, the dismayed Powers agreed to regularize extraterritorial, international government of the municipality of Apia and to stabilize a recognizable native "king"-ship. Under direction by the Powers' consuls a "President of the Council" would supervise the municipality. A "Chief

Justice" would reduce chaos by doing justice between municipality and "king"-dom. A tripartite land commission would determine the thorny question of what sales of natives' land to aliens had been fraudulent. Tripartite responsibility seldom works well. Besides, this arrangement was doomed from the outset: It failed to recognize preponderance of German interests and ambitions. It gave the Powers no general government through which to control and manipulate a centralized native authority. It assumed a native understanding of the idea of "king"-ship workably close to that of whites. Further, the Treaty officials appointed to the new posts were, however well-meaning, astonishingly devious and inept.

In order to understand the complications that Louis encountered and the ingrained instability of the polity to which he was entrusting several thousand pounds of investment, one must struggle with the tangle of Samoan native institutions: The local "extended-family" system heads up in "names"—honorary titles each expressing the prestige of the village granting it to the ablest eligible high chief in behalf of a much larger group of villages. (Suppose certain district clubs of Tammany Hall carried high nominating powers denied most of the others—only, God help us, it is not so simple as that either.) Sometimes several crucial "names" were awarded to the same chief. If, by juggling and threatening, one such "name"-bearer could acquire a striking preponderance of the highest "names," he became "king" of Samoa. In the prewhite past this had actually happened once, but it was never clear that the "king" notion as such was not a whites' importation. The validity of the "name"-monopolist's honors had been little more than acknowledgment of power. Certainly such a "king"-ship, with its hint of centralization, was purely personal in fact and sure to collapse at the death or the discrediting of the "name"-laden "king." I know all this is confusing. So was Samoa, all the more so because the system was based on mere oral tradition, leaving ample room for informal treacheries, desertions, resentment, grudging loyalties, ambitions, and suspicions based on religious feuds—for the London Missionary Society (Congregationalist), English Wesleyan, and French Catholic missions were all strong in Samoa.

When Louis first landed, the Germans had recently brought back from punitive exile and installed as puppet-"king" the chief Malietoa (highest "name") Laupepa, whom, some years before, they had torn down as a tool of Britain and the States. Germany was now alone in holding him up. In his absence, greater physical power and personal (as opposed to hereditary) prestige had come to his two long-standing rivals: Tamasese, whom the Germans had sometimes used to keep Malietoa in line; and Mataafa, proud kinsman of Malietoa's, ablest and personally most impressive of the three. The consequent bewilderment and frustration among natives had recently culminated in Mataafa's men, using arms sold them by British and American traders, repulsing with loss a landing party from the German corvette *Adler*. A vague local notion of a "vice-king," first suggested by an American carpetbagger in the 1870s, enabled Mataafa to insist that Malietoa's power, whatever it was, was invalid unless he were associated with it. This tended to concentrate anti-German feeling behind Mataafa, particularly since, the new President of the Council being a German, the new Treaty government was not implausibly suspect of being a front for the German Firm.

Outright alliance between Britain and the States might have simplified matters. But Mataafa was a "Popee" (Catholic), thus looked at askance by British missions, which had powerful friends in London; the Foreign Office, disliking diversions from more crucial frictions with Germany in Africa, was trying to let Samoa cool off; and local whites were not yet solidly hostile to the Treaty government since, in the unlikely but possible event that it worked, it might be a permanent and welcome check on Germany. Government's flounderings ruined what hope there was. What revenues were collected went for official salaries and government buildings, while the municipality was starved for funds for bridges and court expenses and "king" Malietoa lived in a second-grade native hut over the way from the President's new house. When annoyed by the local newspaper, the government exhausted the treasury by clandestinely buying it—a fact that leaked out only when the gold paid down was found to be still in government wrappings. After the Powers' men-of-war arrested chiefs supporting Mataafa in arms and jailed them in Apia, rumors of a projected rescue moved the government to mine the jail with dynamite *in terrorem*. Then, startled by local disapproval of this singular confession of weakness, the government exiled the prisoners without color of legal justification—and, to a Polynesian, exile is worse than death.

Such highhanded shufflings were well calculated to offend Louis's nose for official indecency. While the house was yet building, he was wading deep in investigation of his new community. His findings were first intended to supply a final section on Samoa of *South Seas*; but, as that scheme lurched to a halt, they became a small book, *A Footnote to History*, published in 1892, which is still a considerable document on South Sea politics. At last Louis was doing able and exhaustive, if sometimes dry, reporting, shrewdly and skilfully weaving official records and first-hand recollections together. His opening diagnosis of Samoa is invaluable, and his necessarily second-hand description of the hurricane is a great document of the sea, a piece of writing that should have—but never has—silenced those doubting his ability in anything but verbal embroidery. His conclusion—that Samoa would know no peace until Mataafa had a sizable place in the sun—was borne out by history when, in 1899, the Germans' first act after taking Western Samoa over was to make Mataafa unrivalled "king." But the content was tactless, intentionally so. Louis's purpose was to rouse opinion "at home" to some healthy interest in English-speaking commitment in these remote islands, and to discredit the Treaty government—which meant defiance of the German influence in Samoa.

While the *Footnote* was preparing and printing, Louis further identified himself with anti-German forces by eloquent protest against the dynamite episode, the purchase of the newspaper, the sequestration of taxes needed by the municipality—all duly gone into at length for the London *Times*. (Taking the chair at a public meeting of irate citizens, he conducted it so well that the customary vote of thanks to the chairman was moved by a previously inimical German.) He also showed a talent for drafting documents of rigid protocol and exquisite incisiveness that would have delighted his former professors of law and unquestionably rankled in the formal bosoms of officialdom as they were meant to. And he clearly recognized the possibility that, once the *Footnote* saw print, officialdom would nail his hide to the wall for being a turbulent nuisance. It was unwise thus to comment publicly on a German Jack-in-office: "Such an official I never remember to have heard of, though I have seen the like, from across the footlights and the orchestra, evolving in similar figures to the strains of Offenbach." [44]

Repercussions from the *Footnote* were lively, if not altogether as expected. The firm of Tauchnitz were prosecuted and fined for reprinting it in Germany, Louis gamely offering to pay half the fine and costs. Its account of a treacherous scheme against Mataafa offhandedly suggested to the American consul by an L.M.S. missionary with political ambitions caused an uproar in the Society's London offices. On returning from a trip "home," the missionary tried to bring suit for libel against Louis. The affair ended when Louis agreed publicly to apologize if a board of his enemy's colleagues should require it after a formal hearing—which they did not.[45] The editor and nominal lessee of the government-purchased newspaper loudly protested Louis's *Times* letters and did secure an apology, studded with skilful reservations, from Louis in the matter of the purchase itself; the last item in the correspondence is dated only three days before Louis died.[46] But the Germans in Samoa were intelligent enough to approve the general honesty and accuracy of the book, though confessing irritation with some of its lashings. The Firm actually asked Louis to dinner to bury the hatchet. When, early in 1893, the President and the Chief Justice left Samoa in self-engendered defeat, Louis had some reason to congratulate himself and Samoa. But he was not vindictive about

. . . the two dwindling stars. Poor devils! I like the one, and the other has a little wife, now lying in! . . . . When I heard that the C.J. was in low spirits and never left his house, I could scarce refrain from going to him.[47]

In the meantime he had kept his personal situation boiling. During most of 1892 and 1893 Mataafa lay behind armed sentries in a politically significant village west of Apia, where, every month or so, Louis defied official frowns by visiting the "beautiful, sweet old fellow," [48] as he found him to be. (Aunt Maggie once went along on such a visit, unhesitatingly jumping her horse over pig-fences en route.) Louis's role was that of one high chief countenancing and advising another, sometimes in efforts to mediate the rebellion, sometimes taking the long view and seeking Mataafa's backing for a coconut-fiber mill to give Samoa another cash crop—which last gave rise to rumors that Louis was arranging to buy arms for the rebels. Impressed with these visits, Mataafa soon accorded Louis "royal" *kava*—the highest honor in Samoan etiquette and of grave political import. It is not surprising that, reading the *Times* and Cusack-Smith's comments on all this, a Foreign Office official noted on the back of a despatch: "Mr. Stevenson would do better if he stuck to novel-writing and left politics alone." [49]

In August 1892, Louis showed real genius for embarrassing officialdom: Lady Jersey, utterly aristocratic wife of the Governor of New South Wales, came visiting Haggard with her daughter and old-school-tie brother, Captain Rupert Leigh. Vivacious, clever, she liked the Stevensons as much as Louis liked her and, though Fanny did not care for the Countess, saying she was too much like Mrs. Hauksbee, she did not show it openly. Haggard was rather a bull in a china shop in relations with his government. Louis was full of the considerable wrongs and marked virtues of Mataafa, then likely to start shooting any day. Somebody suggested that Leigh might visit the rebel "king," strictly incognito, since anybody close to the representative of the sovereign person of Queen Victoria in a major colony could hardly appear to countenance rebels. Lady Jersey determined to go along —which was sheer lunacy. The same reasons that made the visit inappropriate for Leigh meant that she had no business even to think of it.

But prankishness was in the ascendant—Bob Stevenson would instantly have detected the fine old flavor of Libbelism. Louis invented for Lady Jersey an incognito as his cousin, "Amelia Balfour," writing her mysterious notes of instruction in the idiom of Jacobite doings in the Forty-Five with Mataafa cast as "The King over the Water," and commencing a burlesque epic somewhat in the manner of William Morris to commemorate the occasion. Mataafa received the party with special honors for Louis's cousin that gave every indication that he knew very well indeed who the *Tamaitai Sili* (great lady) was. They spent the night and returned next day mischievously certain that

> It is all nonsense that it can be concealed; Miss Amelia Balfour will be at once identified as the Queen of Sydney, as they call her; and I would not in the least wonder if the visit proved the signal of war. . . . the thing wholly suits my book and fits my predilections for Samoa.[50]

The German consul reported home that local gossip said Lady Jersey had given Mataafa much money. She and Haggard added insult to injury by paying a visit to Tamasese, the third "king," and being received by him in uniform; for a wonder, Louis does not seem to have been involved in this second prank. But Libbelism or not, the Countess's escapade had had some meaning. Cusack-Smith wrote home in a sort of agony that, as Louis thought, these antics made war very likely. Moors was reasonably certain—and so was all Samoa—that, if Mataafa had struck at this time, he would have extinguished Malietoa and given the Powers a *fait accompli* to reconcile themselves to. People remembered it next year when Mataafa did start shooting and received a resounding defeat from the Malietoas, who had used the interval to strengthen themselves and their prestige.

I do not know what explaining Lady Jersey and Leigh had
to do on returning to Sydney. But Haggard was in much trouble with his superiors. And, by October, when HMS *Ringarooma*
came into Apia to pick up sealed orders, "the beach" was certain
that they principally concerned arresting and deporting Louis.
Forehandedly Louis called on her commander and made friends
with the ward-room to secure a comfortable trip if rumor was
correct. It was not—not yet.

In late December, however, the High Commissioner of the
Western Pacific, Sir John Thurston, whose duties included the
policing of British subjects outside formal European polities, issued a *Regulation for the Maintenance of Peace and Good Order
in Samoa*, prescribing fine and imprisonment for any British subject guilty of sedition toward the Samoan government and defining sedition as

> . . . all practices, whether by word, deed, or writing, having
> for their object to bring about in Samoa discontent or dissatis-
> faction, public disturbance, civil war, hatred or contempt to-
> ward the King or Government of Samoa or the laws or consti-
> tution of the country, and generally to promote public disorder
> in Samoa.[51]

The impression that this Russian-sounding document was aimed
at Louis was soon so strong that he wrote to ask Colvin for help
in the right quarters. Colvin's strings in London pulled most effectively. By March Lord Rosebery (for the Foreign Office) was
most cordially writing Louis that Cusack-Smith's despatches
gave Whitehall no uneasiness about Tusitala's activity. By April
the Colonial Office had soundly spanked Thurston—told him to
take no steps about the inconvenient Mr. Stevenson without first
consulting his superiors in London, and coldly instructed him to
amend his Regulation into something faintly resembling British
notions of law.[52] This was being in politics with a vengeance,
when government departments intervened in one's behalf against
their own high-echelon officers. But Louis was not tempted to
make it a career. In early 1893, during a stopover at Auckland,

Louis met Sir George Grey, great elder statesman of the Pacific. The old gentleman warmly commended the general tenor of what the amateur had been doing in Samoa, but also cautioned him to refrain from further letters to the British papers. Only once thereafter was that caution disregarded.

When Mataafa's disastrous armed rebellion broke out in July 1893, Louis arranged use of the Apia public hall as hospital and assisted at bloody operations on wounded Mataafa partisans. This was the other side of the drama of war that, when he had passed a Mataafa picket a few days before, had made his spirit "nicker like a stallion." He told Mark Twain:

> . . . I wish you could see my "simple and sunny heaven" now; war has broken out, "they" have long been making it, "they" have worked hard, and here it is—with its concomitants of blackened faces, severed heads and men dying in hospital. . . . the government troops have started a horrid novelty: taking women's heads. If this lead to reprisals, we shall be a fine part of the world. Perhaps the best that could happen would be a complete and immediate suppression of the rebels; but alas! all my friends (bar but a few) are in the rebellion.[53]

Mataafa and his higher chiefs were exiled to the German-controlled Marshall Islands, his minor chiefs were jailed in Apia. Loyally solicitous, aware how deadly a disease homesickness can be to Polynesians, Louis sent a supply of prestige-restoring *kava* and trade cloth, for shirts and *lavalavas*, via Graham Balfour, who visited the Marshalls later that year.

In October 1893, Louis went to Hawaii for a few weeks of change, taking with him as servant Taalolo, the Vailima cook and minor chief in his own right, to see the sights of Honolulu, which was to the South Seas what Paris is to Europe. The boy developed measles before landing, but was out of quarantine in time to look after Louis, who fell ill in his quarters in the Sans Souci boarding house at Waikiki; the next boat brought Fanny to help him home again. In discussing Samoan affairs with the

Honolulu press, Louis showed a sort of oversimplified despair about white encroachment on and shattering of native ways, perhaps heightened by the recent deposition of Queen Liliuokalani by the "missionaries":

> . . . I can see but one way out—to follow the demand of the Samoan people that the Berlin Act be rescinded, while the three Powers withdraw absolutely, and the natives be let alone, and allowed to govern the islands as they choose . . . there would be internal dissensions covering a certain period, . . . it might affect commerce, and certainly the present standing of all foreigners . . . but . . . it is the patient and not the doctor who is in danger. . . . If left alone, the Samoans would continue fighting, just as they do under the tripartite treaty . . . but at least they would fight it out by themselves, without their wars being turned to the advantage of meddling foreigners.[54]

The suggestion has small realism, but much grasp of the problem and considerable objectivity from a man who stood to lose so much if, by a miracle of disinterestedness, the Powers should turn Samoa back to the Samoans. The rack of Colt's rifles at Vailima was not there just for ornament. Several times, as rumors of war blew stronger, they had been cleaned and assigned to various members of the household.

This, though Louis could not have known it, was his last glimpse of the outside world. He spent much of it ill in bed, some of it with old friends or sitting on the veranda at Sans Souci chatting with anybody who came along or playing solitaire or just looking at the sea breaking on the distant reef. For all his illness he made a major point of securing for Taalolo the feature of the trip that he most yearned for—a ride on the narrow-gauge railroad from Honolulu to Pearl Harbor. A local sculptor named Allen Hutchinson did a bad bust of him. The Thistle Club of Honolulu made him an honorary chieftain—he wore the club's tiny silver thistle on his jacket thenceforth—and his speech of acceptance was gracefully ironical and sentimental. The doctor and Fanny persuaded him to abandon the idea of another and more serious speech for a public meeting of the club.

At home in November—a Samoan festival season coinciding with Louis's birthday—he made gestures showing how well he had learned Samoan values. Those minor Mataafa chiefs in the Apia jail were not suffering actual privation, but their quarters, in thatched lean-tos in the courtyard, were not suited to their rank. Rations were sufficient, they collaborated with their genial Austrian jailer, Count Wurmbrand, in policing and discipline, but they stood much in need of countenance and, in defiance of tact, Louis determined to supply that. On November 15, Fanny, Belle, Lloyd, and he drove openly to the jail in a hired carriage to make the prisoners gifts of tobacco and *kava*—the social and political implications far outweighing the value of the presents. It was Le Ona openly confirming his friendship for and support of the defeated.

Next month the prisoners gave a tremendous return feast for Louis and family—in the jail. (This sounds bizarre only to those unacquainted with Polynesia.) The courtyard was heaped with handicrafts, pigs, chickens, fish, *kava*, all brought by the prisoners' families. The highest chief of the lot honored Fanny by calling her name first at *kava*. Then, in token of his high prestige and honorable behavior, the whole mass of things was presented to Louis item by item. Speakers described Louis as their "only friend," saying that they had no money to buy worthy luxuries, such as salt beef and ship's biscuit from traders, but all these things were the work of the chiefs' families' grateful hands— beautiful pieces of *siapo* (bark-cloth), dozens of decorated fans and baskets. . . .

"This," said the high talking-chief, in a typically ironic Samoan idiom of self-depreciation, "is a present from the poor prisoners to the Rich Man."

Louis knew that it was all pregnant with politics. His hosts insisted that he summon help and take all the presents home at once, so that they would make the greatest possible show passing Malietoa's house. There were rumors that this confusing affair—during which the jail gates stood wide, guarded only by a couple of distracted sentries—was a cloak for an armed rising of the Tamasese faction who wanted the Stevensons for hostages. But Louis trusted Mataafa's men, and was moved by it all, as he well might have been:

> . . . one thing sure: no such feast was ever made for a single family, and no such present was ever given to a single white man. It is something to have been the hero of it. And whatever ingredients there were, undoubtedly gratitude was present.[55]

Gratitude soon had a wider basis still: Taalolo's father-in-law, a stout Mataafa man of rank enough to be imprisoned, fell ill in jail. Louis fetched a doctor—probably Dr. Funk, the local general practitioner—to look after him. On the doctor's advice to get the patient into better quarters, Fanny persuaded Wurmbrand to look the other way while she effected a jail-delivery of one. When Wurmbrand lost his job over it, Louis took him up to live at free charges at Vailima and quieted the rest of the hullabaloo by posting bond for the sick man's return, which was duly effected after his recovery. During 1894 the prisoners were gradually released on a sort of sliding-scale amnesty, Taalolo's father-in-law among the last. In September 1894, to thank Louis for upholding their hands, he and a number of former prisoners served notice that they personally—in Samoa chiefs do not willingly do such work—would make him a new road from the cross-island track to the main Vailima stream. The offer was freer than most native promises: Louis was to furnish no food for the workers and make no presents, merely lend necessary tools. And they not only promised it: they performed it.

By early October the road was finished. Louis made a great feast of acceptance for the participants in this drudgery, wrote himself a great speech, with the pious references and elaborate courtesies necessary in Samoan speaking, had a missionary translate it, and read it impressively. The gist of it was the politically neutral point that Samoa's only future lay in working harder and quarreling less; that, if Samoans did not make optimum use of their land, thronging outsiders would take it away. But, in view of the strictly Mataafa character of the guests and of Louis's previous calculated indiscretions, most of Apia was too nervous to accept his invitation to come and grace the occasion.

This has often been stickily misinterpreted as a matter of all Samoa thanking nice, kind Tusitala for his help. By now the reader knows that it was nothing of the sort: Louis's championing of the Mataafas was not likely to rouse gratitude among Malietoas or Tamaseses, so the Road of the Loving Heart was the work of a single faction in temporary eclipse. But—neither must this be lost sight of—the extraordinary nature of the gesture points to extraordinary emotions affecting the chiefs concerned. Faction they might be; certainly the terms in which they may have stated their motives would sound strange to us; but this was a thing that they would not have done spontaneously, or even voluntarily, for any other white man conceivable. Let them speak for themselves: The signboard[56] that they erected at the highway entrance of the road said:

> We bear in mind the surpassing kindness of Mr. R. L. Stevenson and his loving care during our tribulations while in prison. We have therefore prepared a type of gift that will endure without decay forever—the road we have constructed. We are:

LELEI	PALAULI	TUPUOLA	LOTOFAGA
MATAAFA	PALAULI	TUPUOLA	AMAILE
SAIEVAO	SI'UMU	MUNIAIGA	AMAILE
POE	SI'UMU	IFOPO	MANONO
TELESE	SI'UMU	FATIALOFA	LEPA
	LEMUSU	SOLOSOLO	

Six weeks later some of the same men helped to carry Tusitala up Mt. Vaea for burial.

It would be gratifying to tell how the road did endure forever. But Samoans' memories are short and, since Louis died, they have seen several changes of authority and much distracting confusion. In 1946 the new Administrator for the New Zealand Mandate found the road, long superseded by a macadamized affair installed by the Germans, almost lost in new growth. Under the illusion that Tusitala's name still meant much in Samoa, he organized a road-clearing festival, reopened the track with a feast at which Samoan schoolteachers planted rare native trees along its margin—and read them Louis's speech about more work and less bickering. Whatever spark he hoped to arouse failed to glow. Only prison labor now keeps the Road of the Loving Heart open, the plantings are dying of neglect, and few bother to think how appropriate it is that the narrow, smooth cut through the trees is closed by a fine view of the summit of Vaea.

Five years ago the present holder of the Malietoa "name" told me that only very, very old Samoans would normally even remember Louis's name. Now and again alien influence may revive the tradition locally. But, except for his house and tomb, the only striking relic of Louis fifty-eight years later is the current issue of Samoan postage stamps, which shows Vailima on the one-shilling and the tomb on the sixpenny.

Tusitala

> There is something in me worth saying, though I can't find what it is just yet.
>
> —Stevenson to Henley,
> Balfour, *Life:* I, 202

ON HEARING that Louis was to settle permanently in Samoa, Colvin wrote Baxter: ". . . fulfilment of an old fear . . . that it would end in their settling for good in the South Seas . . . Whoever does that is lost . . . as far as the keeping of the powers of his mind and doing work goes." [1] Perhaps this restatement of this invaluable man's belief that nobody could write without regular doses of London fog in his throat was effort to express how deeply he missed Louis, whom he did love like a younger brother. But this apprehension could also have had some straightforward meaning:

In Samoa Louis grew farthest from the egocentricity with which he entered life. This was curious, because here his circumstances were most egocentric, even more so than when he traveled alone through the Cévennes or along the Union Pacific. At the same time that he was living more widely in politics and people, more and more divorcing his own personality from his work, he became focus of a whole group of people dependent largely on him for livelihood and, to an unusual degree, for emotional satisfactions.

The Vailima household was no standard Western family acting as placenta for a second generation gradually to go independent; it was a centripetal colony. Widowed Aunt Maggie doubtless belonged with her only son if she and he both wished her there. Fanny certainly belonged with Louis wherever he was. True also, the Victorian tradition was more patriarchal than ours. It was nearer normal for sons and daughters to weave their lives into those of their parents before marriage or after widowhood. But the closeness with which Belle's and Lloyd's orbits swung round Louis does give an impression of hyperdependency.

The squire of Vailima thought of Lloyd as brother-son; but Lloyd might have been better off, other things being equal, developing himself at a distance, as Louis had in his time. Belle and Joe Strong had been married longer than Louis and Fanny; yet, once they entered the magnetic field in Honolulu, they attached themselves to Louis with a tenacity that, in Belle's case, never lapsed. After Louis died, these people of some talent, considerable flexibility, and unusual experience continued to perform like functions of the dead man—perhaps an index to the strength of his personality, but a curious destiny even if Louis had been the size of Shakespeare. It could have harmed him, as certain biographers hinted it did. I can find no trace of that. But his willingness to become a sort of high-valence atom at the center of this emotional molecule does remind one of the small boy of 17 Heriot Row. If people elected to join the outer fringes of the molecule, Louis was not the man to prevent them. Colvin tended to see sponging in it. With accurate cordiality, Louis came to understand that it was devotion of high value.

When urging Barrie to visit Samoa, Louis sent him thumbnail sketches of the Vailima household, along with a warning that, if Fanny happened to dislike him, his visit would be miserable. Lloyd:

> Six foot, blond, eye-glasses—British eye-glasses, too. Address varying from an elaborate civility to a freezing haughtiness. Decidedly witty. Has seen an enormous amount of the world. Keeps nothing of youth, but some of its intolerance. Unexpected soft streak for the forlorn. When he is good he is very, very good, but when he is cross he is horrid. Of Dutch ancestry, and has spells known in the family as "cold blasts from Holland." Exacting with the boys, and yet they like

him. Rather stiff with his equals, but apt to be very kindly with his inferiors—the only undemonstrative member of the family, which otherwise wears its heart upon both sleeves; and except for my purple patches the only mannered one.

Belle:

Runs me like a baby in a perambulator, sees I'm properly dressed, bought me silk socks, and made me wear them, takes care of me when I'm well, from writing my books to trimming my nails. . . . manages the house and the boys, who are very fond of her. Does all the hair-cutting of the family. Will cut yours and doubtless object to the way you part it. Mine has been re-organised twice.

and Fanny:

She runs the show. Infinitely little, extraordinary wig of grey curls, handsome waxen face like Napoleon's, insane black eyes, boy's hands, tiny bare feet, a cigarette, wild blue native dress, usually spotted with garden mould. In company manners presents the appearance of a little timid and precise old maid of the days of prunes and prisms—you look for the reticule. Hellish energy; relieved by fortnights of entire hibernation. Can make anything from a house to a row, all fine and large of their kind. Doctors everybody, will doctor you, cannot be doctored herself. A violent friend, a brimstone enemy. . . . Is always either loathed or slavishly adored—indifference impossible. . . . Dreams dreams and sees visions.

And looking at himself:

Exceedingly lean, rather ruddy, black eyes, crows-footed, beginning to be grizzled, general appearance of a blasted boy—or blighted youth . . . Past eccentric—obscure and oh we never mention it—present industrious, respectable and fatuously contented. . . . Really knows a good deal but has lived so long with aforesaid family and foremast hands, that you might talk a week to him and never guess it. . . . Name in family, The Tame Celebrity. Cigarettes without intermission, except when coughing or kissing. Hopelessly entangled in apron-strings. Drinks plenty. Curses some. Temper unstable. Manners purple on emergency, but liable to trances. Essentially the common old copy-book gentleman of commerce; if accused of cheating at cards, would feel bound to blow out brains, little as he would like the job. Has been an invalid for ten years, but can boldly claim you cant tell it on him. Given to explaining the Universe—Scotch, sir, Scotch.[2]

All good, economical drawing and invaluable, particularly as to Fanny. But this should be qualified by recalling that, in the same period, he addressed several sets of zealously admiring verses to her, culminating with those used, and probably intended, as the dedication to *Weir of Hermiston*:

> . . . Take thou the writing; thine it is. For who
> Burnished the sword, blew on the drowsy coal,
> Held still the target higher, chary of praise
> And prodigal to counsel—who but thou?
> So now, in the end, if this the least be good,
> If any deed be done, if any fire
> Burn in the imperfect page, the praise be thine.

Louis's and Fanny's symbiosis unquestionably remained vivid down among its roots and juices. But it also seems probable that Louis's spiraling maturity was training his newer twigs into patterns that Fanny found disquietingly unfamiliar. His last years are difficult to understand without seeing him as developing a set of dimensions for which Fanny lacked the formula. Consider his *Fables*:

They have remained quite obscure—partly, I suspect, because awkward to reconcile with the accepted picture of R.L.S., the graceful, slight optimist. In preceding pages I have quoted "The Man and His Friend," that miracle of monosyllables; and tried to epitomize "Something in It" and "The House of Eld." Some of them may have been written in 1874, but content dates at least five as post-*Casco*. Not until 1888 did Louis have enough of them on hand to promise Longmans a volume of them some time in the future. My own belief is that most of them were written or else radically rewritten in Louis's last nine or ten years.[3]

Some are long and highly stylized in what Colvin called "the vein of Celtic mystery,"[4] at any rate set in Hebridean backgrounds—brittle, sharp-boned dreams of the cruel succession of generations and the lean if valid rewards of truth-seeking. Some are short, icicle-clear, silver-bright, arrogant, but sometimes collectedly wistful glimpses of the essential bleak absurdity of the human situation. The best of them are like tales that the serpent might have told Adam after the expulsion to illustrate the new knowledge of Good and Evil—little dramas on the theme that Louis set Colvin in a letter from Bournemouth in that jangled spring of 1887:

> You believe in unbelief; don't, it's not worth while. The world has been going on long enough for us to *know* we are wrong; yet something is meant by everything, even negro slavery had a sense in it, . . . I am, sir, your obedient servant
> > Andrew Crossmyloof
> > Gallio
> > Julius Caesar
> > Archbishop Sharpe
> > My uncle Toby
> > > and
> > The Man in the Moon.
> Everything is true; only the opposite is true too; *you must believe both equally or be damned. . . .*[5]

Jenkin would have recognized and probably mistrusted this surgical Pyrrhonism, which manages simultaneously to burlesque skepticism, faith, spiritual consolation, determinism, free will, humanitarian sympathy, Panglossism, and moral indignation:

There was once a sick man in a burning house to whom there entered a fireman. "Do not save me," said the sick man. "Save those who are strong."

"Will you kindly tell me why?" inquired the fireman, for he was a civil fellow.

"Nothing could possibly be fairer," said the sick man. "The strong should be preferred in all cases, because they 'are of more service in the world."

The fireman pondered a while, for he was a man of some philosophy. "Granted," said he at last, as a part of the roof fell in; "but for the sake of conversation, what would you lay down as the proper service of the strong?"

"Nothing can possibly be easier," said the sick man: "the proper service of the strong is to help the weak."

Again the fireman reflected, for there was nothing hasty about this excellent creature. "I could forgive you being sick," he said at last, as a portion of the wall fell out, "but I cannot bear your being such a fool." And with that he heaved up his fireman's axe, for he was eminently just, and clove the sick man to the bed.

Even the weaker items lack the journalistic jeer that mars Bierce's efforts in the same line. Once one is acquainted with Louis's *Fables*, they recur to him the rest of his life, like the fox that lost his tail and the emperor's new clothes, during flashes of wonder at human antics: the ruefully steadfast missionary . . . the people of the greatest nation in the world who scarcely looked the part . . . the agonized young man covered with yellow paint. . . . Among them they disquietingly illustrate the perils of looking without fear through the one-way window into an amoral cosmos. They must be pregnant indications of what went on in Louis's head as he lay in Bournemouth with his mouth shut tight on seeping blood or weeded sensitive plant at Vailima; and are a long, long way from the inscription on the Portsmouth Square monument. It took Chesterton's skill in para-dox to explain this aspect—which I think fundamental—of this curious brain: ". . . existence was splendid because it was . . . desperate. To Stevenson, the optimist, belong the most frightful epigrams of pessimism. . . . all life was glorious because of them." [6]

Practically all are written with awesome nearness to just precisely the way Louis had conceived the given item. There is no spare word, calorie, or thousandth of millimeter of play in "The Reader and the Book" or a suspicion of uncertainty in the unabashed rhetoric of "The Song of the Morrow."

Fanny considered the *Fables* aberrations that Louis had perversely preserved; perhaps it was her braking that kept the book back until he died. She was correspondingly outraged when Baxter redeemed Louis's promise to Longmans by giving them the manuscripts to publish as posthumous supplement to a new edition of *Jekyll*. Being herself, she naturally saw this as treachery to Louis—the real Louis, meaning *her* Louis, the elder of "my two boys" whose delight in schooner voyages reconciled her to seasickness. Work that so excluded her from sympathy must be unworthily meaningless. It has been hinted that her grounds for objection were often based on reluctance to see Louis startle the primmer segments of his public. Had that been her notion, however, *The Beach of Falesà* would never have seen print.

But there is no blinking the possibility that, during the Samoan period, she also was experiencing shifts in directions already sketched. After seeing in London a doctor who had attended both Louis and Fanny in Sydney, Colvin wrote Baxter that the man had serious misgivings about Fanny's emotional health. The calendar could have been a factor; after all, she was fifty when the *Equator* made Apia. This is all necessarily surmise; but through the flawed medium of letters, reminiscences, and photographs, one seems to see Fanny mechanically hospitable but withdrawing farther than ever from any but people committed to the Louis-molecule; obsessively planning and planting, pleasure become necessary distraction; thickening and looking glummer as the years pass—those late photographs have small resemblance to the woman with the lighted-up face who married Louis—insisting more pretentiously on her contact with the occult. . . . Her appearance was taking on a formidability that eventually made both Richard Le Gallienne and Henry James liken her to "an old grizzled lioness." [7] That leonine effect went well with her growing suspicion, already well founded when she reached Samoa, that somehow to be Louis's wife made her a great woman—or perhaps the other way round.

For loyal, brave, capable, adjustable, and occasionally generous though Fanny was, there was never anything selfless about her devotion to Louis. That is not complaint in his behalf. Perhaps, in a sense that I hope is not cynical, it could have been hers to complain because, after founding his marriage on illness and constant supervision, he regained enough health and strength to resume nearly normal relations with the Samoan world—in a manner of speaking, he changed the rules of the game in the middle. In any case there is certainly too much Chekhov in the figure she presented at Vailima. As Louis lay swiftly dying, Clarke recalled, Fanny stood apart by the foot of the stair, rigid with what I conceive of as the shock of seeing her *raison d'être* struck dead. In some ways this makes her the tragic figure of the two. She had spent all her life trying to manifest her sense of self-importance. In Louis she had found the means and the material best suited to her qualities; and now that was gone in a single frustrating flash.

Louis lived 4000 miles from any colleague in letters of anything like his own stature. He showed no signs of uneasiness because—though it was a bald fact—nobody in Samoa was near his size. His family talked his language, so far as idiom goes, and he needed no more. The quality of his work in this isolation should make one gravely doubt the legend that elbow-rubbing with one's aesthetic peers is essential to avoid intellectual and artistic stagnation. Perhaps letter-writing made the difference.

Certainly the mails were a blessing in more than a mere business sense. At Vailima he yearly dictated or wrote at least the length of the average novel in personal letters: Long journal-

letters to Colvin which he hoped would make a profitable book
for his heirs;[8] long or short letters keeping up with Baxter
(usually including business), Bob, Gosse, James, Lang, Meredith, Low, Payn, Archer, Miss Boodle, Mrs. Fairchild, Mark
Twain, H. B. Baildon (an old schoolmate turned literary);
much, partly business, to Burlingame of the Scribner house, since
Louis's more profitable market was now in the States; to fellow-
writers whom he had never met but had made friends with on
paper: Kipling, Schwob, Haggard, Barrie, Conan Doyle. . . .
These letters are not so ebullient as those of his twenties and
thirties. Now and again the old free-wheeling intimacy appears,
but on the whole this Louis is better organized, more solid, less
outgoing—almost as if scar tissue left by the Henley affair
slightly clogged his emotional joints.

In any case mail day was the great event at Vailima as well
as on "the beach." Books from Lang supplying detail for a new
story; proof from *Scribner's*; magazines and newspapers to
give the illusion of contact with the outside world; worried letters from Colvin; rueful letters from Baxter reporting the low
level of the bank balance; James gently bemoaning Louis's absence but rejoicing in his work; letters from young Austin,
from autograph-seekers (whom Louis usually obliged unless their
manners were too deplorable), cranks, and young people want-
ing "to write." The couple of days before the east-bound steamer
was due were devoted to preparing the outgoing mail. Louis was
now businesslike enough usually to date letters. He even kept a
register of those received and when answered. But now and
again, his replies reassuring Colvin and outlining fatter projects
for Baxter would have to go off hurried and expostulatory because that smoke on the horizon had been a surprise.

Even with the drag of regular mails added to writing, politics, and entertaining, Louis found time for his flageolet, the
melancholy, inept sounds of which were a most familiar sound in
Vailima. His studies at Bournemouth of harmony and counterpoint had come to little, but he often joined Belle's piano and
Lloyd's banjo in a catch-as-catch-can concert to which he at

least contributed original dissonance. Always an early riser—a non-Bohemian touch—he woke about dawn to coffee, or chocolate, and a biscuit, then, in the attitude that St. Gaudens modeled, smoked and made notes for the day's work until general breakfast two or three hours later. After breakfast Belle took his dictation of rough draft, Louis on his feet as a rule, leaning on the table or propped against the wall or pacing swingily as in the Sargent portrait. Since she had no shorthand and he included detailed punctuation, his dictation must have been slow. If well, he had a plunge in the pool before lunch. After lunch and perhaps some music, he pulled in his chair to the pine work table for arduous, interlining revision or redrafting; or read proof or wrote or dictated letters or, when necessary, went down to Apia; after the first year his working about the place slacked off. Before dinner (at six) he bathed and changed and made a cocktail. After dinner he might read to the family and visitors the day's bag of work for applause and comment, or play cards—they were all enthusiastic card-players, often exploring new games out of Hoyle—and then a nightcap of whisky and water sent him to bed between eight and ten.

As "creative" writing goes, this is a steep pace. In the four Samoan years it produced close to 700,000 words of printed copy, all exhaustively revised;[9] with the letters it is easily the annual equivalent of two novels of normal length. Moreover this daily schedule was often broken for days or weeks by travel or political emergency, sometimes by the periods of drying-up that most novelists experience, during which Louis was likely to announce that he was pro tem. an Idiot Boy and spend a day or two pestering people. Symonds expressed to Gosse his wonder that Louis should work instead of lying about under trees as became the traditional South Sea exile. But Louis had no burning need to loaf and invite his soul; by now his soul was not too ill at ease within him.

For Tusitala the writer these years were steadily less confused. They began with much time apparently wasted—cobbling up *South Seas*, writing the *Footnote*, collaborating with Lloyd. But in the end small waste was evident. These false starts, jostlings, and experimentings seem more like prolonged tuning up for a more advanced kind of music:

The Wrecker was born "On board the schooner *Equator*, almost within sight of the Johnstone Islands (if anybody knows where they are)," [10] which sounds strange now in view of the hundreds of thousands of Americans set down for refueling and chow at the Johnston air-base since 1942. Reid's tales of smuggling, piracy, barratry, and maritime fraud had already powerfully reënforced the effect of what Louis had picked up in Honolulu as material for *South Seas*.[11] Now, with Reid's help on the seamanship, Lloyd and Louis planned a long serial to pay for the *Northern Light* by exploiting the strange values of the very seas she was to sail. They worked at it in the *Equator*, in their flimsy huts on Apemama, at Moors's in Apia, in the temporary cottage at Vailima. In 1891-92 *Scribner's* ran it—an episodic, discursive, irresponsibly broken-backed affair with the kinetic clatter of an enthusiastic tap-dancer and, here and there, some highly notable narrative. Louis was almost as annoyed as grateful when, in its day, this outsold *Ballantrae*; few ever look at it now whereas *Ballantrae* survives at least on the margin of things people read.

Its variety of backgrounds precluded integration: art-student Paris, bourgeois Edinburgh, go-getter San Francisco, desert Midway Island, overripe Honolulu, and down-and-out Sydney, as well as glimpses of the Marquesas and a fictitious American state of Muskegon. The Paris and San Francisco sequences are spoiled by overbrashness. But the enigma of the *Flying Scud*—not even posed until a third of the book is read—works admirably among its loose ends and gradual resolutions. Few tail-foremost mystery plots have been better handled. Dodd's narrative of the voyage to Midway is about as near as paper and ink can get to heavy weather at sea. And, as I have written elsewhere, there are some of Conrad's virtues in the blazing catastrophe of Carthew's story, as the interlacing behavior-patterns of a British pettifogger, a stormy Ulsterman, and a Norse berserker suddenly commit the castaways to a nightmare of murdering perfect strangers in cold blood. Successive small decisions—even the matter of whether to take one's money in coin or in drafts on San Francisco—conspire beautifully to dictate the inevitability of massacre.

The Ebb-Tide, begun in 1890, was also intended to be long, but only its opening episode was in good shape in 1893 when Balfour picked it up and insisted that it was a good long novelette as it stood. The finished product shows signs of telescoping haste, but Papeete beach and the drunken, barratry-minded voyage are not bad. And the cream of it is the Cockney beachcomber, part weasel and part worm, drawn from heaven knows what nauseating original, an underprivileged psychopathic personality with few peers in literature. Conrad again comes quickly to mind. He had his own impulses and originalities, but these flavors anticipate *Victory* and *Lord Jim*, though in a crisper handling, as clearly as Sherwood Anderson anticipated Faulkner.

To ascribe wholly to Lloyd the inferior work in these novels is probably unfair. One can readily take his published word that the overworked Paris episodes of *The Wrecker* are primarily Louis's; they are too like *The Story of a Lie* and the fragment *Cannonmills*. But it is hard to believe Lloyd's memory accurate in claiming for himself the voyage to Midway, the character of Nares, and the massacre on the brig. If he wrote like that in 1891, he must soon have experienced severe aesthetic mutation. His first independent publication, a lame short story of the Indian Mutiny sold to *Scribner's* in 1892 (the hundred dollars went to build Vailima a proper chief's house for ceremonies), shows no such skill. Except for a few humorous short stories about the South Seas, his subsequent fiction has little but competent grasp of what editors liked in the days of George Barr McCutcheon. Apparently each collaborator roughed out assigned blocks of narrative for the other to rework, the process continuing until consistency and pace were arrived at. But it seems also to have been Louis who did final draft from stem to stern: ". . . the last copy is all in my hand," [12] he wrote Bob about *Ebb-Tide*.

That explains much. Lloyd was craftsman enough to rough out the voyage to the wreck. But he can hardly have put such quality into the departure of the *Norah Creina*:

> . . . cast off before I got on deck. In the misty obscurity of the first dawn, I saw the tug heading us with glowing fires and blowing smoke, and heard her beat the roughened waters of the bay. Beside us, on her flock of hills, the lighted city towered up and stood swollen in the raw fog. It was strange to see her burn on thus wastefully, with half-quenched luminaries, when the dawn was already strong enough to show me, and to suffer me to recognize, a solitary figure standing on the piles.[13]

Nevertheless collaboration had value for Louis. He was a comradely man; Lloyd had been with him through most of the scenes and details used; no doubt he took an elder-brotherly pride in having the young fellow at work—and not clumsily—alongside. His will left the bulk of his literary properties to Lloyd subject to Fanny's life-interest. Reading the day's work aloud in the evening, he specially watched Lloyd's reactions; once, when Lloyd was too full of admiration to speak quickly about a bit from *Hermiston*, Louis grew half-hysterical with disappointment. The important sums that collaborations brought—*Scribner's* paid $15,000 for serial rights on *The Wrecker*, for instance—went far toward building Vailima. And, without these preliminary handlings of realistic South Seas data, Louis might not have done so well with *The Beach of Falesà* when he sat down to it in September 1891:

His own opinion of the *Beach* is sound as far as it goes:

> . . . the first realistic South Sea story; I mean with real South Sea characters and details of life. Everybody else who has tried that I have seen, got carried away by the romance, and ended in a kind of sugar candy epic, and the whole effect was lost—there was no etching, no human grin, consequently no conviction. Now I have got the smell, and the look of the

thing a good deal. You will know more about the South Seas after you have read my little tale than if you had read a library.[14]

Quiller-Couch objected to its overearly resolution of the second of what seemed to him two equally important issues: Will the hero make good his footing on the island? and how will he treat his native "wife"? Actually the second is no major issue; Louis used Wiltshire's insistence on genuine marriage merely to arouse sympathy for a backhandedly decent man. The only story-line is the conflict between Wiltshire and the party of the brutally treacherous Case and the bombastic Negro and

. . . old Captain Randall, squatting on the floor native fashion, fat and pale, naked to the waist, grey as a badger, and his eyes set with drink. His body was covered with grey hair and crawled over by flies; one was in the corner of his eye—he never heeded; and the mosquitoes hummed about the man like bees. Any clean-minded man would have had the creature out at once and buried him; . . . there I was entertained all day by that remains of man, his tongue stumbling among low old jokes and long old stories, and his own wheezy laughter always ready, so that he had no sense of my depression. He was nipping gin all the while. Sometimes he fell asleep, and awoke again, whimpering and shivering, and every now and again he would ask me why I wanted to marry Uma. "My friend," I was telling myself all day, "you must not come to be an old gentleman like this."

Had *Treasure Island* never been written, the *Beach* would show how clean Louis's narrative could be. It is strange that only now is a movie to be made of it.[15] It even has "sex," unlike most of Louis's more renowned work—a naked-to-the-waist, flower-scented native heroine as lovely as she is loyal. In drawing Uma, he had no reason for his old complaint that his heroines too often turned ugly on him.

Uma had her troubles with editors, however. Louis had Wiltshire quieting her mission-inculcated scruples about living in sin with a mock marriage, certifying her ". . . illegally married . . . for one night only, and Mr. John Wiltshire is at liberty to send her to hell when he pleases." The *Illustrated London News*, serializing the tale, cut out the whole document, indicating only that it was mysteriously abominable. Cassell & Co., publishing it in *Island Nights Entertainments*, sought to disinfect it by the senseless device of making it read ". . . for one week." When later offering abortive *The Go-Between* to the *News* Louis sardonically noted that it ". . . might be lisped at a mothers' meeting." [16]

This glimpse of the late Victorian editor is helpful, because Louis was now embarking on fuller treatment of women characters. It is not quite true that so far he had either eschewed or failed with women: Anastasie Desprez, Alicia Risingham, the Countess von Rosen, all had some life. But his heroines were uniformly stickish—Joan Sedley, the Admiral's daughter, the girl in *The Pavilion on the Links*. Louis, as well as his critics, often pondered this lack, and Fanny often pointed it out to him. In May 1892, telling Colvin of plans for *The Young Chevalier* (most significant in this context and presently to be described), he wrote:

I am afraid my touch is a little broad in a love story; I can't mean one thing and write another. . . . the sentiment being very intense, and already very much handled in letters, positively calls for a little pawing and gracing. With a writer of my prosaic literalness and pertinency of point of view, this all shoves toward grossness—positively even toward the far more damnable *closeness*. This has kept me off the sentiment hitherto, and now I am to try: Lord! . . . with all my romance, I am a realist and a prosaist, and a most fanatical lover of plain physical sensations plainly and expressly rendered; hence my perils. To do love in the same spirit as I did (for instance) D. Balfour's fatigue in the heather; my dear sir, there were grossness ready made![17]

That passage has been interpreted as crass bowing to Victorian prudery—what business has the artist with such values as grossness or its absence? Louis certainly felt that less reticence about erotics would strengthen literature. Only a few weeks before he died he wrote Bob:

> If I had to begin again . . . I believe I should try to honour Sex more religiously. The worst of our education is that Christianity does not recognize and hallow Sex. . . . a terrible hiatus in our modern religions that they cannot see and make venerable that which they ought to see first and hallow most. Well, it is so; I cannot be wiser than my generation.[18]

Here are matured revolutions! Writing to Bob twenty years earlier, young Louis would have been confident of being wiser than his generation with one hand tied behind him.

Nevertheless his emendation of "grossness" to "closeness" restores him to the aesthetic terms in which alone such a matter can be discussed. Twenty years before, while commending Whitman for boldly treating erotics as keystone in the arch of life, he had also noted that no aspect of living is likelier to trip the writer by distracting his reader—too little empathy is as bad as too much, both are high hazards.[19] My own conclusion is that Louis's gingerliness with fictitious love was partly realistic acceptance of the terms of his time—he had small ambition to turn technical innovator[20]—but also came partly of the slowness with which he shed adolescent values.

Had he felt deeper need of erotic plot- and character-values, in whatever set of conventions, he would have long been trying them out, regardless of whether they were ever published; yet he very seldom did so. Or, the other way round, his first decisive impulse to treat fully the erotic values of women came on him in Samoa, scene of striking new maturity in several other respects. Once he tries, his practice so flouts his previous misgivings as to make one doubt their validity. He could still discuss the point in general, as in his letter to Bob quoted above; but the die had long been cast.[21] At any rate, 1892 saw him writing *Catriona*, embarking on *The Young Chevalier*, planning *Sophia Scarlett* (to involve three heroines), and making early drafts of *Weir of Hermiston*—all containing love affairs and each (except *Scarlett*, which was never begun) notable women.

Catriona works out the loose plot-threads of *Kidnapped* with shrewd talk and some good melodrama. Louis liked it: the interpolated tale of Tod Lapraik proverbially rates second in its kind only to Wandering Willie's tale in *Redgauntlet;* and he did solid work in the figures of Prestongrange, ruthless politician-lawyer; James More, wheedling traitor; and Barbara Grant, beautiful and waspish *dea ex machina*. She was woman enough for once, not least because David wavers toward her though author and everybody else destined him for Catriona. But Louis went farther still in the problem that he had long dreaded, including a wry little comedy immersing David and his best beloved in some three simultaneous false positions that force them to share lodgings under pretense of being brother and sister. A slippery project: the young people must remain innocent but worse entangled by the hour, exasperatingly blind without turning stupid, unwillingly coupled but basically delighting to be so. For the sake of ideas still lively in Louis's time and fraught with devastation, they must not only remain chaste but not even consciously contemplate alternatives. Their consequent glow of embarrassment and intimacy is excellently and warmly handled. And the juggling seems to have been technically adequate: The story was serialized in *Atalanta*, a British magazine for girls. What the girls made of David's and Miss Drummond's fundamental trouble is more than I dare guess.

Falesà and *Catriona* were the bridge, perhaps not into the erotic field only. Though one is hardly a novel at all and the other a mere anecdote, both moved away from what Edwin Muir justly labeled the "decorative" aspect of Louis's fiction—the element distinguishing unfavorably between the Durie brothers' duel and Wiltshire's reciprocal ambush of Case in the jungle. Henceforth—never mind the pot-boiling *St. Ives*—Louis's work edges closer and closer to wilfully organic intimacy with life, deeper than the mere vividness, good as it is, of David's troubles in the heather.

Entered on willy-nilly, as essential changes must be, this necessarily involved shudderings and fears and rackings, and took months to complete. In the early October before his death, Louis's intimidated gloom alarmed Colvin:

I know I am at a climacteric for all men who live by their wits, so I do not despair. But the truth is I am pretty near useless in literature, . . . Were it not for my health which made it impossible, I could not find it in my heart to forgive myself that I did not stick to an honest, commonplace trade when I was young, which might now have supported me during these ill years. But do not suppose me to be down in anything else; only, for the nonce, my skill deserts me, such as it is, or was. It was a very little dose of inspiration, and a pretty little trick of style, long lost, improved by the most heroic industry. . . . I am a fictitious article, and have long known it. I am read by journalists, by my fellow-novelists, and by boys; . . . And I look forward confidently to an aftermath; I do not think my health can be so hugely improved without some subsequent improvement in my brains. . . . I cannot take myself seriously as an artist; the limitations are so obvious. I did take myself seriously as a workman as of old, but my practice has fallen off, I am now an idler and cumberer of the ground; . . .[23]

The mood occasionally strikes artists in any medium. Round Christmas 1890, Louis had given Colvin a wonderful example of sudden shifts of climate; on December 27th: "I am worked out and can no more at all"; on December 28th: "I have got unexpectedly to work again and feel quite dandy. Good-bye."[24] But few have Louis's ability to jeer at himself while in the dumps.

The one thing certain about such feelings is that they seldom mean what they purport to. Here they may actually have been the final pang of transition. Within a few days, at least, this "fictitious article," this worked-out wordmonger never of considerable talent, had picked up the rough of *Hermiston* left on the stocks months before and begun to give it the authoritative air of one of the great novels of the nineteenth century.

The fragmentary *Young Chevalier*, begun shortly after *Falesà* and *Catriona*, involved reviving both Alan Breck and Ballantrae. It got little farther than a prologue. But that prologue is extremely notable for opening with a woman utterly remote from the virginities and inhibitions of *Catriona*; she startles the reader as if he had unexpectedly found her in his bed. The man who had long boggled at "sex" now readily evoked a sort of tawny, warm she-genie instantly substantial as a thick braid of hair and as exigent as hunger. The single scene built round her builds like fire. It appears that this Marie-Madeleine Paradou was to have been mere occasion of a quarrel illuminating the principals and then drop out of the story. I doubt if Louis would have had the heart thus to throw her away. But he felt misgivings about plot and proper key, so Marie-Madeleine stopped where she was, deliberately and rosily avid behind the wine-shop counter, with the *mistral* hooting outside and the dust eddying in the cold room. Fanny approved of this scene—further cause to doubt that, as some have surmised, it was she who kept Louis shy of full-dress erotics.

Most of 1893 went toward grinding away at *St. Ives*[25] to fulfil the indiscreet agreement made with McClure at Saranac; reworking *The Ebb-Tide*; drafting an ingratiating biography of the lighthouse Stevensons, large portions of which were never published in collected works; but even this year the fragmentary *Heathercat* gives another glimpse of Louis's seeking a new dimension in fiction. Vigorous, able, and darkly shadowed though the opening of *Ballantrae* may be, it suffers a seizure of dryness and "decoration" set beside the equivalent opening wordage of *Heathercat*. *Ballantrae* has a touch of puppetism and its background is stylized, as if rubbed into simplification by years of repetition. The world of *Heathercat* is all of a piece: the curate daffing with the long-legged wench and the hill-side conventicle drenched by a rain-squall are not far away and long ago but here and now, though the time is the late seventeenth century.

Other signposts appear: In these two last fragments Louis ventured on and brilliantly succeeded in full-scale third-person narrative. *Treasure Island, Kidnapped, Falesà* had all been in the first person. He had used third only in the *New Arabian Nights, The Black Arrow* and shorter narrative, including parts of *Jekyll*. His choice of this more objective form may have shown an urge toward a tool better adapted to multidimensional work. His choice of settings also looks as if he were spiraling back to the Scotland that had printed itself off on the sensitive surfaces of his youth. Having exercised himself on the exotic data of the South Seas, then conjured up, as the *mistral* blew in Avignon, the dusty, sunny old town that had once been his gateway to life, he now trended still farther back—to Swanston Cottage for St. Ives, to the claustrophobic closes of David's Edinburgh, the solan geese whitening the Bass Rock with their droppings, the sandy bents where David and Alan waited for Andy Scougall—the very materials that had first set the boy looking about him. *Heathercat* was the Covenanters' moorlands seen through Cummy's authors:

> . . . solitary hills and morasses, haunted only by the so-called Mountain Wanderers, the dragoons that came in chase of them, the women that wept on their dead bodies, and the wild birds of the moorlands that have cried there since the beginning. It is a land of many rain-clouds; a land of much mute history written there in prehistoric symbols. Strange green raths are to be seen commonly in that country, above all by the kirk-yards; barrows of the dead, standing stones; . . .

Louis bracketed this and *Hermiston* as works ". . . which will either be something different or I have failed. . . . if my mind will keep up to the point it was in a while back, perhaps I can pull it through." [26]

When in September 1894 he set to work at high pitch, his

choice between the two stumps of narrative lay with "the tale of the Lord Justice-Clerk and of his son, young Hermiston, that vanished from men's knowledge." Why he so chose can be only surmised. It may have been because the rough drafts he worked from had already developed all the principal characters more fully in *Hermiston* than in *Heathercat*; or perhaps because the plot-values of *Hermiston* were nearer to his own emotional history. No two people were ever more dissimilar than Thomas Stevenson and Adam Weir. But, always symbolically, often materially, Louis here celebrated his maturity by grasping with new firmness the very shapes of his own ganglia. Having so often written about himself, he was now writing himself. That is what so sharply distinguishes *Hermiston* from the "autobiographical novel"—this is a matter not of self-explanation but of self-texture.

In publishing three successive preliminary drafts of *Hermiston*, Balfour preserved an interesting study of Stevenson the zealous reviser. Some of these versions must be a year apart, but the method, however bettered in detail, is notably consistent, a firm foundation for the new manner: rich, muscular, with leisurely reverberations, easy but not facile, full but not burdened. On the third start some 50,000 words were dictated or reworked at least once.

There have been two schools of thought about this work: The more sanguine—myself included—agree with Edwin Muir, a man of distinctly modern approaches, whose estimate of earlier Stevensons is temperately cautious. He was almost reverent about *Hermiston*:

> . . . he began when he was over forty to speak in the unaffected voice of the great writer. . . . we see in a flash all that he might have become. . . . a noble gentleness and flexibility. The figures exist in a clear dawn, and have the freshness of a morning race, where everyone without effort or distortion is a little above the human scale. . . . they differ from Hardy's characters, tragic in a lesser fashion, by their integral and ac-

tive powers . . . judging him by it, one can almost say that no other writer of his time showed evidence of equal powers.[27]

Even E. F. Benson, who so zealously belittled Louis and leveled at him so many baseless accusations, said that, in *Hermiston*, he ". . . seemed to step within the house of the immortals." [28]

The other school grant that *Hermiston* as it stands is superlatively all very well, but fear that Louis would have botched it, unable to sustain the pace. This is most recently and sympathetically stated by Daiches, who level-headedly tempers informed and extreme admiration with reluctant skepticism. He even suggests that this prognosis is not too tragic, since, like "Kubla Khan," the existing fragment has its own aesthetic completeness. He likens "the quiet passion of the writing" to that of Caldwell and Faulkner—a comparison startling until he makes a supplementary distinction:

> But . . . Stevenson is not writing his story as a preliminary to diagnosis, social or historical, but as result of diagnosis; there is nothing tentative in his understanding of the whole complex of causes, lying in history, heredity and psychology, that produced this crisis and make it the inevitable prelude to tragedy. . . . a mature insight expressed through a style stripped of all superfluous fat.[29]

The issue whether or not, if he had lived, Louis would have kept it singing and trembling and brooding as it began is as fruitless as considering what might have happened if it had not rained before Waterloo. The biographer can merely ask leave to gloat a little over how rewardingly his man now showed that he had learned not so much to be an author as how to write, not so much to be happy as to comprehend, respect, and rejoice in personality. The more that miniature politics apparently distracted him, the less sure he grew that art is the supreme human activity, the better he wrote, the more skilfully he sought such compassionate irony as *Hermiston* shows. It may not be true at all that aesthetic maturity is either condition or cause of emotional maturity; but, if so, Louis's case was the most significant of exceptions.

The women are superb: The elder Kirstie, with the vigor of a woman-Centaur, possessive, shrewd, all of a mother but the fact and the mawkishness; the younger Kirstie, dark and soft but sinewy, femininely barbaric in both dependence and flurries of prideful reluctance; the sure sketch of Mrs. Weir, drawn with a sort of loving exasperation from Louis's own grandmother Smith. There is no word for the massive validity of old Adam Weir—Louis's final reflection of fascination with Raeburn's portrait of Lord Braxfield, the solid, gamey, brutal jurist who became a principal legend of the Scottish bar. But this was no fictionized rewrite of Cockburn's *Memorials*. Louis's long-ripening, pagan respect for personality here works as organically as it does for the likes of himself in young Archie Weir. This is no self-portrait either; but Archie is "the same kind of fool." I suspect that handling Archie was the most illuminating experience of Louis's life.

Day after day during October and November the rough text came off the bolt like the crackly pulling of strong silk, work so rousingly good that Louis's depression could not last. The confidence of his approach is amazing. It takes a bold writer to start the elder Kirstie on the blistering story of the Four Black Brothers, break off to tell the reader that she told it "like one inspired," and then proceed to make her do exactly that; the only parallel that comes to mind is the legend of Babe Ruth pointing out the center-field fence. Evening after evening he read the day's revision aloud, had his nightcap, and went to bed, waking with the sun to deliberate and fondle the unfolding futures of these pregnantly doomed people.

Politics remained relatively quiet. While running so hot a trail, Louis was not likely to return to his financial forebodings. He was writing Baxter, in fact, about the likelihood that, within a few years, capital and royalties should be returning him an annual income of £1000, now that Vailima was so nearly in permanent shape. Much too much has been made of Louis's sense of too heavy economic burdens in 1893-94. His outcries in letters home about "no rest but the grave for Sir Walter" appear to me like one form of rationalization of the strains produced in him by the emotional and aesthetic shifts taking place deep within him.

After the summer's toil, *St. Ives* was almost finished, but the final disposition of that nimble young fellow could wait. . . . Baxter was on his way to Samoa via Suez, bringing the first two volumes of the Edinburgh Edition, subscriptions to which had saved the bank balance. This was the first of the old cronies to come visiting, perhaps only the first. . . . Thanksgiving dinner for the local Americans had gone handsomely. . . . HMS *Wallaroo* was in port. . . . On December 3 the only dark spot was a foreboding fit of Fanny's—something dreadful was about to happen to an intimate of the family's, perhaps Balfour, who was knocking about Micronesia in ratty schooners; such feelings usually came to nothing whatever, but her firm belief in her occult sensitivity prevented her from disguising them. Coming downstairs from his afternoon's work, Louis tried to distract her by talking about a possible lecture tour of the States for revenue; then suggested a game of solitaire, apparently a recognized way of diverting her from gloom; then kept up distractions with a proposal to fetch up a special Burgundy for dinner and make a special salad dressing of his own invention. He was solicitously gay, alive with the overtones of creation. But he had come to the place of the name.

There on the veranda outside the great hall he put his long, bony hands to his head and said sharply: "Oh, what a pain!"—then to Fanny: "Do I look strange?" She lied swiftly: "No," and, with Sosimo's help, guided him to an easy chair within-doors. Aunt Maggie and Belle came at once. Lloyd saddled and rode breakneck for Apia and Dr. Funk. Funk took Lloyd's lathered mount and started up the mountain, Lloyd stole another hitched before a trading store and pounded after. The surgeon of the *Wallaroo* soon joined Funk at Vailima. Louis's breathing was steadily weakening.

Three years before he had amused himself and Annie Ide with the implications of his giving her his birthday: "I may, as you say, live forever; I might, on the other hand, come to pieces like the one-hoss shay at a moment's notice; . . ."[30] He had once told his mother that, after a certain age, it would be touch and go whether the longevity of the Balfours or the low viability of the Stevensons would take possession.

The doctors could promise nothing. A little after eight o'clock, December 3, 1894, with no sign of returning consciousness, Robert Louis Stevenson died on a cot in the hall.

The headmen of Tanugamanono, the village below Vailima, came bringing fine mats, symbols of the village's prestige, to spread over the body. Clarke had arrived and was praying beside the dying man when the end came. The Vailima Catholics sang their own hymns over him, Sosimo watched all night beside the body. By sunrise the Mataafa men were hard at work clearing a switchback path through the high bush up Mt. Vaea. The summit is a room-sized platform, then tree-covered; it was soon cleared and the grave dug in the middle. Dressed in a fine shirt and black trousers, covered with the British ensign from the *Casco*, Louis was carried up—his frailness made the steep climb easier—on Samoan shoulders. Over the grave the Tongan exiles whom he had befriended set up a Tonga-style funeral decoration of mats and streamers.

He very probably did not feel the doctors' swift examinations or hear Clarke's prayers. I hope he was not conscious after his last words. There are many worse ways to die than without knowing there is final occasion for regret, full of the exultation of accomplishment, in the act of affectionate solicitude for one's own.

Five years ago I rose early, in order to avoid the heat of the well-risen sun, and climbed Mt. Vaea from Vailima. Recently cleared again, the trail was easily followed and, since the weather had not been rainy, was slippery only coming down. People who made the climb soon after Louis's death say that they saw the ocean from the summit; by now the growth of trees down the northern slope masks the view except for a gap through which the red roof of Vailima is visible far below.

A concrete slab soon replaced the level grave. On the gabled plinth that surmounts it are bronze plaques—designed by Gelett Burgess, whom Fanny knew in California after Louis's death —that on the east carrying "Requiem," that on the west Ruth's speech to Naomi in Samoan. On the northern short face is a plaque for Fanny, whose ashes are beneath it, decorated with the tiger-lily that she considered her emblem, the hibiscus of the islands, and Louis's verses beginning: "Teacher, tender comrade, wife . . ." By insignificant accident the visitor coming up the trail sees Fanny's plaque first.

Few bother to make the climb nowadays. Western Samoa has only a trickle of tourists. The shrubs on the margin of the clearing bloom with red-leathery flowers, and the plaster sheathing of the concrete has washed away in places. When I was there, the remaining surface carried many fools' names in pencil, some native, mostly Western.

There under the slab lie the long, light, slender bones; the queer, inadequate ribs; the aquiline, dolichocephalic skull. The trend of the skeleton must be as clear as Flint's pointer—due north. Louis was like the fish that, Will o' the Mill noticed, always swam with their heads upstream.

To match the Victorian setting of the story, loose ends and minor characters must be accounted for after the catastrophe:

Baxter heard of Louis's death en route but came on to Samoa anyway. He went home via San Francisco, presently pursued by Fanny's wrath over the publication of the *Fables*. Though he probably knew Louis most intimately of his surviving friends, he did not publish about him at any length. The Stevenson letters that he left to the Savile Club, whence Edwin J. Beinecke procured them for the Yale University Library, have been invaluable.

On hearing of Louis's death Henry James went wailing to

Mrs. Sitwell that it could not, must not be true. He refused to serve as an executor of Louis's literary estate, thus escaping the complications that arose about the official biography and other matters.

Colvin spent several years working on the official biography. His slowness in developing it moved Fanny and Lloyd, after much agitation, to transfer the assignment to Graham Balfour, who completed it in 1901. In the meantime Colvin had published the *Vailima Letters*. After their so-long-delayed marriage in 1903, he and the former Mrs. Sitwell lived on most cultivatedly and harmoniously into the 1920s.

Fanny, Belle, and Lloyd remained at Vailima for some years, during part of which Lloyd served as U. S. vice-consul. Eventually Fanny sold the estate to a Vladivostok merchant who had chosen to retire to Samoa. After the Germans annexed Western Samoa in 1900, the Imperial government took over Vailima as governor's residence.

Fanny visited Europe at least twice more, but lived mostly in California until her death, of cerebral hemorrhage, in 1914. People were most respectful of her in her declining years. She bought or built several houses, including a large town house in San Francisco and a suburban place near Santa Barbara. After Louis's death her writing was confined to biographical reminiscences used in various editions of his works. Belle took her ashes to Samoa to be buried in Louis's grave.

Belle was much with her mother until death parted them. Her second husband was Salisbury Field, playwright and protégé of Fanny's. Her autobiography, *This Life I've Loved*, was recently reissued to celebrate her ninetieth birthday. It naturally has much to say about Louis, in supplement to the *Memories of Vailima* that she wrote with Lloyd and the biographical sketch of Louis that she produced for the Stevenson Society of America. She also wrote a novel, *The Girl from Home*, about Hawaii as she had known it in the gay days of the Royal Crowd.

Lloyd married Katharine Durham, whom he met in Honolulu, in 1896. Two children were born. The marriage terminated in divorce and Lloyd remarried. Between 1905 and 1920 he published numerous light novels and short stories, some based on his enthusiasm for pioneer motoring, and collaborated with Austin Strong on two plays. He also traveled widely and was well known at the Lambs Club in New York. He died in 1947 in California.

Austin Strong went on to successful playwriting in *Three Wise Fools* and *Seventh Heaven*.

After Louis's death his mother returned to Scotland and lived with her sister. She attended a great Stevenson memorial meeting and, with characteristic self-effacingness, would have missed being on the platform if she had not been recognized in the nick of time. In 1897 she contracted a fatal pneumonia at the age of sixty-eight: ". . . thinking she saw her son at the foot of the bed, she exclaimed, 'There is Louis! I must go,' and fell back at once, unconscious, though she did not actually breathe her last until the next day." [31]

Appendix A

The Dialectics of a Reputation

> You often find that a long criticism upon a man, or his
> work, is but a demand that he should be somebody else
> and his work somebody else's work.
>
> —Helps, *The Spanish Conquest in America:* I, 194

BETTER than most people, writers survive themselves,
at least in the Library of Congress. Better than most
writers, Louis survived himself in both reputation and people's
memories of his person. The final form of this survival is yet to
be determined.

Within a few days of his death, Fanny wrote to Mrs. Sitwell
suggesting that London literary people agitate for British annexa-
tion of Samoa, so that Louis's grave might become British soil.
The economic and political future of thousands of turbulent
Polynesians was thus to hinge on the irrelevancy that a famous
and charming writer had chosen to live and die in their islands.

Grief and understandable lack of perspective may excuse the
overtones of canonization in this notion. They continued to vibrate through Fanny, poor, lost woman, until she died. There
was less excuse for others: Quiller-Couch was soon writing: "Put
away books and paper and pen. . . . Stevenson is dead, and now
there is nobody left to write for." [1] Within a few months half
the minor versifiers in the English-speaking world had elegies
in print: Richard Le Gallienne hailed the dead man as "Vergil
of prose!" [2] Bruce Porter as "Our pilot into light!" [3] Within
thirty years every living human being whose cat had patronized
the same veterinarian as Bogue had published dilute memories

of Robert Louis Stevenson. The biographer owes them all thanks for invaluable data, but he must also wonder at many of them as well as at "Q" and Porter. E. F. Benson's inaccurate and venomous study of Stevenson in 1924 was right on one point: the man did suffer "the indignity of being pilloried in stained glass." [4]

By that time many things were changing—literary conventions, approaches to writing, standards of behavior, and the literary attitude toward Stevenson. That last is now in the crucial stage, when a not illiterate woman can say: "How interesting that you are doing a life of Stevenson! I hadn't thought of him since my children read him," as if the subject were Beatrix Potter.

Hegel's private universe of thesis, antithesis, and synthesis, though no favorite of mine, can be useful in aesthetic history. In an applicable context Stevenson once wrote that literary —and other artistic—reputations are often "out of affectation by dogmatism." The instability of such parents causes literary fame to contain within itself the seeds of its own destruction. Overpraise elicits attack and relative neglect. Then—sometimes—comes rediscovery with—sometimes—solider reason to readmit the writer to the canon. In our time this has happened in some degree to Melville, Henry James, Trollope. Utter giants see less of these vicissitudes: Balzac, Tolstoi, Thackeray suffer fluctuations but do not shatter and reshape. It is the "little masters" who vibrate in and out of the light for generations before settling down to presumptive title to so many lines or pages in any given *History of Literature: for Teachers and Students.*

Often wasteful, the process can usefully peel off the personal and the adventitious. But downhill is easy and synthesis by no means inevitable. Otherwise efforts at revival would succeed oftener, and we should do nothing but reread Howells, Swinburne, and Peacock—much good reading, but time is limited. I am not confident that synthesis will descend on the figure that Stevenson now cuts in literary eyes, though I heartily wish it may and consider that, if it does not, the fault will lie with inadequate readers, not with Stevenson. In his case one can be sure only that antithesis has done its worst. If his reputation is ever to turn inside out, digest all his tenable achievements, slough off accretions wished on him by the changing years, and become a new and vigorous organism, it must happen soon.

In editing a complete Henry James-Stevenson correspondence Janet Adam Smith recently deplored the fashion in which Stevenson as person—whether truly conceived or not—has obscured the literary artist of high integrity. Boldly she lumps James and Stevenson as peers of the same literary stratum, their intimacy founded not so much on Louis's charm and James's pouncing sympathies as on shared respect for and grasp of the art to which both were dedicated. To neo-Jamesians this may sound like presumption. It is merely long-delayed recognition, here coming from a well-qualified Jamesian, of the comradely seriousness with which James took the writer of boys' stories and nursery verse whom he knew at Bournemouth, considering *Kidnapped* work of great brilliance and identifying Louis as "the sole and single Anglo-Saxon capable of perceiving" [5] how well the latest James novel was written. Lack of cliquery lends greater weight to this acceptance. Unlike Colvin, Gosse, and Henley, James had not been so long committed to the young Stevenson's literary future that he was unable to see either his merits or his defects without distortion.

In such testimony lies what hope there is of rescuing Stevenson. It will take doing. Trauma has been severe and, in these matters, the cards must lie right to begin with. Said Edwin Muir, with regrettable accuracy: "Stevenson has simply fallen out of the procession. He is still read by the vulgar, but he has joined that band of writers on whom, by tacit consent, the serious critics have nothing to say." [6]

Degeneration visibly began when Gosse wrote Louis that not since Byron went to Greece had a literary adventure so seized the public as his settling in Samoa where, the newspapers understood, he had become some sort of king of savages. An ill-omened comparison: of all sizable writers Byron leaned most on personal gesture to foster literary renown. Borrow thought as much—or said he did—as he watched Byron's funeral procession, concluding that, however much the noble lord owed to his pathological antics, people would always read *Childe Harold*. For an amateur gypsy this was poor fortune-telling. The beautiful, vicious, vaunting person has now so eclipsed the poet that, no matter how biographies of the man multiply, few but earnest students read more of *Childe Harold* than the apostrophe to the ocean. A bilious critic could say that softer but equally specious traits made Stevenson the Byron of children and compilers of reading-lists.

Before his death Stevenson had already been exposed to the hazards of having his essays set as school examples. It was rather like giving a novice-machinist a chronometer to reproduce. True, many of the models on whom he broke himself to pen and paper were subtler still. But subjective choice, however bold, is different from academic prescription, and the consequences were mostly unfortunate: Youngsters with literate futures usually revolt against school examples and may never find for themselves, in the teeth of negative conditioning, that prim school texts of Burke and Hawthorne actually make most rewarding reading. Nor were results much better when more docile spirits were moved to imitate the Stevenson of the earlier essays and travels.

Academic anthologists were significantly prone to give their readers the dulcet experiment of *An Inland Voyage* instead of the sturdier skill of *Silverado*. Such sins of tunnel-vision ended in exhibiting Stevenson as incarnating gay wholesomeness, as wholesomeness was then understood, as the rising generation inevitably gagged at it. And, though his alleged optimism kept him considered pertinent to human life for long after his death, he was gradually being forced into a descent into the nursery, a place even more sinister than the pulpit, whence he may or may not arise on the third day. Belittlingly, dilutingly, and sweetishly the pleasant letters from "the lean man" to "the children in the cellar" helped the emphasis swoon over to "Of speckled eggs the birdie sings," illustrated by Jessie Willcox Smith or Charles Robinson—the perpetrator of those puffed and tallowy urchins wearing rumpled bedsheets and carrying large initial capitals. But wrath is pointless. Worse things have happened to even greater works: consider the usual child's abridgement of *Gulliver*.

Treasure Island also did sad damage. Ah, pirates, my dears, ah, the Spanish Main, ah, pieces of eight and shiver my timbers! The cultivated aunt wishing her small nephew normally but hygienically pirate-minded furnished him with Jim Hawkins's story. Few items of warranted literary standing can compete so well with dime novels or comic books. So *Treasure Island* appeared on children's shelves long before they could savor it—it was written, after all, for the early teens, not the kindergarten—and was left off high-school reading lists (replaced by *The Black Arrow*, since a Stevenson was indicated) because it was a "child's book." [7] Here are remarkable anomalies: Woolly animals and Silver panting aloud as he knifes the honest hand. The patter of little feet and Israel Hands trailing across the deck with the great wound in his thigh and the blood-sticky dirk in his yellow teeth. Pattycake and the stiff-as-a-crucifix deadness of O'Brien lying "across the knees of the man who had killed him, and the quick fishes steering to and fro over both." The movies usually completed the sabotage by casting Jim as a child of nine or ten instead of as a boy in his teens conceivably capable of snatching up a cutlass in the melée at the blockhouse.

Movies have even more to answer for in sabotage of the third Stevenson item still high in public awareness; though perhaps not one in ten who has seen a movie version of *Jekyll* knows who wrote it, any more than they could name the authors of *Dracula* or *Frankenstein*. Resistance as well as ignorance may enter here. A bumble-minded lady to whom "Robert Louis Stevenson" connotes only decalcomania pirates and "Up into the cherry-tree" may have difficulty grasping the astounding fact that the same author provided occasion for the apelike horrors perpetrated by John Barrymore, Fredric March, Spencer Tracy, *et al.* in scenarios smoky with sex in the interpolated orgy scenes.[8] For all its merits and the money that its success brought directly and indirectly, *Jekyll* probably did Louis more harm than good. It boomed him on the basis of sensational effects, and combined with the creeping renown of *Treasure Island* to identify him with literary *genres* of low prestige. Grave observers prone to mistrust popularity and virtuosity found this hard to overlook. Stevenson was hardly cold in his grave when the first peevish exceptions to his literary apotheosis were entered.

The silliness of some admirers contributed much to the violence of the reaction. It was not only that Stevenson was used as moral landmark in works like *Daddy-Long-Legs* and *Mary Ware: the Little Colonel's Chum;* that limp-leather excerpts from the *Vailima Prayers* were lively Christmas items; that aenemic ladies itching "to write" so damply worshipped the memory of the dear, delicate, kind man. Things had been almost equally oozy among some writing professionals. Too many had crowned Louis peer of Scott in romance and Dryden in style, being of that school of critic who must always substitute comparison for analysis. Louis too would probably have found much of this irksomely exaggerated; he had long since written to Will Low:

> It is a blessed thing that, in this forest of art, we can pursue our woodlice and sparrows, *and not catch them*, with almost the same fervour of exhilaration as that with which Sophocles hunted and brought down the Mastodon.[9]

The pity of it was that the indicated correction was too often in the hands of people distortingly eager and ill-natured about it.

It had begun mildly in 1888 with young Barrie's suspicion that Stevenson leaned too much on

> the great work he is to write by and by when the little works are finished. . . . He experiments too long; he is still a boy wondering what he is going to be. . . . It is quite time the great work was begun.[10]

Louis retaliated by heaping the cheeky young fellow with praise of *A Window in Thrums*. Next year the tone was harsher when Steuart—the same who later endowed Louis with a ravishing mistress who never existed—sneered elaborately at Stevenson largely on the grounds that Alan Breck was reminiscent of Rob Roy and that Louis disliked *Tom Jones*.[11] But the heavy shelling did not begin until 1897, when, using his review of Yeats's *The Secret Rose* as occasion for attacking Stevenson, George Moore set one of the major motifs of this reaction opposite in direction and rather more than equal in force:

Animus promptly involved him in some strange statements: In the teeth of John Silver and *Jekyll*, for instance: "[Stevenson] imagined no human soul, and he invented no story that anyone will remember . . ."; in the teeth of the *Odyssey*: ". . . great literature cannot be composed from narratives of perilous adventures." [12] But the gist of it is overstatement of the contention that even Stevenson's best is mere "literary marquetry";[13] this renowned "style," Moore averred, was only a trick of first couching a platitude in the customary words, then deliberately replacing the key-word with a racier substitute—not exactly accusing Stevenson of thumbing a thesaurus but seeing the net effect as if that method had been used. Technically, of course, this is nonsense, but no doubt Moore was pleased thus to dispose of the man who wrote: "The sky itself was of a ruddy, powerful, nameless, changing colour, dark and glossy like a serpent's back. . . ."

In the States the following year John Jay Chapman supplied the extreme case of using Louis's theory of writer-training as a club to beat him with. Because he had recommended playing "sedulous ape" to writers of quality, this strident voice accused him of being merely "the most extraordinary mimic that has ever appeared in literature." [14] It attributed his relative failure with *In the South Seas* to his having lacked "an original to copy from." At once it was easier to share Greenwood's resentment of critics ". . . who begin to find out that [Stevenson's] style was bad. Whether they would have discovered that as readily if he had not told them of his extraordinary pains to acquire a style I doubt; . . ." [15]

The falsity of this Ape-Chapman approach is impossible to demonstrate, for it is immediately perceived or never. One reader is confident, for instance, that what ailed Mark Twain in his Prince-and-Pauper phase was imitation, no doubt unconscious, of Charles Reade; another sees no such influence and never will. Knowing both Stevenson and most of his models well, I am convinced that, by his late twenties, he was as near idiosyncrasy as Sterne before him or Kipling after him. For proof by exception, the patent influence of Meredith spoiled *Prince Otto*. In all common sense, whom does *Treasure Island* or "Pulvis et Umbra" read like? For proof by example, try Frank Swinnerton's well-known study of Stevenson, which, though patronizing about his style, falls again and again into writing identifiable yards away as watered-down Stevenson and nothing else.[16] Query: if this style is a mere tissue of imitations, lacking quality peculiar to itself, how can it be so clearly identifiable when imitated? why does not the reader sensing imitation think rather of Hazlitt, Browne, or Bunyan, instead of Stevenson?

In the second wave the charge of sedulous apery was raised to that of empty stylism. Leading from another citation of Stevenson against himself, Benson summed up in 1925:

> . . . tells himself (and it is probably quite true) that few ever went so far as he who had less natural talent for writing. . . . A style he certainly did achieve, which, at its best, was admirably lucid and picturesque, but it was always a foreign language to him and he never wielded it with ease . . . a forced style, not natural, and he forged it into less an instrument than a fetter. . . . It compelled him, as under the lash, to sacrifice simplicity to the desire to be striking and sonorous, and to arrest attention to what is trivial by some unusual phrase, just as he called attention to himself by outlandish habiliments.[17]

Quotations put in evidence are from the youthful journeyman-work of *Voyage* and *Donkey*, which is sharp practice. No word of the above applies to the passage from "A Christmas Sermon" quoted on p. 276, least of all does the outlandish word-masking triviality appear, for the sentiment was resoundingly nontrivial in 1888. Nor could it conceivably apply to almost any bit in the hurricane chapter of the *Footnote:*

> For the seventh war-ship, the day had come too late; the *Eber* had finished her last cruise; she was to be seen no more save by the eyes of divers. A coral reef is not only an instrument of destruction, but a place of sepulture; the submarine cliff is profoundly undercut, and presents the mouth of a huge antre, in which the bodies of men and the hulls of ships are alike hurled down and buried. The *Eber* had dragged anchors with the rest; her injured screw disabled her from steaming vigorously up; and a little before day, she had struck the front end of the coral, come off, struck again, and gone down stern foremost, oversetting as she went, into the gaping hollow of the reef. Of her whole complement of nearly eighty, four souls were cast alive on the beach; and the bodies of the remainder were, by the voluminous outpourings of the flooded streams, scoured at last from the harbour, and strewed naked on the seaboard of the island.

In any idiom or any century, that is writing.

Soon after Benson, C.E.M. Joad was even using Stevenson as deplorable example for ". . . How to Write Badly," quoting Samuel Butler against him and, for contrast, commending Shaw's dictum: "Effectiveness of assertion is the beginning and the end of style." [18] This currently popular—and practically tonic—attitude toward style was summed up better by the Duchess than by Joad, Butler, and Shaw together: "Take care of the sense and the sounds will take care of themselves." The doctrine was pertinent to the audience that Joad addressed—the readers of a labor newspaper. But more experienced students of such matters might have advised Joad to read William James's "On a Certain

Blindness in Human Beings" for the effect of the contrast between James's excellent lean style (of which, I assume, the Duchess would approve) and the full flavor of Stevenson in the long passages from "The Lantern-Bearers" here used to illustrate James's psychological point. In fact, the founder of pragmatism here publicly hopes that this essay of Stevenson's will be immortal, "both for the truth of its matter and the excellence of its form,"[19] which is notable from a man who managed both to write well and to think hard. In winnowing literature for further illustration, he harnesses Stevenson with Josiah Royce, Wordsworth, Walt Whitman, and Tolstoi . . . fast company for a mere phrase-juggler. It is difficult to be patient with the Joadish assumption that there is no more to style than happy extension of the Duchess's maxim, sound though it is as far as it goes, or with the bland issue-dodging of Shaw's "effectiveness of assertion."[20]

It all leads to a Blefuscudian debate over whether Louis's acute awareness of technical issues, strongest in his youth but always lively, damns him as a literary fiddler. Thomas Beer had no doubts as he used Louis as stalking-horse for ridiculing American fascination with the *fin de siècle:*

> His intellect was not legitimately rebellious at all, . . . So the high place was not for him; but his levity impressed timid, bookish folk as red rashness, and for fourteen years a moving syrup of appreciation supported the gay invalid on its sweetness. . . . His prose chimes gently on, delicately echoing a hundred classic musics, gently dwindles from the recollection as do all imitations, and is now impressive only to people who think that a good prose is written to be read aloud.[21]

In view of the facts about Louis's illness and mental attitudes already in the reader's possession, it is enough to call this obscene and point out that the larger issue concerned hardly needs debate. Obviously "style" cannot be dissected away from content, except in the sense that expert acting can be abstracted from the roles it employs—after all, John Barrymore's and Laurence Olivier's Hamlets were not exactly alike. In parallel, highly expert writing often carries a quality that, though not indispensable to literary stature—consider Dreiser—can heighten susceptible readers' pleasure aside from content as such. The critic addicted to the ascetic, Joadish approach to writing—which often comes of too prolonged early exposure to spurious "fine writing"—should dedicate himself to the useful if limited function of improving the quality of prose in *The Journal of Hydrogenetics.* He will never understand that this quality of "style" may be conspicuous, consciously sought for because the writer consciously values it, without ending in the mawkishness of bad Poe or the petrifaction of Samuel Johnson—both fatal to "effectiveness." Thomas Henry Huxley wrote very well indeed; but that is neither the only nor the most rewarding way to write well. Here is self-conscious, highly mannered, young Stevenson, describing the invalid-exile on the Riviera:

> He is like an enthusiast leading about with him a stolid, indifferent tourist. There is someone by who is out of sympathy with the scene, and is not moved up to the measure of the occasion; and that someone is himself. The world is disenchanted for him. He seems to himself to touch things with muffled hands, and to see them through a veil. His life becomes a palsied fumbling after notes that are silent when he has found and struck them. He cannot recognize that this phlegmatic and unimpressionable body with which he now goes burthened, is the same that he knew heretofore so quick and delicate and alive.[22]

"Effective" enough, almost clinical in accuracy of observation; but you could never write like that by letting the sounds take care of themselves.

Anatole France warned beginners always to excise sentences that immediately rouse in the writer a feeling of glowing success. This sound advice holds good only before cartilage becomes bone, applies to the novice only. The journeyman worth his salt has grown to where he no longer feels this narcissistic glow on any occasion. Instead, working through hard-slashing revision toward "By God, that's what is called for!", he rather feels content sometimes transmuted, come alive and flickering, through spontaneous combinations and higher powers of mannerism and technical tricks. Making gunpowder is a delicate technical trick; the explosion is not. In spite of Barrie, Benson, and Beer, I think Stevenson managed this shift:

> Her husband loved the heels of her feet and the knuckles of her fingers; he loved her like a glutton and a brute; his love hung about her like an atmosphere; one that came by chance into the wine-shop was aware of that passion; and it might be said that by the strength of it the woman had been drugged or spellbound. She knew not if she loved or loathed him; he was always in her eyes like something monstrous—monstrous in his love, monstrous in his person, horrific but imposing in his violence; and her sentiments swung back and forward from desire to sickness.[23]

That, of course, is from semi-rough draft of *The Young Chevalier*. The number of such thwarted beginnings that Louis left is often taken as evidence of his weakness in the building of fiction. With greater staying power, it is said, he would either never have begun or else finished this and *Heathercat* and *The Great North Road*. (I wish he had given them the time and energy absorbed in such tactical errors, also abortive, as *The Owl*, *Henry Shovel*, and *The Castaways of Soledad*.) Here, for a change, is some color of a true bill: ". . . he scamped his plots, but not his sentences." [24] *Kidnapped* stopped coolly in the middle after a sharp structural break between the kidnap-the-heir plot-line and the flee-from-the-law plot-line. *Ballantrae* has that mishandled, overmechanized climax. Those who feared that *Hermiston* might not have held up to its first third had genuine cause for uneasiness. The contrast between these and the high coherence of Louis's better shorter narratives leads even generous critics to attribute to him a limit in narrative stamina like the range of a gun—his wind gave out too soon, forcing him to cobble things up out of tone.[25] To get the most good out of Stevenson one must learn—a thing sometimes necessary with Dostoevski and Thomas Mann too—to forgive him his faults of fundamental structure for the sake of the long, highly integrated stretches in which he does so clangorously well.

Frank Swinnerton's critical study of Stevenson,[26] first published in 1914, tried to be fair, but its author's fundamental mistrust of his subject wrested it into a sort of epitome of all that can be said to disparage the man. Stevenson couldn't depict women— he admitted it himself; never mind the two Kirsties. He could handle only picturesquely eccentric character; never mind Wiltshire and Prestongrange. He founded no school of fertile disciples, so he could have been no genius. He founded a school of disciples that fatally cheapened the romantic novel. . . . As large and small stones heap up, it is plain that Chapman's was the only tenable position: At best this was an able trickster whose tricks amused people for a while, then palled. That classes him where he belongs, with O. Henry and Jerome K. Jerome. Within seven years of Louis's death Shorter had already made the flatly incomprehensible statement: "Any one of [Stevenson's] good stories is not one whit better in style and in vigour than . . . Mr. Stanley Weyman's 'Count Hannibal.' " [27] It is so much easier to recognize what Saintsbury was talking about in calling Louis's work ". . . a combination of literary and story-telling charm that perhaps no writer except Mérimée has ever equalled." [28]

Since personality was part of Stevenson's renown, the attack naturally moved into that sector. After Henley's eruption in 1901, the only iconoclastic notes came from inconspicuous people who had failed to feel Louis's charm, such as Trudeau and Cusack-Smith. The saintly consumptive among his loving brown vassals, the friend of lit-tul children, kept on growing heavenward in shapely smoke like the genie from the bottle and, as the genie must have, losing substance as he grew. In this book Appendix B supplements the previous text in covering what happened when the "debunkers" of the 1920s, working from fragmentary new material, so strained themselves and probability by trying to make Louis sound like a character out of the *Spoon River Anthology*. Clayton Hamilton, who really did know a good deal about Stevenson, backed up Steuart's vicious findings, speaking as expert: ". . . a new image of R.L.S., fully rounded with all his faults and virtues properly proportioned." [29] Several voices of protest were raised against "Mr. Steuart's gloating amplification . . . with foolish and fantastic conjectures and inferences of his own pages long uttered in a kind of fatuous dance of jubilation." [30] But the net effect favored this egregious biographer, who allowed Louis only personal courage, otherwise insisting that such apparently blameless behavior as distinguishing correctly between "shall" and "will," giving a beggar sixpence, or admiring Hazlitt all signified inner emptiness.

The culmination was contributed by E. F. Benson, the personal phase of whose study of Stevenson in 1925 is a rare piece of cultivated Billingsgate that even I, who am naturally indignant at every other sentence, can read with pleasure in its skill with whips of scorpions:

There is some effort toward fairness: "Stevenson was most emphatically not a humbug"; Henley was aiming not at Stevenson but at ". . . those who were turning him into Mary's lamb" (palpably wrong to anybody with Benson's ear for overtones); those who never knew personally the charm that blinded Louis's friends must assume "some quality in him far more divine and august than mere mental charm . . . a love of beauty as intense as any that the highest genius of the race have known, combined with a passionate desire to communicate it." [31] This is either nonsense or sarcasm, but it clears the ground for Benson to settle down contentedly to the feet of clay:

Thus, Louis was callously indifferent to others. His dress ". . . cannot quite escape association with the type which we are accustomed to call 'bounder.' " When writing home that he might be deported from Samoa, he was lying for self-glorification. He highly relished his old-man-of-the-tribe role among cringing women and crawling natives at Vailima, "a very forcing-house for egoism." His depiction of Huish, the unspeakable cockney of

Ebb-Tide, was so successful because of "consonant first-hand knowledge of spiritual experience."

That is about like attributing to Thackeray spiritual consonance with Barry Lyndon on the same grounds. But I have written 150,000 words to no purpose if rebuttal of Benson is necessary. What can have moved the Archbishop of Canterbury's son to such bitter slander of a man he had never known? Again the responsibility probably lies on the posthumous glorification that Louis's less well-advised friends insisted on. Benson's keynote quotes Gosse in what must be the silliest thing ever said of one adult by another: "I ought to remember [Stevenson's] faults, but I protest I can remember none." Such drivel did endow the hapless subject with the "hieratic and beatified smirk" that Benson resented, and its natural effect was to fill too many people with malicious joy when Hellman and Steuart assured the world of letters that it had been an implausible fraud all along. That is the way antithesis sabotages reputations. Benson should nevertheless have been ashamed of himself. So should Leonard Woolf for his urbane surprise at finding—with a cultivated cough—after rereading some Stevenson in 1926, "More pleasure . . . than I had expected." [32]

There it is. Reading Stevenson was soon aesthetic slumming and the "Seraph in chocolate" gave place to a pretentious and clandestinely lecherous poseur who happened to possess some personal bravery. Every year since Swinnerton and Hamilton the ripples from the immediately posthumous reputation have decreased in height. Only recently have such thoughtful studies as those of Miss Janet Adam Smith and David Daiches given hope that interest may revive in terms appropriate to adult readers.

The diagnostic note was struck twenty years ago by Edwin Muir. Never mind his special thesis of a special stultification of Scots literature, for he exempts Stevenson from its shadow: ". . . there is little doubt that had he lived he would have been the first Scottish novelist in the full humanistic tradition." [33] Muir's contribution is to apply to Louis's case the divergence, already under way in his time, away from the writer-as-such toward the Wells-type pamphleteer and the Gissing-George Moore type of amateur clinician. (Or substitute Shaw for Wells, and disciples of Ibsen for Gissing-Moore.) Gissing's dogged pertinence, close to genius; Shaw's unflagging virtuosity with words; Wells's single-edged and humorous energy—I wish I could think of something equally cordial about Moore—all had quality. But that had little enough to do with this shift in literary fashion. It was their content, not their quality, that commended the new trend to those in the right places and, in turn, gradually conditioned them and their successors against the sort of thing that Stevenson represented. The best of fine work can be done in any literary tradition. But it is an unfortunate loss to the sum of culture when a narrowness of taste parochial to any given fashion blacks out excellent work in idioms grown unfashionable. The music-minded are more tolerant, less apt to invidious comparisons, more inclined to accept musicianship whatever the context that manifests it. It is no reproach to nor excuse for neglect of a given composer that he is somewhat dwarfed by Beethoven or that people don't write that kind of music nowadays. Yet the college lecturer does not hesitate to yawn at Stevenson, though to expunge from literature the upper third of his work would leave so huge a hole. We really cannot do without Villon's flight in the snow or Henry Durie's "Who is to tell the old man?" or the tale of Tod Lapraik or the whole voyage of the brig *Covenant* of Dysart—and much of that is in the minor range of Stevenson's excellences.

True, the modern reader has handicaps to overcome if he falls on Stevenson beyond *Treasure Island* and *Jekyll*: for instance, the dominance of individualistic moral issues in his work. Readers born after 1900 are well broken to "problem"-plays and -novels—the phrase is archaic, the thing livelier than ever— which essentially imply condition-contrary-to-fact. Overtly or subtly they insist that revision of social or economic convention would reduce the maladjustments described. But these same people have had inadequate experience with looking at a universe in which what one feels hinges on what one does, not on what is done or has been done to one. Both universes are tenable, both are proper material for fiction. And a valid taste for quality would seek values common to both and disregard variations of fashion, as it can disregard immense differences of idiom in deriving the same shiver of recognition from Falstaff's death, *A Tale of a Tub*, and *Huckleberry Finn*. But that kind of nerve-ends seems to be scantily distributed.

For another difficulty out of the same barrel, Stevenson was, in a rare sense, a writer. That was the quality that kept him so close to Henry James. In our day the writer has become equivalent of the *shaman*—the esoteric, ecstatic scapegoat, supernormal bridge to mysteries over readers' heads, a function sometimes combined with that of the amateur psychiatrist inventing fictitious and overconsistent case-histories for purging the passively unstable. The product must meet a need, else it would not be in such demand, and the better reviews of current novels would not sound so much like adepts discussing the mystical experiences of diverse cults. No doubt it should be the dominant function of writing to do for readers what finger-painting does for unstable children or shock-therapy for the schizoid. But it is significant that the current writer's work, of whatever cryptic depth of *mythos*, would seldom lose much by being reasonably well translated into any European language; whereas, though Stevenson has been widely translated, it can never conceivably have been adequately done.[34]

Beer's sneer at those who think good prose should be written for reading aloud is the point of divergence. "I condemn him to read everything aloud," said Stevenson when asked late in life for advice for the young writer. Only when pen or typewriter is wired in with the ear are the special, essential juices of a language expressed. This does not necessarily lead to foolishly purple prose of the sort Beer doubtless had in mind. Shaw's prefaces are triumphs of a man with an angel's ear for pith and cadence. And translation would sadly mar them. The same would apply to Ring Lardner.

This quality relates to a quality cognate in poetry, which is notoriously damaged by translation. Bunyan, Louis's master, had it to overflowing: " . . . we are always most zealous when Religion goes in his Silver Slippers; we love much to walk with him in the Street, if the Sun shines and the People applaud him." So had Coleridge sometimes, as in this apostil in *The Ancient Mariner*:

> In his loneliness and fixedness, he yearneth toward the journeying moon and the stars that still sojourn, yet still move onward; and everywhere the blue sky belongs to them, and is their appointed rest, and their native country and their own natural homes, which they enter unannounced, as lords that are certainly expected, and yet there is a silent joy at their arrival.

Translation would butcher those; or this from *Weir of Hermiston:*

> One ancestor after another might be seen appearing a moment out of the rain or the hill mist upon his furtive business, speeding home, perhaps, with a paltry booty of lame horses and lean kine, or squealing and dealing death in some moorland feud of the ferrets and the wild cats.

But there is a difference between material that refuses translation solely because of idiosyncrasy of idiom—say Uncle Remus —and material, like the excerpts above, with the untranslatable quality that marks the writer-as-such and, since poetry is nothing at all without it, is more easily recognized in poetry. (It should be unnecessary to point out that I am not talking about "poetical prose," whatever that may be.) Unfortunately for Stevenson and many another author of rich quality, this asset is neither here nor there for the reader who—suiting himself as he has every right to do—wants his fiction to be either a spurious tract for the times or a cathartic and vicarious excursion into psychopathology.

Lack of experience with the essay bars many modern readers from much good Stevenson outside his fiction. Mourning the

demise of this literary form is as pointless as deploring the
disappearance of bootjacks. But, again, it is culturally inconvenient that the fields of comment in which Bacon, Montaigne,
and Hazlitt were so sure-footed and flavorsome are in so many
cases no longer fair game for amateurs. Thus Louis's "The
Character of Dogs" practically ceased to be publishable after
Pavlov's early work. The content of "A Chapter on Dreams"
has been taken over by the psychiatrist; of "Beggars" by the
social service worker; of "Virginibus Puerisque" by, God save
the word, the marriage-counselor. The result has certainly been
better quality of data and theories. But we have paid for that in
widespread inability to savor the "effectiveness of assertion" of
our literary elders in some of its better aspects.

In this bald effort to persuade readers to sandwich some
Stevenson among explorations of other and newer writings, to
claim him more than comfortable standing-room on Parnassus
would be misrepresentation. My tremendous enthusiasm for
much of his prose work cannot be matched, as I have already
indicated, by any such feeling for his verse. He himself called
his formally published verse—*A Child's Garden, Underwoods,
Songs of Travel, Ballads*—mere pithy talk in rhythm. In Trudeau's copy of *Underwoods* he wrote:

> Some day or other ('tis a general curse)
> The wisest author stumbles into verse.[35]

Yet to see the best of it as negligible would be another error.
Standard anthologies usually give him space and notice, justly
enough, in the same category as Kipling, Henley, Poe. In more
fugitive work he often adjusted verses into grace and connotation or found a string of phrases that cling significantly to
the memory:

> The maiden jewels of the rain
> Sit in your dabbled locks again. . . .
>
> There I hung and looked, and there
> In my grey face, faces fair

Shone from under shining hair.
Well I saw the poising head,
But the lips moved and nothing said;
And when lights were in the hall,
Silent moved the dancers all.

Still, O beloved, let me hear
The great bell beating far and near—
The odd, unknown, enchanted gong
That on the road hales men along. . . .
And with a still, aërial sound
Makes all the earth enchanted ground.

He loved great poetry—Virgil, Milton, Marvell—like a mistress, and that very passion kept him from great affection for his own. He would have been first to agree that his literary validity would suffer little if he had never published a line of verse.

But it was very high indeed in other aspects and—the thought is always frustrating—still rising when he died, so it can do without the ultimate versatility. Few of the prose writers who knew their craft best were poets in the same class. This validity of Louis's lay in fascinated industry that warmed words into coming alive in his hands; in devotion so intense that writer and words grew indistinguishable; in intelligent, organic ambition not for himself but for his beloved medium. It all culminated— glowing, eccentric, and whalebone-strong—in the parson's glimpse of Janet trampling the clothes; Pew tapping on the frozen road; Utterson and Poole listening at the laboratory door; the Durie brothers' quarrel; Hermiston hearing of his wife's death. . . . If literary fashion, as arbitrary as the cut of next year's evening gowns, keeps people from reading such things for their own delight and wonder, the more fools they.

Appendix B

Controversy

O<small>N MANY</small> points of fact or interpretation or both this book has sharply disagreed with previous treatments of the subject.

It can do so because it is first to work from access to the full texts of many of Louis's and Fanny's crucial letters and other writings and other sources previously unavailable or unexplored. In order not to clog the general reader with detailed debate, I have usually handled small disagreements in notes, larger ones in this Appendix.

My new evidence or reinterpretation in the light of new evidence undermines two schools of biography of Stevenson: the "family" accounts of him, particularly the reminiscences prefixed to later editions of his works; and the "debunking" biographers of the 1920s, particularly George S. Hellman and John A. Steuart.

In many instances, of course, "family" witnesses, often writing years after the events described, do nothing more heinous than to telescope events that carry different meaning when it is found that they actually occurred at less or greater intervals. In this category falls the misleading implication in such material that Louis and Fanny fell in love at first sight. But there is also occasional suppression, sometimes understandable if regrettable—as when some "family" representatives denounced Clayton Hamilton's account of Andrew Lang telling of his unfavorable first impression of Louis. Fanny's letters and journals of given periods sometimes have accounts of episodes differing markedly from the orthodox "family" versions. The book contains no "family" material of which there is any reason to doubt the accuracy. I may add that I have leaned over backward to omit data relating to people still living in all cases where special pertinence did not demand inclusion in order that Louis be adequately understood.

Controversial points are here discussed approximately in chronological order.

"Claire": After Fanny died in 1914, Belle Strong (by then Mrs. Salisbury Field) sold at auction a mass of Louis's manuscripts, letters, and other memorabilia. Out of these George S. Hellman and various colleagues edited and privately published several volumes of previously unpublished material, including most of what appears as *New Poems* in subsequent editions of Stevenson.

So far this was valuable contribution to knowledge of a most interesting man. But the demon of exegesis tempted Hellman to speculate on the basis of this new material. Thus, he selected and juxtaposed three pieces of newly available verse: An obviously young lyric deploring one's lady-love's ambivalence between love and hate; another mourning an unborn child; a third about separated lovers on the margin of which Louis had penciled "Claire." None is much more specific than the word "love" itself. But this is what Hellman and associates made of them:

. . . hints of a love tragedy of intense passion and suffering acted in Edinburgh in the opening years of Stevenson's manhood. . . . there was apparently only one woman in Stevenson's life who, although he was devoted to her, might yet have had reason to hate him. We know her merely as "Claire," the name inscribed marginally on the manuscript of "Swallows Travel To and Fro," verses which in 1875 were composed with her in mind. She was the Edinburgh girl who was in all probability the prospective mother of that unborn child lamented in the poem "God Gave to Me a Child in Part" referred to above. . . . When (we must believe because of parental objection) he was forced to break with this girl whose status and antecedents may have justified his family's opposition, and when in 1872 he was sent by his parents to the continent, her love may well have changed to the hatred prophesied in the opening lines. . . . (Introduction by William P. Trent to *Poems by Robert Louis Stevenson Hitherto Unpublished.*)

When made public in the *Century* in December 1922, these surmises caused a mild sensation. Soon Hellman had what he took to be confirmation of his guesswork in a letter from Katharine Durham Osbourne, Lloyd's first wife, long divorced from him, who claimed psychic contact with Louis, even though she had never met him alive. She had also quarreled violently with Fanny. Hellman vaguely noted obvious animus but nevertheless published parts of her long and numerous letters set off by her having read his *Century* article, containing this:

I have been told just now—as though it were a secret—by one of the Stevenson relatives about Louis's first and great love. The girl's name was Claire or Clare. . . . a blacksmith's daughter. His smithy was near Swanston cottage. She was in her teens, a beautiful fair haired lassie—with light eyes, and as innocent as Louis himself. They walked and loved in a pleasant wood near the Swanston cottage. (*The True Stevenson:* 72.)

She offered no corroboration from Louis in the spirit-world, but it was all so specific that bolstering was hardly needed. In 1925 Hellman's disclosures were full of Claire.

In the previous year Steuart's highly dilute biography of Louis had built even juicier stories on Hellman's constructions. Steuart's sources were alleged but unidentified Edinburghers who gave him the facts about Claire: It appears that this was a romantic pseudonym; she was really a Kate Drummond, a swooningly dark and lovely Highland girl whom Louis met in an Edinburgh brothel, whence he planned to rescue and marry her.

His parents violently opposed the scheme. Apparently lacking the courage of his convictions, Louis gave her up. Steuart's mysterious informants even showed him the house where the pair met and told him of how the madam often berated and once beat Claire-Kate for wasting time with penniless Louis. Steuart so relished this tale that he soon based a foolish novel, *The Cap of Youth*, on it.

These standards of evidence were obviously low. In her usually accurate biography of Louis published in 1923, Miss Masson called Hellman's construction of Claire " . . . an altogether incorrect deduction . . . The name of Claire . . . is misplaced and misapplied." (*Life* . . . ; 80.) But, since she gave no reasons, it still seemed not unlikely that some fire lay behind the smoke. Like most commentators on Stevenson since Steuart and Hellman published, I too had taken it for granted that, fair or dark, innocent or dissolute, Highland or Lowland, some sort of Claire had existed and, as was strongly hinted, left a damagingly deep mark on Louis.

On obtaining access to the originals of Louis's letters to Mrs. Sitwell, very recently released from Colvin's embargo, in the National Library of Scotland, I was fascinated by finding what looked like the first real documentary evidence of the girl's existence. Soon after returning from Cockfield in 1873, Louis wrote Mrs. Sitwell:

> Of course I am not going on with Claire. I have been out of heart for that; and besides it is difficult to act before the reality. Footlights will not do with the sun; the stage moon and the real lucid moon of one's dark life, look strangely on each other. (Stevenson to Mrs. Sitwell, National Library.)

In editing the letter, Colvin had excised this whole passage. My necessary conclusion was that he knew enough of Claire to wish no hint of her to reach the reading public. Obviously Louis had told Mrs. Sitwell of this recent entanglement of his and now, answering some cautionary inquiry of hers, was reaffirming—

with unusually poor taste for him—a previously stated determination to abandon the affair.

For months I tried vainly to fit this ugly little addition to the Hellman-Steuart story into what I knew of Louis. I even tried—and failed—to convince myself that "Claire" might be a working-title of or character in a story or long poem that Louis had determined to drop in consequence of reorientation due to his meeting Mrs. Sitwell. But that also was mere shaky surmise, perhaps wishful thinking, in any case in a vein already too popular in later accounts of Louis. Elwin's *The Strange Case of Robert Louis Stevenson* (1950) exultantly quoted: "Of course I am not going on with Claire . . . " as the solid evidence of her having existed that it seemed to be.

As long ago as the late 1930s, however, Graham Balfour's widow had encouraged the literary-project theory by telling Roger Lancelyn Green that the allegedly notorious Claire had been only "a character in a novel which Stevenson began to write in the early 1870s and continued under the advice of Mrs. Sitwell, but finally gave up." (Green to *Times Literary Supplement*, published January 26, 1951.) Green (*Tellers of Tales*, 1946, pp. 153–54) expanded this notion for juvenile audiences:

> Mrs. Sitwell soon became his most helpful and sympathetic friend, advising him in all that he did as well as in his writings. He was at this time trying to write novels which he afterwards destroyed as worthless, and on one occasion when he complained to Mrs. Sitwell that he could not describe the reactions of a particular heroine in the story, she suggested that he should write letters to her under the name of "Claire" (the heroine) and she would answer as that character would in real life. This was all very amusing . . . Not knowing the origin of these letters to and from "Claire" many recent biographers of Stevenson have imagined a real love affair between him and a girl of that name.

No doubt picking up this hint, the late Laura L. Hinkley presently stated, adducing no evidence: "Claire was Mrs. Sitwell." (*The Stevensons*, 1950, p. 90).

In devastating substantiation, Green included in the above-mentioned letter to the *Times Literary Supplement* a previously unpublished passage from a letter of Louis's to Mrs. Sitwell that really did rock Claire-Kate on her charming foundations. Internal evidence—Louis mentions cramming for his forthcoming examinations for the Inns of Court—dates this letter, which I have since consulted in full, as early in the relationship:

> I have done my quantum of history, and have just stopped to make my first adition [*sic*] to Claire. I have added some sentences out of this letter, making the meaning clearer of course and trying to better the loose expressions one uses in *really* writing to dear friends,—those sentences about the organ recalling the "perfume" of my past life here, and how the thought of your letter came upon me so strongly.

This obvious reference to a work-in-progress, coupled with the previously quoted passage from a somewhat later letter about giving Claire up, leaves small doubt that Hellman and Steuart were victims of their own ingenuity. My guess had been right, even if wishful. Claire-Kate now became *Claire*, working title as well as central object of a literary project based on Louis's relation to Mrs. Sitwell.

These valuable data did not, however, clear up all ambiguities. Green's suggestion that Mrs. Sitwell wrote back in the character of Claire is incapable of demonstration, since Louis destroyed all her letters of this period. His further suggestion that their correspondence was taken by both parties as at least ostensibly literary exercise for him is extremely difficult to square with his phrase, quoted by Green as above, " . . . in *really* writing to dear friends . . ." This cannot possibly mean more than that, with a certain self-consciousness by no means rare among literary letter-writers, he knows and she knows that passages from his letters may well be used as raw material for the *Claire*-project. Even without that telltale phrase, the further (if shadowy) implication that the fervor of Louis's letters to the lady are little more than tenderly pumped-up rhetoricism, all among sympathetic friends, will not square with the reams of letters that he wrote to her *after* explicitly serving notice that he is giving up *Claire*—there is no change whatever in tone or content after that point; or with the clear implication (cf. *Monsieur Est Bien Jeune* preceding) in the later letters that at least once he broke out of bounds and sought exclusive lover's privileges. Nor, as the reader already knows from examples, were these letters of a tenor that could lead anybody to deduce a "real love affair" imagined by Louis as fictional exercise. Stubbornly, almost pathetically, they renounce explicit, man-to-woman eroticism and deal copiously with both his and Mrs. Sitwell's personal troubles with families. No young writer trying his hand at making love-letters sound plausible would always have signed "Ever your faithful friend/Robert Louis Stevenson."

So far the published record. In some form the literary project stands substantiated, though the constructions on the basis of Green's evidence are not altogether satisfactory. I was less troubled by them because I had known the shape of the missing piece of the puzzle since autumn, 1949. It was the sort of luck that occasionally rewards the researcher for dusty digging. In late 1949 I consulted the originals of Louis's letters to Colvin in the Beinecke Collection, and there turned up one stray—a previously unpublished letter of Louis's to Mrs. Sitwell antedating both "Of course I am not going on with Claire . . ." and "I have done my quantum of history . . ." Very recently returned from the Cockfield idyll, he has been deliriously happy in the thought of Mrs. Sitwell for a night and a day. Since returning he has walked the streets of Edinburgh and dreamed of "showing all these places to you, Claire, some other night."

That single vocative alone not only demolished the poor girl but instantly identified her as more than Green's lay-figure for Louis to practice with. "Claire" was merely the first of the series of emotion-charged pseudonyms that Louis applied to Mrs. Sitwell; later came Consuelo, Madonna, Mother. Apparently first applied to her at Cockfield, it became the natural focus for the slightly fictionalized idealization of Mrs. Sitwell that Louis would be addressing in *Claire*, the literary project. "Swallows travel to and fro . . ." was probably written to the distant Mrs. Sitwell in the first days of his return and docketed "Claire" in pencil—the treacherous detail that set Hellman's mind so busily to work—to indicate that it might be worked into the developing manuscript, just as he planned to work in passages from letters.

This crucial letter, apostrophizing Mrs. Sitwell as Claire, was probably in Colvin's possession when Hellman first published his surmises. But, instead of correctly identifying Claire, Colvin only muttered peevishly and evasively. Why he thus neglected his long-dead friend's reputation, I do not know. By then he was quite old and may have forgotten the facts.

Exit Claire. It seems a pity thus to annihilate what was built up as so attractive a girl. Perhaps there was a dark prostitute whom Louis specially patronized when he had shillings to spare, recollection of whom still floated round Edinburgh when Steuart was snapping up his trifles—though the only one whom Louis specifically mentions was fair. But that is as far as even admitted speculation has a right to go. The moral is that, when biographical ingenuity gets astride of a hint, it is perilously easy to conjure up spirits from the vasty deep. The whole episode lends relish to the subtitle of Hellman's book: *A Study in Clarification*.

Unborn Child: If the verses "God gave to me a child in part . . ." came of an actual episode in Louis's life, this paragraph from a previously unpublished letter of Louis's to Simpson from Hyères in the spring of 1884 is interesting:

I must tell you a joke. A month or two ago, there was an alarm; it looked like family. Prostration: I saw myself financially ruined. I saw the child born sickly, etc. Then, said I, I must look this thing on the good side; proceeded to do so studiously; and with such result that when the alarm passed off—I was inconsolable." (Stevenson to Simpson, Savile Gift.)

On the good scientific principle that, of two possible explanations for a phenomenon, the simpler is sounder, this accounts for the verses far better than a postulated pregnancy in a young lady who did not exist.

Giving Mrs. Will Low as source, Hellman had a tale of Fanny's suffering a miscarriage during one of the Pacific voyages. It is biologically possible, though improbable, that a woman over fifty years old can conceive. Even supposing Mrs. Low a reliable witness, however, Fanny was not altogether so after Louis's death.

A most dubious posthumous legend of an alleged bastard son of Louis's occasionally crops up, most notably in G. B. Stern's *No Son of Mine.* He seems to have been a dark and, I should judge, unstable young man appearing some thirty years ago with a story of having been begotten by Louis on an Aberdeen girl named Margaret Stevenson—which, probably by no coincidence, is a name attributed by Steuart to one of the two Swanston mistresses (see below). Papers that Miss Masson deposited in the 8 Howard Place Museum give the birthplace as Alva, Scotland; her search of the parish records found the father given as one Wilson, a photographer.

Battle of Swanston: Steuart used as weapon against Louis a tale that he developed of how Louis was involved with two different mistresses in the neighborhood of Swanston in 1878 and 1879 coincidentally with his reproaching Burns for being a Don Juan and with his presumably being deeply in love with Fanny. He learned that the two women came to blows in public on one occasion. He strongly implies that his sources on this included both. Baxter and Henley. Baxter I doubt. Henley is another matter, and may have been vindictive enough to have expanded what he knew of Louis's carryings-on to supply this story to

Steuart. Being a great admirer of Henley, who had helped him get his start in writing, Steuart would certainly not have been inclined to doubt anything Henley told him.

Henley's knowledge of Louis's relations with women certainly included acquaintance with one girl with whom Louis was involved; that is clear in a letter of Louis's to him from California mentioning that, among other troubles, he has had a threatening letter from a young lady whom Henley has met personally; he says that he suspects some third party has instigated her to write. Whatever the now undiscoverable facts, Henley left Edinburgh long before Louis met Fanny, so the affair must have predated Louis's falling in love with his future wife. I suspect that the episode, whatever it amounted to, may be connected with a letter of Louis's to Mrs. Sitwell in the spring of 1875, when Henley was in Edinburgh and out of hospital:

> As for the other matter it is over and gone and has done me a service in the going: I have written a very short paper which is the best I have ever done, as I believe firmly. . . . "On the Spirit of Spring." But I do not know if I shall get it printed. I am afraid they will think it too wicked, these good editors. It is a jolly mixture of sensuality and awful pretty sentimentality; and if it isn't Spring taken simply in the fact, I'm a Dutchman. (Stevenson to Mrs. Sitwell, National Library.)

The essay was sent to Colvin, who promptly lost it, possibly out of unconscious discretion. Louis took the loss most nonchalantly for a youngster under the impression that it had been his best work so far.

In view of how unreliable Steuart's sources proved about Claire, I feel well justified in throwing the battling mistresses of Swanston also into the discard. Practically none of either story fits the known or demonstrable facts about Louis's pre-marital carnalities; at most one knows only of (1) the fair, amply constructed prostitute of whom he wrote in a suppressed passage in his experimental autobiography (*cf.* Hellman,

"Stevenson and the Streetwalker," *American Mercury*, July 1936); (2) the girl whom Henley knew, who must thus have postdated the Claire crisis as both Hellman and Steuart date it, who wrote Louis threateningly in late 1879; and (3) the girl who wrote him on the decorated stationery some time before July 1873 (*cf.* p. 47). It may seem absurd to devote so much space to these details. But it is necessary to point out that there is practically no evidence behind long-standing allegations that Louis was a moral coward about Claire, a hypocrite about Burns's amours, and unfaithful to Fanny.

Mrs. Sitwell's Reputation: After hints in previous writings, Hellman took occasion in July 1936 ("Stevenson and the Streetwalker," *American Mercury*) to state his conviction that Mrs. Sitwell

> . . . accepted not only the youth's adoration but also his passion. . . . later, when young Stevenson learned that he was not alone in receiving Mrs. Sitwell's personal favors, the idealism, the fine fervor almost mystically wrought into their association created within him a deep conflict leading to the verge of suicide.

He could never have made this error had he had access to the full texts of Louis's letters to Mrs. Sitwell. Ironically, it was Colvin's and Mrs. Sitwell's conviction that many passages of these were "too sacred and intimate to print" (Masson, *I Can* . . . : 88) which left the way open thus to impugn the lady's virtue. The gist of the relation, as the reader already knows, is that it stayed so dogmatically this side of carnality. Louis shows no trace of suicidal impulse at this period, nor was there any revulsion, such as Hellman hints at, against either the lady or Colvin—if it was meant to imply that Colvin was the one who had been sharing her. Louis's respect for and faith in both never slackened. Years later from Sydney both Fanny and Louis wrote that, if either Colvin or Mrs. Sitwell was in danger of dying, Louis should be summoned in time to reach the bedside—better he should die of the voyage or the British climate than that he should never again see either of his two emotional mainstays.

Dear Head on the Pillow: It is understandable, though perhaps pointless some seventy years after the event and in the middle of the twentieth century, that Fanny's adherents have never admitted that Louis and she anticipated the parson.

In 1915, a year after Fanny died, Hamilton (*On the Trail of Stevenson*, withdrawn edition: 92) first published the essential fact; his sources, whoever they were, had the timing wrong, when he wrote that on meeting at Grez "their affinity was instant and their union immediate and complete." The reader already knows that it was Bob Stevenson who first attracted major attention from Fanny and that it was geographically most unlikely that any consummation of her growing feeling for Louis occurred until at least much later in 1876.

Fanny's heirs protested violently against Hamilton's statement as well as several other passages in his book indicating that Louis had had an unconventional past. The publishers withdrew the book and printed a drastically revised second edition. A number of copies of the withdrawn printing survive. In *The True Stevenson* of 1925 Hellman greatly advanced knowledge of Louis by recounting the story of the withdrawal and, in effect, repeating the suppressed assertions. The fact of these premarital relations is essential to understanding Louis's breach with his family in 1879. But again Hellman overreached his evidence: He developed the theory that Louis broke with his family and went to Fanny out of "the generous impulse of reparation" ("Stevenson and the Streetwalker," *American Mercury*, July 1936); that he answered Fanny's summons because honor-bound to her by having ". . . accepted what, as the saying goes, is a woman's ultimate favor" (*The True Stevenson:* 62); in short, to make an honest woman of her, not for love. The reader already knows from previously unpublished letters of Louis's in my text that he was head over heels in love with her in early 1879, and that, when he left Scotland, neither Fanny nor Louis seems to have been altogether convinced that marriage was the only thing for them.

There is practically no evidence behind the theory, which even Hellman and Steuart could not accept, that it was knowledge of Thomas Stevenson's resources that critically moved Fanny to attach herself to Louis. True, her letters show her overimpressed by the art students' accounts of the great fortune that Louis would inherit if he lived; and true, she sometimes showed consciousness of the advantage of marrying prosperous husbands. But the cold fact is that she sought divorce long before there was any sign whatever of reconciliation with 17 Heriot Row; marriage was definitely planned in December 1879. Unless it be maintained that she was gambling desperately with her whole future, burning her bridges with Osbourne on the remote chance that Thomas Stevenson might soften, it is certain that she married Louis because she loved him and wanted to care for him the rest of his life.

Date of Divorce: Mrs. Anne Roller Issler, whose researches into Louis's California period are invaluable, believes that Fanny's divorce did not occur until shortly before the marriage (*Happier for His Presence*: 142.) The legal record was unfortunately destroyed in the San Francisco Fire of 1906. Her position is based on good oral tradition for the most part. Mine is based on Louis to Baxter from Monterey, postmarked October 15, 1879: ". . . there is to be a private divorce in January, . . ."; and on Louis to Baxter from San Francisco, February 22, 1880, saying that, in consequence of a recent sharp illness of Louis's, Fanny and he had almost got married "right away"—manifestly impossible if her divorce had not already been accomplished. All through these months it is evident in Louis's letters that both Osbourne and Fanny's family, as well as Thomas Stevenson later, had requested as long an interval as possible between divorce and remarriage.

Not even Steuart managed to believe the local gossip that Sam Osbourne gave the bride away at Louis's wedding.

The Burned Prostitute: Hellman (*The True Stevenson:* 100-105 —"Stevenson and the Streetwalker," *American Mercury*, July 1936) makes much of a story attributed to Hamilton (allegedly from Gosse) of how Louis began a novel about a streetwalker and Fanny forced him to burn it. On the incident, Hellman says, Henry James, hearing the story before he met Louis, based his *The Author of Beltraffio*, substituting the unsympathetic wife's arranging the death of her child for Fanny's design against the manuscript. This last is certainly an error: Janet Adam Smith (*Henry James and Robert Louis Stevenson:* 21, fn.) first pointed out that James himself referred the story to an anecdote of J. A. Symonds and wife. Fanny highly approved of *Beltraffio* on publication, an attitude that she was unlikeliest of women to take if there had been any reason to see personal reference in it. There is interesting further evidence in the close correspondence between James's account of Mrs. Ambient in *Beltraffio* and Louis's description of Mrs. Symonds in a letter to Colvin from Davos, previously unpublished:

> . . . for Mrs. S. I have much pity but little sympathy. A stupid woman, married above her, moving daily with people whose talk she doesn't understand. Her position is doubly aggravated by her having the appearance of even genius; so that people continually talk to her over her head, poor soul, to her singular distraction. . . . she has not the patience even to try after ordinary kindness in everyday affairs, but plays a sort of mild Wuthering Heights at bed and board—and is, I think I see, continually sorry for it. No two people were ever less formed to make each other comfortable; happy they could never hope to make each other—the root of that, comprehension, being absent. As you begin to find Mrs. S. entirely out, you begin to think better of both. (Stevenson to Colvin, Beinecke Collection.)

The fact of the manuscript that Louis is said to have burned at Fanny's insistence at Hyères can be neither substantiated nor refuted. It is strange, however, that Louis, who almost always heralded each new literary scheme in letters to friends, fails to mention this one in any surviving letter that I have seen. I suspect that the tale grew up as a garbling of the actual fact of Louis's burning the first draft of *Jekyll* when Fanny disapproved of it so violently and constructively.

Eagle-in-a-Cage: Moors (*With Stevenson in Samoa*: 196-203) hints that, over-harassed by his strong-minded womenfolk at Vailima, Louis grew yearningly interested in buying Nassau Island for a bachelor retreat. Fanny and he had touched there in the *Janet Nichol* and been attracted by its picturesque loneliness; Fanny's Vailima diary makes it clear that the scheme of buying Nassau was as much hers as Louis's. Moors's reputation was not altogether that of a man who would always be a careful witness, and he may well have harbored ill will from the time when, as Belle was determining to divorce Joe Strong, Moors embroiled himself with Fanny and her daughter by siding with Joe.

Hellman, however, took this bait (*The True Stevenson*: 216) and soared away on wings of surmise to find Louis's sense of being overpowered by officious females at Vailima expressed (most subtly) in the bleakness of *The Castaways of Soledad* (a posthumous fragment with strange overtones) and in the subtitles originally attached to "The Bottle Imp" and "The Waif-Woman." Fanny had insisted that Louis refrain from seeking publication for *The Waif-Woman*; Hellman implies that the reason was her sensing that it is a cryptic protest against the warpings and mean decisions into which she had occasionally tricked or cajoled Louis. The stated grounds were that the story was over-derivative—Louis had been reading translations of sagas—and on the whole inferior work. The judgment is not ill justified by the text, which appeared first in *Scribner's* (December 1914) after Fanny's death and is now included in the Vailima and South Seas editions.

This is Hellman's masterpiece of fragile innuendo. There is no other evidence that Louis felt more than normal masculine impatience with Fanny and Belle, and a good deal to show that he warmly appreciated their devotion and usefulness to him.

Works Consulted

This is little more than a check-list for the convenience of possible future researchers. It is not.complete, but it does contain practically all crucial published material on Stevenson, outside his formally published works, as well as a mass of more or less peripheral material.

Letters and other material consulted in original form and unavailable in published form are roughly identified in the running notes by where they may be found. "National Library" is the National Library of Scotland. "8 Howard Place" is the Stevenson museum at that Edinburgh address. "Beinecke Collection" is that of Edwin J. Beinecke, part of which is at Yale University. "Savile Gift" is the mass of Stevenson-to-Baxter letters originally at the Savile Club, now deposited by Mr. Beinecke at Yale. "Widener Collection" is the Harry Elkins Widener Library at Harvard University. "Huntington Library" is the Henry E. Huntington Library at San Marino, Calif.

Adams, Henry
   Henry Adams and His Friends. A Collection of his Unpublished Letters . . . with a Biographical Introduction by Harold Dean Cater. Boston, Houghton Mifflin Co., 1947
   ———*Letters of* . . . (1858–1891). Edited by Worthington Chauncey Ford. Boston, Houghton Mifflin Co., 1930.
Allen, Maryland
   "South Sea Memories of R. L. S.," *Bookman* [N. Y.]; August 1916.
Anderson, David
   The Enchanted Galleon. N. P., privately printed, n.d.
Anonymous
   "Literary Leprosy," *Saturday Review*, November 30, 1901.
   ———"Stevenson From a New Point of View," *Current Opinion*, December 1924.
   ———"Stevenson Unwhitewashed," *Atlantic Monthly*, March 1900.

Archer, William
"In Memoriam: R. L. S.," *New Review*, January 1895.
———"R. L. S. at Skerryvore," *Critic*, November 5, 1887.
Arnold, William Harris
"My Stevensons," *Scribner's*, January 1922.
Ashe, Rev. Matthew J.
"Stevenson's Catholic Leaning," *Catholic World*, November 1942.
Asquith, Margot
The Autobiography of . . . [first printing]. London, Thornton Butterworth, Ltd., n.d.
Aydelotte, Frank
The Oxford Stamp and Other Essays. Articles from the Educational Creed of an American Oxonian. New York, Oxford University Press, 1917.
Baildon, H. Bellyse
Robert Louis Stevenson. A Life Study in Criticism. London, Chatto & Windus, 1901.
Balfour, Graham
The Life of Robert Louis Stevenson. New York, Charles Scribner's Sons, 1901.
———"A South Sea Trader," *Macmillan's*, November 1896.
[Balfour, Mr. and Mrs. J. Craig]
"Robert Louis Stevenson" by Two of His Cousins. *English Illustrated Magazine*, May 1899.
Barnett, David
A Stevenson Study: "Treasure Island." Edinburgh, David Macdonald, Ltd., 1924.
Barrie, J. M.
An Edinburgh Eleven. Pencil Portraits from College Life. New York, Lovell, Coryell & Co., n.d.
———*Margaret Ogilvy*. New York, Charles Scribner's Sons, 1917.
Bay, J. Christian
Echoes of Robert Louis Stevenson. Chicago, Walter M. Hill, 1920.
Beer, Thomas
The Mauve Decade. American Life at the End of the Nineteenth Century. New York, Alfred A. Knopf, Inc., 1926.
Benson, E. F.
As We Were. A Victorian Peep Show. London, Longmans, Green & Co., 1930.

————"The Myth of Robert Louis Stevenson," *London Mercury,* July–August 1925.

Bermann, Richard A.
Home From the Sea. Robert Louis Stevenson in Samoa. Translated by Elizabeth Reynolds Hapgood. Indianapolis, The Bobbs-Merrill Co., n.d.

Billy, André
Les Beaux Jours de Barbizon. Paris, Editions du Lavois, 1947.

Black, Margaret Moyes
Robert Louis Stevenson. Famous Scots Series. Edinburgh, Oliphant Anderson & Ferrier, n.d.

Bland, Henry Mead
Stevenson's California. San Jose, Pacific Short Story Club, n.d.

Bok, Edward W.
The Americanization of Edward Bok. New York, Charles Scribner's Sons, 1922.

————"The Playful Stevenson," *Scribner's*, August 1927.

Bonet-Maury, Gaston
"R. L. Stevenson, Voyageur et Romancier," *Révue des Deux Mondes*, September 1902.

Boodle, Adelaide A.
R. L. S. and His Sine Qua Non. Flashlights from Skerryvore by the Gamekeeper. New York, Charles Scribner's Sons, 1926.

[Brown, Alice and Louise Imogen Guiney]
Robert Louis Stevenson. A study by A. B. with a Prelude and Postlude by L. I. G. Boston, issued for private distribution, 1896.

Brown, George
Pioneer Missionary and Explorer. An Autobiography. London, Hodder & Stoughton, 1908.

Brown, George E.
A Book of R. L. S. Works, Travels, Friends and Commentators. London, Methuen & Co., n.d.

Brown, Horatio F.—*see* Symonds, John Addington

Buchan, John
Pilgrim's Way. An Essay in Recollection. Boston, Houghton Mifflin Co., 1940.

————*Sir Walter Scott*. London, Cassell & Co., Ltd., n.d.

Buckley, Jerome Hamilton
William Ernest Henley. A Study in the "Counter-Decadence" of

the 'Nineties. Princeton, N. J., Princeton University Press, 1945.

Buell, Llewellyn M.
"Eilean Earraid: the Beloved Isle of Robert Louis Stevenson," *Scribner's*, February 1922.

Burgess, Gelett
"An Interview with Mrs. Robert Louis Stevenson," *Bookman* [N. Y.], September 1898.

Burriss, Eli Edward
"The Classical Culture of Robert Louis Stevenson," *Classical Journal*, XX, 271.

Butcher, Alice Mary (Landreth), Lady
Memories of George Meredith. London, Constable & Co., Ltd., 1919.

Calahan, Harold Augustin
Back to Treasure Island. New York, Vanguard Press, n.d.

Canby, Henry Seidel and Frederick Erastus Pierce—*see* Stevenson, Robert Louis

Carré, Jean-Marie
The Frail Warrior. . . . Translated from the French by Eleanor Hard. New York, Coward-McCann, Inc., 1930.

Carrington, James B.
"Another Glimpse of R. L. S.," *Scribner's*, August 1927.

Chalmers, Stephen
The Penny Piper of Saranac. An Episode in Stevenson's Life. With Preface by Lord Guthrie. Boston, Houghton Mifflin Co., 1896.

Chapman, John Jay
Emerson and Other Essays. New York, Moffat, Yard & Co., 1909.

Charteris, the Hon. Evan
John Sargent. New York, Charles Scribner's Sons, 1927.

———*The Life and Letters of Sir Edmund Gosse*. New York, Harper & Brothers, 1931.

Chesterton, G. K.
Robert Louis Stevenson. New York, Dodd, Mead & Co., 1928.

Churchill, William
"Stevenson in the South Sea," *McClure's*, December 1894.

Clarke, W. E.
"Robert Louis Stevenson in Samoa," *Yale Review*, January 1921.

Clifford, Mrs. W. K.
"The Sidney Colvins: Some Personal Recollections," *Bookman*, [London], April 1928.

Colby, Frank Moore
"A Debated Charm," *Bookman* [N. Y.], February 1902.

Collins, Joseph
The Doctor Looks at Biography. New York, George H. Doran Co., n.d.

Colvin, Sidney
Memories & Notes of Persons and Places. 1852–1912. New York, Charles Scribner's Sons, 1921.

———"Robert Louis Stevenson at Hampstead," *Hampstead Annual*, 1902.

———*Robert Louis Stevenson:* His Work and Personality. By . . . , Edmund Gosse, Neil Munro, Charles Lowe, S. R. Crockett, St. John Adcock, Ian Maclaren, W. Robertson Nicoll, Lloyd Osbourne, Alfred Noyes, Eve Blantyre Simpson, Alice Gordon, H. C. Beeching, J. A. Hammerton, Y. Y., and others. London, Hodder & Stoughton, 1924.

———(ed.) "Some Letters of Mrs. R. L. Stevenson and One from Henry James," *Empire Review*, March–April 1924.

Connell, John, pseud. [John Henry Robertson]
W. E. Henley. London, Constable & Co., n.d.

Cooke, Delman Gross
William Dean Howells. A Critical Study. London, Stanley Paul & Co., n.d.

Cooper, Lettice
Robert Louis Stevenson. The English Novelists Series. Denver, Alan Swallow, n.d.

Copeland, Charles Townsend
"Robert Louis Stevenson," *Atlantic Monthly*, April 1895.

Cornford, L. Cope
Robert Louis Stevenson. New York, Dodd, Mead & Co., 1900.

Cowell, Henry J.
Robert Louis Stevenson. An Englishman's Re-Study After Fifty Years of R. L. S. London, Epworth Press, n.d.

Cummins, Saxe—*see* Stevenson, Robert Louis

Cunliffe, J. W.
English Literature During the Last Half Century. New York, Macmillan Co., 1923.

Cunningham, Alison
Cummy's Diary. A Diary Kept by R. L. Stevenson's Nurse . . . while travelling with him on the Continent during 1863. With a Preface and Notes by Robert T. Skinner. London, Chatto & Windus, 1926.

Daiches, David
Robert Louis Stevenson. The Makers of Modern Literature. Norfolk, Connecticut, New Directions Books, n.d.

Dalglish, Doris N.
Presbyterian Pirate. A Portrait of Stevenson. London, Oxford University Press, 1937.

Daplyn, A. J.
"Robert Louis Stevenson at Barbizon," *Chambers's Journal*, Series 7, 1917.

Dark, Sidney
Robert Louis Stevenson. London, Hodder & Stoughton, n.d.

Delebecque, Jacques
"A Propos du Roman d'Aventure: Notes sur quelques ouvrages de R. L. Stevenson," *Mercure de France*, January–February 1921.

Dewar, J. Cumming
Voyage of the Nyanza R. N. Y. C. Being the record of a three years cruise in a schooner yacht in the Atlantic and Pacific and her subsequent shipwreck. Edinburgh, William Blackwood & Sons, 1892.

Dickie, Francis
"The Tragic End of Stevenson's Yacht Casco," *World* Magazine, January 4, 1920.

Doughty, Leonard
"Answering R. L. S.," *Southwest Review*, Autumn 1928.

Doyle, Arthur Conan
Through the Magic Door. New York, McClure Co., 1908.

Droppers, Garritt
"Robert Louis Stevenson," *Harvard Monthly*, March 1887.

Duncan, William Henry, jr.
"Stevenson's Second Visit to America," *Bookman* [N. Y.], January 1900.

Eaton, Charlotte
A Last Memory of Robert Louis Stevenson. New York, Thomas
Y. Crowell, n.d.

Elwin, Malcolm
The Strange Case of Robert Louis Stevenson. London, Macdonald,
1950.

Ewing, Sir Alfred
An Engineer's Outlook. London, Methuen & Co., Ltd., n.d.

Fabre, Frédéric
"Un ami de France: Robert Louis Stevenson dans le Vélay," ex-
trait de la *Révue d'Auvergne,* 1932.

Festetics de Tolna, Comte Rodolphe
Chez les Cannibales. Huit Ans de Croisière dans l'Océan Pacifique
à Bord du Yacht "Le Tolna." Paris, Librairie Plon, 1903.

Field, Isobel Osbourne Strong
Robert Louis Stevenson. Saranac Lake, N. Y., Stevenson Society
of America, 1920.

————*This Life I've Loved.* New York, Longmans, Green & Co.,
1937.

————(with Lloyd Osbourne) *Memories of Vailima.* New York,
Charles Scribner's Sons, 1902.

Fisher, Anne B.
No More A Stranger. Stanford University, Calif., Stanford University Press, n.d.

Fletcher, C. Brunsdon
Stevenson's Germany. The Case Against Germany in the Pacific.
London, William Heinemann, 1920.

Fraser, Marie
In Stevenson's Samoa. Preface by James Payn. London, Smith,
Elder & Co., 1895.

Freeman, John
English Portraits and Essays. London, Hodder & Stoughton,
n.d.

Genung, John Franklin
Stevenson's Attitude to Life. With Readings from his Essays and
Letters. New York, Thomas Y. Crowell, 1901.

Gilder, Jeannette L.
"Stevenson—and After," *Review of Reviews* [U. S.], February
1895.

Gosse, Edmund
Bibliographical Notes on the Writings of Robert Louis Stevenson.
London, privately printed at the Chiswick Press, 1908.
———*Critical Kit-Kats.* New York, Charles Scribner's Sons, 1914.
———*Leaves and Fruit.* New York, Charles Scribner's Sons, 1927.
———*Questions at Issue.* London, William Heinemann, 1893.
———*Silhouettes.* New York, Charles Scribner's Sons, n.d.
———*Some Diversions of a Man of Letters.* London, William Heinemann, 1919.
———"Stevenson's Relations with Children," *Youth's Companion,*
June 13, 1899.
Green, Roger Lancelyn
"Stevenson in Search of a Madonna," *Essays and Studies: 1950.*
Edited by G. Rostrevor Hamilton. London, John Murray,
1950.
Tellers of Tales. Edmund Ward, Leicester, England, 1946.
Greene, Charles S.
"California Artists. II. Joseph D. Strong, Jr." *Overland Monthly,*
May 1896.
Greenwood, Frederick
"An Impression of the Week," *Sphere,* December 7, 1901.
Gregg, Frederick James
"A Unique Collection of Stevenson," *Book Buyer,* April 1899.
Guthrie, James
Robert Louis Stevenson. Some Personal Recollections by the late
Lord Guthrie. Edinburgh, W. Green & Son, Ltd., 1920.
Gwynn, Stephen
Robert Louis Stevenson. London, Macmillan & Co., Ltd., 1939.
Hamerton, Philip Gilbert
Philip Gilbert Hamerton: an Autobiography 1834–1858; and a
Memoir by His Wife. London, Seeley & Co., Ltd., 1897.
Hamilton, Clayton
On the Trail of Stevenson. New York, Doubleday, Page & Co.,
1916.
———"The Real Stevenson at Last," *International Book Review,*
January 1925.
Hammerton, J. A.
On the Track of Stevenson and Elsewhere in Old France. Bristol,
J. W. Arrowsmith, n.d.

————(ed.) *Stevensoniana;* an anecdotal life and appreciation of Robert Louis Stevenson. Edinburgh, John Grant, 1910.

Hampden, John—*see* Stevenson, Robert Louis

Harrison, Birge
"With Stevenson at Grez," *Century*, December 1916.

Hartman, Howard
The Seas Were Mine. Edited by George S. Hellman. New York, Dodd, Mead & Co., 1935.

Hellman, George S.
Lanes of Memory. New York, Alfred A. Knopf, Inc., 1927.

————*The True Stevenson;* A Study in Clarification. Boston, Little, Brown & Co., 1925.

————"R. L. S. and the Streetwalker," *American Mercury*, July 1936.

————"Stevenson and Henry James," *Century*, January 1926.

————"The Stevenson Myth," *Century*, December 1922.

————"Stevenson's Annotated Set of Wordsworth," *Colophon*, VII, 1931.

Henley, William Ernest
Essays. London, Macmillan & Co., Ltd., 1921.

————[Obituary of R. A. M. Stevenson] *Pall Mall Magazine*, July 1900.

————"R. L. S.," *Pall Mall Magazine*, December 1901.

Hervier, Paul-Louis
"Stevenson jugé par son beaufils," *La Nouvelle Révue*, May–June 1922.

Hinkley, Laura L.
The Stevensons; Louis and Fanny. New York, Hastings House, 1950.

Hinsdale, Harriet
Robert Louis Stevenson. A play by . . . Caldwell, Idaho, Caxton Printers, 1947.

Holland, Clive
"Robert Louis Stevenson at Bournemouth," *Chambers's Journal*, December 1934.

Hopkins, Gerard Manley
The Correspondence of . . . and Richard Watson Dixon. London, Oxford University Press, 1935.

Howells, William Dean
Life in Letters of William Dean Howells. Edited by Mildred Howells. Garden City, Doubleday, Doran & Co., Inc., 1928.

Hubbard, Elbert
Robert Louis Stevenson and Fanny Osbourne. New York, Hartford Lunch Co., n.d.

Hutchinson, Allen
"Stevenson's Only Bust from Life," *Scribner's,* August 1926.

Issler, Anne Roller
Happier For His Presence. San Francisco and Robert Louis Stevenson. Stanford University Press, n.d.

———*Our Mountain Hermitage.* N. P., Stanford University Press, n.d.

———*Stevenson at Silverado.* Caldwell, Idaho, Caxton Printers, 1939.

Japp, Alexander H.
Robert Louis Stevenson. A Record, an Estimate and a Memorial. New York, Charles Scribner's Sons, 1905.

Jersey, Margaret Elizabeth (Leigh) Child-Villiers, Countess of
Fifty-One Years of Victorian Life. New York, E. P. Dutton & Co., 1921.

Joad, C. E. M.
The Bookmark. Preface by H. N. Brailsford. London, John Westhouse, n.d.

Johnstone, Arthur
Recollections of Robert Louis Stevenson in the Pacific. London, Chatto & Windus, 1905.

Keable, Robert
Tahiti: Isle of Dreams. London, Hutchinson & Co., 1923.

Keesing, Felix M.
Modern Samoa: Its Government and Changing Life. London, George Allen & Unwin, Ltd., n.d.

Kelman, John, jr.
The Faith of Robert Louis Stevenson. New York, Fleming H. Revell Co., 1903.

Kernahan, Coulson
Wise Men and a Fool. New York, Brentano's, 1901.

Lang, Andrew
Adventures Among Books. London, Longmans, Green & Co., 1905.

——*Essays in Little.* New York, Charles Scribner's Sons, 1907.

——[anonymously] "Robert Louis Stevenson," *Scots Observer*, January 26, 1889.

Lanier, Charles D.
"Robert Louis Stevenson," *Review of Reviews* [U. S.], February 1895.

Lawson, McEwan
On the Bat's Back. The Story of Robert Louis Stevenson. London, Lutterworth Press, n.d.

Leatham, James
The Style of Robert Louis Stevenson. Turriff, Deveron Press, n.d.

Le Gallienne, Richard
The Romantic '90s. New York, Doubleday, Page & Co., 1925.

——*Sleeping Beauty* and Other Fancies. London, John Lane, The Bodley Head, 1900.

Leslie, Mrs. Shane
Girlhood in the Pacific. London, Macdonald & Co., n.d.

Lockett, W. G.
Robert Louis Stevenson at Davos. London, Hurst & Blackett, Ltd., n.d.

Longaker, Mark
Ernest Dowson. Philadelphia, University of Pennsylvania Press, 1944.

Lovett, Richard
James Chalmers; His Autobiography and Letters. New York, Fleming H. Revell Co., n.d.

Low, Will H.
A Chronicle of Friendships, 1873–1900. New York, Charles Scribner's Sons, 1910.

——"A Letter to the Same Young Gentleman," *Scribner's*, September 1888.

——*Stevenson and Margarita.* N. P., n.d.

Lucas, E. V.
The Colvins and Their Friends. New York, Charles Scribner's Sons, 1928.

Luke, Sir Harry
From a South Seas Diary, 1938–1942. London, Nicholson & Watson, 1943.

MacCallum, Thomas Murray
    Adrift in the South Seas. Including Adventures with Robert Louis Stevenson . . . Los Angeles, Wetzel Publishing Co., Inc., n.d.
McCarthy, Justin
    A History of Our Own Times. From 1880 to the Diamond Jubilee. New York, Harper & Brothers, n.d.
McCarthy, Mary
    Handicaps. Six Studies. London, Longmans, Green & Co., n.d.
McClure, Samuel S.
    My Autobiography. New York, Frederick A. Stokes Co., n.d.
MacCulloch, J. A.
    R. L. Stevenson and the Bridge of Allan: with Other Stevenson Essays. Glasgow, John Smith & Son, 1927.
McGaw, Sister Martha Mary
    Stevenson in Hawaii. Honolulu, University of Hawaii Press, 1950.
Mackaness, George
    Robert Louis Stevenson: His Associations with Australia. Sydney, privately printed for the author, 1935.
McLaren, Moray
    The Unpossessed. London, Chapman & Hall, 1949.
————*Stevenson and Edinburgh.* A Centenary Study by . . . London, Chapman & Hall, 1950.
Macpherson, Harriet Dorothea
    R. L. Stevenson: A Study in French Influence. New York, publication of the Institute of French Studies, 1920.
Maitland, Frederic William
    The Life and Letters of Leslie Stephen. New York, G. P. Putnam's Sons, 1908.
Masson, Rosaline
    A Life of Robert Louis Stevenson. New York, Frederick A. Stokes Co., 1923.
————*Poets, Patriots, and Lovers.* Sketches and Memories of Famous People. London, James Clarke & Co., Ltd., n.d.
————(ed.) *I Can Remember Robert Louis Stevenson.* Edinburgh, W. & R. Chambers, 1922.
————*Robert Louis Stevenson.* London, T. C. and E. C. Jack, n.d.
Meredith, George
    Letters of . . . Collected and Edited by His Son. New York, Charles Scribner's Sons, 1912.

Moore, George
[Review of *The Secret Rose*] London *Daily Chronicle*, April 24, 1897.

Moorman, Lewis J.
Tuberculosis and Genius. Chicago, University of Chicago Press, n.d.

Moors, Harry Jay
With Stevenson in Samoa. Boston, Small, Maynard & Co., n.d.

Morley, Christopher
Essays. Garden City, N. Y., Doubleday, Doran & Co., Inc., 1928.

———*Ex Libris Carissimis.* Philadelphia, University of Pennsylvania Press, 1932.

———"A Geometry Notebook," *Saturday Review of Literature*, March 19, 1927.

Morris, David B.
Robert Louis Stevenson and the Scottish Highlanders. Stirling, Eneas Mackay, n.d.

Morse, Hiram G.
Robert Louis Stevenson as I Found Him in His Island Home. N. P., 1902.

Muir, Edwin
"Robert Louis Stevenson," *Modern Scot*, Autumn 1931.

———*Scott and Scotland.* The Predicament of the Scottish Writer. London, George Routledge & Sons, Ltd., 1936.

Munro, D. G. Macleod
The Psychopathology of Tuberculosis. London, Humphrey Milford, Oxford University Press, n.d.

Myers, Frederick W. H.
Human Personality and the Survival of Bodily Death. London, Longmans, Green & Co., 1903.

O'Rell, Max, pseud. (Paul Blouët)
John Bull & Co. The Great Colonial Branches of the Firm: Canada, Australia, New Zealand and South Africa. New York, Cassell Publishing Co., n.d.

Osbourne, Katharine Durham
Robert Louis Stevenson in California. Chicago, A. C. McClurg & Co., 1911.

Osbourne, Lloyd
   An Intimate Portrait of R. L. S. New York, Charles Scribner's Sons, 1924.
Parker, M. W.
   Modern Scottish Writers. Edinburgh, William Hoyt & Co., 1917.
Paul, C. Kegan
   Memories. London, Kegan Paul, Trench, Trübner & Co., 1899.
Pears, Sir Edmund Radcliffe
   "Some Recollections of Robert Louis Stevenson," *Scribner's*, January 1923.
Pennell, Joseph
   [Comment on *A Mountain Town in France*] *The Studio*, Winter 1896–97.
Phelps, William Lyon
   Essays on Modern Novelists. New York, Macmillan Co., 1910.
Pinero, Arthur Wing
   Robert Louis Stevenson as a Dramatist. . . . With an Introduction by Clayton Hamilton. N. P., printed for the Dramatic Museum of Columbia University, 1914.
Pritchett, V. S.—*see* Stevenson, Robert Louis
Proudfit, Isabel
   "The Big Round World," *Psychoanalytic Review*, April 1936.
   ——*The Treasure Hunter.* The Story of Robert Louis Stevenson. New York, Julian Messner, Inc., n.d.
Quiller-Couch, Arthur Thomas
   Adventures in Criticism. New York, G. P. Putnam's Sons, 1925.
Raleigh, Walter
   The Letters of . . . New York, Macmillan Co., 1926.
   ——*Robert Louis Stevenson.* London, Edward Arnold, 1895.
Rice, Richard Ashley
   Robert Louis Stevenson: How to Know Him. Indianapolis, Bobbs-Merrill Co., n.d.
Rivenburgh, Eleanor
   "Stevenson in Hawaii," *Bookman* [N. Y.], October-November-December 1917.
"Robert Louis Stevenson." A *Bookman* Extra Number. London, Hodder & Stoughton, 1913.

Robert Louis Stevenson's Handwriting. Prefatory Note by Gertrude Hills. New York, Edwin J. Beinecke Collection, privately printed, 1940.

Rosenbach, A. S. W. (ed.)
A Catalogue of the Books and Manuscripts of Robert Louis Stevenson in the library of the late Harry Elkins Widener. With a Memoir by . . . Philadelphia, privately printed, 1913.

St. Gaudens, Augustus
The Reminiscences of . . . New York, Century Co., 1896.

Saintsbury, George
A History of 19th Century Literature (1780–1895). London, Macmillan & Co., 1896.

Sadler, Fernande
L'Hôtel Chevillon et Les Artistes de Grez-sur-Loing. [Typescript in my possession]

Safroni-Middleton, A.
"A New View of R. L. S.," *John o' London's Weekly*, January 20, 1950

————*Sailor and Beachcomber.* Confessions of a Life at Sea in Australia and the Islands of the Pacific. London, Grant Richards Ltd., 1915.

Sanchez, Nellie Van de Grift
The Life of Mrs. Robert Louis Stevenson. New York, Charles Scribner's Sons, 1920.

————"Some Stevenson Legends," *Overland Monthly*, January 1930.

Savile Club, The
N. P., privately printed, 1923.

Schwob, Marcel
"R. L. S.," *New Review*, February 1895.

Sharp, William
Literary Geography & Travel Sketches. New York, Duffield & Co., 1912.

Shaw, George Bernard
Dramatic Opinions and Essays with an Apology. New York, Brentano's, 1909.

Sherman, Stuart
Critical Woodcuts. New York, Charles Scribner's Sons, 1926.

————*The Emotional Discovery of America.* New York, Farrar & Rinehart, 1932.

Shipman, Louis Evan
 "Stevenson's First Landing in New York," *Bookbuyer*, February 1896.
Simpson, Eve Blantyre
 Robert Louis Stevenson's Edinburgh Days. London, Hodder & Stoughton, 1914.
 ————*The Stevenson Originals*. New York, Charles Scribner's Sons, n.d.
Sitwell, Sir Osbert
 Great Morning. Boston, Little, Brown & Co., 1947.
Smith, Arthur D. Howden
 Alan Breck Again. New York, Coward-McCann, Inc., 1934.
 ————*Porto Bello Gold*. New York, Brentano's, n.d.
Smith, Janet Adam (*see also* Stevenson, Robert Louis)
 R. L. Stevenson. Great Lives Series. London, Duckworth, n.d.
 ————(ed.) *Henry James and Robert Louis Stevenson*. A Record of Friendship and Criticism. Edited, with an introduction by . . . London, Rupert Hart-Davis, n.d.
Snyder, Alice D.
 "Paradox and Antithesis in Stevenson's Essays," *Journal of English and Germanic Philology*, XIX.
Speculative Society, The History of the . . . (1764–1904). Edinburgh, printed for the Society . . . , 1905.
Steinbeck, John
 "How Edith McGillicuddy Met R. L. S.," *Harper's*, August 1941.
Stephen, Leslie
 Studies of a Biographer. London, Duckworth & Co., 1898.
Stern, G. B.
 No Son of Mine. New York, Macmillan Co., 1948.
Steuart, John A.
 The Cap of Youth, being the love romance of Robert Louis Stevenson. Philadelphia, J. B. Lippincott Co., 1927.
 ————*Letters to Living Authors*. London, Sampson, Low, Marston, Searle & Rivington, 1890.
 ————*Robert Louis Stevenson*. A Critical Biography. Boston, Little, Brown & Co., 1924.
Stevenson, Fanny Van de Grift Osbourne
 The Cruise of the "Janet Nichol" Among the South Sea Islands. A Diary by . . . New York, Charles Scribner's Sons, 1914.

————"The Half-White," *Scribner's,* March 1891.

————"Miss Pringle's Neighbors," *Scribner's,* June 1887.

————"The Nixie," *Scribner's,* March 1888.

————"Too Many Birthdays," *St. Nicholas,* July 1878 (Signed Fanny M. Osborne [*sic*]).

————"Under Sentence of the Law," *McClure's,* June 1893.

Stevenson, Margaret Isabella (Balfour)
From Saranac to the Marquesas and Beyond, being letters written by . . . during 1887–88, to her sister, Jane Whyte Balfour, with a short introduction by George W. Balfour, M.D., LL.D., F. R. S. E. Edited and arranged by Marie Clothilde Balfour. New York, Charles Scribner's Sons, 1903.

————*Letters from Samoa.* 1891–93. Edited and arranged by Marie Clothilde Balfour. New York, Charles Scribner's Sons, 1906.

Stevenson, Robert Louis: Anthologies:
Novels and Stories by. . . . Selected with an Introduction by V. S. Pritchett. London, Pilot Press, Ltd., 1945.

. . . *Collected Poems.* Edited, with an Introduction and Notes, by Janet Adam Smith. London, Rupert Hart-Davis, 1950.

Selected Writings of. . . . With an Introduction by Saxe Cummins. New York, Random House, n.d.

Selections from. . . . Edited by Henry Seidel Canby and Frederick Erastus Pierce. New York, Charles Scribner's Sons, n.d.

The Stevenson Companion. Selected and Arranged with an Introduction by John Hampden. London, Phoenix House, n.d.

Stevenson, Robert Louis: works unavailable in collected editions:
Authors and Publishers. (Unpublished essay in possession of Edwin J. Beinecke.)

————*The Castaways of Soledad.* . . . With an introductory essay by George S. Hellman. Buffalo, N. Y., privately printed, 1928.

————*Confessions of a Unionist.* (Unpublished article in Widener collection; galley proofs.)

————*Five Poems and Letters From . . . to Charles Warren Stoddard,* N. P., privately printed for John M. Patterson, 1924.

————*Four Letters of . . . Concerning the Dramatization of Dr. Jekyll and Mr. Hyde.* Pretoria, printed for private circulation, 1923.

————Fragment on popular press and *crimes passionnels*. (Unpublished; in possession of Edwin J. Beinecke.)

————Fragment on Roux illustrations for *Treasure Island*. (Unpublished; in possession of Edwin J. Beinecke.)

————*Java,* a deleted fragment from the Vailima Letters. . . . Philadelphia, privately printed, n.d.

————*Letters to Charles Baxter* [Edited by Clement Shorter]. . . . N. P. privately printed, n.d.

————*Letters to an Editor* by . . . [Edited by Clement Shorter]. N. P. privately printed, n.d.

————*The Manuscripts of Robert Louis Stevenson's Records of a Family of Engineers: the Unfinished Chapters.* With introduction by J. Christian Bay. Chicago, Walter M. Hill, 1929.

————*Monmouth: A Tragedy.* New York, William Edwin Rudge, 1928.

————*Plain John Wiltshire on the Samoan Situation.* (Unpublished article in letter-form in possession of Huntington Library.)

————*Poems by . . . Hitherto Unpublished.* With introduction and notes by George S. Hellman and William P. Trent. Boston, Bibliophile Society, 1921.

————*. . . Hitherto Unpublished Prose Writings.* Edited by Henry H. Harper. Boston, Bibliophile Society, 1921.

————*A Samoan Scrapbook.* (Unpublished letter-press in possession of Edwin J. Beinecke.)

————"San Carlos Day," . . . with an introduction by George R. Stewart. *Scribner's,* August 1920.

————"The South Seas: Life Under the Equator; Letters From a Leisurely Traveller," *New York Sun,* February 8, 15; March 15, 22, 29; April 5, 12, 19, 26; May 3, 10, 17, 24, 31; June 7, 14, 21, 28; July 5, 12, 25; September 6, 13, 20, 27; October 4, 11, 18, 25; November 1, 8, 15, 22; December 13. All 1891.

————*Stevenson's Workshop.* With 29 ms. Facsimiles. Edited by William P. Trent. Boston, Bibliophile Society, 1921.

————*Three Short Poems.* London, printed for private distribution only, 1898.

Stevenson, Thomas
Christianity Confirmed by Jewish and Heathen Testimony. . . . Edinburgh, Adam & Charles Black, 1884.

Stevenson's Baby Book: being the Record of the Sayings and Doings of Robert Louis Balfour Stevenson . . . San Francisco, printed for John Howell by John Henry Nash, 1922.

Stewart, George R.
"The Real Treasure Island," *University of California Chronicle,* April 1926.

Stoddard, Charles Warren
Exits and Entrances. Boston, Lothrop Publishing Co., n.d.
————"Stevenson's Monterey," *National Magazine,* December 1906.

Strong, Austin
"His Oceanic Majesty's Goldfish," *Atlantic Monthly,* May 1944.
————"The Most Unforgettable Character I've Met," *Reader's Digest,* March 1946.

Stubbs, Laura
Stevenson's Shrine. The Record of a Pilgrimage. London, Alexander Mering, 1903.

Sullivan, Thomas Russell
Passages from the Journal of. . . . 1891–93. Boston, Houghton Mifflin Co., n.d.

Swinnerton, Frank
R. L. Stevenson. A Critical Study. New York, George H. Doran Co., n.d.

Symonds, John Addington
John Addington Symonds. A Biography Compiled from His Papers and Correspondence by Horatio F. Brown. London, John Murray, 1903.
————*Letters and Papers of John Addington Symonds.* Collected and Edited by Horatio F. Brown. New York, Charles Scribner's Sons, 1923.

Taylor, Una
Guests and Memories. Annals of a Seaside Villa. London, Oxford University Press, 1924.

Testimonials in Favour of Robert Louis Stevenson, Advocate. N. P., n.d.

Triggs, W. H.
"R. L. Stevenson as a Samoan Chief," *Cassell's Family Magazine,* February 1895.

Trudeau, Edward Livingston
An Autobiography. New York, Doubleday, Page & Co., 1916.

Twain, Mark, pseud. (Samuel Langhorne Clemens)
Mark Twain's Autobiography. With an Introduction by Albert Bigelow Paine. New York, Harper & Brothers, 1924.

Vallings, Harold
"Stevenson Among the Philistines," *Temple Bar*, February 1901.

van Rensselaer, Mrs. M. G.
"Robert Louis Stevenson and His Writing," *Century*, November 1895.

Vulcan, Jenny
The Story of Robert Louis Stevenson (Tusitala the Tale-Teller). London, Stead's Publishing House, n.d.

Wallace, William
"The Life and Limitations of Stevenson," *Scottish Review*, January 1900.

———"Scotland, Stevenson, and Mr. Henley," *New Liberal Review*, February 1902.

Watt, Francis
Edinburgh and the Lothians. London, Methuen & Co., Ltd., n.d.

———*R. L. S.* New York, Macmillan Co., 1913.

Williamson, Kennedy
W. E. Henley. A Memoir. London, Harold Shaylor, n.d.

Webster, Alexander
R. L. Stevenson and Henry Drummond. London, Essex Hall, 1923.

Wilson, Edmund
"Henley and Faulkner Not at Their Best," *New Yorker*, December 24, 1949.

Woolf, Leonard
Essays on Literature, History, Politics, Etc. London, Hogarth Press, 1927.

Notes

I have used three different editions of Stevenson—not necessarily the best ones—as convenience served. References below to *Letters* invariably mean the South Seas Edition, 32 volumes, New York, Charles Scribner's Sons, 1925. (SS) before a volume number means South Seas Edition. (Vail.) means Vailima Edition, 31 volumes, New York, Charles Scribner's Sons, 1925. (Bigelow-Scott) means the truncated Bigelow-Scott Edition, New York, Bigelow, Brown & Company, n.d.

Prologue and I, 1: *The Gyve Is Riveted*

1. This is Una Taylor's reading (*Guests and Memories:* 356). Misreading Louis's hand, Colvin gives "oil" for "will." (*Letters:* II, 236.)

2. Squire, *Robert Louis Stevenson:* 16.

3. Gower Woodseer of *The Amazing Marriage* was drawn partly from Stevenson as Meredith first knew him. Barrie seems to have considered that some aspects of Sentimental Tommy, particularly the passion for the *mot juste*, were drawn with Stevenson in mind, though the two authors never met personally.

4. Robert was a Stevenson family name. Lewis Balfour was the boy's paternal grandfather. "Balfour" was dropped as Louis approached manhood. For circumstances possibly attending the change from "Lewis" to "Louis," see note 31 below.

5. *Records of a Family of Engineers* (Vail.): XII, 411.

6. The rest of the blazon seems to have been taken from arms borne by other Scots families named Stevenson; the office of Lyon King-at-Arms courteously supplied me with information on this.

7. "Smith opens out his cauld harangues
      On practice and on morals; . . ."

8. The diagnosis is fairly clear. Dr. George Balfour (*From Saranac to the Marquesas:* xvii) says that, after Louis was born, she "developed a patch of fibroid pneumonia in the left lung, with slight hemoptysis"—in terms of the time a strong indication of tuberculosis.

9. This could have been a noncharacteristic diphtheria? It is notable that Louis failed to contract diphtheria when nursing Bob in 1874 and again at Silverado when both Fanny and Lloyd had light cases.

10. Louis's severe swellings and nervous upsets when under treatment with iodides in the '80s hint at thyroid abnormalities.

11. Colvin, *Memories & Notes* . . . : 100.

12. Simpson, *Robert Louis Stevenson's Edinburgh Days:* 211.

13. Stevenson to Mrs. Sitwell, *Letters:* I, 212–13.

14. Guthrie, *Robert Louis Stevenson:* 27.

15. Balfour, *Life* . . . : I, 39.

16. *Memoirs of Himself* (SS):XIII, 274; Balfour, *Life:* I, 39.

17. Smith (*Robert Louis Stevenson:* 17) suggests that late reading is not unusual in children having adults available to read to them.

18. Few Americans know the Metrical Versions; the Twenty-third Psalm is a fair sample of their knotty and original quality:

The Lord's my shepherd, I'll not want, He makes me down to lie
In pastures green; he leadeth me the quiet waters by;
My soul he doth restore again; and me to walk doth make
Within the paths of righteousness ev'n for His own namesake. . . .

Or consider the queernesses of Psalm XXII:

. . . And I was cast upon thy care ev'n from the womb till now;
And from my mother's belly, Lord, my God and guide art thou.
Be not far off, for grief is near, and none to help is found,
Bulls many compass me, strong bulls of Bashan me surround. . . .

19. *Rosa Quo Locorum* . . . (SS):XIII, 241.

20. *Popular Authors* (SS):XVII, 27.

21. Black, *Robert Louis Stevenson:* 24.

22. Mrs. M. I. Stevenson, *From Saranac to the Marquesas:* 234.

23. "Bands" being the token of ordination.

24. Louis's mother recorded this in her Baby Book but again with more amusement than alarm.

25. *Memoirs of Himself* (SS):XIII, 278–9; 282.

26. Gosse (*Leaves and Fruit:* 330) saw fit to doubt that Cummy's

influence on Louis was at all morbid. The son of Gosse's father should have known better.

27. Stevenson to Thomas Stevenson, *Letters:* I, 34.

28. Arnold, "My Stevensons," *Scribner's*, January 1922, quoting an unpublished note to *Kidnapped*.

29. "An Apology for Idlers" (SS):II, 62.

30. Prefatory note to *Memories and Portraits* (SS):XIII.

31. The legend is that Thomas Stevenson's loathing for an Edinburgh radical named Lewis prompted the change of spelling in Louis's name to the French form—in pronunciation the final "s" was always sounded. I am uncertain about this story. An entry of Mrs. Stevenson's in the Baby Book looks extremely like "Louis." Louis's signatures on the books of the Speculative Society are also ambiguous. Still the spirit of the story is *ben trovato* enough.

32. Masson, *I Can Remember* . . . : 3.

33. Across the way from 17 Heriot Row. While at Inverleith Terrace the Stevensons could certainly have acquired a key to the gardens. But children who were habitués did not recall Louis as consistently there. Edinburgh legend regards the miniature island, about as big as a doormat, in the Queen Street Gardens pond as having initiated Louis's fascination with islands in general and as perhaps the germ of *Treasure Island*. If it is important, this is dubious. Louis does not mention it in accounting for his taste for islands in "Memoirs of an Islet."

34. Masson, *Life* . . . : 46–47.

35. A bat shaped like a large, flattened cooking spoon used in the Academy's peculiar game of *hailes*, handling of which calls for high dexterity. I am told that the game is gradually disappearing from the Academy, the only place where it was ever played.

36. In the Swanston Cottage garden Lord Guthrie once found an old gutta-percha golf ball marked "R.L.S." to show that Louis at least experimented with the game. (Guthrie, *Robert Louis Stevenson:* 69.)

37. Simpson, *Robert Louis Stevenson's Edinburgh Days:* 151–52.

38. Stevenson to Archer, *Letters:* III, 77.

39. *Memoirs of Himself* (SS):XIII, 285.

40. Stevenson to Mrs. Fairchild, *Letters:* IV, 102.

41. In Scots this means "obscenity." America has come to use it to mean "sharp practice." (*Cf. American College Dictionary:* 1133.)

42. The sketches show small enough talent, but they are amusingly similar to the figures printed for *Skelt's Juvenile Drama* that was the germ of "A Penny Plain."

43. Stevenson to Crockett, *Letters:* IV, 179.

I, 2: *Changeling*

1. Stevenson to Baxter, Beinecke Collection.

2. "Popular Authors," (SS):XXVII, 28.

3. "A College Magazine," (SS):XIII, 35.

4. Even Sampson, who tends to be sniffy about Stevenson, admits the soundness of this theory of how writing is learned (*Concise Cambridge History:* 852). See Appendix A for further discussion.

5. In an interview given to the Christchurch (N. Z.) *Press* (April 24, 1893) Louis recalled the impression that *The Renaissance* made on him in 1873.

6. Masson, *Life:* 62.

7. Morley, "A Geometry Notebook," *Saturday Review of Literature,* March 19, 1927.

8. Gwynn, *Robert Louis Stevenson:* 65.

9. Masson, *I Can* . . . : 51. Though no genuine classicist, Louis had enough Latin to enjoy Virgil, Horace, Martial, and Saint Augustine in later life as well as when nearer his schooling. He made several loose translations of Martial items and often used Latin tags, usually from Horace, on verses and essays as titles. *Cf.* Burriss ("The Classical Culture of Robert Louis Stevenson," *Classical Journal,* XX, 271) for academic appraisal of his grasp of Latin.

10. Gosse, *Critical Kit-Kats:* 276.

11. Stevenson to Mrs. Sitwell, *Letters:* I, 256–57.

12. Mr. Paul Miller supplied me with a paper on the subject by Mr. J. L. Herries of Edinburgh. It appears that round 1870 Louis was at least nominally secretary of some sort of Edinburgh psychical society.

13. Masson, *Life:* 68.

14. Flora Masson recalled Baxter's breaking a chair at 17 Heriot Row by inelegantly tilting back in it. Imperturbably he picked up

a splinter and handed it to Louis's mother saying: "My dear Mrs. Stevenson, this is what comes of having cheap furniture." (Masson, *I Can . . .* : 129.)

15. Such as this, from Hyères, probably in 1883 (Savile Gift):

Toddy Vale
by Kilrummer

Thomson:

It's done—I'm a dissenter. I kenned fine frae the beginning hoo it was a' to end. I saw there was nae justice for auld Johnstone. The last I tauld ye, they had begun a clash aboot the drink. O sic a disgrace! when, if onything, I rayther drink less nor mair since yon damned scandal about the blue ribbon. I took the scunner as far back as that, Thomson—and O man, I wuss that I had just left the establishment that very day! But no; I was aye loyal like them that went afore me.

Well, the ither day, up comes yon red-headed, pishion-faced creeter—him a minister! "Mr. Johnstone," says he, "I think it my duty to tell 'ee there's a most unpleasant fama aboot you." "Sir," says I, "they take a pleesure to persecute me."

What was't? Man, Thomson, I think shame to write it: NO BONY-FEED WI' THE PLATE. Isn't that peetiful? the auld, auld story! the same, weary, auld, havering claver that they tauld aboot Sandie Sporran—him that was subsekently hanged, ye'll mind. . . .

Whatever, I saw that I was by wi't. Says I "I leave the Kirk"— "Well," says he, "I think ye're perfectly richt" and a wheen mair maist unjeedicial and injudeecious observations. Noo, I'm a Morrisonian and I like it fine. We're a sma' body, but unco' tosh. . . . I'm a great light in the body; much sympathy was felt for me generally amang the mair leeberal o' a' persuasions: A man at my time of life and kent sae lang!

A[r] Johnstone

P.S. I'll hae to pay for the wean. In a so-ca'd Christian country! Mercy me!

16. Stevenson to Baxter, *Letters:* I, 290.

17. *To Charles Baxter: On the Death of their Common Friend, Mr. John Adam, Clerk of Court* (SS):XV, 142.

18. Stevenson to Baxter; *Letters to Charles Baxter.* Internal evi-

dence makes it clear that Shorter was wrong in attributing this to the Samoan period.

19. In Scots "howff" means "haunt"—the American equivalent would be somewhere between "dump" and "joint." A "shebeen" is a tavern depending principally on after-hours, illegal business.

20. Balfour, *Life:* I, 99.

21. Stevenson to Colvin, *Letters:* I, 387.

22. Hellman, "Stevenson and the Streetwalker," *American Mercury*, July 1936.

23. Stevenson to Haddon, *Letters:* II, 87.

24. Stevenson to Haddon, *Letters:* II, 85. *Selections from His Notebook* (SS):XIII, 298.

25. Masson, *I Can* . . . : 171. "W.S.," Writer to the Signet, in Scots law a judicial officer who prepares warrants, writs, etc.

26. *Memoirs of Himself* (SS):XIII, 282.

27. "Stormy Nights," (SS):XV, 249.

28. Stevenson to Mrs. Sitwell, National Library.

29. Chesterton, *Robert Louis Stevenson:* 58–59.

30. Gosse, *Leaves and Fruit:* 327.

31. Masson, *I Can* . . . : 96.

32. CXCII in *New Poems,* (SS):XV, 242. The unwary might see much earlier autobiography in "To Priapus," CXXIV in *New Poems;* actually this is a free translation from Martial.

33. CLXII in *New Poems* (SS):XV, 203.

34. Colvin, *Memories & Notes* . . . : 101.

35. Stevenson to Mrs. Sitwell, National Library.

36. "The Vanquished Knight," (SS):XV, 107.

37. XIII in *New Poems* (SS):XV, 101.

38. "A College Magazine," (SS),XIII, 42.

39. A manuscript of this in the Beinecke Collection is dated July '71 in Louis's hand. "Tho' deep indifference should drowse . . ." which fits into the same pattern, is similarly dated December '70. One of these girls of Louis's stratum may well have been Eve Blantyre Simpson, Sir Walter's sister; the only genuine evidence of this is contained in a still unpublished letter from Louis to Baxter written twenty years later.

40. People attributed to Louis a Scottish accent in later life in proportion to how picturesque they wished to make him sound. Some apparently confuse him with Harry Lauder; others, like Charlotte

Eaton, an American (*A Last Memory of . . .* : 80), say he had "not the slightest Scottish accent." The only expert opinion I have from a surviving witness is that of Dr. Robert Scot-Skirving of Sydney, N.S.W., who knew Louis at the Jenkins' in youth and saw him several times in Sydney in the early 1890s. He says that you could tell he was a Scot, right enough, but gives no hint of the exaggeration of speech sometimes implied. Sometimes, of course, to amuse himself and others, Louis spoke very broad Scots indeed.

41. Ewing, *An Engineer's Notebook*: 250.
42. Gosse, Preface to Pentland Edition: 74.
43. *Memoir of Fleeming Jenkin* (Vail.):XI, 529.
44. *Ibid.*: 531.
45. *Ibid.*: 525.
46. Stevenson to Colvin, *Letters*: II, 106.
47. Henley, *Pall Mall Magazine*, December 1901.

I, 3: *The Gifted Boy*

1. Field, *This Life I've Loved*: 103.
2. Hammerton, *Stevensoniana*: 5.
3. Gosse, Notes to Pentland Edition: 19.
4. "Talk and Talkers," (SS):XIII, 65.
5. Henley, *Essays*: 117–18.
6. Henley, Obituary of R. A. M. Stevenson, *Pall Mall Magazine*, July 1900.
7. Mrs. Fanny V. de G. Stevenson, preface to *New Arabian Nights* (SS):III, xiv.
8. Very probably recalled in the scene with Dudgeon in *St. Ives*.
9. Stevenson to Colvin, *Letters*: I, 157.
10. "Lay Morals," (SS):II, 198–99.
11. LI in *New Poems*, (SS) XV, 130.
12. Muir, *Scott and Scotland*: 85.
13. R. A. M. Stevenson, *Velasquez*: 6.
14. Stevenson to Angus, *Letters*: III, 258.
15. Balfour (*Life:* I, 107 fn.) says only five meetings were held. The founding principles were Liberty, Justice, Reverence; one object was abolition of the House of Lords. *Cf.* letter from Charles

Baxter in *T.P.'s Weekly*, July 21, 1911. In Masson, *I Can* . . . : 46 is a note of Thomas Stevenson's recalling that the draft of the constitution that he saw began "Disregard everything our parents have taught us. . . ."

16. I do not know just when Louis shifted altogether to cigarettes. He was still smoking a pipe at Davos in 1880, though by then cigarettes seem to have dominated.

17. Sampson, *Concise Cambridge History* . . . : 852.

18. Chesterton, *Robert Louis Stevenson*: 68–69.

19. Colvin, *Memories & Notes* . . . : 108.

20. Ferrier was Louis's only special crony in the scheme. Others were G. Scott-Moncrieff and Robert Glasgow Brown, later founder of the short-lived *London*. "A College Magazine" has sketches of both.

21. Stevenson to Mrs. M. I. Stevenson, *Letters:* I, 72.

22. XXX in *New Poems*, (SS):XV, 112.

23. Stevenson to Henley, *Letters:* II, 132.

24. Gwynn, *Robert Louis Stevenson*: 4.

25. Experts tell me that the paper is competent technically. Under probable correction by Thomas Stevenson, a world expert in just this field, it could hardly have helped being so. Two years later, under what I strongly suspect was Jenkin's influence, Louis read a paper on "The Thermal Influence of Forests" before the Royal Society of Edinburgh. No scientific impulse ever had less sequel.

26. Some of Louis's taste for Darwin at least—"I bought Darwin's last book in despair, for I knew I could generally read Darwin" (*Letters:* I, 89)—came of admiration for his excellent style.

27. "A Valentine's Song," (SS):XV, 128.

28. LXXV in *New Poems*, (SS):XV, 148–49.

29. "Prelude," (SS):XV, 106–107.

30. Stevenson to Mrs. Sitwell, National Library.

31. Stevenson to Baxter, part *Letters:* I, 80, 81; part National Library.

32. Stevenson to Mrs. Sitwell, *Letters:* I, 216.

33. Stevenson to Mrs. Sitwell, National Library.

34. Stevenson to Mrs. Sitwell, National Library.

35. Stevenson to Mrs. Sitwell, National Library.

36. Stevenson to Mrs. Sitwell, National Library.

37. Stevenson to Mrs. Sitwell, National Library.

38. Stevenson to Mrs. Sitwell, National Library.
39. Stevenson to Mrs. Sitwell, *Letters:* I, 101.
40. Stevenson to Mrs. Sitwell, National Library.
41. Stevenson to Mrs. M. I. Stevenson, Strong Collection.
42. Stevenson to Mrs. M. I. Stevenson, *Letters:* I, 112. Masson (*Life:* 105) says that Colvin or somebody had told Clark of Louis's troubles at home. This is probably reliable.
43. Masson, *I Can . . . :* 13.

I, 4. *Monsieur Est Bien Jeune*

1. Lucas, *The Colvins and Their Friends:* 336.
2. *Ibid.:* 54. Much of this book is invaluable. Katharine D. Osbourne, who insisted on knowing all there was to know about her husband's family and his stepfather's connections, though she married into the complex after Louis's death, wrote Hellman that Mrs. Sitwell ". . . found the life of a clergyman's wife uninteresting." (*The True Stevenson:* 80.) I am sure that this is nonsense as accounting for the separation. But strenuous efforts to discover what ailed Sitwell have been unavailing. Drink is as likely a guess as any.
3. Louis wrote a prospectus for this venture. Its tone is appropriately but, for him, queerly smug. (Vail. XXIV: 50–52.) Mrs. Sitwell's only readily identifiable literary work is a competent translation of Yriarte, *Venice.* Much of her reviewing is said to have been done for the *Manchester Guardian.*
4. *Memoirs of Himself* (SS):XIII, 290.
5. Clifford, "The Sidney Colvins . . .", *Bookman* (London), April 1928.
6. Lucas, *The Colvins and Their Friends:* 341.
7. Van Rensselaer, "Robert Louis Stevenson and His Writing," *Century*, November 1895.
8. *Memoirs of Himself* (SS):XIII, 291–92.
9. Colvin note in *Letters:* I, 15.
10. Even an amateur researcher has much to complain of about Colvin's editing of the *Letters.* He made excisions with no suspension-points for warning; occasionally changed words; sometimes badly

misread Louis's hand; dismembered letters and reassembled them with paragraphs from other letters. His excisions often leave the impression that the boy was much more egocentric than the full text shows him to have been, and unhappily left the nature of Louis's relation to Mrs. Sitwell open to serious misinterpretation. Beyond that, for all its sins of commission, it cannot be said that his editing produced a distorted impression.

11. Stevenson to Mrs. Sitwell, National Library.
12. Stevenson to Mrs. Sitwell, National Library.
13. Stevenson to Mrs. Sitwell, National Library.
14. Stevenson to Mrs. Sitwell, National Library.
15. Stevenson to Mrs. Sitwell, National Library.
16. Stevenson to Mrs. Sitwell, National Library.
17. Stevenson to Mrs. Sitwell, *Letters:* I, 114.
18. Stevenson to Mrs. Sitwell, National Library.
19. Stevenson to Mrs. Sitwell, *Letters:* I, 113.
20. "Health and Mountains," (SS): XXVII, 160.
21. Stevenson to Mrs. Sitwell, *Letters:* I, 115.
22. Stevenson to Mrs. Sitwell, *Letters:* I, 123, plus original in National Library.
23. Stevenson to Mrs. Sitwell, National Library.
24. Stevenson to Mrs. Sitwell, National Library.
25. "Lay Morals" tells of the ". . . generous, flighty" young man ". . . falling into ill-health . . . sent at great expense to a more favourable climate; . . . When he thought of all the other young men of singular promise . . . who must remain at home to die . . . and how he, by one more unmerited favour, was chosen out from all those others to survive; he felt as if there were no life, no labour, no devotion of soul and body, that could repay and justify these partialities. . . should he die, he saw no means of repaying this huge loan which by the hands of his father, mankind had advanced him for his sickness. . . . So he determined that the advance should be as small as possible; and so long as he continued to doubt his recovery, lived in an upper room and grudged himself all but necessities. But so soon as he began to feel a change for the better, he felt justified in spending more freely, to speed and brighten his return to health, and trusted in the future to lend a help to mankind, as mankind, out of its treasury, had lent a help to him." (SS):II, 164–66.

26. Stevenson to Mrs. Sitwell, *Letters:* I, 125.

27. Stevenson to Mrs. M. I. Stevenson, *Letters:* I, 149.

28. The result was "Notes on the Movements of Young Children" in the *Portfolio*, August 1874—a labored piece but with some shrewd observation in it.

29. "This is my son. He is just nineteen. He is very proud of his mustache. Do try to make it show up well." Louis's mustache was always somewhat straggly and often occasion for ribald comment from his friends. (Stevenson to Mrs. Sitwell, *Letters:* I, 172.)

30. Stevenson to Mrs. Sitwell, National Library.

31. Stevenson to Mrs. Sitwell, National Library. Colvin (note in *Letters:* I, 139) believed that Louis never had the complete story of Pola's parentage. This is strange, since Colvin personally excised the passage containing the above incident. It may be, of course, that Louis had become wary of everything that the Russians said—so wary that Colvin and he had discounted the whole story as merely another Slavic extravagance.

32. Stevenson to Mrs. M. I. Stevenson, *Letters:* I, 139.

33. Stevenson to Mrs. Sitwell, *Letters:* I, 153.

34. Stevenson to Mrs. M. I. Stevenson, *Letters:* I, 141.

35. Stevenson to Mrs. Sitwell, *Letters:* I, 145.

36. Founded on Mme. Zassetsky (Stevenson to Henley, *Letters:* I, 385). As printed the passage was markedly bowdlerized.

37. Stevenson to Mrs. Sitwell, *Letters:* I, 168. "Why, you are simply still a child!"

38. Stevenson to Mrs. Sitwell, *Letters:* I, 155.

39. Lang, *Adventures Among Books:* 42.

40 .Stevenson to Thomas Stevenson, *Letters:* I, 166.

41. Stevenson to Mrs. Sitwell, *Letters:* I, 153.

42. Stevenson to Thomas Stevenson, *Letters:* I, 166.

43. Stevenson to Mrs. Sitwell, National Library. Previously published in Bay, *Echoes of Robert Louis Stevenson*.

44. Stevenson to Colvin, *Letters:* I, 180.

45. Stevenson to Mrs. Sitwell, National Library.

46. Stevenson to Mrs. Sitwell, National Library.

47. Stevenson to Mrs. Sitwell, *Letters:* I, 202.

48. LVI in *New Poems*, (SS): XV, 134–35.

49. Stevenson to Mrs. Sitwell, National Library.

50. Stevenson to Mrs. Sitwell, National Library.

51. Stevenson to Mrs. Sitwell, National Library.

52. Stevenson to Mrs. Sitwell, *Letters:* I, 250–51.

53. The version in the text is that of LXXVII in *New Poems*, (SS): XV, 148. The altered version actually sent to the lady is Stevenson to Mrs. Sitwell, National Library.

54. Stevenson to Mrs. Sitwell, National Library.

55. Masson, *I Can . . . :* 115.

56. Legends attending Louis's abortive legal career include the story that this clerk did not know him by sight, which is likely; and that, when Louis was to make a perfunctory representation in court for a friendly client, he was unable to utter a word, which is not particularly likely.

57. Gosse, *Silhouettes:* 379.

58. The passage dealing with the complications of friendship between men and women, "be it never so unalloyed and innocent," may reflect Louis's current tangles over Mrs. Sitwell.

59. *Vanity Fair*, December 11, 1875. In 1886 Colvin introduced Louis to Browning; nothing of note seems to have resulted.

60. Stevenson to Mrs. Sitwell, National Library.

61. Stevenson to Mrs. Sitwell, National Library.

62. Stevenson to Mrs. Sitwell, *Letters:* I, 211.

63. Stevenson to Mrs. Sitwell, *Letters:* I, 239–40.

64. Balfour, *Life:* II, 49.

65. Will Hickok Low was born in Albany, N. Y. and studied painting in Paris and the Fontainebleau colonies during Louis's time there. In the 1880s and 1890s he was a fairly conspicuous figure in American art, working with John La Farge and having a large hand independently in the decoration of the old Waldorf-Astoria and the Capitol at Albany. Naturally, much of his work looks very pretty-pretty in modern eyes. He is said to have been, to some extent, the original of Loudon Dodd of *The Wrecker*.

66. Gosse (*Critical Kit-Kats:* 276–78) covers the steamer meeting but fails to mention the dinner at Stephen's—why, I do not know. Maitland (*Life and Letters of Leslie Stephen:* 268) is most explicit about it.

67. Louis first signed these famous initials in the *Cornhill*; Balfour (*Life: I*, 168–69) indicates that the privilege of signing even initials was an honor for a beginner. Maitland says that some ingenious people suspected that "R. L. S." stood for "The Real Leslie

Stephen." Louis's "Roads," his first paid contribution (to the *Portfolio*), was signed "L. R. Stoneven."

68. Stevenson to Mrs. Sitwell, *Letters:* I, 249.

69. This was not Louis's fault. From Hyères he offered Henley a commission on sales in view of all he was doing. Henley refused.

70. Stevenson to Mrs. Sitwell, *Letters:* I, 260.

71. Stevenson to Mrs. Sitwell, National Library.

72. Stevenson to Mrs. Sitwell, National Library.

73. Stevenson to Mrs. Sitwell, National Library.

74. Stevenson to Mrs. Sitwell, National Library.

75. Stevenson to Archer, *Letters:* III, 43.

76. "A Song of the Road," (SS): XIV, 72.

77. "Walking Tours," (SS): II, 134.

78. Stevenson to R. A. M. Stevenson, Beinecke Collection. All that came of this scheme was the Borrow-like hero's horse and caravan in *The Pavilion on the Links*.

79. Balfour, *Life:* I, 171.

80. "A Winter's Walk," (SS): XXVII, 126.

81. Stevenson to Colvin, *Letters:* I, 299.

82. "Forest Notes" (SS): XXVII, 154.

83. Australian friends of mine have kindly ascertained that both Martin and the verses actually existed.

84. Stevenson to Martin, *Letters:* I, 313–14.

I, 5. *Better in France*

1. Stevenson to Simoneau, *Letters:* II, 139.

2. Stevenson to Mrs. Sitwell, *Letters:* I, 322.

3. Sullivan, *The Journal of Thomas Russell Sullivan:* 119.

4. Stevenson to Henley, National Library.

5. Stevenson to Henley, National Library.

6. *An Inland Voyage* (Vail.): I, 60.

7. Attwater is supposed to have been partly drawn from A. G. Dew-Smith, a Cambridge scholar whom Louis knew.

8. "Why, you hit me!" . . . "So it would appear!"

9. Colvin, *Memories & Notes* . . . : 110.

10. By a curious coincidence, when I was last in Paris a very bad

movie version of *The Black Arrow* was showing in the theater that now occupies part of the site of the Lavenue's of Louis's day.

11. Joseph Pennell (*The Studio*, Winter, 1896) was quite polite about Louis's sketches of scenery in the Cevennes. To me they show about the same talent as, and less developed skill than, that of the draftsman who does free-hand renderings in the average architect's office. Numerous examples of Louis the graphic artist survive, ranging from sketches of Mentonese done at the age of twelve to drawings of Tahiti done in 1889. All are accurate and intelligent, none (except the Davos woodcuts) done with any grasp.

12. Stevenson to Henley, National Library.

13. The one final burst of imitation was the highly Hazlittean flavor of "Talk and Talkers" in 1881—and all the better for it.

14. "Rudely puffed the winds of heaven; roguishly upclomb the all-destructive urchin; and the cit groped along the wall, suppered but bedless, occult from guidance, and sorrily wading in the kennels." ("A Plea for Gas Lamps," (SS): II, 144.) Or maybe this is doing Louis an injustice. This has a flavor of Carlyle at his worst, and at one point Louis determined to stop reading Carlyle lest he acquire the old gentleman's mannerisms.

15. "Pan's Pipes" (SS): II, 141.

16. I do not mean that Louis had never before had ambitions toward narrative. He wrote many imitative narratives in his adolescence and at least as early as his solitary stay in Menton was planning "The Curate of Anstruther's Bottle," a sort of basic sketch of which is in "The Coast of Fife," one of his *Scribner's* essays. But at this period he first began to strike out satisfactory shapes in narrative.

17. Of the four sections of "Virginibus Puerisque," Section I was unquestionably written before he met Fanny. III (published February 1877) and IV (published May 1879) are very probably post-Fanny. II, the best of the series, did not see publication until the first collection of Louis's essays for a book. Perhaps Stephen found too cynical its rueful approach to matrimony as a courageous swindle on the lady one hopes to marry.

II, 1. *The Blind Bowboy*

1. "The Family," (SS): XV, 213.

2. Sources for the following account of Fanny are principally: Sanchez, *Life of Mrs. Robert Louis Stevenson;* Field, *This Life I've Loved;* Osbourne, *An Intimate Portrait of R. L. S.;* Lucas, *The Colvins and Their Friends;* and Fanny's own letters to Timothy Rearden and Dora Norton Williams. Local checks have also been made.

3. I am told that, though at first one of Beecher's congregation, Jacob later disagreed with the great preacher and turned Universalist. Mrs. Sanchez says that Jacob always refused to hear ill of Beecher during the Tilton scandal.

4. Katharine Durham Osbourne occasionally hinted that Fanny was actually three or four years older still. This date comes from local records as well as from Sanchez; its accuracy is unquestionable.

5. Colvin, *Memories & Notes:* 130.

6. Mrs. Bolton's best-known work seems to have been a hortatory affair called *Paddle Your Own Canoe*—the titular verses of her collected works, which were honored with a preface by General Lew Wallace and a "proem" by James Whitcomb Riley. There may be still more flavor of the period in the "Found Dead":

> "Found dead by the roadside, Augustus Hall,
> With a bottle clasped to his frozen breast;
> He died from drink where he chanced to fall";
> Ran the coroner's verdict, and this was all.
> God only knows the rest . . .

7. All the sisters' marriages paralleled Fanny's in being somehow unusual; she was directly connected with two of them: Elizabeth's man, an army officer, took her to live in frontier forts. Cora's Sam Orr was a Nevada silver man and occasional partner of Sam Osbourne. Nellie met her fate when Fanny took her to Monterey —a Mexican-Spanish barkeeper, Adolfo Sanchez, of excellent local family. Josephine's first husband, George Marshall, was a crony of Sam's, who came back from the Civil War dying of tuberculosis; her second was a banker in Danville, Ind.

8. To save trouble for future researchers, here are the crucial data from state and federal records: Samuel C. Osbourne was mustered into the 46th Indiana on Nov. 14, 1861; resigned May 26, 1862; sold his and Fanny's share of the Vandegrift farm to Jacob Vandegrift for $4000 on Nov. 24, 1862; was mustered into the Indiana Legion on July 9, 1863. George Marshall died at Panama on Jan. 23, 1864, according to the Vandegrift family Bible. The facts as stated in Sanchez' *Life* of Fanny and in *This Life I've Loved* do not check too well with the documented data above.

9. "Lloyd" for John Lloyd, a friend of Sam's, who had befriended Fanny during Sam's expedition to the Coeur d'Alenes, and seems to have been somewhat resentfully in love with her. The boy was called "Sam" until the mid-1880s. I use "Lloyd" to prevent confusion.

10. Harrison, "With Stevenson at Grez," *Century*, December 1916.

11. For reasons best known to herself Fanny told Gelett Burgess after Louis's death that it was not true that she had ever painted. ("An Interview With Mrs. Robert Louis Stevenson," *Bookman* [New York], September 1898.)

12. Harrison, "With Stevenson at Grez," *Century*, December 1916.

13. Bob's greater attraction than Louis's for Fanny in the early stages of the relation is previously undescribed. The source is Fanny's own letters.

14. Balfour, *Life:* I, 160.

15. "Virginibus Puerisque," (SS): II, 30.

16. CXXXVIII in *New Poems*, (SS): XV, 188–89.

17. Stevenson to Henley, National Library.

18. Stevenson to Baxter, Savile Gift.

19. This is published as part of "Reflections and Remarks on Human Life": "I . . . who have hitherto made so poor a business of my life, am now about to embrace the responsibility of another's. We should hesitate to assume command of an army or a trading-smack; shall we not hesitate to become surety for the life and happiness, now and henceforward, of our dearest friend? . . . After that, there is no way left, not even suicide, but to be good. . . ." and so forth—a very interesting example of the way Louis roughed out notions for subtle orchestration in essays.

20. Stevenson to Haddon, *Letters:* II, 86–87.

21. Stevenson to Mrs. Sitwell, National Library.
22. Stevenson to Colvin, Beinecke Collection.
23. Stevenson to Thomas Stevenson, *Letters:* I, 319–20.
24. I have never seen a file of *London*. Its founder, first editor, and proprietor until he died of tubereulosis in 1879 was Robert Glasgow Brown, college friend of Louis's. Lang (*Essays in Little*, 27) called *London* "a quaintly edited weekly paper which nobody read or nobody but the writers in its columns." It lived long enough to acquire a small immortality by publishing the *New Arabian Nights* and some of the worst and the best of Louis's early essays, e.g., "Pan's Pipes" and "A Plea for Gas Lamps." Louis seems to have written for *London* from Paris in its earlier stages, among his contributions being a sketch of Belle Osbourne, for which he got five pounds, and some sort of description of the Paris Bourse. Jenkin roundly scolded Louis for dabbling in this sort of journalism.
25. *Letters to Charles Baxter.*
26. Stevenson to (probably) R. A. M. Stevenson, Strong Collection.
27. Stevenson to Colvin, Beinecke Collection.
28. Stevenson to Colvin, Beinecke Collection.
29. Stevenson to Henley, Savile Gift.
30. Masson, *I Can . . . :* 196. Several years previously the *Encyclopaedia Britannica* had commissioned Louis to do a few articles. His "Béranger" was accepted, his "Burns" rejected as too divergent from generally accepted attitudes toward the subject; the refusal was courteous and the work honorably paid for. No doubt this rejected article, which I have never seen (if it survives), anticipated the longer essay in some respects.
31. Stevenson to Gosse, *Letters:* I, 341.
32. Stevenson to Haddon, *Letters:* II, 194.
33. Baildon, *Robert Louis Stevenson:* 84.

II, 2: *The Gates of Darkness*

1. Stevenson to Henley, National Library.
2. Stevenson to R. A. M. Stevenson, Beinecke Collection.
3. Stevenson to Colvin, *Letters:* I, 351.

4. Stevenson to Baxter, Savile Gift.

5. Thomas Stevenson to Colvin, Beinecke Collection.

6. Stevenson to Henley, National Library.

7. Stevenson to Baxter, Savile Gift.

8. Mrs. Issler (*Happier For His Presence:* 107) shrewdly saw the significance of this fact. For a very minor correction, this is not a "heavy book" but a thinnish pamphlet.

9. Joseph Dwight Strong was a middle-sized, fair-mustached artist, California-born, related to early Hawaiian missionaries, whom philanthropic millionaires sent from San Francisco to study art at Munich. On his return he became popular among San Francisco artists. Fanny mistrusted his developing love affair with Belle, but was apparently willing to use him as intermediary for correspondence with Louis kept secret from Osbourne.

10. Stevenson to Baxter, Savile Gift.

11. Louis would have had a little more money if, early in the summer, he had not instructed Baxter to send £20 to Jacob Vandegrift (Fanny's brother) at Riverside, California. Jake's health was poor and he had moved to Southern California. I do not know whether he was intermediary passing this money on to Fanny or whether she had asked Louis to help out her brother. Another £20 went to Jake from Davos.

12. Charteris, *Life and Letters of Sir Edmund Gosse:* 112.

13. Stevenson to Colvin, Beinecke Collection.

14. Eventually Thomas Stevenson paid the publishers £100 to withdraw the *Emigrant* before publication. It is usually surmised that, in addition to his considering it below Louis's standard, he was also reluctant to have Louis's hardships so conspicuously described. They had been voluntary, of course, but might reflect discredit on the family anyway.

15. *The Amateur Emigrant* (Stone & Kimball, 1895): 54–55.

16. Stevenson to Colvin, *Letters:* I, 350.

17. Stevenson to Henley, National Library. "Paul" is C. Kegan Paul, publisher of Louis's first two books. The long story is presumably "The Story of a Lie." Colvin published part of this letter in *Letters.* It is hopelessly characteristic of his editing that he excised "just bursting into figure but dirty."

18. XCII in *New Poems,* (SS): XV, 160.

19. Stevenson to Colvin, *Letters:* I, 352.

20. Stevenson to Henley, *Letters:* I, 353.
21. *Across the Plains* (Bigelow-Scott): IX, 68.
22. CIII in *New Poems*, (SS): XV, 166.
23. "Monterey," (Bigelow-Scott): IX, 71. Louis's eleven months in California in 1879–80 have been devotedly researched and accounted for by Mrs. Anne B. Fisher in Monterey and Mrs. Anne Roller Issler in San Francisco and the Napa Valley. I rely heavily on both, particularly on Mrs. Issler. Since I have data to which these ladies did not have access when writing, I sometimes disagree with their conclusions, but I have nothing but admiration for their thoroughness and accuracy.
24. Stevenson to Baxter, Savile Gift.
25. One of the few errors of fact in Masson, *Life . . .* is the statement (p. 179) that Louis was "attempting the work of a cowboy on a ranch" when he met this collapse.
26. Stevenson to Colvin, *Letters:* I, 387.
27. Stevenson to Baxter, Savile Gift.
28. Stevenson to Colvin, Beinecke Collection.
29. Stevenson to Simoneau, *Letters:* II, 133.
30. *Scribner's,* August 1920; introduction by George R. Stewart. Louis's by-line was "The Monterey Barbarian."
31. The Widener Collection has a rare exemplar of this.
32. "Monterey," (Bigelow-Scott): IX, 75–76.
33. Collins, *The Doctor Looks at Biography:* 141–43.
34. "Monterey," (Bigelow-Scott): IX, 78.
35. Stevenson to Henley, National Library.
36. Stevenson to Baxter, Savile Gift.
37. Henley to Colvin, Beinecke Collection.
38. Stevenson to Baxter, Savile Gift.
39. Her husband was the original of Speedy in *The Wrecker.* Louis looked up Mrs. Carson when in San Francisco in 1888. She was present as honored guest at the unveiling of the Portsmouth Square monument.
40. Stevenson to Henley, National Library.
41. Issler, *Happier For His Presence:* 92 *et seq.*
42. See Appendix B for Mrs. Issler's disagreement with me on the time of the divorce.
43. Stevenson to Gosse, *Letters:* I, 379.
44. Stevenson to Gosse, *Letters:* I, 366.

45. Stevenson to Colvin, *Letters:* I, 388.

46. California health authorities tell me that it is unlikely that Louis acquired malaria round Monterey or San Francisco. He may have done so while crossing the Middle West in August, for there was then still much malaria in that region. It is just as likely that he had acquired it in France long before, and that some of his difficulties—"my health began to break last winter," quoted in the text—were connected with unrecognized recurring attacks.

47. Stevenson to Gosse, *Letters:* I, 379.

48. This section, in a somewhat expanded form, has been read by an eminent psychiatrist and by a physician specializing in tuberculosis with special interest in its psychiatric aspects. Their exceptions were few, minor, and granted debatable.

49. These attitudes were most closely applied to Louis in Hamilton, *On the Trail of Stevenson:* 69–71: " . . . he always worked most and best in those seasons when he was confined to his bed. Whenever he was well, he played and talked; whenever he was ill he worked and wrote." Hamilton claims that he found Henry James more or less agreeing on this point; see also Raleigh, *Robert Louis Stevenson:* 23. Hamilton was explicit about the alleged hyper-libido of the tuberculous: "In common with many people afflicted with a tendency to tuberculosis, he was troubled, throughout his adolescence, with a superfluity of sexual impulsion." (*On the Trail of Stevenson*, suppressed printing: 132.) See Brown, *International Clinics:* 43rd series, 149, for the extreme scepticism that modern medicine has assumed toward this theory.

50. *The Psycho-pathology of Tuberculosis:* 64–67.

51. Stevenson to R. A. M. Stevenson, *Letters:* II, 82.

52. Balfour, *Life . . .:* I, 253.

53. Brown, *Letters and Papers of John Addington Symonds:* 126.

54. Benjamin, Coleman, and Hornbein, *American Journal of Orthopsychiatry*, October 1948, is a preliminary report of a study on this and related issues: "We have been unable to find any pretuberculous personality features common to all our patients, or even to a large majority of them, either as regards general structure or specific conflict situations. . . . In half of our cases severe emotional conflicts precipitated by actual life situations were present at or shortly before the onset of the clinical tuberculosis . . . strongly supports the often propounded thesis that psychological

factors may play a prominent role in the tuberculous breakdown although it does not prove such factors to be necessary condition for such development."

55. Proudfit, "The Big Round World," *Psychoanalytic Review,* April 1936, is an elaborate and intemperately Freudian description of Louis based primarily on data from the Baby Book that his mother kept of his early years. The troubled layman can only point out that, as in the case of so many psychiatry-minded commentators on Louis, the author is handicapped by imperfect knowledge of the details of Louis's history. For instance, she apparently conceives his travels as always entered on from restlessness—whereas health was usually primary; her attaching high symbolic importance to the double ground-plan of Vailima is unfortunate, since the rectangles were *en échelon*—not, as she conceives them, side by side; it was most distinctly untrue that "Only dark-skinned, gypsy types of women appealed to him; . . ." ; he did not draw and paint "with passionate interest" in childhood, his trials in that line being sporadic and usually connected with literary rather than visual values, etc., etc.

56. Stevenson to Baxter, Beinecke Collection.

57. Stevenson to Henley, *Letters:* I, 386.

58. Stevenson to Jacob Vandegrift, jr., in possession of Mr. Frank A. Thomas.

59. In the *Century.* The book was written at Davos—not, as the marker states, at Silverado. Louis's actual first American publication was a set of poorish verses in the *Atlantic Monthly,* October 1880.

60. This does not put the Russian-Jewish storekeeper of Calistoga in a very favorable light. Louis was much less given than many of his contemporaries, however, to sprinkling his talk and writings with subhuman Jews. When Adelaide Boodle suspected him of anti-Semitism—perhaps from reading *Squatters*—he replied: "What a strange idea to think me a Jew-hater! Isaiah and David and Heine are good enough for me. . . . Were I of Jew blood, I do not think I could ever forgive the Christians; the ghettos would get in my nostrils like mustard or lit gunpowder. . . . I should not be struck at all by Mr. Moss of Bevis Marks. I should still see behind him Moses of the Mount and the Tables and the shining face." (*Letters:* III, 271.)

61. Stevenson to Miss Monroe, *Letters:* III, 31. This, of course, was the Harriet Monroe who founded *Poetry* magazine.

62. Lucas, *The Colvins and Their Friends:* 127–28.

63. *Life in Letters of William Dean Howells:* 332–33. See III, 3, note 9, for further detail on Stevenson and Howells.

64. Masson, *I Can. . . :* 10.

65. Stevenson to Mr. and Mrs. Thomas Stevenson, Beinecke Collection.

66. Masson, (*Life. . . :* 195) says that besom (broom) is figurative Scots for a woman "a little tart in temper . . . 'a handful.'"

67. Stevenson to Cunningham, Masson, *I Can. . . :* 196.

III, 1: *The Magic Mountain*

1. "Letter to a Young Gentleman" . . . , (SS): XXVII, 10.

2. Sanchez, *Life of Mrs. Robert Louis Stevenson:* 86.

3. Vallings, "Stevenson Among the Philistines," *Temple Bar,* February 1901.

4. Osbourne, *An Intimate Portrait of R. L. S.;* 24.

5. Sanchez, *Life of Mrs. Robert Louis Stevenson:* 79.

6. Lockett, *Robert Louis Stevenson at Davos:* 49–50.

7. Colvin preface, *Letters:* I, 4. From 1857 until 1869 Louis's special dog at Heriot Row was Coolin, also a Skye. Louis's Latin epitaph for him is in Masson, *Life:* 73. "The Character of Dogs" has much to say about Coolin.

8. Stevenson to Mrs. Fanny V. de G. Stevenson, Strong Collection.

9. Richard (*Lorna Doone*) Blackmore was appealed to for treatment for Bogue's ears.

10. Gosse, "Stevenson's Relations with Children," *Youth's Companion,* June 15, 1899.

11. Colvin, *Memories & Notes:* 107.

12. Masson, *I Can* . . . : 217–18.

13. Brown, *Letters and Papers of John Addington Symonds:* 130.

14. Brown, *A Book of R. L. S.:* 255.

15. *Cf.* Appendix B for Louis's opinion of Mrs. Symonds.

16. Stevenson to Colvin, *Letters:* II, 14.

17. This, of course, was the occasion for Louis's verses, "In Memoriam: F. A. S.," which often appear in anthologies.

18. Vallings, "Stevenson Among the Philistines," *Temple Bar,* February 1901.

19. This visit has given the present management of the Hôtellerie du Bas-Bréau, successors to Siron, the erroneous impression that it was there that Fanny and Louis first met.

20. Stevenson to Gosse, *Letters:* II, 30–31.

21. This same letter spoils two foolish stories: One, that Louis's mother piously forbade Louis to use oaths in *Treasure Island;* whereas, of course, oaths were automatically taboo in both *Young Folks* and in the general market for books for youngsters that he was trying to tap. In writing ". . . youth and the fond parents have to be consulted," Louis meant not his own parents but parents generally. Two, that one of Henley's grievances against Louis was the theft of Pew out of *Admiral Guinea* for use in *Treasure Island;* actually, Pew was created originally for *Treasure Island.*

22. It was Henderson who moved *Treasure Island* up from the subtitle.

23. Stevenson to Henley, National Library.

24. Stevenson to Gosse, *Letters:* II, 57.

25. Robert Leighton, then on the staff of *Young Folks,* encouraged this by calling the story " . . . a comparative failure . . . did not raise the circulation . . . by a single copy." (Hammerton, *Stevensoniana:* 54–56.) This is, of course, excellent testimony. Leighton printed in the correspondence column of *Young Folks* one letter complaining about *Treasure Island,* to which he answered: "The story is an admirable one, and is as much superior to what are usually distinguished as pirate stories as true power is superior to sham and pretense." This was matched a few weeks later by a commendatory letter. Fanny took as gauge of the relative popularity of serials in *Young Folks* the frequency with which correspondents used the names of their characters as pseudonyms, and on that basis rated both *The Black Arrow* and *Kidnapped* as appealing much more (Vail.: XIII, 4), which was probably justified. But to proceed to thinking *Treasure Island* a liability to the paper, which even Leighton does not claim, is certainly wrong. Failure to illustrate (except the first number) was part of the bargain that left Louis

his book copyright. Henderson continued to run it in relatively favored position, though never on the first page. If its reception had been really bad, he would not have hesitated to drop it in the middle, as he did the following winter with *Sir Claude* when its author petered out under "circumstances which we need not describe in detail." Moreover, if *Treasure Island* had been that bad, the paper would hardly have commissioned *The Black Arrow*.

I enjoyed going back to the original issues of *Young Folks* for *Treasure Island*. Besides Louis, the only discernible contributor of any note was Louisa M. Alcott ("How It All Happened," Christmas number 1881, which had Silver being tipped the black spot.) No. 579 contained "Flint's Pointer" and the following representative sample of serials:

Don Zalva the Brave (lead serial) by Alfred R. Phillips (the paper's standby), author of *Ralpho, Kairon, Desdichado*, etc.: "Loudly did the trumpets sound as the Moorish knights, all clad in polished steel and rich silks and mounted on most beautiful Arab steeds, dashed into the lists. . . ."

Round the World, or, Milo Romer, the Animal King. A Romance of Every Clime. By Captain Frederick Whittaker, author of *Corinda*.

Phyllis and Corydon, or, From the Mountain Shadow to the Footlights. By Mrs. C. A. Read: "The intruder [into the heroine's bedroom] was a woman, tall, thin, and ghost-like. There was not a vestige of colour to be seen in her wrinkled face; the nose and chin nearly met, and her eyes burned with a strange light. . . ."

The Cruise of the Vedette, or, The Strange Fortunes of Max Pennshurst. A Story of American Boy-Life.

Fergus the Foundling, or, The Field of Bannockburn. A Scottish Romance of the Days of Robert the Bruce. By the author of *Theseus, the Hero of Attica; The Young Knight;* etc.

26. Stevenson to Mr. and Mrs. Thomas Stevenson, *Letters:* II, 123.

27. Stevenson to Henley, National Library.

28. Stevenson to Mrs. M. I. Stevenson, *Letters:* II, 236.

29. Stevenson to Henley, National Library.

30. Yeats to Stevenson, in possession of the Osbourne estate.

31. *Cf.* "My First Book," (Vail.: V, xxiv), referring to the pro-

logue to "The Adventures of Sam the Black Fisherman" in *Tales of a Traveller*.

32. *Testimonials in Favour of Robert Louis Stevenson, Advocate*.

33. Balfour, *Life*: I, 227.

34. Lloyd (*An Intimate Portrait of R. L. S.*: 37) wrote that, as a youth, Louis once planned to enlist in the Territorials. Possible but unlikely—there is no other mention of such a scheme.

35. Louis's admiration for Tolstoi seems to have been bestowed on the didactic writings rather than the novels. This was no Russophobia—Louis was mad about Dostoevski in the early French versions.

36. "Stevenson at Play," (SS): XXVII, 374.

37. Stevenson to Henley, *Letters*: II, 89.

38. Stevenson to Henley, National Library.

39. Stevenson to Low, *Letters*: II, 222.

40. Balfour, *Life*: I, 256.

41. Stevenson to Henley, National Library. Mr. Brisk is in *The Pilgrim's Progress* right enough, though there lacking a Christian name: he came courting Mercy in the Second Part.

42. Stevenson to Henley, National Library.

43. Stevenson to Henley, National Library.

44. Stevenson to Henley, National Library.

45. Stevenson to Henley, National Library.

46. Stevenson to Henley, National Library.

47. Stevenson to Henley, *Letters:* II, 81.

48. Balfour, *Life*: I, 238.

III, 2: *Happy Once*

1. The place is lucky still to be standing. During World War II a naval shell pitched into its garden close enough to knock gingerbread work off the rear balcony.

2. Stevenson to Mrs. Sitwell, *Letters*: II, 121.

3. Stevenson to Low, *Letters*: II, 154–55.

4. Stevenson to Colvin, *Letters:* III, 249.

5. Stevenson to Henley, National Library.

6. I have heard gossip about Valentine's having been Louis's mistress, and have traced the probable source of it. Its origin seems to have been Fanny's writing California friends about Valentine's occasional sleeping in Louis's room. Fanny, of course, was the last woman of earth to have failed to be suspicious if any such thing were going on, to write anybody about it if there were any suspicion, or to consent to such an arrangement unless certain everything was proper. Louis's later comment on Valentine's leaving the party at Honolulu does not square with this story either. He would have written far more to Baxter, as a sort of confessional, or said far less. The story may have gained momentum because Hellman took the fugitive "Ne Sit Ancillae Tibi Amor Pudori" to mean that, though he did nothing active about it, Louis had looked on Valentine with indiscreet favor. The assumption is not impressive. The verses show only that somewhere, some time, Louis wrote them of a blonde servant in a house that he lived in. La Solitude had a stair to loiter on, right enough; but, since Valentine was assistant nurse from the start, Louis hardly needed to brush her hand in passing if he wished physical contact. His employing the term "housemaid" leads me to believe that the whole thing sounds much more like Louis at twenty in Heriot Row than Louis at thirty-three in Hyères.

Since I came to the above conclusions, Janet Adam Smith has pointed out (*Robert Louis Stevenson, Collected Poems:* 538) that these verses come from a manuscript book of Louis's in which several other items are dated in the early 1870's. Her notes in this invaluably careful and intelligent compilation are often thus crucially useful.

7. Son of F. H. Yates, early Victorian comedian; veteran hack in farce, fiction, humorous bits; early experimenter with the Victorian equivalent of the gossip column. In 1858 he was expelled from the Garrick Club for an attack on Thackeray in a magazine article, and Dickens's defense of Yates precipitated the long estrangement of the two novelists. In 1883 Yates was prosecuted for criminal libel on the Earl of Lonsdale and was sentenced, after appeal, to four months' imprisonment, of which he served seven weeks.

8. Stevenson to Henley, National Library.

9. Stevenson to Henley, *Letters:* II, 192.

10. Stevenson to R. A. M. Stevenson, National Library.

11. Beinecke Collection.
12. Balfour, *Life:* I, 255.
13. Duncan, "Stevenson's Second Visit to America," *Bookman* (New York), January 1900.
14. Stevenson to Henley, National Library.
15. Stevenson to Miss Cunningham, *Letters:* II, 141.
16. For a literary curiosity, "To Minnie" anticipates T. S. Eliot in its self-consciously poignant use of others' weightier verse as flavoring, though with Louis this never became a habit. It is not important; nor is a different anticipation of Eliot in this bit of Stevenson juvenilia ("Stormy Nights," (SS): XV, 251):

"Why would you hurry me, O evangelist,
  You with the bands and the shilling packet of tracts
  Greatly reduced when taken for distribution? . . . "

17. Sampson, *Concise Cambridge History* . . . : 740.
18. Louis used the background of Royat in *The Enchantress*, an abortive story about a young woman entrapping a youth ruined by gambling. I have never seen the manuscript of this.
19. D. B. Wyndham Lewis, *François Villon:* xiv.
20. Stevenson to Mrs. M. I. Stevenson, *Letters:* II, 176.
21. Stevenson to Mrs. MacMorland, *Letters:* II, 176. This was one of the few people with whom Louis, and particularly Fanny, made good friends at Davos.
22. "Crabbèd Age and Youth," (SS): II, 49–50.
23. Stevenson to Thomas Stevenson, *Letters:* I, 165–66.
24. Stevenson to Henley, National Library.
25. *Hitherto Unpublished Prose Writings.* . . .
26. Stevenson to Colvin, Beinecke Collection.
27. Stevenson to Simoneau, *Letters:* II, 140.
28. Stevenson to Gosse, *Letters:* II, 282.
29. "Virginibus Puerisque," (SS): II, 43.
30. *The Manuscripts of Robert Louis Stevenson's Records of A Family of Engineers:* 52.
31. Japp, *Robert Louis Stevenson:* 144.
32. Sherman, *Critical Woodcuts:* 156–58.
33. "Lay Morals," (SS): II, 152.
34. "Reflections and Remarks on Human Life," (SS): II, 213.
35. Japp, *Robert Louis Stevenson:* 186.

III, 3. *The Tragic Woman and the Flimsy Man*

1. Balfour, *Life:* II, 8.
2. A German land-mine exploding near Skerryvore in 1943 so crazed the structure that it was decided to demolish it. When I visited the site in 1949, nothing was left but the rubble-cluttered, weedy garden and the street name "R. L. Stevenson Avenue" near by.
3. Archer, *The Critic*, November 5, 1887.
4. Stevenson to Henley, National Library.
5. Stevenson to Henley, 8 Howard Place.
6. Stevenson to Henley, National Library.
7. "A Humble Remonstrance," (SS): XIII, 149–50.
8. Students of both owe much to Miss Janet Adam Smith for her *Henry James and Robert Louis Stevenson*, which, with an excellent introduction, collects all the pertinent essays from both in addition to the complete correspondence so far as known.
9. Fairchild was partner in Lee, Higginson & Co. and president of a paper company. He and his wife very probably met the Stevensons in England. He is said to have been interested in American copyright reform and to have helped William Dean Howells to his connection with Harpers after the Osgood firm failed; he certainly knew Howells and introduced him and Louis in New York; they did not get on, though Louis initiated a cordial renewal of the acquaintance from Samoa a few years later. I cannot understand why Fairchild should have commissioned Sargent to paint a man whom he knew only casually, but then Bostonian connections with the arts have always baffled me. Fairchild was, in any case, a generous and useful friend to Louis.
10. This detail seems to have been what inspired the legend that the eccentric Mrs. Stevenson went barefoot to London dinner parties. Sargent's full-face portrait of Louis, as well as his rough sketches of him, is a disappointment.
11. Hammerton, *Stevensoniana:* 151.
12. Meaning Fanny—the phrase is said to come from the presen-

tation copy of *Rab and His Friends* as Dr. Brown inscribed it to
Louis.

13. Boodle, *R.L.S. and his Sine Qua Non*: 9.

14. Gosse, *Critical Kit-Kats*: 296.

15. Charteris, *Life and Letters of Sir Edmund Gosse:* 185.

16. Duncan, "Stevenson's Second Visit to America," *Bookman*
(New York), January 1900.

17. Balfour, *Life*: I, 250.

18. Brown, *John Addington Symonds*: 405. In his *Journals* (346)
André Gide records recantation of the misgivings he felt on first
reading *Jekyll* in English: "Finished the Stevenson. Jekyll's confession is wonderful, and what I wrote yesterday is absurd. If I do not
tear out this page it is for the mortification of rereading it some
day."

19. John Macy (*The Spirit of American Literature*: 38) makes a
parallel point about *Treasure Island:* "If the book were rewritten
so that all the rhythms were knocked out of the sentences, it
would be destroyed for many adults, whereas the essential narrative
would hold the boy almost as well . . . " This point is usually hard
for the young writer to grasp.

20. Actually, the only respectable sums that Louis derived from
the stage came from Sullivan's dramatization of *Jekyll*.

21. Stevenson to James, *Letters:* II, 328.

22. Smith, *Henry James and Robert Louis Stevenson*: 22.

23. London *Morning Post*, December 16, 1901.

24. *The Story of a Lie* (Bigelow-Scott): V, 315.

25. Chesterton, *Robert Louis Stevenson*: 11.

26. These are various salutations on letters of Louis's to Fanny.
Mrs. Fisher (*No More A Stranger*: passim) was in error in taking so
seriously the possibility that Louis habitually called Fanny "Folly."
This seems to have been rather a notion of Lloyd's, and not very
consistent either.

27. "Her speaking voice was low, modulated, and sweet, but
with few inflections, and her husband once compared it to the
pleasantly monotonous flow of a brook running under ice" (Sanchez,
Life of Mrs. Robert Louis Stevenson: 99). This could not possibly
apply to any variety of Hoosier speech. It does sound, however, like
the consequence of determined effort to eliminate local idiosyn-
crasies.

28. "Virginibus Puerisque," (SS): II, 23.
29. "Talk and Talkers," (Vail.): XII, 144.
30. Colvin, *Memories & Notes . . . :* 142–43.
31. Stevenson to Mrs. Jenkin, *Letters:* II, 339–41.
32. Stevenson to Colvin, *Letters:* II, 346.
33. Stevenson to Mrs. Sitwell, *Letters:* I, 215.
34. Stevenson to Colvin, *Letters:* II, 346.
35. Boodle, *R.L.S. and His Sine Qua Non*: 168.

III, 4: *The Gates of Gold*

1. I take Miss Masson's word that, under Scots law, Louis could have refused this arrangement and taken a third of the value of the estate outright, being only surviving child (*Life . . . ,* 254–55). That he did not may mean scrupulous regard for his father's wishes.

2. Stevenson to Henley, *Letters:* II, 347. I leave to better-qualified if incautious theorizers the hint that Louis's lowest emotional ebb coincided with the prelude and postlude of his father's death, and that, once the fact of death was digested, buoyancy was marked.

3. Stevenson to Colvin, Beinecke Collection.

4. Gosse, *Critical Kit-Kats*:297–98. Vallings ("Stevenson Among the Philistines," *Temple Bar*, February 1901) came out of a dispute with Louis about *Our Mutual Friend* with the impression that he felt considerable contempt for Dickens. Actually Louis was a good deal of a Dickensian. He elaborately planned a dramatization of *Great Expectations*, nicknamed Gosse "Wegg," compared a Samoan woman-servant trying to be quiet to Mrs. Nickleby, mentioned that his and Lloyd's scheme for *The Wrecker* was unwittingly like Dickens's techniques in his later novels, etc., etc. It seems to have been Esther Summerson and the Cheeryble Brothers on whom he was especially severe at Davos on this occasion.

5. New York *Herald*, September 9, 1887.

6. At the Fairchilds' Louis met T. R. Sullivan, dramatizer of *Jekyll* for Mansfield. Sullivan gave Fanny and Aunt Maggie his box for the New York opening of *Jekyll*. Lloyd, arriving late from Newport, saw it from the back of the house.

7. Stevenson to Simpson, *Letters:* III, 13. Stevenson to Archer, *Letters:* III, 17.

8. This eventually became the monument-plaque in St. Giles', Edinburgh, with a pen replacing the cigarette. The St. Giles version seems to me much inferior to the circular medallion ornamented by the verses "Youth now flees on feathered foot. . ." that was the earlier version.

St. Gaudens was simultaneously working on his Sherman. Louis asked to meet the tough old general. St. Gaudens's account of the interview is pathetic: The old man's memory was failing, and part of the time he was under the impression that Louis was "one of my boys." But he sharpened up when they got on the subject of military tactics and Stevenson seems to have acquitted himself well talking shop with a man who was unquestionably the nearest he ever came to meeting a first-class general.

9. Balfour, *Life:* II, 35.

10. Eaton, *A Last Memory of Robert Louis Stevenson:* 11.

11. Trudeau, *An Autobiography:* 229.

12. The relation nevertheless was superficially cordial. Later Louis sent Trudeau a complete set of all his books to date, each inscribed separately to a member of the Trudeau household with a couplet of comment; some have already been quoted in the text; other notable items are:

Travels with a Donkey:
> It blew, it rained, it thawed, it snowed, it thundered.
> Which was the Donkey? I have often wondered.

Jekyll and Hyde:
> Trudeau was all the winter at my side.
> I never spied the nose of Mr. Hyde.

13. Stevenson to Fairchild, Beinecke Collection.

14. In Boston she met William James, who told her of his great enthusiasm for Louis and his work. She did not realize at the time that he was brother of Henry James, whom she greatly admired. The philosopher's feeling for Stevenson, whom he had never met, was so warm that he refused to buy less expensive pirated editions of his works. (Colvin note, *Letters:* II, 334.)

15. I do not know how Fanny knew the Storers. They may be

recalled as a wealthy and handsome couple of great social and political ambitions whose indiscretions later involved President Theodore Roosevelt in a most embarrassing tangle.

16. Here are a few out of the first few pages, written supposedly by an American: "I am only vexed he should sometimes talk nonsense." ". . . graduated from the high school." "Panhandle Preference. . . . ."

17. *Silverado Squatters* (Bigelow-Scott): VII, 274.

18. Stevenson to James, *Letters:* III, 8.

19. Barrie was curiously nasty about the *Scribner's* essays, saying of their author (*An Edinburgh Eleven:* 22): " . . . his self-consciousness has become self-satisfaction," going on to hope that they would stay " . . . buried between magazine covers." This apparently was partly suspicion roused by emigration to the vulgar States: " . . . one would like to see him back at Bournemouth writing within high walls." The motif is depressingly familiar. People who knew Louis well, in addition to Barrie, who never met him, were strangely given to wishing him back in a climate that might well have killed him.

20. Stevenson to Gosse, *Letters:* II, 281.

21. San Francisco *Daily Examiner*, June 18, 1888.

22. Stevenson to Miss Boodle, *Letters:* III, 271.

23. Louis may have been encouraged to pursue this line by Droppers's impressive approval of an anticipatory passage in "Pan's Pipes" (*Harvard Monthly*, March 1887.) This was the first solemn criticism of Louis's work published in the States; it seems to have been done at William James's suggestion; *cf.* Colvin note, *Letters:* II, 334.

24. His ability at introspection was proved again at Vailima in 1892 when he wrote F. W. H. Myers, an intelligent pillar of the Society for Psychical Research, an account of some dream-experiences associated with fever that has had little attention and contains much essential Louis: "Experience A. During an illness at Nice I lay awake a whole night in extreme pain. From the beginning of the evening *one part of my mind* became possessed of a notion so grotesque and shapeless that it may best be described as a form of words. I thought the pain was, or was connected with, a wisp or coil of some sort; I knew not of what it consisted or yet where it was, and cared not; only I thought, if the two ends were

brought together, the pain would cease. Now all the time, with *another part of my mind*, which I ventured to think was myself, I was fully alive to the absurdity of this idea, knew it to be a mark of impaired sanity, and was engaged with *my other self* in a perpetual conflict. *Myself* had nothing more at heart than to keep from my wife, who was nursing me, any hint of this ridiculous hallucination; the *other* was bound that she should be told of it and ordered to effect the cure. I believe it must have been well on in the morning before the fever (or *the other fellow*) triumphed, and I called my wife to my bedside, seized her savagely by the wrist, and looking on her with a face of fury, cried 'Why do you not put the two ends together and put me out of pain?'

"Experience B. The other day in Sydney I was seized on a Saturday with a high fever. Early in the afternoon I began to repeat the sound usually written 'mnh,' caught myself in the act, instantly stopped it, and explained to my mother, who was in the room, my reasons for so doing. 'That is the beginning of the mind to wander,' I said, 'and has to be resisted at the outset.' I fell asleep and woke, and for the rest of the night repeated to myself a nonsense word which I could not recall next morning. I had been reading the day before the life of Swift, and all night long one part of my mind (*the other fellow*) kept informing me that I was not repeating the word myself, but was only reading in a book that Swift had so repeated it in his last sickness. The temptation to communicate this nonsense was again strongly felt by *myself* but was on this occasion triumphantly resisted. . . . So much for the two consciousnesses where I can disentangle them; but there is a part of my thoughts that I have more difficulty in attributing. One part of my mind continually bid me remark the transrational felicity of the word, examined all the syllables, showed me that not one was in itself significant, and yet the whole expressed to a nicety a voluminous distress of one in a high fever and his annoyance at and recoil from the attentions of his nurse. It was probably the same part (and for a guess *the other fellow*) who bid me compare it with the nonsense words of Lewis Carroll or the inventions of a lunatic with those of a sane man. But surely it was *myself* (and myself in a perfectly clear-headed state) that kept me trying all night to get the word by heart on the ground that it would afterward be useful in literature if I wanted to deal with mad folk. It must have been *myself* because the *other fellow* believed (or pretended to believe) he was reading the passage in a book where it could always be found when wanted.

"Experience C. The next night *the other fellow* had an explanation ready for my sufferings, of which I can only say that it had something to do with the navy, and that it was sheer undiluted nonsense, had neither end nor beginning, and was insusceptible of being expressed in words. *Myself* knew this; yet I gave way and my watcher was favored with some references to the navy. Not only that: *the other fellow* was annoyed—or I was annoyed on two inconsistent accounts: first, because he had failed to make his meaning comprehensible; and second, because the nurse displayed no interest. The *other fellow* would have liked to explain further; but *myself* was much hurt at having been got into this false position, and would be led no further. . . I have called the one person *myself* and the other the *other fellow*. It was myself who spoke and acted; the other fellow seemed to have no control of the body or the tongue; he could only act through myself, on whom he brought to bear a heavy strain, resisted in the one case, triumphant in the two others. Yet I am tempted to think that I know the other fellow; I am tempted to think he is the dreamer described in the Chapter on Dreams to which you refer." Myers, *Human Personality*. . . . (first published in *Proc. Soc. Psychical Research:* IX, 9 *et seq.*) Louis probably met Myers at the Taylors', where both were frequent visitors.

III, 5: *Case of the Pomeranian Dog*

1. Masson, *Life:* 271. The facts of this episode were largely muffled up until there became available the correspondence about it —the famous "Quarrel Letters"—deposited by Charles Baxter in the Advocates' Library. They were first copiously used by John Connell in *William Ernest Henley* (1949). My selection of Louis's letters in the text includes numerous passages that Connell omitted and considerable material to which he did not have access elsewhere. My disagreements with Connell arise, no doubt, from his understandable impulse to exercise the charity that a biographer

owes his subject. I recognize and cheerfully repudiate the notion that the same could be said of my judgment favorable to Louis. It is probably significant that, reviewing Connell's book (*New Yorker*, December 24, 1949), Edmund Wilson, though lacking thorough acquaintance with the episode, had a marked impression that Henley behaved much worse than Louis.

2. Stevenson to Henley, 8 Howard Place.

3. As editor of the *Magazine of Art*, Henley warmly defended Rodin in the controversy over his "naturalism." Rodin did a fine bust of Henley. Through Henley, Louis met Rodin and occasionally corresponded with him. Rodin's gift to Louis of a cast of *Le Printemps* was set up first at Skerryvore, then at Vailima. Henley later hinted that a scheme for Rodin to do a bust of Louis was dropped because the sculptor had too clearly discerned Louis's spiritual emptiness (*Pall Mall Magazine*, December 1901).

4. The best of hers that I have seen is "Spring and the Wayfarer" in the *Scots Observer*, February 21, 1891:

> ". . .Why she was born or how she was bred
> She knows no more than the thistledown airs
> Ask why the white thorns shake and pass.
> Who is there knows? who is there cares?
> The lost world makes time for playing,
> All may go dancing, dreaming, maying. . . ."

5. John Connell, *William Ernest Henley:* 113–14.

6. Stevenson to Henley "Quarrel Letters," National Library.

7. John Connell, *William Ernest Henley:* 116–17.

8. *Ibid.:* 118.

9. Mrs. de Mattos to Stevenson, "Quarrel Letters," National Library.

10. Stevenson to Baxter, "Quarrel Letters," National Library.

11. Stevenson to Baxter, "Quarrel Letters," National Library.

12. Stevenson to Baxter, "Quarrel Letters," National Library.

13. Stevenson to Baxter, "Quarrel Letters," National Library.

14. Stevenson to Baxter, "Quarrel Letters," National Library.

15. Stevenson to Baxter, Savile Gift.

16. Stevenson to Mrs. Fanny V. de G. Stevenson, *Letters:* III, 57. Colvin read "flaming" for "flimsy."

17. John Connell feels that there was much smugness about

Louis's final letter to Mrs. de Mattos, exhorting her to confess un-scrupulous behavior and ask pardon, which he published in part in *William Ernest Henley:* 126. To me, who know Louis better, the full text sounds like a man relying on monosyllabic formality to keep himself in hand, and indicates very strongly that he still felt that his cousin had betrayed him by distorting or refusing to con-firm facts that he knew her to know as well as he did.

18. Stevenson to Baxter, Savile Gift. The verses to be quoted are at the end of "A Christmas Sermon."

19. Stevenson to Baxter, Savile Gift.

20. Stevenson to Baxter, Savile Gift.

21. Henley, *Poems* (1926): 143.

22. John Connell, *William Ernest Henley:* 364–65.

23. Balfour, *Life:* II, 214.

24. Henley, *Pall Mall Magazine*, December 1901.

25. Sherman, *The Emotional Discovery of America:* 181.

26. Unless otherwise noted, the above extracts are all Henley, *Pall Mall Magazine*, December 1901.

27. Colby, *Bookman* (New York), February 1902.

28. December 16, 1901.

29. "Literary Leprosy," *Saturday Review*, November 30, 1901: "in plain words . . . cowardly and malignant." The writer deplores the sentimental halo growing round Stevenson's memory, but: "Instead of fair criticism . . . we find a case stated against him wholly by innuendo. Anyone who knew Stevenson and his work only by what Mr. Henley has said of him would conceive him a poor creature who sometimes had a trick of talking well, to whom fortune and friends, especially Mr. Henley, were marvellously kind, while he was anything but equally considerate to his friends; and that withal, the half had not been said against him that might have been, had the writer of the article been a less generous man . . . really artistic malice . . . a familiar friend's contribution to his dead friend's literary reputation. Savage criticism would have been generous beside it."

30. Henley, *Poems* (1926): 24.

IV, 1: *The Isles of Voices*

1. Bok, *The Americanization of Edward Bok:* 113–14.
2. San Francisco *Chronicle*, June 8, 1888.
3. Stevenson to Mrs. Fairchild, *Letters:* III, 188.
4. Ballantyne, who had never been in the Islands, described coconuts fresh from the tree as lacking the heavy husk. This error determined him never again to use a background without first-hand acquaintance—hence his trips to lighthouses, voluntary service with firemen, etc.
5. Stevenson to Mrs. Fairchild, *Letters:* III, 187–88; Stevenson to Mrs. Sitwell, *Letters:* 1, 269. Bougainville called Samoa the Navigator Islands in token of the natives' canoes and seamanship. The name persisted until well into the nineteenth century, but is now rarely used.
6. The long fragment that I have seen is not much loss.
7. *The Wrecker* (SS): I, 130.
8. Colvin (*Letters:* 1, 394) says Louis met Stoddard as described in *The Wrecker*. Stoddard says they met at Strong's studio (*Exits and Entrances:* 14).
9. Johnstone, *Recollections of* . . . ; 16 *et seq.*
10. Stevenson to R. A. M. Stevenson, *Letters:* III, 100. Louis was hardly enough of a seaman to afford such crisp opinions. Otis wrote: "With perhaps the exception of the fisherman's stay-sail, all canvas was in due proportion to the yacht's measurements . . . as a vessel she was perfectly safe, and during her long cruise in the South Seas the water never came into her cockpit but once" (Johnstone, *Recollections of* . . . : 16 *et seq.*) At the Marquesas and again at Honolulu, the *Casco* met the *Nyanza,* yacht of the Dewar family. The Dewars and the Stevensons seem to have got on well enough, but there was trouble between their respective crews, partly in consequence of a letter from the *Casco* party published in the Edinburgh press that called the *Nyanza* ugly. (Cf. McGaw, *Stevenson in Hawaii:* 32–33.)
11. Stevenson to Colvin, *Letters:* III, 76.
12. Mrs. M. I. Stevenson, *From Saranac to the Marquesas* . . . : 185.

13. *Ibid.:* 67–68.
14. Stevenson to Baxter, *Letters:* III, 74.
15. "Farewell," (SS): XV, 167.
16. *The Wrecker* (SS): XXI, 189–90.
17. Stevenson to Colvin, *Letters:* 113–14.
18. Stevenson to Baxter, National Library.
19. *In the South Seas* (Vail.): XVI, 15.
20. The Marquesas is one of the three major groups of South Sea Islands that I have never visited. I know most of the rivals with which the group is usually compared for rugged beauty and, from the evidence of photographs and drawings, believe them as lovely as any. The above general description is guided by general knowledge of Polynesian conditions as well as by pictures and written accounts.
21. Stevenson to Colvin, *Letters:* III, 70.
22. In most of the Islands this trend is now reversed. See my *Anatomy of Paradise:* 378–85.
23. "Kanaka" originally meant "man" in Hawaiian; it has cognates in most Polynesian languages. In the Islands it gradually came to mean "native" in a somewhat derogatory sense, even being applied to distinguish Melanesians from whites.
24. In speaking of such chiefs as Moanatini, Moë, etc., it is difficult not to want quotation marks about "prince," "princess," or (in such cases as that of Tembinok') "king." Their authority was often real, in Stevenson's as well as pre-white times, but their relation to their inferiors was not congruent with that of the European subject to a king proper. Europeans applied such titles to South Sea dignitaries before these distinctions were well realized. In Hawaii, however, a monarchy developed from a high chiefly family did to some extent succeed in approximating the European regal institution; hence King Kalakaua does not so much need quotation marks in the next chapter.
25. Stevenson to Colvin, *Letters:* III, 70–72. Stevenson to Payn, *Letters:* III, 132.
26. Mrs. M. I. Stevenson, *From Saranac to the Marquesas . . . :* 115.
27. "Memoirs of an Islet" (SS): XIII, 66.
28. Stevenson to Colvin, *Letters:* III, 73.
29. Mrs. Fanny V. de G. Stevenson to Colvin, *Letters:* III, 84.
30. *Ibid.:* 85.

31. Prepared by soaking chunks of firm, raw fish first in sea water, then in lime-juice, which has a "cooking" effect; eaten with a dip of sea water and coconut cream (expressed from the mature nut), it is very toothsome, rather like superior crabmeat. Only quick-frozen fish should be used among us, to avoid infection with tape-worm.

32. "To an Island Princess" (SS): XIV, 153–54.

33. Stevenson to Baxter, *Letters:* III, 121.

34. The wrap-around skirt (*sulu* in Fiji, *lavalava* in Samoa) con-trived from a length of cloth by missionaries trying to improvise a modest garment for native converts. In Samoa and Tahiti women may wrap it bosom to knee—what the movies call a *sarong,* which is Malay.

35. Sanchez (*Life of Mrs. Robert Louis Stevenson:* 143) has a more picturesque story: Aunt Maggie had a prayer-meeting of natives on the ship. Among prayers offered was one for her safety. Otis, who despised missionaries and their works, said something rude and struck the mainmast with his fist—which sank into a previously unsuspected patch of dry rot. . . . But Louis's letters, otherwise most explicit on the episode, mention no such detail. Otis was too capable to have been so abjectly ignorant of such damage at eye-level. Nor is the incident mentioned in any of Aunt Maggie's highly detailed letters home. I conclude that this is one of the colorful stories added to the Stevenson family legends after Louis's death.

36. Louis never saw Teriitera again. But he had at least one brim-mingly affectionate letter from him; and when, later that year, a hurricane ruined Tahiti's food-crops, the Rich One duly sent £50 to buy tide-over supplies.

37. Stevenson to R. A. M. Stevenson, *Letters:* III, 102.

38. Stevenson to Baxter, *Letters:* III, 99.

IV, 2: *Landfall*

1. Louis first met and was embarrassed by the telephone at Calis-toga in 1880. He liked it no better in Honolulu; during his stay at the Sans Souci at Waikiki in 1893 he wrote a letter to the *Pacific Commercial Advertiser* defending the establishment against be-

ing classed as a "disorderly house" (which it technically was, since it served drinks irregularly) and alleging that the telephone was the only disorderly thing in it: ". . . bleating like a deserted infant from the dining room. I dare never, from a variety of prudential considerations, approach this interesting instrument myself; . . . The introduction of the telephone into our bed and board, into our business and bosoms, partakes of the nature of an intrusion." (*Pacific Commercial Advertiser*, October 6, 1893; from Johnstone, *Recollections of* . . . : 108–109.) Nevertheless *The Wrecker* was one of the first pieces of fiction to use the telephone in its plot, being barely outdated by *A Connecticut Yankee* . . . (1889).

2. "Haole" is Hawaiian for "outsider"—it gradually came to be used to label the white interloper as distinguished from the native proper.

3. Stevenson to Baxter, *Letters:* III, 105.

4. Louis wrote some pretty verses to Kaiulani when she left for Europe with Cleghorn in 1890 on the same ship as Aunt Maggie: *Songs of Travel*, XXX, (SS): XIV, 155.

5. Perhaps it was the King himself. In the discrepancy of tone between Louis's first letter to the *Times* and the parallel material in *A Footnote to History*, there is plain implication that he had not yet heard Joe Strong's account of the embassy in any detail when writing the letter.

6. London *Times*, February 10, 1890.

7. *Scribner's*, March 1891.

8. Stevenson to Mrs. Fanny V. de G. Stevenson, *Letters:* III, 126 –28.

9. Even now, when leprosy is considered much less contagious, it takes resolution to shake hands with a known leper, as I once found.

10. Stevenson to Payn, *Letters:* III, 132.

11. Stevenson to Colvin, *Letters:* III, 130.

12. Johnstone, *Recollections of* . . . : 76–80 et seq.

13. *An Open Letter to the Reverend Dr. Hyde of Honolulu*, (SS): XXVI, 40; 44.

14. So Chatto & Windus sent the royalties from the *Letter* to the Leper Fund. (Stevenson to Colvin, *Letters:* III, 312.)

15. Stevenson to Mrs. Fairchild, *Letters:* III, 186–87. The wounded colleague is unquestionably "Father" Damon, to whom Louis had given apologetic warning of the impending letter to

Hyde (Stevenson to Mrs. M. I. Stevenson, *Letters: III,* 164–65.) There is some indication that his relations with Damon were again cordial in 1893.

16. Stevenson to Colvin, *Letters:* III, 113.

17. Copra is coconut meat dried for packing and shipping; it is the principal cash crop of many South Sea islands.

18. Fanny V. de G. Stevenson to Mrs. Sitwell, *Letters:* III, 107. Later, at least once, she seems to have pined to get back to sea after a long time ashore. (Stevenson to James, *Letters:* III, 180.)

19. Stevenson to Baxter, *Letters:* III, 120; 121.

20. *Pacific Commercial Advertiser,* June 24, 1889.

21. "Trade room" is almost self-explanatory: a space below decks fitted with shelves and counter for display and sales during stops.

22. According to Fanny (*The Wrecker,* preface, [Vail.]: XVII, xxii), Reid wound up in jail in Levuka for selling a vessel he did not own.

23. MacCallum was actually a hold-over from the previous voyage which he had made as deck hand. His *Adrift in the South Seas,* written in his old age, takes cautious sifting, but, after proper discount, gives valuable detail.

24. A quasi-lethal distillate traded to South Seas natives when there were no restrictions on such enterprise.

25. This is the way I read the Stevensons' experience with Tembinok' in the light of general South Seas custom. It is not Louis's.

26. See Note 11 below, in "Tusitala," IV, 4.

27. Stevenson to Colvin, *Letters:* III, 138.

28. Fanny V. de G. Stevenson to Colvin, *Letters:* III, 124–25.

29. Stevenson to Colvin, *Letters:* III, 113.

30. The same ability is evident in *Kidnapped;* only it appears that the modern American student lacks even the vague knowledge of "the Forty-Five" necessary to feel the values of the book. David Daiches tells me that *Kidnapped* baffled his students until he gave them the fundamental story of the two Pretenders.

31. Colvin notes this in *Letters:* III, 264.

32. Colvin to Baxter, Savile Gift. The *Sun* ran thirty-four instalments in its Sunday magazine section, of which only seventeen were included in the eventual book. In England *Black and White*

had the British serialization for £1000, probably less McClure's 20% commission (Colvin to Baxter, Savile Gift).

33. McClure, *My Autobiography:* 192.

34. Stevenson to Colvin, *Letters:* III, 257.

35. Janet Adam Smith (*Robert Louis Stevenson:* 105–106; 109) well defines its objective as " . . . a solid, complete view of his subject, illuminating it from as many angles as possible, not the usual tourist's bundle of snapshot impressions . . . a book that did not need its author's name to commend it," and concludes that it was ". . . the most solid of his general writings, and far from being the least readable."

36. Stevenson to Henley, *Letters:* II, 192.

37. Stevenson to Gosse, *Letters:* II, 281.

38. "The Day After Tomorrow," (SS): II, 252.

39. "Letter to a Young Gentleman . . ."; (SS) XXVII, 6.

40. Stevenson to Schwob, *Letters:* III, 241.

41. Stevenson to Low, *Letters:* IV, 263.

42. *A Footnote to History* (SS): XXVI, 284.

43. Like practically everybody else who knew Louis, Moors wrote about him: *With Stevenson in Samoa* (1910). He says that he went out to meet the *Equator* in consequence of a letter from Joe Strong telling him of the Stevensons' probable presence in her. Since Strong too was in the ship it is curious that Moors does not mention him as one of the party nor make it clear that the letter of introduction was superfluous. The reason may be that Moors is known to have sided with Strong later when Belle was determining to divorce her husband—an attitude that badly strained relations between Moors and Vailima. In general Moors's material must be approached with caution. His memory obviously played him false in several instances—for instance, his account of how McClure came to San Francisco to persuade Louis to do the South Sea letters, and of how Moors himself midwifed the arrangement with McClure that permitted Louis to drop the letters; as well as such errors as saying that Louis visited Easter Island, etc., etc.

44. Balfour, *Life:* II, 141.

45. Stevenson to Baxter, *Letters:* III, 175.

46. In the South Seas, from British influence, "bush" means wilderness with substantial growth of vegetation.

47. The figures are from Triggs in *Cassell's,* Vol. 21, 183. This

reputable journalist sent his text to Louis for correction, so the amounts are probably reliable, though Louis may not have had too accurate an idea himself of the whole cost of Vailima. Fanny told the Colvins that the cost was ten Chile dollars an acre, then about £1/8/4.

48. Stevenson to Lady Taylor, *Letters:* III, 153.

49. "Vailima" means "five streams." Four were all that the place actually afforded, but Louis liked the sound and insisted on "five."

50. Stevenson to James, *Letters:* III, 179.

51. Stevenson to Colvin, Beinecke Collection.

52. Stevenson to Mrs. Sitwell, National Library.

IV, 3: *Le Ona*

1. Low (*A Chronicle of Friendships:* 400) says that Stevenson and La Farge had met casually in the Century Association in 1888.

2. *Letters of Henry Adams:* passim.

3. Sanchez (*Life of Mrs. Robert Louis Stevenson:* 219) tells of how Louis reveled in this legend, describing the lady as a Moroccan and "black but a damned fine woman."

4. *Henry Adams and His Friends:* 201–202.

5. Samoa has no malaria, but does have a great mosquito-transmitted hazard in filariasis, which, in exaggerated stages, produces elephantiasis. Fanny made some fairly shrewd guesses about the disease in her Vailima diary. Most whites living in Samoa for some years are to some extent infected.

6. "Taro" is a fleshy-bulbed plant, cousin of Jack-in-the-pulpit, that supplies principal carbohydrates in many South Sea Islands.

7. Stevenson to Meredith, *Letters:* IV, 227.

8. Stevenson to Colvin, *Letters:* IV, 113; Stevenson to Miss Taylor, *Letters:* IV, 117.

9. "The Woodman," (SS): XIV, 165–67.

10. Hammerton, *Stevensoniana:* 100.

11. "Lavalava" is equivalent to the Tahitian *pareu;* see above, Note 34 in "The Isles of Voices," IV, 1.

12. Stevenson to Colvin, *Letters:* IV, 164.

13. Stevenson to Colvin, *Letters:* IV, 167.

14. Fraser, *In Stevenson's Samoa:* 24.

15. Mulligan to State Department, December 5, 1894.

16. Cusack-Smith to Lord Salisbury, July 19, 1892; Foreign Office 58/274, Despatch 23.

17. Stevenson to Colvin, *Letters:* IV, 100.   *

18. "Tutuila" (SS) XXVI, 52.

19. "Papalagi" (pronounced *'palangi*) means the outsider, usually the white man, or the place he comes from.

20. I have seen this called first publication of *The Bottle Imp.* The actual first was in *Black and White,* March 28 and April 4, 1891. I have also seen Louis reproached for stealing the plot from an old German folk tale. He acknowledged the debt both in the original subtitle of the story ("A Cue from an Old Melodrama") and in a note usually published with it crediting "a piece once made popular by the redoubtable O. Smith." Fanny says that O. Smith was author of an absurd transpontine melodrama on this theme that Louis acquired from Sir Percy Shelley's collection of such things for private theatricals: no doubt Smith got it from the German tale, whatever it may be (Preface to Volume XV, Vailima Edition: 271–72).

21. Similarly Islanders tend to think of all pictures, whether photographs, drawings, or what not, as representing actual scenes and events. Thus the Biblical lantern-slides that the Stevensons showed on Makin produced something of a religious revival. Backsliding local skeptics were confounded by actually seeing Moses in the bulrushes, and so forth.

22. Mrs. M. I. Stevenson, *From Saranac to the Marquesas:* 247.

23. Sanchez, *Life of Mrs. Robert Louis Stevenson:* 192.

24. Clarke states that he recruited the Vailima servants, using his own prestige to reassure their relatives ("Robert Louis Stevenson in Samoa," *Yale Review,* January 1921). He probably did so with the Protestants early among them, but is most unlikely that he, being an eminent Protestant, had anything to do with the Catholics who gradually came to predominate on the Vailima staff.

25. Undated interview in the San Francisco *Examiner* in the Harry Elkins Widener collection.

26. Stevenson to Colvin, *Letters:* IV, 239–40.

27. Stevenson to Colvin, *Letters:* IV, 55. There is some doubt

whether "Tusitala" was coined specially to identify Louis, the first professional writer of whom Samoans had been aware, or whether it already existed in the language. For the translation, Mr. F. J. H. Grattan of the Department of Native Affairs in Samoa tells me that "writer of books" is not close to the original sense nor yet "teller of tales." *Tala* in Samoan seems to mean an elaborate rumor as well as a story. Samoans now use it to identify any professional writer. I was startled to hear myself called "tusitala" in Samoan villages.

28. "Kava" is the root of a kind of pepper plant which is ceremoniously grated or chewed and steeped in water; the infusion is then drunk in ceremonies significant of the drinker's relative prestige in the community. Many claim that it is cooling; others that, in quantity enough, it is intoxicating.

29. Stevenson to Colvin, *Letters:* III, 288.

30. "The Family," (SS) XV, 219.

31. *Across the Plains,* (Bigelow-Scott): IX, 60.

32. Masson, *I Can . . . :* 282–83.

33. Stevenson to Colvin, *Letters:* IV, 28–29.

34. Balfour, *Life:* II, 227.

35. *The Presbyterian Monthly,* April 1, 1893: "I thought when I came here that perhaps a text would be suitable. The first text that occurred to me was this: 'Is Saul also among the prophets?' . . . I am an old and, I hope I may be allowed to say, a very good Presbyterian, the proof of which is that I have sat out a sermon of one hour and thirty minutes. It was delivered at the parish church of Wick and, by remarkable coincidence, the parish church is still standing in support of my statement. . . ."

36. Stevenson to Miss Boodle, *Letters:* IV, 294–95.

37. Stevenson to Colvin, *Letters:* IV, 300.

38. Stevenson to Barrie, *Letters:* IV, 306.

39. *Songs of Travel,* (SS): XIV, 150.

40. *A Footnote to History,* (SS): XXVI, 157.

41. Stevenson to Colvin, *Letters:* III, 289.

42. Stevenson to Colvin, *Letters:* III, 304.

43. Stevenson to Colvin, *Letters:* IV, 171.

44. London *Times,* November 17, 1891.

45. This was the Rev. Arthur E. Claxton, whose account of knowing Stevenson (*Chambers's Journal,* October 1922) had no

hint of this feud. To save future researchers trouble, here is a summary of available facts: According to a memorandum of Haggard's (FO 58/266, Public Record Office), Claxton hoped to be another Shirley Baker. He was Native Advocate before the Land Commission set up by the Berlin Act to settle Samoan land claims. On July 18, 1891, while discussing Samoan affairs with Harold M. Sewall, the American consul, he speculated provocatively about the possibility of arresting Mataafa if the rebel chief came to Apia in consequence of a letter of invitation that Sewall had recently written. Sewall renounced the idea of such treachery. Claxton suggested that it be done in a manner to lay suspicion on the Germans. Louis put the story in *A Footnote* in a form implying that the scheme had been the principal occasion of Claxton's call on Sewall. Probably in consequence of this damaging tale, Claxton was asked to resign from his post as Native Advocate after his return from London, where a letter of Moors's to the L. M. S. had preceded him and got him into hot water. His threatened suit was technically impossible because Carruthers, Moors's attorney, would not take the case and Moors had hastily retained in behalf of Stevenson the only other lawyer in Apia. By April 1892, Claxton had left Apia, alleging that it was necessary for his wife's health. Sewall was by then back in the States. His letter describing the interview was a crucial document at the mission hearing. It substantially confirmed Louis's account but left Claxton the technical loophole of having been merely speculating out loud, not directly proposing a course of action. In his article Claxton claimed that, on leaving Samoa, he had received from Louis a letter introducing him to Charles Baxter, which was never presented. If this is not altogether a lie— and the reverend gentleman seems to have been a rather untrustworthy witness—this may have been a matter of identifying his counsel in case Claxton should bring suit in Britain. Moors, *With Stevenson in Samoa*, is well enough documented on this affair to be trustworthy for once.

46. Chatfield's letter to the London *Times* (printed January 11, 1893) ends: "It seems to me that, had Mr. Stevenson employed his time and exercised his undoubted talents in his legitimate business, instead of dabbling in Samoan politics and discovering mare's nests in the administration of their official functions by the Chief Justice of Samoa, and the President of the Municipal Council and Ad-

viser of the King, he would have gained more legitimate *kudos* and have avoided the egregious mistakes and exaggerations of ordinary events which his letters to the *Times* demonstrate. Mr. Stevenson is, I confidently assert, no friend to Samoa, although he poses as the champion of the oppressed and long-suffering inhabitants." His rebuttal is elaborate; but, particularly on the two strangest antics of the Government—the dynamite under the jail and the secret purchase of the newspaper—most unimpressive. The effect he leaves is that all of the bad judgment that Louis imputed and nine-tenths of the actual facts can stand unaltered. The occasion of Louis's apology was a letter to Chatfield from former German Consul Stuebel (whom Louis highly respected) taking some of the edge off the newspaper-purchase story. Characteristically, Louis's letter to Chatfield takes a great deal of trouble to assure his accuser that there is no reason why their public differences should flaw cordial social relations between Chatfield's and Louis's family.

47. Stevenson to Colvin, *Letters:* IV, 46.

48. Stevenson to Colvin, *Letters:* IV, 44.

49. Endorsement (initials illegible) on FO 58/266, Document 23 (political).

50. Stevenson to Colvin, *Letters:* IV, 90.

51. No. 1 of 1892/ A REGULATION/ . . . FOR THE MAINTENANCE OF PEACE AND GOOD ORDER IN SAMOA . . . Office of the High Commissioner for the Western Pacific, Suva, Fiji; supplied me by the courtesy of Mr. Leonard G. Usher, Public Information Officer. Dated December 29, 1892.

52. Ripon to Thurston, April 14, 1893. E. F. Benson ("The Myth of Robert Louis Stevenson") saw fit to imply that Louis's fear of deportation was mere childish display of an exaggerated idea of his own importance. The correspondence in the files of both the Colonial Office and the Foreign Office leaves no doubt whatever that Thurston's intentions were pretty grim until his superiors cooled him off. Benson probably got this notion from Claxton's account (Masson, *I Can Remember* . . . : 252) of Thurston's telling him in Sydney that he had consistently felt that deporting Stevenson would be a mistake.

53. Stevenson to Mark Twain, in the Mark Twain papers at the University of California.

54. Johnstone, *Recollections of* . . . : 92.

55. Stevenson to Colvin, *Letters:* IV, 254.

56. The Samoan names subscribed are those of the chiefs opposite their native districts. This Mataafa was not the exiled "king" but a minor chief whose name was accented somewhat differently. This is not the usual translation, but one, more literal and more accurate, supplied me by Mr. F. J. H. Grattan, of the Native Affairs Department, Trusteeship of Western Samoa.

IV, 4: *Tusitala*

1. Colvin to Baxter, Beinecke Collection.

2. These quotations are all Stevenson to Barrie; source is largely Brown, *A Book of R. L. S.*, plus excisions supplied out of Masson, *Life* . . . : 331. Brown pages are 188; 251; 236–37.

3. Says Colvin (preface to the first edition of *Fables*): "Among the multitude of new interests and images which filled his mind during the last six years of his life, he seems to have given little thought to the proposed book of fables. . . . That collection, as it stood at the time of his death, was certainly not what its author had meant it to be. It may even be doubted whether it would have seen the light had he lived; . . ." See Colvin's note in *Letters*, (SS): I, 203–204 for his guess as to which items may have been begun in 1874; also Louis himself (*Letters:* I, 205) about "my *Fables*." The trouble is that this could conceivably refer to his review of Lytton's *Fables in Song*. Gosse says (preface to Pentland Edition) that Louis *began* the *Fables* at Bournemouth in 1887. Balfour (*Life* . . . : II, 171) implies that "The Song of the Morrow" originated in Samoa. It certainly has the air of being out of the same barrel as "The Waif-Woman" and "The Isle of Voices" in technical handling.

4. Colvin note, *Letters:* I, 204.

5. Stevenson to Colvin, Beinecke Collection.

6. Quoted in Snyder, "Paradox and Antithesis in Stevenson's Essays," *Journal of English and Germanic Philology:* XIX (1920), 542.

7. Lucas, *The Colvins and Their Friends:* 276.

8. They did, when published, with Colvinish emendations and

excisions, as *Vailima Letters*, in 1895. Later Colvin twice expanded the collection, ending with the full four volumes of *Letters* used in this biography.

9. This includes: *Island Nights Entertainments; Catriona; A Footnote to History; Ebb-Tide; Weir of Hermiston; St. Ives; Waif-Woman;* the false starts of *Heathercat* and *Young Chevalier;* and some allowance for final work on *The Wrecker* and later parts of *South Seas.*

10. *The Wrecker*, (SS): XXI, 421.

11. The extent to which *The Wrecker* was founded on the actual episode of the wreck of the *Wandering Minstrel* on Midway Island is best judged after reading *John Cameron's Odyssey*, including Farrell's intelligent and extensive notes. The crux of the Louis-Lloyd plot—a sea captain's forcing castaways to pay all their resources for rescue—may well have been (as Farrell surmises) told Louis by Captain Walker. Certainly Fanny (Prefatory Note to *The Wrecker*, Vailima edition: 6–7) states pretty flatly that Louis got such a story about the *Minstrel* in Honolulu. Otherwise there is little about the *Minstrel* story, except the setting on Midway, to connect it with the novel.

12. Stevenson to R. A. M. Stevenson, *Letters:* IV, 321.

13. *The Wrecker*, (SS): XXI, 187.

14. Stevenson to Colvin, *Letters:* III, 292.

15. According to press releases, Universal-International is planning a film-version of the *Beach* under title of *Pantang.* So far as I can find out, this is the first time it has been filmed. Louis revived the hero of the *Beach* in drafting (apparently for submission to Henley's *Scots Observer*) a long letter, never published, entitled *Plain John Wiltshire on the Samoan Situation.* The manuscript is in the Huntington Library.

16. Stevenson to Shorter, *Letters to an Editor.*

17. Stevenson to Colvin, *Letters:* IV, 48.

18. Stevenson to R. A. M. Stevenson, *Letters:* IV, 323.

19. "In his desire to accept all facts loyally and simply, it fell within [Whitman's] program to speak at some length and with some plainness on what is, for I really do not know what reason, the most delicate of subjects. Seeing in that one of the most serious and interesting parts of life, he was aggrieved that it should be looked upon as ridiculous or shameful. . . . We may be thoroughly

conscious that his end is improving; that it would be a good thing if a window were opened on these close privacies of life; . . . But . . . we feel that he was not the man for so difficult an enterprise . . . where, by a little more art, we might have been solemnized ourselves, it is too often Whitman alone who is solemn in the face of an audience somewhat indecorously amused." (*Familiar Studies*, [Vail.]: II, 141–42.)

20. Louis's widest excursions into forms experimental for his time were his free verses, acknowledgedly somewhat in imitation of Baudelaire's *Petits Poèmes en Prose*, done in the same spring that produced the lost "On the Spirit of Spring" that was so improperly pagan (see Appendix B). They appear in *New Poems*, (SS): CXCII, CXCII (II), CXCV, CXCVI, CXCVIII, No doubt it is significant that these also contain the most overt eroticism in all Louis's surviving works.

21. There is small reason to flaw a consistent picture of a whole man with odd and somewhat lip-licking efforts, to make a point of Louis's occasional vivid appreciation of women's appearance. A case in point is the effort to find significance in the excisions that Colvin made (in Stevenson to Colvin, *Letters*: III, 280–81) in Louis's comments on the beauty of a Samoan woman servant. The cuts then made have actually been privately reprinted as if invaluable—whereas, though it was old-maidish of Colvin to cut, they do not materially alter the tenor of Louis's remarks.

22. Entitled *David Balfour* in American publication.

23. Stevenson to Colvin, *Letters*: IV, 326–27.

24. Stevenson to Colvin, *Letters*: III, 232.

25. *St. Ives* was almost finished when Louis died. Because magazine serialization had already begun, Quiller-Couch finished it along plot lines that Louis had already laid out, involving the fantastic balloon escape and the Yankee privateer. Few claim much quality for *St. Ives*, though it is a good hack job and does show the vividness with which Louis could recall Edinburgh and environs. It is interesting, however, for the contrast—proving that there is always a difference between the best chalk and the worst cheese—between the handling of Louis's sections and that of Quiller-Couch's.

26. Stevenson to R. A. M. Stevenson, *Letters*: IV, 287.

27. Muir, "Robert Louis Stevenson," *Modern Scot*, Autumn 1931, 201.

28. Benson, *As We Were:* 275–76. In connection with *Weir of Hermiston* it is interesting to note that Louis was coming to his forty-fourth birthday and that—although such studies may be suspect—scientific investigation once showed the average age of novelists finishing their masterpieces to be forty-six.
29. Daiches, *Robert Louis Stevenson:* 118.
30. Stevenson to Miss Ide, *Letters:* III, 308.
31. *From Saranac to the Marquesas. . .* : xix.

Appendix A:
Dialectics of a Reputation

1. Quiller-Couch, *Adventures in Criticism:* 96.
2. Hammerton, *Stevensoniana:* 283.
3. *Ibid.:* 281.
4. Benson, "The Myth of Robert Louis Stevenson," *London Mercury*, July-August 1925.
5. Smith, *Henry James and Robert Louis Stevenson:* 188.
6. Muir, "Robert Louis Stevenson," *Modern Scot*, Autumn 1931.
7. The final ignominy was: In one of the rival versions of Hans und Fritz that have infested American comic strips for the last forty years an intermittent phenomenon has been a sparse crew of pirates headed by a top-shaped, peg-legged individual called John Silver. For a curious parallel, consider the survival in the old Happy Hooligan strip of an occasional character called Hawkshaw the Detective, sole relict of Tom Taylor's classic Victorian drama, *The Ticket-of-Leave Man.*
8. Movie scenarios are usually based not directly on the book but on Sullivan's stage version. Hollywood has tried many other Stevenson stories, too often in low-budget productions with small excuse for existence. The first of which I can find record is *A Lodging for the Night* done early by D. W. Griffith (Lloyd Douglas, *Not So Long Ago:* 60). The earliest I remember seeing was a *Treasure Island* with Shirley Mason as Jim; the best an *Ebb-Tide* in the mid-thirties, with, I think, Percy Marmont in it; Paramount seems to have done it again in 1947 as *Adventure Island*. A *Kidnapped* was

released in 1948. As I write, a *Catriona* is said to be in production in
England. A marvelously mangled *Black Arrow* and a silly *St. Ives* are
also recent. Others of which the Museum of Modern Art has record
are *The Bottle Imp* (1917); *The Suicide Club* (as *Trouble for Two*)
(1936); *The Wrecker* (1933). Universal-International has announced
plans to produce *The Beach of Falesà*. As the most popular item,
Treasure Island has taken the worst beating. The Walt Disney production released in late 1950 made the usual mistake of casting Jim
as a child instead of a vigorous youth in mid-teens; had Silver mug-
ging and rasping in complete defiance of character; but particularly
distinguished itself by carefully throwing away the story's best
sound-movie scenes, such as the squawking of the parrot in the
dark blockhouse, Ben Gunn's imitating Flint's dying hail, and Billy
Bones singing *Fifteen Men* in the inn parlor. In 1938, I learn, the
Russians did a *Treasure Island*, making Jim a girl named Jenny with
whom Dr. Livesey falls in love, and adding political interest by mix-
ing in an Irish rebellion. In consequence of this job the head of the
Soviet film industry was cashiered and, I hope, sent to Siberia, because erroneous political feeling had moved him to show his Irish
rebels as adventurers, not heroes. The juvenile audiences who saw
the picture before its withdrawal are said to have been divided between applauding the pirates and denouncing them as "bandits."
(New York *Times*, January 17, 1938.)

9. Stevenson to Low, *Letters:* III, 162.

10. Barrie, *An Edinburgh Eleven:* 117–20.

11. This is not to be taken too hard, however, since Steuart's
Letters to Living Authors also condescends almost comically to
most of his contemporaries except Tolstoi. His implication that
Louis saw too little merit in Fielding is unjustified: Fielding appears
in a list of Louis's early favorites (Balfour, *Life:* I, 117), but he seems
to have preferred *Joseph Andrews* and *Amelia* to *Tom Jones*,
which he called " . . . a novel of which the respectable profess that
they could stand the dulness of it if it were not so blackguardly, and
the more honest admit they could stand the blackguardism if it
were not so dull." ("Some Gentlemen in Fiction," (SS): XXVII, 84);
later, ". . . dirty, dull, and false." When Louis describes to Henley
a list of books that a certain London publisher had been donkey
enough to turn down, it included an item that certainly shows
that he had the hang of Fielding's merits: this is a newly discovered

Fielding novel called *Solomon Crabb:* "I am enjoying Solomon Crabb extremely; Solomon's capital adventure with the two highwaymen and Squire Trecothick and Parson Vance; it is as good, I think, as anything in *Joseph Andrews.* I have just come to the part where the highwayman with the black patch over his eye has tricked poor Solomon into his place, and the squire and the parson are hearing the evidence. . . . Constable Muddon is as good as Dogberry and Verges put together; when he takes Solomon to the cage, and the highwayman gives him Solomon's own guinea for his pains, and kisses Mrs. Muddon, and just then up drives Lord Conybeare, and instead of helping Solomon, calls him all the rascals in Christendom!—O Henry Fielding, Henry Fielding!" (Stevenson to Henley, *Letters:* II, 72). For that matter, the Fielding and Richardson episode in the fugitive *Stevenson's Companion to the Cook Book* (SS): XXVII, 339-41 reeks wonderfully of the essential Fielding.

12. London *Daily Chronicle*, April 24, 1897.

13. I have no idea why Moore was so angry. There is no indication that he ever met Louis, so it can hardly have been personal spite. Chesterton guesses, a little lyrically, that Moore may have resented Louis's being " . . . possessed . . . and indeed the incarnation of, that intangible spiritual lightness, that sixth sense of literature, which is sometimes called humour and sometimes humility." (*Pall Mall Magazine*, September 1901.)

14. Chapman, *Emerson and Other Essays:* 221.

15. Greenwood, *The Sphere*, December 7, 1901.

16. E. g., pp. 83–84: "All style which is so intricately patterned, so reliant upon its music, its rhythm, its balance, gratifies the ear in the way that old dance music gratifies the ear. The minuet and the saraband, stately as they are, have their slow phrases, and flow to their resolution with immemorial dignity; they are patterns of closely-woven figured style, than which we could hardly have an illustration more fit. . . . in Stevenson's writing there is no violence to old airs and old order. . . .You may find in it an amazing variety of pitch and cadence; but at length the care that has made it betrays the artificer; at length the reader will look in vain for the rough word." Without influence from Stevenson, of whom I assume Swinnerton had just been reading a great deal in preparation for this book, the first sentence could have run: "Anything so complicated in pattern, so far committed to music, rhythm, and balance,

pleases in a fashion recalling old dance music"—and so forth.

Rice, *Stevenson and How to Know Him,* and Aydelotte, *The Oxford Stamp*: 189, have sound comment on the Ape-Chapman theory.

17. Benson, "The Myth of Robert Louis Stevenson," *London Mercury*, July-August 1925.

18. Joad, *The Bookmark*: 91; 94-95.

19. James, *Selected Papers on Philosophy*: 4.

20. The point is all the weaker for Shaw's articulate admiration for the way Stevenson wrote (*Dramatic Opinions and Essays*: I, 90, 94; II, 171). In this article Joad too is unable to resist quoting Stevenson against himself: " . . . though we are mighty fine fellows nowadays, we cannot write like Hazlitt." As a matter of picayune fact, Joad's quotation is inaccurate, though he did not alter the sense. The original is "Walking Tours," (SS): II, 137.

21. Beer, *The Mauve Decade*: 177-78. Internal evidence hints that Beer had just been reading Hellman, Steuart, and Miss Masson's *I Can Remember Robert Louis Stevenson*. He seems to have been inadequately acquainted with Stevenson's work, making an inexcusable error, "the castaway of Falesà" (p. 178), and giving an effect of complete ignorance (or ignoring) of the work of Stevenson's last seven or eight years.

22. "Ordered South," (SS): II, 73.

23. *The Young Chevalier* (SS): XXVIII, 196.

24. Hammerton, *Stevensoniana*: 173.

25. Swinnerton, *Robert Louis Stevenson*: 104.

26. Arnold Bennett said of Swinnerton's book on Stevenson: "Since its appearance Stevenson's reputation has never been the same." (Quoted in a Doran advertisement in *International Book Review*, June 1924.)

27. Hammerton, *Stevensoniana*: 213.

28. Saintsbury, *History of Nineteenth Century Literature*: 339.

29. Hamilton "The Real Stevenson at Last," *International Book Review*, January 1925.

30. Sherman, *The Emotional Discovery of America*: 181.

31. Benson, "The Myth of Robert Louis Stevenson," *London Mercury*, July-August 1925.

32. Woolf, *Essays on Literature*: 29-43.

33. Muir, "Robert Louis Stevenson," *Modern Scot*, Autumn 1931.

34. Aydelotte (*The Oxford Stamp:* 49) shrewdly testifies: ". . . . the person who reads one of Stevenson's essays with a foreigner . . . will be amazed at the number of colloquial phrases . . . which will cause the foreigner to stumble."

35. Duncan, "Stevenson's Second Visit to America," *Bookman* (New York), January 1900.

General Index

Adams, Henry, 369–72
Aegean Islands, 234, 280
Ah Fu (cook), 318, 327, 342, 344, 347, 349
Ainsworth, W. Harrison, 29
Alabama Claims, 125
America's interests in the Pacific, 332–33, 369; in Samoa, 394 ff.
Anderson, Sherwood, 419
Apemama Island, 345–48
Apia harbor, 358–59
Apia jail, 402, 404–405
Appin murder, 352
Archer, Thomas, 19
Archer, William, 19, 240–41, 416
Arnold, Matthew, 62
Arrick, 381, 387
Asquith, Lady, 191
Athenaeum Club, 268, 285, 371
Atalanta, 424
Atlantic Monthly, 180
atolls, 318–20

Babington, Rev. Churchill, 74, 79, 84, 201
Babington, Mrs. Churchill (Maud Balfour), 67, 74, 79, 82, 84
Bacon, Francis, 454
Baildon, H. B., 416
Baker, Shirley, 346, 381
"Baker's," *see* Saranac
Balfour of Burleigh, 26
Balfour family, 4–5
Balfour, George (uncle), 4, 172, 173, 182, 262
Balfour, Graham (cousin), 200, 309, 357, 387, 402, 428, 431, 434, 460
   The Life of Robert Louis Stevenson, 295–96, 434

Balfour, James (uncle), 5
Balfour, John (uncle), 4
Balfour, Rev. Dr. Lewis (grandfather), 4, 5, 6, 12, 24, 38, 63, 173
Balfour, Margaret Isabella, *see* Stevenson, Mrs. Thomas
Balfour, Maud (cousin), *see* Babington, Mrs. Churchill
Ballantyne, *The Coral Island*, 305
Balzac, H. de, 59, 113, 206, 437
Bancroft, *History of the United States*, 160
Bandmann, Dan, 279
Barbauld, Anna Letitia, 220
Barbizon, 117–18, 21
Barrie, J. M., 298, 391, 409, 416, 441, 447
   A Window in Thrums, 442
Barrymore, John, 440, 445
Baudelaire, *Fleurs du mal*, 29, 32, 47, 59, 113
Baxter, Charles, 40–42, 48, 59, 61, 99, 145, 155, 213, 214, 215, 250, 259, 263, 281, 284, 287, 288, 289, 292, 294, 295, 304, 414, 431, 433, 464
   mentioned: 69, 80, 141, 142, 153, 154, 162, 163, 168, 169, 172, 176, 185–86, 189, 283, 291, 293, 311, 330, 342–43, 387, 408, 414, 416, 430, 468
Beecher, Rev. Henry Ward, 126, 127
Beer, Thomas, 445, 447, 452
Beinecke Collection, 333
Bennet, Dr., 85
Benson, E. F., 429, 437, 444, 447, 449–50
Béranger, Pierre de, 113

Index of Works